Philosophy for AS and A2 is the definitive textbook for students of Advanced Subsidiary or Advanced Level courses, structured directly around the specification of the AQA – the only exam board to offer these courses. Following a lively foreword by Nigel Warburton, author of *Philosophy: The Basics*, a team of experienced teachers devote a chapter each to the six themes covered by the syllabus:

AS
- Theory of Knowledge
- Moral Philosophy
- Philosophy of Religion

A2
- Philosophy of Mind
- Political Philosophy
- Philosophy of Science

Each of the six themed chapters includes:

- A list of key concepts, to introduce students to the topic
- Bite-size sections corresponding to the syllabus topics
- Actual exam questions from previous years
- Suggested discussion questions to promote debate
- Text-boxes with helpful summaries, case-studies and examples
- An annotated further reading list directing students towards the best articles, books and websites
- A comprehensive glossary, providing a handy reference point

There is a final chapter on exam preparation, designed to help students get to grips with the examination board requirements.

Philosophy for AS and A2 is written by a team of expert teachers based at Heythrop College – part of the University of London – which specialises in teaching philosophy and theology.

The editors: Elizabeth Burns is an experienced teacher of both GCSE and A Level, and **Stephen Law** is the author of three bestselling philosophy books: *The Philosophy Files, The Outer Limits* and *The Philosophy Gym.* **The contributors:** Michael Lacewing, Patrick Riordan, Janice Thomas and Nicholas Wilson.

EDITED BY ELIZABETH BURNS AND STEPHEN LAW

philosophy
FOR AS AND A2

Routledge
Taylor & Francis Group

LONDON AND NEW YORK

First published 2004
by Routledge
2 Park Square, Milton Park, Oxon OX14 4RN

Simultaneously published in the USA and Canada
by Routledge
270 Madison Ave, New York, NY 10016

Routledge is an imprint of the Taylor & Francis Group, an informa business

© 2004 Elizabeth Burns, Stephen Law, Michael Lacewing,
Patrick Riordan, Janice Thomas, Nicholas Wilson

Reprinted 2005 (twice), 2006 (twice)

Foreword © 2004 Nigel Warburton

Typeset in Berling by
M Rules
Printed and bound in Great Britain by
Bell and Bain Ltd, Glasgow

British Library Cataloguing in Publication Data
A catalogue record for this book is available from the British Library

Library of Congress Cataloging in Publication Data
Philosophy for AS and A2/edited by Elizabeth Burns and Stephen Law. – 1st ed.
    p. cm.
    Includes bibliographical references and index.
      1. Philosophy–Textbooks. I. Burns, Elizabeth, 1963– . II. Law, Stephen.
III. Title: Philosophy for advanced subsidiary and advanced leve
    B74.P49 2004
    107'.6–dc 22   2003027166

ISBN10: 0–415–33562–0 Hbk
ISBN10: 0–415–33563–9 Pbk
ISBN13: 978–0–415–33562–1 Hbk
ISBN13: 978–0–415–33563–8 Pbk

CONTENTS

Contents

Contents

Contents

•list of contributors

Elizabeth Burns

Elizabeth lectures in Philosophy of Religion and is Dean of Undergraduate Studies at Heythrop College, University of London. Her publications include articles on revisionist Christianity and several subject guides for the University of London External B.D.

Michael Lacewing

Michael lectures on Moral Philosophy and the Philosophy of Mind at Heythrop College. He is interested in the implications of psychoanalytic theories of human nature for ethics, and is working on a book on the emotions. He regularly gives talks to schools and sixth form conferences.

Patrick Riordan

Patrick lectures on Political Philosophy at Heythrop College. His books include *A Politics of the Common Good*, and *Philosophical Perspectives on People Power* which is about the distinctive Philippine experience of democracy. Patrick has been a Visiting Professor in the Philippines on several occasions.

Janice Thomas

Janice lectures on the History of Modern Philosophy and the Philosophy of Mind, and is Head of the Department of Philosophy at Heythrop College. She has published widely on subjects ranging from personal identity and the logic of intending to Mill's philosophy of mind and the consciousness of non-human animals.

Nicholas Wilson

Nicholas has taught philosophy at undergraduate level for several years. His research interests are primarily in the Philosophy of Science and the Philosophy of Language and Logic. He is currently a Tutorial Assistant at Heythrop College and a Teaching Fellow in the Department of Philosophy at King's College London.

˙foreword

Studying philosophy should be exciting and perhaps a little disturbing. Exciting because it can open up new perspectives on the world and ourselves and provide powerful tools for clear thinking in a wide range of contexts. Disturbing, perhaps, because when taken seriously, philosophy takes very little for granted. You may find that philosophy challenges what you have always believed. If you believe in God, for example, thinking about the supposed proofs and disproofs of God's existence can be unnerving (though it may ultimately also be reassuring). Philosophy can even challenge your perceptual beliefs. How do you know that you are really reading this book now and not, for example, lying in bed asleep dreaming that you are reading the book, or else plugged into some kind of experience machine, like the one in *The Matrix*? If you want to keep your assumptions intact, philosophy is probably not the subject for you. If, however, you want to develop your ability to think independently about a range of puzzling yet important questions, and to study and engage with the thought of some of the world's greatest thinkers, philosophy can be an empowering and intellectually liberating subject.

I wasn't able to study philosophy formally until I went to university, and even then began it as a subsidiary subject. I have to admit that it took me some time to work out what my teachers were getting at. Like many of my fellow undergraduates, I had very little idea of what I was letting myself in for when I attended my first lecture, even though I'd struggled through (and occasionally nodded off over) Bertrand Russell's *The Problems of Philosophy* the summer before my first university term.

The AS and A2 levels in philosophy didn't exist back then in the early 1980s. Students in Britain are now more fortunate than I was in that they can study philosophy to quite a high level before committing to the subject at university. The A level is demanding enough to give anyone studying it seriously an excellent grounding in the subject. Students are also much luckier than we were in the range and quality of introductory books that jostle for their attention in the bookshops (these include several excellent books by the co-editor of this book, Stephen Law). When I began teaching A level philosophy while finishing my Ph.D., there were, almost unbelievably, only two or three introductions to philosophy readily available. In the absence of a book that was pitched at an appropriate level for intelligent sixth-formers, I expanded and rewrote some of my teaching notes into the book *Philosophy: The Basics* (London: Routledge, 4th edn 2004). Part of my aim was to write the book I wished I'd been able to pick up when I was 16. It was also intended to give newcomers to the subject a framework for understanding the subject in their first year at university. Now there are half a dozen books at least that I'd wholeheartedly recommend to a sixth-former (or anyone else) interested in learning something about the subject. My personal list, in approximate order of difficulty, would include: Thomas Nagel's *What Does It All Mean?* (Oxford: Oxford University Press, 1987), Stephen Law's *The Philosophy Gym* (London: Headline, 2003), Edward Craig's *Philosophy: A Very Short Introduction* (Oxford: Oxford University Press, 2002), and Simon Blackburn's *Think: A Compelling Introduction to Philosophy* (Oxford: Oxford University Press, 2001).

The present book is different from those I've just mentioned in that it follows very closely the AS and A2 level syllabus. It is also written by a range of authors, each concentrating on their own specialist subject. University philosophers have been rather slow off the mark in providing teaching materials for the AS and A2 level. It is very heartening that the philosophers of Heythrop College, which is part of London University, have devoted the time and energy to create this textbook. Its strengths should be obvious. The authors' experience as teachers is demonstrated in the clarity of their explanations, something which is almost unnoticeable when done well, but which, as you will find if you read more widely in philosophy, is not as common as you might hope.

My advice to you is to read this book closely, but read it actively. Don't see yourself as passively absorbing its content. Try to think critically about what is written here. Philosophy should never be regurgitation. Nor is it a matter of strolling through a museum of dry and dusty ideas. Studying philosophy is learning to philosophise, not just learning what other people have said. Use your own examples, think it through from your own point of view, perhaps disagree with some of the authors here. Engage critically with what you read. What may not be obvious while you are immersed in the detail is that when you study philosophy you aren't simply learning a body of ideas, what you are doing is learning to think for yourself about some of the most profound questions we can ask.

Nigel Warburton

The Open University

•acknowledgements

Some of the material in Chapter 3 has been adapted and developed from material originally produced for the Bachelor of Divinity by distance learning offered by the University of London External Programme (www.londonexternal.ac.uk).

introduction

Michael Lacewing and Elizabeth Burns

● WHY STUDY PHILOSOPHY?

In recent years, interest in studying philosophy at A Level has increased dramatically.

But why are people interested in philosophy? What use is the study of philosophy? The answers may include some of the following:

1. Subject matter: The questions that philosophy investigates are some of the most profound that we can ask. What can we know about the world we live in, and is certainty important? Is right and wrong 'simply' a matter of culture? Is it rational to believe in God? Are we just animals which have evolved, or do we have a spiritual dimension which will survive the death of our bodies?

2. Independent thought: Doing philosophy is an excellent training in thinking for yourself. Many people are quick to say that what people believe, especially on such philosophical matters as ethics or religion, depends on their upbringing. But very few people say this about themselves. Does what you think about abortion, or miracles, come straight from your parents and teachers? Or do you think you have good reasons to believe what you do? If you aren't thinking for yourself already, doing philosophy will provide you with the perfect opportunity.

3. Character: Because it encourages open-mindedness, doing philosophy can actually change your character. It can help you mature in your thoughts about and relations with people who are different from you, whether they are people you meet or authors you read. It can give you not just new thoughts, but new ways of thinking – about yourself, about others, about the world.

4. Reasoning: Doing philosophy is not easy. It is difficult to understand the arguments and the ideas. As with doing anything that is difficult, you develop new skills which make it easier with practice. Some of the skills that doing philosophy can teach you are:

- understanding the relations between ideas: how one idea can imply another or contradict it
- the ability to spot flaws in arguments
- the ability to construct arguments
- imagination: coming up with novel solutions and ideas
- communication and conversation: philosophy is done through discussion and debate.

● AS AND A2 PHILOSOPHY

At the time of writing, there is only one syllabus for AS and A2 philosophy, set by the AQA. Each qualification is comprised of three units of study, as follows:

AS

Unit 1: Theory of Knowledge

Unit 2: *either* Moral Philosophy *or* Philosophy of Religion

Unit 3: selections from *one* of the following set texts:

- Plato, *The Republic*
- Descartes, *Meditations*
- Marx and Engels, *The German Ideology*
- Sartre, *Existentialism and Humanism*

A2

Unit 4: *either* Philosophy of Mind *or* Political Philosophy *or* Philosophy of Science

Unit 5: selections from *one* of the following set texts:

- Aristotle, *Nicomachean Ethics*
- Hume, *An Enquiry Concerning Human Understanding*
- Mill, *On Liberty*
- Nietzsche, *Beyond Good and Evil*

- Russell, *The Problems of Philosophy*
- Ayer, *Language, Truth and Logic*

Unit 6: Synoptic Study: a long essay on one of 12 studies that either bring together the thought of two different philosophers (comparative studies) or the thought of one philosopher in relation to one particular topic (complementary studies).

Each course has a similar structure in that one unit is compulsory (Theory of Knowledge and the Synoptic Study), one unit is a set text, and the remaining unit allows a choice of topic. This is a good combination for learning philosophy.

First, Unit 1, the Theory of Knowledge, with its arguments about what we know and how we can justify our beliefs, is a natural foundation for all of philosophy. We cannot argue about whether God exists, for example, unless we have some idea of how we could justify believing such a claim.

The range of options that are available in Units 2 and 4 are indicative of the Big Questions which philosophy tackles, including: What is right and wrong? Does God exist? How do our minds relate to our brains? What is it to live in freedom? and How does science work to produce knowledge? Studying any of the issues that these units explore exposes you to the breadth and depth of philosophical argument and therefore gives you a good idea of what philosophy really grapples with, what it tries to do.

Units 3 and 5 introduce another side to philosophy. Philosophy works with ideas, and ideas are communicated through texts. Learning how to read a text, how to really understand what the author wanted to communicate, is therefore very important. But when ideas are not obvious, the interpretation of the text becomes no easy matter. These two units encourage you to be sympathetic to texts and to be precise in your interpretation of them. In part, they are about the importance of language to arguments and the implications of saying one thing, rather than another that sounds quite similar. But they are much more than this. The texts that have been chosen are among the most influential that have ever been written. In studying them, you are introduced to examples of philosophy done at its very best. They demonstrate how ideas hang together, and how a whole view of the world is developed through the interconnections of ideas.

Unit 6 gives you the chance to demonstrate your skill at making such connections. Units 1–5 test your knowledge, either of arguments for or against a particular idea or of what a particular philosopher said. For Unit 6, this is not the main focus. It is true that there is more knowledge to be gained, for you will study one or two philosophers or issues in greater depth. But the main test is of your ability to think deeply about two philosophers, or a philosopher and an issue, that you have learned about separately, and to bring them together so that you see the implications of one unit for another. More than any other unit, this is an exercise in making connections and evaluating the results. It is the unit that creates an organic whole out of the other units.

● ABOUT THIS BOOK

This book covers the syllabus for Units 1 and 2 of the AS, and Unit 4 of the A2. There is a chapter on each of the six topics: Theory of Knowledge, Moral Philosophy, Philosophy of Religion, Philosophy of Mind, Political Philosophy, and Philosophy of Science. Each of these chapters contains questions for discussion, placed throughout the text to stimulate understanding and reflection. Each chapter also contains past exam questions, given at the end of the section in which the material relevant to the question is discussed, and a glossary providing concise definitions of key terms. Words that appear in the glossary are in bold type the first time they are used in the text. The final chapter offers guidance on how to prepare for and do well in the examinations.

● RECOMMENDED READING

You will find some suggestions for further reading in the Foreword to this book. Three longer and more demanding introductions to philosophy, each a model of clarity, are M. Hollis's *Invitation to Philosophy* (Oxford: Blackwell, 1997), A. Morton's *Philosophy in Practice* (Oxford: Blackwell, 1995), and J. Teichman's *Philosophy: A Beginner's Guide* (Oxford: Blackwell, 1991). You may also find a philosophical dictionary helpful. Particularly recommended is Simon Blackburn's *The Oxford Dictionary of Philosophy* (Oxford: Oxford University Press, 1996).

1

theory of knowledge

UNIT 1   Janice Thomas

KEY CONCEPTS ⊙

- ⊙ knowledge
- ⊙ justification
- ⊙ rationalism
- ⊙ empiricism
- ⊙ scepticism
- ⊙ a priori and a posteriori knowledge
- ⊙ reliable methods
- ⊙ coherence
- ⊙ foundationalism
- ⊙ naive realism
- ⊙ representative realism
- ⊙ idealism
- ⊙ phenomenalism

● INTRODUCTION

Plato was one of the earliest philosophers in western thought to discuss the nature of knowledge. At the beginning of the dialogue called the *Theaetetus*, Plato pictures Socrates asking a fellow teacher to introduce him to his brightest new student. Socrates asks the student (the Theaetetus of the title) what he thinks knowledge is. Not surprisingly Theaetetus has a few false starts. At first he suggests that knowledge is all the subjects he is taught by his teacher: such subjects as astronomy, natural history, mathematics and so on.

Socrates quickly helps Theaetetus see that all of these, although they are indeed *kinds* of knowledge, are just examples. Astronomy is knowledge of the stars and planets. Natural history is knowledge of animals and plants. But Socrates is looking for the nature of knowledge in general, independent of the particular concerns of this or that subject matter. He wants to know what makes any proposition at all, which someone might find in any science or context whatever, count as knowledge.

The Theory of Knowledge (the branch of philosophy also called **epistemology**) continues to take as one of its main aims the attempt to give an account of the nature of knowledge in general, just as Socrates and Plato tried to do. A number of difficult questions need to be addressed before we can be sure that any particular **belief** we hear expressed is *knowledge*, whatever the subject matter involved:

- Where does the supposed knowledge come from (reason? experience? some other source?)?
- Does the person who holds it believe it?
- Is it true?
- What is the nature of the justification that could or should be given in support of that belief?
- Are there any sceptical arguments that could threaten that supposed knowledge?
- Are there conclusive arguments that would defeat any and all such sceptical arguments?
- How reliable is the method – often sense perception – by which that belief was acquired?

These are very complex questions. They are also connected with each other in numerous subtle ways. Making a start on answering them requires realising that – although we often take ourselves to know things, whether in the various sciences or in everyday life – not all our beliefs are adequately justified. Even with the beliefs about which we feel most certain it is not always correct to think that we have a right to believe them.

The word 'belief' in Theory of Knowledge

In ordinary conversation, talk of a person's beliefs is usually meant to refer to that person's religious, moral, political or even perhaps aesthetic convictions. They are often matters of faith rather than ones where proof or evidence is thought to be available or even relevant. Beliefs in non-philosophical talk are generally 'very firmly held convictions about very important matters'.

On the contrary, when philosophers talk about 'a belief', what is meant is 'any fact of the matter or proposition which might be held to be true'. So among your beliefs in this sense might be the belief

- that it is Monday
- that it is windy today
- that water boils at 100 degrees Celsius at sea level
- that you were born more than ten years ago
- that overeating causes obesity
- that $2 + 2 = 4$

and so forth. A belief in this sense could be something utterly trivial as well as something serious. It could be something general or something particular. It could be something that might not have been true. (If weather fronts had behaved differently, today could have been calm rather than windy.) But equally, of course, a belief could be something that could not have been otherwise, something guaranteed true by logic (e.g. If A is taller than B and B is taller than C then A is taller than C.) The important thing is that beliefs have **truth value**. They are capable of being true or false.

We are about to embark on an exploration of the questions listed above. The intention is to draw out their implications and articulate the difficulties they raise. Philosophers specialising in Theory of Knowledge sometimes despair of giving a credible and well-defended account of the knowledge we all ordinarily and unreflectively take ourselves to have. You should try, as you make your study of epistemology, to form a reasoned judgement about whether the sceptic's despair has any sort of warrant.

● EMPIRICISM AND RATIONALISM

Assume for the moment that at least some of our beliefs (in the sense of 'belief' described in the box) are known to be true. This is to make the assumption that there is such a thing as knowledge at all, that we do know some things however trivial. Later in this chapter we will encounter sceptics who seriously maintain that we have no knowledge whatsoever. For the present we are going to assume that such sceptics can be defeated somehow.

Suppose you have some beliefs you are convinced are true and therefore that you know them. Asked what their source is (how you came by them) you might wonder how to avoid a false start similar to Theaetetus' false start mentioned earlier. The natural answer might seem to be something like 'Well, I know it's Monday because I looked at the calendar' or 'I can see that it's windy by looking out the window.' But would that take us very far in a philosophical enquiry of the sort we are doing?

Perhaps surprisingly, many philosophers have thought this natural approach is actually a good way to start. For we can in fact generalise fruitfully from such examples. In each of these two cases, different as they are in some ways, we come up with a belief that is a promising candidate to be knowledge simply by looking and seeing. Looking and seeing (indeed, using all of your senses) is one – very important – form of experience. These two examples thus suggest that one (very general) source of at least some knowledge is experience.

Of course it hardly needs saying that not every proposition suggested by or derived from experience constitutes knowledge. Some beliefs suggested by some experiences are not even true so they cannot be knowledge. Seeing the landscape through a window spattered with water droplets I may say 'It's raining' when in fact the rain stopped some time ago. Part of my experience seems to teach me that it is raining but in this case what I learn from (that part of) my experience is not knowledge but a mistake.

Here is a different example. If I know that a particular friend is taller than me and I hear that her younger brother has grown taller than her then I easily infer, even without seeing him, that her brother is taller than me as well. I do not need to see him to know that he is taller than me. This is not something I am taught by experience. Rather, it is a piece of knowledge whose source is reasoning. I *could* have learned it by visual comparison or measurement. But in the example as I told it simple reasoning was enough, independent of any investigation using my senses, to ascertain the truth.

The two sources of knowledge that have now been introduced – reasoning and experience – have been associated with two great movements or approaches in the history of philosophy.

Rationalism in its most extreme form is the view that all knowledge is ultimately derived from or depends upon truths obtained by the employment of unaided reason alone.

Empiricism in its most extreme form is the view that all knowledge is ultimately derived from or consists in truths obtained from experience alone.

It is doubtful whether anyone has ever been a rationalist or an empiricist in these extreme forms. History of philosophy textbooks and commentaries traditionally list the seventeenth-century philosophers René Descartes (1596–1650), Baruch Spinoza (1632–77) and Gottfried Leibniz (1646–1716) under the heading 'Rationalists'. Sometimes Plato (428–348 BC) and Immanuel Kant (1724–1804) are grouped with them under the same heading. Similarly John Locke (1632–1704), George Berkeley (1685–1753) and David Hume (1711–76) are often described as 'the British Empiricists'. Shortly we shall see that these titles need careful qualification if they are to be applied appropriately to any of the philosophers named.

 ## QUESTION FOR DISCUSSION

Are there any possible sources of knowledge other than reason or experience?

Rationalism

The reason why I have said that perhaps, strictly speaking, none of the philosophers just listed deserves the unqualified title 'rationalist' is because there are a number of distinct notions or principles associated with the term 'rationalism'. Most of the philosophers labelled rationalists subscribe to only a subset of those principles or notions, not to all of them.

Here is a list of some of the main doctrines that have at different times been associated with the title rationalist:

- that it is possible to attain knowledge of the existence of things through the exercise of reason alone
- that some knowledge is innate (known from birth)
- that all knowledge is part of a single deductive system and that all phenomena can be explained within this system
- that empirically acquired knowledge (if there is any) is less certain and inferior in status to deductively acquired knowledge
- that rationalist views are opposed to those of the empiricists.

Knowledge of existence

In some ways Descartes is the paradigmatic rationalist. Famously, he believes that at least his own existence can be known by the exercise of reason alone. Indeed, anyone who follows the procedure of systematic doubt that he describes in the *Meditations* can reason with complete certainty to his or her own existence. For as Descartes realised, however hard you try to doubt or question your own existence or to imagine that you don't really exist but are just dreaming or being tricked into believing that you do, it is always certain that *something* must exist to do that very doubting or questioning. There must be a dupe to *be* duped, a dreamer who dreams his own existence.

Descartes also holds that the existence of God can be proven by deductive argument involving only his innate ideas and premises he takes to be self-evident. This argument makes no appeal to sensory information or to experience.

Innate knowledge

However, it would be controversial to say that Descartes – paradigmatic rationalist though he is – holds in a straightforward way any of the *other* four strands of rationalism summarised above.

For instance, it might be argued that Descartes does not believe in innate knowledge. As mentioned just above, it is certainly true that he thinks we all have a number of 'innate ideas': he thinks, for example, that we are all born with an innate idea of God. We may, however, need to reach the age of reason before we are able to employ our inborn ideas in a clear way in any of our thoughts and reflections.

And in any event an idea does not by itself constitute knowledge. Remember that knowledge requires truth. To know something is to know that something is the case. And it is only propositions or beliefs that can have a truth value. That is, only propositions can be true or false. So Descartes's belief in innate ideas cannot be read, without further argument, as a belief in innate knowledge.

It has to be admitted that some readers think Descartes's innate ideas are not just the single atoms of thought I have been taking them to be but, rather, that each of them incorporates several elements in a way that makes it more like a proposition than a single, uncombined notion or concept. So perhaps, after all, Descartes does subscribe to the view that we have some innate knowledge. This is a matter of interpretation. The important thing to realise at this point is that Descartes's status as a rationalist does not depend on his believing that there is such a thing as innate knowledge.

Truth requires propositions

A single idea on its own, not combined with any other idea, cannot be either true or false. To see what this means suppose I come up to you and say 'oranges'. Is what I have said true or false? You know what I am talking about. You know that oranges are a citrus fruit, orange in colour, tasting a certain way, and so forth. But have I said anything you could evaluate as being either true or false when I utter my single word, 'oranges'?

Obviously not. I would have to combine 'oranges' with some other idea, perhaps the predicate '. . . are fruits' or a subject like 'I am allergic to . . .', before I would have said anything that had a chance of being true (or false either).

Other philosophers on the other hand would count themselves as rationalists precisely because they do believe in innate knowledge. Among contemporary philosophers the American, Noam Chomsky, is well known for subscribing to a particular innatist doctrine. He is an expert in linguistics and his linguistic innatism holds that human beings, however different the natural languages that they learn as babies, share an innate 'deep grammar'. In other words he believes that, as a species, we have innate knowledge of the general grammatical principles governing production of all human languages, however different the surface features of those languages. We are born knowing which very general grammatical rules to follow as soon as we begin turning the very many bits of language we hear as newborn infants into utterances of our own.

Chomsky associates his linguistic innatism with classical rationalism and identifies himself explicitly with Descartes and Leibniz. He regards them as his philosophical ancestors in – as he interprets them – claiming that important areas of human knowledge are inborn.

Plato is another philosopher who is often described as a rationalist because of his doctrine that all knowledge worthy of the name is innate. This is not the place to explore Plato's doctrine in detail. Suffice it to say that on his view souls exist before they are incarnated in human beings. Before their time as embodied humans begins they are made acquainted with the eternal Platonic Ideas (or Forms), knowledge of which constitutes all the knowledge there is, on Plato's view. (How this acquaintance is achieved is mysterious and the subject of much speculation by commentators.)

Knowledge for Plato is thus inborn in the sense that it is already there in the newborn's mind even though it is made obscure and difficult to access by the effects of the soul's being united with the body. But the unique features of his epistemology just described mean that Plato, alone in the history of philosophy, is *both* an innatist and a thinker who believes that all knowledge is acquired in the course of – a very special kind of non-sensory, pre-natal – experience.

❓ QUESTION FOR DISCUSSION

Are there any pieces or sorts of knowledge which you were born knowing?

Knowledge as a deductive system

Another thread in rationalism is the suggestion that knowledge forms a deductive system, so that reason in the narrow sense of 'deductive power' or 'capacity to draw inferences' is all that is needed to acquire knowledge. This view could involve holding that *all* knowledge is enclosed in a deductive system. But it could also take the weaker form of holding that important truths of, for example, metaphysics, logic and morality are knowable but only by deducing them from other known truths. On such a weaker view there would also be the possibility of obtaining other knowledge from other sources (most likely, experience).

Of course deduction has to start somewhere. This is perhaps one reason why belief in inborn or innate knowledge is often held to be a part of rationalism. But the starting point for deducing all the rest of knowledge need not be something known innately. For Descartes, for example, it is the knowledge of his own existence, itself a piece of knowledge gained by reasoning and not known innately, which for him acts as the foundation of the rest of what can be known.

What is needed by the rationalist **foundationalist** is not a truth that you are born knowing but rather a truth that can be known independently of experience. This is what the logicians call a piece of ***a priori*** knowledge. To know something *a priori* is to know it without doing any research, without doing a field study or going into the lab, without doing any experiments. Indeed, *a priori* knowledge is knowledge of propositions that *could not* be proved or confirmed observationally. There is no experimental or sensory evidence you could assemble to show that such a proposition is true or to justify your belief in it.

Good candidates for knowability *a priori* are what logicians call **necessary truths**. These are ones that could not – logically could not – fail to be true. To understand such a truth is to see that it could not fail to be the case. Geometry and logic provide numerous examples of such necessary truths which can be known *a priori*. So the example used above involving the 'taller than' relation can be known independently of any experience to express a necessary truth and that is why it is rightly said to be knowable *a priori*. (If *A* is taller than *B* and *B* is taller than C, *A cannot fail to be* taller than C.) Likewise, truths of arithmetic like 2 + 2 = 4 are knowable *a priori* because they can be seen straight off to state necessities. Arithmetic truths like this could not state a falsehood without changing the meanings of the symbols used to express them.

It should be noted that 'necessary truth' and 'known *a priori*' are not synonyms. They do not mean the same thing even if some truths that are necessary – meaning that they *could not* be false – happen also to give us examples of *a priori* knowledge. Some necessities are knowable only **a posteriori**. They cannot be known to be true without some help or support from experience but they state necessities nonetheless.

For example, to discover that what the ancients called 'the morning star' is the very same heavenly body as the one they called 'the evening star' you need what is called 'empirical evidence'; you must have used your senses. So this knowledge is *a posteriori* knowledge even though the proposition you know (that the morning star is the very same thing as the evening star) is something that must be true since a thing's identity with itself is something necessary, something it could not possibly escape.

 ## QUESTION FOR DISCUSSION

Can you think of any other examples (other than identity statements) of truths that are knowable only *a posteriori* although they are necessary truths?

Related examination question

(Part a) Explain and briefly illustrate the meaning of *a priori* and *a posteriori* knowledge. *(6 marks) (2001)*

Contrasts with empiricism

Rationalists believe that most of our knowledge comes from reason unassisted by the senses. But they also think that any knowledge that does come – or appears to come – through the senses is inferior to what reason teaches. Plato, as we have seen, believes that all knowledge comes from pre-natal acquaintance with the Ideas and that the senses can give us, at best, right opinion. Similarly, Descartes argues that reason alone gives us doubt-proof certainty.

But it is a serious misapprehension to think that rationalism and empiricism are necessarily mutually exclusive stances. Descartes also believed in the value of empirical research, in every discipline or science from physics and physiology to optics and musicology. He did not dismiss knowledge gained through the senses. Rather he regarded the deliverances of reason as *necessary prerequisites* to the safe acquisition of empirical knowledge. Reason must give me knowledge that a non-deceiving God exists before I can legitimately trust and claim to know what my senses tell me.

And if we are looking for scepticism about the possibility of gaining knowledge of truths through **inductive reasoning** built up from sensory observations, we will find it – not so much among the classical rationalists – but rather in the writings of Hume, the most celebrated of the British Empiricists. His quarrel with the rationalists was not with their respect for reason and demonstration but with their conviction that metaphysical and moral principles, every bit as much as mathematical and logical propositions, could be given justifications by reason.

Related examination questions

(Part a) Briefly explain what is meant by rationalism. *(6 marks) (2002)*

(Part b) Explain and illustrate the rationalist view that some concepts are *not* drawn from experience. *(15 marks) (2003)*

Empiricism

There is certainly a contrast between empiricism and rationalism. But this is not so much a contrast between diametrically opposed principles as a (sometimes quite profound) difference in emphasis. In what follows I will give an account of the empiricist stance by contrasting the central doctrines of empiricism with the views referred to in the previous section as five 'strands' of rationalist thought.

No innate ideas or knowledge

To begin with, then, empiricists differ from some rationalists in believing that all ideas come from experience. For some empiricists there are no innate ideas. The mind is a blank tablet (a *tabula rasa*) at birth. Thus the truths or propositions that make up our knowledge consist of ideas that have come to us exclusively through our senses. There is no such thing as inborn knowledge.

It should be noted, however, that empiricists recognise some form of inner sense as well as the outer senses (sight, hearing and the rest). This means that they accept that experience includes more than just sense perception. Introspection reveals a wealth of emotions, sensations, feelings and memories, which shape our knowledge of things.

That said, however, it must be admitted that the empiricist stance can be summarised without too much caricature in two simple slogans rooted firmly in the sensory realm: 'seeing is believing' and 'nothing in the mind that has not first been in the senses'.

The rejection of reason?

The definition of extreme empiricism offered above (p. 9) suggests that such an extremist would differ from rationalists in claiming that there is no such thing as *a priori* knowledge, that all knowledge is *a posteriori* (it comes from experience).

This seems so obviously false, however (think of all the truths proven in Euclidean geometry), that we should not be surprised if we are unable to find any actual philosopher who ever held this extreme view. If innate ideas and knowledge are rejected and thus experience is regarded as the only source of ideas it is still possible for an empiricist to believe that some or even all knowledge is founded in or supported by reason.

Locke, for example, offers a theory of knowledge that maintains that all ideas come from experience but that all knowledge consists in discovering, with the use of reason, which ideas 'agree' with each other and which do not. Thus, officially, Locke accepts as knowledge only necessary truths that can be known *a priori*.

However, he also maintains that experience and experiment teach us many 'right opinions' about the world studied by the physical sciences. So although he stops short of calling such empirically discovered truth 'knowledge' he deserves to be regarded as an empiricist not only for his rejection of innate ideas but for his pioneering allegiance to the capacity of empirical science to justify (as 'right opinion') our claim to the truth of our beliefs about matters of fact. And unlike Plato, Locke is a great respecter of right opinion – especially that provided by empirical science!

Berkeley and Hume also have an allegiance to empirical as opposed to 'armchair' science and endorse its capacity to provide us with true beliefs about the world. Berkeley is famous, or perhaps notorious, for having denied the distinction between sensory appearance and reality (see below p. 38). He maintains that things are constituted by the ideas my senses give me when I see, hear and touch them. There is nothing more to know about the real nature of the objects of the senses than is given in sense experience.

Hume is also notorious. In his case it is for his scepticism about the possibility of our having knowledge about any of what he calls 'matters of fact'. 'Matters of fact' are those propositions that are not demonstrable, i.e. they are not knowable *a priori* or guaranteed by logic. Experience urges us to accept them as true and they would thus be *a posteriori* knowledge – if they were known.

But Hume's matters of fact cannot be known, on his view. And this is precisely because they cannot be demonstrated. For example, experience may teach me that bread is nourishing but there is no logical inference by which I can demonstrate (prove) the fact. Hume would say 'and rightly so', for logic certainly does not rule out the possibility that the next piece of bread I eat might fail to provide any nourishment at all.

However, Hume's allegiance to empirical science is shown by his devising rules for using inductive reasoning so as to have – if not knowledge of matters of scientific fact – the most highly probable and trustworthy opinions. Such opinions are, on Hume's view, safe guides to action. They are also ones that we are both wise to follow and prevented from ignoring by human nature.

Reason cannot prove the existence of anything

Hume's empiricism does not show itself in a reluctance to acknowledge that some of our knowledge comes from reason for, as we have seen, he is quick to make that acknowledgement. Rather he is an empiricist because he denies that reason is capable of justifying our acceptance of numerous important (metaphysical) beliefs. These include:

- belief in the existence of the external world
- belief in necessary causal connections in nature
- belief in the existence of the self
- belief in the existence of either material or immaterial substance.

Unfortunately, as we have also seen, Hume does not believe that sensory evidence can establish the existence of any of these things either.

Hume's empiricist predecessors (i.e. Locke and Berkeley) on the other hand seem inclined to think

- either that we sense material things immediately and are thus justified in believing in their existence (Berkeley)
- or at least that our senses provide us with sensations from which we can infer the existence of material things as the causes of those sensations (Locke).

In the latter case Locke might say that we have only 'right opinion' but he never seriously questions that we are justified in believing in the existence of the material world of which we have sensory experience.

Hume's extreme scepticism has seemed to many to be an inevitable outcome of empiricism, one that Locke and after him Berkeley avoided only by blinding themselves to the implications of their shared notion of a perceptual idea. For the empiricist notion of a perceptual idea is the notion of a non-material entity which stands in for the material thing or property of which it is an idea. If sense perception can only furnish us with intermediaries, entities which are not the material objects themselves about which we are trying to know, there is always the chance that those intermediaries may fail to represent the world accurately. We will see below that this simple line of thought underpins all the standard forms of epistemological scepticism.

Related examination question

(Part c) Assess empiricism. *(24 marks) (2003)*

● KNOWLEDGE AND JUSTIFICATION

If one of your firmly held beliefs is challenged how should you go about trying to justify it? We ordinarily assume that any proposition of which we feel certain is true. But my conviction, no matter how strong, that a particular belief of mine is true is not, and should not be, enough to convince me or anyone else that I am justified in holding it. For certainty is an emotional or subjective state of the would-be knower. It is not an evidential state. And even if knowing too is a mental state it is not the same sort of mental state. My feeling of certainty should never count all by itself as evidence for the truth of the proposition to which I subscribe.

Certainty is not equivalent to knowledge

To see that certainty and knowledge do not amount to the same thing consider the following two examples:

Imagine a bigot who thinks members of a particular race or religion are inferior to other people. No matter how certain he is about the inferiority of those he looks down on you are bound to think that his certainty does not amount to knowledge. His certainty gives no justification or support to his (bigoted) belief.

Now consider a very able but very nervous student. She has worked hard and revised diligently. During the examination she may be so nervous that she feels wholly uncertain of the truth of what she is writing even though her excellent answers secure her a high mark. Her knowledge is not in any way diminished by her temporary uncertainty.

Clearly, the ideal state of affairs would be if certainty and knowledge were always found together. It is true that they have no intrinsic connection with each other. It would, however, be highly rational and desirable for people always to feel most sure of what they are genuinely entitled to claim to know. But certainty is no guarantee of knowledge. So how can we be sure that what we believe we also know?

Since Plato's time it has been held that knowing is not a subjective matter. It is at least a matter of being *justified* in a belief, of having what is sometimes called (in a phrase popularised by A. J. Ayer (1910–89)) 'a *right* to be sure' (Ayer 1956: 31ff.). Here are a number of objective criteria which have been proposed for distinguishing genuinely justified belief from that which, however strong, lacks justification:

- quantity and quality of evidence
- predictive and explanatory power
- reasonableness and probability
- acquisition by a reliable method
- deducibility or inferability from foundational pieces of knowledge
- coherence with a body of accepted beliefs
- immunity to doubt.

I will now look in detail at each of these proposed criteria in turn.

Quantity and quality of evidence

Any proposition I believe on good evidence is prima facie one about which I have a right to be sure, something I am justified in believing. We could all give a fairly full list of the sorts of things that should count as good evidence and be taken seriously in any forum, for example a court of law:

- witnessing the event myself or receiving information from a reliable witness
- photographs, sound recordings, documents, DNA samples, fingerprints or other physical evidence that attests to what happened
- the word of a competent authority: one with the training, experience and expertise to make judgements in such a matter
- the use of appropriately sophisticated or refined equipment for making any relevant observations or tests
- sufficient numbers of tests or observations under differing circumstances producing the same results with no counter-instances.

This list makes no pretence to be exhaustive. In different circumstances different criteria might prove relevant or even crucial. What matters is that these are the sorts of evidential requirements that most of us would readily mention as needing to be met before a claim to know would be justified. At least some or all of these would need to be produced by anyone trying to justify any knowledge claim.

And the more such criteria are met the more we should be inclined to say the knowledge claim is supported or justified to a high degree or even that it is conclusively justified. These remarks may seem very commonsensical and uncontroversial – almost too obvious to mention. Later on we will look at the views of radical sceptics, those who say that even knowledge claims that meet all these criteria and more are insufficiently justified. At that point it will be worth remembering how undeniable these points seemed here.

Predictive and explanatory power

In the previous section, the notion of a belief's being 'justified to a high degree' appeared. This hints at a difference between the *truth* of beliefs and their *justification*, which is very important to note explicitly. If you believe a proposition it must be either true or false and that exhausts the possibilities. But a belief may be justified to different degrees. When it is highly justified we say that it is 'reasonable' or perhaps 'well warranted'.

It is important to note also that even a very highly justified belief might fail to be true and thus fail to be knowledge. The other side of this coin is that a true belief you happen to hold by accident or on insufficient grounds would not be knowledge even though it is true. True belief and knowledge need not coincide.

Now it seems only common sense that a belief will be justified just to the extent that that belief allows or helps us to predict and explain relevant phenomena. This seems right either in everyday life or in science. Suppose the belief I am claiming is true is that the walls of my kitchen are yellow. You would expect to see yellow walls when you enter that room. Again, if you claim to know that I have been painting, your claim is supported by the fact that, if true, that proposition would neatly explain why my hands and clothes are covered with wet paint.

Here is another example. If an astronomer believes some proposition that is suggested by a particular astronomical theory, his belief will be supported by the occurrence of a planetary movement predicted by that theory. The movement of that planet will be explained by the astronomer's theory.

Reasonableness and probability

Reasonableness and probability, like the two criteria just discussed, are not by themselves conclusive. Obviously they are also to some extent relative. This does not mean that they cannot be part of a satisfactory case in support of the correctness or truth of some proposition. They can thus, together with evidence that other criteria from the list are met, provide a high degree of justification for believing that proposition.

For example, the British climate is such that weather predictions are very difficult to make at any time of year. Nonetheless I would be justified in believing that there will be rain in the Midlands sometime in the next four months. This is because past experience teaches that rain is highly probable. Rainfall statistics show that there has never been any four-month period since records began when that part of the country has been completely without rain. It is highly reasonable to be guided by the Met. Office records in such a case.

Reliable methods of belief acquisition

If the method by which you acquired a particular belief is a method which, in general, reliably produces true beliefs it seems very reasonable to trust that belief. Such a belief seems highly justified and that in turn gives you good grounds for claiming knowledge.

For example, if you have looked up the time of an exam on the printed timetable issued by the examination board you should feel very confident about your belief about the time of that exam. Having used a reliable method of belief formation you have a very high degree of justification for your belief. Asked if you know when that exam is going to be, you are likely to say you do know.

But which methods of acquiring beliefs are the reliable ones? The natural first response to this question is 'The ones that always give us true beliefs!' However, a method's track record turns out, on reflection, not to be a very good indicator for our purposes. This is because, as was pointed out earlier, some true beliefs can fail to be knowledge precisely because it is possible to hold, on poor grounds or no grounds at all, a belief that just *happens* to be true. That is to say, it is all too possible to be right by a kind of accident or luck.

Consider the following example. Imagine a soothsayer who makes predictions about the outcomes of sporting events by reading tea leaves. Ten times out of ten he successfully names the winners on the basis of the arrangement of leaves in the bottom of his teacup. Since his method of coming up with the winners' names has a 100 per cent success rate it would surely count as a reliable method if generating truths were all that mattered for judging reliability.

Yet it is impossible to see how there could be any causal connection whatever between the outcome of a distant sporting event and the pattern of some tea leaves. The reasonable view would appear to be that the successful predictions are a result of nothing but accident or coincidence.

Using a reliable method of acquiring true beliefs, if such a method can be found, is an excellent way of obtaining highly justified beliefs. But the example just given shows that we need some way of identifying reliable methods of belief-acquisition independently of their 'truth ratio', as it has been called. Appeal to 'reliable methods' does not take us beyond the notions of good evidence, reasonableness and probability, predictive and explanatory power, which we have already looked at. For these are the criteria that we have to employ when judging which methods of belief-acquisition or formation are plausibly regarded as the reliable ones, whose use justifies us in subscribing to a belief.

QUESTIONS FOR DISCUSSION

What does good justification consist in? How can you be sure that you are justified in accepting the beliefs or propositions you take to be true?

Foundational pieces of knowledge

Some epistemologists would say that what is needed to ground or justify many of our beliefs is that they have the right relationship to other beliefs that we possess, namely our foundational beliefs or pieces of knowledge. Foundational beliefs on this view are ones that need no further support because they are known straight off to be true. They carry their truth 'on their surface' so to speak and so can act as the foundations upon which the edifice of knowledge is erected. For the foundationalist, all other justified beliefs are justified because they depend upon or are derived from the foundational propositions.

The phrases 'known straight off' or 'carry their truth on their surface' are not very precise. Some foundationalists mean by such phrases that basic beliefs must guarantee their own truth by being necessary truths, ones that are **incorrigible**. (This means they are not the sort of thing that is capable of being corrected.) Others think there are basic beliefs that are corrigible or fallible but are nonetheless somehow self-certifying or self-justifying. Their self-justification may be held to consist in the fact that they have been obtained using a generally reliable method and that there is no evidence against them. The risk they carry of being mistaken or untrue is utterly minimal.

 ## QUESTIONS FOR DISCUSSION

What is the difference between a foundational truth that is necessary and one that is fallible? Can you think of any examples?

So, historically, foundationalists differ from each other in the (types of) propositions they regard as foundational. For example, many analytic philosophers of the early twentieth century were persuaded that certain kinds of sensory reports can be known in a 'straight off', non-derived way. To them, reports like 'I see a red patch' or 'This seems smooth to me' seemed such simple expressions of what is given immediately in sense experience that they must be good candidates to be utterly basic or foundational beliefs. They seem to lie beyond the possibility of support by anything else. No further justification need or could be given for believing them.

The view just described takes **sense data** (the basic bits of experience given to the subject in sense perception) to furnish the elements upon which other beliefs depend. So my basic knowledge that I see something green and brown might serve, on such a foundationalist view, as the basis or premise from which I might infer that there is a tree.

Descartes, as we have seen, does not accord a foundational role to sense data. He does, however, regard at least the proposition 'I think therefore I am' as a non-derivative truth, which is basic in the sense that it cannot be doubted. Since it is indubitable, it can serve as a pattern for other truths. Any proposition as clear and distinct as 'I think therefore I am' is equally to be trusted, on Descartes's view. Even empirical beliefs can be justified if they come to me as a result of the exercise of the senses I have been given by a god who does not deceive. And I can know that such a god exists because I can reason to that conclusion from the innate contents of my mind including my innate idea of God.

Various though the different types of foundationalism are, they share a central structural feature. For each such view there are only two kinds of beliefs. There are the fundamental, underived beliefs. There are also the less fundamental, derived or dependent beliefs supported by the fundamental beliefs. To be justified in believing one of the dependent or derived beliefs is to see how that belief is supported or generated by the fundamental true belief on which it rests.

Foundationalism of whatever sort has a picture of our knowledge as involving chains of justification. Derived knowledge rests on basic beliefs. Basic beliefs certify their own truth in some way and thus justify themselves. Thus, for foundationalism, if there is anything at all that is rightly called 'knowledge' it must be either foundational itself or based on some foundational knowledge. So the existence of any knowledge at all implies the existence of basic foundational knowledge. This gives us what is sometimes called the 'infinite regress argument' for foundationalism:

- If every justified belief were justified by inferring it from some other justified belief there would have to be an infinite regress (an unending succession) of justifications.
- But an infinite regress is impossible.
- So, if there is any knowledge at all there must be some beliefs that are self-justifying or foundational.

This suggests the two main criticisms which have been levelled at foundationalist theories of knowledge. First, there is the question of whether the foundationalist can give a convincing account of the nature of the inferential connection or dependence that he claims exists between basic and derived beliefs. Second, there is the question of how the foundationalist's basic beliefs manage to be intrinsically credible or self-certifying in the strong sense that the foundationalist needs.

Coherence

The second difficult question just raised is particularly difficult for the foundationalist who regards reports of a subject's sense data or sensory experiences as the paradigm foundational propositions or basic beliefs. This is the question of how there can be intrinsically credible, self-certifying beliefs or propositions. For sense data reports such as 'I see a red patch' or 'This feels smooth to me' do not pretend to be **self-evident truths**.

The difference between the self-evident and the obvious

A self-evident truth, as philosophers use this term, is one that is true in virtue of logic. It could not fail to be true. In order to know that it is true all you need do is understand what it is saying. This means that the set of self-evident truths does not coincide with the set of obvious truths. For example, if you are standing unsheltered in open country in the middle of a force nine gale it will be obvious that it is windy. But if you then say 'It is windy' you are not uttering a proposition whose truth is guaranteed by logic. That proposition is a **contingent truth**. That it is windy is not a logical necessity – the weather could easily have been different. How it *is* is not how it logically *had to be*. It is obvious, but not self-evident, that it is windy.

Now consider an example invented by Quine and Ullian (Quine and Ullian 1970: 22–3). (They use the term 'demonstrable' as I use 'self-evident'.)

'If you help none who help themselves you do not help yourself.'

That this proposition is true is hardly obvious. Indeed it isn't even obvious what it means. Understanding it may take several readings. When you do succeed in working out what it is saying, however, you should see that it cannot fail to be true. It is self-evident in that to understand it is to see its logical necessity.

Sense data reports (sometimes called 'observation statements') may sometimes be obvious but they are not self-evident. The immediacy they possess is that of individual subjective experience. Their claims to be self-certifying or intrinsically credible rest on that immediacy together with their simplicity. Those who suggest them as candidates to be beliefs that are basic or foundational for all the rest of our knowledge are asking, 'How could I be wrong to trust a belief as unmediated and simple as "I see a red patch" or "This seems smooth to me"?'

Another way of expressing this question is 'How could I be mistaken in simply reporting how things seem to me?' As we shall see, radical sceptics find it all too easy to raise doubts about supposedly basic beliefs that are not self-evident and rely – as all reports of appearances do – only on the authority of introspection.

Those epistemologists who are worried about the capacity of foundationalism to give a credible account of the basis and structure of our knowledge often turn to coherence as either an additional or an alternative way of providing justification for our beliefs. The sort of coherence they have in mind is the coherence beliefs can have with one another. It seems a reasonable suggestion that our beliefs do not stand or fall in isolation. Foundationalism is on the right track in seeing beliefs as related to one another in a system.

But it is wrong to think we must view this system as linear and one-directional. The foundationalist regards every justified belief as either justified by another, which is in turn justified by a further belief, etc., or as being itself an intrinsically credible point at which a chain of justification can terminate.

In contrast, the coherentist defines justification, not in terms of chains of dependency, but in terms of relations of mutual support. At any given time we have many beliefs that we accept as true. Accepting a new belief is a matter of examining the 'fit' between the new proposition and those already accepted as true. We are justified in accepting a new belief that coheres with our existing belief set. A net with many interconnections or an ecosystem with many different niches – either of these gives a better analogy in terms of which to understand our belief sets than does the image of a number of mutually independent chains.

But what does coherence actually amount to? Obviously propositions that contradict one another are not coherent with one another. But coherentists mean something much richer by their notion of coherence than 'bare absence of contradiction'. Coherent beliefs are not merely ones that are not in head-on conflict. They lend each other support in a mutually reinforcing system. A foundationalist might, like Descartes, take seriously the idea of building up a system of justified beliefs one element at a time, perhaps even starting with a single proposition. But a coherentist views a belief system as a large set of beliefs that must be acquired, if not all at once, then at least largely at one time.

What criticisms challenge the coherentist view of justification? I have already raised one of the main difficulties: the difficulty of specifying in full detail and with precision exactly what the coherence relation consists in.

A second difficulty is the worry that a complete belief system might have a serious competitor. It seems easy to imagine the following. There are two distinct sets of mutually coherent beliefs, which are equally extensive and systematic. Each seems to accommodate basic observation reports equally well but they differ crucially. The nature of the world of which one system of beliefs purports to give us knowledge is very different from the world pictured by the other.

If coherence is the sole criterion of a justified belief surely each belief in each of the imagined rival systems is equally justified and has an equal chance of giving us truth about the world. Yet there is only one world and surely we are not justified in having contradictory beliefs about it?

This is perhaps why many reject such strong coherentism in favour of a weaker coherentism. This is one that looks to sense perception, memory, even some kinds of intuition as additional sources of justification complementary to that afforded by coherence.

 ## QUESTIONS FOR DISCUSSION

What is a coherence theory of justification? What are its strengths and weaknesses?

The tripartite definition of knowledge

So far I have been assuming that knowledge and highly justified belief go together. It is time to examine that assumption in some detail. Traditionally, propositional knowledge (which is the only kind in question in this chapter) has been defined as justified true belief. The three elements must all be present if a proposition *p* which the subject claims to know is to be judged a genuine piece of knowledge for that subject.

Belief is required only in the sense that the subject would assent to *p* if asked. The nervous examinee mentioned above would count as believing her answers because they were the ones she wrote, however un-confidently, in response to those questions.

Truth must be present in all but the most peripheral examples. In fact, it takes considerable ingenuity to think of a case where one could know something which was not the case. After all, why seek knowledge unless we take it to give us insight into the way things actually are?

However, it might be worth considering briefly one such example. A schoolboy in ancient Greece who is asked to say where the gods live replies that they live on Mount Olympus. Arguably it is right to say that he *knows* the answer. It may be that we feel sure that no such gods ever existed or lived anywhere. Nonetheless the boy had knowledge in that he was fully justified in his belief and got the answer right according to the standards then prevailing.

In general, however, knowledge involves truth and belief. But clearly, justification carries most of the weight in the tripartite definition of knowledge. This is one reason why there are theories of knowledge corresponding to each of the broad types of justification we have looked at. There are reliabilists, foundationalists and coherentists about knowledge as there are about belief.

The tripartite definition has held sway ever since Plato and deservedly so. Truth, belief and justification are all crucial features of knowledge. Equally important, but perhaps less attended to, however, are the relations that hold between these three features for any particular would-be knower. This last point came sharply into focus in 1963 when Edmund Gettier published his celebrated challenge to the tripartite definition in an article called 'Is justified true belief knowledge?'

Gettier's position, argued for by the use of counter-examples, is that a given subject might be justified in believing a true proposition and still fail to know that proposition. The subject might fail to have knowledge because his believing the true proposition in question might be an accident rather than a result of the justification he possesses. Gettier's challenge could be expressed as the view that truth, belief and justification, while they are all **necessary** for knowledge, are not jointly **sufficient**. Some other condition or conditions must be added to the definition of knowledge.

The simpler of Gettier's examples goes roughly as follows. Imagine a short-listed candidate for a job (Mr Smith) who overhears the president of the company say that one of the other candidates (Mr Jones) will be hired. Waiting to be interviewed, Smith watches Jones count his change at the drinks machine. Gloomily he reasons, 'Jones is going to get the job and Jones has ten coins in his pocket. Therefore the successful candidate has ten coins in his pocket.'

Does he know that the successful candidate has ten coins in his pocket? As it happens, the belief he has is true but only because he himself, surprisingly, is offered the job and, unknown to him, he has ten coins, uncounted, in his own pocket. His belief in the proposition that the successful candidate has ten coins in his pocket is a justified belief since he deduced it validly from two propositions he was justified in believing. There is nothing wrong with his reasoning. But it seems clear that he does not have knowledge of that proposition, justified and true though his belief is.

Since Gettier's famous challenge, epistemologists have laboured to repair or amend the tripartite definition. Some have suggested that *justification* needs more, ever more subtle, criteria and conditions. Others have suggested further conditions to add to the traditional three. Others still, as mentioned above, have said that the *right* relation must exist between the belief's truth and the subject's belief.

So it has been said that there is knowledge only when the truth of the belief in question is causally responsible for the subject's believing it. If the truth of *p* is not at least part of the explanation of *why* I believe *p* then my belief in *p* is not knowledge. Later in this chapter we will see how attempts to meet Gettier counter-examples like the one above have merged with many recent attempts to disarm radical scepticism.

 # QUESTION FOR DISCUSSION

What further condition or conditions could be added to truth, belief and justification to make a satisfactory definition of knowledge?

Related examination question

(Part c) Assess the view that justified true belief is *not* the same as knowledge. *(24 marks) (2002)*

● KNOWLEDGE AND SCEPTICISM

A radical sceptic might object at this point that most of the discussion of justification and knowledge so far has been a waste of time and energy. In the opinion of the most radical sort of sceptic there is no belief that is sufficiently justified to count as knowledge. This is because he is not prepared to call any proposition *that can be doubted* knowledge. And he is convinced that there are no propositions that cannot be called into doubt.

Philosophical doubt

Even the sorts of axioms and basic premises that rationalist foundationalists wish to start from are vulnerable to the doubt which this severest of philosophical sceptics employs. For this kind of doubt is hyperbolic (i.e. extremely exaggerated) doubt. Descartes called such doubt, when he made use of it in the *Meditations*, 'metaphysical doubt', meaning that it went beyond mere ordinary feelings of uncertainty or psychological doubt. This kind of doubt is a tool designed to test our knowledge to the limit. It involves suspending judgement on anything that it is logically possible to suspend judgement about.

Famously, Descartes concluded that his *cogito ergo* sum was proof against this metaphysical doubt, so he did not rest in scepticism. But some sceptics find it possible to suspend judgement even here. They would say that experience by itself does not give knowledge. All knowledge involves the application of concepts and background information to experience. The best-entrenched concept may turn out to be vulnerable to conceptual revision.

'Witches', 'demons', the names of Greek gods, were once thought to be concepts and referring expressions in good standing. Now they are thought to have failed ever to refer to anything real. Perhaps the same could happen even to concepts like that of a thinker or a subject of experience.

Perhaps easier to grasp, or at least to agree with, is the caution of the philosophical sceptic whose philosophical doubt falls on the observation reports talked about in the section on foundationalism above. For surely it is true that I could always be mistaken in thinking I am seeing something red or feeling something smooth?

If, like this sort of sceptic, we refuse the title of knowledge to anything vulnerable to this kind of hyperbolic doubt there will be very few, if any, beliefs we are entitled to call knowledge.

Global scepticism

There are philosophers who think, on just such grounds, that there is no such thing as knowledge. One title for this view is **global scepticism**. The global sceptic holds that no belief is immune to this sort of corrosive doubt, that no belief is sufficiently justified to count as knowledge.

It is sometimes thought that the global sceptic can be easily refuted. The sceptic who claimed to *know* that there was no such thing as knowledge would be defeated out of his own mouth. He would be claiming knowledge that there is no knowledge.

However, global scepticism is not so easily dealt with. Its challenge is, as in Descartes's case, mainly aimed at those who wish to defend the view that some kinds of knowledge exist. Its purpose is to make defenders of knowledge produce successful *arguments* for their position.

So the global sceptic can simply deny that there is any view or belief that lies outside the reach of doubt – including his own view that there is no knowledge. Now the burden of proof falls on the anti-sceptic. How is the anti-sceptic to respond? One minimal move I can make is to argue that it is not logically possible that all my beliefs be false or mistaken together. Some of the propositions I believe and take myself to be justified in believing must be true and thus known by me even if I do not know which ones.

An argument against one kind of global scepticism

To see that it is not logically possible for all your beliefs to be mistaken together, consider a belief that seems highly justified. For anyone reading this, the belief 'I am not at the North Pole' seems likely to be true and believed on excellent grounds. Now imagine with the sceptic that this belief of yours is mistaken, i.e. not true. If it is not true then that implies that it *is* true that you are at the North Pole.

But consider your belief that you are not at the South Pole. If this second belief is mistaken, that implies that it *is* true that you are at the South Pole.

Now put your two original beliefs together. You believe that you are not at the North Pole and that you are not at the South Pole. At least one of these beliefs must be true. There is no way for them *both* to be false simultaneously since there is no way you could be at both Poles at the same time. (Of course they can both be *true* together!)

So, if global scepticism is the view that all my beliefs might be false together, global scepticism is wrong.

Unfortunately for the anti-sceptic there is another version of global scepticism that is more robust. It might be agreed that all my beliefs cannot be false together but this hardly matters since I can never know which among any set of beliefs are the ones that are actually true. Of any single one of my beliefs I cannot know that it is correct. So each of my beliefs in turn might be mistaken and can be doubted even if all of them together cannot be. And, thus, I do not have knowledge of any one of them.

Related examination question

(Part a) Briefly explain what is meant by global (or total) scepticism. *(6 marks)* *(2003)*

QUESTION FOR DISCUSSION

Should the fact that I can doubt any empirical proposition anyone cares to mention make me despair of ever having knowledge of matters of fact?

Externalism and internalism about knowledge

Some epistemologists would take the view at this point that the sceptic's position is not as threatening as might at first be thought. What is called an **externalist** about knowledge would say that it is not necessary in order to have knowledge that the knower in question know that he knows. Knowledge is not a matter of the state of mind of the knower. It is a matter of the conditions for knowledge obtaining. It is a matter of the knower being justified in the right way in believing something true.

For the externalist, as long as the subject is related in the right way to the belief whose truth he is convinced of, and to the circumstances and relations that supply the justification of his belief, that is enough for knowledge. Conditions external to the knower – or at least independent of his awareness of their holding – make it true that a particular subject's particular belief on a particular occasion is knowledge. If it is justified, non-accidentally true belief, it is knowledge. This is so whether the knower knows that he knows or not.

Unsurprisingly the contrasting view about knowledge labelled **internalism** is more threatened by the kind of global scepticism we have been examining. For the internalist, knowledge consists of awareness that the conditions for knowledge are met in the given case. On this view a subject *S* knows *p* only if

- *p* is true
- *S* believes that p
- *S* is justified in believing *p*, and
- *there is no element of luck or accident in S's believing p on the basis of the justification he knows himself to have.*

At this point it becomes apparent that the sceptic's ground has been vastly strengthened by Gettier's challenge. For on reflection we can see that an element of luck or accident could be involved in practically every conceivable example of a piece of knowledge that we might think we possess. Two examples should suffice to clarify this point:

First, suppose I am looking at a vase on the table and claim to know the truth of the proposition (*p*), 'There is a vase on the table', based on my perception. Ordinarily we would take clear visual perception of something under standard conditions to justify a perceptual claim. So *p* might seem the most uncontroversial piece of knowledge I could claim to have.

However, a sceptic could argue that – even if he grants the truth of *p* – my belief in it does not amount to knowledge despite my very good sensory evidence. For I have not ruled out the possibility that what I am seeing is a cunning hologram of a vase located just in front of (and obscuring my view of) the vase that is actually there. I have not defeated the possibility that my justified belief in my true proposition is mere accident. So I do not have knowledge.

Here is a second example. After days lost in the desert without water you have become blinded by the glare and are also beginning to hallucinate. You see an oasis in the distance and think 'At last, there is water.' Do you know that there is water there? Even if it is true that there is water exactly where you think you see it, it could be that you are right simply by freak accident. The possibility that you are just a lucky blind hallucinator defeats your claim to know the true justified belief that you possess.

For the internalist, knowledge requires not just *actually* non-accidental justified true belief. It requires non-accidental justified true belief *that is not defeated* by the possibility of any such contrived circumstances as those described in the two examples. Since the number of such contrived possible defeating circumstances is limited only by the very generous bounds of human imagination, knowledge for the internalist looks increasingly beyond everyone's reach.

 # QUESTIONS FOR DISCUSSION

Does externalism provide a safe route out of radical scepticism? Could one be an internalist and still escape scepticism?

The argument from illusion

The two examples just given and the sceptical consequences they are designed to support are in a way comparatively novel and exotic. Remember that they are aimed only at propositions conceded by the sceptic to be *true* and *highly justified* for the subject who believes them. Yet the sceptic has his reasons for thinking they nonetheless fail to be knowledge.

But there are a number of familiar sceptical arguments aiming to capitalise on our sense of our own imperfect capacity to acquire genuine knowledge. They aim to make us doubt by comparing our present circumstances to ones in which we have turned out to be mistaken in the past although we then thought ourselves justified. This section will explain the so-called 'argument from illusion'. In the next two sections we will look at arguments to do with dreaming and the possibility of deception.

The argument from illusion is often used by sceptics about our knowledge of the **external world** (more on this shortly). It is designed specifically to undermine our trust in our senses. This argument can be broken down into three main steps. First the sceptic asks 'What is it of which I am immediately aware in sense experience?' He wants to get me to agree that the immediate objects of perception are what philosophers call 'sense data'. The Latin word 'data' (or 'datum' in the singular) means 'given'.

A sense datum is thus a simple piece of sensory given, for example a patch of red colour I see is a visual sense datum and a sweet sound I hear is an auditory sense datum. It seems difficult to resist the claim that what we are immediately aware of in sense perception are our sense data. The term was coined as a general label for exactly that.

Moreover, think of all the ways in which I could be wrong about my present experience. There are lots of illusions or misapprehensions I could be under. For example:

- A large jumbo jet in the distance looks small.
- If my hand is cold then water that is only lukewarm may feel hot to me.
- If the conditions, for example the lighting, were non-standard I might see, say, a purple object as black.
- If I am in an unusual condition – dehydrated, drugged, ill – everything may seem blurry to me.
- If I experience a mirage or other hallucination or an after-image I may have a rich array of sense data that have no external cause at all.

Yet surely, in all these cases, *something* really has the sensory features I wrongly attribute to the world. Something is really small, hot, black, blurry or whatever. The sceptic argues that in all these cases there must be sense data that are distinct from both the subject and the things in the world. That is, there must be sense data to have the sensory features the world only seems to have.

If I agree that I am aware of sense data in cases of illusion or misperception, then the sceptic will move to the second step in his argument. This consists in pointing out that it is the best policy, all other things being equal, to give a single account of all relevantly similar phenomena. We have agreed that cases of *mis*perception are best accounted for in terms of sense data mediating between the perceiver and the world. We should therefore agree that sense data mediate between perceiver and world in *all* cases of perception, even ones where there is no mistake. The latter are called **veridical perceptions**, meaning 'truth-telling ones' or 'ones that tend to lead the perceiver to make a correct judgement about the nature of the thing perceived'.

The third and final step in the argument from illusion is as follows. We have agreed that sense perception always consists in sense data mediating between a perceiver and the world. These sense data are usually seen as a special sort of mental entities. But whatever their metaphysical status they are intermediaries. Their role is to represent the character of the things in the world outside the subject. And any intermediary can be either a faithful representative or a misleading one.

We know from cases of illusion and misapprehension that sense data sometimes mislead. Perhaps most sense data are veridical but how can we ever know? In the nature of the case, there is no position from which we can see (or otherwise sense) whether our sense data match the world or not. There is no perspective from which we can see whether or not they are faithful representatives.

This is because we must always use our senses in perception and they in turn always employ sense data. They seem (or so the sceptic would have us believe) to make a kind of veil which falls between us and the world, preventing us from telling the nature of the world. For all we know, occasionally or even all the time, there could be nothing beyond this **veil of perception**. Our sense data might be all there is.

 ## QUESTIONS FOR DISCUSSION

What is the argument from illusion? What do sceptics take it to prove? Can it be defeated?

Dreaming

Many philosophers, famously including Descartes, have raised a sceptical puzzle regarding dreaming. This puzzle could be neatly put in terms of the point just reached in the previous section, the point that our sense data could, for all we know, be all there is.

We have all had the experience of waking from a dream to discover that something we thought we were seeing, hearing or otherwise sensing was not really there. While we were asleep our experience was exactly as if we were seeing or hearing whatever it was. But now we have woken up to find that we were in a sense deluded.

The sceptic reminds us of this universal experience of mistaking the non-veridical seemings or sense data of dreams for veridical ones. Then he asks how I can ever be sure I am not now dreaming so that any sense data I may be experiencing are just the deceptive sense data of dreams.

Now we all know the difference between dreams and reality. The problem is that at any given point we have no test that we can apply to tell whether our present experience is a dream. For example, a dreamer can dream that she is pinching herself and thus establishing that she is awake. In fact, a dreamer can dream that he is applying *any* test of wakefulness that might be devised.

So the sceptic seems to have a good case for saying that no one ever knows anything on the evidence of his or her senses. My sense data might always be the products of dreaming rather than genuine waking experience.

Deception

The argument from deception is another sceptical hypothesis which works in much the same way as the previous two. But, according to Descartes's version at least, it calls into doubt not just knowledge based on sensory reports but also the necessary truths of logic and mathematics. This is the hypothesis that for all I know someone may be deceiving me into believing even propositions that I think myself most justified in believing.

Descartes invented the notion of an arch-deceiver: an omnipotent and malign being bent on deceiving me in as many of my beliefs as possible. So, for example, I may think I am seeing some very familiar material object in good light when I am healthy and my eyes are in good working order. But it is logically possible that all the while the object does not exist and I am just being tricked into thinking I am seeing it. Perhaps *nothing* material exists and I am just an immaterial mind subject to a massive, systematic deception.

It must be said that Descartes does not believe that there is such an arch-deceiver. God would not allow such a being to exist. However, as far as what is logically possible goes, it does seem that we can never rule out *a priori* that any of our beliefs might be being caused, not by its apparent cause, but by trickery. So this sceptical argument too seems to give the radical sceptic's position a powerful support.

Recently, radical sceptics have employed a sceptical device, the 'brain in a vat hypothesis', which has much in common with Descartes's arch-deceiver. The sceptic asks anyone who thinks he can know about his surroundings how he knows that he is not a brain which has been removed from its skull and body by a mad scientist, put into a vat of life-preserving chemicals and hooked up to a giant computer which feeds it sense data exactly as if it were still connected to working eyes, ears, taste buds, etc. A brain in a vat would be massively deluded about its real environment. It would believe, quite wrongly, that it was seeing, hearing and otherwise sensing the world through a complete living human body. It would not know it was just the comparatively small mass of material making up a human brain.

 ## QUESTION FOR DISCUSSION

Is there any way to establish that you are not a brain in a vat who is massively deluded about the world it seems to you that you are experiencing?

● KNOWLEDGE AND THE EXTERNAL WORLD

In their most powerful forms the sceptical arguments discussed in the previous three subsections exploit the view that we do not experience the external world immediately. The proponent of the argument from illusion explicitly argues that sense perception always involves intermediaries or sense data which represent the world to the perceiver. The other two arguments presume that private experiences are independent of what they are experiences *of*, so that the two might fail to match. But must we concede that we always experience the world indirectly, through sense data?

Realism

What philosophers of perception sometimes call 'naive realism' is the view that, contrary to what the sceptic thinks, we do perceive ordinary objects as they are, immediately and directly and without sense data or any element of inference or interpretation. The word 'naive' is not a criticism. It is there to signify that this view is held by the ordinary person in the street who has never engaged in philosophical reflection about perceptual knowledge. Naive realism is offered as the view of common sense.

A philosopher who adopts naive realism is saying that the pre-philosophical view is right, or at least has more to be said for it than the sort of view we have been looking at above. And it certainly does seem to answer to common sense in its claim that, at least in a large percentage of cases, contact with the world through the senses does *feel* as if it is direct and unmediated.

Certainly there seems something wrong with the 'veil of perception' view that regards sense data as screens or blindfolds that lie between the perceiver and the world. For a start it should be noted that there are different kinds and degrees of immediacy and also different ways in which an intermediary or representative can perform its function.

Think of the difference between attending a cup final yourself and being told about it by a lucky spectator. The first-hand experience has much more of one type of immediacy.

On the other hand, think of the difference between seeing a match from near the back of the stands and watching it on television. The televised match comes to you through your television set and numerous technical intermediaries – different camera angles, close up lenses, slow-motion replays and so forth. Yet these very interventions and devices make the experience more immediate. Certainly they ensure that you have more accurate knowledge of what happened than does the distant spectator.

The same could be said for the presence of my reading glasses, without which knowledge of the words I am reading would be impossible. There is no reason to feel that, if sense data are in fact part of the process of sense perception, they by their very existence make knowledge of the external world either doubtful or impossible. In fact the existence of these intermediaries could be regarded as essential.

It is a sense of the rightness of this last point that accounts for the existence of another realist view called 'representative realism'. This is, in fact, the view of sense perception as always involving sense data that the argument from illusion promotes. But the representative realist says that the sceptic is wrong. Sense perception can and does give us knowledge of the external world. One version of representative realism argues that sense perception gives me knowledge of an external object if my sense data representing that object are *caused, in the right sort of way, by the object in question.*

For example, suppose the following things are true. Your sense data are exactly as if you are seeing a cat on the mat. Also it is the case, in a perfectly straightforward way, that the cat on the mat is the cause of your having those very sense data. Light reflected off the cat travels to your eye and affects the optic nerve sending appropriate messages to your brain. In this situation the representative realist just mentioned would hold that it is right to say that you know the cat is on the mat.

However, think again of the example given above of seeing a vase on the table. It could be that the hologram that is in fact seen was only created at that exact spot in order to trick the viewer into wrongly thinking she knew of the existence of a vase on the table when she did not. In that case, in a way, the real vase *is* part of the cause of the perceiver's sense data. It is part of the causal chain running from the intentions in the trickster's mind through the setting up of just that hologram to the production of the deceptive sense data in the perceiver's mind.

We know in this case, as was said earlier, that the perceiver does *not* know the vase is there and thus that the causal chain here is deviant. But how, in general, are deviant causal chains to be recognised as such? We seem to need a method for identifying them that is independent of our knowledge of which causal chains do, and which do not, produce genuine knowledge. But there seems to be no such independent method. So representative realism fails unless such a method can be found.

Related examination questions

(Part a) Identify *two* differences between naive realism and representative realism. *(6 marks) (2003)*

(Part b) Explain and illustrate *one* criticism of naive realism. *(15 marks) (2003)*

(Part c) Assess representative realism. *(24 marks) (2003)*

Idealism

External world scepticism is sometimes expressed very briefly as the view that we have no guarantee that appearance and reality coincide. Without such a guarantee we have no knowledge of the world. All we can ever know are appearances. We never get beyond our sense data.

Berkeley is one philosopher whose response to the threat posed by such scepticism is to deny that there is a distinction between appearance and reality. If reality simply consists of appearances and nothing else, we can know that things are exactly as our senses tell us they are. This is to make the deliverances of the senses immune to sceptical challenge by becoming what philosophers call an idealist.

It is important to try to keep clear what the metaphysical position known as idealism is (as opposed to its main rival, **materialism**). It is also important to distinguish realism about the external world from its opposite, anti-realism.

Idealism is the theory that reality consists solely of ideas and the minds in which they exist. Materialism is the view that the fundamental character of reality is material (i.e. that things occupy space and are mind-independent). For the idealist there are no mind-independent things. For the materialist, whatever the nature of mind, there are also material things which would exist even if all the minds went out of existence.

Realism is the theory that things really are, in general, as they seem. They would be that way whether or not any perceiver came along to perceive them as being that way. Naive realism and representative realism agree in thinking that sense perception acquaints us with a reality whose nature does not depend on our interpretation or perception of it, i.e. an external world.

As we shall see, idealism is also a realist theory. For Berkeley, the ideas constituting what we think of as the objective physical world do not depend on any human mind or interpretation for their existence or nature. They are just as real as matter is for the naive realist or the representative realist. Which is to say that for any human subject – as far as Berkeley is concerned – the real objects with which he is acquainted by sense experience are not products of his imagination. They are *idea-l* (of the nature of ideas) but they are not brought into existence by his mind. Instead they depend for their existence on the mind of God.

Anti-realism in this context is the view that there is no fact of the matter about what the perceptible world is like. Rather the world is how we have, collectively, decided to interpret it as being. Berkeley's idealism is definitely not anti-realist in this sense.

It is easy to sympathise with Berkeley's motivation for his idealism. We have seen that the radical sceptic has a battery of arguments which seem to prove it possible that even substantial numbers of sensory reports about the appearances of things do not add up to knowledge of the existence and nature of the external world. Berkeley rightly accuses his predecessors, like Locke, of taking liberties in assuming that their empirical evidence is sufficient to entitle them to infer the existence and nature of material objects when that evidence consists only of appearances.

The troubles afflicting idealism are very numerous, however, and very difficult to overcome. Here we can mention only a few of the most serious. One is that Berkeley does not seem to have a way of accommodating in his theory the notion of a genuinely public world. If the apple in my hand consists of the ideas or sense data I experience when I look at, smell, touch and feel it, how can you see exactly the same apple or receive it from my hand?

Also, if everything in the physical world consists of God's ideas, what happened at creation? Presumably God had to make his ideas different in some way from the ideas which he had of the as-yet-uncreated world before he brought it into existence. He had to turn 'mere' ideas in his mind into ideas that would be *perceptible* by the as-yet-uncreated minds of humans.

 ## QUESTION FOR DISCUSSION

How can Berkeley be both an idealist and a realist – are these two notions not opposites?

Related examination questions

(Part a) Identify *two* differences between idealism and representative realism. *(6 marks) (2001)*

(Part c) Assess the view that only minds and their ideas exist. *(24 marks) (2001)*

Phenomenalism

Phenomenalism is the theory that all propositions about the material world can be translated without remainder into propositions about actual or possible sense experiences. Another way to put this is to say that all external-world propositions can be inferred from or analysed into propositions about appearances.

If phenomenalism were correct then the problem of external-world scepticism would seem to be solved without going quite the length of adopting idealism. Phenomenalism does not say that material things consist of ideas, perceptions or sense experiences. It says that material things consist of whatever it takes to be capable of being sensed, to be able to be the objects of sensory experience.

So adequate experience of the right sorts of sense data should be enough to establish the existence and nature of an object in the external world able to be responsible for a subject's perceiving such a thing.

But how many and which exact sense data would count as adequate? Once again it seems that the sceptic is able to counter the anti-sceptical suggestion. For no number of sense-data statements (propositions about actual sense experiences or hypothetical statements about possible perceptions) would together be enough to *entail* the conclusion that a material object of a certain kind exists. There is no logical contradiction between any number of reports along the lines of 'I am experiencing something red and round and smooth and shiny and tomato-shaped' (said by numerous people) and the proposition 'There is no tomato on the table.'

It might take ingenuity to explain how so many observers could be deluded but there is not and should not be thought to be any entailment between statements about appearances and statements about how things actually are. For if there were, then illusions and delusions would be logically impossible. And we know from experience that this is not so.

Related examination question

(Part c) Assess phenomenalism. *(24 marks) (2002)*

REFERENCES

Ayer, A. J. (1956) *The Problem of Knowledge*, Harmondsworth: Penguin.
Quine, W. V. O. and Ullian, J. S. (1970) *The Web of Belief*, New York: Random House.

RECOMMENDED READING

● Audi, R. (1998) *Epistemology: A Contemporary Introduction to the Theory of Knowledge* (London: Routledge) is a very accessible, clear, introductory text.

● Ayer, A. J. *The Problem of Knowledge* and Russell, B. *The Problems of Philosophy* are both classics of twentieth-century philosophical writing about many of the central problems of epistemology. Both are written in a clear, engaging style.

● Baggini, J. and Fosl, P. (2003) *The Philosopher's Toolkit* (Oxford: Blackwell) is a very good compendium of clear explanations of concepts and arguments, which any student of philosophy new or old would find useful.

● Dancy, J. and Sosa, E. (eds) (1997) *A Companion to Epistemology* (Oxford: Blackwell) is an excellent encyclopaedic reference work with an astonishing amount of useful material about different aspects of the subject in one volume.

● Lehrer, K. (1990) *Theory of Knowledge* (London: Routledge) is another good introduction, which should be accessible to readers who are less familiar with the theory of knowledge.

● Williams, M. (2001) *Problems of Knowledge* (Oxford: Oxford University Press) is an excellent introduction, if a bit less easy than Audi.

GLOSSARY

a posteriori **knowledge** – Knowledge which cannot be known to be true without some help or support from experience.

a priori **knowledge** – Knowledge which requires no confirmation from experience and, indeed, *could not* be proved or confirmed by observation. Many, though not all, necessary truths are knowable *a priori*, for example, '*A* is *A*'.

belief – Any fact of the matter or proposition, whether trivial or serious, that might be held to be true.

contingent truth – One that might have been otherwise. For example, it is a contingent truth that it is sunny today; the weather could easily have been otherwise.

empiricism – In its most extreme form this is the view that all knowledge is ultimately derived from or consists in truths obtained from experience alone.

epistemology – An alternative name for the Theory of Knowledge, i.e. the branch of philosophy that studies what we can know and how we know it.

external world – The world outside my own mind about which my bodily senses furnish me with information. This may be held to include my own body since my senses give me sense data about my body as well as about my mind's wider environment.

externalism and internalism about knowledge – The externalist believes that someone might meet all the conditions necessary for possession of knowledge without realising that this was the case, without knowing that he knows. As long as the subject is justified in the right way in believing something true he is rightly said to have knowledge. The internalist will say, however, that the true knower knows that all the conditions for knowledge have been met. This means that he knows that any element of 'getting hold of the truth by accident' has been defeated in this case. Arguably, however, the elimination of all possibility of accident from any given putative case of knowledge is impossible.

foundationalism – The view that knowledge forms a system that is like a building resting on a foundation. The foundational beliefs support themselves, they are self-justifying. They do not need – nor could they have – further justification. All other beliefs are derived from, and receive their justification from, the foundational beliefs.

global scepticism – The global sceptic holds that no belief is immune to the all-corrosive doubt that Descartes called 'metaphysical' doubt. Thus, on this view, no belief is sufficiently justified to count as knowledge.

idealism – The theory that reality consists solely of ideas and the minds in which they exist. For the idealist there are no mind-independent things. In contrast, the materialist believes that, whatever the nature of mind, there are also material things which would exist even if all the minds went out of existence.

incorrigible propositions – If there are any such, they are ones that are literally 'uncorrectable', beyond the reach of correction. A typical example offered is 'That appears red to me.' It is difficult to see how such a report of immediate experience could be mistaken, thus *capable* of being corrected.

inductive reasoning – That form of reasoning or inference that argues that if all previously observed *A*s have been *B*s, and no previously observed *A*s have failed to be *B*s, future *A*s are likely to be *B*s as well.

materialism – The view that the fundamental character of reality is material (i.e. whatever basic things there are occupy space and are mind-independent). For the materialist, material things could exist even in the absence of all minds.

necessary and sufficient conditions – Necessary conditions of *p* are ones without which *p* would not occur. Sufficient conditions of *p* are ones that are enough to produce *p*. All of a thing's necessary conditions must obtain if it is to exist but a *single* sufficient condition guarantees that what it is sufficient for obtains.

necessary truths – These are ones that could not – logically could not – fail to be true. To understand such a truth is to see that it could not fail to be the case.

phenomenalism – The theory that all propositions about the material world can be translated without remainder into propositions about actual or possible sense experiences. For example, the proposition 'There is a cat on the mat' says no more than 'If anyone were to look at the mat (or feel it, etc.) he or she would have sense experiences of seeing (feeling) a cat.'

rationalism – In its most extreme form this is the view that all knowledge is ultimately derived from or depends upon truths obtained by the employment of unaided reason alone.

self-evident truths – A self-evident truth is one that is true in virtue of logic. It could not fail to be true. In order to know that it is true all you need do is understand what it is saying. However, this means that the set of self-evident truths does not coincide with the set of obvious truths. A proposition might be obviously true (like 'It's raining' said in a downpour) but not self-evident (it is contingent, not necessary). Alternatively, a proposition might be self-evident (to understand it is to see its logical necessity) but not obvious (to someone who had not worked out what it meant).

sense data – The basic bits of experience given to the subject in sense perception (the singular is 'a single sense datum').

truth value – The truth value of a proposition *p* is the answer to the question 'Is *p* true?' If the answer is 'Yes, *p* is true' then *p*'s truth value is 'true'. If *p* is false then its truth value is 'false'.

veil of perception – A metaphorical barrier (veil) that perceptions and sense data themselves are said to constitute between a perceiver and the object of perception so that the perceiver may make false judgements about what she perceives.

veridical perceptions and sensations – Ones that 'tell the truth' about the things they are perceptions or sensations *of*. Veridical perceptions make me disposed to judge correctly about the world. In contrast, non-veridical perceptions and sensations are misleading.

2

moral philosophy

UNIT 2   Michael Lacewing

KEY CONCEPTS ◗

- good
- bad
- right
- wrong
- practical ethics
- normative ethics
- meta-ethics
- utilitarianism
- happiness
- deontology
- duty
- virtue
- abortion
- euthanasia
- speciesism
- cognitivism
- moral realism
- intuitionism
- naturalism
- non-cognitivism
- emotivism
- prescriptivism
- relativism

● INTRODUCTION

Moral philosophy is the attempt to think critically about right and wrong, good and bad. There are three different ways we can think about these ideas.

First, we can think about whether a particular action or type of action is right or wrong. Is abortion right or wrong? Is euthanasia right or wrong? Is it right to treat other animals as food? This type of thinking is **practical ethics**.

How are we to find the answers to these types of questions? **Normative ethics**, the second way to think about right and wrong, good and bad, develops general theories about what is right and what is good, which we can use in practical cases. One such theory, **utilitarianism**, claims that the only thing that is good is happiness. Everything else that is good is only good because it contributes to happiness. It also claims that the right thing to do is whatever will bring about the most good, i.e. the most happiness. By contrast, **deontological** theories claim that some actions, e.g. murder, are just wrong, no matter how happy it might make people. It claims that what is right is not to be defined in terms of what is good. You have probably heard both these views expressed in conversation. A third view we will look at is **virtue theory**. This claims that the question 'What is a good person?' is more fundamental than the question 'What should I do?' If you knew what it was to be a good person, then you would know what a good person would do. A good person leads a good life. So in order to know what sort of person a good person is, we need to understand what a good life for people is.

The third way to think critically about right and wrong, good and bad, is **meta-ethics**. *Meta-* is a Greek word meaning 'above', 'beyond', or 'after'. In this case, meta-ethics is the study of the *very ideas* of right and wrong, good and bad, the concepts that ethics takes for granted. For example, if I say that abortion is wrong, am I making a statement that can be true or false in the same way that it is a true (or false) statement that you are holding this book in your hand? Or am I expressing a command, such as 'Do not commit abortion'? Or am I expressing a feeling, perhaps one that is shared with other people, but still just a feeling? Meta-ethics investigates whether terms like 'right' and 'wrong', 'good' and 'bad', correspond to facts about the world or whether they are simply expressions of human feeling.

Practical ethics is about what it is right or wrong to *do*, considering a particular type of action. Normative ethics provides *theories* about what is good or bad and what it is right or wrong to do in general. Meta-ethics is not about what to do at all; it is about the nature of the *concepts* 'right' and 'wrong', 'good' and 'bad', what they mean, and what their origin is.

A final note: throughout this chapter I talk about actions being right or wrong, good or bad. But of course, failing to act in a particular way can be just as good or bad as acting in a particular way. There are some actions that we should not fail to do, like feeding our children, and some actions we should never normally do, like murder. So whenever I talk of 'actions', I mean to cover 'omissions' as well.

● NORMATIVE ETHICS

Deontological views

Deontologists believe that what is right or wrong is a matter of **duty**. We have moral duties to do things that it is right to do and moral duties not to do things that it is wrong to do. So far this might sound obvious. But what is 'duty'?

Deontologists deny that whether something is right or wrong depends on its consequences (see 'One example, three theories' on p. 47). A good way to understand deontological views, therefore, is by looking at the importance they give to actions in their own right, independent of consequences. It is something about any particular action that makes it right or wrong *in itself*. How can we tell whether an action is right or wrong in itself?

Intuitionists believe that there are many things that can make an action right or wrong, and we have to use our moral intuition to tell what these are. We shall discuss intuitionism further in the section 'META-ETHICS: COGNITIVISM'. Other theories derive duties from reason or from the commands of God.

God and duty

One reason for believing that certain types of action are right or wrong in themselves is that God has commanded us to do or not to do them. In order to discover what is right and wrong, we need to discover what God has commanded. There are different ways that we might come to know what God commands. One way is through divine revelation: at some point, God has actually told somebody, and, very often, they have written it down as scripture. This is the model of the Ten Commandments. Each commandment tells us that a particular action is right or wrong ('Honour your parents', 'Do not commit adultery', and so on), and the tradition is that God revealed these moral laws to Moses.

Another way is through **natural law**. St Thomas Aquinas (1225–74) argued that we can discover what is right and wrong through nature: through the way the natural world is and through human nature, especially reason. For example, every action that we want to do, we want to do for some end or purpose, something that we find good about it (even if we are mistaken). It is natural, then, to desire what is good. This is part of natural law, that we seek what is good. Likewise, reason naturally seeks knowledge and truth, and when applied to actions, reason seeks harmony with other people. Our desires and our reason were created by God to seek what is good, and this is the way that we come to learn what God has commanded as right or wrong. This is not always easy, since this knowledge may require careful thought and wisdom or even further revelation from God.

One example, three theories

My friend has not done her homework on time, and in order to avoid getting into trouble, she has decided to stay at home, pretending that she is sick. She can get the homework done today and bring it tomorrow, and then no one will know that she didn't do it on time. She has asked me to lie for her, to tell the teacher that she is sick. Should I lie?

An act utilitarian might say that lying in this case is not wrong, because no one is hurt. In fact, it will save my friend from getting into trouble. If no other harm is done (let's suppose I'm a good liar and won't get caught), lying might not only be permissible, I would be wrong not to lie. But an act utilitarian could also say this doesn't take the longer-term consequences into account. This act might encourage both me and my friend to take lying too lightly, and we will lie in the future when it does have bad consequences. If this is true, I shouldn't lie.

A deontologist would say that we shouldn't look at the consequences of the lie, we should look at lying – the action – itself. If we have a moral duty not to lie, and deontologists normally argue we do, then we should not lie, even though the consequences of telling the truth may be more painful.

A virtue theorist would consider the virtues of honesty and of loyalty to one's friends. Someone who is honest does not lie over trivial matters. And loyalty to my friend means I have her good at heart; if I lie for her, am I encouraging her not to take responsibility for her choices? She will also miss a day of school. Perhaps I would be a better friend if I support her in coming to school and telling the truth.

Certain types of action, then, are in accordance with human nature and reason, and these are morally right. Other types of action are wrong, because they are not in accordance with human nature and reason. For example, Aquinas argues that lying goes against the nature of reason to seek the truth and that sexual practices that are not related to procreation go against the natural use of our reproductive organs.

Kant: duties are determined by reason

Immanuel Kant (1724–1804) argued that moral principles could be derived from practical reason (reasoning applied to practical matters) alone; no other standard, such as human nature or God's commands, is necessary. To understand his claim, we need to put some premises in place.

First, Kant believed that, as rational animals, we don't just 'do things', we make choices. Whenever we make a choice, we act on a **maxim**. Maxims are our personal principles that guide our choices, e.g. 'to have as much fun as possible', 'to marry only someone I truly love'. All our choices have some maxim or other behind them, which explains our reasons for that particular choice.

Second, morality is a set of 'laws' – rules, principles – that are the same for everyone and that apply to everyone. If this is true, it must be possible that everyone could act morally (even if it is very unlikely that they will).

Kant uses this idea to devise a clever test for whether acting on a particular maxim is right or wrong. Here's an example of how it works: Let us say that you want a gift to take to a party, but you can't afford it, so you steal it from the shop. What maxim have you acted on? Something like: 'If I can't afford something I want, I will steal it.' Kant says this can only be the right thing to do if everyone could do it, because it must be possible for everyone to do what is right. In his terms, 'Act only on that maxim through which you can at the same time will that it should become a universal law' (Kant 1991: 84).

If we could all just help ourselves to whatever we wanted, the idea of 'owning' things would disappear. But if I don't own something – because nobody owns anything – you can't really 'steal' it from me. You can only steal something if it isn't yours. Stealing assumes that people own things, and people can only own things if they don't all go around helping themselves whenever they want. So it is logically impossible for everyone to steal things just because they can't afford them. And so stealing the gift is wrong.

Kant called his test the 'Categorical Imperative'. An imperative is just a command. Morality commands us to act in certain ways. The command is categorical because we can't take it or leave it. It is not just morally wrong to disobey, Kant thought, it is also irrational. It must be possible for all rational animals to choose to behave rationally. So choosing to behave in a way that it is impossible for everyone to follow is irrational. So we must obey the Categorical Imperative because it is irrational not to.

So now we know what our duty is. It is our duty only to act on maxims that can be universalised.

It is very important to realise that Kant does *not* claim that an action (e.g. stealing) is wrong because we wouldn't like the consequences if everyone did it. His test is not whether we would like our personal maxim to be a universal law. His test is whether we could choose for our personal maxim to be a universal law. His test is about what it is possible to choose, not what we like to choose.

 # QUESTIONS FOR DISCUSSION

What is the Categorical Imperative? Why does Kant claim it is irrational to disobey the Categorical Imperative?

Now for Kant the idea of 'duty' applies not only to right actions, but also to a particular kind of motive. Much of the time we do things just because we want to; and most of these things it is also morally permissible to do. Since we are doing them just because we want to, there is nothing particularly praiseworthy about doing them. Kant argued that our actions are morally worthy *only* if we do them 'from a sense of duty', i.e. we do them because it is our duty to do them. Our motive is to comply with what it is our duty to do. Kant compares two shopkeepers who both give correct change. The first is honest because he is scared of being caught if he tries to cheat his customers. The second is honest because it is morally right to be honest. Both do what is morally right. But only the second, says Kant, deserves our praise.

Criticisms of Kant's theory

There have been many criticisms of Kant's theory. I shall consider just three popular ones here.

First, couldn't any action be justified on Kant's theory, as long as we phrase the maxim cleverly? In stealing the gift, I could claim that my maxim is 'To steal gifts from large shops and when there are seven letters in my name (Michael)'. Universalising this maxim, only people with seven letters in their name can steal only gifts and only from large shops. The case would apply so rarely that there would be no general breakdown in the concept of private property. So it would be perfectly possible for this law to apply to everyone. Kant's response is that his theory is concerned with my *actual* maxim, not some made-up one. It is not actually part of my choice that my name has seven letters, or perhaps even that it is a gift I steal (some people do, however, have 'principles' about only stealing from large shops). If I am honest with myself, I have to admit that it is a question of my taking what I want when I can't afford it. For Kant's test to work, we must be honest with ourselves about what our maxims are.

Second, Kant's test delivers some strange results. Say I am a hard-working shop assistant, who hates the work. One happy Saturday I win the lottery, and I vow 'never to sell anything to anyone again, but only ever to buy'. This is perhaps eccentric, but it doesn't seem morally wrong. But it cannot be universalised. If no one ever sold things, how could anyone buy them? It is logically impossible, which makes it wrong according to Kant's test. So perhaps it is not always wrong to do things that require other people to do the opposite. But then how can we tell when we must universalise our maxims, and when it is all right if they cannot be universalised?

Third, Kant is wrong about good motives. Surely, if I do something nice for you, like visit you in hospital, because I like you, that is also a morally worthy action. Much of the time we do good things because we feel warmly towards the people we benefit. Kant denies that this motive is good enough. We have to want to benefit people because it is our duty to do so. Some philosophers have thought that this doctrine, putting duty above feelings in our motives, is somehow inhuman.

There is one aspect of deontology that I haven't discussed yet, namely the importance of respect. I will say more about this when discussing euthanasia.

Related examination question

(Part b) Explain and illustrate *one* criticism of a deontological approach to ethics. *(15 marks) (2003)*

Utilitarianism

Jeremy Bentham (1748–1832) is usually thought of as the father of utilitarianism. His main principle of ethics, which is known as the 'principle of utility' or 'greatest happiness principle', is 'that principle which approves or disapproves of every action whatsoever, according to the tendency which it appears to have to augment or diminish the happiness of the party whose interest is in question' (Bentham 1962: 34). Or again, 'that principle which states the greatest happiness of all those whose interest is in question, as being the right and proper . . . end of human action' (p. 33, n. 1).

If we simplify this a little, we can say that utilitarianism claims that happiness is the only good, and that an action is right if it leads to the greatest happiness of all those it affects, i.e. if it *maximises* happiness. Otherwise, the action is wrong. (This definition is only true for **act utilitarianism**. I will consider **rule utilitarianism** later.) The greatest happiness should be the goal of our actions, what we hope to bring about. Our actions are judged not 'in themselves', but in terms of what *consequences* they have.

It is important to notice that 'greatest happiness' is comparative (great, greater, greatest). If an action leads to the greatest happiness of those it affects, no other action taken at that time could have led to greater happiness. So an action is right only if, out of all the actions you could have done, this action leads to more happiness than any other.

Hedonistic and ideal utilitarianism

Bentham's idea of happiness is pleasure and the absence of pain. This theory of happiness is called **hedonism**. Bentham thought that it is possible to measure pleasures and pains and add them up on a single scale. His scheme for doing this is the 'felicific calculus'. If a pleasure is more intense, will last longer, is more certain to occur, will happen sooner rather than later, or will produce in turn many other pleasures and few pains, it counts for more. In thinking what to do, you also need to take into account how many people will be affected (the more you affect positively, and the fewer you affect negatively, the better). The total amount of happiness produced is the sum total of everyone's pleasures produced minus the sum total of everyone's pains. Whichever action produces the greatest happiness is the right action.

John Stuart Mill (1806–73), the son of James Mill, a close friend and disciple of Jeremy Bentham, rejected Bentham's ideas on happiness. He pointed out that there is a deeper dimension to human experience, which is missing in Bentham's account. There is no mention of love of honour, beauty, order, or freedom, and 'If [Bentham] thought at all of any of the deeper feelings of human nature, it was but as idiosyncrasies of taste' (Mill 1962a: 101).

Rather than all types of pleasure being of equal weight, Mill thought that some pleasures – the pleasures of thought, feeling, and imagination – were 'higher' than others. As long as our physical needs are met, Mill claims, we would prefer to experience a **higher pleasure** over any amount of lower pleasure. And this is what makes it a higher pleasure, that everyone who is 'competently acquainted' with both sorts of pleasure prefers this pleasure to another sort of pleasure. In introducing this distinction between higher and lower pleasures, Mill rejects the felicific calculus, and adds the element of quality to the quantitative analysis of happiness that Bentham puts forward.

Another way Mill argues for his theory of higher pleasures is by comparing a human being with a pig. As human beings, we are able to experience pleasures of deep personal relationships, art, and creative thought that pigs are not. But these very capacities also mean we can experience terrible pain, boredom, dissatisfaction. Yet we don't think that this possibility would be a good reason for choosing to be a well-looked-after pig, rather than a human being. 'It is better to be a human being dissatisfied than a pig satisfied' (Mill 1962b: 260). This must mean that quantity of pleasure is not the only factor in our happiness. The quality of the pleasure is important, too.

Some philosophers have argued that Mill's idea of higher pleasures actually introduces *ideals* into his account of happiness, so that happiness is composed of more than pleasure and the absence of pain. It is not the pleasure the ideal brings that is important, but the ideal itself. This interpretation or development of Mill's theory is known as 'ideal utilitarianism'.

Related examination question

(Part a) Briefly distinguish between ideal and hedonistic utilitarianism. *(6 marks)* *(2003)*

Preference and negative utilitarianism

A third variation on utilitarianism claims that it is not happiness as pleasure that we should try to maximise. It is the satisfaction of people's *preferences*. There are two reasons usually given for preferring talk about preferences to talk about pleasure. First, it is more difficult to know how much pleasure someone experiences than whether their preference has been satisfied. So it is easier to count up preference satisfaction than pleasure. Second, it can be right to satisfy someone's preferences even when he doesn't know this has happened, and so doesn't derive any pleasure from it. For example, I can want you to look after my ant farm when I die. Suppose you don't derive any pleasure from looking after ants, but you don't mind either, and suppose ants don't experience pleasure either. According to preference utilitarianism, you should still look after my ants, rather than kill them, even though no one gets any pleasure from it.

A fourth variation, known as 'negative utilitarianism', claims that maximising the good – happiness – is not as important as minimising the bad – suffering and unhappiness. On Bentham's formulation, these are supposedly the same thing (to decrease pain is to increase happiness). But negative utilitarianism counts suffering more heavily than happiness. Our main priority, in acting morally, is to decrease the suffering in the world. Bentham, by contrast, would give equal priority to decreasing suffering and increasing pleasure.

Act and rule utilitarianism

So far we have considered the greatest happiness principle as applying to actions. Act utilitarianism, we have said, states that an action is right if it maximises happiness. But this faces two important objections.

First, how can we know or work out the consequences of an action, to discover whether it maximises happiness or not? If the felicific calculus – or anything like it – isn't ridiculous, it is at least very difficult actually to apply. How do I know exactly how happy each person affected by my action will be? However, notice that Bentham does not say that an action is right if it *actually* maximises happiness. He says it is right according to 'the tendency which it appears to have' to maximise happiness. We don't need to be able to work things out precisely. An action is right if we can reasonably expect that it will maximise happiness.

This still means we have to be able to work things out roughly. Mill thought this was still too demanding. Happiness is 'much too complex and indefinite' (Mill 1962a: 119) a standard to apply directly to actions. But we don't need to try, Mill claimed, because over time people have automatically, through trial and error, worked out which actions tend to produce happiness. This is what our inherited moral rules actually are: 'tell the truth', 'don't steal', and 'keep your promises' are embodiments of the wisdom of humanity, while lying, theft, and false promising tend to lead to unhappiness.

Mill called these moral rules 'secondary principles' (Mill 1962b: 278). It is only in cases of conflict between secondary principles (e.g. if by telling the truth you break your promise) that we need to apply the greatest happiness principle directly. Some philosophers argue that Mill's secondary principles are rules of thumb, i.e. not strict rules that we must follow, but helpful guidance in our thoughts about what to do.

The second criticism of act utilitarianism is that no type of action is ruled out as immoral. If torturing a small child produces the greatest happiness, then it is right to torture a small child. Suppose I am part of a group of child abusers who really enjoy torturing small children. But, for whatever reason, we only find and torture abandoned children. Only the child suffers pain (no one else knows about our activities). But we all derive a great deal of happiness. So more happiness is produced by our torturing the child than not, so it is morally right. This is clearly the wrong answer.

If we didn't apply the greatest happiness principle to actions, neither of these criticisms would work. Rule utilitarians argue that we should adopt those rules which, if everybody followed them, would lead to the greatest happiness (compared to any other rules). An action is right if it complies with those rules.

Clearly, the rule forbidding torture of children will cause more happiness if everyone followed it than the rule allowing torture of children. So it is wrong to torture children.

An objection to rule utilitarianism is that it amounts to 'rule-fetishism'. The point of the rules is to bring about the greatest happiness. But what if I know that, for example, lying in a particular situation will produce more happiness than telling the truth? It seems pointless to tell the truth, causing unhappiness, just because a rule says we should tell the truth, when the whole point of following that rule was to bring about happiness. It seems that there should be an exception to the rule in this case. But then whenever a particular action causes more happiness by breaking a rule than by following it, we should do that action. And then we are back with act utilitarianism, weighing up the consequences of each action in turn.

I end with an objection that applies to all utilitarian theories. They weigh the unhappiness of one person against the happiness of another, whether this is in deciding which action to do or which rule to adopt. We are not concerned with people as individuals, but as 'receptacles' for happiness. The distribution of that happiness – who gets happy by how much – is irrelevant. The objection is that this does not show the proper respect to people that they deserve as individuals.

 # QUESTIONS FOR DISCUSSION

What are the main differences between act and rule utilitarianism? Which theory is more plausible? Can any form of utilitarianism successfully answer the objections raised above?

Virtue theory

The distinct claim of virtue theory is that the question 'How shall I be?' comes before the question 'What should I do?' We can only know what to do when we have figured out what type of person a morally good, or virtuous, person is. An action is right, roughly, if it is an action that a virtuous person would do. A virtuous person is someone who has the **virtues**, morally good traits of character. A right action, then, will express morally good traits of character, and this is what makes it right. Telling the truth expresses honesty, standing up to a bully expresses courage, and so on. Our main aim, therefore, should be to develop the virtues, because then we will know what it is right to do and we will want to do it.

Plato's theory

In his most famous work *The Republic*, Plato (*c.*429–*c.*347 BC) argued that the soul has three 'parts': reason, *thumos* or 'spirit', and desire. (We don't have a good word to translate what Plato meant by *thumos*. But we still sometimes use the word 'spirit' in a similar sense, when we say that an athlete showed real spirit, or that a politician gave a spirited response to criticism.) Each part has its own distinct virtue, and there is a fourth virtue for the soul as a whole. The virtue of reason is wisdom (sometimes translated as prudence), the virtue of spirit is courage, the virtue of desire is self-control. If reason rules the soul with wisdom, so that spirit moves us to courageously do what is right, and we only desire what is right, then the soul as a whole is just.

Plato developed this theory in response to the question 'Why should we be just?' Is the only reason not to cheat people because we might get caught? Plato argued that justice was its own reward, and that to understand why we should be just, we need to understand what justice is. A just person, who – of course – would not act unjustly, is someone with a just soul. When our souls are just, they are in the right state, every part as it is meant to be, 'healthy'. And if my soul is in a bad, unhealthy state, the person who suffers most is me. The desire for material wealth that leads me to cheat someone, for example, is out of control. If my desires are out of control, I can feel 'driven', 'forced' to do things by the strength of those desires. If I brought them under control, I would not want to act unjustly. And this state of the soul would be good for me; I will be calm and able to choose well.

But how do I know that cheating someone is wrong (unjust) in the first place? Plato argued that if you are wise, then you know what is good and what is bad. There are 'eternal Forms' for good and bad, and wisdom is knowledge of these (see the Analogy of the Cave, discussed in book VII). It is very unclear in Plato's argument, though, how having knowledge of something as abstract as the Forms can really help us in practical life.

These four virtues – wisdom, courage, self-control, and justice – became known as the 'cardinal' virtues. Plato put a lot of emphasis on the role of reason in the virtuous person. Later Christian thinkers, in particular Aquinas, developing a remark made by St Paul (1 Corinthians 13: 13) added three 'theological' virtues: faith, hope and charity (or self-giving love). These put less emphasis on reason, but are still concerned with the state of someone's soul.

Aristotle's theory

What we are still lacking, though, is a general account of what a virtue is. Perhaps the most detailed, and certainly the most popular model for contemporary theories, is offered by Aristotle (384–322 BC), a pupil of Plato. Both Plato and Aristotle thought that virtues are qualities of a person that help him to 'flourish' or 'live well'. By this, they meant 'in accordance with human nature'. For Plato, as we have seen, this means that each part of the human soul must perform its designated task well, and in particular, reason must be in charge. Aristotle agreed, as he also believed that reason is central to human nature. But he placed more emphasis than Plato on training (rather than curbing) our emotions, so that we automatically react and want to act in the best way.

Aristotle argued that there are two types of virtue, virtues of the intellect and virtues of character. A virtue of character is a character trait that disposes us to feel desires and emotions 'well', rather than 'badly'. By 'well', he meant 'at the right times, with reference to the right objects, towards the right people, with the right motive, and in the right way' (Aristotle 1980: 38; 1106b). Of the different virtues of intellect – such as quick thinking and general intelligence – the one we are concerned with in ethics is *practical wisdom*. It is practical wisdom that allows us to know what right is in each case.

A car driver has just deliberately swerved in front of your friend's car. Your friend beeped, and the other driver has stopped his car, got out, and has started swearing at your friend. What's the right thing to do? You probably feel angry and a bit scared. Are you feeling these emotions 'well'? Being angry towards a bully who is insulting a friend seems the right time, object, and person. But your anger could be too strong and motivate you to start a fight, in which case you are not feeling it in the right way. Or if you are too afraid, you might want to say something, but not be able to. To understand the right way to feel anger and fear, we need to understand the situation more: was this a once-off, or does this driver generally terrorise the neighbourhood? Is this person just a bad driver, or a bully you have come across before on other occasions? And to know what to do, you need to know yourself: if you say something, will you say it in a way that is helpful, or will you just be provocative, making the situation worse? Someone who is virtuous also has practical wisdom, which Aristotle says only comes with experience, and a wise person understands situations and how they develop, and what all the options are.

In this situation, you could feel angry or fearful too much or too little, 'and in both cases not well' (Aristotle 1980: 38; 1106b). Aristotle defended the 'doctrine of the mean', the idea that a virtuous response or action is 'intermediate'. Just as there is a right time, object, person, etc. at which to feel angry (or any emotion), some people can feel angry too often, regarding too many objects, (perhaps they take a critical comment as an insult), and towards too many people or maybe whenever they get angry, they get very angry, even at minor things. Other people can feel angry not often enough, with regard to too few objects and people (perhaps they don't understand how people are taking advantage of them). Aristotle's doctrine of the mean does *not* claim that when you get angry, you should only ever be moderately angry. You should be as angry as the situation demands, which can be very angry.

Someone who gets angry 'too much' is short-tempered. We don't have a name for someone who gets angry too little. Someone who has the virtue relating to anger is good-tempered. The virtue is the 'intermediate' state between the two vices of 'too much' and 'too little'. Many virtues fit this model, Aristotle argues. Some, like good temper, work with feelings. Other virtues, like honesty, work with motives for actions. Telling the truth 'too much' is tactlessness. Telling it 'too little' is lying when you shouldn't. The virtue of honesty involves telling the truth at the right times, to the right people, etc.

But, even if it is true, the doctrine of the mean isn't much help practically. First, 'too much' and 'too little' aren't quantities on a single scale. The list of 'right time, right object, right person, right motive, right way' shows that things are much more complicated than that. Second, to know whether a character trait or action is 'intermediate' is just to know it is virtuous. How often should we get angry, and how angry should we get? There is no independent sense of 'intermediate' that can help us answer these questions.

Criticisms of virtue theory

This leads to the main criticism of virtue theory. It cannot provide enough guidance about what to do. If I am not a virtuous person, telling me to do what a virtuous person would do doesn't help me know what to do. This criticism is a little unfair, since virtue theory is not intended to be applied to actions directly in this way. It doesn't aim to provide an exact method for making decisions. But it can provide some guidance by helping us think about situations in terms of the virtues, rather than only duties or consequences.

What about cases in which virtues seem to conflict? Loyalty can require we stick up for our friends. If I get angry with the driver who insulted my friend, is that 'too much' anger but the right amount of loyalty to my friend? But if I don't get angry, is that 'too little' loyalty to my friend? Even if we can resolve this apparent conflict of virtues, will all such conflicts disappear? For example, when someone has done something wrong, and we are putting it right, can we show justice and mercy, or do we have to choose?

QUESTIONS FOR DISCUSSION

What is Aristotle's doctrine of the mean? Which theory of virtue provides more guidance about what to do, Plato's or Aristotle's? Why?

Two final points on Aristotle's theory will bring out some differences between his ideas and our common-sense understanding of virtue. First, as we noted above, Aristotle and Plato thought that being virtuous was beneficial for the virtuous person. This was because they believed that human beings, as rational animals, live the best lives (best for themselves) when they act rationally. And Aristotle argued that being virtuous just is living rationally, because you do and feel things at the right time, etc., which is determined by the rational virtue of practical wisdom. By contrast, we sometimes feel that a virtuous life may not be a good life for the person living it.

Second, we all find it easiest to act according to our own character. Because a virtuous person has a virtuous character, he or she finds it easy to do the right thing. For Aristotle, only when the right thing comes naturally is it properly a virtuous action. By contrast, we often feel that someone who finds it difficult to do the right thing but does it anyway shows virtue. Aristotle would call this person 'strong-willed', but not virtuous.

Related examination questions

(Part a) Identify and briefly describe *two* virtues. *(6 marks) (2001)*

(Part c) Assess whether it is useful to focus on virtue in order to explain why we should be moral. *(24 marks) (2001)*

(Part c) Assess virtue theory. *(24 marks) (2003)*

● PRACTICAL ETHICS

Euthanasia

The *New Oxford Dictionary of English* defines 'euthanasia' as 'the painless killing of a patient suffering from an incurable and painful disease or in an irreversible coma'. 'Euthanasia' comes from two Greek words, *eu-*, a prefix meaning 'good' or 'well', and *thanatos*, meaning 'death'. Literally speaking, when someone undergoes euthanasia, his or her death is good. Normally, for death to be good, living would need to be worse than death. We can understand that the two conditions the definition describes – incurable, painful disease and irreversible coma – are two of the most important ways living can be worse than dying. In these cases, we might say life is not worth living. This is why euthanasia is also called 'mercy killing'.

Types of euthanasia

We can distinguish six types of euthanasia. In involuntary euthanasia the patient does not want to die. In nonvoluntary euthanasia the patient has not expressed his or her choice. This may happen if the patient is too young to express choices; it has been usual practice to allow some infants with terrible congenital diseases, such as Tay-Sachs, to die. Or the patient might not be able to express choices now – because of being in a coma or mentally impaired through senile dementia – and did not express a choice earlier. In voluntary euthanasia the patient wants to die and has expressed this choice.

Each of these three types can be either active or passive. In active euthanasia the patient is killed, for instance by a lethal injection. In passive euthanasia the patient is allowed to die, for instance by withholding treatment for the disease that then kills her.

Passive euthanasia does not fit the definition given at the outset, because it involves letting the patient die rather than killing him. It also doesn't fit because the death can sometimes be very painful and prolonged. Active euthanasia, by contrast, is almost always painless, since very high (fatal) doses of painkillers can be given with the injection.

When, if at all, is euthanasia justified?

People commonly agree that, because it is important for us to be able to make choices about things that are important to us, involuntary euthanasia will almost always turn out to be wrong. But does this also mean we must respect the choice for euthanasia? Is voluntary euthanasia always right?

We need to first distinguish the question of whether voluntary euthanasia can be morally permissible from the question of whether it should be legalised. One of the most common arguments against euthanasia relies on the possible abuses that could happen. Patients might feel pressured into agreeing to euthanasia by families that didn't want to look after them or by doctors who wanted to use the hospital resources for other patients. Alternatively, patients who felt depressed and unable to see how to live a meaningful life despite their illness may choose euthanasia, when with help they could have become less depressed.

Is there a genuine distinction between killing someone and letting her die?

An act utilitarian may argue not. In both cases, the person dies. All that matters is that she doesn't suffer. However, other theories argue there is. Not killing someone is related to the virtue and duties of justice. Justice requires that we respect people, their choices and rights. Not letting someone die is related to the virtue and duties of charity. Charity requires that we help other people's lives go well.

People all over the world are dying from hunger or disease who could have been prevented from dying. It is difficult to argue that because you did not give more to charity you have done something as bad as if you had actually killed them yourself.

There are some cases in which letting someone die is equivalent to killing him. The clearest case is when you have a duty to provide food or medicine to someone and you do not. For example, a parent who didn't give her child food would be guilty of murder. In such a case, both justice and charity require the same thing, and so there is no practical difference between killing and letting someone die.

Is there a practical difference in the case of euthanasia? Many doctors think that administering lethal injections goes against the idea and duties of practising medicine. However, in addition to the duty to protect the lives of their patients, doctors also have the duty to do what is best for their patients, including relieving pain. One way of trying to respect both duties at once is to allow the patient to die while doing everything possible to ensure her death is painless. Some people argue that the duty to protect life does not involve the duty to prolong life for as long as possible, if the quality of life is very poor. Therefore, doctors are not failing in their duty to protect life by allowing patients to die when they can only expect a very poor quality of life.

Some deontologists argue that we have a duty not to kill human beings, even if the person who dies requests it. This is one interpretation of the idea of the sanctity of life, that we must respect someone's right to life even when he wants to die. Because deontology draws a distinction between killing someone and letting him die, these deontologists may allow passive euthanasia, but not active euthanasia.

These are important points. However, both Switzerland and the Netherlands have legalised euthanasia, and there is no firm evidence of such abuses occurring on a wide scale. But the question of whether euthanasia should be legal is not our question here, and it is important to remember that the argument from abuses is not an argument against the view that voluntary euthanasia is morally permissible.

One argument against voluntary euthanasia is inspired by Kant. He argued that suicide is wrong. He said that there is a contradiction in choosing one's death out of desire for the best for oneself. Our self-love is what keeps us alive, and it would be a contradiction if it also sought to destroy life (1991: 85). But this is a poor argument, because there is no contradiction if our self-love seeks life when life is best and seeks death when death is best (as in euthanasia). This way our self-love always seeks the best for us.

An argument for voluntary euthanasia inspired by Kant claims that rationality is what bestows dignity on human beings, and we must respect people's dignity. Therefore, humans being who may lose their dignity and their rationality through illness and pain may legitimately request euthanasia. We respect and protect their dignity by helping them die in circumstances of their own choosing. This is one of the most powerful arguments for voluntary euthanasia.

 # QUESTIONS FOR DISCUSSION

What reasons are there to think that active euthanasia is wrong, but passive euthanasia is not wrong? Are they persuasive?

Related examination questions

(Part a) Briefly distinguish between active and passive euthanasia. *(6 marks) (2002)*

(Part b) Outline and illustrate *one* deontological argument for preserving life, with reference to *one* of the following moral issues: abortion, animal rights, euthanasia. *(15 marks) (2002)*

(Part b) Explain how, in any *one* situation, killing might be seen as a virtuous act. *(15 marks) (2001)*

(The latter two questions are also relevant to a later section and so are repeated there.)

Abortion

Abortion is the termination of a pregnancy. We usually use the term to refer to the deliberate termination of a pregnancy, but in medicine, a miscarriage is also called a 'spontaneous abortion'. We will be concerned with deliberate abortion.

A woman becomes pregnant when a sperm fertilises one of her eggs ('conception'). The fertilised egg is a 'zygote' until it implants in the wall of her uterus, five to seven days later. It is now called an 'embryo', until eight weeks old, when it is called a 'fetus'. However, I shall use the term 'fetus' for the developing organism at all stages from conception to birth.

What is the moral status of the fetus?

Many of the arguments for abortion focus on the moral status of the fetus. Most of the current debate is about whether a woman who was not raped and whose life is not threatened by being pregnant can be right to have an abortion. People who oppose abortion usually claim that the fetus has a right to life, because it is a human being and all human beings have a right to life. This is a deontological argument. But why should we think that all human beings have a right to life? Many people don't think that animals have a right to life, since they are happy to eat them; what is special about being human?

One thing that would make us special is that we have a soul, while animals do not. If true, this is a very strong objection to abortion. The traditional point at which we are said to acquire souls is at conception. We are going to stay just with arguments that are not theological, but two facts are worth noting. First, two-thirds of zygotes are spontaneously aborted, i.e. rejected naturally by the uterus. If each is made special by the presence of a soul, that seems a moral tragedy. Second, some types of contraception, such as the IUD (intra-uterine device) and certain types of contraceptive pill, work by changing the lining of the uterus so that fertilised eggs cannot implant in it. These methods of contraception do not stop eggs from being fertilised. If abortion is wrong because a being with a soul is prevented from developing, then these types of contraception are equally wrong.

Once we allow that abortion immediately after conception is permissible, we are faced with the difficulty of trying to find a point to draw the line. The fetus develops a little each day, day on day, until it is born, and after that, the child develops a little, day on day, until it is an adult with reason and rights. So how is it possible to say 'Now the fetus does not have a right to life, now it does'? At any point where we draw the line, the fetus is not very different just before this point and just after this point.

One way to solve this difficulty is to consider why human beings might have a right to life. What is special about being human? The things that come to mind – such as reason, the use of language, the depth of our emotional experience, our self-awareness, our ability to distinguish right and wrong – are not things that a fetus has (yet). But many other human beings, including those with severe mental disabilities and senile dementia, also don't have these characteristics. But we do not normally think it is permissible to kill them.

There is one important characteristic we do all share, and that a fetus acquires at around 20–4 weeks, and that is **sentience**. Sentience is the primitive consciousness of perception, pleasure and pain. If the right to life depends on sentience, then a fetus begins to have a right to life at around 20 weeks, but not before. Of course, as we noted above, we cannot say precisely when. Sentience develops at different speeds in different fetuses. But we should err on the side of caution, and it seems that fetuses do not, in general, develop sentience until 20 weeks old. However, if we choose this quality as the basis for a right to life, it means that many animals have a right to life as well because they are sentient (see next section).

But even sentience does not give the fetus a right to life in the first 20 weeks after conception, and most abortions take place within that period. If the fetus does not have the characteristics that give someone a right to life, we might argue that, unlike animals, it will have them if it is allowed to develop. It has a right to life now because it has the *potential* to become a person with a right to life in the future. But this is a bad argument.

First, the sperm and the egg that combined to form the fetus also had the potential to become a person. If it is potential that matters, then contraception of any form would be as wrong as abortion. An obvious reply to this is that the sperm and egg don't form a natural 'unit' for us to ascribe potential to. However, this reply must give us some reason to think it is only the potential of natural units that matters.

Second, it is not normal to treat potential as though it was already realised. Someone who has only the potential to become a teacher is not yet a teacher, and should not be put in charge of lessons. Someone who has the potential to become a millionaire cannot spend the money yet.

One important stage in the realisation of the potential of the fetus is at *viability*. This occurs when the fetus is sufficiently developed to be capable of surviving outside the uterus. With the advance of technology, viability is becoming earlier and earlier, though it is still considerably later than sentience. After viability the fetus could be delivered, kept alive outside the woman's body, and put up for adoption. This could make it wrong to abort the fetus.

QUESTIONS FOR DISCUSSION

Does the fact that a fetus will become a human being give it a right to life? Why or why not? What reasons are there to think that sentience is a morally important property?

On what other grounds, if any, might abortion be permissible?

We have so far only considered deontological arguments. Act utilitarianism asks us to consider the balance of pleasure and pain, or of preferences, in the two situations of abortion and giving birth. Normally we believe it is better to be alive than not alive. So the future life of the fetus must weigh very heavily in its favour, and certainly outweigh the inconvenience to the woman of carrying the pregnancy to term and then putting the baby up for adoption. But there is a question whether the future experience or preferences of the fetus count, because before sentience it is not yet a being with the ability to experience pleasure and pain. Utilitarianism doesn't give us an obvious answer as to what to do about future beings.

Virtue theory takes a very different approach. The discussion so far seems to treat women as containers for a fetus rather than creators of a life out of their own bodies. The *meaning* of pregnancy and abortion are not explored.

Rosalind Hursthouse argues that to think of an abortion as though the fetus does not matter is callous and shows a lack of appreciation for the type of being a fetus is – that it is quite literally one's flesh and blood, developing from oneself (Hursthouse 1992). It shows the wrong attitude to human life, death and parenthood. But this doesn't automatically make all abortions wrong. If a woman wants an abortion because she fears she cannot afford to feed the child or because she has a very demanding job and may neglect it, this is not a callous thought. However, the fact that she prioritises her job above children may indicate that her priorities in life are wrong, that she hasn't understood the value of parenthood. But it depends on the particular case. It may be that the woman leads a very worthwhile, fulfilling life, and cannot fit motherhood into the other activities that make her life as good as it is. For virtue ethics, then, each abortion is an individual case, involving an individual woman in a unique set of circumstances. And so each case must be judged by its own merits.

Related examination questions

(Part b) Outline and illustrate *one* deontological argument for preserving life, with reference to *one* of the following moral issues: abortion, animal rights, euthanasia. *(15 marks) (2002)*

(Part b) Explain how, in any *one* situation, killing might be seen as a virtuous act. *(15 marks) (2001)*

Animal rights

Most people believe that it is morally permissible to rear and kill animals for food and clothing and to experiment on them, at least for medical if not cosmetic purposes. Is this view defensible?

Peter Singer: a utilitarian argument

Peter Singer is a utilitarian. In *Animal Liberation* (1975), he argued that the way we commonly treat animals is not morally justifiable. We do not think that it is right to treat women worse than men just because they are women (this is sexism), nor to treat blacks worse than whites (this is racism). Likewise, it is wrong to treat animals differently just because they are not human. This is 'speciesism'.

There is a disanalogy here. With women and men, blacks and whites, there is no difference in those important capacities – reason, the use of language, the depth of our emotional experience, our self-awareness, our ability to distinguish right and wrong – that make a being a person. But there is a difference between human beings and animals regarding all of these.

Singer argues that these differences are not relevant when it comes to the important capacity that human beings and animals share, namely sentience. He quotes Bentham: 'The question is not, Can they reason? nor Can they *talk*? but, *Can they suffer?*' (Bentham 1962: ch. XVIII, sect. 1, note). How can we defend causing suffering to animals when we would think it wrong to cause suffering to people? For a utilitarian, an act (or rule) is wrong if it produces more suffering than an alternative. Who is suffering is irrelevant. When it comes to suffering, animals should be treated as equal to people.

Does this mean that we should become vegetarian, avoid wearing leather, and protest against animal experiments? Not necessarily.

There is first the question of the utilitarian calculation: would stopping animal experiments reduce the amount of (animal) suffering in the world more than it would increase (human) suffering?

Second, the utilitarian position only objects to suffering, not to killing. This leads to the 'container' view of life: an animal's life is only valuable because of the happiness it contains. If you painlessly kill that animal and bring another animal into being (as is done when rearing animals), you haven't reduced the total amount of happiness in the world. Singer's position implies not vegetarianism, but making sure that animals are happy when they are alive and slaughtering them painlessly.

This would make eating meat much more expensive, because animals would have to be kept in much better conditions, but it would not make it morally wrong per se. It is wrong at the moment, because animals are not treated as well as they could be.

But if killing animals is permissible on this theory, what about babies? We don't think that killing babies, using them for food or experiments, is morally permissible, yet babies are no different in their psychological capacities from many animals.

Deontological arguments

Deontologists will argue that killing human beings is wrong because they have a right to life. Having rights is related to our rationality and choices; rights to life, liberty, and property protect the 'space' that we need in order to make choices and live our lives as rational beings. Animals aren't rational and don't make free choices the way we do, so they don't have rights.

But babies also aren't rational and don't make free choices (yet) and some people with severe mental disabilities never do. If they have a right to life, and do not have different psychological capacities from certain animals, then to deny those animals a right to life would be speciesist. The problem is this: if you pick some special property only human beings have to justify a right to life, some human beings won't have it. If you pick a property all human beings have to justify a right to life, then some animals have it as well.

Tom Regan argues that to have a right to life, a creature only needs to be a 'subject of a life' (Regan 1983: 243). By this he means it has beliefs, desires, emotions, perception, memory, the ability to act (though not necessarily free choice), and a psychological identity over time. If a creature has these abilities, there is a way its life goes for it, and this matters to it. A right to life protects this. Although we can't know exactly which animals meet this criterion, we can be sure that almost all mammals (including humans) over the age of one do so.

Because these animals have a right to life, Regan argues, we cannot kill them for any reason less important than saving life. Because we do not need to eat meat or wear leather to live, we should not use animals for these purposes. Regan also argues that an animal's right to life is equal to a human being's. We do not normally discriminate between 'more valuable' and 'less valuable' human lives, even though some people are capable of much greater things than others. So we should not discriminate between 'more valuable' human lives and 'less valuable' animal lives. The right to life is equal for all subjects of a life. This means we cannot justify medical experiments that involve killing animals by the human lives the experiment may help save. We should be no more willing to use and kill animals than human beings.

For some people, these conclusions indicate that something must have gone wrong in the argument. After all, isn't it 'natural' that we eat animals, and isn't using them for clothing and medical purposes just an extension of this? But when it comes to human beings, it is difficult to know what is 'natural'. It is easier to say that tribal people who hunt animals in the wild for food are doing something 'natural' than that our practices of factory farming, such as keeping 20,000 chickens in a single enclosure, are 'natural'.

We should notice that the views we have discussed may not object to tribal hunting. The animal lives as good a life as its species might normally live, and its flesh brings celebration and pleasure. This is not true for the factory-farmed animals we eat every day. And the lack of alternative to meat for a healthy diet for many tribal people may be considered a legitimate reason to eat animals.

 ## QUESTIONS FOR DISCUSSION

What implications do the utilitarian and deontological arguments against eating animals have for our current practices? Which argument against eating animals is more persuasive, the utilitarian or the deontological? Why?

An argument from virtue ethics

But is the speciesism argument valid in the first place? Virtue ethics encourages us to think further about human 'nature' and our place in the natural world. It notes that 'speciesism' isn't the only case where we 'naturally' privilege those closest to us. We also privilege our families and friends, and we are loyal to the places we grow up and the companies we work for. None of this seems morally objectionable. Perhaps it is not *just* the capacities of the being that determine how we should treat it, but also our relationship to it. There is a moral importance to bonding, the creation of special ties with particular others. Our bond to other human beings is special because we share humanity.

The capacities of a being are very important, however. To treat another being that is rational as though it is not rational is to show it disrespect. Not to recognise that it can suffer is to show a lack of compassion. To treat a living creature as a meat-growing machine or experimental object is likewise to display a relationship with it that resembles selfishness, because we reduce it from what it is in itself to something that exists only for our sake.

But what does this mean for whether eating meat and medical experiments on animals are wrong? Virtue ethics has left us without a clear answer, but a sense of the difficulty of the question.

> **❙ Related examination question**
>
> ❙ (Part c) Assess whether utilitarianism can help us decide if it is ever morally right to kill. *(24 marks) (2002)*

● META-ETHICS: COGNITIVISM

Meta-ethics is the study of ethical concepts, such as right and wrong, good and bad, and of sentences that use these concepts. **Cognitivism** is the view that we can have moral knowledge. One main cognitivist theory, **moral realism**, claims that good and bad are properties of situations and people, right and wrong are properties of actions. Just as people can be 1.5 metres tall or good at maths, they can be good or bad. Just as actions can be done in 10 minutes or done from greed, they can right or wrong. These moral properties are a genuine part of the world. This is the type of cognitivism we will discuss.

Utilitarians, virtue ethicists and deontologists can be cognitivists if they believe the claims they make amount to knowledge. If they are cognitivists, many are likely to be moral realists. But Kant is a different type of cognitivist. He does not believe that moral concepts pick out properties in the world. Instead, moral judgements are derived from pure practical reason. His position is that moral knowledge is like mathematical knowledge: we can know mathematical truths, such as 4 + 2 = 6, but many people do not think that numbers exist in the world. These truths are a product of reason, not part of reality.

Intuitionism

Intuitionism is the realist theory that we come to know about moral properties by 'intuition', rather than by 'pure' reason or by our senses. It is most associated with two British philosophers, G. E. Moore (1873–1958) and W. D. Ross (1877–1940).

Moore and the naturalistic fallacy

In *Principia Ethica* (1903), Moore argued against ethical **naturalism**. Naturalism is the claim that moral properties are in fact natural properties. For example, a preference utilitarian might say that what is bad about murder *just is* the frustration of the victim's preferences. Goodness is maximising the satisfaction of people's preferences. And whether people's preferences are satisfied is a natural (psychological) fact.

Moore called the attempt to equate goodness to some natural property, such as preference satisfaction, the 'naturalistic fallacy'. Goodness, he claimed, is a simple and unanalysable property. It cannot be defined in terms of anything else. Something similar, he thought, could be said about colours. Blue is a simple property, and no one can explain what blue is, you have to see it for yourself to understand what blue is. But unlike colours, goodness is a non-natural property. It is not part of the natural world of atoms that makes up all we (literally) see. But it is part of reality. (If we have souls, these aren't part of the natural world, but they are part of reality.)

Moore's main argument for believing that it is a **fallacy** – a mistake – to identify goodness with a natural property has been called the 'open question' argument. If goodness just is happiness, then it wouldn't make sense to ask 'Is it good to make people happy?' This would be like asking 'Is making people happy making people happy?' This second question isn't a real question (the answer has to be 'yes'), but 'Is it good to make people happy?' is a real question: the answer can logically be 'yes' or 'no'. And so goodness cannot be happiness. The argument is the same whatever we substitute for happiness. 'Is x good?' is always a real question while 'Is x x?' is not. And so goodness cannot be any other property.

This argument doesn't work. Here is a similar argument. 'The property of being water cannot be any property in the world, such as the property of being H_2O. If it was then the question 'Is water H_2O?' would not make sense – it would be like asking 'Is H_2O H_2O?' But it does make sense. So water is a simple, unanalysable property.' This is not right, as water *just is* H_2O.

The reason the argument doesn't work is that it confuses concepts and properties. As we have just seen, two different concepts – water and H_2O – can pick out the same property in the world. (You learnt about water long before you knew it was H_2O; during this time, you had the concept of water, but not the concept of H_2O. So they are different concepts, but they both refer to the same thing.) Likewise, the concept 'goodness' is a different concept from 'happiness', but perhaps they are exactly the same property in the world. We may doubt this for other reasons, e.g. because beauty is also good, and beauty is a different property from happiness. The point is that the open question argument does not show that they are different.

❓ QUESTIONS FOR DISCUSSION

What is the 'naturalistic fallacy'? Do Moore's arguments against the naturalistic fallacy succeed? Why or why not?

'Intuition'

Even though his argument that goodness is unanalysable is bad, perhaps Moore is right to say that goodness is a non-natural property. After all, for something to be good or right does seem to be quite different from its being heavy or 'over there'. (I discuss this further in the next section.) If values are non-natural properties, how do we know about them? Moore's answer is 'intuition'. Basic judgements about what is good, e.g. pleasure, beauty, etc., are intuitions. They are **self-evident** judgements (see 'Intuitionism and self-evident judgements'). Moore thought it was self-evident that pleasure and the enjoyment of beauty are good and that maximising pleasure is right.

Moore's idea of an 'intuition' seems quite mysterious, especially because Moore claims that moral properties are not natural properties. All our usual ways of knowing things – through our senses or through the operations of reason – are no good here. Some recent philosophers, especially virtue theorists, have argued that it is our *emotions*, together with practical wisdom, that give us this kind of intuitive knowledge. If our emotional responses are virtuous, then they intuit the moral values a situation has. For example, if I am courageous in sport, then I can feel pain or fear – which tells me something bad is happening or may happen – yet I continue to push myself anyway, because I also feel the importance and good of achievement. Virtuous feelings are actually types of cognition – cognitions of values. This theory may claim values are natural properties or agree with Moore that they are non-natural properties.

Ross and prima facie duties

W. D. Ross was a deontologist, and argued that it was self-evident that certain types of actions, which he named **prima facie** duties (1930: 29), were right. He

Intuitionism and self-evident judgements

A self-evident judgement has no other evidence or proof but its own plausibility. This doesn't necessarily mean that everyone can immediately see that it is true. 'Self-evident' is not the same as 'obvious'. Our ability to make these judgements needs to develop first, and we need to consider the question very carefully. But if we do, we will see that the judgement is true.

The difficulty with 'self-evident' judgements is that people disagree about whether they are true or not. Moore thought it was self-evident that pleasure is good and that maximising the good is right. Ross, on the other hand, thought it was self-evident that there are times when it is wrong to maximise pleasure. He argued that it was self-evident that certain dutiful actions, such as fulfilling a promise, are right. The problem is, because the judgements are supposed to be self-evident, we cannot give any further reasons for believing them.

But this doesn't mean we can reject the idea of self-evidence. Suppose we *could* give reasons for thinking that pleasure is good, for example it's good because it forms part of a flourishing life for human beings. Is it self-evident that being part of a flourishing life makes something good? If not, we need to give a further reason for this judgement. And we can ask the same question of any further reason we give. And so on, forever. It seems that if judgements about what is good are not self-evident, then judgements about what counts as a reason for thinking something is good must be.

Some philosophers suggest an alternative: judgements about what counts as a reason depend upon a particular set of beliefs that are not being questioned at the moment. When we then question those beliefs, we can give reasons for believing any one belief or judgement at once, but must in turn assume others. This way no judgement is self-evident, because it can be supported by others. Why should we believe *any* of the judgements in the set? Because the set as a whole is coherent and makes sense of our experience.

listed seven classes of prima facie duties: duties of fidelity (such as keeping a promise), duties of reparation (when we have done something wrong), duties of gratitude, duties of justice, duties of beneficence (helping others), duties of self-improvement, and duties of non-maleficence (not harming others). These duties can sometimes conflict with each other, and one may override the other. That is why Ross called them 'prima facie duties' – they are duties 'at first sight'. In cases of conflict, one will give way and no longer be a duty in that situation.

As we have seen, utilitarians (Moore), deontologists (Ross), and virtue ethicists can be intuitionists. What is common to all these positions are the claims that moral values are real and known through intuition. One of the main difficulties with intuitionism is knowing how we can resolve arguments between people whose intuitions disagree. Perhaps intuitions are not knowledge of reality, but just expressions of people's feelings. We will see that the non-cognitivist theory of emotivism claims just this.

Moral realism

Moral realism is perhaps the 'default' or 'common-sense' position on ethics for many people. Many people believe that things really are right or wrong; it is not our beliefs that make them right or wrong. People are, of course, also aware of cultural differences in moral beliefs, a fact that can lead some to give up moral realism for **relativism** (see 'Relativism' in the next section). But tolerance of cultural differences tends to be quite limited, and many people continue to hold on to a number of moral absolutes. For example, very few people seem to think that because murder of members of other tribes, or female circumcision, or sati (where widows are expected to throw themselves on the funeral pyre of their husbands) is morally permitted in some tribal societies, that makes murder, or female circumcision, or sati right, even in those societies.

The moral realist believes that statements like 'Euthanasia is not wrong' are expressions of beliefs, which can be true or false. Whether such statements are true or false depends on the way that the world is, on what properties an action, person, or situation – such as euthanasia – actually has. They must 'fit the facts'.

Facts and values

What sort of facts? Moore's argument for the naturalistic fallacy tries to draw a distinction between natural facts, which we know through our senses, and moral values, which we know through intuition. But Moore still believed there were 'facts' about these values, i.e. he believed that moral properties existed as part of reality, and that beliefs about moral properties could be true or false. He simply rejected the idea that facts about moral values could be deduced from any other kind of facts.

The puzzle is how a value can be *any* type of fact. Values are related to evaluations. If no one valued anything, would there be any values? Facts are part of the world. The fact that dinosaurs roamed the earth millions of years ago would be true whether anyone had found out about it or not. But it is more difficult to believe that values 'exist' quite independently of us and our talk about values.

This contrast is unfair. There are lots of facts – for example, facts about being in love, or facts about music – that 'depend' on human beings and their activities (there would be no love if no one loved anything). But they are still facts, because they are independent of our judgements, and made true by the way the world, in this case the human world, is. You can make mistakes about whether someone is in love or whether a piece of music is baroque or classical.

This response is helpful, but values still seem different from the examples given. When two people disagree over a matter of fact, whether it is about the natural world (dinosaurs) or the human world (love), we normally know how we could prove the matter one way or the other. Facts are things that can be shown to be true. But if two people agree over all the facts about abortion, say, but still disagree about whether it is right, we cannot appeal to any more 'facts' in the same way. What we would call 'the facts' seem to be *all* agreed, but the dispute about values remains. Value judgements always go beyond the facts. Of course, the realist will say there is one fact that has not been agreed upon, namely whether abortion is right or wrong. But the case brings out the point that disagreeing about values seems to be quite different from disagreeing about facts. So values aren't facts.

Moral facts are reasons

Realists respond by pointing out that there is more of a connection between facts and values than this argument suggests. Notice that we always appeal to the facts when we are trying to justify a moral judgement. If there were no connection, this would seem silly. But we can give *reasons* that support our moral claims, for example that eating meat is wrong, because of the suffering it causes to animals. This reason – that our practice of eating meat causes animal suffering – is a factual claim, about a way that the world is. It is either true or false that the practice of eating meat causes suffering to animals. This may be hard to prove, but we know roughly *how* to prove it.

The model is this: '"Eating meat causes animal suffering" is a reason to believe "Eating meat is wrong".'

In general terms, '"Fact *x*" is a reason to believe "Moral judgement *y*".'

So far, so good. Now the moral realist claims that this relation 'is a reason to believe' is true or false. Either fact *x* is a reason to believe moral judgement *y* or it is not. Compare reasons for other types of belief. If the measurement of radiometric decay indicates that dinosaur bone fossils are 65 million years old, this is a reason to believe that dinosaurs lived on earth 65 million years ago. It is not *proof*, perhaps, but it is a reason. (Reasons can come in different strengths; there can be good reasons, really good reasons, and proof. Bad reasons are not actually reasons at all.) The result of radiometric dating of dinosaur bones is a reason to think dinosaurs lived on earth 65 million years ago, whether you think it is a reason or not. Facts about reasons are objective, just like facts about the natural world. But facts about reasons are another *type* of fact.

What type? Well, it is not a fact that science can discover. There is no scientific investigation into what reasons there are. But this doesn't mean it is not part of reality. Philosophers would say facts about reasons are **normative** facts. They are facts about justification and reasoning.

Moral realists claim there are facts about the reasons we give for our moral judgements. Like all facts, these facts about reasons are part of the way the world is. How does this help moral realism? Let's go back to the example of abortion. We said that the two people agree on all the 'facts' about abortion, but disagree on whether it is wrong. What we meant, says the realist, is that they agree on all the natural facts, but we forgot about the facts about reasons. For example, is the fact that the fetus will become a human being a (strong) reason for thinking abortion is wrong? The answer to this question, claims realism, is factual, a fact about a reason. So the two people don't agree on all the facts, because they don't agree on the normative facts. One of them is making a mistake, because they are not seeing certain natural facts as reasons at all or, at least, not seeing them as strong reasons, when they are reasons or strong reasons. If two people agree on all the natural facts *and* all the normative facts, then they will also agree on the value. So we can understand values as a type of fact.

Moral realism accepts that it can be very difficult to establish whether a natural fact constitutes a reason for believing something is right or wrong, and how strong this reason is. But this is the case in all types of investigation into reality. We must always 'weigh up the facts' when making judgements about what to believe. This 'weighing up' is an attempt to discover the facts about reasons. Moral judgements – judgements about moral values – are judgements about normative facts.

I said earlier that utilitarians, deontologists and virtue ethicists can all be moral realists. For example, hedonist utilitarians claim that pleasure always gives us a reason to try to create it (it is good), and pain always gives us a reason to try to avoid it. They also claim that there is always more reason to bring about more pleasure than less (this is right). Virtue ethicists, on the other hand, claim that certain facts about being human mean that a certain way of living is the best, most flourishing life. We therefore have reason to develop our characters in ways that allow us to live like this, and meet our and other people's needs.

 # QUESTIONS FOR DISCUSSION

Should we make a distinction between facts and values? What implications does such a distinction have for moral realism?

Related examination question

(Part b) Explain and illustrate the cognitivist view that we can know moral facts. *(15 marks) (2003)*

Associated problems

We have already discussed three objections that are often made to moral realism. We shall finish this discussion before looking at three other objections.

Three quick objections

The first objection we have discussed is the difference between facts and values, the gap that Moore noted with his open question argument and that non-cognitivists argue for (see 'META-ETHICS: NON-COGNITIVISM' below). The point can be put concisely: no fact can logically entail a moral value. This objection is sometimes also known as the 'is–ought gap'. We have seen the realist's response: whether a natural fact counts as a reason for believing a certain value judgement is itself a matter of objective fact (it is a normative fact). Perhaps it is true that natural facts don't logically *entail* value judgements. This is because 'entailment' is one kind of normative fact, like 'proof'. But there are others, like 'evidence for' and 'reason for'.

A second objection we have already discussed is the claim that moral disputes cannot be resolved by appeals to facts, that judgements of value always go beyond the facts. The realist's reply here is that this is true if you are only talking about natural facts. But there are other types of fact that people are disagreeing on, namely normative facts. If we resolved the disagreement about both natural facts and normative facts, people would agree on the moral judgement as well. The moral realist can also accept that we cannot resolve disagreements about normative facts just by appealing to natural facts. A modern form of intuitionism might claim that we discover facts about reasons through a kind of intuition.

A third objection is known as the argument from 'queerness'. Isn't the idea of values existing in the world like facts a very strange notion? And how we are supposed to come to know these values seems very strange too. But realists will deny that they claim anything queer at all. If all realists thought values existed as Platonic Forms, perhaps the argument from queerness would have some force. But we have seen that values can be understood in terms of normative facts. And it seems we need these even to do science, because the idea of a natural fact (the results of radiometric dating) being a reason to believe another fact (when dinosaurs existed) is needed wherever we have beliefs. So normative facts aren't strange. As for how we come to know about values, as indicated in the discussion of intuitionism, one possible reply is 'through emotional cognition', a combination of emotional sensitivity with right reasoning. It is through virtue and practical wisdom that we come to an understanding of moral reasons.

Related examination question

(Part c) Assess the view that we can't get an 'ought' from an 'is'. *(24 marks) (2003)*

Three long objections

The first new objection questions why we should believe that our intuitions (of values directly, or of certain facts being reasons for certain value judgements) are *beliefs* at all. They might actually be expressions of feeling, or a matter of choice. I shall not discuss this now, since the sections in 'META-ETHICS: NON-COGNITIVISM' below present these theories.

There are two further objections to look at. One is the question of relativism. The other is the question of the relation between moral values and motivation.

Relativism

Different cultures have different moral beliefs and practices. If moral realism is correct, then some moral beliefs are true, and others are false. We measure our morality against the way the world is. The realist claims that different cultures are all aiming to get at the *truth* about ethics, just as scientists are trying to find out the truth about the world.

The relativist claims that this makes it difficult to understand why such a variety of cultural practices have existed. Why have different cultures come up with different moral answers? Where they disagree, how can we explain why at least one culture has 'got it wrong'? Why couldn't people in that culture see what was right and do that? The realist's story doesn't sit well with an understanding of the history of a culture and how its ethical practices developed.

Relativism understands ethical claims to be part of a culture, not part of reality; ethical practices have developed to help people find their way around a social world. But there are many social worlds, many cultures, and they have developed different ways of doing things. And so there is no ethical truth beyond culture. There is no single truth to ethics.

Realists have three responses. First, they can say that different ethical practices reflect the different particular conditions in which different cultures are situated, but not different ethical principles. For example, the Inuit used to abandon their old people on ice flows to die, while we try to keep them alive for as long as possible. But this doesn't mean killing old people is right for the Inuit and wrong for us. The practice is simply due to the harsh conditions of survival in which the Inuit lived. It would be right for us if we lived in their conditions, and wrong for them if they lived in ours.

Second, realists draw attention to just how many general ethical principles and virtues different cultures share. For example, most cultures have prohibitions on killing, lying, and theft, and encourage care of the weak.

Third, realists draw attention to moral progress. We have become more humane than in the past, and there is greater agreement about moral judgements than before. This is because we are discovering real moral truths.

But are these answers persuasive?

Moral judgements guide our behaviour. If I think pleasure is good, I aim to bring about pleasure. If I think abortion is wrong, I will not commit or encourage others to commit abortion. This motivating aspect of moral judgements seems puzzling if the moral realist is correct. A fact, in and of itself, doesn't lead to action. It seems that I need to *care* about the fact, and then the motivating force comes from the caring. For example, the fact that it is raining doesn't motivate me to pick up my umbrella unless I don't want to get wet. How then does 'Abortion is wrong' motivate me to act unless I care about right and wrong? But surely, claims this objection, statements about right and wrong, good and bad are motivating in their own right.

But are they? questions the moral realist. This objection doesn't work otherwise. There certainly seem to be people – and perhaps all of us at certain times, e.g. when we are depressed – for whom statements about morality are not motivating. They just don't care about morality; they can understand that an action is morally wrong, but this doesn't affect their behaviour. Moral judgements, then, are only motivating to people who care about morality. Since most of us do most of the time, it is easy to think that the judgements are motivating on their own.

Related examination questions

(Part a) Briefly explain *two* reasons for believing that there are no moral facts. *(6 marks) (2002)*

(Part b) Describe and illustrate *one* account of how moral language can guide or influence action. *(15 marks) (2001)*

● META-ETHICS: NON-COGNITIVISM

Non-cognitivism maintains that there is no ethical knowledge, because ethical judgements are not statements that can be true or false. In this way, non-cognitivists draw a sharp distinction between facts and values.

Emotivism

The principle of verification and Ayer's theory

In the 1930s, a school of philosophy arose called logical positivism. The cornerstone of its beliefs was the principle of verification. This claims that a statement only has a meaning if it is either (1) **analytic** or (2) empirically verifiable. An analytic statement is true (or false) just in virtue of the meanings of the words. For instance, 'a bachelor is an unmarried man' is analytically true, while 'a square has three sides' is analytically false. A statement is empirically verifiable if **empirical** evidence would go towards establishing that the statement is true or false. For example, if I say 'the moon is made of green cheese', we can check this by scientific investigation. If I say 'the universe has 600 trillion planets', we can't check this by scientific investigation in practice, but we can do so *in principle*. We know how to show whether it is true or false, so it is 'verifiable' even though we can't actually verify it.

The principle of verification entails that many types of statement, for example, statements about right and wrong, beauty, and God, are *meaningless*. They are neither true nor false, because they do not actually state anything. If I say 'murder is wrong', there is no empirical investigation we can do to show this. We can show that murder causes grief and pain, or that it is often done out of anger. But we cannot demonstrate, in the same way, that it is *wrong*. To say 'murder is wrong' is not, therefore, to say anything that can be true or false.

We can see how this theory relates to Moore's intuitionism (see p. 70). Moore claimed that basic moral judgements are self-evident and that good is a non-natural property. Both claims imply that moral judgements cannot be shown to be true or false by empirical investigation. But Moore believed that moral judgements are nevertheless true or false, because they are about non-natural properties. For the logical positivists, however, if empirical investigation can't settle the truth of moral judgements, they are meaningless.

So if ethical statements don't state truths, and are therefore literally meaningless, what do they do? In his book *Language, Truth and Logic* (1936: ch. 6), the logical positivist A. J. Ayer argued that ethical judgements express feelings: 'If I say to someone, "You acted wrongly in stealing that money" . . . I am simply evincing my moral disapproval of it. It is as if I had said, "You stole that money," in a peculiar tone of horror' (p. 142). Our 'intuitions', as Moore would describe them, are simply our feelings of approval or disapproval. Feelings are not cognitions of value, and value does not exist independently of our feelings.

The main difficulty with logical positivism is that according to the principle of verification, the principle of verification is meaningless. The claim that 'a statement only has meaning if it is analytic or can be verified empirically' is not analytic and cannot be verified empirically. What empirical evidence can we produce to show that it is true? None. But if the principle of verification is meaningless, then what it claims cannot be true. So it does not give us any reason to believe that the claims of ethics are meaningless.

Stevenson's theory

Fortunately for Ayer, his theory of ethics, known as emotivism, does not depend on the principle of verification. Charles Stevenson did not use the principle of verification nor claim that the only types of meaning are descriptive and analytic meaning. In his book *Ethics and Language* (1944), he discussed the *emotive* meanings of words, which is a different type of meaning again. The sentence 'You stole that money' has a purely descriptive meaning, namely that you took money that did not belong to you without permission from the owner. But it can be used with an emotive meaning ('You *stole* that money!'), a meaning that expresses disapproval. Many moral terms ('steal', 'honesty', 'respect') have both descriptive and emotive meanings. The central ones, though, 'right', 'wrong', 'good' and 'bad' only have emotive meanings.

Stevenson analyses emotive meaning by connecting meaning to *use*. The purpose of moral judgements is not to state facts. 'Good' and 'right' are not names of properties (natural or non-natural). We use moral terms and moral judgements to express our feelings and to influence the feelings and actions of other people. When we use the terms 'good' and 'right', we express our approval.

This claim is the essence of emotivism. And it is a strong claim. Surely the whole point of ethics is to influence how we behave. Words with emotive meaning do just that. The view that 'right' and 'good' are the names of properties (whether natural or non-natural) makes their meanings descriptive, not emotive. But, as we saw above (p. 78), this makes it difficult to see why we should care about moral facts. Why should I care that the act was wrong any more than I should care that it was done at 3.30 p.m.? According to moral realism, they are both just properties of the act. Emotivism, by contrast, connects caring, approving, disapproving, with the very meaning of ethical words.

Related examination questions

(Part a) Briefly explain what is meant by the claim that moral language is used to express feelings rather than to describe facts. *(6 marks) (2001)*

(Part b) Describe and illustrate *one* account of how moral language can guide or influence action. *(15 marks) (2001)*

Emotivism and moral disagreement

One of the most powerful objections to emotivism is that it seems to entail a very unsatisfactory view of ethical discussion. If I say 'abortion is wrong' and you say 'abortion is right', I am just expressing my disapproval of it and you are expressing your approval. I'm just saying 'Boo! to abortion' and you're saying 'Hurrah! for abortion'. This is just like cheering for our own team; there is no *discussion*, no *reasoning*, going on at all. Even worse, emotivism claims that we are trying to influence other people's feelings and actions. But trying to influence people without reasoning is just a form of manipulation.

Ayer thought this objection partly false, partly true. It is false because emotivists claim that there is a lot more to ethical discussion: the facts. When arguing over animal rights, say, we are constantly drawing facts to each other's attention. I point out how much animals suffer in factory farms. You point out how much more sophisticated human beings are than animals. And so on. In fact, says Ayer, *all* the discussion is about the facts. If we both agree on the facts, but still disagree morally, there is no more discussion that can take place. And this is why the objection is true – but not an objection. When all the facts are in, there is nothing left to discuss. (We saw the realist's response to this on p. 76.)

The disagreement that remains, Stevenson argued, is not a disagreement over any fact. It is a disagreement in attitude. It is a practical disagreement; no one can live both by the attitude that 'eating meat is wrong' and by the attitude that 'eating meat is right'.

Prescriptivism

R. M. Hare believed that emotivism had identified some important mistakes in moral realism, but he argued that it gave the wrong account of the meaning of moral words. Moral words are not descriptive and emotive in meaning; they are descriptive and *prescriptive* (Hare 1952). This difference meant that he was able, he claimed, to give a more persuasive account of moral discussion that allowed a greater role for reason.

Prescriptive meaning

Prescriptive meaning works like commands, also known as imperatives. If I say 'Leave the room', I am telling you to do something. Hare argued that if I say 'Eating meat is wrong', I am saying 'Don't eat meat'. In claiming that moral judgements are like imperatives, Hare's theory is like Kant's (see p. 48). The emotivists were right to claim that the purpose of moral judgements is to guide how we act. And commands do exactly that: they tell us how to act.

There is a difference between commanding – or telling – someone how to act, and trying to get them to act that way. We saw that emotivism is open to the objection that it makes ethical discussion a matter of manipulation. Hare's theory sees the 'guiding' aspect of ethics as a matter of prescription, rather than a matter of influencing someone through emotion. This makes ethical discussion more straightforward and rational.

So what is prescriptive meaning? We use the word 'good', says Hare, when we want to *commend* something to someone. We can talk about good chocolate, good teachers, and good people. In each case, we are saying the chocolate, teacher, or person is praiseworthy in some way. In each case, there is a set of standards that we are implicitly relying on. Good chocolate is rich in the taste of cocoa. A good teacher can explain new ideas clearly and create enthusiasm in her students. A good person – well, a good person is someone who is the way we should try to be as people. A virtue theorist would say a good person is someone who has the virtues. Just as there are certain traits a teacher should have to be a good teacher, there are certain traits a person should have to be a good person.

Whenever we use the word 'good', Hare claims, we always use it in relation to a set of standards. After all, if you say 'Martin Luther King was really good', whether you mean 'good as a speaker' or 'good as a father' or 'good as a person' depends on the context. But you must mean 'good as . . .' something. There are different sets of standards for being a good speaker, a good father, and a good person.

When we use 'good' to mean 'morally good', we are appealing to a set of standards that apply to someone as a person. If we say that an action is a good action or a right action, we mean it is an action that complies with the standards for how someone should act to be a good person. There is a slight difference of emphasis between 'good action' and 'right action': 'good action' *commends* the action without necessarily *commanding* it; we are saying it should be praised, but not necessarily that you *have* to do it to be a good person. If we say an action is the 'right action', then we are commanding it; it is a guideline for behaviour that people should follow.

So the prescriptive meaning of 'good' relates to the fact that it commends. What about its descriptive meaning? This comes from the set of standards that is being assumed. Its descriptive meaning picks up on the qualities that the something must have to be a good . . . (speaker, father, coffee pot, desk, whatever).

 ## QUESTIONS FOR DISCUSSION

What is the difference between descriptive and prescriptive meaning? What does the word 'good' mean?

How moral language works

Because 'good' is always used in relation to a set of standards, it always has a descriptive meaning. And since we usually use 'good' to commend, we generally use it with prescriptive meaning as well. But we do not always use it with prescriptive meaning. Take the dog show Crufts. The judges have a set of standards for each type of dog, and will say things like 'What a wonderful poodle!' You might agree that, as poodles go, that poodle has it all, but really you prefer your poodles rugged and scruffy. So if you say 'OK, so it's a good poodle', you aren't commending the poodle, you are just acknowledging that it is fluffy, dainty, and so on. We might capture this by saying 'So it's a "good" poodle.'

This can happen with any word that both commends and describes; we can use it just to describe and not commend or disapprove. Take moral words like 'steal' or 'honesty'. We often use the word 'honest' to commend someone. But I can say 'If you weren't so honest, we could have got away with that!' This is an expression of annoyance, not praise. I'm using 'honest' in a purely descriptive way. This even works with 'good person'. I can agree that a 'good person' is one who is honest, kind, just, etc. But I can still think that good people are not to be commended, because, as Woody Allen said, 'Good people sleep better than bad people, but bad people enjoy the waking hours more.'

Hare is making a point similar to that of the emotivists: that descriptive meaning and prescriptive meaning are logically distinct. And when we use words with a moral meaning, we use them with a prescriptive meaning. This means that nothing about being honest (e.g. telling the truth: descriptive meaning) can make me commend honesty (think that telling the truth is how to behave: prescriptive). More generally, nothing about the facts – of abortion, euthanasia, animal suffering – can logically entail that abortion is wrong, say, or that euthanasia is right. We are, in this way, *free* in the prescriptions that we make.

However, Hare argues that this freedom is rationally constrained. As we saw, prescriptions relate to a set of standards. And a standard applies to something in virtue of the properties it has; for example chocolate is good if it has a rich taste of cocoa. So if one bar of chocolate is good chocolate because it has a rich taste of cocoa, then another bar of chocolate that has the same taste must also be good chocolate. Whenever we apply a standard, we are logically committed to making the same judgement of two things that match the standard in the same way. If I say this chocolate is good but that chocolate is not, I must think that there is some relevant difference between the two.

When it comes to moral judgements, the same is true. We can choose what standards we live by, but standards always work in a certain way. I think that it is wrong for you to steal from me, because it infringes my rights of ownership. Therefore I must think that it is wrong for me to steal from you, because it infringes your rights of ownership – unless I can say that there is some relevant difference between the two cases. Hare argues that the simple fact that in one case *you* steal from *me* and in the other case *I* steal from *you* is not a relevant difference; both actions infringe rights of ownership. Because this was the reason I gave in the first case, and the same fact is true in the second case, I must accept that the same judgement applies in the second case.

Prescriptivism and emotivism

How does Hare's theory improve on emotivism? Emotivists thought that the only role for reason in ethical discussion is establishing the facts. Hare has developed two more ways in which reason is part of ethical discourse.

First, we can argue about consistency. For example, in his argument regarding animals, Singer claimed that there was no relevant difference between the suffering of people and the suffering of animals. If we are going to say that causing the suffering of people is wrong, we are committed to saying the suffering of animals is wrong – unless we can find a relevant difference. Establishing whether there are any relevant differences is another role for reason.

Second, we can infer prescriptions from other prescriptions. A famous argument against abortion says 'Taking an innocent human life is wrong. Abortion is the taking of an innocent human life. Therefore abortion is wrong.' This is a valid argument, even if we rephrase it as Hare would understand it: 'Do not take innocent human life. Abortion is the taking of an innocent human life. Therefore, do not commit abortion.' To disagree with the conclusion, we must disagree with at least one premise. And so our prescriptions are logically related to one another. So we can use reason to discuss these relations.

Related examination questions

(Part a) Identify *one* similarity and *one* difference between emotivism and prescriptivism. *(6 marks) (2003)*

(Part b) Explain and illustrate the view that moral language is prescriptive. *(15 marks) (2002)*

Associated problems

What is the role of reason in ethics?

We have already discussed one objection to non-cognitivism, namely that it cannot account for our use of reasoning in moral discussion. The non-cognitivist response is simply to rebut the objection. Moral disagreements can be, and often are, about facts. When they are not about facts, Hare argues, moral disagreements can also be about the consistency in applying certain standards, and about how one standard can imply another. Stevenson argues a parallel point: that moral disagreements can be about whether one moral attitude excludes another in the sense that no one can live by both at the same time.

We can develop this last point further. People do not have feelings or make choices in isolation. The attitudes we adopt have implications for other attitudes and mental states. If I disapprove of an action, I must also have certain beliefs about it (my reasons for disapproving, such as that it causes pain) and certain desires towards it (such as wanting to prevent it), and as Hare argued, I must have similar feelings about similar actions. Moral disagreement, then, can be about the relations between different feelings that we have. For example, deciding whether abortion is right or wrong is complicated because there are many feelings involved, sympathy towards the mother, sympathy towards the fetus, feelings about human life, death, and parenthood. It is difficult to work out how these feelings can all be acted upon, and that is why people disagree.

Form and content

Two further, and very important, difficulties that non-cognitivism faces relate to the fact that it doesn't place limits on what we can approve or disapprove of. The first difficulty stems from the fact that non-cognitivism identifies moral judgements with a particular *type* of judgement, rather than a particular *content*. Emotivism equates moral judgement to the expression of moral approval or disapproval (and related emotions). Prescriptivism equates it to an expression of principle that applies to people as people. But isn't morality about sympathy, loyalty, courage, happiness, and so on?

It must be true to say, as non-cognitivism does, that moral judgements are special or different in some way. This is shown, for instance, in the close relation between making a moral judgement and being motivated to act on it. But is the special nature of moral judgements to be explained just in terms of their *form* (emotional expression or universal prescription), or are they special because of their *content*, i.e. what it is they are about?

This question becomes clearer when we consider the second, related difficulty. Because non-cognitivists understand moral judgements in terms of their form, not their content, they seem to allow that anything could be morally approved or disapproved of or chosen as a principle of action. I could disapprove of people under 1.6 metres tall or choose to live by the principle that we must maximise the number of florists living in Kensington. But the idea of morality is not so unrestricted. It must relate in some way to what is good for people (or more broadly, animals, the environment, God). If we don't at least try to relate our feelings of approval and disapproval or our choice of principles to this, those feelings and choices cannot qualify as 'moral'. Not just any set of expressions of approval or principles can count as 'morality'. Values are not so detached from facts – about human nature, for instance – that we can understand any system of principles or feelings as embodying a system of moral values.

How can the non-cognitivist explain this? According to the non-cognitivist, we explain moral values in terms of feelings or choices. But the objection shows that we have to presuppose certain ideas about moral values in order to understand feelings or choices as relating to morality at all. It is not just a matter of the form of the judgement.

We need to ask whether we can value anything we choose to. Non-cognitivism claims first, that a judgement is a value judgement if it has a particular form; and second, that value judgements 'create' values rather than 'discover' them. For the moral realist, our value judgements are a reflection of values that exist independently. For the non-cognitivist, values are a reflection of our value judgements. It follows that, if values depend entirely on our will, we could value anything we chose to. But this is difficult to make sense of. Outside certain limits, we would consider people mad rather than thinking that they just had a different set of values from ours.

Imagine that someone did believe in maximising the number of florists in Kensington, and all her 'moral' feelings and actions related to this: she is willing to do anything to pursue her goal (even murder), she tries to stop florists from closing down, she tries to change the law to protect florists in Kensington, she feels no disapproval towards theft, lying, disloyalty, no approval of kindness or courage – unless they relate to florists in Kensington. Such a person would be classed as a psychopath. As I said above, the limits of what we understand as 'morality' relate to what we can understand as relating to what is good for human beings (or more broadly, animals, the environment, God).

One way non-cognitivists can respond is by making use of those facts about human beings that limit our idea of morality. It is precisely because human beings have certain needs, have a particular nature, that we do not value things that are not related to human (animal, etc.) welfare. And this is just a natural fact about human beings. 'Valuing' is an activity of the will, but the will is guided by its nature. In truth, there is no *logical* restriction on possible 'moralities', but there is a considerable *factual* one. We are all set up, by evolution perhaps, to value actions and people in particular, familiar sorts of ways. This is why we call only particular sets of feelings or principles 'moral'. The objection doesn't prove that there are facts about morality that our feelings or choices must answer to. It only shows that a common human nature underlies our feelings and choices. But it is still these feelings and choices that create morality.

Nihilism

A fourth objection to non-cognitivism is that it entails that there are no values, so anything goes. This is known as **nihilism**. If morality is the product of my feelings and choices, then morality has no authority over me. I can do whatever I like, as long as I don't get caught. 'Morality' becomes no more than a matter of taste, and taste cannot be shown to be right or wrong ('de gustibus non disputandum': taste cannot be disputed).

Non-cognitivists argue that this is either an unfair simplification of their theories or a straightforward misunderstanding. The adoption of nihilism is itself a choice or expression of feeling, and one that moral people will disapprove of morally. The view that there are no moral values is one particular moral position, and comes into conflict with the moral feelings and choices of other moral positions. The theory that moral values are a reflection of our feelings does not imply that we should stop having moral feelings. Nihilism is not 'more correct', but a cynical and immature view of life (note the emotionally expressive evaluative words). And so we should have disapproving moral feelings towards anyone who advocates that morality is just a matter of taste.

Non-cognitivism and tolerance

Many people think that non-cognitivism implies a certain kind of tolerance. If morality is a reflection of our choices or feelings, and my choices or feelings are different from yours, then who are you to tell me that my morality is wrong? Non-cognitivism implies tolerance, they claim, because no one can correct anyone else.

Tolerance can appear to be a virtue, but it can also be a vice. Should we tolerate every view, including racism, sexism, female circumcision? Doesn't morality require that we 'take a stand' against what is wrong? Can non-cognitivism allow for this?

The objection is based on a mistake, because non-cognitivism does not entail tolerance for two reasons. First, tolerance is itself a moral value. 'You ought to tolerate other people's values, because there are no moral values' is self-contradictory. If there are no moral values, then there is nothing I 'ought' to do. We only ought to be tolerant if tolerance is a good or right thing to be. So, turning the tables, who are you to tell someone else to be tolerant? This is no different from saying that someone ought not to eat meat or ought not to be racist. It is a moral claim. Non-cognitivism doesn't entail that we ought to be tolerant or that we ought not to be tolerant.

Second, if my morality is different from yours, then not only will I disagree with you about whether a particular action is right or wrong, I may also disapprove of people who disagree with me and try to persuade them to change their mind. Or, I might feel that tolerance is a moral value, so I feel I should tolerate their different values. But this tolerance will have its limits. Very few people think that tolerance is a more important value than preventing a racist murder, say.

For these same reasons, non-cognitivism does not imply relativism. To claim that moral judgements can be right for you and wrong for me because we have different cultures is itself a moral claim. If I feel approval towards a particular action, I may disapprove of people who behave as if the action is wrong. How tolerant I am of other cultures depends entirely on whether I think such tolerance is a good thing.

But can I really justify interfering with how other people behave just because their actions don't accord with my feelings or choices? This seems very petty. But this isn't the reason I am interfering, claims the non-cognitivist. It is not because it offends me, but because they are being racist or cruel or cowardly or whatever.

The difference between non-cognitivism and moral realism is this: for the non-cognitivist, that I think racist discrimination is a good reason to prevent an action is an expression of my moral feelings. For the realist, that this is a good reason to interfere is a normative fact. The realist claims to have the backing of reality.

Moral progress

A final objection to non-cognitivism is that it does not allow for the idea of moral progress. If there is no moral reality, then our moral beliefs or feelings cannot become better or worse. Obviously, they have changed; people used to believe that slavery was morally acceptable and now they do not. But how can non-cognitivism say that this is *progress*? There are two responses non-cognitivists can give.

First, as we noticed when discussing the place of reason in moral debate, non-cognitivists can claim that there can be very real improvements in people's moral views if they become more rational. This can happen in several different ways. First, people may come to know certain facts that they didn't know before. In the case of slavery, people believed many things about slaves that were not true (one popular false belief was that they were stupid). Moral progress here means basing one's moral feelings or principles on the facts, not mistakes. Second, people can become more consistent, more willing to universalise their principles. Some utilitarians, such as Peter Singer, argue that if we were consistent in our feelings about preventing suffering, we would not eat meat. If he is right, then this would be moral progress. Third, people can become more coherent in their moral judgements. Many of us have moral feelings that come into conflict with each other, e.g. over abortion. Moral progress here would be a matter of working out the implications of our views, and changing what needed changing to make them coherent with each other.

Because people are ignorant, do not always think logically, and have not resolved the conflicts between their different feelings, the non-cognitivist can say that there is plenty of room for moral progress. But moral progress just means becoming more rational in our moral thinking, not becoming more 'correct' in our moral judgements.

A second response that non-cognitivists can make to the objection from moral progress is this: If I disapprove of the moral feelings or principles of societies in the past and approve of the moral feelings and principles of society in the present, then I will also say that we have made moral progress. Society has moved from moral principles that were bad (i.e. principles I disapprove of) to moral principles that are good (i.e. principles I approve of). That is what moral progress is.

This response means that moral progress is only visible from a particular moral point of view. If you disagree with me, you might claim that today's moral principles are much worse than those 200 years ago and so we have not made moral progress. But this is now just the familiar problem of moral disagreement or relativism, and we saw how the non-cognitivist answered these problems above. The problem of moral progress is just another example of these problems.

Related examination questions

(Part c) Assess the view that moral beliefs are a matter of personal decisions, preferences and tastes. *(24 marks) (2001)*

(Part c) Assess emotivism. *(24 marks) (2002)*

(Part c) Assess the view that we can't get an 'ought' from an 'is'. *(24 marks) (2003)*

REFERENCES

Aquinas (1998) [1485] *Summa Theologica*, excerpts reprinted in McInerny, R. (ed.) *Thomas Aquinas, Selected Writings*, Harmondsworth: Penguin.

Aristotle (1980) [*c.* 325 BC] *The Nicomachean Ethics*, ed. David Ross, Oxford: Oxford University Press.

Ayer, A. J. (1936) *Language, Truth and Logic*, London: Victor Gollancz.

Bentham, J. (1962) [1789] *Introduction to the Principles of Morals and Legislation*, reprinted in Mill, J. S. *Utilitarianism*, ed. Mary Warnock, London: Fontana.

Hare, R. M. (1952) *The Language of Morals*, Oxford: Clarendon Press.

Hursthouse, R. (1992) 'Virtue theory and abortion', *Philosophy and Public Affairs* 21, 223–46.

Kant, I. (1991) [1785] *Groundwork of the Metaphysic of Morals*, translated and analysed by Paton, H. J. as *The Moral Law*, London: Routledge.

Mill, J. S. (1962a) [1838] 'Bentham', London and Westminster Review, reprinted in Mill, J. S. *Utilitarianism*, ed. Mary Warnock, London: Fontana.

——(1962b) [1863] *Utilitarianism*, reprinted in Mill, J. S. *Utilitarianism*, ed. Mary Warnock, London: Fontana.

Moore, G. E. (1903) *Principia Ethica*, Cambridge: Cambridge University Press.

Plato (2000) [c. 360 BCE] *The Republic*, ed. G. R. F. Ferrari, trans. Tom Griffith, Cambridge: Cambridge University Press.

Regan, T. (1983) *The Case for Animal Rights*, Berkeley: University of California Press.

Ross, W. D. (1930) *The Right and the Good*, Oxford: Oxford University Press.

Singer, P. (1975) *Animal Liberation*, New York: Random House.

Stevenson, C. L. (1944) *Ethics and Language*, New Haven, Conn.: Yale University Press.

● ◖ **RECOMMENDED READING** ◗

● A lively, engaging, and quick introduction to the main issues of ethics, written in a very clear style, is Simon Blackburn's *Being Good* (Oxford: Oxford University Press, 2001). At the opposite end in terms of length is Peter Singer's edited collection of introductory essays *A Companion to Ethics* (Oxford: Blackwell, 1991), an irreplaceable resource. Each essay, written for the beginner, is an excellent survey of a single topic. One of the clearest, mid-length introductions to ethics is James Rachels's *The Elements of Moral Philosophy*, 3rd edn (Boston: McGraw-Hill, 1999). He considers normative theories in relation to practical issues. With more detail, Piers Benn's *Ethics* (London: UCL Press, 1998) is a careful and accurate introduction across the whole range of normative and meta-ethical issues. And Richard Norman's *The Moral Philosophers* (Oxford: Clarendon Press, 1983) is one of the best introductions to the normative and meta-ethical theories of ethics via the great philosophers who held them. It also includes a good discussion of moral realism, defending it against the powerful attack that can be found in the first two chapters of John Mackie's *Ethics: Inventing Right and Wrong* (Harmondsworth: Penguin, 1977). Bernard Williams's *Morality* (Cambridge: Cambridge University Press, 1976) includes difficult, but excellent, discussions of subjectivism, relativism, the idea of 'good', and utilitarianism. His joint book with John Smart, *Utilitarianism: For and Against* (London: Cambridge University Press, 1973) is one of the most informative discussions of utilitarianism: its structure, its motives, and its problems.

Finally, on practical ethics, two classic works, both defending a utilitarian standpoint but discussing a wide range of arguments, are Peter Singer's shorter and clearer *Practical Ethics*, 2nd edn (Cambridge: Cambridge University Press, 1993) and Jonathan Glover's more detailed *Causing Death and Saving Lives* (Harmondsworth: Penguin, 1977).

GLOSSARY

act utilitarianism – The normative moral theory that claims (1) happiness is the only good, and (2) an action is only right if it leads to greater happiness than (or at least equal happiness to) any other action possible in that situation, i.e. if it maximises happiness.

analytic – An analytic statement is true (or false) in virtue of the meanings of the words. For instance, 'If I'm heavier than you, you are lighter than me' is analytically true, while 'a square has three sides' is analytically false.

cognitivism – The meta-ethical theory that we can have moral knowledge. Many cognitivists are also moral realists, although Kant is an exception. He believed moral knowledge could be deduced from pure reason.

deontology – The normative moral theory that whether an action is right or wrong is determined by the properties of the action, and not, for example, by its consequences.

duty – The idea that an action is morally obligatory or required. It is the central moral concept of deontology.

empirical – Relating to or deriving from experience, especially sense experience, but also including experimental scientific investigation, even if it involves special instruments.

fallacy – A pattern of poor reasoning. A fallacious argument or theory is one that is mistaken in some way.

hedonism – Hedonism can mean either of two different claims: (1) happiness is the only good, or (2) happiness is pleasure and the absence of pain. Utilitarianism, as defended by Bentham, is a hedonic theory in both senses.

higher pleasure – If one type of pleasure, e.g. reading literature, is preferred to another type of pleasure, e.g. drinking alcohol, by almost everyone who has experience of both, then it is the higher pleasure. Mill argued that higher pleasures are more valuable to human beings than lower pleasures, and contribute more to their happiness. He believed that pleasures of thought, feeling, and imagination were higher pleasures while pleasures of the body were lower pleasures.

intuitionism – The cognitivist meta-ethical theory that claims we come to know moral truths through 'intuition', rather than pure reason or the senses. It is associated with the view that moral properties are not natural properties we can know about in any other way.

maxim – A personal principle that guides our choices, e.g. 'to have as much fun as possible', 'to marry only someone I truly love'. Our choices usually have some maxim or other behind them, which explains our reasons for that particular choice. Kant claimed that only maxims that everyone could live by are morally acceptable.

meta-ethics – The study of the meaning and nature of moral concepts, such as 'right' and 'good', and moral statements, such as 'Abortion is wrong'. Among other things, meta-ethics debates whether morality is objective or subjective and whether there can be moral knowledge.

moral realism – The cognitivist meta-ethical theory that claims that moral properties are a genuine part of the world, e.g. good and bad are properties of situations and people, right and wrong are properties of actions. Statements about moral properties can be true or false, and so there are moral facts.

natural law – The normative moral theory that

claims that a basic set of principles for reasoning about what to do (practical reason) has been laid down by God or can be derived from facts about human nature and the natural world.

naturalism – The meta-ethical theory that moral properties are, or are determined by, natural properties. It is a type of moral realism.

nihilism – The meta-ethical theory that there are no moral values, that morality is a fiction. It is sometimes thought to be entailed by non-cognitivism.

non-cognitivism – The meta-ethical theory that maintains that there is no ethical knowledge, because moral judgements are not statements that can be true or false. Moral judgements are expressions of emotion or attitudes, or prescriptions about what to do. Non-cognitivists draw a sharp distinction between between facts and values.

normative – Relating to 'norms', rules or reasons for conduct.

normative ethics – General theories about what is good and what types of action or codes of action are right. Normative ethical theories can provide guidance in practical cases.

practical ethics – The branch of philosophy that discusses whether a particular action or type of action, e.g. abortion, is right or wrong.

prima facie – At first sight, correct or accepted until shown otherwise. Ross argued that certain types of action are duties that we ought to perform unless they conflict with something more important. He called these prima facie duties.

relativism – The meta-ethical theory that morality is created by cultures or societies, and so the rightness or wrongness of moral claims is 'relative' to particular cultures or societies. There is no truth about morality independent of what cultures and societies actually think.

rule utilitarianism – The normative moral theory that claims (1) happiness is the only good, and (2) an action is right if it complies with rules which, if everybody followed them, would lead to the greatest happiness (compared to any other rules).

self-evident – A self-evident judgement has no other evidence or proof but its own plausibility. This doesn't necessarily mean that everyone can immediately see that it is true. 'Self-evident' is not the same as 'obvious'. However, the only way we can come to know the judgement is true is by considering it.

sentience – Primitive consciousness of perception, pleasure and pain.

utilitarianism – The family of normative moral theories that claim the only thing that is good is happiness, and the sole criterion for right and wrong is the maximisation of happiness. See also **act utilitarianism** and **rule utilitarianism**.

virtue – Usually, a morally good trait of character. Aristotle argued that virtues dispose us to feel desires and emotions 'well', rather than 'badly'. By 'well', he meant 'at the right times, with reference to the right objects, towards the right people, with the right motive, and in the right way' (Aristotle 1980: 38).

virtue theory – The normative moral theory that claims that the question 'What is a good person?' is more fundamental than the question 'What should I do?' Virtue theorists therefore develop theories about what it is to be a good person. An action is right, roughly, if it is an action that a virtuous person would do.

3

philosophy of religion

UNIT 2 Elizabeth Burns

Key concepts ○

- personal
- omnipresent
- creator and sustainer of the universe
- transcendent
- omniscient
- omnipotent
- perfectly good
- analogy
- verification
- falsification
- language-game
- cosmological argument
- teleological argument
- argument from religious experience
- ontological argument
- Pascal's wager
- Reformed epistemology
- the problem of evil
- miracles
- divine command ethics

● INTRODUCTION

Philosophy of religion uses the tools of philosophy to try to work out the meaning of religious beliefs and whether they might, in some sense, be true. If there is a God who requires us to live in a certain way, who helps us in times of trouble or gives us the hope of a life after death, this could make a big difference to our lives. So we need to know whether it's rational to make such claims.

● THE MEANING AND JUSTIFICATION OF RELIGIOUS CONCEPTS

Conceptions of God

We will begin by considering the various ways in which God has been described: his **attributes** or **properties**. These include 'personal', **'omnipresent'** (present at all places and (possibly) at all times), 'creator and sustainer of the universe', **'transcendent'** (outside the universe and (possibly) outside time), **'omniscient'** (all-knowing), **'omnipotent'**(all-powerful), and 'perfectly good'. In each case, we need to ask whether we can give a **coherent** account of what we mean when we say that God has that property – whether we can, for example, spell out what it means to say that God is omnipotent without saying anything that seems to contradict other things we want to say about God or about the world.

Personal

What is a person? There is much disagreement about this, but, broadly speaking, a person may be said to be at least some of the following:

- an individual substance: something which exists separately from other persons
- a collection of desires, beliefs, and sensations. This is sometimes called 'the bundle theory'.
- rational: able to acquire knowledge and use it to make decisions
- able to act by free choice
- aware of and able to communicate with other persons
- able to form relationships with other persons
- worthy of dignity and respect.

All of these may be – and have been – applied to God.

However, some scholars make a distinction between saying that God is a person and saying that God is personal. For example, Brian Davies argues that 'God is personal' means that God has knowledge and will (he makes choices), and is active. But this is not the same as saying that God is a person; Davies notes that the phrase 'God is a person' is not found in the Bible or the creeds, and says that we should not talk about God 'as if he were the man in the next street'. People are associated with 'bodies and parents and food and drink and sex and society and death' but God is 'bodiless and immortal or eternal' (in Davies 2000: 560–1).

 # QUESTION FOR DISCUSSION

Davies says that God has knowledge and will, and is active. But are there other ways in which we could say that God is personal without implying that he is like 'the man in the next street'?

Omnipresent

An omnipresent God is present at all places, and, if God is timeless, at all times. But God is not present in the same way as physical objects are present. For Thomas Aquinas (*c.*1224–74) (1920), God is present in all places and at all times because his power, knowledge and **essence** (nature) extend to all places and all times.

Creator and sustainer of the universe

The God of the Bible is portrayed as creator of the world and everything in it (Genesis 1–2), but not usually as responsible for its continued existence. However, traditional western theology has held that God both created and sustains the universe, and that these activities are, in effect, the same; God's creation is continuous. This belief was derived from the view that God is timeless; if time does not pass for God, his act of creation is occurring at every moment of the history of the universe.

Hugh J. McCann (in Quinn and Taliaferro 1999) argues that the natural world cannot sustain itself. Scientific laws describe the characteristics and processes of natural things, but there is no natural process that explains how things continue to exist, and for this we need God. Although scripture sometimes seems to suggest that God is more active at some times than others – in sending Jesus to first-century Palestine, for example – this is simply because some of God's acts make his concern especially clear to us, and because some of them may involve departures from the natural order of events. It would be contradictory for an unchanging God to intervene in our world only occasionally; since he cannot change, he must be continuously involved. It would also be contradictory for a loving God to intervene only occasionally; his concern for his creation means that he is involved with everything that happens.

Transcendent

A transcendent God is outside the universe, and may be outside our temporal system (Aquinas held both of these views). If God is timeless, it may be objected that he cannot act within our temporal world. But Nicholas Wolterstorff (in Peterson et al. 2001) suggests that, on Aquinas' view, God's actions affect events in time even though they are not themselves events in time. For example, although God may have enabled the Israelites to escape from Egypt in 1225 BC, God's action did not occur in 1225 BC. Events that are past, present or future from our perspective occur simultaneously from God's perspective.

Omniscient

To say that God is omniscient is to say that he is all-knowing. The meaning of this depends on whether we say that God is timeless, or that he exists everlastingly within time.

If God is timeless, his omniscience means that he sees, and therefore knows about, all the events of time (which, from our point of view, are past, present and future) simultaneously. Boethius (c.480–525) (in Davies 2000) said that this is like a man standing on a mountain seeing all the events on the road beneath him.

However, if God knows about our future actions before we perform them, this suggests that we cannot be free. If God knows that I will go hang-gliding next Tuesday, then, it would seem, I can't choose to play croquet instead. More importantly, if God knows that I will murder the Prime Minister next Tuesday then I can't do otherwise. I am therefore not responsible for my actions.

One way to respond to problems of this kind is simply to admit that human beings do not have free will. Alternatively, we could say that we do have the freedom to choose our actions, but that this freedom is limited by our natures – the kind of people we are – and our backgrounds – our upbringing, and the situations in which we find ourselves. For example, suppose I choose croquet rather than hang-gliding next Tuesday. I might think that my choice is completely free; I could just as easily have chosen hang-gliding. But someone who knows me well, and knows that I am a very cautious and anxious kind of person with family responsibilities, will not be at all surprised at my choice. This kind of freedom is called **liberty of spontaneity**. On this view, the fact that God timelessly sees what I will do next Tuesday does not matter because my freedom is so limited; what I think of as a free choice could be accurately anticipated by someone – like God – who understands me completely.

Someone who wanted to say that our choices are completely free – that we have **liberty of indifference** – could appeal to Boethius. He suggests that, although

God sees all human decisions and actions in one simultaneous present, this is not the same as saying that his knowledge **determines** our actions. We are therefore responsible for them and will be rewarded or punished, as appropriate. For example, Boethius says, if I know that a man is walking, the fact that I know this does not affect his freedom to do it. In the same way, if God sees all human actions as they occur, this does not affect our freedom to choose what we do.

 ## QUESTION FOR DISCUSSION

If God sees our actions as they happen, do you think that our actions can be genuinely free?

Two definitions of human freedom

- Liberty of spontaneity: We are free to choose our actions, but our freedom is limited by our natures and our backgrounds.
- Liberty of indifference: We are completely free to choose our actions.

If God exists everlastingly within time, his omniscience means that he knows everything about the past and the present, and everything about the future which his knowledge about the past and present enables him to predict. So, if human beings have only liberty of spontaneity, an everlasting God still knows what we will choose to do in the future. However, if we have liberty of indifference – genuine freedom – some say that an everlasting God cannot know our future choices because the future hasn't happened yet (e.g. Swinburne 1993). Others (e.g. Nelson Pike, in Peterson et al. 2001) think that, somehow, an everlasting God can know our future choices. But Pike seems to suggest that we are not free to make God's knowledge about the future false – which places constraints on human freedom and responsibility once more.

Omnipotent

To say that God is omnipotent is to say that he is all-powerful. Broadly speaking, there are two views about what this means:

- God is able to bring about anything that is **logically possible** (Aquinas and Swinburne). So he could not bring about the existence of a square circle, for example, because the creation of such a thing is not logically possible.

- As with the first view, God is able to bring about anything logically possible, but, in addition, he could have created a world in which what we take to be contradictions were not contradictions (William of Ockham (c. 1285–1349), and possibly René Descartes (1596–1650), discussed in Hughes 1995). So, although it is not logically possible for there to be a square circle in our world, God could have created a world in which the laws of logic were different, in which there could have been a square circle. Notice that this is not the same as saying that God is able to bring about things that are logically impossible in our world.

Even if we don't have to say that an omnipotent God can bring about things that are logically impossible in our world, it would appear that there are other things he can't do which, as an omnipotent being, we would expect him to be able to do. For example, the famous 'paradox of the stone' asks whether God could create a stone too heavy for him to lift. If he could not do this, there would be something which he could not do, i.e. create the stone. But if he could do this, there would still be something he could not do, i.e. lift the stone. (There are a number of variations on this paradox: for example, could God create a bowl of porridge too big for him to eat?)

Leaving aside the problem that, on most views, God does not have a body with which to lift stones (or consume porridge), various solutions to this problem have been put forward. Some have suggested that God could not make the stone. Although there is no contradiction in saying that a *human being* could create a stone that he or she could not lift, there is a contradiction in saying that *God* could make a stone that he could not lift – because it would be contradictory for an omnipotent being to make a thing too heavy for him to lift (George Mavrodes, in Peterson et al. 2001). Others have suggested that God could make the stone. He could choose not to lift it, thereby choosing not to destroy his own omnipotence (Swinburne 1993). Or we could say that, if God cannot lift the stone, there is no such thing as the power to lift the stone and God therefore cannot be expected to have this power. Or God could make an ordinary stone and promise never to move it. So he would be unable to lift it not because he lacked power but because to lift it would be to break his promise (Thomas V. Morris, in Davies 2000).

 QUESTION FOR DISCUSSION

We have looked at four possible solutions to the paradox of the stone. Which of these do you think is the best?

Perfectly good

Broadly speaking, God may be perfectly good in one, or perhaps both, of two senses. In the **metaphysical** sense of goodness, God's perfect goodness means that he is complete; he has no deficiency of any kind. In the moral sense of goodness, God's perfect goodness entails that he has no moral deficiency; he is perfectly benevolent, just, wise, and so on.

If God's goodness is moral goodness, this raises the question: Does God decide what is morally good, or is God good because he conforms to a standard of goodness that exists independently of himself? Debate about this question has a long history going back to Plato's *Euthyphro* dilemma. We will discuss it further in the final section of this chapter.

Related examination questions

(Part a) Identify and briefly describe *two* of God's properties. *(6 marks) (2001)*

(Part a) Briefly explain what is meant by any *two* of the following terms: transcendence, omnipotence, omniscience, omnipresence, perfect goodness. *(6 marks) (2002)*

Combining God's attributes

We have noted a number of difficulties in working out the meaning of some of God's attributes. Additional problems seem to arise when we consider God's attributes in combination. Perhaps the most significant of these is the problem of evil. This states that, if God creates and sustains a world containing evil, and is both omniscient (and therefore knows about the evil) and omnipotent (and therefore has the power to prevent or alleviate it), how can we also say that he is perfectly good?

One possible solution is to deny one or more of God's attributes.

QUESTION FOR DISCUSSION

Consider each of the following attributes in turn: creator/sustainer of the universe, omniscient, omnipotent, perfectly good. How might the denial of each attribute help us to solve the problem of evil?

Another possible solution is to modify one or more of God's attributes.

QUESTION FOR DISCUSSION

Considering the same attributes again, how might each be modified to help us solve the problem of evil?

Further solutions to the problem of evil will be considered later in this chapter.

Related examination question

(Part b) Explain *one* philosophical problem that arises when combining two or more of God's properties. *(15 marks) (2001)*

The nature of religious language

Religious language as analogical

Some of the difficulties in understanding the meaning of God's attributes could, perhaps, be avoided by saying that these attributes must be understood **analogically**.

Aquinas thought that words could not be ascribed to God and his creation **univocally**; i.e. their meaning when applied to God could not be the same as their meaning when applied to his creation. If the word 'good' means the same in 'God is good' as in 'Katherine is good', this implies that God is no better than the things he has created; he is just a sort of 'super-person'.

Aquinas also thought that words could not be ascribed to God and his creation **equivocally**; i.e. their meaning when applied to God could not be completely different from their meaning when applied to his creation. If the meaning of the word 'good' in 'God is good' is completely different from the meaning it has in 'Katherine is good', there seems to be no way to work out what it means to say 'God is good'.

Aquinas therefore argued that God's attributes can be understood analogically. Terms that are used analogically of God are used in a sense related to, but not the same as, the sense in which they are applied to our human world. In the previous section, we saw that God may be said to be personal and present in senses that are similar to but not the same as the senses in which a human being may be personal or present. For Aquinas, the meaning of terms used analogically could be 'stretched' in one of two ways. If, when we say that God is good, we are using an analogy of attribution, we mean that God is the source and cause of the goodness we see in the world. And if, when we say that God is good, we are using an analogy of proportionality, we mean that the way in which God is good is related to the way in which human beings are good. So, 'God is good in whatever way it is appropriate for God to be good' (Vardy 1999: 38).

Neither understanding of the use of analogy is without difficulties. In saying 'God is good', religious believers usually mean more than 'God is the cause of goodness', and, if God is good in whatever way it is appropriate for God to be good, this tells us little about God's goodness if we don't know how it is appropriate for God to be good.

Verification

Since it is difficult to explain the meaning of religious language, by the beginning of the twentieth century some scholars had begun to say that religious language has no meaning at all – that statements about God are meaningless.

In the 1920s, a group of philosophers who became known as the Vienna Circle and later as logical positivists developed a theory of meaning, a method for distinguishing between sense and nonsense, called the **verification principle**.

The 'strong' verification principle

In its first formulation, sometimes known as the 'strong' version, the verification principle claims that a meaningful statement is either **analytic** or **empirically verifiable**. An analytic statement is made true by the meanings of the words. In the classic example, 'A bachelor is an unmarried man', if we analyse the word 'bachelor' we find that this means 'an unmarried man'; so the statement must be true. A statement that is empirically verifiable is one that can be shown by experience to be true (e.g. 'There are some cars in the car park'), or one which we could, in principle, show by experience to be true even if we cannot do so at the moment. (A. J. Ayer, borrowing from Moritz Schlick, suggested as an example of this, 'There are mountains on the farther side of the moon' (1971: 49).)

According to the strong verification principle, any statement that is neither analytic nor empirically verifiable is meaningless. It therefore appears to rule out many of the statements made by religious believers.

However, this version of the verification principle also rules out many other statements that we usually regard as meaningful. For example, we can't show by experience that all flamingoes are pink because, no matter how many flamingoes we observe, it is always possible that there is, somewhere, a flamingo that is blue. It was therefore necessary to modify the verification principle.

The 'weak' verification principle

According to the 'weak' verification principle, a meaningful statement is one that is either analytic or shown by experience to be probably true.

This version of the principle allows us to say that the statement 'All flamingoes are pink' is meaningful on the grounds that experience suggests that all flamingoes are pink, even if we can never prove this conclusively. However, for Ayer, 'no statement which refers to a "reality" transcending the limits of all possible sense-experience can possibly have any literal significance' (1971: 46).

 ## QUESTION FOR DISCUSSION

Is the word 'literal' significant here?

Responses to the verification principle

Some scholars have suggested that we should reject the verification principle because, even in its weak version, the principle itself cannot be verified. The verification principle tells us that a meaningful statement is one that experience shows us is probably true; but, so the objection goes, experience cannot tell us this. This is because there are some statements (Davies (1993) suggests those about life after death, for example) that do seem to be meaningful but cannot be shown by experience to be probably true.

Others have argued that religious beliefs *can* be verified by experience. Later in his life, even Ayer seems to have allowed appeals to mystical experience, saying that he did not wish 'to restrict experience to sense experience'. He said that he wouldn't 'mind at all counting what might be called introspectible experiences or feelings; mystical experiences, if you like' (quoted in Charles Taliaferro 1998: 99). And John Hick (1990a) has argued that our beliefs about religion will be verified at the end of our lives. He tells a parable of two people walking along a road, one of whom believes that it leads to the Celestial City, while the other sees the journey as an 'aimless ramble'. When they reach the end of the journey, it will be clear that one of them was right and the other wrong. Similarly, Hick says, at the end of our lives our beliefs about religion will be verified (or not) when we either experience some form of life after death or cease to exist. This is known as eschatological verification.

QUESTION FOR DISCUSSION

To what extent do you consider these to be effective responses to the challenge of the verification principle?

The 'strong' verification principle:

A meaningful statement is either analytic or empirically verifiable.

The 'weak' verification principle:

A meaningful statement is either analytic or can be shown by experience to be probably true.

Two responses

- We should reject the verification principle because the principle itself cannot be shown by experience to be probably true.
- Religious beliefs *can* be verified by experience.

Falsification

As we have seen, some scholars have argued that statements about religious belief are nonsense because they cannot be verified. A closely related view is that statements about religious belief are nonsense because they cannot be **falsified**; in other words, believers are unwilling to allow anything to count against them.

The theory asserting that, for a statement to be meaningful, we must be able to say what would make it false, was initially developed by the philosopher of science Karl Popper. It was applied to religious belief by Antony Flew in his contribution to a discussion that became known as the *University* debate.

Flew and falsification

Flew tells a parable, based on a similar story from John Wisdom's paper 'Gods', of two explorers who come across a clearing in the jungle. One says that there is an invisible gardener, but the other denies this. They conduct various tests to try to detect a gardener; they set up an electric fence and patrol with bloodhounds, but no gardener is ever found. But still the first man maintains that there is a gardener: 'a gardener, invisible, intangible, insensible to electric shocks, a gardener who has no scent and makes no sound, a gardener who comes secretly to look after the garden which he loves' (Flew, in Hick 1990b: 367). But, the second man responds, 'Just how does what you call an invisible, intangible, eternally elusive gardener differ from an imaginary gardener or even from no gardener at all?' (p. 367). He objects that the definition of 'gardener' has been qualified to such an extent that it no longer has any meaning. The gardener-hypothesis has been 'killed by inches, the death by a thousand qualifications' (p. 368).

Similarly, Flew claims, religious believers respond to objections to their beliefs by qualifying those beliefs until they no longer have any meaning. For example, a believer might say that 'God loves us as a Father loves his children.' Faced with the objection that God appears to show no concern for a child dying of inoperable throat cancer, the believer might respond that God's love is 'not a merely human love' or that it is 'an inscrutable love'. But, Flew says, what is such love worth? What would have to happen for us to say that God does not love us – or even that he does not exist?

Hare's objection to falsification

R. M. Hare (in Hick 1990b) responds by telling a parable about a madman who thinks that all dons (university lecturers) want to kill him. No amount of evidence to the contrary can dissuade him from this belief; he will not allow anything to count against it. But the difference between his view of dons and our view of dons is simply that the madman has an insane **blik** (a word invented by Hare meaning, broadly speaking, a view held without reasons), and we have a sane one. Hare argues that neither view about dons can be falsified; there is nothing that would conclusively show either view to be mistaken. Therefore, he suggests, our view of dons is simply a matter of personal feeling, or choice.

However, it could be objected that Hare's parable actually supports Flew's falsification theory. The madman's belief is meaningless precisely because it is not falsifiable – because he will not allow anything to count against it. By contrast, our own view about dons *is* falsifiable. If every don I met aimed a loaded gun at my head, I would have reason to believe that at least some dons wanted to kill me. But since I have never, to my knowledge, met a don with murderous intentions, my belief that dons have no desire to kill me has not been falsified. So, the madman's view of dons is irrational, but ours is not.

Mitchell's response

Basil Mitchell (in Hick 1990b) responds to Flew by suggesting that the **theist** does recognise the fact of pain as counting against the assertion that God loves human beings. But he does not allow it to count decisively. Mitchell tells a parable about a member of the resistance in an occupied country who meets a stranger. The stranger tells him that he is on the side of the resistance and that he must have faith in him, no matter what happens. The resistance member is deeply impressed by the stranger and decides to trust him. Subsequently, even when the stranger seems to be acting for the enemy, the resistance member believes that he is on his own side. Similarly, the believer who trusts God continues to believe that God loves human beings, despite the many examples of evil in the world. Thus, Mitchell argues, the God-hypothesis cannot be falsified because there are good reasons for accepting it; they counteract any statements that might seem to falsify statements about religious belief.

 ## QUESTION FOR DISCUSSION

Do you think that Christianity would be falsified if it could be proved, beyond reasonable doubt, that Jesus never lived, that he was a habitual liar, that he suffered from delusions, or that he did not rise from the dead?

Falsification

For a statement to be meaningful, we must be able to say what would make it false.

Objections

- Hare: some of our beliefs are 'bliks': there are no reasons for them and they cannot be shown to be false.
- Mitchell: some things do count against religious beliefs, but these are not decisive because there are stronger reasons for accepting these beliefs. Therefore, religious beliefs cannot be falsified.

Language-games

The so-called **language-game** theory was derived from the later philosophy of Ludwig Wittgenstein, particularly his *Philosophical Investigations*. It has been applied to religious belief by a number of scholars, but perhaps most notably by D. Z. Phillips. Wittgenstein's philosophy is notoriously difficult to interpret; what follows is therefore my attempt to give a clear and systematic account of his view, but some scholars may disagree with my interpretation.

Wittgenstein said that we cannot assume that words refer to objectively-existing things; rather, words acquire meaning from the way in which they are used. The philosopher's task is to describe the way we use language, not to ask questions about whether or not things exist.

According to this theory, there are many different kinds of language, each associated with a different kind of activity. Each kind of language is called a language-game. Games have their own distinctive vocabularies and rules, which are learned by participants, and are neither true nor false. The same is true of languages. One list of language-games includes 'asking, thanking, cursing, greeting, praying' (Wittgenstein 1958: §23). As Beverly Clack and Brian R. Clack (1998) point out, Wittgenstein never describes religion in its entirety as a language-game, but this description has been used by others (e.g. Phillips).

The activity with which a language-game is associated is called a **form of life**. To understand the meaning of a word, we must understand not only the part it plays in its language-game, but also its purpose in the relevant form of life. For example, talk of the love of God must be understood not only in the context of other things that are said about God, but also by looking at what it means in practice. Again, Wittgenstein does not describe religion in its entirety as a form of life, but others (e.g. Keightley 1976) have suggested that this application of Wittgenstein's theory cannot be ruled out.

Since language-games are distinct from each other, the statements of one language-game cannot be criticised on the grounds that they conflict with the statements of another. This would be like a football player criticising a rugby player for handling the ball. So, for example, we might say that the story of Adam and Eve does not conflict with scientific theories about the origin of the world because religion and science are two different language-games (Hick 1990a); they are just two different ways of thinking, speaking and acting.

Although, according to Wittgenstein, the philosopher's task is to describe the way we use language, the language-game theory does not rule out the possibility that religion is concerned with a deity who exists outside of the language-game; the philosopher simply does not ask questions about this. However, Phillips seems to have developed Wittgenstein's view in a **non-realist** way. For Phillips, God is not a personal, active being; rather, God is found in the language people learn when they learn about religion. Knowledge of God is not knowledge of an objectively-existing supreme being, but knowledge of how to use religious concepts. And God does not intervene in the world in response to prayers; instead, believers pray in order to understand their own and others' difficulties, working out how best to deal with them or cope with them (Phillips 1981).

Objections to the application of the language-game theory to religious belief

Objections to the application of the language-game theory to religious belief include the following (but note that these objections may apply more to the views of those who have developed Wittgenstein's views than to Wittgenstein himself):

- '[T]he Neo-Wittgensteinian theory of religious language is that it is not (as it professes to be) an account of . . . ordinary religious language use but rather is a proposal for a radical new interpretation of religious utterances' (Hick 1990a: 98).
- Religious language and the religious form of life cannot be separated from other languages and forms of life:

> When the religious believer says that God created the heavens and the earth, that God raised Jesus from the dead or that God answered his prayers for healing, he implies there are connections between religious language and the language we use to describe nature, history and the daily events of our lives.
>
> (Evans 1982: 153)

- Such an interpretation of religious belief is relativist: each community constructs its own truths, and no view is true or false independently of the community in which it is used (Baggini 2002).

 ## QUESTION FOR DISCUSSION

What might be the possible consequences of relativism about religious beliefs?

Related examination questions

(Part c) Assess the view that talk about God is unintelligible. *(24 marks) (2001)*

(Part c) Assess whether religious language is meaningful. *(24 marks) (2003)*

● ARGUMENTS FOR THE EXISTENCE OF GOD

We have considered definitions of some of God's attributes, and how – and indeed whether – the language in which we describe God makes sense. We now examine four arguments which may – or may not – support belief in the God we have attempted to describe.

The cosmological argument

The **cosmological argument** is based on the assumption that the existence of the world, or some aspect of it, needs to be explained. The activity of God is said to provide this explanation.

Aquinas' cosmological arguments

The first three of Aquinas' (1920) Five Ways (arguments for the existence of God) are forms of the cosmological argument. (The Fourth Way is a form of the moral argument, and the Fifth is a version of the teleological argument.)

- The First Way argues that there must be a first cause of all change, since nothing changes itself and there cannot be a series of things each of which is changed by another, which is changed by another . . . and so on, without end.
- The Second Way argues that there must be a first cause of everything that exists, which is not itself caused to exist by anything else.
- The Third Way argues that there must be a **necessary** (here meaning not dependent on anything else) cause of all **contingent** things (things that may not have existed). If there had been no necessary cause, there would have been nothing to bring contingent things into existence and there would have been nothing now, and this is clearly not the case.

In each case, Aquinas argues, the cause is what all people call God.

Objections to the cosmological argument

Various objections to the cosmological argument have been raised. Four of the most important are as follows:

First, why could there not be an infinite series of causes of change, existence and contingent things? Why do we have to say that each series of causes began at some point? This is known as the problem of infinite regress.

Davies (1993) responds that, even if we say that each causal series goes back to infinity, we still need to find a cause of the whole series.

The second objection could be seen as a response to Davies. Although things in the world have causes, why do we need to say that there must be a cause of the universe as a whole? This objection was first raised by David Hume (1711–76) (1980), and illustrated by Bertrand Russell, who said that, although every person has a mother, this does not mean that the human race as a whole has a mother. Russell says, 'I should say that the universe is just there, and that's all' (1967: 139).

QUESTION FOR DISCUSSION

J. L. Mackie asks what reason there might be for making God 'the one exception to the supposed need for something else to depend on' (in Peterson et al. 2001: 215). Could this be applied to Russell's argument about the universe?

Third, it could be argued that no version of the cosmological argument gives us reason to believe in a single first cause; a different God could have been responsible for each planet, for example.

It may be possible to respond to this objection by appealing to **Ockham's razor**, a rule derived from the writings of Ockham, which states that 'entities are not to be multiplied without necessity'. In other words, we should accept the simplest explanation. Applied to the cosmological argument, this would mean that if a single first cause is an adequate explanation for the existence of the world, we shouldn't introduce further first causes unless there is some need to do so.

Finally, even if we accept that there must be a first cause of change, existence and contingent things, the cosmological argument seems to give us no reason to suppose that this cause has the full range of attributes that God is usually said to possess. For example, the argument gives us no reason to believe that the first cause is omniscient. And although the argument does imply that the first cause must be very powerful, this is not to say that it is omnipotent (*all*-powerful).

Nevertheless, it may be possible to find support for God's other attributes in other arguments for his existence. We therefore turn to the next of these: the teleological argument.

Related examination question

(Part c) Assess the cosmological argument. *(24 marks) (2003)*

The teleological argument

The **teleological argument** claims that the existence of God explains why the world appears to have been designed. ('Teleological' comes from the Greek *telos*, which means 'end', 'purpose', or 'design'.) Broadly speaking, there are three types of teleological argument: those that argue that particular things in the world seem to have been designed for a purpose, those that argue that the world seems to have been designed to function in a regular way, and those that argue that the world seems to have been 'fine-tuned' to support life and that, had any one of many things been slightly different, we would not have been here to appreciate it. In this section, we will look at one example of the first type (William Paley (1743–1805)), and one example of the second, which also contains elements of the third (Swinburne 1991).

Design in the sense of purpose

Paley gives us perhaps the most famous version of the argument in his *Natural Theology*, or *Evidences of the Existence and Attributes of the Deity collected from the Appearance of Nature*. Paley says that if he found a stone on a heath, he would be justified in saying that it might always have been there. But, he says:

> suppose I had found a watch upon the ground, and it should be inquired how the watch happened to be in that place: I should hardly think of the answer which I had before given, that . . . the watch might have always have been there.
>
> (in Klemke 1992: 32)

Paley thinks that, in such a situation, we would conclude that it had been put together for a purpose and that it must therefore have had a maker.

Paley claims that we would come to this conclusion even if we had never seen a watch made, if we had never known someone who could make one, if we could not make one ourselves or even understand how it was made, if the watch sometimes went wrong, or if there were some parts of the watch whose purpose we were unable to deduce.

We would not think that it was just one of a number of possible combinations of physical matter, that it contained within itself a principle that organised its various parts, that the mechanism was just a trick to make us think that the watch was designed, or that the design was the result of the laws of nature. We would still think that the watch had been designed, even if we knew nothing at all about how or why this had been done.

Similarly, Paley suggests, the natural world contains many instances of apparent design. For example, a bird's wings are made in such a way that it is able to fly, and the fins of a fish enable it to swim. Paley concludes that there must have been a designer of the world. The designer must have been a person, and that person is God.

Design in the sense of regularity

Swinburne gives us an example of a 'teleological argument from the temporal order of the world' (1991: 136). He argues that simple laws govern almost everything. For example, the law of gravity ensures that stones will fall, and the law of chemical cohesion ensures that desks hold together. The universe might have been chaotic, but it is not, and this requires an explanation.

Swinburne argues that it cannot be explained by science. Science can explain why particular phenomena behave in the way that they do – for example why an electron exerts the attractive force it does. But it cannot explain why phenomena behave in such a regular way. Therefore, he argues, there must be 'an agent of great power and knowledge' (p. 141) who causes phenomena to behave in this way.

Hume's objections

The classic critique of the design argument is found in Hume's *Dialogues Concerning Natural Religion*, published in 1779, twenty-three years before Paley's statement of the argument.

Swinburne (in Davies 2000) identifies eight objections made by Hume, all of which occur in the *Dialogues*, with the exception of the first, which comes from the earlier *Enquiry Concerning Human Understanding*:

1 We can only ascribe to a cause whatever qualities are needed to produce the effect. So the design argument, if it works, proves only the existence of a design-producing being. We cannot also say that this being has any of the other attributes traditionally ascribed to God.

Davies's (1993) response is that the designer of the universe must be powerful to achieve its effect, incorporeal (without a body) because it lies outside the universe, and purposive because it produces order. He suggests that, even if God is thought to have more attributes than these, we can argue that the design argument provides at least some support for his existence.

2 We cannot infer from the fact that examples of order in the universe have human causes that order in the universe as a whole has a cause, because the universe is unique. In other words, the analogy does not work because we have no way of knowing whether order and its explanations within the universe are in any way like order and its explanation in the universe as a whole.

Davies suggests that it is not unreasonable to ask questions about the origin of something unique. Scientists try to account for things – such as the human race – which are unique. And even if there is only one universe, it does share some of its properties with other things; for example, like many of its parts, it changes, is composed of material elements, and exhibits regularity. (In fact, as we saw earlier, Paley has already used a similar argument. He says that we would assume that a watch was designed even if we had never seen one before. The existence of watches points to the existence of watchmakers because watches exhibit regularity.)

3 If the world was designed, who designed the designer?

Swinburne suggests that the existence of the designer does not need to be explained because 'scientists have always thought it reasonable to postulate entities merely to explain effects, so long as the postulated entities accounted simply and coherently for the characteristics of the effects' (1991: 282). Thus, Davies argues, there is no reason to suppose that the cause of order exhibits the kind of order which requires an explanation external to itself. Just as human thoughts are causes of order but are ordered in themselves, so the order in the world is caused by thoughts of God which require no external explanation for their orderliness.

4 The argument makes God too anthropomorphic, i.e. too much like a human being.

Davies argues that, if God is the explanation of the world, he cannot be like the thing his existence explains; he does not have to share all the attributes of human designers. Swinburne says that, in order to control the regularities in the universe, God must be free, rational and very powerful, but that he cannot have a body since this would restrict his influence to a limited part of the universe, and we need him to explain scientific laws which operate in the world as a whole.

5 Why should there be only one designer? Many people work together to build a house or a ship, etc.

It has already been suggested that God does not have to share all the attributes of human designers (point (4) above). Davies notes that, although order is often produced by groups of human beings, this does not imply that every instance of order must be produced by a group.

As Swinburne points out, Hume is aware of 'the obvious counter-objection to his suggestion', i.e. Ockham's razor, which, as we saw in connection with the cosmological argument, requires that entities are not to be multiplied without necessity. Applied to the teleological argument, it leads to the conclusion that there is no reason to say that there is more than one designer. Hume thinks that this does not apply to his argument, however, because we do not know whether there is a god with enough power to order the whole universe. But Swinburne thinks that it does apply, whether or not we have such knowledge. Further, he suggests that, if the universe were ordered by several deities, we would expect to see 'the characteristic marks of the handiwork of different deities in different parts of the universe' (1991: 284). For example, there might be an inverse square law of gravity in one place, and a law just short of being an inverse square law in another.

6 Why can we not regard the universe as a living organism, which grows and reproduces in a regular manner, rather than as something like a machine or artefact?

Swinburne suggests that this objection does apply to design in the sense of purpose, but that it does not apply to design in the sense of regularity: 'The seed only produces the plant because of the continued operation of the laws of biochemistry' (p. 284).

7 The universe could be the result of chance; i.e. there are periods of chaos and order and we are currently living in a period of order.

But, even if the universe is the result of chance, it could be argued that we still need to explain the present order. According to Swinburne, the view that the universe is the result of chance becomes less plausible as time progresses and order remains.

8 Swinburne also notes that the *Dialogues* contain a substantial presentation of the argument that the world contains evil and that, if God designed the world, he is either not totally good or not omnipotent. But Swinburne suggests that this does not affect the teleological argument because it does not attempt to show that God is good or omnipotent.

Davies does appear to regard the existence of evil as a problem for the teleological argument but suggests that evil things can also be designed. For Davies, someone who accepts the teleological argument does not have to say that every particular thing works together for the good of other particular things.

 ## QUESTION FOR DISCUSSION

Are you convinced by the responses to these objections? Look again at (3) and (8) in particular.

Further objections

The argument from purpose

Since the publication of Charles Darwin's *The Origin of Species by Means of Natural Selection* in 1859, some (e.g. Richard Dawkins) have argued that we no longer need God to explain the way in which the natural world seems to be so well suited to its purposes. According to Darwin, the current state of the universe is merely the result of the struggle for survival; those organisms that were unable to adapt to their environments simply did not survive.

However, arguments from regularity such as Swinburne's are not vulnerable to this objection. Although the theory of evolution explains the apparent design of individual living things, it does not explain why the world works in accordance with laws of nature. One can simply say that evolution is the means by which God enables plants and animals to develop in such a way that they are best suited to their purposes, and that the existence of God is needed to explain the regular workings of laws of nature.

The argument from regularity

Nevertheless, it can be objected that, if God designs by means of natural selection, he has chosen a method that causes considerable suffering to those creatures who have failed to adapt adequately to their surroundings.

We could also object that the expectation of an intelligent cause does not guarantee that there is one; the presence of order could be just a brute fact. But Davies says that there are many other cases in which we do accept the existence of an intelligent designer as an explanation of order when there is no other explanation. For example, if a sequence of musical notes results in a symphony, we generally conclude that they were ordered by a composer.

Alternatively, we could argue that, if the universe were not regular, we would not be here to observe it. Therefore, the fact that we are here is not particularly surprising and so does not stand in need of any special explanation. In order to refute this objection, Swinburne (1991) constructs the example of a man who will be killed unless a card-shuffling machine draws an ace of hearts from each of ten packs of cards. The machine does draw ten aces of hearts and the victim thinks the machine has been rigged, but his kidnapper says that the outcome is not remarkable since he would not have lived to see it if any other cards had been drawn. But, Swinburne suggests, the victim is right; even though he could not have seen any alternative outcome, a draw of ten aces of hearts is still extraordinary and needs an explanation.

Related examination questions

(Part a) Briefly explain what is meant when an argument is described as 'teleological'. *(6 marks) (2001)*

(Part b) Outline and illustrate how the teleological argument for the existence of God uses analogy. *(15 marks) (2001)*

(Part c) Assess what can be concluded from the teleological argument. *(24 marks) (2001)*

The argument from religious experience

So far, we have examined two arguments that infer God's existence from some aspect of the world. In this section, we will consider the claim that it is possible to have more specific experiences of God or his effects, and that such experiences constitute evidence for his existence.

What is a religious experience?

Types of religious experience

Swinburne (1991) identifies five kinds of religious experience, two public and three private.

The two types of public experience are:

- those in which God, or God's action, is identified in a public object or scene, such as the night sky
- those that occur as a result of unusual public events, e.g. the appearance of the risen Jesus to his disciples (Luke 24: 36–49).

The three types of private experience are:

- those that an individual can describe using normal language, e.g. Joseph's dream that an angel appeared and spoke to him (Matthew 1: 20–1)
- sensations that cannot be described in normal language, e.g. mystical experiences
- those in which the individual has no sensations, but is directly aware of God (Swinburne does not describe these as mystical experiences, but others, e.g. William P. Alston (in Peterson et al. 2001), do so.)

The characteristics of mystical experience

William James suggests that there are four marks that enable us to identify a mystical experience:

- **ineffability**: It cannot be described in words; it can only be felt. It must be experienced to be understood.
- **noetic** quality: Although it is like a state of feeling, it is also a state of knowledge. It communicates a truth or truths that cannot be communicated in any other way.
- transiency: It does not last more than an hour or two.
- passivity: It sometimes causes a feeling of being controlled by a higher power.

James considers a number of examples of mystical experience, including those of Hindus who have undergone training in yoga: the 'experimental union of the individual with the divine'. Diet, posture, breathing, concentration and moral discipline lead disciples to a state known as *samadhi*, in which they learn that the mind has a higher state, beyond reason and above consciousness and in which there is no sense of self. In this state, they see the Truth and know themselves for what they really are, 'free, immortal, omnipotent, loosed from the finite, and its contrasts of good and evil altogether, and identical with the Atman or Universal Soul' (in Peterson et al. 2001: 13).

Alston argues that, since God is spiritual, mystical experiences that are non-sensory are more likely to present God as he is. Alston says that we cannot adequately describe some of the things in the world that we claim to perceive directly and therefore have to resort to analogy. For example, I might be able to describe my **perception** of someone only by saying 'She looks like Susie'. So, although we cannot describe direct perceptions of God, it is quite legitimate to claim that we have such perceptions.

Can we use religious experience to prove God's existence?

Swinburne argues that, in judging whether or not a religious experience is a genuine experience of God, we should apply the Principle of Credulity and the Principle of Testimony.

The Principle of Credulity

The Principle of Credulity states that, unless there is some special reason for doubt, we should accept that 'How things seem to be is good grounds for a belief about how things are' (Swinburne 1991: 254).

There are four things that might make us doubt that the way things seem to be indicates how things are:

1   The conditions or the person have been found in the past to be unreliable. For example, past experience may suggest that it is unwise to trust perceptions made under the influence of LSD, or by a particular person.
2   Similar perceptual claims have proved false. For example, if a person claims that he has read ordinary-size print at a great distance but cannot do this on other occasions, it is likely that his original claim was false.
3   Background evidence suggests that it is very probable that the thing perceived was not present. For example, a claim to have seen John in the corridor might be doubted if there were others in the corridor looking for John who did not see him.
4   Although the perception is genuine, it was not caused by the thing thought to have been perceived. For example, a person may genuinely have seen someone in the corridor who looked like John, but his perception may have been of an actor dressed like John.

Swinburne suggests that these may be applied to religious experiences as follows:

1   Claims to have had a religious experience are not usually doubted on these grounds. Most religious experiences are had by those who have not taken drugs and are generally regarded as reliable.
2   This challenge would be effective if it could be shown that alleged religious experiences are generally unreliable. This could be done if there were a good proof of God's non-existence – but there is not.

Some suggest that religious experiences are unreliable because they support conflicting beliefs. Swinburne responds that God may be known by different names to people of different cultures. In cases where there is a genuine conflict – a Jew would not accept an experience of Christ, for example – if the opponent can give good reasons for regarding the experience as false, the person who had the experience must either withdraw the claim or 'describe it in a less committed way' (1991: 266); for example, the claim could be to have been aware of some supernatural, but unidentified, being.

 QUESTION FOR DISCUSSION

Do you think the suggestion that God may be known by different names to people of different cultures constitutes a reasonable response to the objection that religious experiences are unreliable because they support conflicting beliefs? Give reasons for your answer.

> Another way to suggest that alleged religious experiences are generally unreliable is to say that those who have such experiences have not had the kind of experiences that are needed to make such claims probably true. For example, it might be argued that a claim to have recognised a person is only likely to be correct if you have previously perceived that person in some way and been told who he is, or if you have been given a detailed description of him. But Swinburne suggests that a description of God as an omnipotent, omniscient and perfectly free person may enable us to recognise him, and, even if we find it difficult to recognise power, knowledge or freedom in human persons, we might be able to recognise extreme degrees of them.

3 This challenge would be effective if it could be shown that, very probably, God was not there to be perceived, but, as Swinburne has already suggested, this cannot be done.

4 This challenge would be effective if it could be shown that alleged experiences of God were caused by something other than God. But, if God is omnipresent and the sustainer of all causal processes, *whatever* brings about an experience of God will, ultimately, be caused by God. It could only be shown that these alleged experiences were not caused by God if it could be shown that God does not exist.

Thus, Swinburne concludes, we should accept alleged experiences of God as genuine unless it is much more probable that God does not exist. And, he claims, the balance of probability may be tipped in favour of the genuineness of religious experiences if there is evidence that others have such experiences.

The Principle of Testimony

According to Swinburne's Principle of Testimony, unless there is some special reason for doubt we should accept that the experiences of others are as they report them. Most of our beliefs about the world are based on the perceptions of others. We might doubt someone's perception if we had evidence that, either generally or in that particular case, they were misremembering, exaggerating, or lying. But, in most cases, none of these applies. In the case of religious experience, we can test whether they do apply by examining the person's life-style after the experience. If they act as if there is a God, it is likely that the experience was genuine. Although believing on the basis of others' experiences is not as good a reason for belief as believing on the basis of one's own experience, many of our beliefs about the world *are* based on the reports of others and, particularly when many people claim to have had the same experience, it is reasonable for us to accept their testimony.

So, if we accept the testimony of others (the Principle of Testimony) this may make it probable that God exists and show that there is no overriding reason to reject our own experience as genuine (the Principle of Credulity). Someone who has not had an experience of God will have less evidence for God's existence, but he or she will still have the testimony of others on which to base such a belief.

Swinburne's Principle of Credulity: Unless there is some special reason for doubt, we should accept that how things seem to be is good grounds for belief about how things are.

Swinburne's Principle of Testimony: Unless there is some special reason for doubt, we should accept that the experiences of others are as they report them.

Responses to the Principle of Credulity

In support of the fourth challenge to the Principle of Credulity, that alleged experiences of God are caused by something other than God. Wayne Proudfoot (in Peterson et al. 2001) argues that such experiences can be explained in historical or cultural terms. He suggests that religious experiences are shaped by the religious traditions within which they occur, and within the particular forms of the tradition that shaped the person and his or her experience.

Michael Martin suggests that religious experiences are caused not by external realities but by the workings of people's minds – the psychological hypothesis. The use of drugs and alcohol, mental illness and sleep deprivation provide experiences that are not trusted because they do not give us a coherent account of an external reality and '[r]eligious experiences are like those induced by drugs, alcohol, mental illness, and sleep deprivation: they tell no uniform or coherent story, and there is no plausible theory to account for discrepancies among them' (in Peterson et al. 2001: 45).

QUESTION FOR DISCUSSION

Do you agree with Martin that there is no plausible way to explain why some religious experiences seem to be incompatible with others? Look again at Swinburne's arguments in response to the second challenge to the Principle of Credulity.

The Negative Principle of Credulity

Martin suggests that, if experiences of God are grounds for belief in the existence of God, experiences of the absence of God are good grounds for belief that God does not exist. So if we accept the Principle of Credulity we also have to accept the Negative Principle of Credulity, according to which 'If it seems . . . to a subject S that x is absent, then probably x is absent' (in Peterson et al. 2001: 52).

Swinburne argues that we cannot experience the absence of God because we do not know under what conditions God would appear if he existed. But Martin suggests that, if we do not know this, this would also mean that we cannot experience the presence of God.

So perhaps a better response to this objection is suggested by Davies (1993: 127), who says that the fact that some claim to have experienced the absence of God does not mean that those who have experienced God are wrong. Two groups of people may hunt for the same animal. The first may see it and the second fail to find it, but this does not mean that the first group was mistaken.

Responses to the Principle of Testimony

As we saw above, Swinburne argues that we can test whether a person's experience is likely to be genuine by examining their life-style after the experience – whether, in the case of a religious experience, the person acts as if there is a God. However, Martin suggests, '[o]ne could have a vision of God and yet, on account of weakness of will or the overpowering or dreadful nature of the vision, degenerate morally' (in Peterson et al. 2001: 46). In addition, it is quite possible that someone might show moral improvement after an illusory religious experience.

 # QUESTION FOR DISCUSSION

To what extent do Martin's objections to the Principle of Testimony invalidate claims to have experienced God?

Related examination questions

(Part b) Outline and illustrate *two* characteristics of a religious experience. *(15 marks) (2003)*

(Part b) Outline and illustrate *two* criticisms of the argument from religious experience. *(15 marks) (2002)*

The ontological argument

We have examined several arguments based on some feature of the world or human experience – arguments that are *a posteriori*: after, or based on, experience. We now turn to an argument that begins with human thought – an argument that is *a priori*: before, or prior to, experience.

Broadly speaking, the **ontological argument** claims that existence is part of the definition of God and that God must therefore exist.

Anselm's ontological argument(s)

The ontological argument originated with Anselm (1033–1109). In chapter 2 of his *Proslogion*, he defines God as 'that than which nothing greater can be conceived' (thought of) and argues that even the fool mentioned in Psalm 14:1 can have this concept in his mind. However, he continues, if the concept exists only in the mind it cannot be that than which nothing greater can be conceived, because then there would be something greater – the same concept existing in reality. Therefore, that than which nothing greater can be conceived cannot exist only in the mind; it must exist in reality as well.

In chapter 3 of the *Proslogion*, Anselm argues that, although a person can be thought not to exist, the same is not true of God; he exists necessarily. This is because, if God did not exist necessarily, he would not be that than which nothing greater can be conceived.

It is important to realise that Anselm is using 'necessary' in a sense different from the sense in which Aquinas uses the word in his Third Way. As we saw, in the Third Way, God's necessity means that he is not dependent on anything else. For Anselm, however, something exists necessarily if its non-existence would be self-contradictory. Necessity of this kind is often called logical necessity.

Some scholars (e.g. Norman Malcolm) have argued that *Proslogion* chapter 3 gives a different version of the argument from that found in *Proslogion* chapter 2.

However, others (e.g. Davies 1993) have argued that the so-called second form of the argument is simply a further explanation of the first; Anselm is just making it clear that, since the definition of God includes necessary existence, God cannot not exist.

Gaunilo's objection

Writing 'On behalf of the fool', Gaunilo of Marmoutier raises several objections to Anselm's argument. In the most well-known of these, he tries to show that Anselm's argument is absurd by using it to prove the existence of a perfect island. His argument is as follows:

- Some say that there is a 'lost island', which is superior in every way to islands inhabited by human beings.
- But it would be ridiculous to argue that this island must exist on the grounds that if it exists only in the mind it is not 'more excellent than other lands' (Anselm 1962: 308–9).

In his reply to Gaunilo, Anselm says that 'of God alone it can be said that it is impossible to conceive of his non-existence' (1962: 319). This is because, as Anselm has shown in chapter 3 of his *Proslogion*, only God exists necessarily.

A second response has been made by Alvin Plantinga (in Peterson et al. 2001), who has suggested that the idea of a greatest possible island is incoherent because, no matter how many palm trees (or whatever) the island has, it is always possible for it to have more. The same is not true of God. A being cannot be more powerful than omnipotent, or more knowing than omniscient, so it makes sense to describe an omnipotent, omniscient (etc.) being as perfect, whereas it makes no sense to describe any island as perfect, because any island can be improved still further.

Descartes's ontological argument

Descartes (in Davies 2000) argues that God is 'a supremely perfect being' and that existence is a perfection: a desirable attribute that it is better to have than to lack. Therefore, existence cannot be separated from God, just as having three angles cannot be separated from the essence of a triangle, and the idea of a mountain cannot be separated from the idea of a valley.

Kant's objections to Descartes

Immanuel Kant (1724–1804) made two famous objections to Descartes's version of the ontological argument. First, he says that '[t]o posit a triangle [i.e.

say that it exists], and yet to reject its three angles, is self-contradictory; but there is no contradiction in rejecting the triangle together with its three angles. The same holds true of the concept of an absolutely necessary being' (in Davies 2000: 338). That is, although it may be contradictory to say that God exists without some of the attributes that he must have in order to be God, it is not contradictory to say that God, with all his attributes, does not exist.

Davies (1993) says that Anselm is not trying to argue that God exists on the grounds that existence must be included in the definition of God; rather, he is arguing that something than which nothing greater can be conceived cannot exist only in the mind. However, it could be argued that the two arguments are equivalent. If the concept of something than which nothing greater can be conceived must include existence and therefore cannot exist only in the mind, this amounts to saying that God exists because existence must be included in the definition of God.

 ## QUESTION FOR DISCUSSION

Do you agree that the two arguments are equivalent?

Kant's second objection is that existence cannot be a perfection because it is not a real **predicate**, an attribute of something that tells us more about it. A hundred existing thalers (a thaler was a unit of German currency) do not contain any more thalers than 100 possible thalers.

However, we could argue that 'exists' is only different from other kinds of predicate in that it describes something not described by other predicates. And this must be true of every predicate. This 'something' differs from that which is described by other predicates in that anything that does not have this particular property also lacks all other properties. But 'exists' is not the only property the absence of which also rules out other properties. For example, something that does not possess the property of being male cannot possess the property of being a father. So, we could suggest, the difference between 'exists' and other properties is simply one of degree. The absence of the property of existence simply rules out a larger number of other properties (i.e. all of them) than the absence of any other property. So perhaps we *can* say that existence is a real predicate – that it does tell us something about an object.

The ontological argument and non-realism

As we have seen, it is difficult for someone who accepts the ontological argument to show that the concept of God exists objectively. However, if, as some non-realists suggest, God is simply a concept in the minds of believers, then it may be possible to argue that the ontological argument does, indeed, prove the existence of God.

Related examination questions

(Part a) Briefly explain *one* difference between the ontological and teleological arguments for the existence of God. *(6 marks) (2003)*

(Part b) Outline and illustrate *one* criticism of the ontological argument for the existence of God. *(15 marks) (2003)*

Arguments for God's existence

A posteriori arguments (based on experience)

- cosmological argument: God explains the existence of the world or some aspect of it.
- teleological argument: God explains the purpose or regularity in the universe.
- argument from religious experience: Religious experiences are evidence for God's existence.

A priori argument (prior to experience: based on thought)

- ontological argument: Since (necessary) existence is part of the definition of God, God must exist.

● FAITH, REASON AND BELIEF

We have examined a range of arguments for the existence of God. However, we saw that none of these arguments provides conclusive proof of the existence of an objectively-existing personal deity. For some scholars, this does not matter, as they think that faith does not depend upon arguments. They hold that there are some things that cannot be known by reason, but that it is nonetheless reasonable to choose to believe them.

Pascal's wager

In his *Pensées*, Blaise Pascal argues that, if there is a God, he is beyond our comprehension, and we are therefore unable to give rational arguments for belief. However, he suggests that it is reasonable to wager that God exists. We have to choose one way or the other: in favour of God, or against him. And, Pascal says, if you wager that God exists, 'if you win, you win everything; if you lose, you lose nothing. Wager that he exists then, without hesitating!' (in Stump and Murray 1999: 298).

But what of the person who says: 'I am made in such a way that I cannot believe'? Pascal replies that the inability to believe arises from the feelings. Such a person should therefore try to change these feelings by behaving as if he believed; by taking holy waters and having masses said he will eventually come to believe naturally.

Pascal says that no harm will come to a person from following this course of action. He says, 'You will be faithful, honest, humble, grateful, doing good, a sincere and true friend. It is, of course, true; you will not take part in corrupt pleasure, in glory, in the pleasures of high living. But will you not have others?' (in Stump and Murray 1999: 300).

 # QUESTION FOR DISCUSSION

To what extent does reason feature in Pascal's account of faith?

Objections to Pascal's wager

There are a number of possible objections to Pascal's wager. These include:

1 Pascal is appealing to self-interest.

George Schlesinger replies that Pascal's wager was only a first step. Once the wager has been made the wagerer is instructed to behave as if he believed, in the hope of attaining genuine belief in God.

Schlesinger admits that we could still object to this on the grounds that, no matter how desirable the end result, it is achieved by appealing to selfish motives; the person who eventually believes may live a good life in the process of attaining that belief, but he does so only because he wants to attain some good for himself.

But Schlesinger replies that almost every act fulfils some wish; even a philanthropist could be satisfying the need to reach the pinnacle of 'other-directedness'. He suggests that an action is deplorable only when it harms others or oneself by preventing the striving after higher-order pleasures. And the pleasure that Pascal recommends is of the highest order; so, if craving for this pleasure is counted as greed, then it is 'a noble greed that is to be acclaimed' (in Stump and Murray 1999: 303).

2 Pascal seems to present us with only two options. But there are many others. 'How is the wagerer to assess the relative benefits associated with betting on Osiris, Baal, Dagon, Zeus, or Blodenwedd?' (p. 304). This is sometimes referred to as the 'many gods' objection.

Schlesinger's responses to the 'many gods' objection include:

(a) Some choices are more probable than others.

So, he argues, it makes more sense to wager on a God who is faithful, just and right whose attributes 'resonate with our nobler sentiments', than it does to wager on 'an unprincipled, arbitrarily acting, wanton god' (p. 307).

(b) It is reasonable to prefer the simplest hypothesis.

The theistic hypothesis is the simplest because it is the only one that can be expressed in terms of a single predicate; to describe God, the theist need only say that he is an absolutely perfect being. By contrast,

> though there is a large body of ancient Greek literature concerning Zeus, there are still many aspects of Zeus's character that remain unknown to us. We know for instance that he was sometimes asleep, but we have no idea how many hours of sleep he needed and what effect sleeplessness had on him. We also know that he ate and drank, but not how much or whether he occasionally overgorged himself or how long he could go without any food at all.
>
> (in Stump and Murray 1999: 308)

❓ QUESTION FOR DISCUSSION

Do you agree that theism is the simplest hypothesis?

Related examination question

(Part a) Briefly outline Pascal's wager. *(6 marks) (2002)*

Reformed epistemology

In the previous section, we saw that there are some religious beliefs that can be accepted only on the basis of faith, but that it might be rational to accept these beliefs on the basis of faith.

Philosophers known as 'Reformed epistemologists' have argued that there are some religious beliefs that must be accepted on the basis of our experience of God, and that all other religious beliefs are dependent on these beliefs. Such beliefs are known as **properly basic** – they are beliefs on which other beliefs depend, and which can be accepted without proof.

Plantinga

Plantinga is, perhaps, the best known proponent of Reformed epistemology. Following the theologian Herman Bavinck, he says that theologians in the Reformed tradition reject **natural theology** (arguments for God's existence) because:

- People do not, as a matter of fact, believe in God on the basis of arguments for his existence.
- Belief in God can be rational without arguments for God's existence.
- It is not possible to come to belief on the basis of arguments because the arguments of natural theology do not work.
- Scripture begins with God as the starting point, and the believer should do the same.
- We believe in the existence of the self and the **external world** without arguments, so it is acceptable to believe in God without arguments (in Peterson et al. 2001: 330–1).

Plantinga cites the view of John Calvin (1509–64) that there is 'a sense of deity inscribed in the hearts of all' (quoted in Peterson et al. 2001: 331) and that it is sin that prevents us from being aware of the deity: many of us cannot believe because we are sinful.

Further, God 'not only sowed in men's minds that seed of religion . . . but revealed himself and daily discloses himself in the whole workmanship of the universe. As a consequence men cannot open their eyes without being compelled to see him' (p. 332). Calvin says of the heavens that

> [e]ven the common fold and the most untutored, who have been taught only by the aid of the eyes, cannot be unaware of the excellence of divine art, for it reveals itself in this innumerable and yet well-ordered variety of the heavenly host.

> (in Peterson et al. 2001: 332)

QUESTION FOR DISCUSSION

Does this imply that Calvin and Plantinga accept a version of the teleological argument?

Plantinga suggests that no argument is implied; in such circumstances, Calvin claimed, the person simply knows that God exists.

Following Calvin again, Plantinga claims that it is not simply the case that the Christian does not need arguments; he ought not to believe on the basis of argument because, if he does, his faith will be unstable.

Thus, according to Plantinga, the Reformers thought that belief in God can be taken as basic: a person is rational to believe in God without arguments, and without basing this belief on any other beliefs.

The Great Pumpkin objection

Plantinga defends Reformed epistemology against the objection that, if belief in God is properly basic, why cannot any belief be properly basic – such as the belief that the Great Pumpkin returns every Halloween? Or that if I flap my arms hard enough, I will be able to fly around the room?

Plantinga says that Reformed epistemology does not allow us to hold that beliefs such as these are properly basic. Although some propositions seem self-evident when they are not, 'it would be irrational to take as basic the denial of a proposition that seems self-evident to you' (in Peterson et al. 2001: 339). For example, Plantinga says that, if it seems to you that you see a tree, it would be irrational to take as basic the proposition that you do not see a tree.

There are, he thinks, no arguments showing us what is and is not properly basic. But we can tell the difference between propositions that are and are not properly basic by collecting examples of statements that are properly basic and those that are not. By examining these statements, we can work out how to decide what makes a belief properly basic.

So, for Plantinga, the Reformed epistemologist can say that belief in the Great Pumpkin is not properly basic, even though he or she holds that belief in God is properly basic. But he or she must say that there is a relevant difference between the two beliefs, and there are plenty of these. For example, the Reformed epistemologist can say, like Calvin, that God has implanted in us a natural tendency to see his work in the world, and that the same cannot be said of the Great Pumpkin – because there is no Great Pumpkin, and there is no natural tendency to accept beliefs about the Great Pumpkin.

QUESTION FOR DISCUSSION

Do you think that this is a good response to the 'Great Pumpkin objection'?

Objections to Reformed epistemology

For Reformed epistemologists, it is an awareness of God that enables them to say that belief in God is properly basic. But this awareness of God is open to the objections to religious experience that we considered above. For example, Robert Pargetter (in Peterson et al. 2001) considers the possibility that some experiences are brought about by the circumstances in which they occur, or that, in the same situation, some people will experience God while others will not.

Other scholars argue that there are **defeaters** (i.e. things that count against a belief to the extent that we must reject it) for the basic belief that God exists. These include the fact that many people do not believe in God, explanations of religious belief as psychological projections, and the existence of many religions. However, perhaps the most significant potential defeater is the problem of evil. Although Plantinga has argued that no one has yet constructed a successful argument for God's non-existence based on the existence of evil, William Hasker thinks that the problem of evil does constitute a defeater for theistic belief.

Replies to these two objections might consist of detailed responses to the objections raised: trying to explain why a good God might allow evil, for example. In addition, Hasker suggests, we could appeal to various arguments for the existence of God and argue that, taken together, they support the view that the overall evidence is more in favour of God's existence than against it (in Peterson et al. 2001: 353).

Fideism

Fideism may be defined as the view that religious beliefs cannot be assessed by reason. If views that reject natural theology may be called fideistic, the views of Wittgenstein and his followers and the Reformed epistemologists may also be termed fideistic in this sense (Terence Penelhum in Quinn and Taliaferro 1999).

However, a more radical form of fideism, which not only rejects natural theology but stresses the paradoxical nature of faith has been widely associated with Sören Kierkegaard (1813–55). Although recent scholarship has suggested that this may not be an accurate representation of Kierkegaard's own view, he does seem to have put forward such a view when writing under the pseudonym of Johannes Climacus in his book *Concluding Unscientific Postscript*.

Climacus argues that attempting to find God by means of reason can take a great deal of time, and that this time is wasted since a person has no belief while undertaking the search. The person may die tomorrow without finding God, but even if he does not, belief in God is not something to be accepted 'if convenient' but something to be accepted at any price. While objective knowledge

> rambles comfortably on by way of the long road of approximation without being impelled by the urge of passion, subjective knowledge counts every delay a deadly peril, and the decision so infinitely important and so instantly pressing that it is as if the opportunity had already passed.
>
> (in Peterson et al. 2001: 96)

For Climacus, the passion with which a person believes is more important than the objective truth of the beliefs. He argues that someone who goes to the house of the true God with a true understanding of God but prays in a false spirit has less truth than the person who prays to the image of an idol with passion: he prays truthfully, even though he worships an idol. Truth is an objective uncertainty held passionately. Climacus suggests that attempting to find God by contemplating nature may lead him to see omnipotence and wisdom, but will also show him much else that will lead to objective uncertainty. But, he says, faith embraces uncertainty with a passion. Such faith is a risk – but without risk there can be no faith. To preserve his faith, Climacus says that he must hold fast the objective uncertainty, 'so as to remain out upon the deep, over seventy fathoms of water, still preserving my faith' (p. 98).

Objections to fideism

Of the various possible objections to fideism, two, perhaps, are particularly significant. First, if faith requires us to commit ourselves to our beliefs without using reason, how do we decide which beliefs to commit ourselves to? There are many different belief-systems from which to choose. Secondly, belief that is not subjected to critical analysis can sometimes have terrible consequences. For example, in 1977, the Reverend Jim Jones claimed to be a living God with a divine message and convinced his community, Jonestown, to commit mass suicide in the hope of attaining a better life after death.

Peterson et al. suggest that faith can be tested by reason without losing the faith itself. Although Luther thought that Copernican astronomy (which showed that it is the earth which moves and not the sun, as is assumed in the Bible, e.g. Joshua 10: 12–14) was a threat to faith, few people now think that astronomy damages faith. Indeed, many come to believe that some of their views about God are logically contradictory without losing their faith. Further, for a religious belief-system to be taken seriously by a reasonable person, it must be possible to test it for logical consistency and truth. Evans suggests that there is no reason to believe that God wishes us to suppress our critical faculties; our ability to think is a gift from God and it is therefore reasonable to assume that he intended us to use it (1982: 21).

Related examination questions

(Part a) Briefly explain the view that faith is opposed to reason. *(6 marks) (2003)*

(Part c) Assess the role of faith in supporting religious belief. *(24 marks) (2002)*

● THE IMPLICATIONS OF GOD'S EXISTENCE

The problem of evil

The so-called problem of evil represents, for many people, either the biggest challenge to their religious faith, or the clearest reason for rejecting belief in God. Broadly speaking, the problem is as follows:

The world contains two kinds of evil:

- moral evil: evil brought about by the actions of human beings – torture, for example, and
- natural evil: all that is evil in the physical universe, such as earthquakes and diseases.

But if God is omniscient, omnipotent and good, why does evil exist? If God knows about the suffering caused by evil, has the power to prevent it, and does not wish human beings to suffer, why does the world contain evil?

It seems that the two statements:

- There is evil in the world, and
- God exists

are contradictory.

In general terms, there are two ways in which people have attempted to solve the problem:

- by denying or modifying one of the attributes in question
- by constructing a defence or **theodicy** (derived from the Greek *theos*, 'God', and *dikē*, 'righteous'), a technical term for attempts to solve the problem of evil.

The Free Will Defence

The Free Will Defence (FWD) is an attempt to explain the existence of moral evil (although some versions also use a form of the defence to explain natural evil).

Perhaps one of the best-known versions is put forward by Plantinga. He admits that there is a contradiction between God's attributes of omniscience, omnipotence and goodness if it is held that there are no limits to what an omnipotent being can do, and that a good being always eliminates evil as far as it can. But Plantinga observes that few would argue that God can bring about logically impossible states of affairs or cause necessarily false propositions to be true. He therefore considers the following modifications:

* There are no nonlogical limits to what an omnipotent being can do.
* An omniscient and omnipotent good being eliminates every evil that it can properly eliminate.

He argues that there are some evils that cannot be eliminated without eliminating goods that outweigh them. For example, suffering and adversity may lead to 'a heroism that inspires others and creates a good situation out of a bad one' (in Peterson et al. 2001: 282–3).

Thus, Plantinga concludes, there is no explicit contradiction between statements asserting God's omniscience, omnipotence and goodness. So those who say that there is a contradiction between these statements must mean that a contradiction is *implied*.

Plantinga says that we could argue that this is not the case because there is a good reason why an omniscient, omnipotent, good God does not eliminate evil. He cites Augustine's view that 'the creature is more excellent which sins by free will than that which does not sin only because it has no free will' (quoted by Plantinga, in Peterson et al. 2001: 285). For Augustine, 'God can create a more perfect universe by permitting evil' (p. 286). Plantinga accepts a version of this view, although he distinguishes between his own Free Will Defence, which says what God's reason for permitting evil might possibly be, and a Free Will Theodicy, which attempts to say what God's reason for permitting evil is.

The FWD, according to Plantinga, tries to show that there may be goodness that God cannot bring about without permitting evil. Plantinga argues that a world containing free creatures who perform more good than evil actions is more valuable than a world that contains no free creatures. God can create free creatures, but he cannot cause or determine them to do only what is right. In exercising their freedom, some of these creatures go wrong, and this is the source of moral evil. However, Plantinga says, '[t]he fact that free creatures sometimes go wrong . . . counts neither against God's omnipotence nor against his goodness; for he could have forestalled the occurrence of moral evil only by removing the possibility of moral good' (pp. 287–8).

Plantinga considers the following objections to his view:

1   Freedom and determinism are compatible (sometimes called the **compatibilist** position and most notably argued by Flew (in Flew and Macintyre 1955)). In other words, God could have created creatures who were free, but also determined by God to do only what is right. (Note that, for Flew, a free creature is one who has liberty of spontaneity; see p. 97.)

Plantinga says that this objection seems quite implausible; we might just as well say that being in jail doesn't limit our freedom because if we were not in jail we would be free to come and go as we pleased.

❓ QUESTION FOR DISCUSSION

Do you think that this is a good response to the objection?

2   An omnipotent God could create a world in which creatures are genuinely free to do wrong but never in fact do so (this is Mackie's view (in Peterson et al. 2001)). A good God would create the best of all possible worlds. Since it would have been possible to create a world in which creatures freely choose to do good and this world is not such a world, there cannot be a good God.

In response, Plantinga argues that it would not have been possible for God to create a world in which Curley Smith, a corrupt mayor of Boston, produces moral order but no moral evil. 'Every world God can actualise is such that if Curley is significantly free in it, he takes at least one wrong action' (in Peterson et al. 2001: 299). In other words, Plantinga says, Curley suffers from **transworld depravity**; and, if a person suffers from it, 'then it wasn't in God's power to actualise any world in which that person is significantly free but does no wrong' (p. 300).

Plantinga argues that everybody suffers from transworld depravity. Therefore, it would not have been possible for even an omnipotent being to create a world in which creatures never chose to perform morally wrong actions. So, 'the price for creating a world in which they produce moral good is creating one in which they also produce moral evil' (p. 300).

Responses to the Free Will Defence

We can only accept the FWD if we agree that a world of genuinely free agents (i.e. those with liberty of indifference, as opposed to liberty of spontaneity) is better than one of automata (beings or things which act/move in accordance with a 'programme'; they cannot think for themselves), even at the price of much suffering. Davies (1993) suggests that most people do accept this, and that we normally think well of those who allow others freedom.

Vardy (1992) suggests that whether or not we think that God could have created human beings who make genuinely free choices in favour of the good on every occasion hinges on our view of God's omnipotence; if God is able to do things that are logically impossible, then he may be able to create beings who always freely choose to do what is good.

However, even if we accept the assumption of the FWD that a free act cannot be caused by God, Flew (quoted in Davies 1993) points out that, according to classical theism, God is the first cause lying behind all causal processes, both past and present. And this means that God must ultimately be responsible for the evil caused by human beings.

Davies responds that, although God brings into existence and sustains the things determining human behaviour, he is not, himself, the cause of that behaviour. God makes free human actions possible, but he is not the cause of those actions.

Hick's Irenaean theodicy

As we noted above, although the FWD focuses on the existence of moral evil, some versions also use a form of the defence to explain natural evil. For example, for Augustine, natural evil is the consequence either of **the fall** of human beings or of the fall of angelic beings who exert an evil influence on the earth. Hick's view encompasses moral evil, but, he claims, it also provides a better explanation for the existence of natural evil.

Hick rejects the view of Plantinga and others on the grounds that, even if their argument is sound (and he later suggests that it is not), it is based on an Augustinian theodicy. Hick argues that most people now regard the story of Adam and Eve and the fall as myth rather than history, accepting instead that humanity evolved from lower forms of life and emerged in a morally, spiritually and culturally primitive state. They also reject the idea that natural evil is the consequence of a human or angelic fall.

❓ QUESTION FOR DISCUSSION

Do you think that these are good reasons for rejecting the FWD?

Instead, on the basis of the thought of Irenaeus, Hick constructs a theodicy based on a two-stage conception of the creation of humankind. At the first stage, human beings are created in the 'image' of God: they are 'intelligent, ethical and religious animals' (in Peterson et al. 2001: 304) with the potential for knowledge of and relationship with God. The second stage is a process of 'soul-making': a gradual process of further growth and development, in which humans are brought, through their own free responses, into what Irenaeus called the divine 'likeness'; the human animal gradually becomes a child of God.

Hick says that we were created in this way; firstly to preserve our freedom. God has created the world and human beings in such a way that his existence is not 'overwhelmingly evident' to us. There is an **epistemic distance** between human beings and God, a distance between the little we know about God and the state of having complete knowledge of God. The world is 'religiously ambiguous' so that there is 'freedom to open or close oneself to the dawning awareness of God which is experienced naturally by the religious animal' (in Peterson et al. 2001: 305). We are free 'to acknowledge and worship God' or 'to doubt the reality of God' (p. 305), so that we have the possibility of coming freely to know and love our Maker.

Secondly, Hick argues that freely chosen goodness is more valuable than ready-made virtues. He thinks that Flew and Mackie were correct to argue that God could have created free beings who always choose the good, and suggests that he did so in the case of Jesus Christ. But Hick argues that

> virtues which have been formed within the agent as a hard-won deposit of her own right decisions in situations of challenge and temptation, are intrinsically more valuable than virtues created within her ready made and without any effort on her own part.
>
> (in Peterson et al. 2001: 306)

God therefore created imperfect creatures who would attain the more valuable kind of goodness through their own free choices.

Hick argues that the many examples of human sin support the view that human beings are self-regarding animals. But the many examples of human goodness support the view that God is gradually creating children of God. A world in which people can suffer is an appropriate environment for the second stage of creation. In a world in which no one could suffer – in which, for example, someone who fell off a high building floated unharmed to the ground, or bullets became insubstantial when fired at a human being – no action could be morally wrong and there could therefore be no moral choices. But, in the world as it is, we can develop courage and determination, and in our relationships we can develop the values of 'mutual love and care, of self-sacrifice for others, and of commitment to a common good' (in Peterson et al. 2001: 310).

Hick acknowledges that the main threat to this view comes from the amount and intensity of moral and natural evil. However, he says that our judgements about the intensity of natural evil are relative. If an agonising death from cancer were thought to be the worst thing there is, in a world without cancer something else would then rank as the worst form of natural evil. This would be removed, and so on, until no natural evil remained. But then we would have an environment that could not lead to moral growth. Likewise, if we experienced misfortune in proportion to our wrongdoings, right actions would be done only to bring health and prosperity, and not purely because they are right. So, 'God's good purpose enfolds the entire process of this world . . . and . . . even amidst tragic calamity and suffering we are still within the sphere of God's love and moving towards God's kingdom' (in Peterson et al. 2001: 313).

Hick acknowledges that the person-making process is not completed on earth and that his theodicy must therefore presuppose survival of death and a period of further living and growing towards the end state. He also argues that it is only if the whole human race is saved that the sins and sufferings of 'the entire human race throughout all history' (p. 314) can be justified.

Responses to Hick

We have seen that Hick argues that the consequences justify God's actions. However, Peterson et al. (1998) consider the following objections to his view:

- The epistemic distance between human beings and God could have been maintained at less cost. Even if we agree that the epistemic distance is a good thing and that suffering contributes to this by making God's existence less obvious, is it necessary that there should be *so much* suffering in order to achieve this?
- There is insufficient evidence to support the view that there is a soul-making process.
- If the soul-making process does exist, does the goal justify the means used to achieve it? This doubt is also the conclusion reached by Ivan Karamazov in his famous speech to Alyosha in Dostoyevsky's *The Brothers Karamazov*. He says: 'if the sufferings of children go to make up the sum of sufferings which is

necessary for the purchase of truth, then I say beforehand that the entire truth is not worth such a price' (1958: 287).

A further objection is considered by Clack and Clack (1998):

- If evil will be righted in the future, why fight against present evils?

 ## QUESTION FOR DISCUSSION

How might Hick respond to these objections? Do you find such responses convincing?

The 'reasonableness of the existence of God' defence

In this section we have examined two attempts to explain how an omniscient, omnipotent and good God could allow the existence of evil. However, Davies suggests that, even if we cannot understand the reasons why evil exists, we might still have good reasons for thinking that God exists. We would therefore have to conclude that both evil and God exist and that the existence of evil does not make the existence of God impossible. Indeed, Davies suggests, it might be argued that we should not expect to be able to understand the reason for suffering: 'For what falls within the plan of an omnipotent, omniscient God will be something understood only by what is omnipotent and omniscient' (1993: 40).

QUESTION FOR DISCUSSION

Do you agree with Davies that there might be reasons to believe in God's existence that are stronger than the argument for God's non-existence based on suffering?

Related examination question

(Part c) Assess whether the existence of moral evil casts doubt on the existence of God. *(24 marks) (2002)*.

Miracles

There are various definitions of 'miracle'. These include:

- a violation of the laws of nature (Hume 1975). Examples of this might be Jesus' turning water into wine, walking on water, and resurrection.
- an event that does not violate the laws of nature, but that is directly brought about by a god, sometimes referred to as a coincidence miracle. To illustrate this, R. F. Holland (1965) tells the story of a child playing on a railway line as a train approaches. The train driver faints, the brake is applied automatically, and the train stops a few feet from the child. The child's mother thanks God for a miracle.
- an inexplicable event that believers consider to have religious significance. As an example of this, Gareth Moore (1988) asks us to imagine an injured child at the foot of a mountain. There is a landslide and a large boulder begins to roll down the mountain. However, just before it reaches the child, it stops in mid-air and hovers 15 cm above him. Many tests are carried out, but no cause is ever found. Although the event is regarded as a miracle, and God is said to have saved the boy's life, this does not mean that somebody or something held the boulder up, preventing it from crushing the boy. It was a miracle because there was no cause for the boulder not to fall on the boy.

Objections to belief in miracles defined as coincidences or inexplicable events

In the case of coincidence miracles, Mackie has objected that 'the interpretation of the event as a miracle is much weaker than the rival natural explanation' (in Peterson et al. 2001: 443). So, although it may have been extraordinary good luck that the train driver fainted and thereby involuntarily applied the brakes just in time to save the child, it was just that – good luck. No doubt you can think of many examples of accidents in which those involved were not so lucky.

For miracles of both kinds, it might be objected that these are not usually what is understood by a miracle. In the first case, no natural laws are violated, and, in the second, the event is not caused by God. In the case of miracles as inexplicable events, it is difficult to understand the sense in which such miracles may be regarded as having religious significance. What does it add to our understanding of an event apparently without a cause to say that it was brought about (although not in a causal sense) by God?

QUESTION FOR DISCUSSION

How could someone respond to these objections?

Hume's objections to belief in miracles defined as violations of laws of nature

Hume (1975) argues that belief in miracles is not rational; we should proportion our belief to the available evidence. However, the available testimony regarding miracles is poor. He argues that, in the whole of history, there has never been a miracle that has been attested by a sufficiently large number of witnesses of good sense, education and learning, with a reputation to lose if they should be found to be telling lies.

Secondly, he suggests, human nature loves the fantastic. People enjoy the miraculous accounts of travellers, with descriptions of sea and land monsters. Similarly, religious people, in their enthusiasm to promote a holy cause, may imagine that they see things that are not real. There have been many examples of forged miracles, prophecies and supernatural events, detected either by contrary evidence or by their absurdity.

Thirdly, Hume claims that miracles occur chiefly among 'ignorant and barbarous nations'; if they do occur amongst civilised people, they have been received from 'ignorant and barbarous ancestors'. Such people tend to assume that there is a supernatural cause of battles, revolutions, diseases, famine and death, but, in our more enlightened times, we know that there is nothing mysterious or supernatural involved.

Finally, Hume notes that different religions report different miracles. Therefore, he says, none of them is true. He says that it is impossible that the religions of ancient Rome, Turkey, Siam, and China should all be true. Therefore, any miracle from any of these religions discredits the other religions and the miracles that allegedly occur within them.

Comments on Hume's definition of miracle

Some scholars have questioned whether we need to say that a miracle violates a natural law. According to William Lane Craig, there are three main views of natural law:

- The regularity theory – laws of nature are not really laws but just 'generalised descriptions of the way things happen in the world' (in Davies 1998: 153). A natural law simply describes whatever happens in nature. So, if unexpected events occur, these are simply incorporated into the description.

- The nomic necessity theory – laws are not only descriptive, they also tell us what can and cannot happen. But they must take into account everything that does happen, and so must be revised if an unexpected event occurs. However, if a law is inaccurate because God is acting, 'the law is neither violated nor revised' (p. 153). On this view, miracles are defined as 'naturally impossible events . . . events which cannot be produced by the natural causes operative at a certain time and place' (p. 154).
- The causal dispositions theory – natural laws tell us about the way in which various kinds of things affect other kinds of things; e.g. 'salt has a disposition to dissolve in water' (p. 154). If God acted to prevent salt from dissolving in water, the law would not be violated because salt would still have a disposition to dissolve in water. So a miracle is not a violation of a law of nature but 'an event which results from causal interference with a natural propensity which is so strong that only a supernatural agent could impede it' (p. 154).

Craig argues that none of these views supports the view that a miracle is a violation of a law of nature. Rather, miracles are 'naturally (or physically) impossible events, events which at certain times and places cannot be produced by the relevant natural causes' (p. 154).

 ## QUESTION FOR DISCUSSION

To what extent would Craig's view, if correct, support belief in miracles?

Replies to Hume's objections

The possibility of miracles

Craig suggests that it would only be rational to deny the possibility of miracles if one had good grounds for believing in atheism. He argues that Hume 'incorrectly assumes that miracles are highly improbable' (in Davies 1998: 155) and suggests that the resurrection of Jesus is not improbable in the light of evidence such as the post-mortem appearances, the empty tomb, and the disciples' belief that Jesus had risen from the dead.

The reliability of testimony

In response to Hume's first objection, Davies (1993) asks how many witnesses constitute 'a sufficient number'. And what counts as good sense, education and learning? In addition, Hume does not show that people are always swayed by their love of the fantastic. There may be some instances in which this is so, but it seems implausible to suggest that every person who claims to have seen a miracle has been swayed by love of the wonderful. Thirdly, it may sometimes be reasonable to accept testimony that conflicts with what seems to us to be probable or possible. For example, Thomas Sherlock says that it would be unreasonable for a man who lived in a hot climate to reject our testimony that rivers can sometimes be solid (quoted in Davies 1993: 206).

Vardy (1999) points out that Hume only deals with others' reports of miracles; he might have believed in miracles if he had experienced one himself. However, Mackie (in Peterson et al. 2001) argues that even if one has observed a miracle oneself, one could have misobserved it, or may be misremembering or deceiving oneself. Vardy also suggests that, when Hume was writing, miracles were supported only by word-of-mouth reports whereas, today, miracles are sometimes supported by scientific evidence. But even these could be simply extraordinary events (Vardy admits they could be just evidence of the power of the human mind) with no religious significance. For us to be certain of their religious significance, they would need to be clearly connected with a religious cause, such as prayer.

Davies acknowledges that, even if we agree that, until now, our experience has not supported belief in miracles, it is still not impossible that miracles could happen at some time in the future. However, it is possible that we are mistaken in thinking that natural laws have never been violated (or that naturally or physically impossible events have never occurred), just as we would be mistaken in thinking, on the basis of inadequate investigation, that whales are not mammals (Plantinga, quoted in Davies 1993: 207).

Conflicting accounts

Davies suggests that it is not impossible that the miracles of two religious traditions could both be true. However, if the miracles of two religions supported contradictory truth-claims, this would count against the truth of at least one of those miracles.

A further objection

A further objection to belief in miracles is that, if God intervenes in the world, it could be argued that he is guilty of arbitrariness. He seems to help individuals with (sometimes) trivial problems, but to ignore major disasters – such as the murder of 6 million Jews (Maurice Wiles, quoted in Vardy 1999: 208–9). Davies points out that, for Aquinas, a miracle is not an *intervention* by God because God is always present. Nevertheless, the question of why God brings about miracles only on some occasions remains.

QUESTION FOR DISCUSSION

If it cannot be *demonstrated* that miracles, defined as violations of laws of nature, occur, do you think it is reasonable to believe that they do?

Related examination question

(Part b) Outline and illustrate *one* reason for doubting that miracles occur. *(15 marks) (2002)*

Religion and morality: divine command ethics

In our discussion of God's perfect goodness, we noted the question: Does God determine what is morally good, or is God good because he conforms to a standard of goodness that exists independently of himself?

The view that whatever God commands is morally good is known as divine command ethics (DCE). Janine Marie Idziak (in Quinn and Taliaferro 1999) cites the following arguments in support of it:

- The Bible contains various examples of an immoral act being made right by a divine command; for example, God commanded Abraham to sacrifice his son.
- Conformity to the divine will is an important theme of Christian spiritual life; for example, in his late medieval work *The Imitation of Christ* Thomas à Kempis describes Christ telling a disciple to accept his will without argument or complaint.
- John Locke (1632–1704) argued that, since God created us, we must live in accordance with his will.

  An objection to this argument is that the fact that *A* made *B* is not a good reason for *B* to obey *A*, as B. L. Haines's hypothetical case of a couple who have children in order to use them as child prostitutes and live off their earnings illustrates. A reply might be that we should obey God not just because he has made us but because, as Karl Barth suggests, he has given himself to us, he chooses to be with us, and he has taken our place and taken up our cause.

- We should obey God's commands because he has the power to enforce them.

However, 'might' does not 'make right'; a tyrant may have great power, but this does not mean that it is right for us to obey him. Others have therefore modified this argument, saying instead that to reject DCE compromises and limits God's power because this makes God subject to something not in his power. But some theists accept that divine power *can* be limited in this way; it is not necessarily an imperfection to be bound to what is independently good.

• If God is the first cause of everything, he is also the cause of goodness.

Objections to divine command ethics

Idziak lists the following objections to DCE:

• Theists may disagree about the content of divine law, e.g. whether capital punishment is required, whether birth control, abortion and homosexuality are permissible. So how do we decide what God commands? Some theists say that the Bible is the source of knowledge of divine commands, while others look to official Church teachings, or revelation. But some are sceptical about these sources of knowledge. Another suggestion, made by Patterson Brown (quoted by Idziak), is that we can infer through reason what God would command.
• If being good is doing what God wills, 'God is good' means 'God does what God wills'. So how do we describe what it is for God to be good? R. M. Adams (quoted by Idziak) suggests that to call God good is to express a favourable emotional attitude towards him and to ascribe to him qualities regarded as virtuous.

 # QUESTIONS FOR DISCUSSION

On what grounds would someone express a favourable emotional attitude towards God? And how would someone recognise which qualities to ascribe to him?

• DCE have counterintuitive consequences. If God commanded theft, adultery, rape, cruelty for its own sake, the torturing of children, or the hatred of God, these would become right.

The most plausible response to this, according to Idziak, is that God's commands are in keeping with his nature and character. Therefore, he will not command such things.

❓ QUESTION FOR DISCUSSION

If God exists, in the light of the arguments given above, do you think it is more plausible to say that God determines what is morally good, or that God is good because he conforms to a standard of goodness that exists independently of himself?

● **REFERENCES**

Anselm (1962) *St Anselm: Basic Writings*, trans. S. N. Deane, La Salle, Ill.: Open Court Publishing Company.

Aquinas, Thomas (1920) *Summa Theologica*, trans. Fathers of the English Dominican Province, 2nd edn. Available online: <http:www.newadvent.org/summa>

Ayer, A. J. (1971) *Language, Truth and Logic*, 2nd edn, Harmondsworth: Penguin.

Baggini, Julian (2002) *Philosophy: Key Themes*, Basingstoke: Palgrave Macmillan.

Clack, Beverly and Clack, Brian R. (1998) *The Philosophy of Religion: A Critical Introduction*, Cambridge: Polity Press.

Davies; Brian (1993) *An Introduction to the Philosophy of Religion*, Oxford: Oxford University Press.

—— (ed.) (1998) *Philosophy of Religion: A Guide to the Subject*, London: Cassell.

—— (ed.) (2000) *Philosophy of Religion: A Guide and Anthology*, Oxford: Oxford University Press.

Dostoyevsky, Fyodor (1958) *The Brothers Karamazov*, trans. David Magarshack, Harmondsworth: Penguin.

Evans, C. Stephen (1982) *Philosophy of Religion: Thinking about Faith*, Leicester: InterVarsity Press.

—— (2002) *Pocket Dictionary of Apologetics and Philosophy of Religion*, Leicester: InterVarsity Press.

Flew, Antony and Macintyre, Alasdair (eds) (1955) *New Essays in Philosophical Theology*, London: SCM Press.

Hick, John (1990a) *Philosophy of Religion*, 4th edn, Englewood Cliffs, NJ: Prentice Hall.

—— (ed.) (1990b) *Classical and Contemporary Readings in the Philosophy of Religion*, Englewood Cliffs, NJ: Prentice Hall.

Holland, R. F. (1965) 'The miraculous', in Phillips, D. Z. (ed.) *Religion and Understanding*, Oxford: Blackwell.

Hughes, Gerard J. (1995) *The Nature of God*, London: Routledge.

Hume, David (1975) *Enquiry Concering Human Understanding*, ed. L. A. Selby-Bigge, Oxford: Clarendon Press.

—— (1980) *Dialogues Concerning Natural Religion*, ed. Richard H. Popkin, Indianapolis: Hackett Publishing Company.

Keightley, A. (1976) *Wittgenstein, Grammar and God*, London: Epworth Press.

Klemke, E. D. (ed.) (1992) *To Believe or Not to Believe: Readings in the Philosophy of Religion*, Orlando: Harcourt Brace Jovanovich, College Publishers.

Moore, Gareth (1988) *Believing in God: A Philosophical Essay*, Edinburgh: T. & T. Clark.

Peterson, Michael, Hasker, William, Reichenbach, Bruce and Basinger, David (1998) *Reason and Religious Belief: An Introduction to the Philosophy of Religion*, 2nd edn, Oxford: Oxford University Press.

Peterson, Michael, Hasker, William, Reichenbach, Bruce and Basinger, David (eds) (2001) *Philosophy of Religion: Selected Readings*, 2nd edn, Oxford: Oxford University Press.

Phillips, D. Z. (1981) *The Concept of Prayer*, Oxford: Blackwell.

Quinn, Phillip L. and Taliaferro, Charles (eds) (1999) *A Companion to Philosophy of Religion*, Oxford: Blackwell.

Russell, Bertrand (1967) *Why I Am Not a Christian*, London: George Allen and Unwin.

Stump, Eleonore and Murray, Michael J. (eds) (1999) *Philosophy of Religion: The Big Questions*, Oxford: Blackwell.

Swinburne, Richard (1991) *The Existence of God*, Oxford: Clarendon Press.

—— (1993) *The Coherence of Theism*, Oxford: Clarendon Press.

Taliaferro, Charles (1998) *Contemporary Philosophy of Religion*, Oxford: Blackwell.

Vardy, Peter (1992) *The Puzzle of Evil*, London: Fount.

—— (1999) *The Puzzle of God*, 3rd edn, London: Fount.

Wittgenstein, L. (1958) *Philosophical Investigations*, Oxford: Blackwell.

RECOMMENDED READING

Useful introductions to the philosophy of religion include:

● Clack, Beverly and Clack, Brian R. (1998) *The Philosophy of Religion: A Critical introduction*, Cambridge: Polity Press.

● Davies, Brian (1993) *An Introduction to the Philosophy of Religion*, Oxford: Oxford University Press.

● Hick, John (1990) *Philosophy of Religion*, 4th edn, Englewood Cliffs, NJ: Prentice Hall.

● Jackson, Roy (2001) *The God of Philosophy: An Introduction to the Philosophy of Religion*, Sutton: The Philosopher's Magazine.

- Peterson, Michael, Hasker, William, Reichenbach, Bruce and Basinger, David (1998) *Reason and Religious Belief: An Introduction to the Philosophy of Religion*, 2nd edn, Oxford: Oxford University Press.

- Vardy, Peter (1999) *The Puzzle of God*, 3rd edn, London: Fount.

The following dictionary is also recommended:

- Evans, C. Stephen (2002) *Pocket Dictionary of Apologetics and Philosophy of Religion*, Leicester: InterVarsity Press.

GLOSSARY

This glossary provides brief definitions of some of the key terms used in this chapter. Note that, for some terms, the precise definition is a matter of dispute.

analogical – Having a meaning which is similar to but not the same as.

analytic – A statement made true by the meanings of the words; in the classic example, 'A bachelor is an unmarried man', if we analyse the word 'bachelor' we find that this means 'an unmarried man'; so the statement must be true.

a posteriori – After, or based on, experience.

a priori – Before, or prior to, experience.

attributes of God – Descriptions or properties such as 'omniscient', 'omnipotent', etc.

blik – A view held without reasons (a term invented by R. M. Hare).

coherent – In a coherent description the parts of it fit together (and perhaps support each other) without contradictions.

compatibilism – The view that freedom and determinism are compatible.

contingent – Describes something that is dependent on something else and therefore may not have existed.

cosmological argument – Argues that the existence of the world or some aspect of it is explained by the existence of God.

defeater – Something that counts against a belief, to the extent that we must reject the belief.

determinism – The view that all events are 'fixed', either because they are the unavoidable outcome of past events, or because they have been created in this way by God.

empirically verifiable – Describes a statement that can be shown by experience to be true.

epistemic distance – The distance between the little we know about God and the state of having complete knowledge of God.

equivocal – Having different meanings in different contexts. For example, 'bank' can refer to a river bank, or to the place where I keep my money.

essence – God's essence or nature consists of all the attributes or properties essential to him, which he must have in order to be God.

external world – The world existing independently of human experience.

fall, the – The fall from perfection of the human race following the sin of Adam and Eve.

falsification – The theory that a statement has meaning only if we are able to say what would show it to be false.

fideism – The view that religious belief need not or must not be analysed by reason.

form of life – An activity or set of practices.

immanent – Involved within the world.

ineffable – Cannot be described.

language-game – A system of language associated with an activity, with its own distinctive vocabulary and rules.

liberty of indifference – Genuine freedom of action.

liberty of spontaneity – Apparent freedom of action; our actions are chosen, but our choices are constrained by our backgrounds and our natures, and are therefore predictable.

logically possible – Not involving a contradiction.

metaphysics – The branch of philosophy concerned with the nature of reality; literally, that which is beyond physics.

natural theology – Arguments for God's existence.

necessary – Not dependent on anything else. Something is logically necessary if its non-existence would be self-contradictory.

noetic – Concerned with knowledge.

non-realist – Not committed to something existing independently of individuals or communities. Applied to religion, this usually means that God exists only within the language believers use to talk about him; he is a useful concept, but has no objective reality.

Ockham's razor – A rule stating that entities are not to be multiplied needlessly; in other words, the simplest explanation is the best.

omnipotent – All-powerful.

omnipresent – Present at all places and, perhaps, at all times.

omniscient – All-knowing.

ontological argument – Argues that (necessary) existence is part of the definition of God and that God must therefore exist.

pantheism – The belief that God and the world are the same.

perception – An impression of the world gained through one or more of the senses.

predicate – An attribute of something that tells us more about it.

properly basic – Describes beliefs on which other beliefs depend, and which can be accepted without proof.

properties of God – See **attributes of God**.

substance – Something that exists objectively, in its own right.

teleological argument – Argues that the apparent design of the world is explained by the existence of God.

theist – Someone who believes in God.

theodicy – An attempt to explain why God permits evil.

transcendent – Outside or beyond our world or experience.

transworld depravity – The tendency to perform at least one wrong action in any possible world.

univocal – Having the same meaning in two different contexts. For example, if 'good' is being used univocally, 'God is good' and 'Katherine is good' means that God and Katherine are both good in the same sense.

verification principle – Says that a meaningful statement is either analytic or empirically verifiable ('strong' version), or that a meaningful statement is either analytic or can be shown by experience to be probably true ('weak' version).

4

philosophy of mind

UNIT 4   Janice Thomas

KEY CONCEPTS ●

- substance dualism
- materialism
- privacy and privileged access
- subjectivity
- qualia ('what it's like-ness')
- intentionality ('aboutness')
- anomalous monism
- phenomenology
- logical behaviourism
- numerical and qualitative identity
- eliminative materialism
- functionalism
- multiple realisability
- inverted spectrum hypothesis

- reductionism
- occasionalism
- epiphenomenalism
- parallelism
- interactionism
- mental causation
- solipsism
- Turing Test
- thought experiment
- argument from analogy
- inference to the best explanation
- criteria of identity
- bodily continuity
- psychological continuity

● INTRODUCTION

If you are reading this book and thinking about its contents you have both a body (furnished with eyes) and a mind. There may seem to be no great philosophical mystery about what eyes or a human body are. But what is a mind? And what is the relationship between mind and body? There are many metaphysical theories about the nature of mind and body. For example, substance dualism maintains that mind and body are two, utterly metaphysically distinct, kinds of substance. Materialism maintains that only material substance exists. Both of these views cannot be right, but how can we decide between them?

Attempts to answer the most central metaphysical questions about the nature of mind – like the ones just mentioned – always seem to bring in their train related epistemological questions and puzzles. How, if at all, can we have knowledge of minds, our own or those of others? What is the nature of persons and their identity over time and how is personal identity to be known? Philosophy of Mind aims to help us reach defensible views about ourselves and our fundamental nature by tackling these questions and trying to answer them in as clear and rational a way as possible.

● APPROACHES TO MENTALITY AND THE NATURE OF MIND

Distinguishing the mental from the physical

Asked to list a good number of your physical states and properties and then to do the same with your mental states and properties, you would be unlikely to find it difficult. It is surprisingly easy to give examples of both your physical and your mental states, identifying them correctly as one or the other. The physical list would contain 'passport properties' like your eye and hair colour, height, weight, scars, birthmarks and so on. On the mental list would be feelings, perceptions, sensations, present thoughts, memories, plans, etc.

Defining a term by giving a list of items to which that term applies is called 'defining by enumeration'. Can we do better than mere enumeration in defining the mental and distinguishing it from the physical? Can we make a principled distinction based on **criteria** that are adequate to the task?

The following are all criteria that have been proposed as distinctive marks of the mental:

- lack of spatial features
- immediacy, privileged and infallible access (privacy, certainty)

- subjectivity, qualia, feelings, sensations ('what it's like-ness')
- intentionality ('aboutness')
- anomalousness.

I will look at each of these in turn.

Lack of spatial features

Physical events, processes and things are all located in space. They all happen *somewhere*. If you are in the audience at a live concert, the musicians are physically nearby. Sensory and neural processes are happening in your eardrums and brain. But is your *experience* of the music happening anywhere? Could a neurosurgeon find it inside your skull? How wide or tall might it be? How much would it weigh?

These questions might well strike you as ones it would be silly to try to answer. You might reasonably wonder whether it even makes sense to talk about mental states and events having spatial properties.

Privileged access

But other features are also distinctive of the mental. With a little thought you will quickly realise that you have privileged and immediate access to your own mental states. Others have to watch your facial expression or behaviour to guess what you are thinking and feeling. They may have to move to your location to see and hear what you are sensing. Even then, they can only infer that you sensed what they now sense.

But you know immediately, without having to check any evidence, what is going on in your mind. Your thoughts and sensations are private to you. And this means that you have unique authority (**first person authority**) about them. You are infallible with respect to your mental states.

In contrast, anyone can know things about your body every bit as readily as you do. Indeed, a doctor might well know what you can only guess, e.g. that your ankle is not just sprained but broken.

Subjectivity

Someone else might have the same **type** of headache as you are now experiencing or you might have a headache of the same type on a different occasion. But the **token** sensations and feelings that you alone have at the moment or on any particular occasion are unique to that occasion and to you. They are also endowed with what is known as **phenomenology**. This is a fancy term for the subjective or felt qualities that your sensations and feelings seem to you to have. There is something each of them is like for you. There is a way (or several ways) each of your feelings feels. You are aware of the tartness of the taste of the marmalade as you take a mouthful of toast, the brightness of the blue as you look out the window at the sky, the dull throbbing of a particular pain.

These subjective 'feels' or **qualia** as they are sometimes called, these ways that your sensations feel to you, are their phenomenology. Purely physical things do not experience phenomenology; they do not have the wherewithal with which to have feeling. Since a rock or a piece of furniture has no feelings or sensations there is nothing it feels like to be a rock or a piece of furniture. To some it has seemed that only minds can have subjective experience, that phenomenology or 'what it's like-ness' is the criterion of the mental.

Intentionality

Mental states, or at any rate some of them, have another striking feature not mentioned so far. Thoughts, beliefs, hopes, fears, wishes, desires and so forth are all directed at something. They are all *about* their subject matter. This 'aboutness' is sometimes called 'representational character' and sometimes **intentionality**.

Intentionality in this sense is nothing to do with actions being done intentionally or on purpose. The intentionality that is sometimes said to be distinctive of the mental is the directedness or intentness of the mind on its object. If I have a thought about my grandmother that thought is directed upon or about my grandmother. If I think of dragons my thought is directed (intent) upon dragons. A thought can be about an object whether or not that thing exists now or has ever existed.

Anomalousness

A fourth suggestion about what is distinctive of the mental is Donald Davidson's view that the realm of the mental is, in a way, lawless. He argues that there are no scientific laws relating mental events to one another or to physical events.

It seems true that anything that happens in the physical realm is related by scientific laws to whatever caused it and whatever it, in turn, causes. So, if a stone of a certain weight is dropped a certain distance the force with which it hits the ground can be predicted, calculated and exactly explained because the whole physical event is governed by precise physical laws.

But minds behave differently. You may fly off the handle when someone insults you on one occasion and, on another, even though you are insulted in exactly the same way, you may remain calm and ignore the insult. We can even imagine that you might be in exactly the same overall brain state on both occasions and yet both your feelings and your actions might be different. There are no laws by which mental events, as such, can be predicted or explained.

On Davidson's view the mental is **anomalous**. There are no laws connecting mental events with each other and with physical events. Psychological events, considered as such, escape the net of scientific law. And this is what marks the mental off from the rest of physical reality.

❓ QUESTIONS FOR DISCUSSION

Which of the five criteria of the mental outlined so far seems to you the best candidate to be the distinctive mark of mentality? What criticisms could be addressed to each suggested criterion?

The claim of each of these five criteria to be the mark of the mental has been disputed. No one holds that these features are not important. Nor is it denied that at least the first four characterise many mental states and events. But critics remain unconvinced that they are features *exclusive to* or *distinctive of* mentality:

- Many items that are not mental events or states cannot rightly be said to have spatial location or features. Think of, for example, geometrical theorems or television series.
- There are mental states that seem more accessible to others than to oneself. (E.g. Is it love or just infatuation you are feeling?)
- Some philosophers argue vigorously against the existence of subjective phenomenological feels, or 'qualia', as they are sometimes called. They do not, however, wish to deny the reality of conscious mentality.
- Maps, pictures and stories have intentionality in that they are obviously about what they represent but they are evidently not mental states.
- And the theory that mental events are anomalous is a much disputed and perhaps an empirical one, which awaits further research.

Related examination question

(Part a) Describe and illustrate two ways in which mental states allegedly differ from brain states. *(18 marks) (2002)*

Theories concerning the nature of mind

The two main metaphysical theories of the nature of mind to be considered here are dualism and materialism. The two sorts of dualism to be discussed are substance dualism and property dualism. We will then look at the following materialist theories: behaviourism, identity theory, and functionalism.

Dualism

Substance dualism

Plato and Descartes were both substance dualists. They both believed that there are two kinds of substance, which are fundamentally different in their essence. The two substances are, of course, body and mind (or soul). The two great philosophers shared at least one argument for the view that the physical and the mental are essentially different.

Both saw mind as simple and indivisible but body as composite and divisible. Since things with opposed properties cannot be identical (one and the same thing) Plato and Descartes both concluded on this argument alone that mind and body must be distinct.

They also each had a number of further arguments for dualism. We cannot look at all of them here but should at least mention the main one usually attributed to Descartes. This is the argument from dubitability:

- I can doubt whether I have a body or indeed whether any material bodies exist.
- For all I know I may be nothing but an immaterial mind or spirit being fooled into thinking that there are physical bodies (one of which is mine) and that I have sense organs to supply me with the sensations (sights, sounds, etc.) I am experiencing.
- Famously, however, I cannot doubt the existence of the experiencing subject or mind having those sensations.
- So my body has a property my mind does not have. Its existence can be doubted by me though I cannot doubt that my mind (the subject of all my thoughts) exists.
- A single substance cannot at the same time be dubitable by me and fail to be so. So my indubitable mind and dubitable body must be distinct substances.

Out-of-body experiences as evidence for substance dualism

Sometimes people who have been near death (in an accident or serious surgical operation) report having had an amazing experience while apparently unconscious. The experience is one of leaving the body and floating above it. Then the person may report having travelled down a long tunnel towards a white light and perhaps heard the voice of a long-dead relative before 'returning to this world' and waking up in the old familiar body.

If a subject can move to a location in space distinct from that of his or her body then that body and subject must be distinct substances. They must be two substances not one.

So 'out-of-body experiences', as they are called, would be good evidence for substance dualism *if* there were good evidence for out-of-body experiences. The question, of course, is whether feeling exactly as if you have left your body and viewed it from a distance can be shown to be a veridical feeling as opposed to a very persuasive hallucination.

There are numerous arguments for dualism but as yet none that is invulnerable to criticism. That I can doubt the existence of my body but not my mind, for example, is a seriously flawed argument.

An argument *of exactly the same form* would take us from true premises to what is certainly a false conclusion. Here is an example: Superman's strength is indubitable. But everyone doubts Clark Kent is strong. Since Superman has indubitable strength and Clark Kent's strength is dubitable, Superman is not Clark Kent. This conclusion we know is false. But the premises are true. So the argument that seems to go from those premises to that conclusion cannot be valid. The form of this argument is not a valid one. So the argument from dubitability, being of exactly the same form, fails to prove substance dualism.

Related examination question

(Part a) Describe and illustrate *two* criticisms of dualism. *(18 marks) (2003)*

Property dualism

This, as the name suggests, is the view that mental and physical properties are fundamentally distinct. There is only one sort of substance but it has two basic sorts of properties. Mental properties cannot be reduced to physical ones or vice versa.

On such a view, minds are not substances of a different metaphysical type from physical bodies. So property dualism can and does often combine with a materialist view of mind.

But having a particular mental property is not simply equivalent to being in a particular physical state, for example a particular brain state. For the property dualist, mental properties (sometimes described as 'higher-level properties') constitute an autonomous domain, which resists reduction to the physical domain.

Materialism

Behaviourism

If the arguments for substance dualism seem flawed and unpersuasive, the natural next place to look for a defensible philosophical account of mind may be some form of materialism. In the mid-twentieth century many philosophers of mind, influenced by behaviourism in psychology, turned to philosophical or logical behaviourism.

Behaviourism in psychology is the view that psychology's proper business is the scientific explanation, prediction and control of behaviour. 'Scientific' in this context means 'concentrating on what can be publicly observed and studied, i.e. behaviour and reactions to stimuli'. What cannot be observed can only be the subject of speculation. Appealing to inner states (let alone immaterial substances) is explanatorily pointless and unscientific.

Behaviourism in philosophy rejects the existence of mysterious inner states that are unverifiable because they are in principle inaccessible to empirical research. It says instead that words for states of mind signify nothing but the behaviour that common sense usually regards as associated with those states. So, in its earliest formulation, the behaviourist account of pain, for example, is that it just consists in wincing, crying out ('that hurts') and pulling away from the source of injury. There is no role for an inner state of 'being in pain'.

Early critics pointed out that this view, as sketched so far, is flawed in the following way. If pain is *defined* as pain behaviour the injured stoic (who does not wince, cry, etc.) is not in pain at all and the actor who pretends pain by behaving appropriately actually *is* in pain. The behaviourist's definition cannot be correct.

Behaviourists responded to this stoicism/pretence objection by adding an important qualification. The stoic *is* in pain, despite the lack of appropriate behaviour, because he *has a disposition* to wince, etc. He is simply not choosing to act as he is disposed to do. The actor lacks that disposition, and so is not in pain, whatever pain behaviour he imitates.

But even this logical behaviourism, with its resort to talk of the subject's dispositions, has failed to make many converts. There are three main reasons. First, there is our intuitive conviction that we do have inner states. Most people feel that introspection gives us good evidence of actual, occurrent mental states that do not simply boil down to impulses towards characteristic behaviour. These states, we feel, cannot be equivalent to our behaviour, because they *cause* our behaviour.

Second, there is the belief most people also share, that two people could be dispositionally and behaviourally identical and yet could have different subjective states. Perhaps when you and I both look at a Christmas tree and say 'That is green' the experience of colour you are having is qualitatively the same as the experience I have when I see ripe tomatoes. If our psychological states can differ although we share dispositions and behaviour there must be more to psychological states than the behaviourist concedes.

The third problem for the logical behaviourist is the impossibility of defining mental states in exclusively physical terms. Behaviour is all capable of purely physical description. But things like 'being frightened' and 'being in pain' are not. Consider the following example. If I meet a bear in the forest my being frightened might take the form of standing stock still. But what I do might not be fear behaviour at all. Not moving could as easily be courage or recklessness. Reference to my other mental states (for example, my desire to block the bear's route to the children or ignorance of how dangerous bears are) is needed. Mental states cannot be accurately read off from behaviour alone. Nor can they be defined without reference to other beliefs and sensations.

 # QUESTION FOR DISCUSSION

What is logical behaviourism? Give at least three reasons why it might be held to be an inadequate theory of the nature of mind.

▌ Related examination question

(Part b) Assess the view that talk about mental states is talk about actual or potential behaviour. *(32 marks) (2002)*

Identity theory

The identity theory of mind (sometimes called 'central state materialism') arose partly out of dissatisfaction with logical behaviourism. It seemed to go against common sense to say that my being in pain or afraid is nothing but my being disposed to wince or flee.

Surely if a substance is disposed to behave a certain way we think this is because some of its properties make it prone to behave so. For example, 'Glass is fragile' means 'Glass is disposed to shatter easily'. But we assume that this disposition is a result of some internal or molecular-level properties of the glass.

Similarly, identity theorists hold that dispositions to pain behaviour are explicable in terms of actual occurrent inner states or properties of the subject. The label 'central state materialists' refers to their view about which occurrent inner states or properties should be regarded as mental states and properties. Their answer, of course, is that states of the brain and central nervous system (central material states) cause or dispose us to certain characteristic behaviours. Mental states *just are* brain states.

The previous sentence also explains the label 'identity theorists'. The identity in question is the kind of strict, **numerical identity** that links, say, George Eliot and Marianne Evans (the nineteenth-century author). Numerical identity is 'countability as one'. George Eliot just *is* Marianne Evans. There are not two authors but one author with two names.

Similarly, the identity theory of mind says that there are not two things when I burn my finger: first, a brain state triggered by activity in nerves running from my finger to my brain and second, a sensation of pain. Rather, there is just one state, which is both a state of my brain and a mental state or sensation.

The identity theory has at least four features to recommend it:

- It is economical: it posits no extra, mysterious immaterial substances or states.
- It improves on behaviourism in the ways already described. Instead of positing unexplained general dispositions it identifies psychological states with brain states in a way designed to improve our understanding of both.

- It aims for an account that is like scientific accounts of phenomena. For example, identifying mental states with brain states is, superficially at least, very like the chemist's identification of water with H_2O or the physicist's identification of heat with molecular motion. This analogy with scientific reductions suggests that we will understand mental states better for seeing that fundamentally they are nothing but states of the brain.
- It solves the problem of mind/body interaction. This will be discussed in the next section of this chapter.

There are at least two main criticisms of the identity theory. The first is called 'the chauvinism objection'. Recall that the identity theory – at least in the early version we have been considering – identifies mental states like pain, fear, sensory states, etc. with brain states. But which brain states? The states in question must be the brain states of the subjects whose mental states we know about through their reports and our own experience. So, for this view, pain, fear, etc. are nothing but *human* brain states.

But most of us would want at least to leave open for debate the possibility that non-human animals can sometimes be in states like pain, fear, joy, seeing something round or tasting something sweet. However, if there is nothing more to fear, for example, than being in a particular type of human brain state then this means only humans can experience fear. Likewise for all other types of mental states, if they are defined exclusively in terms of the types of brain states that are thought to realise those mental states for humans.

If fear is nothing but a particular type of human brain state, computers, robots, god, angels, Martians and any other non-human subjects you might be able to think of cannot feel fear. They have the wrong types of brain states – or perhaps no brains at all. The identity theory is chauvinist. It says that psychological states can only occur in humans.

I said that there were two main objections to the identity theory. The second objection follows on from what has just been said. So far the only version of the identity theory to have been discussed is the one that identifies *types* of mental state with *types* of brain state. But it is an empirical matter whether even two humans who take themselves to be experiencing the same mental state are in the same type of brain state or not.

And the evidence from neurological research seems to be that, surprisingly, brain state types do not correlate highly with mental state types. You and I may be experiencing the same fear but be in very different types of neural states. You might experience the same fear today and a year from now and your neurological state could be very different on the two occasions.

Related examination question

(Part b) Assess the view that the mind is the brain. *(32 marks) (2003)*

Type–type identity theory, as it is called, is chauvinistic and seems to lack empirical support. However, there is a second sort of identity theory, which identifies token brain states with token mental states. This means that individual instances of brain state types are identified with individual instances of mental state types. On this view, for example, your very particular token brain state at the moment is all there is to the particular token mental state you are presently experiencing. This token–token identity theory seems to preserve the advantages of identity theory but avoid the second objection.

 # QUESTIONS FOR DISCUSSION

What is the difference in meaning between the phrases 'type of brain state' and 'token brain state'? What is the difference between the type–type identity theory and the token–token identity theory?

Functionalism

But is there a way to avoid the chauvinism objection? 'Functionalism' or 'causal role identity theory' claims as one of its virtues to be able to overcome the chauvinism objection. It does this by deploying the notion of **multiple realisability**.

This notion is easy to explain in terms of a humble object like a mousetrap. Some mousetraps are made of wood and metal and work with a spring, often killing the mouse. Others are made of plastic and simply lure the mouse harmlessly into captivity. They are equally mousetraps. Each uses materials strong enough to catch a mouse and a successful design for the job. 'Being a mousetrap' is a functional property. It can be realised in many different ways.

Again, anything toxic to living organisms can be a poison. Different poisons do their unpleasant work by different means, attacking and disabling the organism in many different ways. 'Being a poison' is a functional property.

Mousetraps and poisons can each be realised in many different structures and substances. Functionalism in the philosophy of mind says that mental states, too, are functional properties. They can be realised in a wide variety of physical materials and structures. Human pain, for example, is realised in certain human brain states. Dogs, cats, even goldfish have very different brains so their pain is realised, if at all, in very different physical properties from ours. Perhaps Martian pain, as David Lewis suggests, is realised in hydraulic mechanisms in the Martians' feet (Lewis 1983: 123).

Multiple realisability solves the chauvinism problem. We and our pets and the Martians share the same psychological properties (which are functional properties) and yet differ very much physically. This is because psychological features are defined not in terms of what they are identical with physically but in terms of what they *do*, the causal role they occupy.

Take the example of pain. When I burn my finger this injury sets up a chain of physical events, which are causally related each to the next. First my nerves transfer impulses to my brain. Then whatever state my brain is in is causally responsible for initiating muscular activity which, in this case, means that my finger is pulled back from the flame. The functionalist says that the brain state that is caused by the injury and in turn causes withdrawal from the flame is occupying the causal role of pain; it is (identical with) my pain in this case.

In another species of subject a different sort of physical state (brain or otherwise) would be caused by bodily injury and be responsible for producing avoidance of the injurious circumstance. That state would be pain for that species.

Functionalism solves the problem of chauvinism. Has it any view about the difference of opinion between type and token identity theories? Empirical research will eventually establish the truth or otherwise of claims that this or that type of mental state correlates with a specific type of human brain state. Whatever the results of that research, functionalism will be content. Functional properties could be realised by types as well as their tokens.

 # QUESTION FOR DISCUSSION

How does functionalism solve the chauvinism objection to the identity theory of mind?

But functionalism is not invulnerable to criticism. Earlier I mentioned a possibility which, if it is genuine, can be used to pose a threat to functionalist materialist views. This possibility involves what is called the **inverted spectrum hypothesis**.

You and I both look at a Christmas tree and say 'That is green.' But, so the hypothesis goes, it is genuinely possible that the phenomenological feel of our two experiences is different. No one will ever know, but our psychological states differ. Perhaps something similar differentiates your colour experiences from mine round the whole spectrum. (Hence the name 'inverted spectrum hypothesis'.)

But functionalism defines mental states in terms of functional role. All there is to seeing green on this view is looking at things agreed to be green and identifying them as green. 'Seeing green' in both of us is a state caused by looking at a green thing, which in turn causes utterances of 'That is green.' Filling that causal role is all there is to being that sensation. So functionalism has to say that the inverted spectrum hypothesis does not name a genuine possibility.

If a theory implies that something is impossible when in fact that thing is genuinely possible the theory is false. If the 'inverted spectrum hypothesis' names a genuine possibility, functionalism is false.

 # QUESTION FOR DISCUSSION

What is the inverted spectrum hypothesis and what threat does it pose to functionalism?

Other theories

Believe it or not there are many more arguments for and against each of the materialist theories given so far. There are also further materialist theories of mind, which have not yet been described. There are views that argue that mental states, properties and events supervene on, without being reducible to, physical states, properties and events. There are also reductionist views.

One of these is **eliminative materialism** which, as the name implies, says that reference to mental states like sensations and beliefs is literally false since no such items really exist. Reference to them could and would be eliminated from a mature scientific vocabulary for describing and explaining human life. Talk of such mental or intentional items survives as part of a rough and ready theory (**folk psychology**), which explains people's actions and enables us to make predictions about them in an everyday way. Such talk could, however, never be refined into a scientific and acceptable theory.

'Folk psychological' talk of beliefs, desires, sensations and emotions will eventually have to give way to descriptions of what is really going on in people's heads, namely neuronal firings of different patterns and intensities. Any supposed mental states that cannot be re-described in terms of the sorts of physical states and events just mentioned are misleading fictions and they should be eliminated from our talk about the mind.

Another materialist theory, which has so far only been mentioned indirectly, is Davidson's anomalous monism. It is called a 'monism', as you would guess, because it recognises only one kind of substance, namely matter. It is non-reductionist because it regards mental and psychological states and events as real states and occurrences that cannot be re-described in purely physical terms without losing something important.

Davidson's theory is called 'anomalous' monism because, as mentioned above, it argues that the mental cannot be captured in the net of scientific law. There are no psycho-physical laws. Nor are there laws relating the psychological to the psychological. The arguments Davidson gives for these claims are perhaps too complex for a brief introduction. Below, when talking about Davidson's views on mental causation, I will try to explain more of his position in terms of examples.

Finally, it is appropriate to mention that some philosophers of mind think mentality (consciousness, subjectivity) is just another, very special, biological property like digestion or respiration. In this they share a lot of ground with the eliminativists. Others think conscious states lie forever shrouded in mystery: perhaps a species of physical states but one we are somehow doomed, by the very nature of human cognition, never to understand.

● THE MIND/BODY PROBLEM

The relationship between mentality and physicality

Different theories of the nature of mind generate different views of the relationship between mentality and physicality. You might at first think that, if substance dualism is correct, the relationship should be something like that between two mutually independent physical objects. Each has its own nature and characteristics which determine the nature of the relationship between them – including whether they can interact causally at all and, if so, in what ways. Dualism sees mind as a distinct, autonomous substance capable of existing even in the absence of all material substances but capable of entering into relations with bodies on an equal footing.

However, immaterial substance is exactly what the name implies. It is something wholly lacking in spatial location, dimensions, mass and motion. So it has no qualities by which it could move, impress or otherwise affect anything physical. Nor can it be physically affected. Although most dualists believe that minds affect and are affected by bodies they have no explanation to offer of how this could be accomplished. Immaterial substances lie outside the realm and the reach of physical forces. Even Descartes admitted he had failed to give an adequate account of mind/body interaction.

The assorted varieties of materialism might be thought to have the advantage here. If there *is* only the physical realm then anything real is physical (including the mental). If the mental is really just one part or aspect of the physical then it should be able to act upon other physical things and be acted upon by them in turn.

This could be true even if the mental depends for its existence on the existence and nature of certain physical things. There is nothing in the notion of existential dependence itself that precludes the dependent thing from having an effect on what it depends on. (Think of our dependence on the air we breathe and the food we eat. We can and do affect them both in numerous ways.)

But some materialist views do not recognise minds or mental states as things or entities at all. Rather, they see the mental as merely an aspect of the physical, something capable of being affected by the physical but not of exerting any sort of influence in return.

The appearance of mind/body interaction

Substance dualism regards mind and body as utterly metaphysically different. So the awkward problem of trying to explain at least the appearance of mind/body interaction might seem to be particularly acute for dualism.

Occasionalism

One explanation offered by dualists in the past is occasionalism. This is the view that when my body seems to be affecting my mind or vice versa this is really just a special kind of coincidence. For example, in sense perception, when I see a tree this is not a case of a physical object inexplicably having an effect on my immaterial mind. Rather, what happens is that God produces in my mind a sensation that corresponds to the object reflecting light into my eye at the moment. Similarly, going the other way, on the occasion of my wanting a drink God makes my hand reach to pick up my glass.

Occasionalism seems a desperate expedient. It begins by accepting that mind and body do not interact at all which, of course, goes right against common sense. And defending occasionalism would require independent support for the claim that a quite specific kind of god exists. That is, a god capable of producing innumerable seeming causes and effects yet unwilling or unable to endow our minds with the capacity to be affected by or to affect physical things.

Epiphenomenalism

Another dualist response to the demand for an explanation of the appearance of mind/body interaction is to say that the mental is **epiphenomenal**. This means that it is real and is caused by the physical. However, it is not a part of the world we all see, feel and interact with. It can have no real effect on that world although it may appear to. It is just an impotent by-product.

For the epiphenomenalist it is right to say, for example, that sense perception (a physical process) gives us sensations and ideas (conscious states). Other physical processes cause feelings and desires. Dehydration and lack of food, for example, cause thirst and hunger. But none of my sensations and ideas, feelings and desires can have any effect on the physical world which includes my body.

If it seems to me that the feeling of thirst makes me pick up my glass, that is just a mistake. It is events in my nervous system that are the whole cause of the muscle movements involved. Physical events are part of a closed system consisting exclusively of physical causes and effects. We will return to this view when discussing mental causation below.

Parallelism

Another account that dualists sometimes give of the relationship between mind and body is parallelism. Like occasionalism, this view denies that mind and body actually interact but focuses on the fact that mental states and events are very highly and systematically correlated with physical ones.

What explains this systematic correlation? Since it is not interaction between minds and bodies it must be a cause common to them both, namely the will of God. Just as the chiming of my clock is not the cause of the arrival of my punctual student so the blue physical object in front of me is not the cause of my sensation of blue. The chiming and its correlated arrival are both caused by the fact that it is four o'clock. The fact that there is a blue object located just there is caused, like the fact that I have a sensation of blue just now, by the immensely complex pre-programming of God at creation.

Interactionism

Many would describe parallelism as every bit as desperate a view as the occasionalist's. In fact neither of these views seems to give an adequate explanation of apparent interaction which would satisfy common sense. Nor does epiphenomenalism, despite its belief in the reality and distinctness of the mental.

We all feel that we have immediate experience of our thoughts affecting our bodies (in deliberate action) and of our bodies and the physical affecting our minds (in sense perception). The sort of interactionism that Descartes is usually held to subscribe to, though he feels (rightly) that he has not explained it adequately, seems the most defensible as well as the simplest view. Surely minds and bodies do, really, interact.

But how is this possible if mind and body are so unlike? They have nothing in common that could give one leverage on the other. Moreover, it seems to defy another part of common sense to suggest that something immaterial could inject any impetus into the closed system of physical causes. Nor is it possible to see how physical energy could leave the system to affect the immaterial mind.

 ## QUESTION FOR DISCUSSION

What makes it so difficult to give a philosophical account of mind/body interaction?

Mental causation

Behaviourism again

It seems that dualism cannot explain how body and mind affect one another. All right, it might be said, so much the worse for dualism. Many have responded to dualism's apparent inability to explain mind/body interaction – or even the appearance of it – by rejecting dualism on that ground alone and turning to materialism.

But the mind/body problem is in fact no easier for materialists to deal with than it is for Cartesians. Take, for example, the behaviourist way of dealing with it. Logical behaviourists, remember, claim that mental states are all defined in terms of types of behaviour and dispositions to behave in specific ways. They are inclined to deny that mental states are anything other than patterns of behaviour.

Certainly they would deny that an individual mind like that of Shakespeare, for example, was a thing he possessed. The phrase 'Shakespeare's mind', for a behaviourist, does not denote a thing with which Shakespeare's body could have an interactive relationship. It refers to his extraordinary command of language, his creative imagination, his understanding of human psychology, his dramatic genius, etc.

Behaviourism views the problem of mind/body interaction not as a real problem, which can be solved, but as a pseudo-problem, which needs to be exposed and dissolved. But this way of dealing with the mind/body problem is not very convincing. My mind may not be an entity with causal powers distinct from those of my body but many of my individual thoughts, sensations and feelings certainly seem to me to be causally responsible for bodily movements I make.

For example, surely it is the pain I feel on burning my finger that makes me pull my hand away from the flame and it is my headache that causes me to reach for the aspirin. Again, my decision to go for a walk causes me to get to my feet and the sight of the dog looking eager makes me fetch his collar and lead. The behaviourist owes us an account of the introspective certainty at least some people have that their mental states are causally efficacious.

Identity theories and functionalism again

Behaviourism denies that there are minds or mental states over and above the subject's physical body. So too, in a way, do identity theories and functionalism. But these theories do not, like behaviourism, deny that mental states are distinct from behaviour and dispositions to behave. If my pain, headache, decision and sensation of sight (mentioned in the last paragraph) are each identical with or realised by some state of my brain or central nervous system, surely that gives an answer to the problem of mind/body interaction.

Those mental states, being at the same time physical states, are not causally impotent as immaterial Cartesian mental states cannot help being. They are able to interact with my body as any other physical states interact with my body. They interact with it physically.

This answer faces a difficulty that is referred to in some writings on philosophy of mind as 'the problem of mental causation'. This problem goes as follows. Every physical event has a complete physical cause. Consider my picking up the dog's lead as I get ready to take him for a walk. The movements of my hand and arm as I reach for and grasp the lead are all caused by different nerve impulses initiating different muscle movements. These nerve impulses in turn have complete physical causes in the sense that those causes are obviously adequate to produce the results they do. And these causes have in their turn complete causes (perhaps other neural activity) and so on.

But this means that, in the present case, there is no room for my decision to take the dog for a walk to be even part of the cause of my picking up the lead. That action had, remember, a *complete physical* cause.

Could my mental state – my decision – perhaps have had a causal role further down the causal chain leading back from the physical causes of my picking up the lead? But this suggestion cannot really help. For how could a mental state intervene and act as a cause at *any* point on that chain? Would a mental state acting on a muscle or a nerve or a collection of brain cells not all equally be telekinesis (the immediate action of the mental on the physical)? Telekinesis is rightly regarded by most people with as much scepticism as telepathy, extrasensory perception and other supposed psychic phenomena.

Materialists respond to this point in a number of different ways. The eliminativist will simply regard his case as proven. No dualist or non-reductionist position can successfully account for mental causation. This is because there are no mental causes, only physical ones.

Perhaps surprisingly, various epiphenomenalists agree with the eliminativists in this. So, some who believe in the reality of qualia or conscious subjective states over and above material states and events agree that these mental states (regarded by them simply as by-products of certain physical events) can have no effect on our actions.

Identity theorists of various kinds, including functionalists and Davidsonian anomalous monists, reply by insisting that mental events can and do cause actions. For, surely, we are aware very frequently of acting on reasons and, equally surely, reasons are mental states. To act on reasons is for some of one's mental states to cause just those reasonable actions.

How is this accomplished? The identity theorists point to the fact (as they see it) that every mental event is also a physical event in the brain. It is *as* physical states or events that mental events exercise causal power. Davidson particularly has urged this straightforward response to the mental causation problem.

Davidson's critics have complained that his answer still leaves the mental state causally impotent. A brain state, which also happens to be (psychologically speaking) a decision or a reason, may cause muscle movements. But it does so only in virtue of its being a physical state, not in virtue of being a mental state. Its physical properties do all the work. Its mental properties are idle.

The soprano analogy

The supposed causal impotence of the mental can be understood in terms of the following analogy invented by Fred Dretske (Dretske 1989: 1–2). Imagine an opera singer whose top notes can shatter glass. She might be persuaded to sing an aria and substitute the words 'Shatter, oh shatter!' so that this is what she is singing when she hits her highest notes. Suppose that a glass placed for the occasion shatters when she sings this phrase. It is not the meaning of her words that breaks the glass. It would have shattered even had she been singing 'Oh, do not shatter!' It is the physical properties of what she sings that break the glass, not the meaning of her words. Similarly, it is the physical properties of my brain state, not the (meaning of the) decision it embodies, that cause my body to move.

Even for the monistic materialist, the mind/body interaction problem (or problem of mental causation) remains as intractable as ever.

Related examination question

(Part b) Assess whether theories of the relationship between mind and body have successfully accounted for mental causation. *(32 marks) (2002)*

● KNOWLEDGE OF SELF AND SELF-CONSCIOUSNESS

Privacy and the meaning of psychological terms

In listing criteria of the mental (above, pp. 150–1) I mentioned the view that mental states are distinguished from physical states by being immediately, infallibly known, and private. Even if this does not seem to you what is most distinctive of the mental you are likely to think that introspection nonetheless does in fact give us immediate knowledge of our mental states.

Our subjective states (beliefs, hopes, fears, etc., as well as feelings and sensations such as pains) constitute our inner lives. We ordinarily think that we have private access to them and, indeed, that they are private in a strong and inescapable way.

No one else can feel my pains or have my sensations. No one can see what green looks like to me. Also, I am authoritative about my inner states. No one can correct my judgements about them.

The converse seems true as well. I cannot feel my neighbour's pain or experience what green looks like to him or her. I am able to sympathise with a friend's pain when I see the cut on his arm but that is because I have had cuts myself and I know what my cuts have felt like. I do not really know what he is feeling.

But if all this is so, a philosophical difficulty of some size seems to follow. We have words in our public language for most, if not all, of the concepts with which we classify our inner states. If the previous two paragraphs are correct, 'pain', 'fear', 'hope', 'feeling of relief', 'sensation of green' – all these and innumerable others – would seem to be words and phrases for private objects. That is to say they denote and get their sense from objects that only one person can experience.

How can I be sure that the word 'pain' means in your mouth what it does in mine? We might have thought that each person's position with respect to our shared language of mental contents was impeccable. Each of us has immediate and infallible experience of his or her own mental exemplars which give meaning to the psychological vocabulary.

But I have no way of knowing whether I have got hold of the right mental exemplar (from my private store) which corresponds to the one which any fellow speaker may be using to give meaning to the word he happens to be using. The strong suggestion is that this cannot possibly be how the words for mental concepts get their meaning. The language of mental states must work differently.

The answer seems to be that we rely on public actions and behaviour, at least partly as the behaviourist claims, in order to generate a language adequate to describing and referring to events in our inner lives. (And remember that we are talking about such mundane 'inner events' as 'seeing a green tree' and 'feeling the pain of a cut'. This is not particularly a worry about 'inner events or states' of a mystical, arcane or mysterious kind.)

We learn the meaning of words and phrases like 'hurts' and 'looks green' not by looking in on a private experience and trying to hang a label on it. Rather, children are taught, when enduring a new scrape or cut, that the word for what is making them cry and wince is 'hurt' or 'sting'. Again, we are taught what 'sensation of green' means by being helped to memorise colour words and then told which things look green, which look red, etc., when colour is the obvious variable between one observed thing and the next.

However, the behaviourist has not, after all, been vindicated. This view of how public words for psychological states get their meaning does not say that psychological terms refer to behaviour or that inner states are nothing but dispositions to behave in certain ways. It does not say that there are no inner states.

Rather, what is being said is that terms for (private) mental states are defined in terms of the behaviour to which those states give rise. This, of course, includes verbal behaviour. So 'sensation of green' means 'whatever experience disposes its subject to describe the object seen as green in colour'. It does not mean 'whatever experience feels sufficiently like *this*' – said of some private sensory state being introspected.

 ## QUESTION FOR DISCUSSION

How do the terms for mental states that occur in ordinary natural languages get their meaning?

Self-knowledge and self-consciousness

The previous subsection questioned the traditional British Empiricist view that my infallibly known private mental states (in their terms, my 'ideas') have the role of standing as meanings for psychological words. It seems right to conclude that I do not know the senses of mental terms by introspection.

It may, however, still be the case that introspection does give me knowledge of the states or events themselves that are denoted by these terms.

The difference between sense and reference: two meanings of 'meaning'

Gottlob Frege (1848–1925) famously pointed out that there is a difference between the **sense** of a term and its **reference** or denotation (Frege 1970: 56–78). The sense gives us directions, a 'recipe' for finding things to which that term applies. The reference of a term is the group or class of all those things the recipe could be used to pick out.

So, for example, the sense of the term 'pencil' is something like 'writing implement that makes marks with lead'. Find all the things in the room that match that description and you will have used the sense of the word to gather together its (local) reference or denotation: the collection of pencils in the room.

Do I know anything else through introspection besides the contents of my mind, e.g. the feeling of what is denoted by the phrase 'my pain' or the nature of 'my sensation of green'? To Locke and many others it has seemed that one very important thing I can know introspectively besides the subjective, conscious states I experience is the subject, consciousness or self that is experiencing them. After all, isn't it my *self* that I am immediately aware of in *self*-consciousness?

To this last question Hume gave the emphatic answer 'no!' He said 'For my part, when I enter most intimately into what I call *myself*, I always stumble on some perception or other . . . I never catch *myself* at anytime without a perception, and never can observe anything but the perception' (Hume 1978: 252). In episodes of introspection, Hume thought, we only experience one or another of our thoughts, feelings, sensations, emotions, etc. There is no entity, over and above those conscious states, no possessor of those states, which I can know by looking inward.

For Hume the only thing worthy of the name of 'self' or 'subject of experiences' was the whole bundle or collection of mental contents or experiences themselves which make up my experiential history. Today philosophers still debate whether Locke's confident assertion (of his ability to know himself in introspection) or Hume's denial (of the existence of a self to be known) comes closer to capturing the truth. Is self-consciousness best regarded as awareness of a subject, together with the ideas it is having, grasped in one single mental view? Or is it better thought of as simply a special sort of attention to the mind's ideas and activities? Or is it something different from either of these?

I do appear to have unchallengeable knowledge of who is doing or thinking or feeling whatever it is *I* am doing, thinking, feeling at the moment. I cannot misidentify the subject of my own psychological states. For example, I cannot wonder whether the headache I am feeling right now is mine or not.

But certainty about ownership does not guarantee accuracy about every aspect of the psychological state I know to be mine. So, in an example already used above, someone else may be better able to tell than you are whether you are in love or just infatuated. Or think of the difference a journalist might fail to detect on some occasion between her sense of her duty to tell the public the truth and her desire to embarrass a particular celebrity.

Introspection tells us some truths about ourselves. It gives us infallible knowledge of some aspects of our experiences and conscious states (especially whose they are). But introspection does not tell us the whole truth about our inner life.

QUESTION FOR DISCUSSION

What knowledge can introspection give you about your inner life?

● KNOWLEDGE OF OTHERS

The problem of other minds

Solipsism is the sceptical view that nothing outside your own mind exists. You may reject such extreme scepticism where the external world in general is concerned. But you may feel nonetheless that there is room for doubt whether there are any minds other than your own. This weaker version of solipsism is referred to as 'the problem of other minds' and that is the subject of this subsection.

Once again we begin from the privacy of the mental. Mental privacy, in addition to the other effects we have attributed to it, is the source of the problem of other minds. To say that you have special, private access to your mental states is simply to say that no one other than you can know immediately of the existence and contents of your mind. And that goes for everyone. Each person's inner life is hidden from everyone else. That being the case, however, how can I know that anyone else has a mind?

But can the leap from certainty about oneself to confidence about the existence and contents of other minds really be such a big one? Most people don't doubt that their parents, siblings and friends (i.e. other humans at least) are thinkers and perceiving subjects just like themselves. Is it naive to think this? Should we insist on more evidence? And what sort of evidence could there be?

We might think first of the evidence we use constantly in everyday contexts to ascribe mental states to others. Their winces and groans tell us other people are in pain. Facial expressions, from joyous smiles to grimaces to terrified glances, give us grounds for ascribing happiness, misery and fear.

And, most of all, we talk to them and are answered. Verbal behaviour – otherwise known as 'what people say'! – is often our best guide to what they think, believe, feel, desire and so on. Even if we sometimes make errors, so that we get some of their thoughts and feelings wrong, surely we know from their speaking at all that they do think and feel something.

Or so it seems. But the serious sceptic about other minds would indeed condemn anyone who relies on such evidence as naive. For everyone is aware that cunning fakery is all too easy to contrive. It is not too fanciful to imagine robotic constructions that ape human facial expressions and human behaviour of all sorts, including speech.

And everyone has at times been tempted to attribute mental states to computers and other sophisticated machines (even though these are clearly not human) on the evidence of their output of language. Similarly, many people feel inclined on occasion to attribute psychological states like sensations and beliefs to non-human animals, whether pets or cunning creatures seen in the wild. Yet careful thinkers are unlikely to take behavioural evidence of the sort mentioned as conclusive justification for attributing minds to non-humans, whether beasts or machines.

And if not to beasts and machines then why to other humans? So it doesn't look as if scepticism about other minds is as easy to vanquish as we could wish.

Related examination question

(Part a) Describe and illustrate how solipsism is possible. *(18 marks) (2003)*

Flexibility and language use

The two criteria of mindedness that Descartes offered in the *Discourse on Method* (Descartes 1985: 141) were

- capacity to act in a highly flexible and adaptable way
- use of language.

Many creatures and machines, on Descartes's view, have remarkable abilities. Clocks can tell the time better than we can 'with all our wisdom'. Automatons can be made to produce words in differing contexts. Creatures of different species use complex ruses to capture prey. Birds fly in formation. Many animals can be trained to perform complicated tasks, even to utter words.

But it is not so much what animals and machines can do as what they cannot do that is important. Although Descartes was well aware that many animals use signs of different kinds, he distinguished such animal signal- and sign-making from genuine language (even 'sign-language'). He held that animals never use their signs to express anything other than one of their own 'passions'. (This term means for Descartes 'sensations, drives and feelings' such as hunger, thirst, lust, fear, pain, pleasure and so on.)

A creature with a mind (only humans on Descartes's view) can express much more than just his or her passions. Thoughts and feelings about absent things and people, the past, the future, sport, art, religion, morality, etc. can all form the subject matter of genuine language. But no animal, Descartes thinks, has ever put thoughts about these things into any of its signs.

Equally, he thinks no machine has been or could be made which would be capable of genuine language use including answering questions and conversing appropriately. In our time, many researchers in the field of artificial intelligence have thought this opinion of Descartes's incorrect. Next we will look at a test devised to see who is right.

 ## QUESTIONS FOR DISCUSSION

What are Descartes's two tests for mindedness? How effective are they?

The Turing Test

Alan Turing was a mathematical logician whose work was pivotal in the development of the theory of computation and so of artificial intelligence. He invented what he called the 'imitation game'. Philosophers of mind have adapted the game (including its name, which is now 'the Turing Test') to produce a test of genuine mindedness for computers.

An up-to-date version of the test could work as follows. Imagine that you are chatting on the internet with two respondents whom you have never met. These are separate conversations. You are told that one of the respondents is another person but that the other is a computer which has been programmed to try to trick you into thinking it is a person.

The human respondent answers with whatever answers come to mind. He or she tries to help you. The computer is programmed to give answers like those a human might give. If eventually you give up, unable to identify which of the respondents is which, then this shows that the computer has a mind.

No computer-plus-program yet tested has passed and proved itself minded. To do so the performance of the computer running its program would have to meet both of Descartes's criteria. It would have to be flexible and adaptable. It would have to be able to give genuine-seeming answers (whether true or not) appropriate to a range of questions across a broad selection of very different subject matters. Otherwise you would easily guess that it was just a machine.

Related examination question

(Part a) Describe and illustrate *one* way of deciding whether some machines (e.g. robots, computers, etc.) have minds. *(18 marks) (2002)*

The Chinese room

There are numerous different criticisms of the Turing Test. Here is one oft-voiced one. Many critics have been convinced that no computer could ever qualify as a mind simply in virtue of running a program, however sophisticated. Perhaps a computer could *simulate* a mind in the sense that it could act *as if* it had beliefs, sensations, etc. but it would not really have these things.

This criticism says that, because the Turing Test is a behavioural test for mindedness, it is always possible that a machine could meet the test although it had no mind. Its behaviour could be good enough to fool the tester and yet there would be no mind behind the behaviour.

John Searle is one critic whose version of this criticism has found many friends. His criticism takes the form of a **thought experiment** (Searle 1981: 282–306). Imagine that you are locked in a room and given an instruction manual. The manual gives you instructions that are all a bit like the following: 'When you receive a symbol shaped like this and one shaped like that, find symbols shaped thus and so and pass them on.'

The symbols you receive come through one slot in the wall and you are to post out through a second slot the symbols your instructions tell you to pass on. The symbols (of which you have a huge supply of many different shapes) are all characters of written Chinese. But you know no Chinese whether written or spoken. Your task is just to receive batches of symbols through one slot and select batches of other symbols on the basis of their shape alone, which you then pass on through the other slot.

Unknown to you, Chinese speakers outside the room regard the batches of symbols they pass in as questions. The batches of symbols you pass out seem to them to be answers. You are just moving symbols around according to English rules about the shapes of the symbols. Searle's claim, with which many agree, is that no one performing the tasks required of the occupant of the Chinese room would have or ever achieve any understanding of Chinese.

Searle's main point is that the Chinese room and its occupant function as a computer running a program. Outsiders may be fooled into thinking this computer is a mind that understands Chinese. If you are the occupant, however, you will know that there is no understanding of Chinese in the Chinese room. You will know this because you will be aware that you do not understand Chinese, do not know what the supposed questions are about and do not understand the answers.

Not everyone is convinced by Searle's thought experiment. Some have suggested that the room, symbols and occupant together form a system that *does* understand Chinese. Although one part of that system does not have the relevant understanding, this does not establish Searle's case against the view of mind or understanding as the running of a program by a computer.

 ## QUESTION FOR DISCUSSION

Is there anything more to genuine understanding than running a program?

Defeating the other minds sceptic

The argument from analogy

The counter-argument to Searle just sketched seems very implausible. This may be because the system consisting of you, the batches of symbols and the room does not seem like the kind of thing that could be conscious or have understanding and beliefs.

The intuition behind this criticism of the counter-argument is that there is a way which things with minds look. And there is a kind of thing that has a mind, beliefs and understanding and we expect successful candidates for the title 'mind' to be of that kind. The relevant kind of thing, of course, is a human being.

Not that all minded things need be human. But you may find yourself beginning to be worn down by the sceptic's constant harping on the possibility that whatever apparently minded behaviour you observe, you might be being tricked. You may feel that the way to resist this assault on your ordinary beliefs is to find at least some minimum certainty – at least one 'other mind' you can know to exist – and work up from there.

And there is one thing you *know* has a mind. The so-called 'argument from analogy for other minds' starts from this fact: you know that *you* have a mind. You also know what you look like and how you usually act when you are experiencing various psychological states. You know too that there are other beings around you who bear considerable similarity to you in many respects. These similarities include having a body of a certain type, numerous facial expressions and gestures, actions, speech, etc., in types of situations you are familiar with from your own case. The argument, then, consists in drawing an analogy between your case and that of a fellow human. Since you resemble each other in all the respects listed and many more, surely you also resemble each other in each having a mind.

If this argument works, it establishes the existence of vast numbers of minds since apparently any human being could be taken as your analogue. And it can seem initially a very persuasive argument. However, many philosophers find it less than satisfactory.

One reason for this dissatisfaction is the kind of argument it is. An argument from analogy can never **entail** its conclusion. It invites its hearer to notice similarities and infer unseen ones but the hearer may judge differently and decline the invitation. Again, wherever there are analogies there are also always disanalogies, which may seem more significant to some thinkers than to others.

A second reason for dissatisfaction follows on from the first. In order to be powerful and difficult to resist, an analogy needs to be based on as broad a base as possible. The argument from analogy for other minds, however, rests on only one case – your own. You are taking your own case to be typical. But what is your warrant for that? Using an example of George Graham's, isn't this a bit like supposing all bears are white on the basis of observing a single bear (a polar bear)? (Graham 1998: 53).

Third, and finally, there is the worry that the argument from analogy relies too heavily on superficial similarities and resemblance. Behaviours and bodily features vary extremely widely from one race or culture to the next. It could be that this test for mindedness would fail to pick out, not just the machines and non-human animals (if any) that have minds, but many of the minded humans as well. It would fail to pick out the humans who didn't happen to look very much like you.

 # QUESTION FOR DISCUSSION

What is the argument from analogy for other minds and what are its weaknesses?

Inference to the best explanation

It was dissatisfaction with what he called 'mere argument from analogy' that led John Stuart Mill (1806–73) to devise a related, and much better, argument for other minds. Mill's argument is of a type which, a century later, would come to be known as 'an argument or **inference to the best explanation**'.

Inference to the best explanation

As the name suggests, an inference to the best explanation takes the phenomenon to be explained and tries to devise the best possible theory to account for that phenomenon. Success consists in finding an account that covers every puzzling aspect of the phenomenon, uses the simplest set of hypotheses and makes the fewest assumptions, including assumptions about what kinds of things exist.

Success also involves coming up with an account that is satisfying in another way. No matter how mechanically and methodically it accounts for each feature of the phenomenon to be explained, if a purported explanation is intuitively implausible or too contrived it will not deserve to defeat its rivals. 'A wizard did it using magic' would be a beautifully simple and completely adequate explanation of many things. But it does not satisfy because it stretches credulity too far. To appeal to magic is not to explain. It is to abandon the search for an explanation.

What is important about this notion for our present purposes is this. Once you have found the best possible explanation of something, that is enough to establish the reality of any entities whose existence has to be assumed in order for that explanation to be true.

Mill noticed that there were two chains of events, one involving himself and one involving other humans, which seemed strikingly and significantly the same. One was the causal chain whose first link was his body being affected by certain sorts of things. This lead to his having certain feelings and thoughts (the second link). This in turn caused him to act in certain ways (the third link).

The other chain was the same sorts of circumstances affecting the body of another person followed by the other person acting in the same ways Mill would act in such circumstances.

An example of the sort of thing Mill was thinking of might be you dropping a brick on your foot. The brick affects your body which gives rise to feelings of pain which in turn makes you rub your foot. (You are aware of all three.) Then you see your friend drop a brick on his foot and start rubbing his foot just as you did. (You are aware of two events with a gap.)

The best explanation of the two causal sequences you observe being so similar is that your friend's chain has a second link just like yours, which you can't observe. The best explanation of your friend's rubbing his foot in that way is that he, like you, has a mind with feelings that can be caused by injury and can cause behaviour designed to cure the pain. He too has feelings, caused by the injury, that prompt the rubbing. So he too has a mind in which there can be feelings.

Mill's argument is similar to the argument from analogy but it improves on it. He does not just base his belief in other minds on the fact that he himself has a mind and that other people resemble him. He bases it on a lifetime of scientific observation of causal chains. He draws an inductive inference from many past cases of resemblance between, on the one hand, causal chains all of whose links were observed and, on the other, similar chains with a missing link. Such past resemblances have been best explained by assuming that the missing cause, despite not being observed, did occur.

Mill also makes the highly plausible methodological assumption that members of the same species will share large numbers of features. So he is not arguing from features of himself that could, for all he knows, be untypical, like facial expressions or superficial appearance.

Many present-day philosophers of mind accept the inference to the best explanation argument for other minds. Like Mill they are aware that it is logically possible that something else, other than the presence of a mind, could be responsible for actions like your friend's rubbing his foot when injured. But they also agree with Mill that there is no obligation to canvas all the logically possible explanations that ingenuity could contrive. In fact, when a perfectly credible and adequate explanation that covers all the data is readily available we should not look further. The credible explanation is the most rational alternative to accept.

Related examination question

(Part b) Assess solutions to the problem of other minds. *(32 marks) (2003)*

● PERSONS

In the first part of this section we will look at some of the suggestions that philosophers have made about what conditions must be met by anything aspiring to be called a person. Then we will turn to the question: What are the **necessary and sufficient conditions** for remaining the same person over a period of time?

What is a person?

It might seem that the answer to the question in the title is all too simple. Someone might say 'Persons are human beings. The two expressions are just synonyms.'

But remembering Frege's distinction between sense and reference (see above, p. 171 and Glossary) we might want to change this simple answer for a more precise one. 'Person' and 'human being' clearly have different senses. The second expression is the name of a particular species of animal. It is an open question whether the first expression is restricted in application to the members of a particular species or not.

Perhaps 'person' and 'human being' are like 'creature with a heart' and 'creature with kidneys'. These last two expressions have the same reference: they pick out exactly the same things. But they clearly do not have the same sense. This is an example of Quine's (Quine 1961: 21).

So what is the sense of the term 'person'? Some would say that a person is any being with a mind of a certain degree of sophistication. This leaves the door open to such possible beings as aliens, angels and God. If a being in any of these three categories existed we might feel that we wished to recognise that being as a person.

Certainly we sometimes attribute *personality* to non-human animals but it may be that no one intends by such attributions anything like what would be intended by attribution of the term 'person'. Though most people believe many non-human animals have sufficient mental capacities to feel pain and a number of other conscious states there seems also to be general agreement that it requires more mental sophistication than this to qualify as a person.

If we found any machine that could pass the Turing Test and seemed able to meet Descartes's two criteria for mindedness we might at least consider calling such a machine a person.

The tentative tone of the points made so far ('perhaps', 'may seem', etc.) shows that it is by no means obvious which beings are persons. There is also a question of who is to decide what counts as a person. Who or what would have authority to give *the* definition of 'person'? Is this a question about English usage, which could be solved by looking in the dictionary or perhaps taking a survey of how people believe they use the term?

The dictionary and such a survey *might* help with answering our present question. But it is possible to take the view that the concept of a person is less an artefact of convention or agreement and more like the concept of a triangle.

Triangles have intrinsic features that exist to be discovered whether anyone discovers them or not. People might never have thought about triangles or hit on the notion of such a thing. It would still have been timelessly true that the sum of the interior angles of a triangle is equivalent to two right angles. From now on I will adopt the view that the concept of a person, likewise, contains features that are not invented by anyone but are there to be discovered by analysis of an appropriate kind.

To the general idea of mental sophistication or intelligence noted above we can add

- capacity for a certain range of emotions and feelings
- ability to remember past events and to anticipate and plan as well as to think about what is not available in present sense perception
- capacity to make evaluative (moral, aesthetic, religious) responses and judgements
- capacity for abstract thought
- capacity to use language
- self-consciousness and subjectivity.

You may feel that this list misses out some important features. For example, the capacity to enter into certain sorts of relationship with other persons is sometimes suggested as a feature that should be mentioned.

This list contains numerous capacities and potentials. And this is unsurprising since no one is exercising all his or her 'person features' at once or throughout his or her life. Human persons all begin life with many of these capacities not yet developed to even the most rudimentary degree. Also, alas, many of these capacities fall away to some extent in later life, sometimes disastrously so.

So far we have been looking for features *sufficient* for being a person. Are the properties or capacities already mentioned also *necessary* so that we would not allow that a being who lacked them was a person? The thought that this would be unduly restrictive makes writers such as David Wiggins (1980: 171) define persons as members of a class, *typical members of which* have these and related capacities. We would not want to say that a sufferer from Alzheimer's disease was no longer a person even after many of these capacities had deteriorated beyond recovery.

Similarly, it seems to me, the newborn and the severely mentally disabled should be counted among the persons. This is so even though their potential to develop 'person features' and 'person capacities' has not yet been realised or will, unfortunately, never be so.

Wiggins believes that the only persons are living organisms but does not believe that the human species necessarily is (or will always be) the only one whose members are persons. Other thinkers believe that there could be machine persons if robotics and computer science advance as we can imagine they might. Still others think we might find further types of persons on other planets or in heaven.

If you are a substance dualist you will say that the necessary and sufficient condition for being a person is being an immaterial substance. There is clearly room for debate, not just about what features are necessary to being a person, but – even when that is agreed – about which are the actual and possible persons.

 # QUESTION FOR DISCUSSION

What features are necessary and sufficient for being a person?

The problem of personal identity over time

The philosophers' problem of personal identity over time is sometimes described as the search for criteria of identity for persons. This can be a helpful description provided two things are kept in mind. The first is the meaning of 'criteria' in this context. The second is the meaning of 'personal identity'.

Two meanings of 'criterion'

The term 'criteria' ('criterion' is the singular) can mean either of two things. It can mean 'tests for the presence of some sort of thing'. Or it can mean 'the essential features constituting the nature of something'. For example, one criterion (in the sense of 'test') of who is the guilty party may be having the same fingerprints as the person who did the deed. And one criterion of some substance's being an acid is that it turns blue litmus paper red.

The criterion of being a criminal (what makes it true that the criminal is a criminal) is being the one who committed the crime – whether or not anyone ever finds out. What makes an acid an acid is something about the substance's chemical constitution. An acid will have this nature (will meet this criterion) whether anyone ever discovers its nature or not.

When philosophers talk about criteria of personal identity they are talking about what makes a person encountered on one occasion the very same person as a person encountered on another occasion. It is the *nature* of personal identity that is in question. It is the criterion of personal identity in the sense of 'the necessary and sufficient conditions of personal identity' that philosophers are seeking.

QUESTION FOR DISCUSSION

What are the two senses of 'criterion'? What examples can you think of to illustrate each sense?

Two kinds of identity

The sort of identity in question is what is called strict or numerical identity. This means 'countability as one'. So identical twins, since there are two of them, are not numerically identical. If twins are very similar they could rightly be described as **qualitatively identical**. They share very many properties but they are not numerically identical. Numerical identity is a relationship that a thing can have only with itself.

When philosophers look for criteria of personal identity, then, they are looking for whatever a person must retain to remain one single individual over time. The problem of personal identity is best viewed as a puzzle in philosophical logic. It is a completely general question about the logic of numerical identity where a complex kind of entity is concerned. It is not about your own personality or 'finding your inner self'.

Bodily continuity

The philosophical problem of identity over time for any sort of thing arises because things do not stay the same as time passes. Things alter – sometimes very greatly. And, of course, sometimes things change in such a way that we say they have gone out of existence. The question is, how much change and what kind of change constitute existence change?

Some things undergo numerous alterations during a long lifetime and then go out of existence by dying. Others go out of existence if only very slight change occurs. For example, a rise in temperature of only a few degrees will make an ice cube go out of existence.

When looking for the criteria of identity over time of any kind of thing, common sense suggests that you think about what it took to be a thing of that kind in the first place. This is because, intuitively, it seems that all the thing need do to stay numerically one and the same over time is to retain those essential features. So, for example, an apple goes on being the same apple as long as it retains those features it had to have to be an apple in the first place. In the case of the apple we might say, very crudely, that it had to be a fruit that was picked from an apple tree.

Now is the time to recall the difficulties we had (and the degree of success too) in saying what being a person involves. Earlier we saw that some thinkers regard being an animal of a particular species as both necessary and sufficient for being a person. Others feel that having some or all of a certain list of capacities and potentials is essential for personhood – although there is plenty of debate about which exact capacities and features belong on the list. And there are, as well, thinkers who maintain that only being (or having) an immaterial soul/mind entitles its possessor to be called a person.

So one of the most resilient philosophical theories of personal identity maintains that all you need do in order to remain numerically the same person as you are now is to remain the same living human being. Whatever changes occur to your living body, and however severe they may be, you will still be you.

You may suffer the ravages of degenerative disease or a terrible physical accident. You may go through profound psychological changes such as amnesia or mental illness, conquering an addiction or undergoing a religious conversion. As long as you remain the same living human being – whether you remember who you are or not – that fact alone guarantees that you remain the same person.

The theory just introduced says that keeping the same living body – bodily continuity – is *sufficient* for personal identity. Is it also *necessary*? Could some future person who didn't have your body be you?

It is sometimes held that what we value in personal persistence (our own or that of others) is not the persistence of the body per se. Rather we think that our 'person features' depend on the body (or, at least, need *a* body) to survive. In particular we care about the capacities referred to in the list above and we believe that they would not be retained if the living brain were lost. This makes us prize the living body – in particular the brain – as the 'vehicle' of personal identity.

However, if another vehicle existed that might be good enough. Someone who thinks this way would say that bodily continuity is sufficient for personal identity but not necessary. Something else could do the same job of keeping you you.

Psychological continuity

Several thoughts – and numerous questions – follow naturally from the points made in the previous paragraph. One is that we seem to have shifted from one of the possible views about what a person is to another. Instead of looking for criteria of numerical identity for human beings we are now concerned with criteria of identity for conscious subjects, i.e. the things that can have the capacities on our list of 'person features'. You should ask yourself whether this seems a good change of focus or a mistaken one.

As was noted above, conscious subjects are, in principle, not restricted to human or even any sort of animal beings. Aliens, angels, androids – we can at least imagine conscious subjects of all these types. And perhaps we should recall the immaterial substances many people believe in. Those who think immaterial substances not just genuinely possible but real regard them as very numerous since, according to believers, every one of us has one.

The person you are (meaning the conscious subject you are) may as a matter of present fact depend for its persistence on your actual living body and in particular your brain. This, however, does not mean that it could not survive the death of that body or the loss of that brain if another vehicle could be found to sustain it. Perhaps a replacement brain (or whole body), in this life or the next, could perform the task of sustaining the person you are.

Locke was one of the earliest philosophers to articulate a theory of personal identity using such a psychological criterion. His idea was that the persistent person was not any sort of substance, either material or immaterial. Rather it was a conscious self. For Locke, as far as you can cast back the net of conscious memory and self-awareness, so far stretches the person you are.

This notion is sometimes abbreviated to the title 'the memory criterion' of personal identity. However, Locke was not just interested in memories. His idea of what makes a persisting person comes much closer to what modern writers call 'psychological continuity'. This includes not just memories but the awareness we have, in recalling past actions and events, of ourselves being active and involved in those occurrences.

For someone who adopts Locke's view of the person, keeping the same living body is neither sufficient nor necessary for personal identity. What matters is keeping the same consciousness. What is both necessary and sufficient for staying you is that you continue to be able to be aware of the events and feelings of your past with that same self-consciousness that you had when they occurred.

With such a criterion of personal identity a thinker can accommodate such notions as that of reincarnation, swapping bodies with another person, survival of death, resurrection and possession of one person's body by another. The same living body could host successive persons. It could house one person by day and a different one by night. If the same human body is neither necessary nor sufficient for being the same person it becomes irrelevant to personal identity.

What matters instead, however, is psychological continuity. A Lockean view has to admit that the person is lost or broken if the right consciousness and memories are lost or that continuity is otherwise crucially interrupted. An amnesiac becomes a second, different person, not just one unfortunate person who has forgotten who he is. Someone with false memory syndrome becomes the person whose experiences he thinks he remembers.

 ## Question for discussion

Does psychological continuity provide the best criterion of personal identity?

Even if a modified Lockean psychological continuity view of persons could somehow escape these last two objections there would be a further major difficulty for such a view to face. If it is logically possible that one substitute or replacement vehicle of personal identity could be created or found to carry all your memories, personality, self-consciousness, etc., then it is logically possible that *more than one* could be found. For ask yourself what would be the obvious way to come up with the needed replacement.

Surely the obvious way would be to copy, down to the minutest detail, the brain that is at the moment the vehicle of your identity. Doubtless, the difficulties of making such a copy are innumerable and insuperable. But the logical possibility seems real enough. The trouble is that an agency capable of making one such copy could presumably make two. And the problem with this suggestion is that both copies would have an equal claim to be the earlier person whose brain was copied.

But the two copies could not both be you surviving in a copy. If there were two of them they could not both be numerically identical with the earlier you. And what if earlier you was still in existence? Copies – even divine, post-mortem copies – cannot be quite the correct answer to the puzzle of personal identity.

Conclusion

This has been a whistlestop tour of logical puzzles raised by the idea of personal identity. It has left numerous questions unanswered and should only be regarded as an introduction to the subject. It will have been successful if you have begun seriously to question what it is that is crucial to being the person you are.

Remember that this is not a question about your individual personality, character and psychology. Rather it is the question about what makes you *or any person whatsoever* a person and not another type of thing, however similar.

The only uncontroversial examples of persons we have at our disposal in this discussion also happen to be human beings. But we have seen that a single individual can exemplify many different sorts or kinds of thing (simultaneously and for different periods of its existence). We must know what kind of thing it is whose identity we are trying to trace before we can decide which are the correct criteria of identity for a thing of that kind.

Perhaps you will conclude that only humans are and can be persons. Perhaps not. Perhaps you will adopt the bodily criterion, perhaps the criterion of psychological continuity. Whichever view you decide to support, remember that emphatic declarations of your preferred opinion are not what is needed to establish a philosophical view. You need to support your position with argument.

REFERENCES

Descartes, R. (1985) [1637] *Discourse on Method*, in Cottingham, J., Stoothoff, R. and Murdoch, D. (eds and trans.) *The Philosophical Writings of Descartes*, vol. I, Cambridge: Cambridge University Press.

Dretske, F. (1989) 'Reasons and causes', in Tomberlin, J. (ed.) *Philosophical Perspectives*, vol. 3: *Philosophy of Mind and Action Theory*, Atascadero, Calif.: Ridgeview.

Frege, G. (1970) [1892] 'On sense and reference', in Geach, P. and Black, M. (eds and trans.) *Translations from the Philosophical Writings of Gottlob Frege*, Oxford: Blackwell.

Graham, G. (1998) *The Philosophy of Mind*, 2nd edn, Oxford: Blackwell.

Hume, D. (1978) [1739] *A Treatise of Human Nature*, 2nd edn, ed. L. A. Selby-Bigge and P. H. Nidditch, Oxford: Clarendon Press.

Lewis, D. (1983) 'Mad pain and Martian pain', in his *Philosophical Papers*, Oxford: Oxford University Press.

Quine, W. V. O. (1961) 'Two dogmas of empiricism', *From a Logical Point of View*, Cambridge, Mass.: Harvard University Press. First published in *Philosophical Review* 60 (1951).

Searle, J. (1981) 'Minds, brains and programs', in Haugeland, J. (ed.) *Mind Design*, Cambridge, Mass.: MIT/Bradford Books.

Wiggins, D. (1980) *Sameness and Substance*, Oxford: Blackwell.

RECOMMENDED READING

- George Graham's book mentioned above is a very approachable and engaging introduction to many of the topics dealt with in this chapter.

- Crane, T. (1995) *The Mechanical Mind* (Harmondsworth: Penguin) is another excellent introduction to topics on the border between Philosophy of Mind and Philosophy of Cognitive Science.

● Guttenplan, S. *(1994) A Companion to the Philosophy of Mind* (Oxford: Blackwell). This is an indispensable reference work with entries on many of the concepts and topics covered in the Mind syllabus.

● Heil, J. (1998) *Philosophy of Mind: A Contemporary Introduction*, London: Routledge.

● Kim, J. (1996) *Philosophy of Mind*, Boulder, Colo.: Westview Press.

● Smith, P. and Jones, O. R. (1986) *The Philosophy of Mind: An Introduction*, Cambridge: Cambridge University Press.

The above three are solid, introductory textbooks written in a clear and well organised way with the beginner in mind.

GLOSSARY

anomalous – The word (meaning 'lawless') refers to Donald Davidson's view that there are no strict laws relating mental states to physical states or to other psychological states. Anomalous monism (Davidson's term) is a view in philosophy of mind that opposes substance dualism and maintains that there is only one sort of substance, namely matter.

criterion (s.), **criteria** (pl.) – This term has two distinct uses in philosophical writing. Sometimes a criterion is a test. So, for example, the criterion of being an acid is that it turns blue litmus paper red. The criterion used for identifying person *x* may be that she has the right (*x*'s!) fingerprints. But 'criterion' can also mean 'necessary and sufficient condition(s) for'. So the criterion of being an acid is 'being a substance that can transfer a proton to another substance' (anything with that nature is an acid). Similarly, the criterion of personal identity (what defines the nature of personal identity) may be thought to be 'keeping the same living body'.

eliminative materialism – The theory that reference to mental states like sensations and beliefs is literally false since no such items really exist. Eliminativists think that it would be better not to use terms that purportedly denote mental states. Rather, these terms should be eliminated from our vocabulary wherever possible.

entail – A conclusion is entailed by its premises when it is deduced from them by a valid argument. The premises *make* the conclusion true (because they are true themselves and the argument is valid).

epiphenomenalism – The view that mental states, though real and often caused by bodily occurrences and states, can have no effects.

first person authority – Our ability to know our own subjective states, feelings, etc. immediately, with greater certainty than we possess about the physical world and (arguably) with greater certainty than anyone else has about them.

folk psychology – The conceptual scheme or theory that we all use to interpret, understand and predict each others' behaviour by reference to others' beliefs and desires, without recourse to 'scientific psychology'.

inference to the best explanation – A form of argument, as its name suggests, where the conclusion is accepted because it seems to offer the best explanation of the phenomenon or happening being examined. It may make reference to items that are unobserved or unobservable and, if so, this can be taken to provide a good case for the existence of those items despite their not being observed or observable.

intentionality – The 'aboutness' or 'representational character' of thoughts and other psychological states. The way in which a mental state, 'in someone's head' as we say, can refer to, represent or stand for something in the world.

inverted spectrum hypothesis – The suggestion that it is possible that your experience when you look at something red is qualitatively exactly like mine when I look at something green – and so on round the spectrum.

multiple realisability – The ability of some individuals or types of individuals to be 'realised' or rendered by things of different types. The standard examples are a mousetrap or a poison. Mousetraps can be made to any of numerous designs in a range of different materials. A poison can be any one of numerous substances that are toxic to living creatures in numerous ways. Functionalists believe mental states, similarly, can be realised many different ways in numerous different physical or other materials.

necessary and sufficient conditions – Necessary conditions of *p* are ones without which *p* would not occur. Sufficient conditions of *p* are ones that are enough to produce *p*. All of a thing's necessary conditions must obtain if it is to exist but a *single* sufficient condition guarantees that what it is sufficient for obtains.

numerical and qualitative identity – Two things that resemble each other in all their qualities are still two not one. Qualitative identity is the sort enjoyed by so-called identical twins, assembly-line light-bulbs, pairs of pins, etc. Numerical identity (sometimes called 'strict identity') is the identity a thing has with itself. It is countability as one thing.

phenomenology – The term used by philosophers to refer to the experiential qualities, the subjective or felt qualities that feelings and sensations are perceived to have.

There is something each token sensation is like for its subject. This is its phenomenology or 'phenomenological feel'.

qualia (pl.), **quale** (s.) – The experiential qualities or subjective phenomenological feels of subjective (mental) states. For example, the sharpness of the taste of lemon or the throbbing quality of a particular pain.

sense and reference (or denotation) – The sense of a term gives us some sort of direction, a 'recipe', for finding things to which that term applies. This may be done by listing properties of that kind of thing or by naming necessary and sufficient conditions. The reference of a term is the group or class of all those things the recipe could be used to pick out.

solipsism, problem of other minds – Solipsism is the belief that nothing whatever exists outside your own mind. Even if you are satisfied that there is a world of material objects you may still feel the need of a solution to the problem of other minds. That is, you may still want a convincing argument to establish the existence of *minds* other than your own.

thought experiment – An imaginative thought experiment is a tool used frequently in philosophy to try to find the limits or elasticity of certain concepts. For example, imagine a perfect molecule-for-molecule living copy of someone on earth being made on the other side of the universe. Is the copy the same person as the original (now newly arrived from earth)? Or is the copy a new person? This thought experiment has been thought by some to help us to understand the limits of our concept of a person.

type and token – There are two tokens of the word 'and' in this entry – the one in quotation marks is in ordinary print, the other is in bold. There is only one word type of which the two tokens are instances.

5

political philosophy

UNIT 4   Patrick Riordan

KEY CONCEPTS ⟩

- ⟩ the state
- ⟩ politics
- ⟩ conflict
- ⟩ persuasion
- ⟩ coercion
- ⟩ power
- ⟩ authority

- ⟩ legitimacy
- ⟩ obligation
- ⟩ law
- ⟩ directive and coercive force
- ⟩ constitutive and regulative rules
- ⟩ positive and negative freedom
- ⟩ rights: liberties and claim-rights

● INTRODUCTION

Political issues have always been important for philosophy. Questions such as 'What sort of social order is necessary to enable people to achieve a good life?' link **politics** to other areas of philosophy. Questions like this require clarification of basic issues such as: What is the best life possible for human beings? (ethics), What kind of being is the human such that it must explore questions about its good? (**philosophical anthropology**, philosophy of mind), Is there a common human nature and how is it known? (**ontology, epistemology**). The purely political questions cannot be divorced from questions in other disciplines of philosophy. The Dialogues of Plato (427–347 BC), especially *The Republic*, illustrate this fact. The broad range of philosophical questions from ontology to ethics contributes to the common search for a life that is worth living.

This search is carried on wherever humans become aware of their responsibility for the situation in which they live. The question about the best life possible and how it might be achieved in social cooperation is always asked within a particular context. The values, concepts and criteria available for dealing with the question are not always the same, however. The abstract terminology of political philosophy can give the impression that philosophers in different times and places are talking about the same reality, but that could be misleading.

For instance, terms such as 'community', 'society', **state**, are frequently used, as are terms such as **authority**, **law**, and **obligation**. That these terms can be used in abstraction from any concrete and specific set of institutions and relationships at some point in their history can lead one to think that there is some reality termed 'state', which can be investigated and known, and that there is some other reality termed 'society', equally knowable apart altogether from any specific society.

When we pursue such questions, we are caught in a tension between two poles. On the one hand, we want to avoid any uncritical acceptance of the status quo, which assumes:

* that the way things are is the way they have to be; and
* that the way people traditionally describe and explain the way things are is correct.

On the other hand, because some abstraction is necessary, we need to be careful not to distance ourselves too much from our actual social reality. If our investigations are to contribute to finding a life that is worth living, we have to remain rooted in our concrete historical situation.

The dangers of failing to manage this tension between distance and involvement are the alternatives of **utopianism** on the one hand, or **idealisation** on the other. Utopianism is the glorification of an ideal but unrealisable social order in which problems are solved; this need not be as naive as it sounds, since it can take the form of a highly sophisticated intellectual account of a well-functioning system – one, however, that will never exist. The other danger is the glorification of a particular historical social order as the realisation of the human aspirations for a life worth living. The idealisation of the particular has taken many forms in history, including Germany's Third Reich, and the Stalinist Soviet Union. Imperialism and nationalism provide other examples.

> **Important distinction: possible dangers in political philosophy**
>
> **Utopianism:** the glorification of a non-existent, non-achievable regime
>
> **Idealisation:** the glorification of an actual, historical regime

The question about the kind of social order that will enable us to achieve a good life is usually provoked by some problem. It might be the experience of **conflict** between competing interest groups, or different political parties. The existence of different practical objectives (join the euro, or remain with sterling?) as well as different ways of evaluating the same evidence (was the war against Saddam Hussein warranted?) can challenge us. We have to clarify how we describe and evaluate situations, and then how we can deal with the fact that there are people who disagree with our descriptions and evaluations, and oppose our plans. Clearly, it is not just a matter of disagreement, as if a good discussion might lead us to agree to differ. There is conflict in that people's chances of achieving their objectives and realising their own vision of the good life are restricted by what others do in the pursuit of theirs.

Conflict occurs when the goals pursued by individuals or groups are mutually incompatible or mutually frustrating. For instance, traditionally, the Unionists of Northern Ireland want to remain in the United Kingdom, while the Nationalists of Northern Ireland want to be part of a united Ireland. These goals are not compatible. Similarly, the public ownership of the railway is incompatible with the privatisation of the railway. Adopting the euro is incompatible with maintaining the pound. It is not merely that people disagree on these issues; they are also actively involved in trying to bring about their preferred state of affairs, and so they mutually impede one another.

> **Important distinction**
>
> **Disagreement:** opinions are contradictory.
>
> **Conflict:** goals are mutually incompatible or frustrating.

What contribution can political philosophy make to such situations? Philosophy can clarify the concepts that are used, the values that are operative in people's commitments, and the arguments that they present in promoting their case. This work should have some influence on the quality of political activity and debate. However, philosophers are also citizens of their states and members of their own societies. Sometimes they will go beyond this work of clarification, and take sides in particular debates. Where the line is to be drawn, if at all, between professional analysis and practical commitment, is a matter of dispute between philosophers, and a personal challenge for each one.

Descriptive and normative philosophy

We can distinguish between the **descriptive** and the **normative** modes of speaking. The descriptive is saying what is the case, the normative is saying what ought to be the case, or what is good or bad about what is the case. Take the example of speaking about a state. In a descriptive mode, philosophy can report that in a certain state, perhaps Sweden, the state's main function is the promotion of social justice. Analysis of the relevant conception of justice will follow whatever people in Sweden think that justice is. A normative position might assert that the state's main function ought to be the provision and achievement of social justice. When we speak normatively, we appeal to standards that allow us to assess the performance of states as more or less adequate in relation to those standards.

The normative approach can be further distinguished in a minimalist and a maximalist stance. In the minimalist approach, minimum standards are formulated below which no state ought to fall, for instance, in the respect for human rights. In the maximalist approach, ideal standards might be formulated that no state would ever comprehensively achieve, but that it might meaningfully aspire to, for instance, securing a decent quality of life for all its citizens. This is hardly exhaustible, since the standards of what constitutes a decent quality of life change over time, as expectations are expanded under pressure from achievement.

Important distinction

Descriptive: empirical account of what is the case

Normative: prescriptive account of what ought to be the case

Normative distinguished further:

Minimalist: standards below which one should not fall

Maximalist: ideal as the standard, although not achievable

QUESTIONS FOR DISCUSSION

What examples of conflict are you familiar with? What is the problem with being utopian in politics? If our political system is a good one, what could be wrong with idealising it? Should political philosophers be politically active? Can we avoid being normative in talking about politics? Is it possible to be purely descriptive in politics without any normative aspect?

● IDEOLOGIES

The word **ideology** is used in different senses which reflect the tension between the descriptive and the normative. In one sense it identifies a body of thought held by a group of people, which they rely on to guide their action. Ideology is distinguished both from science, which might also have application in technology, and from common sense. Both technology and common sense guide action also, but ideology is relevant to political action. Any group of people who share a common view of their situation and act in the political forum to preserve it or change it in accord with their values can be said to have an ideology in this sense. In this usage, there is no automatic claim that the ideas expressed in ideologies are valid or true.

In contrast, the notion of ideology as used by Karl Marx (1818–83) is evaluative. For Marx, ideologies are bodies of ideas, which, although false, give the impression of mediating reality. They protect the interests of the dominant class, and function in its exercise of **power**. A typical Marxist example of ideology is the notion of natural rights, linked to the idea of the individual human being. Those who assert a natural right to private property, for instance, are deluded. There is no such reality, according to Marx, but this false way of thinking succeeds in persuading people because of its apparent universality, claiming a right for every human being. Those who accept the idea effectively support the interests of property owners, who, on Marx's view, comprise the dominant class in society.

> **Important distinction: two meanings of 'ideology'**
>
> **Descriptive:** presenting others' ideas without comment
>
> **Normative:** with a negative evaluation of others' ideas

If we use the notion of ideology in a purely descriptive sense, we can identify different practical programmes whereby different groups attempt to shape social order according to their convictions and values. **Liberalism, socialism, communism, conservatism, nationalism** and **anarchism**, are examples. One could add **republicanism**, feminism, religious fundamentalism, environmentalism, **democracy** and **theocracy**.

❓ QUESTIONS FOR DISCUSSION

Where is the limit to be drawn in listing ideologies? Is vegetarianism to be counted as an ideology? What about anti-globalisation? Does there have to be a sufficiently organised political movement with a distinctive set of ideas to constitute an ideology?

Ideologies, practical and theoretical

As well as the practical programmes to which political parties and other groups are committed, there are theoretical attempts to articulate in a coherent and grounded manner the essential ideas of the various 'isms'. It is important to remember that the theoretical presentation of ideas does not mean that those who use the relevant label actually share the views formulated by the political theorist. For instance, those who consider themselves conservatives and perhaps subscribe to the policies of the Conservative Party do not necessarily hold conservative ideas as formulated by some thinker such as Edmund Burke (1729–97) or Michael Oakeshott.

Important distinctions

Ideology as a political movement: e.g. conservatism

Ideology as a theoretical presentation: e.g. Oakeshott's account of conservatism

---

The clarification and assessment of the ideas used by ideologies is an important task of political philosophy. Not only are the concepts such as law and freedom used in different ways by the ideological theorists but they lead to polar opposition on some important issues. When discussing these issues, the political philosopher must also be aware that the terminology and language she uses may well be linked to a specific ideology. Special attention is required to ensure that the critical distance of philosophy is maintained and that it does not lose its independence to some particular ideology.

Ideologies: individualist or communal

Ideologies can be compared with one another in different ways. Do they give priority of emphasis to the individual or to the communal, to liberty or to authority, to liberty or to equality, to the maintenance of established order or to its radical change, to the control of the economy or to the freedom of the market?

A major division in the forms of political ideology is to be found between those that emphasise the individual, and those that give preference to the social. This is reflected in the history of modern political thought. The English philosophers Thomas Hobbes (1588–1679) and John Locke (1632–1704) exemplify **individualism** in their accounts of the origins and nature of political order. They each begin with a description of the human individual existing outside of society. They then consider the steps that would have to be taken for such an individual to enter into social arrangements with others of his kind. Hobbes thinks that it is the need for security, given the threat that each poses to the other, that drives people to agree with one another to accept limitations on their freedom, to be supervised by an all-powerful sovereign. Locke argues that people would take steps to ensure the protection of their rights, since the absence of a settled, known law, an impartial judge, and an effective executive power, mean that protection and securing of rights is haphazard and arbitrary. So he considers that individuals as he describes them would agree to the creation of limited government with powers to make law, adjudicate disputes and enforce the law.

Jean-Jacques Rousseau (1712–78) in France and Karl Marx in Germany (from 1850 in London) criticised this individualistic emphasis. Common to Rousseau and Marx is the view that the individual of liberal political thought is a social product. Another similarity in their thought is the search for a social and political order in which the communal nature of the human is fundamental.

Rousseau lamented the element of cold, calculating reason that was supposed to be the basis of involvement in society, and pointed instead to the bonds of affection and belonging that linked people to one another and to their communities. He reinterpreted the solutions offered by Hobbes and Locke in terms of factors such as envy, greed, resentment, hatred, shame and the desire to dominate, rather than rational self-interest. In his own proposed solution he imagined a form of social order in which people would not be subject to domination by others but would remain free, in control of their own lives. His thought survives in forms of **civic republicanism**, which aspires to an absence of all forms of domination, so that citizens participate in self-government on a basis of equality.

Marx saw the emphasis on the isolated individual as the result of a process of **alienation**. Humans, who share the same physical neediness and capacities for working to meet those needs, instead of being united by their common fate and seeing one another as fellows, became divided and learned to see each other as competitor and threat. The basic dynamic of this alienation was driven by the division of human productive energies along the fault line of property: those who controlled productive property, the owners of capital, and those who had nothing to trade except their labour power, the class of workers, the **proletariat**.

Liberalism

Liberal political ideologies give priority to individual freedom. A fundamental conviction of liberalism is that a rational account of the sources and nature of political authority can be given, on the basis of an analysis of the rights, or the interests, or the aspiration for justice, or the practical rationality of the individual. Once successfully developed, this account will provide a rational grounding of obligation to obey the law, on the one hand, and of the **legitimacy** of state power on the other. Liberal political philosophers offer many such attempts, but none has yet achieved universal acceptance. John Rawls, Robert Nozick, Ronald Dworkin and Joseph Raz are examples.

Liberalism in politics is sometimes linked to economic liberalism, in which the individual's freedom of economic activity as entrepreneur, investor, or worker is respected. Liberal ideologies favour facilitation of economic freedom on the assumption that people will only want to enter into contracts with one another (to buy and sell goods and services, and to sell and buy labour) if they expect to benefit in some way. No one should be prevented by state interference from improving his position by his own free activity, according to the economic liberal. As to the question of whether the free market will provide for the basic needs of all, the liberal usually replies that if someone wants something, they will be prepared to pay for it, and where there is a willingness to buy, sellers will soon take advantage of it. Reliance on the free market is also claimed to be much more efficient than direct control of production and distribution. This polarisation of ideologies has a contemporary application in the debates about the privatisation of government services, from the railways to the National Health Service.

Liberalism holds that people fare best when they are left free to pursue their own interests without interference from the state. A regime based on freedom will foster toleration so that the widest possible expression of opinion will lead to the development of knowledge and the elimination of error, myth and superstition. Eventually, political communities will be able to regulate their lives on rational and defensible foundations. Liberal theorists attempt to establish such foundations in terms of rights, or justice, or equality, or welfare.

In the absence of success in generating universal agreement on rational foundations for the state, liberalism contents itself with the management of conflict so that no one's ideas of the good are imposed on others.

Socialism

Marx's thought inspired many socialist and labour movements, with a variety of political ideologies. The most successful of these in terms of winning political control were the Marxist Leninists of the Soviet Union, and the Maoist Marxists of China. Other varieties of socialism included the social democratic parties of Western Europe, as well as some anti-statist groups, who were also linked to anarchist movements.

Just as liberalism emphasises the freedoms of economic agents in the market as the key to achieving material well-being, so socialist ideologies give priority to the communal interest and advocate the social control of economic activity so as to ensure achievement of communal goals, such as full employment and provision of basic needs for all: food, housing, health care, and education.

Socialism considers the human as essentially social, and so aspires to forms of political organisation that directly reflect this social reality. The details of the socialist vision reflect the features that need to be overcome in order to realise the dream. For Marxist socialists, it requires the abolition of private property, labour for wages, and the division of labour, those forms of the organisation of production that most divide people from one another and alienate them from their social nature. For other socialists the main feature to be overcome is hierarchy, so that the allocations of power that allow some to dominate others will be replaced by an equality in which all will rule together.

Communitarianism

Communitarian positions are based on the view that the human person is always situated in some social context, and that it is impossible to conceive of an individual capable of forming plans and of acting rationally who has not learned to do so within a web of social relationships. They reject the idea of the unencumbered individual as found in liberal thought, i.e. a person without ties and commitments to others.

Some develop this criticism of liberal philosophy into a political ideology, aiming at a situation where a society with shared values and practices would be able to realise these through the application of political power. However, the problem with such an ideology is that it is almost impossible to find homogeneous societies with shared values that can take on the task of ruling themselves.

Nationalism

Nationalism could also be included under the listing of ideologies on the social end of the spectrum, because of the emphasis on the nation. However, nationalisms have taken different political forms, some embracing liberalism, some republicanism and others some form of socialism and even totalitarianism.

Nationalism assumes that humankind is essentially divided into nations, and each nation has a right of self-determination. Criteria for identifying a nation are: a common language, genetic relatedness, shared history and culture, occupation of a distinct and shared territory, and the willingness to identify oneself as a member of the nation.

But these criteria do not provide clarity in deciding who is included and who is excluded from the nation. Are the French speakers of Belgium to be included in the nation of France? Are the immigrants from former African colonies like Algeria and Senegal to be excluded from the nation? What about the children of these immigrants, born and reared in France? Clear lines of division cannot be drawn, and the attempt to do so has sometimes led to racist discrimination and even genocide.

Anarchism

Not all ideologies accept the state as necessary for achieving their values. Some socialist positions anticipate a 'withering away' of the state, as the functions of planning and control are increasingly done by people at grass-roots level. At the other pole, anarchists deny the need for any state, considering that any exercise of political power is an infringement of human freedom. The anarchist position is an extreme form of the liberal individualist position. Some libertarian thinkers, for instance Nozick, rely on a statement of anarchy as a default position, relative to which they build up their defence of the state.

Anarchism typically presents itself as a critique of state power, and can usually rely on a description of abuses to establish its own credentials. But it cannot point to any society that has managed without the institutions of rule. In a world in which anarchy prevailed, there would be no political theory of anarchism. In the absence of established states there would be no need to formulate this critique of the state. The aspiration to achieve a form of social existence without domination of any kind is attractive, but the inevitability of political power sets a limit to what might be practicable. The anarchist idea keeps alive the question of whether political power can be exercised without domination.

Anarchists view the state as evil, since the coercive power involved in the politics of the state both infringes people's liberties, and corrupts those who hold it. Both those who are subject to power and those who exercise it are harmed by it. Anarchists therefore reject the ordinary political processes for achieving power. Their ideology remains utopian.

All of these ideologies have a view on the nature of the state and its relation to society, the sources and nature of political power, and the purposes for which it might be used. Related ideas such as authority, legitimacy, obligation, are also treated differently by the various ideologies. Since ideologies differ from one another, depending on whether they give priority to the individual or to the social, they will consequently have different understandings of human freedom, rights, law, justice, welfare and the common good. The self-presentation by any ideology can appear plausible, and even convincing, but the study of political philosophy should help to put any claim in perspective, and to show how the plausibility of its ideas depends on the basic assumptions of the ideology.

 ## QUESTIONS FOR DISCUSSION

Which ideologies are most realistic? Is success in achieving political power the best indicator of an ideology's worth? Which ideologies are most in danger of utopianism? Which are most likely to idealise some existing regime? Do we have any choice about the ideology we espouse, or is our ideology a product of the way in which we are brought up and taught to think? Which ideologies are incompatible and which are capable of being combined with one another?

● FREEDOM

Negative and positive freedom

Negative and positive freedoms are sometimes distinguished as 'freedom from' and 'freedom to'. A cyclist spins the oiled wheel on its axle to check that there is no friction or interference with the movement. The spinning wheel is a good image to clarify the negative and positive senses of freedom.

Negative freedom is the absence of interference or restraint whereby the wheel is free to revolve on its axle. The application of the brakes is the corresponding image for the restraints that limit freedom. This sense of freedom is also called liberty, typically by Thomas Hobbes, who defined it as the absence of restraint.

The bicycle wheel also illustrates the notion of positive freedom. The wheel is designed to revolve on its axle and so carry the rider forward. Mostly we take the design for granted and check to see that it works as it should. But that it should work in a certain way, and that it has the capacity for certain functions – these are the elements of positive freedom. A bicycle is not designed to float, or to fly; its functions, specified by its design, determine what it is free to do.

When applied to human freedoms this distinction is matched with corresponding notions of law. Thomas Hobbes gave priority to the notion of negative freedom, called it liberty, and defined law as the form of constraint that would put a brake on a person's freedom of movement. Law from this perspective always has a negative connotation, since it always functions to limit anyone's sphere of action (e.g. you may not drive on the right hand side of the road in the UK). Law might be necessary, in order to allow people to live together in peace – without law, the unlimited freedoms of people would pose too great a mutual threat, Hobbes thought – but law seems to be a necessary evil.

Law is seen as a source of freedom by those who emphasise the positive notion. If freedom is a capacity to function in an appropriate way, then our freedoms are specified in a social and political context by the functions we may exercise, and these are expressed and secured in law. This is law in a much wider sense than purely criminal law, with its prohibitions (forbidding murder, theft, perjury, rape, etc.). It includes constitutional law and social norms.

Some ideologies regard law, not as a source of positive freedoms, but as an instrument to be used to effect human fulfilment. They argue that if the capacity of humans to rule themselves and to direct their own lives free from the distorting influences of irrational elements like emotion, passion, or addiction is a key to their fulfilment, then the law could and should be used to direct people to this form of fulfilment. This is the ideal of autonomy as human fulfilment. While there is an important point in the understanding of freedom as mastery of oneself, there is a real danger in the ideologies that consider it an appropriate function of state law to make people autonomous in this sense. Isaiah Berlin and other critics have attacked this understanding of positive freedom when it is linked to state interventionist power.

Constitutive and regulative rules

There is a useful distinction between **constitutive and regulative rules**. Some rules are constitutive, e.g. they make football the game that it is; they define the purposes, such as scoring goals, and delimit the conditions within which the purposes are to be pursued, as, for instance, in the description of the field of play. Other rules are regulative, defining infringements and assigning appropriate penalties. The constitutive rules of the game correspond to the positive view of law and freedom: they create the possibility of functioning. The regulative rules correspond to the negative view of law and freedom: they restrict what any player in the game is free to do. Other social activities can provide examples, such as the financial markets. There are constitutive rules that establish the conventions, defining what money, credit, interest, lending rates, derivatives, etc. are. These rules make a market in money possible. Regulatory provisions specify what would count as an infringement, such as fraud, or defaulting on a loan.

> **Important distinction concerning freedom and law**
>
> Constitutive rules make the social activity possible, e.g. dealing in money. Law in this sense enables positive freedom.
>
> Regulative rules restrict what one may do, e.g. fraud in the market. Law in this sense restricts negative freedom.

While some ideologies give exclusive attention to either positive or negative freedom, the example from football shows that both are important. Sometimes the emphasis must be on negative freedom. There are some social contexts in which it is appropriate to consider the law simply as a restriction of people's freedoms, especially where there are reasons to be suspicious of the state's use of its power. Debates about anti-terrorism legislation provide recent examples. Sometimes the emphasis must be on positive freedom. There are occasions when it is possible to consider the functioning of the law as a whole and to evaluate the adequacy of legal arrangements in facilitating the achievement of common purposes. An example is the debate in the Constitutional Convention in the Philippines, prior to the adoption of the new constitution in 1987, as to whether the country would be best served by a presidential or a parliamentary system. South Africa, after the end of apartheid, provides another example.

Familiar freedoms such as the freedom of speech, or the freedom of religion, as well as being freedoms from interference (negative), can also be understood as positive freedoms, assuring people that they can pursue their fundamental desires to find out the truth about matters and to pursue their ideals.

Given a history in which many states have abused their power, it is understandable that liberal ideologies sometimes emphasise the importance of protecting liberty against state power. At the other pole there are conservative movements that are inclined to see an excess of liberty as a risk, and who stress instead the importance of a supportive social context in which people can realise their potential. The challenge is to find ways of empowering people without taking from them their responsibility to identify and pursue their own good.

Rousseau recognised the danger that the exercise of freedom might lead a person to a loss of real freedom through being subject to another. An analogy is the process whereby a person becomes addicted to nicotine, alcohol or drugs. The first decision to use the substance might be freely made but the choices lead to a loss of freedom in compulsive consumption. An example from democratic politics might be a voter's decision to accept the temptation offered by a politician who attempts to buy her vote with promises such as reduced taxation or preferential treatment. Collusion with the temptation might be freely made but it may have the effect of giving power to a corrupt party which will continue to work with the same methods, resulting in a loss of political freedom for the citizens. Rousseau considered that citizens, once made aware of this danger of losing their freedom, would be prepared to accept **coercion** to prevent its occurrence; in his words, they would choose 'to be forced to be free'. The freedom Rousseau's citizens value is not the freedom to choose this or that, but the freedom to rule themselves.

Freedom involves the capacity to effect choices, choices that are put into effect, as distinct from a listing of preferences. Advocates of positive freedom warn against allowing images of consumer choice to dominate our understanding of this central human capacity. The choices whereby we shape our own lives and our characters are not like the choice of soap brands or beers in a supermarket. What is similar is the existence of options – choose this or that, take it or leave it. But what is distinctive of life-forming choices are:

- that they require commitment to be put into effect, and
- they inevitably change us in ways that consumer choices cannot.

Decisions such as whether to choose a particular career, take a particular job or marry a chosen partner require commitment, and they shape us and our lives. They become part of our personal history, as the opening up of pathways leading to further choices. If I choose to study a particular set of subjects at a particular university, then that opens the way to further choices that I will have to make, and inevitably excludes some other choices.

Similarly, our political context structures our lives by conditioning our positive freedoms. So it is conceivable that a political regime might protect negative freedoms, with minimal restrictions on people's freedom of action, while at the same time the options for action might be severely restricted. This might happen where economic liberalism ensures that state interference in the market is kept to a minimum, but commercial interests effectively determine for people what their options are for consumption or entertainment. People are free to choose, but only from the limited options that vested interests make available to them.

QUESTIONS FOR DISCUSSION

What are the constitutive rules for politics? What regulative rules operate? Is there a difference between these rules, and the constitutive and regulative rules for society? Is it sufficient to protect negative liberty in the confidence that success in doing so will automatically guarantee freedom in the positive sense?

Related examination questions

(Part a) Describe and illustrate *two* differences between negative freedom and positive freedom. *(18 marks) (2003)*

(Part b) Assess whether laws should attempt to uphold the moral standards of society. *(32 marks) (2003)*

Rights

In 1948, the Universal Declaration of Human Rights articulated minimum standards of achievement to be subscribed to by the international community of states. Given the well-attested violations of human rights in our world (e.g. as reported by organisations such as Amnesty International, Rights Watch, and others), along with the inflation of rights language such that every possible demand is now expressed as a right, what does it mean to have a right, and what rights do people have?

Philosophy draws our attention to the problems associated with the way in which we formulate these questions. We spontaneously use the language of possession when talking about rights – rights are things one has. This tendency even led Locke to use the word 'property' when speaking about the set of rights to life, liberty and estates, for the securing of which people were willing to make compacts with one another to form societies under government: 'the reason men enter society is the protection of their property' according to Locke. Resisting this tendency to think in terms of things owned, some philosophers regard rights as the capacities to function in social and political contexts.

A classification of rights originally made by Wesley Hohfeld (1879–1918) lists four types:

- I have a *liberty* to do something, if I am not prevented by some duty from doing it.

- I have a *claim-right* to something, if there is another person who has a duty to provide or protect that something for me.
- I have a *power*, if the law designates me as an officer with responsibility to perform some function.
- I have an *immunity*, if the law frees me from the obligation to submit to the legally assigned power of another.

Rights can be distinguished as liberties and claim-rights, but these are not necessarily separate. Legal systems that recognise liberties also create duties obliging some others, including the state, to respect liberties through non-interference or other forms of protection. Accordingly, the recognised liberties are protected through claim-rights.

The notion of right in each case is dependent on the existence of law. Law is the source of duty or obligation that might restrict a liberty in the first instance, or that might specify a duty allowing others a claim-right in the second instance. The simplest cases for understanding rights are the rights created by human-made law in the civil laws of states. Legal systems having the backing of the coercive power of a state provide remedies for violations of rights. Those whose rights are infringed have some means available to them to have their case heard. Many thinkers maintain that the talk of rights is only meaningful where they are actionable, i.e. where people have recourse to courts to have the wrong redressed.

As well as positive rights created by state law, we also speak of natural or human rights. These appeal to moral or natural law. This appeal is controversial, since, first, not all agree that there is such a thing as moral or natural law, and second, those willing to speak of a natural or moral law do not necessarily agree on its contents. Even where people can agree on the meaning of a human or natural right, there remains the difficulty that such rights are not actionable until codified in some form of positive law. This difficulty played a large role in the debates prior to the adoption of the Universal Declaration of Human Rights.

 ## QUESTIONS FOR DISCUSSION

Which natural rights do we have? What rights does the Universal Declaration assert on our behalf? Are they liberties or claim-rights? For instance, is the right to work a liberty, or is it a claim-right? If a claim-right, who has the duty to employ us?

Balancing individuals' interests and the common good

The rhetoric of moral or human or natural rights is often used to argue that certain liberties and claims ought to be recognised in positive law and made enforceable. Hence, campaigns on behalf of special interest groups frequently present their case in terms of rights. Is there a natural or moral right to assistance in committing suicide? Those who wish to have it legalised are campaigning for the creation of relevant legal rights. Similarly, campaigns to have the law changed so that the partnerships of homosexuals might be considered as legal marriages, or that homosexual couples might be entitled to adopt children, are aimed at the creation of legal rights. Not infrequently the argument will be made in terms of an assumed moral right.

When are the assertions of previously unrecognised moral rights warranted? When are society and the state obliged to respect the asserted right and to make the provisions required, including changes in the law? These questions cannot be definitively answered. Consider discussions about whether the NHS should have to provide infertility treatment for couples who are unable to have children, and similar controversial cases such as the provision of Viagra, the opportunity to select the sex of a child, or the provision of cosmetic surgery. Before the law can incorporate a standardised way of handling such cases there has to be a political discussion, since the conflict involved reveals that the interests of all concerned cannot all equally be satisfied.

In the process of trying to establish what legal rights ought to be instituted, the rights that people claim to have are sometimes invoked as if they were trumps overriding all other considerations. But other factors such as those of cost, proportion to other needs, fairness in the distribution of benefits and costs, impact on other aspects of the social fabric, consequences from allowing precedent, are also politically significant. These other concerns are often grouped together under a heading such as the common good, or as utilitarians will typically do it, under the umbrella notion of social utility or the general welfare.

The proposal to introduce identity cards is a relevant issue. Many of the arguments in favour of the proposal point to features of public utility: the need to manage efficiently the issue of refugees and asylum seekers, to control abuse of social welfare, to facilitate the detection of crime. On the other hand, the arguments against the proposal stress the greater power that would be put in the hands of the state, which would pose a threat to individual liberty.

Mill's harm principle

John Stuart Mill's (1806–73) principle that the prevention of harm to others is the only legitimate basis for the restriction of liberty is helpful in this discussion. The possibility that my activity might harm others, or indeed might harm society as a whole, would warrant interference by the state. That I might be in danger of harming myself would not be sufficient reason to restrict my liberty, according to Mill. This is a useful principle and provides a clear test for when constraints might be imposed on negative liberty. However, the principle itself does not resolve the dilemmas that arise from the difficulty of deciding what harms should be prevented and how much harm. My interests are harmed when the construction of an airport (extra runways at Heathrow, Stansted, Gatwick) reduces the value of my property, but do such harms constitute sufficient reason to prevent the construction? Am I harmed when my interests are damaged? My hearing may suffer from exposure to loud noise – deafness is certainly a harm – but is the drop in value of my property a harm in the same sense?

Related examination questions

(Part a) Describe and illustrate *two* circumstances in which the notion of social utility might conflict with the possession of a natural right. *(18 marks) (2002)*

(Part b) Assess explanations of the relationship between law and rights. *(32 marks) (2002)*

● LAW

Philosophers disagree on what are the essential elements of law. Their views can be located along a spectrum from minimalist to maximalist theories, and these can be contrasted in terms of six fundamental tenets.

Minimalist theories of law

A1   The central case of law is the law of a state.

A2   The law of a state is independent of morality and can be understood without reference to morality.

A3   Law is essentially a set of commands expressing the lawmaker's will.

A4   The state claims a monopoly on the use of force within a territory. With the backing of force, state law guarantees a minimum of peace and security for its citizens.

A5   The force of law depends on the lawgiver's ability to enforce the law.

A6 The basis of obligation is coercion, the assurance that one will be punished for failure to comply with the law's requirements.

At the other end of the spectrum are theories of law based on the following more inclusive principles.

Maximalist theories of law

B1 There are many types of law in human experience, and the law of a state should be understood in the context of other types, such as moral law, natural law, divine law, customary law, and international law.

B2 The law of a state is related to morality in a complex manner, so that it cannot be understood fully without reference to morality.

B3 Law is a product of reason, not will. Its function is to achieve order in a social complex, such that the good of the social whole is achieved.

B4 The state has the responsibility of guiding social interaction through legislation, such that the common good is achieved, or at least not damaged. A minimum of peace and security is a precondition for the achievement of the common good.

B5 The force of law is twofold, directive and coercive. The **directive force** of law is the power to persuade, flowing from the good sense of the arrangements that the law directs. The **coercive force** of law is linked to the threat of sanction.

B6 Insofar as the law's requirements are reasonable in relation to the common good of the relevant community, they lay obligations on the citizens who are capable of understanding the purpose of the law, and who acknowledge their own responsibility in relation to that purpose.

These two positions are different, but more like narrower and broader concentric circles than polar opposites. The maximalist position can incorporate the elements of the minimalist position, while rejecting the exclusions it entails. The theory that acknowledges law's relation to morality can accept the fact that large areas of the law function independently of morality, just as it can accept the fact that for many people the only force exercised by the law is that of coercion. Typically, the minimalist position is helpful in finding agreement, even among people who otherwise disagree with one another about questions of the good and the common good.

The emphasis on the directive force of law linked to its function in relation to the common good ties in with an understanding of positive freedom. Law in this sense facilitates the achievement by citizens of their good, which they pursue in collaboration with one another in society. On the other hand, the acknowledgement of the coercive force of the law and its function in guaranteeing a minimum of peace and security is consistent with an emphasis on negative freedom. The threat that law is understood to pose to the liberties of citizens is considered warranted to the extent that the law is a necessary means to secure the space in civil society in which liberty will have scope for action.

Unjust law

There is the possibility that the law might be unjust, and therefore that it could no longer succeed in persuading citizens to accept its directive force. Law might be unjust if it is defective in one of the following areas:

- If the law serves, not the **common good**, but the sectional good of the lawmaker, or the ruling class, it is unjust. If the law discriminates between people such that the liberties of some are subordinated to the liberties of others, then it is evidently unjust.
- If the law comes from some source other than from the legitimate lawmakers, then it cannot command the obedience of citizens. Lack of legitimacy can render a law unjust.
- If **equity** is violated, the law is unjust. This concerns not so much a structural imbalance in the law, as the unfair application of the law. The law is applied unfairly if cases similar to one another in relevant respects are not treated similarly.

The first reason is intelligible only to someone who holds a more than minimalist theory of law. Theorists who reject the connection between law and morality on the one hand, and law and the common good on the other, ridicule the discussion of unjust law. If the lawmaker has made her will known, and if she is powerful enough to enforce the law, then the law is binding, because its coercive force is effective.

This criticism misses the point. The maximalist position does not deny that the coercive force of the law remains effective even if the directive force evaporates owing to some significant defect. That a citizen may have no choice but to submit to tyrannical force is undeniable. The question, however, is whether the citizen should consider herself obligated by regulations that have the appearance of law but are seriously defective in some relevant respect.

Civil disobedience

There is no easy argument from the establishment of significant injustice in the law to a conclusion warranting civil disobedience, or even revolution. For the maximalist theorist, the resort to civil disobedience or other forms of protest or rejection would have to be argued for in terms of several considerations, only one of which is the injustice of the law. The probability of success, the likelihood of creating greater harm than the harm already caused, and the impact of one's actions on others are also relevant considerations.

In industrial relations unions can threaten to strike, to signal to the employers the seriousness of the issues requiring negotiation and settlement. Strikes are forms of agitation that inevitably involve harm, but fall short of violence in the strict sense. Although the right to strike is recognised as providing workers with some recourse against unfair conditions, strikes have become subject to legislation so as to ensure that unions do not abuse their power and effect greater harm on parties not directly involved in the dispute. Since government is one of the biggest employers in modern states, of police and security forces as well as civil and public servants, the right to strike is denied in some situations to those groups who provide essential services, and whose power if uncontrolled might pose a threat to public safety. Alternatives to strike action have to be sought to allow such groups as fire brigades and members of the military and the police to express grievances. The willingness of citizens in these functions to accept the restrictions on their civil liberties depends on the good functioning of the alternative systems for managing conflict.

 ## QUESTIONS FOR DISCUSSION

Is the right to strike a natural right? Is the state warranted in denying the right to strike to some of its employees? Does social utility or the common good justify overriding the rights of some workers in this context? What are the limits to civil disobedience? For instance, in issues such as environmental protection, or the protection of animals, are protestors justified in disrupting society in order to make their point? When are the limits of justification reached?

Conflict and protest

Liberal democratic regimes accept the inevitability of conflict, rooted in divergence of interests and of world-views. The conflict is carried out in peaceful ways, which resemble the use of argument rather than the use of force. The competition for power is carried on in elections and in parliamentary debates.

In addition to the standard forms of participation in political action, democratic systems also allow for forms of public protest including marches and demonstrations. The exercise of the recognised rights to public assembly and to protest can be abused, and can lead to rioting, violence and random destruction of property. Neo-Nazis or extreme nationalists have provoked racial violence. On occasion, football supporters can unwittingly give cover to organised groups intending to provoke rioting and violence between opposing fans. The mobilisation of large numbers to protest against elements of globalisation in the context of G-8 meetings has sometimes resulted in street fighting and destruction of property. The extent to which the style of policing has provoked the excess in all these cases is debated. The difficult line to draw is where the civil right to peaceful assembly, absolutely essential to protect democracy itself, is exercised in such a way that it leads to violence and destruction. Where the exercise of freedom of speech infringes on the rights of others to their reputation, to be protected from libel, to be free from incitement to hatred, it is evident that limits must be drawn. There is no blueprint available for such eventualities, but prudential judgement and discretion on the part of responsible people is required.

Punishment

The coercive force of the law depends on the threat of punishment. **Punishment** is the final stage in a process of response to crime. Those who break the law have to be caught, tried, and convicted, before they can be punished. It is important to remember this process as the context in which punishment is administered.

Punishment is something deliberately done by a disinterested person acting in a representative capacity, for instance, a prison officer implementing the sentence imposed by a court. The two elements of disinterest and representation distinguish punishment from revenge. The traffic warden who fines me for parking in the wrong place is not acting out of some personal animosity (or at least should not be doing so), but is implementing the traffic regulations on behalf of the local council. By contrast, revenge is the reaction of a victim or of someone personally involved with a victim of a crime, and so is motivated by strong emotion, directed against the supposed perpetrator.

In being punished, those convicted of breaking the law are usually deprived of some good, e.g. money, freedom of movement, the company of others, respect, self-respect, reputation, and in the extreme cases, physical well-being and ultimately life.

If punishment consists in the deliberate harming of the interests of another, if it involves deliberately taking good things away from people against their will, how can it be justified? If society harms people's interests in punishing them, is it not repeating the same kind of wrongdoing as was present in the crime?

Different answers are given to these questions. The justification of punishment depends on how the point of punishment is understood. We can imagine typical remarks which reflect the various theories of punishment:

Internal deterrence

'That will teach him! He needs to be taught a lesson.'

The lesson that the person punished is supposed to learn is that it does not pay to break the law, and so in the future when he is tempted to repeat the crime he will have reason not to do so. When punishment is spoken of as correction, it relies on a similar theory, rooted in the context of education and training in which children are corrected, so that they learn not to repeat their misbehaviour or their mistakes.

External deterrence

'I'm going to make an example of you.'

An exemplary sentence is imposed as a warning to others that crime does not pay. The convicted criminal is punished in order to deter others. It is a matter of debate whether punishment in fact deters. In such discussions it is important to remember that punishment follows on detection and apprehension. It is worth asking if the likelihood of detection is more of a **deterrent** than the severity of the punishment.

Social protection

'She ought to be locked up! Society needs to be protected from the likes of her. We're not safe while she's around!'

The point of punishment on this view is social defence, the protection of society and of victims of further possible crimes. This rationale for punishment is sometimes labelled incapacitation, removing from the convict the capacity to harm others, as for instance someone convicted of driving under the influence of alcohol might have to forfeit her driver's licence.

Reform, rehabilitation

'They need help. When you know their background, you can understand what they do.'

Crime is understood in this approach as anti-social behaviour, and punishment as a reaction by society is acceptable on this view only if it rehabilitates the criminal, reforming him so that he can return to society and play a normal, law-abiding role.

Retribution, restoration

'Criminals can't be allowed get away with it. Wrongs must be righted, the punishment must fit the crime.'

Punishment on this view is intended to restore something that had been disrupted by the crime. For instance, it might be thought that by breaking the law, the criminal has infringed someone's rights; this has disturbed the balance of fairness between the members of society. Punishment is an attempt to restore the order of just relations between people, including the victim, the perpetrator, and others who accept the restriction of their freedom and abide by the law. Penalties in sport reflect this rationale of punishment. Infringements of the rules are penalised by a referee (disinterested person acting in a representative capacity), who thereby removes from the offending team the unfair advantage gained by the foul, and compensates the opposing team for the disadvantage caused by the foul.

The first four theories are often grouped together since they all focus on the consequences of punishment: deterrence, defence or rehabilitation. They look to the future, in contrast to retribution and restoration theories, which are backward looking.

None of the first four theories can stand on its own as a justification of punishment, because none can answer the following critical questions:

- Why is it only the convicted criminal who may be punished?
- Why is it good for the convict to be punished?

Suppose, for example, we knew that by choosing someone at random and making an example of him by public flogging we could effectively put an end to illegal parking in our cities. Would we be justified in doing so? Reliance on the theory of external deterrence alone would seem to suggest that we would be justified.

Would we be justified in locking up those people whom we judge to be potential criminals, since this would be an effective way to protect society? Would we be justified in allowing reformatories and psychiatric hospitals to lock up the maladjusted in the hope of reforming them, using the best scientific techniques available? Exclusive reliance on the relevant theories would seem to justify these strategies, assuming that they would be effective.

Supporters of the deterrence, defence and rehabilitation theories add the 'retributive principle', meaning by it the specification that only convicted criminals may be punished, in order to deal with this difficulty. But this suggests that there is some element of **retribution** or **restoration** that is essential for understanding the point and therefore the justification of punishment.

Another weakness of the forward looking theories is their difficulty in making the punishment fit the crime. Should we keep prisoners locked up until they are reformed, no matter how minor the offence? Should we enlarge fines and prison sentences until the crime rate is negligible? Even if they could be effective, these suggestions go against our sense of fairness, and this indicates that consequences alone cannot justify the activity of punishment.

Restorative theories explain punishment as good for the convict, because she is thereby restored to a context of fairness as a member of society, and existence in society on fair terms is considered a good for anyone. Retributive theories also show how the punishment must be in proportion to the crime in order that fairness is achieved in the restored balance. So there is a basis for limiting punishment. Of course, society must have some sense of its own values and their priorities in order to be able to apply just punishment in these terms, as for instance with the question of the relative seriousness of crimes against the person and crimes against property.

Related examination questions

(Part a) Describe and illustrate *two* criticisms of the view that punishment should be used as a deterrent. *(18 marks) (2003)*

(Part b) Assess whether we have an obligation to obey an unjust law. *(32 marks) (2003)*

● AUTHORITY

Power

In basic physics, power is defined as the ability to do work. Work in turn is understood as the overcoming of inertia, the resistance offered by mass and weight. In social and political contexts, power is the ability to move people, i.e. the ability to get other people to do what one wants. There is a resistance to be overcome: it is the resistance offered by their will; they have their own projects and want to spend their time pursuing their own plans.

Power is exercised in two contrasting ways, **persuasion** and coercion. Persuasion provides arguments that people can accept as giving them reasons to do freely what they are asked to do. When persuaded, those who cooperate do so willingly, having their own reasons for doing what they are asked to do. At the other pole, cooperation is given reluctantly and unwillingly, and people are coerced against their will to do what they are told. Coercion is the effect of the threat or exercise of force.

Between these two poles of persuasion and coercion are many instances in which the factors are combined. Trades unions rely on an element of coercion when they threaten industrial action in order to bring the employers to the negotiating table. Not everything that seems to be persuasion is in fact such. Blackmail, browbeating, bullying, manipulation, can all appear to be forms of talking, but they are much more like coercion than persuasion to the extent that they deny people the genuine opportunity of freely choosing not to cooperate.

> **Important distinction: forms of power in evoking cooperation**
>
> **Persuasion:** people have their own reasons for cooperating.
>
> **Coercion:** threat of force elicits reluctant and resentful compliance.

As is evident from the existence of police forces, armies, courts and prisons, states rely on an element of coercion. A fundamental concern of political philosophy is the clarification of the grounds on which the state might elicit our willing cooperation. What reasons might be provided to convince us that the state's power over us is legitimate, that we are obligated to obey its laws and directives, and that we have good reason to bear costs so as to ensure its survival? These are the typical questions of political philosophy, which can be given different answers depending on the ideological standpoint adopted.

The constitution of a state specifies the allocation of power, its division and distribution, and how it is acquired and transferred. This definition does not presume that the constitution is written. There are many instances of social power that are not directly related to the political in the narrow sense of institutionalised state power. It is important to recognise this so as to locate state power within a broad social horizon. Examples are the capability of advertisers, journalists, educators, preachers, as well as peer-group and other social pressures to influence people to behave in certain ways.

 ## QUESTIONS FOR DISCUSSION

Do the other instances of power function without reliance on any element of coercion? Are they purely persuasive? How can we distinguish manipulation, for instance through subliminal suggestion, from coercion?

Authority

In his analysis of different constitutions Aristotle (384–322 BC) evaluated some constitutions as better than others. One criterion was whether rule is conducted in the interests of the rulers or for the common good. Applying this criterion we can ask if we would prefer to be governed by people who attempt to enlist our willing cooperation by persuasion, showing us how rule is in our interests also (the common good), or by people who rely exclusively on coercion by threatening the use of force? To be deprived of the opportunity of challenging those who govern us by asking for reasons why we should cooperate is to be deprived of a significant aspect of our humanity. To be treated as beings who have to be coerced into action is to be treated as less than human.

People usually cooperate without having to rehearse the whole set of reasons for their action. They rely on a short cut, and point to the law, or tradition, or precedent, or the directives of an official, to explain themselves. Reliance on such a short cut is the recognition of authority. Instead of considering all the reasons that might be given in answer to the question, 'Why should I do what the Prime Minister is proposing to me?', I might simply answer that I choose to comply precisely because it is the Prime Minister who is proposing the course of action. Or, in response to the question 'Why should I obey the law?' I reply: 'Because it is the law!' Strictly speaking, this is not a reason for action, but a replacement of reasons with authority. This must seem regrettable to any philosopher who considers that a person is truly free only when she conforms to rules that she gives herself. Jean-Jacques Rousseau and Immanuel Kant (1724–1804) both emphasised the freedom involved in obeying a law one gives oneself. But from another perspective, it is a valuable social institution which allows for action in response to problems.

If we consider the law in a society as the memory of solutions to problems of coordination, then it can be relied upon to provide guidance for the future. What worked before can work again, and because of the expectation that the same solutions will be applied, people can anticipate the fact and plan accordingly. A large part of barristers' work is the provision of advice on what their clients can expect would be the decisions of courts. Law is then authoritative, providing a short cut to a path of action for which the reasons need not be given in detail. This authoritative function of law is clear because it is explicit, but reliance on custom or on tradition is also a short-circuiting of the process of giving reasons.

There are several types of authority, and it is located in various places. In modern political systems that also exhibit the rule of law, the instances of authority and their sources are clearly identifiable. Constitutions allocate power in a society, and specify the means for its exercise, how it can be transferred and the conditions under which it might cease to be. In a state with a written constitution, the text itself is an authority. In a state with an unwritten constitution, practice and tradition are authorities. Similarly, the body charged with definitive interpretation of the text is an authority, for instance, the law lords, or a Supreme Court. In all of these cases, citizens will habitually rely on appeal to such authority to reach conclusions about the best or proper way to act, without having to rehearse the whole range of reasons. Among the types of authority are persons who are holders of office whose functions and powers are specified by texts or traditions. As well as individual officers, there are groups, such as Parliament, Congress, courts, councils and committees, whose functions and powers are also specified by texts or traditions. The texts and traditions are authorities also, but are in turn products of other groups and persons.

In the examples of authorities given above, anyone who recognises an authority and relies on it for guidance for action can reliably assume that others do so too. For certain authorities, the recognition involves an acknowledgement that the authority has a right to be obeyed. And as a person considers herself bound by the authoritative rule, so she expects that others will acknowledge their own obligation in respect of the authority. So, for instance, if I come upon the scene of a crash on a motorway, and find that there are police officers redirecting the traffic, then I spontaneously follow their direction, presuming that they know best, given their estimation of the nature of the obstacle, and presuming also that even if their solution is not ideal, it is best for all involved that some clear and consistent strategy be followed. Not only do I conform, without entering into long discussions about the nature of the problem and possible solutions, but I expect others to conform out of an acceptance of the authority of the police officers, i.e. their entitlement to be obeyed. In fact, those who slow down to form their own view of the crash scene make the problem worse and impede the work of rescue and recovery.

There are other instances of authority in our societies where it cannot be assumed that the authority is commonly recognised. An authority might be recognised within a specific section of the population. In these cases appeal to the authority will not be helpful in handling conflict that crosses community boundaries. One obvious example is that of the diversity of religions, where religious groups have their own sacred texts and recognise authoritative instances for interpreting the texts, and guiding the life of their communities. Another example is the appeal to science, expertise or professional knowledge. Science functions as an authority for people who themselves do not engage in the relevant discipline, and indeed scientists themselves must accept some things as authorities since no one reconstructs the whole history of scientific discovery (log tables, periodic table of the elements, etc.). People rely on guidance by professionals in certain areas of their lives. The professionals are authorities in that they provide short cuts to guided action for their clients, who are freed of the need to conduct the whole process of argumentation that might otherwise be necessary. These are examples of people who are authorities, or have personal authority rooted in their competence or knowledge, but are not necessarily in authority, holding some office with its defined powers and responsibilities.

Important distinction of persons as authorities

A person *in authority* is a holder of a position of leadership, who can give guidance, and adjudication in conflict situations.

An authority is a person who has some specialised competence or knowledge on which others can rely for guidance.

Legitimacy

Authority has both advantages and disadvantages. Authority is a convenient social institution which allows for relative speed and efficiency in responding to problems and in coordinating social action. Authority allows for the accumulated experience of a community to be a resource for handling problems. The disadvantages include the prevention of innovation. Because it short-circuits argument, authority is in danger of preventing communal learning by insisting on giving well-worn answers to new questions. When relying on authority we tend to interpret events in terms of precedent, with the resulting danger that nothing really new can occur.

The reliance on authority poses a threat to individual liberty, requiring individuals to suspend their own judgement in favour of the established procedures. It is in the face of this threat that the personal liberties such as the freedom of conscience, freedom of religion, the right to free speech and to peaceful assembly have been so strongly asserted. Given this ambiguous nature of authority as both useful and dangerous, the test of legitimacy is used to maintain a measure of control over authority.

The test of legitimacy is the challenge to an authority to answer the question why it should be accepted as a reliable source of guidance in a specific area of life. The challenge can be addressed to a text, a precedent, a tradition, an officer or a council. Max Weber's (1864–1920) distinctions of the sources of authority are helpful in mapping the process of legitimation of those in authority. He identifies three sources of authoritative rule:

- rational-legal, the form familiar to us from modern states that rely on the rule of law, and whose law is codified
- traditional, where authority is hereditary
- charismatic, where the qualities of character of a leader provide followers with sufficient grounds for accepting her as authoritative.

For the third type, the issue of legitimacy does not arise for those who accept the rule of the leader. The decision to follow the leadership of one whose claim to be obeyed is purely the force of her own personality is at the same time an acknowledgement by the followers of the entitlement of the leader to their obedience.

In the second type, entitlement to be accepted as the authoritative ruler is established by appeal to some traditional rule of succession, and the histories of royal families provide examples of how complex this might be in particular circumstances. When monarchs die without direct descendants, the issue of legitimate succession becomes urgent. Those prepared to obey the king or queen must be able to identify clearly who is in authority.

In the first type as sketched by Weber, the entitlement to be in authority is established according to rules that can be argued for in a rational way. In our modern states, the challenge to establish legitimacy for a state or regime is first answered in legal terms, by showing how the allocation of office and power had taken place according to the prescribed rules. But what legitimates the rules?

Liberal political philosophies in particular have attempted to sketch hypothetical valid arguments to provide legitimacy, but also to delineate the boundaries of legitimacy for state power. In most cases the arguments rely on some supposed starting point, such as the hypothetical covenants, compacts or original agreements to form society. All such arguments are weak to the extent that they rely on a supposed original agreement, because no such agreement ever took place. Society and state as we now have them did not originate in an agreement or original compact. Even the USA, which might appear to be an example of a society under government created where no previous society existed, could not have come into existence without the practice and experience of self-government in the colonies under the English monarchy.

Obligation

Accounts of obligation can be summarised in the following list:

- consent of the governed
- original covenant, contract or compact
- achievement of the general will
- care for the common good
- the provision of justice, including the protection of rights.

Coercion, compliance rooted in the threat of punishment, is absent from this list. Coercion can effect compliance, but it can hardly be the reason that people would be able to give for their having a duty to obey the law. The sense of being obligated is a sense of duty, coupled with a recognition that others are entitled to expect, and not merely predict, one's obedience.

Liberal theories of various hues locate the source of obligation in the consent of the governed. Their assumption is that free people are only bound by such obligations as they freely take on. However, anarchists and others point out that people do not have the opportunity to assent freely to such regulations as are the product of modern legislatures, such as tax laws, health and safety regulations, etc. Against this objection it is argued that either the original act of consent to the form of government as contained in the original covenant or compact implies consent to the consequences of the establishment of government, or the continued existence of people within the jurisdiction and their enjoyment of its advantages imply tacit consent.

Where political order is assumed to be rooted in covenants, or compacts, or contracts, entered into by people who thereby create society under law, the obligation to obey the law is derived from this original commitment. For instance, in Hobbes's account, the original agreement among people to create a sovereign who would ensure their mutual non-aggression entails a consent to whatever the sovereign should enact to ensure the conditions for their peaceful and prosperous coexistence. In fact, Hobbes excludes the possibility that subjects might have any grounds for criticising the acts of the legislator.

Locke explicitly limits the powers of government in terms of the rights of the compacting citizens: the only reason people would consent to relinquish some of their liberties would be for the sake of a greater security in the enjoyment of their properties, by which he means the set of rights to life, liberty and possessions.

Both Hobbes and Locke attempt to build into their theories such cases where the original consent had never been expressly given. Hobbes pointed to the case in which a conquered people agree to surrender to the conqueror, thereby consenting to accept the conqueror as the sovereign, in return for having their lives spared. Locke allows for the possibility of tacit consent, not expressly given, but legible in the acceptance of the benefits of existence under government. But these cases are difficult to analyse. Is it possible to speak of consent in any form where no alternative exists to the course of action that people are assumed to have consented to? Those who cannot emigrate owing to lack of resources or opportunity can hardly be said to have consented to the regime in which they continue to exist, even if they continue to enjoy whatever benefits the regime provides.

On the assumption that the purpose of the state is to protect and promote the common good, the legitimation of the state will depend on the state's success in achieving this purpose. If the common good is the good of all and of the whole, as distinct from the sectional good of particular groups or individuals, the application of this criterion will require some clarification of the good of all. For instance, if the protection of human rights is a common good of all citizens, then this standard of legitimation will assess the state's performance in preserving the rights of all. This links in with the discussion of the directive force of the law in an earlier section, where we had an example of an argument that rooted the obligation of the citizen to obey in the law's service of the common good.

A utilitarian version of this grounding of obligation would speak in terms of general welfare or utility, rather than the common good. If the purpose of the state, and of its law, is described in summary fashion as the securing of public well-being, or general welfare, on the assumption that there is some way of measuring them, then these purposes will specify the grounds for obligation. The state's failure to achieve its proper purpose undermines the obligation of citizens to comply.

Rousseau uses the curious language of the general will, and it is difficult to establish what exactly is meant. However, at a basic level we can interpret it to mean that a people forming society under government would want to have its well-being secured and protected by the state. The will of the people is the general will, intending the public welfare, or the common good, or the good of all, rather than the protection of the interests of some privileged subgroup. In these terms obligation is grounded in the relationship between the will of the individual citizen and the general will. The citizen assumes the obligation to put the good of all above her own private good.

Related examination questions

(Part a) Describe and illustrate *two* types of authority. *(18 marks) (2002)*

(Part b) Assess the view that the distinction between authority and power does not survive close examination. *(32 marks) (2002)*

● THE STATE

The state sets itself apart from all other organisations and institutions in the following ways:

- It claims for itself the control of all legitimate use of force within its territory, and so will act to disarm others or prevent them from using force.
- It claims jurisdiction over all people who happen to be within its territory, whether or not they are citizens of the state or have consented to its authority.
- It claims the entitlement to license and regulate the activities of all other institutions and organisations within its territory.
- It claims to represent the people, the country and its institutions in international relations.

The universality of the claims made, applying to all persons and all other organisations within the territory, along with the willingness to make these claims effective through coercion, characterise the state. These features apply, whatever structures of government or legislation are relied upon, whether the constitution is written or unwritten, whether a parliamentary or a presidential system, whether common law or civil law system, whether a federal system or a single state. However, the form they take in any state will depend on its particular history.

Government

The constitution of a state provides for the allocation of power, and specifies and limits the powers allocated. At any time the government is that group within the state which holds the assigned power of ruling. There is national government, and local government. Sometimes the term 'government' is used in a narrow sense to identify the holders of executive power: at national level, the Prime Minister and cabinet in a parliamentary system, or the President and cabinet in a presidential system. It can be used in a broader sense to include also the holders of legislative power, which is the majority in Parliament or in the Houses of Congress.

Political and non-political forms of rule

There are forms of human association that do not presuppose conflict. Examples are military and religious groups. In military bodies, the command structure and the culture of military discipline and obedience ensure unity and coordination of action, and, in some religious organisations, commitment to the same values ensures harmony. Such organisations require a form of rule or government, but one whose purpose is the guidance of the whole to the common end. There have been attempts in history to govern states on the model of such unity and harmony. Some ideologies presuppose harmony and the absence of conflict, such as the self-governance by the people as outlined in Rousseau's *The Social Contract*, in which even political parties are frowned upon because of their tendency to introduce disharmony and sectional interest. Marxist theory expects that all conflict will be ended once the class war has been brought to an end by the victory of the proletariat.

Some regimes are prepared to implement extreme measures in order to ensure unity and harmony, and they exhibit the reliance on force in extreme forms: genocide, ethnic cleansing, the denial of human rights, the imposition of repressive laws, the terrorisation of the population. Can states that rely on such forms of rule be called political in the proper sense? Is tyranny a form of political rule?

Political forms of state rule in the full sense are those

- that accept that conflict is the ever-present context in which government is to be exercised, and
- that commit themselves to handling conflict by negotiation, conciliation and persuasion.

This fuller sense of politics can be used as a standard for evaluating other forms of rule. So while it can be meaningful to use the term 'political' in a loose way to refer to all instances of conflict in states, different forms for the handling of conflict can be evaluated as better or worse, depending on the extent to which they rely on the exercise of force or on some form of persuasion.

The state's functions and services

What are the functions of the state, and what services do we expect it to provide? Linked to the state's monopoly of the use of force is the guarantee of internal and external security. Defence from outside aggression, as well as the maintenance of police and court and penal systems to deal with violence against persons and property, as well as against the state itself internally, belong to the minimum services expected of any state. Hobbes draws our attention to the fact that civil society in the broad sense – 'commodious living', industry, trade, agriculture, public building, the sciences, culture and the arts – is only possible where people can enjoy the minimum of security guaranteed by a powerful state strong enough to threaten punishment effectively.

Locke's specification of the relevant role of the state is designed to protect the citizen from an excessive use of the state's power. While the citizen's rights to life, liberty and estates are guaranteed over against others, they must also be assured against the state itself and its officers. More recent versions of Locke's position, such as that presented by Nozick (*Anarchy, State and Utopia*) take a more radical stance and, assuming anarchy as the default position, attempt to show that only a minimal state could be legitimate.

At the other end of a spectrum from this limited specification of the functions of the state are ideologies that attribute to the state a more comprehensive set of functions. The ancient Greeks, Plato and Aristotle, provide examples of the comprehensive perspective. They see the state as exercising a moral function in relation to its citizens and as providing an all-embracing form of life. Plato in *The Republic* could imagine an ideal city as one in which the rulers, by virtue of their superior knowledge, could select people for the functions for which they were naturally suited, and thereby ensure both that everyone would contribute to the common life according to their own specialised capacities and that everyone would achieve the kind and degree of virtue that was necessary for their own function. The overall effect would be the achievement of social harmony in a city that managed its diversity without conflict.

Aristotle also proposed a highly moral agenda for the Greek political community. He assumed his Athenian listeners would agree that the citizens of any city such as Athens would be concerned about the character of their fellow citizens. So they would design their institutions and their laws to train citizens in the virtues needed in order to live well.

The high moral ideal of politics as articulated by Plato and Aristotle did not survive into the modern period. Augustine (354–430), observing the collapse of the Roman empire, was very conscious of the ambiguous nature of state power. On the one hand, he recognised the necessity of some authority with control of coercive force so as to limit the destructive capacity of human envy, greed, lust for power and the desire to dominate others. On the other hand, he pointed out that the same forces that threatened harm and destruction and needed to be controlled were the very ones employed in exercising control. The same corrupted motivation of desiring to dominate others was as likely to be expressed in the pursuit and exercise of state power as in disruptive elements against which the peace and safety of society required protection. A result of Augustine's analysis was a rejection of a naively idealistic view of the moral task of ruling.

Machiavelli (1469–1527) dealt another blow to the high moral ideal of political rule. As part of his book of advice addressed to princes this experienced Florentine civil servant highlighted what was obvious to all political leaders, that the pursuit and the increase of power were the precondition for achieving all other goals of ruling. Furthermore, he maintained that a ruler could not succeed in the pursuit of power if he were too squeamish about the means to be employed. Any prince who allowed himself to be bound by a strict moral code requiring truth-telling, the keeping of promises, and respect for the lives and property of others, would not have the necessary scope for action required to defend and retain his power. And without power, no other goal could be ambitioned.

We can summarise the scepticism with which any claim to a high moral purpose in politics would now be met:

- Who claims to know the good for others, and how can they justify this claim? How can it be true that they know the good for others, when those others do not all accept the claim?
- We do not expect that anyone is so virtuous that he can be trusted with unlimited power over others. All those who pursue power must themselves be subject to control, and limits must be placed on the power they are allowed to exercise.
- The nature of state power is such that it must rely on coercion. Those who exercise this coercive power are also in danger of giving free rein to their tendency of wanting to dominate others.

Despite the accumulated wisdom expressed in this rejection of an idealistic politics, the modern period has seen the resurgence of naive optimism with regard to politics. This is evident in the attempt to establish reason in place of the traditional foundations of social order. It is also evident in the totalitarian experiments of the twentieth century. Rooted in secular ideologies, Communism and National Socialism represented for their followers new versions of a high moral ideal.

- The Enlightenment was associated with rationalism in politics, with the expectation that it would be possible to create social and political order based on reason, to which free and reasonable citizens could give their assent.
- Communism aimed at the elimination of all social conflict by the victory of the proletariat which would bring class warfare to an end. The abolition of the basis of class warfare by the state's control of all means of production would remove the cause of all conflict.
- National Socialism promised to fulfil the destiny of the German people, which required that the *Führer* and the party controlled all aspects of social, economic and political life.

State provision of social welfare

Our modern states not only function to protect rights and preserve liberty. They are also involved in the provision of a broad range of services, from education to health care to social welfare. While libertarians and economic liberals in particular will argue that the state's involvement in such services should be restricted as much as possible, there are other arguments that can be made in their favour. For instance, a **utilitarian** position could argue for the duty of the state to provide welfare services including education, health care and social security so as to ensure the general welfare of society. The point of providing the services could also be formulated in terms of preventing conflict by ensuring that the needs and the interests of all members of society are satisfied up to a minimum level. This could be seen as much as a contribution to preventing violence against persons and property as is the deterrent effect of the existence of a penal system.

Liberals point to the danger of the violation of the individual's rights, as might occur where there is forced transfer of resources through redistributive taxation. Some say that citizens are then forced to work to support others. However, liberal arguments can also be made to justify the state's involvement in providing some welfare services, beyond the minimum functions of security. So, for instance, every citizen of a liberal democratic regime can be presumed to have an interest in ensuring that fellow citizens are sufficiently literate and well informed to be able to participate responsibly in the political process. Further, coerced transfers can be accepted where there is no reasonable possibility that the necessary service might be provided on the open market. This applies to so-called public goods, such as defence, construction of a dam, maintenance of a power supply or a transport system, where investment in these things could not be economical on the open market. And the protection of public health – the prevention of epidemics, dangerous transmissible diseases and the avoidance of other threats such as those posed by radiation – can also be accepted on liberal premises, even though its implementation might require intrusion on personal liberties.

Ideologies that give a high value to equality as well as liberty are faced with a difficult trade-off problem. The more the state through its services attempts to diminish the inequalities of access to resources or the inequalities of opportunity, the more it is in danger of restricting the liberties of some through taxation and redistribution. Those who wish to uphold both values will not be able to avoid this trade-off, and there is no clear guideline as to how the dilemma might be resolved.

REFERENCES

Aristotle (1992) *The Politics*, trans. T. A. Sinclair, Harmondsworth: Penguin.
Berlin, I. (1969) 'Two concepts of liberty', in *Four Essays on Liberty*, Oxford: Oxford University Press.
Hobbes, T. (1968) [1651] *Leviathan*, ed. C. B. MacPherson, Harmondsworth: Penguin.
Locke, J. (1988) [1690] *Two Treatises of Government*, ed. P. Laslett, Cambridge: Cambridge University Press.
Machiavelli, N. (1961) *The Prince*, ed. G. Bull, Harmondsworth: Penguin.
Marx, K. (1975) *Early Writings*, ed. L. Colletti, Harmondsworth: Penguin.
Mill, J. S. (1962) [1859] *On Liberty*, in M. Warnock (ed.) *Utilitarianism and Other Writings*, Glasgow: Collins.
Nozick, R. (1974) *Anarchy, State and Utopia*, Oxford: Blackwell.
Plato (1955) *The Republic*, ed. H. P. D. Lee, Harmondsworth: Penguin.
Rawls, J. (1971) *A Theory of Justice*, Oxford: Oxford University Press.
Rousseau, J.-J. (1973) [1762] *The Social Contract* and *Discourses*, ed. G. D. H. Cole, London: J. M. Dent.
Weber, M. (1946) *From Max Weber*, ed. H. H. Gerth and C. Wright Mills, Oxford: Oxford University Press.

RECOMMENDED READING

- Kenneth Minogue has written the little book *Politics*, in Oxford University Press's 'Very Short Introduction' series (1995). It has the advantage of being readable, and very short.

- Not so short is Andrew Heywood's *Political Ideologies: An Introduction*, 3rd edition (Basingstoke: Palgrave Macmillan, 2003). Heywood is an A Level Chief Examiner in Government and Politics, and he has written similar introductory textbooks such as *Politics* (1997), *Political Theory* (1999) (both published by Macmillan), and *Key Concepts in Politics* (Basingstoke: Palgrave, 2000).

- Jonathan Wolff is Professor of Philosophy at University College London. He teaches political philosophy and has produced a very readable introductory book intended for undergraduate students, but A Level students should find it readable also: *An Introduction to Political Philosophy* (Oxford: Oxford University Press, 1996).

- A more thematic approach, but also readable, is D. D. Raphael's *Problems of Political Philosophy,* 2nd edition (Basingstoke: Palgrave, 1990).

- Another thematic approach can be found in Adam Swift's *Political Philosophy: A Beginners' Guide for Students and Politicians* (Oxford: Polity, 2001). Swift concentrates on the themes of social justice, liberty, equality and community, and manages to condense many wide-ranging debates in clear and succinct discussions.

- On the questions of law, Simon Lee's *Law and Morals: Warnock, Gillick and Beyond* (Oxford: Oxford University Press, 1986) is a short and readable survey of the relevant debates.

GLOSSARY

alienation – Literally, making other, as in the transfer of property something is handed over to another. In political philosophy self-alienation means giving oneself into the power of another, so that people and societies, when alienated, are deprived of their proper independence and the control of their own lives.

anarchism – Anarchists deny the need for a state, and view any exercise of political power as an infringement of human freedom. They aspire to social existence in freedom and equality, without domination of any kind.

authority – An authority is a person, institution or text that people accept as privileged in providing guidance for their beliefs or their actions. Authority is personal when rooted in the competence of the person (e.g. a scientist). It is official when rooted in the office or function held and exercised by the person (e.g. a judge).

civic republicanism – An ideology that aspires to eliminate all forms of domination, so that citizens achieve their freedom by participating in self-government on a basis of equality.

coercion – Coercion is the effect of the threat or exercise of force. Cooperation is given reluctantly when people are coerced against their will to do what they are told.

common good – The good for the sake of which people cooperate in society. It is the good of the political community as a whole, which includes the welfare of individual members, but is not reducible to an aggregate of their particular goods.

communism – A version of socialism that sees the communal ownership of the social means of production, distribution and exchange – land, capital in the form of factories and machinery, financial institutions such as banks – as the key to solving problems of inequality and injustice.

communitarianism – Communitarians want the shared values and practices of a society to be supported and implemented through the application of political power. They consider community values rather than individual autonomy to be the guiding principle in politics.

conflict – Conflict occurs when the goals pursued by individuals or groups are incompatible or mutually frustrating.

conservatism – Conservatives oppose radical change and want to preserve established society as incorporating important values and achievements.

democracy – Democracy is government by the people, which may be either direct, when citizens participate directly in ruling, or representative, when citizens delegate power to elected representatives in a congress or parliament.

descriptive – In this mode philosophy contents itself with saying what is the case.

deterrence – The attempt to prevent a certain activity by adding socially imposed undesirable effects to its consequences.

epistemology – The branch of philosophy that examines questions about knowledge and how it can be acquired.

equity – Fairness in the law and in its application.

force, directive and coercive – The law relies on two forces for achieving the intended reasonable arrangement of a social complex: the directive force arises from the reasonableness of the arrangements proposed, and the coercive force arises from the sanctions that are threatened.

idealisation – The glorification of a particular society in history as the fulfilment of all human hopes for a life worth living, the best that can be achieved.

ideology – In a descriptive sense an ideology is a body of thought held by a group of people, which they rely on to guide their action. In a normative sense ideology is evaluated negatively, as a body of ideas, which, although false, gives the illusion of truth.

individualism – A doctrine that maintains that human society is to be understood as an artefact, deliberately constructed for the purpose of satisfying the needs or interests of individuals, conceived of as existing apart from, prior to, or independent of society.

law – Law is an instrument for the reasonable arrangement of a social complex so that the complex as a whole and the elements that make it up achieve the purpose for which they cooperate. The law is made and promulgated by those in the social complex who have the responsibility to do so.

legitimacy – Authority is legitimate when it can provide a satisfactory answer to the challenge to explain why it should be accepted as a reliable source of guidance in a specific area of life.

liberalism – Liberal political ideologies give priority to individual freedom. They are convinced that a rational account of the sources and nature of political authority can be given, through an analysis of the freedom, rights, or interests of the individual.

libertarianism – This is an exaggerated form of liberalism which, instead of giving priority to freedom, makes it the absolute value overriding all others. The individual as self-owner is to be allowed an unrestricted scope for action, unhindered by government.

nationalism – Nationalism assumes that humankind is essentially divided into nations, and each nation has a right of self-determination. Criteria for identifying a nation are: a common language, genetic relatedness, shared history and culture, occupation of a distinct territory, and the willingness to identify oneself as a member of the nation.

negative and positive freedom – Familiar freedoms such as the freedom of speech, as well as being freedoms from interference (negative), are freedoms of people to pursue their interests in finding out the truth about matters and to pursue their ideals (positive).

normative – In this mode philosophy evaluates, speaking about what is good and bad, and what ought, and ought not, to be the case. When we speak normatively, we appeal to standards that allow us to evaluate things, persons, institutions, actions and performances.

obligation – The sense of being obligated is a sense of having a duty, for instance, to obey the law, coupled with a recognition that others are entitled to expect, and not merely predict, one's obedience.

ontology – The branch of philosophy dealing with being, the composition of reality.

persuasion – Persuasion provides reasons that people can accept as giving them grounds to do freely what they are asked to do. When persuaded, those who cooperate do so willingly, having their own reasons for doing what they are asked to do.

philosophical anthropology – The branch of philosophy dealing with the broad range of questions about the nature of the human, and of the human person. Philosophy of mind deals with a subset of these topics.

politics – Politics is a form of rule in states based on a commitment to handle inevitable conflict by persuasion and conciliation rather than by the use of force and coercion. Not all forms of rule can be called political in this full sense.

power – In social and political contexts, power is the ability to get other people to do what one wants. It is exercised either by coercion or by persuasion or by some combination of the two.

prescriptive – Saying what is or is not to be done.

proletariat – Marx's word for the class of workers, those who have nothing to sell except their labour power.

punishment – In being punished, those convicted of breaking the law are usually deprived of some good. Unlike revenge, punishment is administered by a disinterested person acting in a representative capacity, for instance, a prison officer implementing the sentence imposed by a court.

republicanism – This ideology considers that sovereignty lies with the people, rather than with monarchy, and that government should be by the people, whether in direct or representative democracy.

restoration – A theory of punishment that sees it as restoring the just order of relationships that had been disturbed by the crime.

retribution – A way of explaining punishment by analogy with market exchanges. In punishment someone convicted of breaking the law is made to pay back to society whatever benefit had been gained in the crime.

rights: liberties and claim-rights – Rights are moral claims that people make on one another. They claim a liberty when they invoke a duty not to be interfered with, and when they invoke a duty to be provided with some thing or service, they assert a claim-right.

rules, constitutive and regulative – Constitutive rules make some social activity possible, e.g. financial markets. Regulative rules restrict what is permissible within the constituted activity, e.g. fraud.

socialism – Socialist ideologies give priority to communal interest and advocate the social control of economic activity so as to ensure achievement of common goals, chief among which is the satisfaction of basic needs of all the citizens.

state – The state is an organisation distinct from all others in claiming for itself the control of all legitimate use of force within its territory, and in claiming the entitlement to regulate the activities of all other organisations within its territory. Its primary purpose is to safeguard the rights of people and to ensure the conditions that will allow them to pursue a good life for themselves. To this end it has the means for making, applying and enforcing law, as well as the means for ensuring internal and external security and defence.

theocracy – Theocracies are regimes of government that claim divinely given principles, laws or policies as their basis of legitimacy.

utilitarianism – The view that the best political system, regime or policy is the one that leads to the best overall consequences. In early versions the consequences were calculated in terms of pleasure and pain, hence, reference to 'the greatest happiness of the greatest number'.

utopianism – The glorification of an ideal but unrealisable social order in which all problems are solved and harmony, peace and justice prevail.

6

philosophy of science

UNIT 4   Nicholas Wilson

KEY CONCEPTS ◗

- ◗ induction
- ◗ deduction
- ◗ the hypothetico-deductive method
- ◗ reductionism
- ◗ falsificationism
- ◗ scientific revolution

- ◗ paradigm shift
- ◗ scientific law
- ◗ constant conjunction
- ◗ theory-ladenness
- ◗ research programme

● INTRODUCTION

Science is involved in most of our everyday activities. Its benefits are all around us: new medicines, televisions, computers, aeroplanes, the latest gadgets, new materials, and so on. All of this is the result of the practices and progress of the scientific community. The philosophy of science is the study of those scientific practices. Broadly speaking, it is the study of what science is, how it develops, and what we know from it. In this chapter, five main areas in the philosophy of science are critically discussed:

- scientific method (what scientists do and how they think)
- the nature of scientific development (how science changes over time)
- scientific knowledge and the aims of science (what we know in science and what science should be like)
- the objectivity of science (whether science is always objectively justified)
- natural and social science (the differences between natural sciences such as physics and biology and social sciences such as history and sociology).

● SCIENTIFIC METHOD

Practising scientists investigate the empirical world in particular, systematic ways. These ways are closely tied in with certain scientific modes of thinking and reasoning about the world. In this section, those practices and forms of reasoning are described and critically examined.

The role of observation, experiment and measurement in science

Following the ideas of Francis Bacon (1561–1626) and John Stuart Mill (1806–73), practising scientists are commonly thought to operate in the following way. First, scientists carry out a careful observation of the empirical world and come across a phenomenon requiring an explanation. Then they make a guess or 'hypothesis' to explain what they have observed. Together with other assumptions, this hypothesis will have certain consequences which scientists can use to make predictions of future phenomena. Then, by taking measurements of and conducting experiments on what they have seen and on their predictions (and by making further observations), their hypothesis is either verified ('confirmed') or falsified. If it is falsified, the hypothesis is rejected and another hypothesis is put forward to explain the phenomenon. If it is verified, the hypothesis acquires the status of a theory which, when general enough and adequately supported by other experiments, can become scientific law (e.g. Newton's law of gravitation). When a number of closely related scientific laws are discovered, a scientific field (or sphere of scientific knowledge, investigation or specialisation) is formed. (This account is vastly oversimplified and is philosophically objectionable in several ways.)

Let us look at an example of this behaviour in practice. It has long been observed that certain kinds of materials burn. Roughly, before the eighteenth century, scientists tried to explain this phenomenon by hypothesising that materials that burn possess a combustible substance called 'phlogiston'. They hypothesised that this substance, phlogiston, is released during burning, characteristically causing the material to turn black. To test this hypothesis, scientists predicted that a material would decrease in weight after burning (owing to the loss of phlogiston). Further experimentation and measurement proved this prediction incorrect. Typically, materials show an *increase* in weight after burning. So the 'phlogiston theory' was falsified.

Later, towards the end of the eighteenth century, a French scientist called Antoine Lavoisier (1743–94) formulated the alternative hypothesis that burning is the addition of a gaseous substance, oxygen, to a body. On this basis, he predicted that a material would typically weigh more after burning than before. Since this prediction turned out to be true, to that extent Lavoisier's theory was confirmed. After further extensive tests and experiments, this hypothesis turned out to have quite a bit of evidence in favour of it and it developed into an accepted truth (or law). The 'oxygen theory' of combustion is now an established part of our scientific knowledge.

Induction

Inductive reasoning

Scientists who follow the practice described above for investigating nature often use **inductive reasoning**. Inductive reasoning is one of two kinds of reasoning also used in everyday thought. The other is **deductive reasoning** (see p. 239 for more on deductive reasoning). There are various forms of inductive reasoning, but here we shall focus on simple enumerative induction, which starts with the premise that one kind of phenomenon has always been observed to follow another and ends with the conclusion that the former phenomenon will *always* follow the latter.

Here are three examples of inductive reasoning:

1 Premise: I have observed the sun rise every day for years.
   Conclusion: The sun will rise tomorrow.

2 Premise: All sodium observed so far glows orange when heated.
   Conclusion: All sodium glows orange when heated.

3 Premise: All the swans I have seen so far are white.
   Conclusion: All swans are white.

The general form of the inductive argument in each case can be represented as follows:

Premise: n number of *A*s have been observed so far to be *B*s (for some number n).
Conclusion: All *A*s are *B*s.

There are two important characteristics of induction. First, inductive arguments are not infallible. In example (3), for instance, the premise may be true but the conclusion is false. In Australia, (most) swans are black. So (even good) inductive arguments with true premises do not have to have true conclusions. Second, two ways in which inductive arguments can be good arguments is by being **inductively forceful** and/or **inductively sound**. An inductive argument is inductively forceful if, given no other information relevant to the truth or falsity of the conclusion, it is more reasonable to expect the conclusion to be true than false. For example, if every person you know of so far who has taken arsenic has died shortly afterwards, then, with no further information about the circumstances of their death(s), it is more reasonable to believe that arsenic is fatal to humans than not. (Inductive forcefulness depends on a number of features of inductive arguments, including how big the sample of As is, how representative the sample is of the total population of As, and so on.) An inductive argument is inductively sound if it is inductively forceful and if its premises are true.

The main points about induction

- In enumerative induction, the premise of the inductive argument is a generalisation about a sample of a certain population. The conclusion of the inductive argument can either be a generalisation from the sample about the total population (e.g. all emeralds are green) or an assertion about a particular future event (e.g. the next emerald I see will be green).
- Inductive reasoning is fallible. A (good) inductive argument can have true premises and a false conclusion.
- An inductive argument is inductively forceful to the extent that, only given the information in the premises, the conclusion is more likely to be true than false. An inductive argument is inductively sound if it is inductively forceful and if its premises are true.

The Problem of Induction

One of the most important points about induction mentioned above is that even good inductive arguments are not always infallible. Inductive arguments do not have premises the truth of which guarantees the truth of the conclusion. Aware of this, David Hume (1711–76) (1978: Book I, part III, and 1975: sections IV and

v) raised an important question: If inductive arguments are not deductively valid, what reason is there for thinking that inductive arguments will work in the future? For example, even if all the sodium in the past has glowed orange when it has been heated, who is to say it will not glow green on some future occasion? The **Problem of Induction** is how to justify inductive arguments, that is, how to explain why inductive arguments like (1)–(3) are *good* arguments. Since a great deal of our everyday reasoning and the reasoning of scientists involves induction, the Problem of Induction threatens our knowledge in many areas. It is therefore important to know whether in using induction we are behaving rationally (or not).

 ## QUESTIONS FOR DISCUSSION

What is induction? What is the Problem of Induction?

Attempted solutions

An inductive principle

One possible response to the Problem of Induction is to supplement inductive arguments with the following principle:

Principle: For some number n, if n number of *A*s have so far been observed to be *B*s, then all *A*s are *B*s.

(Hans Reichenbach (1891–1953) advocates the use of such a principle in *Experience and Prediction*.) If such a principle were employable in inductive arguments as a premise, then inductive arguments would no longer be fallible since if both premises were true, the conclusion would automatically and necessarily follow from them. If it is true that whenever a million pieces of a substance glow a certain colour when heated then all of them do, and if it is true that a million pieces of sodium have glowed green when heated in the past, then it deductively follows that all sodium glows green when heated.

But even ignoring how big the number n has to be to render the principle probable, there is a distinct problem using it here to justify induction. The problem is what justification there is for believing the principle. It is not just obviously true. It is a generalisation and requires some kind of support. And since it is a generalisation, it will require induction as a support. But since induction is precisely what we are trying to justify, the principle assumes exactly that which we want to rationalise. In other words, this solution is **circular**.

Inductive arguments for induction

Another way of responding to the Problem of Induction is to rely on experience. This response says that inductive arguments are rational forms of reasoning because they have worked in the past. And since they have worked in the past, it is reasonable to expect that they will work in the future. After all, in the past we thought induction would work in the future and we were right!

But this response assumes that induction is justified because it has worked in the past (and so will work in the future). But induction just *is* arguing from the past to the future. So this response says that arguing from the past to the future will work in the future because it has worked in the past. So the problem with this response is that it assumes that induction has been justified in the past in order to justify induction working in the future. Like the last response, then, this one is also circular.

Using probability

A third, non-circular, solution is to use probability. This solution maintains that inductive arguments are best seen as only asserting *probable* conclusions and not certain ones. Thus an argument such as (1) should really be phrased as (4):

4 Premise: I have observed the sun rise every day for years.
   Conclusion: The sun will *probably* rise tomorrow.

It can then be said that whilst an argument like (1) is not necessarily justified since we can never really know inductive conclusions for certain, an argument like (4) is justified because it only asserts a probable conclusion.

But there are difficulties with such a solution. A chief problem is that it merely changes the terminology of the original problem and therefore does not provide a genuine solution to it. The original problem was how to provide a justification for an argument such as (1). This solution just replaces the conclusion of (1) with the conclusion of (4). Now, it may be easier to provide a justification for (1) than (4). (What would that look like anyway?) But that does not mean that we no longer need a justification for (1). For we still use arguments with certain conclusions like (1) all the time. So all this solution seems to offer is another problem (which is how to provide a justification for (4)).

Rational by definition

Peter Strawson, in his *Introduction to Logical Theory* (ch. 9), offers a fourth kind of reply to the Problem of Induction. According to Strawson, the terms 'rational' and 'reasonable' derive their meanings from paradigmatic (clear-cut) uses of them. That is to say, Strawson thought that those terms acquired the meanings they do because of the ways they are used in clear-cut cases of rationality/ irrationality and reasonableness/unreasonableness. (In the same way, you might have originally learnt the meaning of the word 'red' by seeing clear examples of its application and by hearing people refer to those examples as 'red'. This is called a 'paradigm case argument'.)

Strawson's crucial claim is that two paradigmatic cases in which the terms 'rational' and 'reasonable' are clearly correctly applied (and from which they derive their meanings) are deduction and induction. So, if any kind of reasoning is to be called 'rational' or 'reasonable', deduction and induction are (since we use them all the time). Therefore, Strawson argues, the Problem of Induction, in one sense, does not have a substantial answer. If the premises of an inductive argument are known to be true, he says, it is not necessary to justify the claim that it is reasonable to expect the conclusion to be true because it is part of the very concept of reasonableness that such an argument is justified.

A difficulty for Strawson's account is the presupposition that how ordinary people are inclined to use terms is always right. True, we may come to understand the meanings of certain terms such as 'red' from paradigm cases in which they are correctly or incorrectly applied, e.g. post-boxes, London buses, etc. But even assuming that this is the case with the terms 'rational' and 'reasonable', it is still possible for someone to understand a term and *misapply* it, that is, apply it incorrectly. For example, if I am colour blind, I might mistake a red light for a green one. So Strawson needs to say more about his linguistic theory of these terms if his argument is to be made plausible.

 QUESTION FOR DISCUSSION

Which attempt to justify induction is most successful in your view?

> **Related examination question**
>
> (Part a) Describe and illustrate the Problem of Induction. *(18 marks) (2003)*

Deduction

Deductive reasoning

Deductive reasoning is the other principal kind of reasoning commonly studied by philosophers. Unlike inductive reasoning, deductive reasoning is reasoning which, if valid, uses premises whose truth guarantees the truth of the conclusion. In a deductively valid argument, it would be self-contradictory to accept the truth of premises and at the same time deny the conclusion.

Here are three examples of deductive reasoning:

5 Premise: All philosophers are eccentric.
    Premise: Socrates was a philosopher.
    Conclusion: Socrates was eccentric.

6 Premise: If this liquid is water, it is drinkable.
    Premise: This liquid is drinkable.
    Conclusion: It is water.

7 Premise: Not all cats have tails.
    Premise: Some tail-less cats are black.
    Conclusion: Not all black cats have tails.

There are two ways in which deductive arguments can be good arguments: (a) if they are **deductively valid** and/or (b) if they are **deductively sound**. An argument is deductively valid if it has premises whose truth guarantees the truth of the conclusion. In a deductively valid argument, it is impossible for the premises to be true and the conclusion false. Only (5) and (7) in the above examples are deductively valid because, in each case, if the premises are true, the conclusion has to be true. For (5), if it is true that all philosophers are eccentric and that Socrates was a philosopher, then it *has* to be true that Socrates was eccentric. For (7), if it is true that not all cats have tails, i.e. that some cats don't have tails, and if it is true that some of those tail-less cats are black, then there must be some black, tail-less cats. But (6) is not deductively valid. If it is true that if this liquid is water, it is drinkable and if it is true that this liquid is drinkable, it does *not* follow that it is water. For there are many drinkable liquids other than water.

A deductive argument is deductively sound if it is deductively valid and if its premises are true. In the above examples, (7) definitely has true premises. (Arguably, (5) does not, because there might be at least one philosopher who is not eccentric!) Since (7) is also deductively valid, (7) is also deductively sound. It is true that not all cats have tails. And it is true that some tail-less cats are black. And it does follow that not all black cats have tails.

 # QUESTIONS FOR DISCUSSION

What is the difference between induction and deduction? What makes for a good deductive argument?

The hypothetico-deductive method of confirmation

Deductive arguments like (5), (6) and (7) are also used in the **hypothetico-deductive method** of confirmation (advocated by Karl Popper). According to this theory, scientific confirmation does not involve induction. (As a result, a big advantage of this view is that Hume's worries about induction do not arise.) Instead, on this view, science proceeds by first tentatively putting forward a hypothesis (or conjecture) about an event and then confirming that hypothesis (or not) when it, along with various other statements, deductively entails a datum. (Also see Popper's related falsificationist theory on p. 244.) This method is called 'the hypothetico-deductive method' of confirmation because it begins with a hypothesis and deduces empirically testable consequences from it. For example, the hypothesis that the pressure was low this morning may be confirmed when it rains in the afternoon since that hypothesis, together with other statements (e.g. the humidity was high), deductively entails its raining. This view of science contrasts with induction. In induction, we first observe certain instances of something and then form a generalisation. In the hypothetico-deductive method, we first propose a hypothesis and then, after deducing its consequences, test it empirically by observation.

But the hypothetico-deductive method (H-D theory) of confirmation has its problems. The theory supplies no account of the reasoning that leads scientists to their theories in the first place. The only reasoning the H-D theorist considers is that which takes place after the construction of the theory. But surely scientists don't first arrive at their theories by means of a non-rational stab-in-the-dark only then to consider what observational support there might be for them. Scientists are rationally led to their theories by the observational data. Laws are got by inference from what is observed. The H-D theory, by itself, cannot account for this. According to the H-D theory, the fundamental inference is always from higher level laws to observation statements, not the other way round.

> Deductive arguments can be deductively valid and/or deductively sound. An argument is deductively valid if it is impossible for premises to be true and the conclusion false. An argument is deductively sound if it is impossible for the premises to be true and the conclusion false and if the premises are true.

┌─ ─ ─ ─ ─ ─ ─ ─ ─ ─ ─ ─ ─ ─ ─ ─ ─ ─ ─ ┐

❙ Related examination question

❙ (Part a) Describe and illustrate the hypothetico-deductive method in science. *(18 marks) (2002)*

└ ─ ─ ─ ─ ─ ─ ─ ─ ─ ─ ─ ─ ─ ─ ─ ─ ─ ─ ─ ┘

● THE NATURE OF SCIENTIFIC DEVELOPMENT

Few scientists would deny that science has made progress over the last, say, 500 years. We know more things about electricity, the human body, radio waves, viruses, and so on. What is more controversial is *how* science has developed and progressed over time. Here we examine three different theories about the nature of scientific development: **reductionism**, **falsificationism** and **relativism**.

Reductionism

One common, intuitive view shared by many scientists and people alike is reductionism. According to reductionists, the progress and development of science, thought of as a body of scientific knowledge, is linear, cumulative and convergent. Reductionists usually support this claim as follows:

1 Scientific progress is linear because scientists are chiefly engaged in formulating, testing and verifying (or falsifying) *new* and *original* scientific theories, hypotheses, and so on. These theories and hypotheses are 'new' because they are not, at that time, part of the established body of scientific knowledge. For example, the theory mentioned on p.235 that burning is the addition of a gaseous substance, oxygen, to a body was substantially different from the phlogiston theory that had preceded it.

2 Science is cumulative because, as new and original scientific theories are developed and introduced into the scientific arena, they are incorporated into the established body of scientific knowledge and add to it. In this way, scientific knowledge accumulates. Thus the oxygen-addition theory of burning added to what scientists knew about combustion in the fifteenth century and increased the body of scientific knowledge about it at that time.

3 Lastly, according to reductionism, science is convergent because, as science progresses, it is thought to approach and tend towards an ideal, single, correct body of scientific knowledge. According to reductionists, theories, laws and even different branches of science are in principle reducible to one another. Eventually, it is hoped, they will be reducible to one, single, unifying 'science of everything'. Two commonly used examples of this convergent view of scientific progress are: (a) the absorption of Galileo's law of falling bodies into

the more widely encompassing Newtonian mechanics and (b) the major shift made early last century from Newton's gravitational theory (and laws of motion) to Einstein's more 'General' Theory of Relativity. Einstein's theory is not only closer to the 'truth', but also covers more facts. (Because of (1), (2) and (3), reductionism may thus be said to compare science to an expanding collection of Chinese boxes.)

Few would deny that some of the ideas put forward by reductionists are correct. For example, few would deny that one aim of scientists is and has been to attain new or unknown information about the empirical world. Moreover, few would deny that, when new scientific information about the world is discovered, it becomes incorporated into what is already known. Indeed, most would affirm that we possess more scientific knowledge today than we ever did.

However, there are at least a couple of problems with reductionism. One problem, voiced by Paul Feyerabend, is that it is simply not true that Galilean physics was 'reduced' to physics of a Newtonian kind. For example, Feyerabend says, one basic law of Galilean physics was that the acceleration of a body falling towards the earth is constant over any finite vertical interval near the earth's surface. However, this law is not deducible from any law or set of laws in Newtonian physics. In Newtonian physics, since the acceleration towards each other of two bodies increases with decreasing distance, a body falling towards the earth would show an increased acceleration as it approaches the earth's surface. (Precise assessment of this objection requires a more detailed investigation into both Newtonian and Galilean frameworks and into the exact nature of the reduction proposed.)

A second, similar problem occurs with the reduction of Newtonian mechanics to Einstein's General Theory of Relativity. In this case, Feyerabend argues, the reason the former cannot be reduced to the latter is that there is a significant difference in the meaning of the concepts involved in either theory. For example, in Newtonian mechanics, the concept of *length* is a concept of a relation between objects that is independent of the motion of the observer and gravitational fields. By comparison, in Einsteinian theory, length is a relation whose value is dependent upon gravitational fields and the motion of the observer. So a proposed reductionist transition from Newtonian mechanics to Einsteinian theory would involve a transition in the meaning of the concept 'length' (and other spatio-temporal concepts). Another way to phrase this is to say that 'classical Newtonian length' and 'Einsteinian relativistic length' are **incommensurable** notions. (See p. 246 for a fuller explanation of incommensurability.) Feyerabend also argues that classical mechanics cannot be reduced to quantum mechanics and that classical thermodynamics cannot be reduced to statistical mechanics. (Reductionists might reply to this that different concepts of length could also be reduced. But this would need some substantial argumentation.)

Falsificationism

A different view of scientific progress is Karl Popper's falsificationist theory. According to Popper, the standard induction-based view (p. 235) of what scientists do is incorrect. On this standard view, what scientists are usually thought to be doing is observing the empirical world (heating a piece of copper), formulating hypotheses to explain it (oxygen has been added to the copper) and then making inductive generalisations about objects of that type (the burning of any object involves the addition of oxygen to it). Instead, according to Popper, what scientists do (or what they should do if they are good scientists) is begin by formulating various hypotheses (or 'conjectures') and then try to falsify them by making predictions, further observations and measurements. If the conjecture is falsified, it is refuted and scientists will seek some alternative. But if the conjecture turns out not to be shown to be incorrect by experience, then it remains a conjecture and an undefeated one. Persistently undefeated conjectures, on Popper's view, should generally be accepted. Science moves forward by incorporating more and more persistently undefeated conjectures.

According to this view of scientific progress, then, science consists of a series of conjectures and refutations. One hypothesis is put forward after another to explain an event and it is then either falsified and refuted, in which case another hypothesis is put forward, or not, in which case it stands for the time being. This raises the questions of what distinguishes science from non-science and why science should be thought to be better as an explanation or more valuable than other practices such as astrology or Greek mythology.

Popper's answer to this question – which he called the problem of demarcation – was that science is falsifiable but that astrology, superstition and the like are not. So, for example, the theory that combustion is the release of a substance called 'phlogiston' is a testable theory because it entails that a burnt substance will decrease in weight after burning. But the astrological theory that Capricorns will prosper in their personal relationships on Wednesdays is not (clearly) testable. For even if the marriage of one Capricorn to another ends on a Wednesday, the astrologer who has made the prediction can always say that the end of the relationship is for the best and that both parties will find greater happiness in the future. Doing this seems to make the astrological claim unfalsifiable.

Popper's account of scientific development can be criticised in at least three ways. First, Popper's view of how scientists work in practice only supplies us with a picture of how scientists come to acquire negative knowledge (knowledge of what is not the case). It does not give us a picture of positive scientific knowledge. For example, on Popper's account, scientists came to falsify the hypothesis that all swans are white through empirical investigation. Scientists then possessed the negative knowledge that it is not true that all swans are white. But Popper does not tell how we have acquired bits of positive knowledge – for example, the knowledge that all emeralds are green or that all bodies remain at rest or in uniform motion in a straight line unless acted upon by some force (Newton's first law). So Popper's theory needs to be supplemented somehow.

Second, whilst Popper's theory provides an adequate account of how scientific research starts out at the level of conjecture, it does not tell us much about the rest of the scientific process. Popper is right that as scientific research begins conjectures are put forward to explain some phenomenon and, as not all conjectures turn out true, they are sometimes falsified. (Einstein's General Theory of Relativity started out like this. It was initially met with widespread scepticism.) But Popper does not go further than this. For after some conjectures are refuted and superior alternatives are proposed, evidence will accumulate for some and not for others. Eventually, the best ones will acquire the status of established truths. (This evolution was also true for Einstein's General Theory.) Popper's account does not cover this stage of the scientific process in as much detail as it might.

A third criticism has been put forward by Thomas Kuhn (1922–). According to Kuhn, most theories are inadequate or incomplete in some way and so are vulnerable to counter-example and falsification. So, on Kuhn's view, most theories will eventually be falsified and hence should be rejected. But this is ridiculous, Kuhn maintains. What scientists should be doing when a hypothesis is rejected is not just finding another one but examining *why* it has been rejected. If it is known why it has been falsified, then it is possible to determine whether (or not) some close alternative should replace it, what kind of alternative or whether the research programme should be abandoned altogether. But in order to do this, Kuhn says, we need to know what kind of theory fits the facts better rather than just which theories have counter-examples. So what we really need is a combined verification–falsification procedure rather than Popper's sole falsification one.

❓ QUESTIONS FOR DISCUSSION

Summarise reductionism and falsificationism. Which view has the greater problems?

Relativism

The third theory of scientific progress and development we shall look at is Thomas Kuhn's. According to Kuhn, there are two distinct stages of scientific development. First, there is what scientists usually do. Kuhn calls this 'normal science'. Normal science consists of practising scientists operating within a standard, community-shared scientific framework (or **paradigm**) and treating anomalies and counter-examples to it as problems to be resolved from within the paradigm rather than as challenges to it. Typically, the scientific framework that is taken for granted is the only plausible one at the time. For example, in the nineteenth century, the accepted standard framework in physics within which scientists worked was Newtonian mechanics.

Then, when normal science reaches 'maturity', there is 'revolutionary science'. According to Kuhn, revolutionary science occurs when scientists have lost confidence in the accepted paradigm and begin to question it. For example, if scientists become aware of a substantial lack of 'fit' between the standard theory and certain data or if a second, rival theory arises that does not have many of the problems of the first, then another paradigm replaces the first and there is a **paradigm shift**. One example of this is the shift from Newtonian mechanics to Einsteinian theory in the early part of the last century.

On this view, then, science develops in stages. It begins with the conservative and ideological activity of scientists who accept theories dogmatically and work within them. It eventually leads to a scientific crisis or breakdown, which develops into a change of vision or paradigm. (Kuhn calls this a 'transfer of allegiance' or 'conversion experience'.)

One peculiar consequence of Kuhn's account is that scientific theories cannot be rationally and objectively compared to each other. In other words, they are incommensurable. This is because, according to Kuhn, a paradigm shift involves a change not only in scientific theory, assumptions, claims, etc. but also in the definitions of central terms in those theories, etc. For example, consider two theories of falling: Anaximenes' theory of falling, according to which the earth is a flattish disc suspended in empty space and objects fall in a line perpendicular to and through the disc; and Aristotle's theory of falling, according to which the earth is a sphere in a universe organised out of concentric shells and objects fall towards the centre of those shells. In Anaximenes' theory, the term 'fall' means something like 'go perpendicularly towards the disc' and in Aristotle's the term means something different, i.e. 'go towards the shell centre'. If an object was dropped and it 'fell' to the ground, both scientists would claim their theory had predicted that event. So it is hard to know how to compare and rank the two theories. (Feyerabend (1968) has also argued that the term 'warm' has a different meaning in kinetic theory (referring to molecular movement and energy) from that in everyday, non-scientific language.)

So, on Kuhn's account, successive theories cannot be compared with one another since it is not possible to compare two theories that do not share the same language or meanings. One potential problem with this consequence is that Kuhn seems committed to a relativism about scientific change and development. Relativism is the counterintuitive view that since it is impossible to compare any two successive scientific theories (or paradigms), it is also not possible to say that one theory is better than another or that either theory is really truer than the other. Kuhn says, of scientists, that 'granting that neither theory of a historical pair is true, they nonetheless seek a sense in which the latter is a better approximation to the truth. I believe that nothing of the sort can be found' (Kuhn 1970: 265).

Kuhn responds to the charge of relativism in a couple of ways. He denies that he believes that 'scientific development is, like biological evolution, unidirectional and irreversible. One scientific theory is not as good as another for doing what scientists normally do' (1970: 264). So there is some question about what Kuhn actually believes.

Second, Kuhn says, to hold that, say, field theory is closer to the truth than the old matter-and-force theory is to hold that the ultimate constituents of the universe are more like fields than they are matter or forces. But how could we possibly know this? We have no idea what the ultimate constituents of the universe are like. So we have no idea which theory is closer to the truth. (Moreover, according to Kuhn, there are unclarities in the expression 'more like the truth'. For example, there do not seem to be any clear criteria for applying it to one thing rather than another.)

The three main views about the development of science

- Reductionism (the intuitive view): The progress and development of science is linear, cumulative and convergent. Objections: Reductionism is not convincing in some cases, e.g. Galilean to Newtonian mechanics.
- Falsificationism (Popper): Science proceeds by conjecture, falsification, then alternative conjecture. Objections: No account of positive scientific knowledge; no examination of why conjectures fail (Kuhn).
- Relativism (Kuhn): Science moves from normal science to revolutionary science in paradigm shifts. Objections: Entails theory incommensurability and relativism.

▌Related examination questions

▌(Part b) Assess the view that progress in science is achieved through refuting scientific theories. *(32 marks) (2002)*

(Part a) Describe and illustrate *two* ways in which the objectivity of science might be challenged. (*18 marks) (2002)*

(Part a) Describe and illustrate *one* explanation of how scientific revolutions occur. *(18 marks) (2003)*

● SCIENTIFIC KNOWLEDGE AND THE AIMS OF SCIENCE

What do we know in science and what do we merely assume or believe to be true because it works? What is it for a scientific theory to work? What do we want a scientific theory to be like? In this section, three issues are looked at: (1) Do we *know* that scientific theories about things we have never seen ('unobservables') are true? Or are they just useful instruments for making predictions about observable phenomena? (2) What do scientific laws describe? Necessary connections in the world? Or just regularities between events that happen to occur at the same time? (3) What should and does science aim for? What do practising scientists ideally seek in formulating a scientific theory?

Realism and instrumentalism

Many scientific claims refer to entities that cannot be directly seen or observed by the naked eye. For example, radio waves, quarks and viruses. Moreover, such claims are often thought to constitute scientific knowledge. But if such entities cannot be directly seen, how is it that what we claim to know about them constitutes knowledge rather than mere guesswork or probability?

Here we examine two views about the status of scientific theories of unobservable entities: **realism** and **instrumentalism**.

According to realists, we can and do know certain facts about unobservable entities, even though we have never directly seen them. For example, according to realists, the kinetic theory of gases – the theory that gases consist of particles of negligible size moving at random and undergoing elastic collisions – is known by scientists to be true, even though no one has ever directly seen or perceived any one of these particles. Furthermore, realists think that *observable* facts provide more than adequate evidence for the existence of such entities and, therefore, that facts about such entities are in principle knowable. For instance, events such as a kettle whistling or a light coming on after a switch has been flicked provide evidence for the existence of gas molecules and electricity. The realist position, then, is that much of science correctly describes how the world really is (as opposed to how we perceive it) and that the terms used in scientific theories correctly pick out real objects in that world.

By contrast, according to instrumentalists, scientific theories are not necessarily true descriptions of the world but rather function as useful 'instruments' with which scientists can perform important calculations and manipulate the world. For example, an instrumentalist may think that the kinetic theory of gases, whilst not being a literal and true description of the world of gases, is still an extremely useful tool, allowing us to predict and explain many observable facts about gases: for example, variations in the temperature, pressure and volume of a gas under certain conditions. Instrumentalists may also think that science, whether giving a correct description of the world or not, certainly neither aims to provide nor does provide us with knowledge about unobservable entities. If instrumentalism is correct, then, it is not legitimate for us to believe a theory that tells us that chairs consist of atoms. But it should nevertheless be accepted since such a theory is explanatorily useful and predictively powerful.

There are three main arguments for realism: the argument from unification, the argument from prediction and the argument from explanation. The first argument – the argument from unification – maintains that scientists typically attempt to unify different types of scientific theory into one, single 'theory of everything'. For example, the replacement of Newton's laws by Einstein's General Theory of Relativity is sometimes said to be a clear example of when one theory became absorbed into another. Since this effort by scientists to unify everything would not work (and would not be working) unless scientific theories correctly described reality, it follows that science must consist of mainly accurate descriptions of the real world. (Moreover, the problem for the instrumentalist is that 'saving the phenomena' is not preserved under conjunction, i.e. if we have two contradicting theories that are both individually good at predicting phenomena, then we would not expect their conjunction to be good at predicting.)

The argument from prediction points out that scientists are often able to predict the occurrence of certain unexpected phenomena on the basis of their theories. For example, Einstein predicted, on the basis of his theory of relativity, that light would bend near the sun. This prediction was tested and verified in 1919 by an eclipse of the sun. The argument from prediction asks how such predictions would be possible if the theories on which they are based were not known to be true.

Finally, the argument from explanation asserts that if scientific theories about unobservables were not known to be true, then it would not be possible for scientists to explain observable phenomena using them. For example, scientists can explain an increase in the pressure of a heated gas in an enclosed container by talking about the behaviour of unobservable particles making up the gas. This explanation would not be available if a particular theory about unobservable objects, namely the kinetic theory of gases, were false. So realism must be true.

There are several ways instrumentalists can respond to each argument. First, the argument from unification. There are two possible replies here:

1 Instrumentalists may deny that what the unification in science aims at, or should aim at, is the unifying of different, true scientific theories into one true theory. Rather, they may claim, it aims at the unifying of different scientific instruments into one all-encompassing 'super-instrument' with which to solve any problem. In this way, instrumentalists can offer a different account of the unification of science from realists.

2 A second, more direct instrumentalist response is to say that unification is not necessary for science at all. Instead, what is happening is not the convergence of many different theories into one, single over-arching theory but their convergence into several, non-convergent theories, which deal with different scientific fields. Such instrumentalists might say that there will be one individual, unified theory for physics, one theory for biology, one theory for chemistry, and so on. So instrumentalists may also respond to the realist's argument by denying the assumption that science is progressing towards a single, unified theory.

Second, the argument from prediction. There are the same two lines of reply open to the instrumentalist in this case too: (1) The first response agrees with the realist that scientists successfully predict future phenomena. They then deny that this is because they rely on theories that are known to be true. Rather, it is because the *point* of a good scientific theory is that it can predict things. (2) Instrumentalists may also flatly deny that scientists successfully predict things. They may argue that since there have been just as many unsuccessful predictions of phenomena (if not more) as successful ones, the whole enterprise of prediction is merely a fluke. The reason why it *seems as if* science produces more correct statements about the future than not is because we notice the correct predictions more since those are the ones we are interested in. (This line of reply does not appear as plausible as the first one since scientific prediction does not seem to be just a chance matter.)

Third and last, the argument from explanation. Some instrumentalists claim here that explanation is not really an essential feature of scientific practice. Instead, they argue, the essential feature of scientific practice is to provide us with useful tools with which to manipulate the observable world. Other instrumentalists accept that explanation is an aim of science but deny that explanatory power is a (good) guide to truth.

The main independent positive argument for instrumentalism is that because past scientific theories eventually turned out to be false, our current theories (probably) will too. There are lots of examples to support this argument: those who thought the earth was flat, those who believed that atoms were indivisible, Newtonians and so on. The chief problem with such an argument is that theories are overturned at different rates in different scientific areas. So whilst in some areas – e.g. evolution and particle physics – one theory replaces another at a relatively rapid rate, in other areas this does not happen – for example, with the theory that water is H_2O. So, even if this argument were right, it would only possibly apply to some areas in science and not others.

 ## QUESTION FOR DISCUSSION

Critically discuss arguments for a realist view of scientific objectivity.

Scientific laws

Scientific laws play an integral role in scientific practice. This naturally raises the question: What are scientific laws? Consider the statements that when mercury is heated to 356.5°C, it boils and that when I watch England play football, they lose (when I have only seen England play twice and they have lost both times). Why is the first a scientific law but not the second?

In this section, we critically discuss two theories of scientific laws: theories that view laws as **necessary connections** and theories that see them as describing **constant conjunctions**.

Laws as necessary connections

One intuitively appealing theory of scientific laws is that scientific laws state necessary connections between events. There is a necessary connection between two events A and B if B would or could not occur unless A did. In other words, if events A and B are necessarily connected, if A does not occur, then neither would/could B. For example, take the scientific law that mercury boils at 356.5°C. This view maintains that these two events – the temperature being (at least) 356.5°C and mercury's boiling – are necessarily connected to one another in virtue of the fact that if the temperature were not at least 356.5°C, mercury would (or could) not boil. It is a law because of the necessary nature of the link between these two events. By contrast, the statement that whenever I watch England play football, they lose is not a scientific law because, although they lose every time I see them play, my seeing them play is not necessarily connected to their losing. They would (could) have lost even if I had not seen them play. And they might have won in spite of the fact that I was there.

Hume had a couple of objections to such a theory. First, he asked, What evidence is there for the existence of such necessary connections between particular kinds of events? After all, we never directly see or observe them. For example, Hume said, when one billiard ball hits another (which then goes off at a predictable angle), all we see are the two billiard balls and the impact. We do not see any necessary link between the two that tells us what will happen in situations of this kind.

Second, Hume argued, if scientific laws described necessary connections between particular kinds of events, then those necessary connections would be knowable *a priori* (without investigating the empirical world). But scientific laws are not knowable *a priori*. Scientists do have to examine the outside world in order to discover what laws there are. So, Hume argued, scientific laws cannot describe necessary connections.

Neither argument is wholly persuasive. As for Hume's first argument, the fact that we cannot directly perceive necessary connections occurring in nature is not sufficient to show either that they do not exist or that we cannot talk sensibly about them. Moreover, there is plenty of indirect evidence for their existence. For example, mercury has *never* boiled at under 356.5°C (at standard pressures). So Hume must strengthen his objection to show the non-existence of necessary connections.

Regarding Hume's second argument, Saul Kripke (1980: Lectures 1 and 2) has argued persuasively that not all necessities are knowable *a priori*. For example, many philosophers are convinced that it is necessary that the morning star is the evening star because there is no possible situation in which that planet is not identical with itself. And they are also convinced that such a statement is also not knowable *a priori*. If the same were true for scientific laws, then Hume would be wrong to argue that they should be *a priori* just because they are necessary.

Laws as constant conjunctions

In contrast with this, Hume denies that scientific laws describe necessary connections between events. Instead, according to Hume, scientific laws merely describe regularities between events (or 'constant conjunctions'). A cause and effect are constantly conjoined to one another if events like the cause are always followed by events like the effect. For example, the event of the temperature of mercury being raised to 356.5°C and the event of its boiling are constantly conjoined because events of the first type are always followed by events of the second (under normal pressure, etc.). So on this view, scientific laws merely serve to elucidate patterns and regularities in nature rather than anything stronger.

An immediate problem for such a view is that it fails to clearly distinguish between all laws and all accidents. For example, on this view, the statement that whenever I watch England play football, they lose describes a law since the two events – England playing football and me watching them – are (so far) constantly conjoined. But this statement is clearly no law. As a result, some Humeans have modified their theory so as to exclude accidents such as this from scientific laws.

Two such theories are:

1 Laws as generalisations. This theory states that the important thing about scientific laws is that they are general enough. They need to contain terms and descriptions that pick out a wide range of things. For example, the statements that when England play, they lose and that this glass of mercury will boil at 356.5°C are too particular to be laws because they involve terms that refer to particular things ('England', 'this glass'). But the statement that mercury boils at that temperature is general enough to count as a law. (The problem with this theory is that it is possible to formulate laws using expressions that are particular. For example, the statement that any substance like the stuff in this glass boils at 356.5°C contains particular expressions but looks like a law.)

2 Counterfactual conditional theory. According to this theory, a statement counts as a law if it supports **counterfactual conditionals**. A counterfactual conditional is a statement of the form 'If such-and-such had happened, then so-and-so would have occurred' where the such-and-such part of the statement did *not* actually happen. For example, the following sentence is a counterfactual conditional: 'If Hitler had never been born, there would have been one less evil person in the world.'

On this view, then, the statement that mercury boils at 356.5°C is a law because it supports the true counterfactual conditional 'If this glass of mercury had not been heated to 356.5°C, it would not have boiled.' By contrast, the statement that whenever I watch England play football, they lose (when I have only seen England play twice and they lost both times) is not a scientific law because the sentence 'If I had not watched England play, they would not have lost' is not true. (The problem with this theory is that so far there is no clear philosophical explanation of when counterfactuals are true or false. Is the statement that if Hitler had not been born, there would not have been a Second World War true or false? Without such an account, this response merely creates another problem rather than solving one.)

The aims of science

Practising scientists naturally aim for a number of theoretical and practical ideals when constructing scientific theories. Six of these ideals are: truth, simplicity, coherence, explanation, prediction and action.

1 The most obvious ideal is truth. Ultimately, for scientists and other researchers, the primary goal is to provide a *correct* description of what is really out there. The problem with this ideal is that it is not always possible to test scientific theories in a simple and clear manner that yields a 'true' or 'false' outcome. This is sometimes because they are just too general to be tested or because they talk about the behaviour of unobservables or simply because they are too complicated or vague. By contrast, a sentence such as 'It will rain today' is specific and clearly defined and has a simple verification procedure to determine its truth or falsity.

For this reason, philosophers of science often employ a distinct notion of **verisimilitude** or 'approximate truth'. Popper appeals to this notion in his falsificationist theory of scientific development (p. 244). According to Popper, the degree of verisimilitude of a theory is the extent to which the theory corresponds to the totality of real facts (rather than just some of them). So although a scientific theory might be strictly 'false' in the sense that it has been disconfirmed by a few contradictory instances, it may still be legitimately said to be a good approximation to the truth because it explains many other facts. For example, although there are counter-examples to Newton's theory of mechanics (e.g. the movement of very small objects does not fit in with his theory), it may still be legitimately said to be superior to Galileo's theory because it is able to explain a greater realm of facts. 'Newton's theory continues to explain more facts than did the others; to explain them with greater precision; and to unify the previously unconnected problems of celestial and terrestrial mechanics' (Popper 1972a: 236). (Remember that instrumentalists might disagree that truth and verisimilitude are aims of science.)

2 Another desirable feature of scientific theories is simplicity. The degree of simplicity of a theory involves several distinct concepts. For example, it at least involves the following: the number of entities postulated, the number of facts used and assumptions made, the nature of the laws involved, its symmetry, its 'elegance' (by which is meant roughly how neatly the theory works), the simplicity of deriving predictions from it, and so on. How simple a theory is will depend on the extent to which it possesses characteristics such as these. (For more on these notions, see Popper 1972b: 138.)

3 Scientists also prefer their theories to be coherent. The coherence of a theory is determined by the extent to which that theory fits in with other theories related to it. For example, the hypothesis that it rained today fits in better with the facts that there is a soaking umbrella in front of me and that the washing has been taken in than it does with the facts that my cat hates umbrellas and that $2 + 2 = 4$. If there are two theories that explain the same phenomena, have roughly the same predictive powers and are confirmed to approximately the same degrees by experimental data, then scientists would prefer the one with the greater coherence (with other known theories).

However, despite coherence playing a definite role in the determination of the value of a scientific theory, there are also certain difficulties in including it in such a judgement: (a) One difficulty is that the criterion of coherence might occasionally seem to be at odds with the criterion of truth. For it seems quite possible to conceive of a theory that is perfectly coherent but that does not correspond to reality at all because it is false. (b) Another difficulty is that the criterion itself is circular. For if the coherence of a theory is determined by the extent to which that theory fits in with other theories and if the coherence of those other theories is similarly judged by their coherence with the original theory, then it is not possible to use any theory as a definite starting point. (c) Also, the very notion of coherence is obscure. Does it merely involve logical consistency? Or do other theories have to imply or make probable the hypothesised theory? What else is involved?

4 A scientific theory should also be able to explain and predict certain kinds of phenomena. We want to know why things happen. So, at a fundamental level, a scientific explanation of some event should involve an account of *why* that event occurred (possibly including an account of why *other* events did not occur). For this reason, it is sometimes thought that there is a symmetry between scientific explanation and prediction. In scientific explanation, we have an account of why something had to happen. In scientific prediction, we are told why something *will* happen. On Hempel's hypothetico-deductive model, another way to put this is to say that, in scientific explanation, we already know what the explanandum is and are trying to give the explanans. In prediction, we already have the explanans (current and past facts) and want to know what will happen (the explanandum). Science is also judged by its practical application, i.e. what actions we can take on the basis of our explanations and predictions. That is to say, science is also valued according to how successful scientists are in the light of what they (and we) want to achieve. (The nature of scientific explanation has also been discussed in some detail on p. 264.)

Main revision points

- Two opposing views about unobservables are: (a) Realism: the view that we can and do know certain facts about unobservable entities, even though we have never directly seen them; and (b) Instrumentalism: the view that scientific theories are not necessarily true descriptions of the world but rather function as useful 'instruments' for making predictions. The three main arguments for realism are the arguments from unification, explanation and prediction. The main argument for instrumentalism is the argument from the falsity of past theories.
- Scientific laws can be seen either as stating constant conjunctions (Hume), in which case it might be added that they must be general enough or support counterfactual conditionals, or as stating necessary connections.
- Practising scientists aim for a number of theoretical and practical ideals when constructing scientific theories. Six of these ideals are: truth, simplicity, coherence, explanation, prediction and action.

 QUESTIONS FOR DISCUSSION

What are the problems with the two views about scientific laws? What are the principal aims of science?

Related examination question

(Part b) Assess the instrumentalist view of scientific theory. *(32 marks) (2002)*

● THE OBJECTIVITY OF SCIENCE

It is widely thought that science is objectively justified. We think that the picture of the world provided for us by scientists is, by and large, a correct description of a reality independent of our perceptions. At the same time, however, there are a number of reasons for thinking this view about the objectivity of science to be mistaken. Below, three problem areas for the objectivity of science are looked at: problems concerning observation and categorisation in science, problems concerning scientific methodology and, lastly, problems concerning what is researched.

Problems concerning observation and categorisation

The belief that scientific theories are justified objectively is closely associated with the belief that scientific theories are justified by observation. After all, it is observation that gives us direct and immediate access to the empirical world. But if, as some philosophers of science claim, observation is **theory-laden**, i.e. (partially) determined by what our theories are, then the objectivity of many scientific claims may be threatened.

One claim used to support the view that observation is theory-laden is the view that perceptual experience is influenced by theory. This view is often defended by pointing out a number of cases in which our perceptual beliefs change, sometimes dramatically, without any change in the perceptual stimulus. A famous example of this is the duck/rabbit drawing. This is a drawing that some people see as a duck, others see as a rabbit and that many people can see as both a duck and a rabbit.

Another well-known example is the Müller–Lyer illusion.

The illusion revolves around the fact that some people report that the second line looks longer than the first even though the lines are in fact of equal length. (Measure them!) Moreover, many individuals continue to perceive the lines as having different lengths even after they have been told that they are really the same. By contrast, some researchers claim that certain groups of people such as certain types of people in Africa do not suffer from such illusions. Examples such as these are supposed to demonstrate that 'theory' (context, background beliefs, previous experience, etc.) partly determines what we currently experience.

Two problems with the above argument are as follows: First, even if it is true that experience is sometimes permeated by theory, there are still limits to the flexibility with which the experience is interpreted. So, for example, whilst we can interpret the duck/rabbit drawing as either a duck or a rabbit, we cannot see it as the Eiffel Tower or a car. This suggests that even if there are situations in which a visual stimulus is ambiguous, it does not mean that it could be seen as anything at all.

Second, ambiguous stimuli are relatively rare and usually only occur when the stimulus is seen in poor or non-ideal conditions. For example, Galileo drew two moons rather than two rings round his representation of Saturn when he was looking at it through a telescope much less advanced than our current versions. (However, this point does not apply to the Müller–Lyer illustration and the duck/rabbit drawing. Moreover, in certain circumstances, a stimulus is interpretable in different ways even when the conditions are ideal. For example, a straight stick may still appear bent when half in water even if in perfect lighting, in front of an expert observer, and so on.)

Another distinct problem with objectivity concerns categorisation. In contrast with Popper (pp. 244–5), John Stuart Mill thought that scientists should begin their investigations of nature by using induction. Further, he believed, scientists should also begin by assuming that all their initial inductions with true premises are true.

However, Mill thought that it would quickly be realised that most of the initial simple inductions that are made – the low-level ones – would need substantial modification. For example, it was quickly realised that low-level inferences about the colour of all members of a species from a number of instances of it would turn out to be false. This was the case with the inductively supported statement that all swans are white.

Despite this, Mill observed, such generalisations do work in other kinds of cases. For example, generalisations about the broad anatomical structure of all members of a species from a sample of them are generally reliable. So inductions made in this case do provide strong support for their conclusions. Mill concluded that after a period of time we would eventually get a better idea of which inductive practices were justified and which were not. We rely on statements of a high level of generality such as the statement that there is generally invariance of broad anatomical features amongst members of a species to determine which lower-level generalisations will come out true.

 ## QUESTION FOR DISCUSSION

Is it true that scientific observation is dependent on theory and that scientific observation is not therefore neutral or objective?

Problems concerning methodology

A second problem for the objectivity of science involves the objectivity of the *methodology* of scientists. One problem with the objectivity of the methodology of scientists is that scientific practice appears to be at least partly guided by the scientific theory of the time. This claim is defended by Popper (1972b). According to Popper, scientific practice does not merely consist in random collections of observations and data. Rather, he argues, it is a principled, logical procedure in which scientists search for particular kinds of data, which they can then use to test their theories. For example, if I have a theory saying that all swans are white, then it would not be sensible to gather any and all data that came my way (e.g. what colour my office is, where I put my shoes). Instead, I should gather data appropriate to determining the truth or falsity of my theory. Indeed, if science were more haphazard than this and not guided in some way, it would prove extremely difficult and time-consuming to verify or falsify any scientific theory at all.

Popper's intention is that this argument has two elements to it. First, he says, it suggests that it is impossible to make observations and collect data without being guided by some theory or other. Second, he says, even if that were possible, it would be useless as a theory-testing procedure since merely looking at the world randomly would not help to confirm or disconfirm any particular hypothesis.

However, Popper might seem incorrect to say that the fact that our attention is typically directed to specific things by theories straightforwardly means that science is not objective. Popper is right that if scientists did behave in this manner, our search for knowledge and appropriate evidence would be much more focused and restricted than it should otherwise be. We could only test theories. We could not come across new and interesting phenomena that might lead to a change in conventional science/scientific theory or a 'paradigm shift' (see pp. 245–7 on Kuhn). But Popper is wrong that our observations are *always* directed like this.

The process leading up to the discovery of X-rays is a good example of this. In 1895, a German physicist named Wilhelm Röntgen switched on a vacuum tube designed to emit cathode rays. Röntgen intended to test whether or not cathode rays thus emitted were capable of penetrating lead, at what distance, whether they could penetrate other materials, and so on. To his surprise, when he turned the vacuum tube on, a screen coated with a particular substance glowed some distance away. Investigating the phenomenon, he found that not only did the screen glow even when various objects were positioned in between the tube and the screen (except thick lead) but also that when he put a thin piece of lead in between the two, he could see the dark outline of the bones in his hand.

260 philosophy for **AS** and **A2**

Further experiments led him to name the new phenomenon 'Agens' or 'X-rays'. But this discovery was not produced by any theory-directed data-gathering. Röntgen was not testing any particular theory to do with glowing screens. Rather, he just happened to be looking in that direction when he was observing the vacuum tube. (So some room should be made for the view that progress is made when conventional methodologies are ignored.)

However, Popper is correct to emphasise that we would not normally notice a variety of phenomena unless there existed some mechanism driving us to do so. But this does not mean that the mechanism should be identified with some theory or other. For example, we are far more aware of bright colours and loud noises than their dull and quiet correlates even though it is likely that no 'theory' in any proper sense of the term is driving us to do this. Rather, it is more plausible that we have been primed as humans to notice such things in order to aid our survival.

Two further facts can be added to this point: (1) Even when we are fully conscious of the fact that bright colours and loud noises in a particular setting are not important (to our survival) and so are not worth paying attention to, it is still very difficult to ignore them completely; (2) Even non-human animals notice such phenomena and surely they are not directed by anything that can be called a 'theory'.

Problems concerning research

A third area of difficulty concerns problems about the objectivity of scientific research. The work of the philosopher of science Imre Lakatos is important in this area. According to Lakatos (1978), assessment in science and in scientific research should not (and usually is not) the assessment of a particular theory or set of theories or even the internal assessment of rival theories. Rather, it is the assessment of the comparative merits of rival research programmes. Research programmes consist of a central claim, a variety of auxiliary assumptions related to that claim and a number of techniques and methods for solving problems. According to Lakatos, one research programme is worse than a rival one within a scientific field if it is 'degenerative' compared to that rival. A research programme is degenerative if its proponents merely add untestable theories and hypotheses to it in order to cope with further recalcitrant data and evidence. By contrast, a programme is progressive if it makes progress by being able to explain and predict new phenomena. Lakatos also says that even a degenerating, implausible research programme with many **ad hoc** hypotheses and unnecessarily supplementary assumptions may be accepted if it is the only programme available.

Here's an example. The research programme centred around Copernicus involved Copernicus's central claim that the planets revolve around the sun, and various auxiliary assumptions – for example, that circles are perfect and that the planets' orbits are circular. Later, Kepler rejected the assumption that planets travel in circular orbits and assumed in its place that they move in elliptical revolutions. This move was not degenerative since by replacing Copernicus's assumption, Kepler was able to make a number of novel predictions which Copernicus had not. By contrast, Ptolemy's research programme based on the idea that the earth is the centre of the universe became increasingly degenerative (as opposed to progressive) because all its advocates appeared to do was supplement the theory with further unfalsifiable claims to account for contradictory experience and observation.

A further, interesting, feature of Lakatos's theory is that he refuses to be explicit about the circumstances under which a research programme has been falsified and should be rejected. The reason for this, he says, is that it is possible for a research programme to disappear and come back into favour for external reasons. One example he uses is the Copernican theory of planets. This theory was originally hypothesised by a Greek philosopher called Aristarchus of Samos. Aristarchus abandoned his theory because of what he thought was strong countervailing evidence. Later, in the sixteeth century, when technology and knowledge had greatly advanced and, importantly, when the telescope had been invented, it was revived by Copernicus. So, according to Lakatos, scientific programmes also depend to a large extent on external factors such as the timing of inventions and the stage of technology.

Thus, Lakatos concludes, it is sometimes rational for scientists to pursue research programmes even if they are obviously degenerative. For it may be that such programmes become progressive in time and with a change in external circumstances. As long as most of the scientists in a community share the aim of discovering true scientific theories, there is nothing wrong with being engaged in such programmes. To this end, Lakatos believes that two other types of external factors should help in deterring degenerative programmes: funding bodies and journals. Funding bodies should discourage scientists from pursuing degenerative research programmes by allocating money to the progressive ones. Journals should refuse to publish papers from degenerative programmes and should adopt a style that tallies with progressive ones.

However, there are also problems with Lakatos's theory. Lakatos has been criticised by Feyerabend for being excessively vague about what is good and what is bad science. Lakatos does not lay down any specific criteria for when a research programme has gone bad. According to Feyerabend, Lakatos's theory implies that a scientist could be working on a hopeless research programme full of unnecessary, ad hoc hypotheses entailing predictions that are either falsified or are unfalsifiable and still could be acting rationally. Lakatos may argue, says Feyerabend, that the scientist is nevertheless rational because the programme might not have had enough time to develop (e.g. Aristarchus's theory). Moreover, his account may even entail that funding bodies would be justified in giving funding to such a programme and that journals might be rational in publishing papers produced from it.

Feyerabend is right that Lakatos has not laid down precise rules for determining whether or not a particular research programme is rational. And Lakatos's account is sometimes couched in vague remarks which do not seem to commit him to one idea of rationality rather than another. But it is wrong to think that this means that Lakatos's theory implies that anything is rational, however bad. For instance, Lakatos says that it would be irrational to allow a programme to degenerate over, say, a thousand years. Moreover, he also says that while funding bodies and journals may disagree in some cases and allow papers to be published from degenerating programmes, this will not always be the case and much of the time they will agree (on what is good and bad).

Three main problem areas for the objectivity of science

- Problems concerning observation and categorisation in science: the view that observation is theory-laden is supported by examples such as the duck/rabbit drawing and the Müller–Lyer illusion. But these examples do not necessarily mean that observation is *completely* theory-dictated or that it is always dictated by some 'theory' or other.
- Problems concerning scientific methodology: the view that scientific practice is partly guided by the scientific theory of the time has been defended by Popper, who argues that science would otherwise be a pointless matter of random information-gathering. However, the invention of X-rays shows that progress is sometimes made when conventional methodologies are ignored.
- Problems concerning what is researched: the view that research is impacted by both internal factors and external ones is supported by Lakatos's theory of research programmes. Lakatos says that research is determined both by how degenerative a programme is (compared to its rivals) and by factors such as technology, funding bodies and journals.

QUESTIONS FOR DISCUSSION

What are the major problems concerning the objectivity of science? Do those problems really imply that science is not objective?

● NATURAL AND SOCIAL SCIENCE

A distinction is often drawn between what are called 'natural sciences' such as physics, chemistry and biology and 'social sciences' such as history and sociology. In this section, we compare and contrast the two kinds of science and expose some of similarities and differences between both.

Similarities and differences

Methodology, theory-formation and confirmation

The work of Popper and Kuhn have had a major impact on views about the methodology and formation of theories in the social sciences. According to Popper, the theory of falsificationism applies equally to the natural sciences and the social ones. So, according to Popper, methodology in the social sciences principally involves putting forward a conjecture (e.g. the socio-political theory that institutions like universities chiefly arose because they helped to preserve class structures in society), and trying to falsify it. Those conjectures that stand the test should be accepted (at that time). Those that do not are falsified and should be rejected.

Popper also believed that falsificationism could serve as a criterion of whether (or not) a theory or field in the social sciences should properly be called 'scientific'. If a social scientific theory could not in principle be falsified, it did not count as science proper. If it could in principle be falsified, it did count as science. (For example, Popper thought that Marxist theory and Freudian theory would fail this criterion since he believed that both kinds of theory were unfalsifiable.)

Popper also thought that many theories in social science were incorrect. So, on Popper's view, social science as a whole faced a dilemma. Either the particular field or theory was falsifiable, in which case, Popper thought, it had already been falsified, or would be, and so should be rejected. Or the field could not be falsified, in which case it did not count as science.

It is true that many theories in the social sciences appear to have been refuted. Marxist theory appeared false because the proletariat revolution did not occur in the West. Freudian theory seemed to have problems because Freud's diagnoses did not have the desired effects on his patients. And it is true that, in many of these cases, such theories were made 'unfalsifiable' by merely adding to the theory so as to preserve its basic structure. The West did not experience a revolution because of the extreme exploitation of the Third World working classes. Freud's diagnoses did not have the desired effects because of other factors in the patients' lives.

But there are nevertheless problems with Popper's criterion. For example, sometimes it may be entirely reasonable when holding a theory in the face of countervailing evidence to reject an auxiliary assumption of it and replace that assumption with another. According to Popper, this would be making the theory unfalsifiable, but it may merely make it a better theory.

Explanation

Few philosophers would deny the applicability of the hypothetico-deductive model to the natural sciences (p. 241). What is more controversial is Hempel's application of it to the social sciences (see Hempel 1968). According to Hempel, the correct explanation of a social phenomenon, e.g. a historical, political or economic event, will involve appeal both to the particular facts preceding the event and to general principles that tie the events together. For example, the explanation of a particular capitalist crisis (e.g. Wall Street crashing) might presuppose both the particular facts leading up to that event and the general principle that capitalist crises in a society are due to the capitalist structure of that society.

A serious problem with Hempel's theory, though, is that it runs the risk of reducing every field into one. Thus, if Hempel is right, sociology might be reduced to psychology and psychology to biology and eventually biology to physics. But whilst this kind of reduction might have some degree of plausibility in the case of natural sciences, it is much less plausible for 'looser' subjects such as history and politics. For if they too were so reducible, then it might seem that supposedly 'free' human actions could be reduced to mere casual chains in physics. Counterintuitively, we would then lack free will.

Objectivity

A final difference between natural and social science lies in different views on their objectivity. As we discussed previously, in the case of natural science, there are problems about the objectivity of natural science concerning observation and categorisation (pp. 257–8), concerning scientific methodology (pp. 259–60) and concerning what is researched (pp. 260–2). In the case of social science, the problems are more closely connected to societal differences.

Social relativism

Social relativism is the view that what is right, correct, reasonable, acceptable, etc. in a society depends on the society in which the action, belief, etc. is placed. For example, it might be thought that how one should behave after eating is partly a matter of the particular manners of the society one is in. Burping after a meal might be rude in one society but complimentary or neutral in another.

But there are at least two problems with such a view. First, it is unclear what is meant by a 'society'. There are numerous ways of dividing up the population of, say, Britain into groups: by job types (teacher, banker, lawyer), by national differences (English, Welsh, Scots), by regional differences (Cornwall, Essex, Lancashire), by religious or cultural beliefs (Jews, Hindus, atheists), and so on. Which of these group divisions should be used to divide up societies? Or is a society merely a group of people in a particular geographical area? If so, then which area or areas?

This leads on to the second problem with social relativism. For if relativism is a true theory about societies that behave differently from one another, then surely it also applies to smaller groups that behave differently. And so surely it also applies to individual people who behave differently. Why should social relativism only apply to large groups that act differently? So social relativism implies that what is right, correct, reasonable, acceptable, etc. for one *person* depends on who that person is. The main problem with this is that, whilst cross-cultural relativism may be fashionable in some groups, not many will want to commit themselves to a full-blooded *individual* relativism.

 # QUESTIONS FOR DISCUSSION

What are the main differences between the natural and social sciences? Are they significant?

Related examination question

(Part b) Assess the extent to which scientific method is appropriate in the social sciences. *(32 marks) (2003)*

● **REFERENCES**

Ayer, A. J. (1971) *Language, Truth and Logic*, 2nd edn, Harmondsworth: Penguin.

Bacon, F. (1960) [1620] *Novum Organum* in Anderson, F. H. (ed.) *The New Organon and Related Writings*, New York: Liberal Arts Press.

Feyerabend, P. (1968) 'How to be a good empiricist', in Nidditch, P. H. (ed.) *The Philosophy of Science*, Oxford: Oxford University Press.

——(1988) *Against Method*, New York: Verso.

Hempel, C. G. (1968) 'Explanation in science and history', in Nidditch, P. H. (ed.) *The Philosophy of Science*, Oxford: Oxford University Press.

Hume, D. (1975) [1748] *An Enquiry Concerning Human Understanding*, 3rd edn, ed. L. A. Selby-Bigge and P. H. Nidditch, Oxford: Clarendon Press.

——(1978) [1739] *A Treatise of Human Nature*, 2nd edn, ed. L. A. Selby-Bigge and P. H. Nidditch, Oxford: Clarendon Press.

Kripke, S. (1980) *Naming and Necessity*, Oxford: Blackwell.

Kuhn, T. S. (1962) *The Structure of Scientific Revolutions*, Chicago: University of Chicago Press.

—— (1970) 'Reflections on my critics', in Lakatos, I. and Musgrave, A. (eds) *Criticism and the Growth of Knowledge*, Cambridge: Cambridge University Press.

Lakatos, I. (1978) *Philosophical Papers,* vol. 1: *The Methodology of Scientific Research Programmes*, Cambridge: Cambridge University Press.

Mill, J. S. (1843) *A System of Logic*, London: Longmans Green.

Popper, K. R. (1972a) *Conjectures and Refutations*, 4th edn, London: Routledge.

—— (1972b) *The Logic of Scientific Discovery*, rev. edn, London: Hutchinson.

Reichenbach, H. (1962) *Experience and Prediction*, Chicago: University of Chicago Press.

Russell, B. (1959) *The Problems of Philosophy*, Oxford: Oxford University Press.

Strawson, P. F. (1952) *Introduction to Logical Theory*, London: Methuen.

● **RECOMMENDED READING**

● Goodman, N. (1973) *Fact, Fiction and Forecast*, 3rd edn (New York: Bobbs-Merrill). The locus classicus of the famous 'grue paradox' and the starting point of many discussions of induction.

● Grayling, A. C. (1995) *Philosophy: A Guide to the Subject* (Oxford: Oxford University Press). An excellent general introduction to the philosophy of science.

● Hempel, C. G. (1965) *Aspects of Scientific Explanation* (New York: Collier-Macmillan). Statement of the problems of confirmation and the 'paradox of the ravens'.

● O'Hear, A. (1989) *An Introduction to the Philosophy of Science* (Oxford: Clarendon Press). Chatty, detailed historical introduction to the subject.

● Papineau, D. (1996) *The Philosophy of Science* (Oxford: Oxford University Press). Contains many valuable essays on topics on philosophy of science and methodology.

● Popper, K. R. (1979) *Objective Knowledge: An Evolutionary Approach* (Oxford: Oxford University Press). Statement of Popper's view that science proceeds not by induction but by hypotheses and falsifications.

● Ruben, D.-H. (ed.) (1993) *Explanation* (Oxford: Oxford University Press). A recent collection of essays on explanation, some hard but all useful.

● Russell, B. (1912) *Problems of Philosophy* (London: Williams and Norgate), ch. 6. A simple, interesting description of the Problem of Induction.

● Swinburne, R. (ed.) (1974) *The Justification of Induction* (Oxford: Oxford University Press). A diverse and interesting recent collection of essays on induction.

GLOSSARY

ad hoc (literally: for that purpose) – A belief, assumption, response to an objection, etc. is ad hoc if the only real reason it has been put forward is for theoretical purposes, e.g. to defend some theory from attack (rather than to explain some phenomenon).

a priori – A statement is knowable *a priori* if it can be known without investigating the empirical world, e.g. that 2 + 2 = 4.

circular – An argument is circular if it assumes or presupposes the conclusion in one of its premises.

constant conjunction – A cause and effect are constantly conjoined if events like the cause are always followed by events like the effect.

counterfactual conditional – A counterfactual conditional is a statement of the form 'If such-and-such had happened, then so-and-so would have occurred' where the such-and-such part of the statement did *not* actually happen. For example, the following sentence is a counterfactual conditional: 'If Hitler had never been born, then there would not have been a Second World War.'

deductive reasoning, deductively valid, deductively sound – Deductive reasoning is reasoning which, if valid, uses premises whose truth guarantees the truth of the conclusion. In a deductively valid argument, it is impossible for the premises to be true and the conclusion false. A deductive argument is deductively sound if it is deductively valid and if its premises are true.

falsificationism – Karl Popper's view that science proceeds not by induction but by proposed conjecture, falsification, then alternative conjecture.

hypothetico-deductive method – The hypothetico-deductive method of scientific explanation explains an event by citing the initial, prior conditions to the event and certain relevant laws.

incommensurable – Two theories are incommensurable if they cannot be rationally and objectively compared to each other.

inductive reasoning, **inductively forceful**, **inductively sound** – An argument that starts with the premise that one kind of phenomenon has always followed another and ends with the conclusion that the former phenomenon is *always* followed by the latter. An inductive argument is inductively forceful if, given no other information relevant to the truth or falsity of the conclusion, it is more reasonable to expect the conclusion to be true than false. An inductive argument is inductively sound if it is inductively forceful and if its premises are true.

instrumentalism – The view that scientific theories are not necessarily true descriptions of the world but rather function as useful 'instruments' with which scientists can perform important calculations and manipulate the world.

necessary connection – There is a necessary connection between two events *A* and *B* if *B* would or could not occur unless *A* did.

paradigm, paradigm shift – A paradigm is a standard, community-shared scientific framework within which scientists treat anomalies and counter-examples as problems to be resolved from within the framework rather than as challenges to it. A paradigm shift occurs when scientists become aware of a substantial lack of 'fit' between the standard theory and certain data or if a second, rival theory arises that does not have many of the problems of the first. It eventually leads to a scientific crisis or breakdown, which develops into a change of vision or paradigm.

Problem of Induction – The problem of how to justify inductive arguments, that is, how to explain why it is rational to believe, say, that all emeralds are green just because they have appeared green in the past. Since a great deal of our everyday reasoning is inductive, the Problem of Induction purports to threaten our knowledge in many areas.

realism – The view that we can and do know certain scientific facts about unobservable entities, even though we have never directly seen them.

reductionism – The view that the progress and development of science, thought of as a body of scientific knowledge, is linear (involves adding new theories to old), cumulative (adds up) and convergent (is heading towards a single, unified theory of everything).

relativism – Thomas Kuhn's view that science moves in paradigm shifts (see **paradigm, paradigm shift**).

social relativism – The view that what is right, correct, reasonable, acceptable, etc. in a society depends on the society in which the action, belief, etc. is placed.

theory-laden – A process is theory-laden if it is partially determined by what our theories are.

verisimilitude (literally, 'approximate truth') – The degree of verisimilitude of a theory is the extent to which the theory corresponds to the totality of real facts (rather than just some of them).

7

preparing for the examination

Michael Lacewing

● INTRODUCTION

To get good exam results, you need to have a good sense of what the exam will be like and what the examiners are looking for, and to revise in a way that will help you prepare to answer the questions well. This probably sounds obvious, but in fact, many students do not think about the exam itself, only about what might come up. There is a big difference. This chapter will provide you with some guidance on how to approach your exams in a way that will help get you the best results you can. It is divided into three sections: revision, understanding the question, and exam technique.

Throughout the chapter, I will highlight revision points and exam tips. You can find these collected together at the end of the chapter.

● REVISION: KNOWING WHAT THE EXAMINERS ARE LOOKING FOR

There are lots of memory tricks for learning information for exams. This chapter isn't about those. Revision isn't just about learning information, but also about learning how to use that information well in the exam. Being able to do this isn't a question of memory, but of directed revision and concentration in the exam.

It may sound obvious, but in order to know how best to answer the exam questions, you need to think about how they are marked. The examiners mark your answers according to three principles, known as 'Assessment Objectives' (AOs). They are:

AO1 *Knowledge and understanding*: how well do you know and understand the central debates for an particular issue, the theoretical positions philosophers have defended, and the arguments they use to defend them? For units 3 and 5, how well do you understand the extract of text and its place in the philosopher's thought?

AO2 *Selection and application*: how well do you select relevant ideas, concepts, examples, and arguments that you encountered in the material or text you studied? How well do you use these ideas and examples to construct an answer that is coherent and relevant to the question asked? Are you able to present a good example that illustrates the point you want to make?

AO3 *Interpretation and evaluation*: how well do you interpret, evaluate, and analyse the arguments that you have read? Do you understand whether an argument succeeds or fails and why? How well do you compare arguments and counter-arguments to weigh up what the most plausible position is?

In addition, you will be marked on the clarity and accuracy of your language.

You can use these AOs to help guide your revision. AO1 leads straight to the first revision point:

> **R1** Learn the theories. Who said what? What terms and concepts did they use? What arguments did they use to defend their positions?

This, you may think, is challenging enough! But AO2 means that you also need to be able to *use* your knowledge. Knowing all about utilitarianism, say, won't help you if you write it all down in answer to a question about Kant. Knowing what is relevant is a special kind of knowledge, which involves thinking carefully about what you know about the theories in relation to the question asked. The best way to learn what is relevant is to practise answering questions, either exam questions or questions you make up for yourself or a friend. Try to make up questions that are similar to the exam questions, using the same 'key words' (I'll talk about these in the next section). Practising answering different questions on the same topic helps keep your knowledge flexible, because you have to think of just the right bit of information that will answer the question.

> **R2** Practise applying your knowledge by answering questions about it. The best questions to practise with are past exam questions, but you can also make up questions for yourself.

An important part of being able to apply your knowledge is coming up with relevant examples. You can either remember good examples you have read, or create your own. In either case, you should know precisely what point the example is making. An irrelevant example demonstrates that you don't really know what you are talking about.

> **R3** Prepare examples beforehand, rather than try to invent them in the exam. If you can use your own, that's great (you'll get extra marks if they are good). But they must be short and they must make the right point; so try them out on your friends and teachers first.

What of AO3? How do you revise for 'interpretation and evaluation'? This AO tests you on how well you can relate and compare arguments to overall theories and to other arguments. The best way to prepare for it is to spend time *thinking* about the arguments and issues. Thinking is quite different from knowing about. You might know Descartes's arguments against empirical knowledge (doubting the senses, dreaming, the evil demon), but you may never have stopped to really work out whether you think they are any good.

AO3 encourages you to do two things. One is to relate a particular argument to a philosopher's overall theory, to understand the relation between the parts and the whole. The second is to reflect on what a particular argument actually demonstrates, and whether there are counter-arguments that are better. Now this is what secondary sources – commentators on Plato, Descartes, etc. – try to do. So if you are working on a particular argument by Descartes, say, be guided by what the commentators have to say. Work through the arguments so that you understand for yourself the pros and cons of each viewpoint. As a minimum, be able to argue both for and against a particular view. Even if you can't come to a firm conclusion about which viewpoint is right, try to come to a firm conclusion about why the different points each seem right in their own way, and why it is difficult to choose. Philosophy is not about knowing the 'right answers', it is about understanding why an answer *might* be right and why it is difficult to know.

> **R4** Think reflectively about the arguments and issues. Practise arguing for and against a particular view. Using commentators where appropriate, think about which arguments are better, and why. Think about the place and importance of arguments in a philosopher's overall viewpoint.

These first four revision points relate to taking in and understanding information. There are two more points that will help you organise the information, learn it better, and prepare you for answering exam questions.

A good way of organising your information is to create answer outlines or web-diagrams for particular issues. (A web-diagram is a way to present a structure of ideas; each idea is in a bubble or at a node, with connections between ideas shown by lines drawn between the nodes. One or two ideas are often central, with other ideas coming off.) For example, if you are doing Unit 2 Philosophy of Religion, you could create an outline or web-diagram for the teleological (design) argument for the existence of God. Think about the essential points, and organize them, perhaps like this:

1 What is 'design'?
2 What is the classical design argument and who has presented it?
3 What is the modern version, and how is it different?
4 Who argued against the design argument, and what did they say?
5 What are its main strengths and weaknesses? Does the modern version answer some of the criticisms of the classical version?
6 What is your conclusion, and why?

With an outline like this, you should be able to answer any question that comes up on the design argument.

> **R5** Create structured outlines or web-diagrams for particular issues. Try to cover all the main points.

Finally, once you've organized your notes into an outline or web-diagram, time yourself writing exam answers. Start by using your outline, relying on your memory to fill in the details. Then practise by memorising the outline as well, and doing it as though it were an actual exam. You might be surprised at how quickly one hour goes by. You'll find that you need to be very focused – but this is what the examiners are looking for, answers that are thoughtful but to the point.

> **R6** Practise writing timed answers. Use your notes at first, but then practise without them.

There is one more thing which is important to revision that I haven't yet talked about: the structure of the questions and how the marks are awarded can help you to decide what to focus on. This is what we'll look at next.

● THE STRUCTURE OF THE EXAMS

Different units have different types of exam. If the examples given below aren't from papers you are doing, don't worry. The point of the examples is to show you the *structure* of the questions and the *marks* assigned to each part. The structure and the way the marks are divided up are the same for each question within a particular unit, whichever option or set text you are taking.

AS exams

Each of the exams lasts for one hour. For Units 1 and 2, you must answer one question from a choice of two in the area you studied. In Unit 1, this is Theory of Knowledge. In Unit 2, this is either Moral Philosophy or Philosophy of Religion. Each question is structured in exactly the same way. Here is an example from Unit 1, Theory of Knowledge (from 2001):

1   Total for this question: 45 marks

    (a) Explain and briefly illustrate the meaning of *a priori* and *a posteriori* knowledge. *(6 marks)*

    (b) Identify and explain two reasons why empiricism may lead to scepticism concerning the *extent* of our knowledge. *(15 marks)*

    (c) Assess the view that all of our *concepts* are derived from experience. *(24 marks)*

The questions for Unit 3 (set text) are slightly different. First, you don't have a choice – only one question is asked on each set text, and you may have studied just one set text, so you have to answer that question. Each question gives a quotation from the set text, and then asks a series of questions all structured the same way. Here is an example (from 2001):

2 Text: Descartes's *Meditations*   Total for this question: 45 marks

Study the following passage and then answer <u>all</u> parts of Question 2.

. . .

    (a)   With close reference to the passage above:
        (i)   Identify what Descartes understands by 'God'. *(2 marks)*
        (ii)   To what conclusion does a consideration of divine attributes lead Descartes? *(2 marks)*
        (iii) Briefly explain how a consideration of 'infinity' leads Descartes to conclude that God exists. *(6 marks)*
    (b)   Describe how Descartes distinguishes intellect from the imagination. *(10 marks)*
    (c)   Critically discuss Descartes's attempt to show that his mind is independent of his body. *(25 marks)*

A2 exams

The exams for Units 4 and 5 last for one hour. Unit 4 (either Philosophy of Mind, Political Philosophy or Philosophy of Science) is like Unit 2, in that you must answer one question from a choice of two from the option you studied. Here is an example of how the questions are structured (from Philosophy of Mind 2002):

1   Total for this question: 50 marks

    (a)   Describe and illustrate two ways in which mental states allegedly differ from brain states. *(18 marks)*
    (b)   Assess whether theories of the relationship between mind and body have successfully accounted for mental causation. *(32 marks)*

Unit 5 (set text) is like Unit 3. Only one question is set on each text, so you have to answer the question on the text you studied. Here is an example (from 2002):

2 Text: Hume's *An Enquiry Concerning Human Understanding*
                                                    Total for this question: 50 marks

Study the following extract and then answer <u>all</u> parts of Question 2.

. . .

(a) With close reference to the passage above:
    (i) Identify <u>one</u> regular cause and <u>one</u> irregular cause. *(2 marks)*
    (ii) Briefly explain Hume's position regarding probability. *(6 marks)*
    (iii) Suggest and briefly develop <u>one</u> criticism of Hume's account of probability. *(6 marks)*
(b) Outline Hume's distinction between impressions and ideas and <u>one</u> conclusion he draws from it. *(11 marks)*
(c) Evaluate Hume's attempt to solve the problem of free will and determinism. *(25 marks)*

Unit 6 is examined by a long essay of 3,000–4,000 words, which you write over a number of supervised sessions lasting four hours altogether. There will be a choice of 12 questions, and your teacher will help you to select the best question for you.

● UNDERSTANDING THE QUESTION: GIVING THE EXAMINERS WHAT THEY WANT

The key to doing well in an exam is understanding the question. I don't just mean understanding the *topic* of the question, like 'empiricism' or Hume's theory of probability. Of course, this is very important. But you also need to understand what the question is asking you to *do*. And this is related, in a very strict way, to the three Assessment Objectives I discussed earlier. This section is on how exam questions 'work'.

Command words

If you look at the examples of questions above, you will see that they start with different 'command words', such as 'explain', 'illustrate', 'identify', 'describe', 'outline', 'assess', 'critically discuss' and 'evaluate'. Obeying these instructions is crucially important to getting a good mark. If you are asked to 'describe how two mental states allegedly differ from brain states', and you argue that 'mental states don't differ from brain states because . . .' then you will fail to gain marks. And the same is true if you are asked to 'assess whether theories of the relationship between mind and body have successfully accounted for mental causation' and you only describe and illustrate what those theories actually claim.

These different command words relate to the different Assessment Objectives. The words 'describe' and 'identify' relate to AO1, *knowledge and understanding*.

You are being asked simply to say what the theories say. The words 'explain', 'illustrate', and 'outline' relate to AO1 and AO2. You are being asked to demonstrate your knowledge in a way that requires *selection and application*. Explanations and illustrations are only good if they are relevant, and set the points you make in a context. The words 'assess', 'evaluate', and 'critically discuss' relate to AO3, *interpretation and evaluation*. Of course, you'll have to show relevant knowledge, too, but you need to go beyond this to weighing up the arguments.

The key to understanding what the question is asking, and so to getting a good mark, is to take notice of the command words.

Question structure

Notice that the different command words always appear in the same parts of the question. So, in Units 1 and 2, 'describe' always appears in part (a), 'assess' always appears in part (c). This is because the marks given for each part of the question relate to a particular AO in a very strict way. You don't really need to worry about the exact correlation. If you follow the command word instructions, you won't go far wrong. But if you want to know, there is a table at the end of this chapter. Here are some rough generalisations that will help.

In the AS units, the marks for AO1 (knowledge and understanding) are distributed throughout parts (a), (b), and (c). The marks for AO2 (selection and application) are distributed in parts (b) and (c). All the marks for AO3 (interpretation and evaluation) are in part (c). In total, there are 18 marks available for AO1, 18 marks available for AO2, and 9 marks available for AO3.

In A2 Unit 4, the marks for AO1 and AO2 are distributed equally across (a) and (b), and all the marks for AO3 are in part (b). Overall, there are 17 marks for AO1, 17 marks for AO2, and 16 marks for AO3. In Unit 5, the division of marks isn't so rigid, although marks for AO3 are still concentrated towards the final parts of the question. Overall, there are 16 marks for AO1, 16 marks for AO2, and 18 marks for AO3. In Unit 6, overall there are 10 marks for AO1, 20 marks for AO2, and 30 marks for AO3.

Why is this important? For the same reason that the command words are important. It tells you what you should be doing. If all the marks are for AO1 (knowledge and understanding), there is no point spending any time evaluating. And if there are 9 marks for AO3 (interpretation and evaluation), then no matter how clearly you describe the theories and arguments, you cannot get a good mark for the question if you do not also evaluate them.

There is another reason this distribution of marks is important. It can help guide your revision. In A2 exams, there are many more marks available for AO3, especially in the long essay, than there are in AS exams. This means you need to spend more time concentrating on evaluating the arguments that you've studied.

● EXAM TECHNIQUE: GETTING THE BEST RESULT YOU CAN

If you've understood the question structure beforehand, and know what to expect in the exam, the question paper will not seem so daunting. You'll have a good idea about how to proceed, and a sense of how the parts of the question are testing different aspects of your knowledge. This section gives you some tips on how to approach the questions when you are actually in the exam.

Exams are very exciting, whether in a good way or a bad way! It can be helpful, therefore, to take your time at the beginning, not to rush into your answers, but to plan your way. The tips I give below are roughly in the order that you might apply them when taking the exam. You might be surprised at the number of things it can be worth doing before you write anything at all.

It is important to decide carefully which question to answer, and this means reading the whole of each question before making your decision. In Unit 1 Theory of Knowledge, this just means reading both questions. In Units 2 and 4, it means identifying the two questions that are relevant to you, and reading through them both. You might find that although you know the answer to part (a), you aren't sure about part (c). If you don't read the whole question first, but just start your answer to part (a) straight away, you could end up wishing you had answered the other question.

In Units 3 and 5, after identifying the right set text, there is only one question that will be relevant. But you should still read the whole question first. This is because you will need to think how long to spend on each part. If you discover that you are less sure of an answer to one part, you may want to leave a little bit of extra time for tackling that section.

E1 Read through all the relevant questions before starting your answer. This will help you to decide which question you can answer best overall, taking into account all the parts, and will also help you to decide how long to spend on each part.

As I've already indicated, once you've decided which question to do, you need to think how long to spend on each part. Here the marks available for each part should be your guide. You have 60 minutes for the exam, and there are 45 or 50 marks available. If you allow five minutes for making some notes at the beginning and five minutes to check over your answer at the end, then you've got one minute per mark. That means, for example, that in the AS Unit 1 exam, you should spend around five minutes on part (a), 15 minutes on part (b), and 25 minutes on part (c). However, you'll probably find that each part is a little harder than the last, so you may want to spend up to 30 minutes on part (c), and cut down (a) and (b) a little. And you may find that you know the answer to one part better than another, so you may want to leave a little more time for the part you find difficult.

The marks also give you an idea about how much you should write. If there are just two marks, then a single precise sentence will often be enough. If there are six marks, then three or four sentences is often enough. With the longer answers, something around 500 words is good for the AS exams, and around 750 words for the A2 exams.

> **E2** The number of marks available for each part should be a rough guide to how long you spend on it and how much you should write. But allow a little extra time for the later parts and parts you find difficult.

Before you start to write your answer to any part, read the question again very closely. There are two things to look out for. First, notice the command words, and remind yourself what they are asking for. In part (a) of the example for Unit 4 above, you are asked to 'Describe and illustrate two ways in which mental states allegedly differ from brain states.' If you only describe, and do not provide examples, then you won't get full marks. Second, notice the precise phrasing of the question. For example, in part (c) of the example for Unit 1 above, the question asks you to 'Assess the view that all of our *concepts* are derived from experience.' This is different from the question of whether all of our *knowledge* is derived from experience. Noticing this will help you keep your answer relevant.

Because an exam is exciting (good or bad), many people have a tendency to notice only what the question is about, e.g. empiricism or Descartes's views on God. They don't notice the rest of the words in the question. But the question is never 'so tell me everything you know about empiricism'! *Every word counts.*

E3 Before starting your answer, read the question again very closely. Take note of every word, and especially the 'command word' that tells you what to do.

You are now ready to start answering the question. But, especially with the longer answers (parts (b) and (c)), many people find it is worth organizing their thoughts first. What are you going to say, in what order? This is particularly important with questions that involve evaluation, since arguments require that you present ideas in a logical order. If you've memorised an outline or a web-diagram, quickly write it out at the beginning so that you note down all the points. It is very easy to forget something or go off at a tangent once you are stuck into the arguments. Having an outline or web-diagram to work from will help you keep your answer relevant and structured. It will also remind you how much you still want to cover, so it can help you pace yourself better. However, you might discover, as you develop your answer, that parts of the outline or diagram are irrelevant or just don't fit. Don't worry; the outline is only there as a guide.

E4 Before you start your answer, especially if it will be comparatively long, it can be worth writing out your outline or web-diagram first. This can help remind you of the key points you want to make, and the order in which you want to make them.

All the questions ask for examples at some point. Finding and using a good example is very important. Good examples are concise and relevant, and support your argument. But you need to explain why they support your argument. An example is an illustration, not an argument.

E5 Keep your examples short and make sure they support the point you want to make. Always explain how they support your point.

Because philosophy is about the logical relationship of ideas, there are a number of rules of thumb about presentation. Here are four important ones.

E6 Four rules of thumb:

(a) Don't use a 'technical term', like 'the greatest happiness principle' or 'the ontological argument', without saying what it means.
(b) Describe a theory, at least briefly, before evaluating it. If you have described it in answer to a previous part, that is fine.
(c) Keep related ideas together. If you have a thought later on, add a footnote indicating where in the answer you want it to be read.
(d) Don't state the conclusion to an argument before you've discussed the argument, especially if you are going to present objections to that conclusion. You can state what the argument hopes to show, but don't state it *as* a conclusion.

Finally, it is very easy to forget something, or say it in an unclear way. Leave time to check your answer at the end. You might find you can add a sentence here or there to connect two ideas together more clearly, or that some word is left undefined. These little things can make a big difference to the mark.

E7 Leave time to check your answer at the end. You may want to add a helpful sentence here and there.

● REVISION TIPS

R1. Learn the theories. Who said what? What terms and concepts did they use? What arguments did they use to defend their positions?

R2. Practise applying your knowledge by answering questions about it. The best questions to practise with are past exam questions, but you can also make up questions for yourself.

R3. Prepare examples beforehand, rather than try to invent them in the exam. If you can use your own, that's great (you'll get extra marks if they are good). But they must be short and they must make the right point; so try them out on your friends and teachers first.

R4. Think reflectively about the arguments and issues. Practise arguing for and against a particular view. Using commentators where appropriate, think about which arguments are better, and why. Think about the place and importance of arguments in a philosopher's overall viewpoint.

R5. Create structured outlines or web-diagrams for particular issues. Try to cover all the main points.

R6. Practise writing timed answers. Use your notes at first, but then practise without them.

● EXAM TIPS

E1. Read through all the relevant questions before starting your answer. This will help you to decide which question you can answer best overall, taking into account all the parts, and will also help you to decide how long to spend on each part.

E2. The number of marks available for each part should be a rough guide to how long you spend on it and how much you should write. But allow a little extra time for the later parts and parts you find difficult.

E3. Before starting your answer, read the question again very closely. Take note of every word, and especially the 'command word' that tells you what to do.

E4. Before you start your answer, especially if it will be comparatively long, it can be worth writing out your outline or web-diagram first. This can help remind you of the key points you want to make, and the order in which you want to make them.

E5. Keep your examples short and make sure they support the point you want to make. Always explain how they support your point.

E6. Four rules of thumb:

(a) Don't use a 'technical term', like 'the greatest happiness principle' or 'the ontological argument', without saying what it means.

(b) Describe a theory, at least briefly, before evaluating it. If you have described it in answer to a previous part, that is fine.

(c) Keep related ideas together. If you have a thought later on, add a footnote indicating where in the answer you want it to be read.

(d) Don't state the conclusion to an argument before you've discussed the argument, especially if you are going to present objections to that conclusion. You can state what the argument hopes to show, but don't state it *as* a conclusion.

E7. Leave time to check your answer at the end. You may want to add a helpful sentence here and there.

● MARKING SCHEME

Here's how the Assessment Objectives relate to the marks:

AS

Units 1, 2

(a) 6 marks for AO1
(b) 6 marks for AO1, 9 marks for AO2
(c) 6 marks for AO1, 9 marks for AO2, 9 marks for AO3

Unit 3

The mark allocation is not quite as strict, but roughly as follows:

(a) (i) 2 marks for AO1; (ii) 2 marks for AO1; (iii) 4 marks for AO1, 2 marks for AO2
(b) 4 marks for AO1, 6 marks for AO2
(c) 6 marks for AO1, 10 marks for AO2, 9 marks for AO3

A2

Unit 4

(a) 9 marks for AO1, 9 marks for AO2
(b) 8 marks for AO1, 8 marks for AO2, 16 marks for AO3

Unit 5

The division of marks between AOs isn't so rigid. Overall, there are 16 marks for AO1, 16 marks for AO2, and 18 marks for AO3. As with the other units, points for AO3 are mostly concentrated in part (c).

Unit 6

In the overall division of marks, there are 10 marks for AO1, 20 marks for AO2, and 30 marks for AO3.

INDEX

Philosophy:
The Essential Study Guide

Nigel Warburton, Open University, UK

Philosophy: The Essential Study Guide is a compact and straightforward guide to the skills needed to study philosophy, written by Nigel Warburton, best-selling author of *Philosophy: The Basics*. The four main skills covered by the book are:

• READING philosophy

• LISTENING to philosophy

• DISCUSSING philosophy

• WRITING philosophy

Philosophy: The Essential Study Guide is an indispensable guide for anyone getting to grips with their first philosophy course.

Hb: 0-415-34179-5
Pb: 0-415-34180-9

4th Edition
Philosophy: The Basics

Nigel Warburton, The Open University

'After ten years and three previous editions, this is still the best book of its kind.' – *Don Cupitt, University of Cambridge*

Nigel Warburton's best-selling book gently eases the reader into the world of philosophy. Each chapter considers a key area of philosophy, explaining and exploring the basic ideas and themes.

For the fourth edition, Warburton has added new sections to several chapters, revised others and brought the further reading sections up to date. If you've ever asked what is philosophy, or whether the world is really the way you think it is, then this is the book for you.

Hb: 0-415-32772-5
Pb: 0-415-32773-3

2nd Edition
Philosophy: Basic Readings

Edited by **Nigel Warburton**, The Open University

Nigel Warburton brings philosophy to life with an imaginative selection of philosophical writings on key topics. *Philosophy: Basic Readings* is structured around the same key themes as its companion volume, *Philosophy: The Basics*, but is also ideal for independent use on any undergraduate introductory philosophy course.

The second edition has been revised and expanded to include sixteen new readings, including:

* Thomas Nagel, What is Philosophy?

* Peter Singer, Moral Experts

* Ronald Dworkin, A New Map of Censorship

* Oliver Sacks, The Lost Mariner

Hb: 0-415-33797-6
Pb: 0-415-33798-4

2nd Edition
Philosophy: The Classics

Nigel Warburton, Open University, UK

'The challenge is to convey to the modern reader the perennial freshness of ideas. Nigel Warburton rises to the challenge with admirable skill.' – *The Times*

Nigel Warburton takes us on a guided tour through philosophy's greatest works including Plato's *Republic*, Aristotle's *Nicomachean Ethics*, Descartes' *Meditations*, Hume's *Enquiry Concerning Human Understanding*, Mill's *On Liberty*, and Marx & Engels' *German Ideology*. Each chapter explores a key classic text, identifying and explaining core themes as well as subjecting them to critical scrutiny.

Hb: 0-415-23997-4
Pb: 0-415-23998-2

2nd Edition
101 Philosophy Problems

Martin Cohen, Centre for Applied Ethics, Australia

'**Introduces philosophy in a novel way.**' – *Times Higher Education Supplement*

'**It's surprising how few [philosophy] introductions actually try and get their readers to join in.** *101 Philosophy Problems* **is an all too rare example of a book that does just that.**' – *Philosophers' Magazine*

Now in its second edition, this ever-engaging, humorous and extremely popular book challenges readers to think philosophically about everyday dilemmas. *101 Philosophy Problems* will stimulate hours of lively philosophical debate.

Hb: 0-415-26128-7
Pb: 0-415-26129-5

101 Ethical Dilemmas

Martin Cohen, Centre for Applied Ethics, Australia

'**A chatty, jokey journey through philosophical dilemmas ancient and modern.**' – *New Scientist*

'**101 Ethical Dilemmas is witty, clever, imaginative, pithy and sweeping in scope.**' – *David Resnik,* author of *The Ethics of Science*

From DIY babies and breeding experiments, by way of ethically dubious chemical factories and the 'School of Terror', before finally ending up in the 'Twinkies courtroom drama' and Newgate Prison, there is a dilemma for everyone here.

This book may not help you become a good person, but at least you will have had a good think about it...

Hb: 0-415-26126-0
Pb: 0-415-26127-9

Philosophy goes to the Movies

Christopher Falzon, University of Newcastle, Australia

'*Philosophy goes to the Movies* introduces philosophy through film ... Given the importance of the visual and powerful new movies, we can only look forward to more books like Falzon's.' – *Times Higher Education Supplement*

Philosophy goes to the Movies is a new kind of introduction to philosophy that makes use of movies including *The Matrix*, *Antz*, *Total Recall* and *Cinema Paradiso*, to explore philosophical ideas.

Ideal for the beginner, this book guides the student through philosophy using lively and illuminating cinematic examples. It will also appeal to anyone interested in the philosophical dimensions of cinema.

Hb: 0-415-23740-8
Pb: 0-415-23741-6

Paradoxes from A to Z

Michael Clark, University of Nottingham, UK

'An entertaining junkshop of mind-troubling problems.'
– *The Guardian*

This essential guide to paradoxes takes the reader on a lively tour of puzzles that have taxed thinkers from Zeno to Galileo and Lewis Carroll to Bertrand Russell.

Clark discusses each paradox in non-technical terms, considering its significance and looking at likely solutions. A refreshing alternative to traditional philosophical introductions, *Paradoxes from A to Z* is guaranteed to stimulate and entertain.

Hb: 0-415-22808-5
Pb: 0-415-22809-3

2nd Edition
Routledge Philosophy GuideBook to Plato and the *Republic*

Nickolas Pappas, The City College of New York, USA

'Admirably clear and accessible ... Throughout one gets the sense of a skilful lecturer who is adept at rendering Plato's thoughts into terms that contemporary students will understand.' – *Mind*

Hb: 0-415-29996-9
Pb: 0-415-29997-7

Routledge Philosophy GuideBook to Descartes and the *Meditations*

Gary Hatfield, University of Pennsylvania, USA

In this Routledge Philosophy GuideBook, Gary Hatfield guides the reader through the text of the Meditations, providing commentary and analysis throughout. He assesses Descartes' importance in the history of philosophy and his continuing relevance to contemporary thought.

Hb: 0-415-11192-7
Pb: 0-415-11193-5

Also available in the series:

Routledge Philosophy GuideBook to Aristotle on Ethics

Gerard Hughes

Hb: 0-415-22186-2
Pb: 0-415-22187-0

Routledge Philosophy GuideBook to Hume on Knowledge

Harold W. Noonan

Hb: 0-415-15046-9
Pb: 0-415-15047-7

Routledge Philosophy Guidebook to Mill on Liberty

Jonathan Riley

Hb: 0-415-14188-5
Pb: 0-415-14189-3

Routledge Philosophy GuideBook to Nietzsche on Morality

Brian Leiter

Hb: 0-415-15284-4
Pb: 0-415-15285-2

Introducing

Research Methodology

Introducing
Research Methodology

A Beginner's Guide to Doing a Research Project

UWE FLICK

Los Angeles | London | New Delhi
Singapore | Washington DC

© Uwe Flick 2011

Originally published under the title SOZIALFORSCHUNG
Copyright © 2009 by Rowohlt Verlag GmbH, Reinbek bei Hamburg

First published 2011
Reprinted 2011

SAGE Publications Ltd
1 Oliver's Yard
55 City Road
London EC1Y 1SP

SAGE Publications Inc.
2455 Teller Road
Thousand Oaks, California 91320

SAGE Publications India Pvt Ltd
B 1/I 1 Mohan Cooperative Industrial Area
Mathura Road, New Delhi 110 044
India

SAGE Publications Asia-Pacific Pte Ltd
33 Pekin Street #02–01
Far East Square
Singapore 048763

Library of Congress Control Number: 2010936663

British Library Cataloguing in Publication data

A catalogue record for this book is available from the British Library
Library of Congress

ISBN 978-1-84920-780-5
ISBN 978-1-84920-781-2 (pbk)

Typeset by C&M Digitals (P) Ltd, Chennai, India
Printed and bound in Great Britain by the MPG Books Group
Printed on paper from sustainable resources

Contents

Table of Contents

List of Boxes

List of Figures

List of Tables

About the Author

Uwe Flick is trained as a psychologist and sociologist. He is Professor of Qualitative Research at Alice Salomon University of Applied Sciences in Berlin, Germany. Previously, he was Adjunct Professor at the Memorial University of Newfoundland at St. John's, Canada and has been a Lecturer at the Free University of Berlin in Research Methodology, a Reader and Assistant Professor at the Technical University of Berlin in Qualitative Methods and Evaluation, and Associate Professor and Head of the Department of Medical Sociology at the Hannover Medical School. He has held visiting appointments at the London School of Economics, the Ecole des Hautes Etudes en Sciences Sociales in Paris, at Cambridge University (UK), Memorial University of St. John's (Canada), University of Lisbon (Portugal), University of Vienna (Austria), in Italy and Sweden, and at the School of Psychology at Massey University, Auckland (NZ). His main research interests are qualitative methods, health and homelessness, sleep problems in nursing homes and social representations in the fields of individual and public health. He is author of *An Introduction to Qualitative Research – Fourth Edition* (London: Sage 2009), *Designing Qualitative Research* (London: Sage 2008) and *Managing Quality in Qualitative Research* (London: Sage 2008) and editor of *The SAGE Qualitative Research Kit* (London: Sage 2007), *A Companion to Qualitative Research* (London: Sage 2004), and of *Psychology of the Social* (Cambridge: Cambridge University Press, 1998).

Preface

Two main developments have shaped the context of this book. First, the political and practical relevance of social research has grown. Empirically based knowledge on such issues as the gap between the poor and the rich, changes in the incidence of diseases and the effects of social disadvantage provide the basis for decision-making, both in policy and in professional practice.

Second, an increasing number of university programs include either introductory or advanced training in the principles and methods of social research. In most cases this covers questions not only of how to understand existing research, but also of how to conduct research projects (of whatever scale). Sometimes this training is embedded in a course or research-based teaching. Often, however, the research project forms a basis for the final (masters, bachelor, doctoral) thesis and the students may be more or less working on their own whilst planning and running their research projects.

Background to the Book

Two background experiences have informed the writing of this book. First, there is my own experience of conducting social research in several fields (including health, youth studies, technological change, ageing and sleep): this experience has taught me a good deal about the problems that arise in research and how to deal with them. Second, there is my experience of teaching social research methods to students and doing social research projects with them. This experience has taken several forms, including research-based teaching, seminar projects, and supervising numerous bachelor, master's and PhD theses. This work has helped me to discover which examples of other researchers' work most serve to inform what research is about.

Aims of the Book

This book is designed to help readers who are embarking on social research projects. There are, of course, numerous resources on social research already available, including some comprehensive textbooks. For introducing social research, however, comprehensiveness is not necessarily a virtue. Comprehensive treatments tend to be bulky and unwieldy and they can be overwhelming in the detail they present.

In contrast, this book aims to provide the reader with a concise overview. It outlines the most important approaches likely to be used in social research projects. And it provides a good deal of practical information on how to proceed with a project. It also includes guidance on, and reference to, further sources on the subject.

Overview of the Book

The first part of the book will give you an *orientation* to the field of social research. It focuses on issues that come into play as one begins to approach a research project. Chapter 1 provides an introductory overview of what social research is, what you can do with it – and what you can't. Chapter 2 shows how research questions originate and how they can be developed and refined. It considers research questions in the context of both qualitative and quantitative research. This chapter also outlines the role of hypotheses. Chapter 3 shows how to find existing research literature and how to use it in your own project.

The second part of the book deals with *planning and designing* a research project. The fourth chapter provides a short overview of the major steps involved in the research process (for both quantitative and qualitative research). Chapter 5 focuses on the design of quantitative and of qualitative research. First, it provides guidance on how to develop a research proposal and a timescale for your project. In the next step, it discusses key research designs in quantitative and qualitative research. The last part deals with sampling – the selection of participants. Some of the major strategies of sampling are described. The sixth chapter outlines the selection of methods and approaches to be used for pursuing your own research question. A central focus is on the decisions you will need to make at various stages of the research process.

In the third part of the book we turn to the business of *working with data*. Methods of data collection are the focus of Chapter 7. Surveys, interviews, observation and the use of existing datasets and documents are all discussed here and issues concerning measurement and documentation are outlined. The analysis of quantitative and qualitative data is the topic of Chapter 8. This chapter introduces content analysis, descriptive statistics and qualitative analysis, as well as case studies and the development of typologies. Chapter 9 focuses on the options for and limitations of doing social research on the Internet (e-research) in the era of Web 2.0. Chapter 10 discusses the limitations of the various methods in quantitative and qualitative research and of each approach in general. Furthermore it considers ways of combining approaches through triangulation, mixed methods and integrated research, which are presented as alternatives.

The fourth and final part of the book addresses issues of *reflection* about your project as a whole and *writing* about its results. Chapter 11 focuses on evaluation of empirical studies in quantitative and qualitative research. Criteria for evaluation in both areas, as well as questions of generalization, are discussed. Chapter 12 outlines issues of research ethics in quantitative and qualitative research, including data protection, codes of ethics and the role of ethics committees. The final chapter discusses issues of writing about research. It describes how results in qualitative and quantitative research can be presented and, in particular, how to provide feedback to participants and how to use results in practical contexts and in wider debates.

Features of the Book

Every chapter begins with a *list of objectives*. These specify what I hope you will learn from each chapter. A *navigator* through a research project is also provided so that you can see at a glance how each chapter fits into the whole. To illustrate, the navigator for Chapter 1 is shown here.

Table   The navigator

You are here in your project →	Orientation	• What is social research? • Research question • Literature review
	Planning and design	• Planning research • Designing research • Deciding methods
	Working with data	• Gathering data • Analyzing data • E-research • Integrated research
	Reflection and writing	• Evaluating research • Ethics • Writing and using research

Case studies and other material are provided throughout in boxes to illustrate methodological issues. At the end of each chapter you will find a *checklist* of what you should keep in mind whilst planning and conducting a research project. These checklists provide readily accessible guidance that can be referred to over and over again as your project progresses. *Key points* and suggestions for *further reading* conclude every chapter. A *glossary* explaining the most important terms and concepts used in the text is included at the end of the book.

I hope this book will stimulate your curiosity about doing a social research project and, by guiding you through such a project, show you that doing a research project can be an enjoyable and exciting experience.

PART I
ORIENTATION

Part I of this book has two aims. First, it seeks to introduce social research in general. It considers what social research is, what distinguishes it, what forms it takes, and how it can (and cannot) be used. These are the topics of Chapter 1.

Second, it seeks to lay a foundation for your own research project. In particular, it introduces the issues of research questions, hypotheses and research literature. Chapter 2 focuses on research questions. It considers what a research question is and how such questions may be developed. This chapter also considers hypotheses – what they are and how and when they are useful.

Chapter 3 considers research literature. It outlines the nature of research literature and how it can – and should – inform the planning of your own research project.

These three chapters together also introduce a theme that runs throughout the book, namely the distinction and the relationship between qualitative and quantitative research.

CHAPTER 1
WHY SOCIAL RESEARCH?

Chapter Overview

Chapter Objectives

This chapter is designed to help you:

- gain an introductory understanding of social research
- begin to see the similarities and differences between qualitative and quantitative research
- appreciate (a) the tasks social research has, (b) what social research can achieve, and (c) what aims you can achieve through it.

Table 1.1 Navigator for Chapter 1

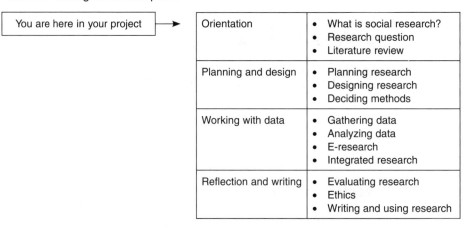

You are here in your project →	Orientation	• What is social research? • Research question • Literature review
	Planning and design	• Planning research • Designing research • Deciding methods
	Working with data	• Gathering data • Analyzing data • E-research • Integrated research
	Reflection and writing	• Evaluating research • Ethics • Writing and using research

What Is Social Research?

Increasingly, science and research – their approaches and results – inform public life. They help to provide a basis for political and practical decision-making. This applies across the range of sciences – not only to natural science and medicine, but to social science too. Our first task here is to clarify what is distinctive about social research.

Everyday Life and Science

Many of the issues and phenomena with which social research engages also play a role in everyday life. Consider, for example, one issue that is obviously highly relevant to everyday life, namely health. For the most part, health becomes an explicit issue in everyday life only when health-related problems occur or are threatening individuals. Symptoms produce an urge to react and we start to look for solutions, causes and explanations. If necessary, we may go to see a doctor and maybe end up changing our habits and behaviors – for example, by taking more exercise.

This search for causes and explanations, and people's own experiences, often lead to the development of everyday theories (for example: 'An apple a day keeps the doctor away'). Such theories are not necessarily spelled out explicitly: they often remain implicit. The question of whether everyday explanations and theories are correct or not is usually tested pragmatically: do they contribute to solving problems and reducing symptoms or not? If such knowledge allows the problem at hand to be solved, it has fulfilled its purpose. Then it is not relevant whether such explanations apply to other people or in general. In this context, scientific knowledge (for example, that smoking increases the risk of cancer) is often picked up from the media.

Health, health problems, and how people deal with them constitute issues for social research too. But in social science we take a different approach. Analysis of problems is foregrounded and study becomes more systematic. This aims at breaking up routines in order to prevent harmful behaviors – for example the relation between specific behaviors (like smoking) and specific health problems (such as the likelihood of falling ill with cancer). To achieve such an aim, we need to create a situation free of pressure to act. For example, you will plan a longer period for analyzing the problem, without the pressure of immediately finding a solution for it. Here, knowledge results not from intuition, but from examination of scientific theories. The development of such theories involves a process of explicitly spelling out and testing relations, which is based on using research methods (like a systematic review of the literature or a survey). For both aims – the developing and testing of theories – the methods of social research are used. The resulting knowledge is abstracted from the concrete example and further developed in the direction of general relations. Unlike in everyday life, here the generalization of knowledge is more important than solving a concrete problem in the single case.

Everyday knowledge and problem-solving can of course become the starting points for theory development and empirical research. We may ask, for example, which types of everyday explanations for a specific disease can be identified in interviews with patients.

Table 1.2 presents the differences between everyday knowledge and practices on the one hand, and science and research on the other. It does so on three levels, namely (1) the context of knowledge development, (2) the ways of developing knowledge and the state of the knowledge which is produced, and (3) the mutual relations between everyday knowledge and science.

What, then, characterizes social research in dealing with such issues? Here we may itemize a number of characteristics, each of which is explored further in this book. They are:

- Social research approaches issues in a systematic and above all empirical way.
- For this purpose, you will develop research questions (see Chapter 2).
- For answering these questions, you will collect and analyze data.
- You will collect and analyze these data by using research methods (see Chapters 7 and 8).
- The results are intended to be generalized beyond the examples (cases, samples etc.) that were studied (see Chapter 11).

Table 1.2 Everyday knowledge and science

	Everyday knowledge and practices	Science and research
Context of knowledge (production)	Pressure to act Solving of problems is the priority: • routines are not put to question • reflection in case of practical problems	Relief from a pressure to act Analyzing of problems is the priority: • systematic analysis • routines are put to question and broken down
Ways of knowledge (production)	Intuition Implicit development of theories Experience-driven development of theories Pragmatic testing of theories Check of solutions for problems	Use of scientific theories Explicit development of theories Methods-driven development of theories Methods-based testing of theories Use of research methods
State of knowledge	Concrete, referring to the particular situations	Abstract and generalizing
Relation of everyday knowledge and science	Everyday knowledge can be used as starting points for theory development and empirical research	Everyday knowledge is increasingly influenced by scientific theories and results of research

- From the systematic use of research methods and their results, you will derive descriptions or explanations of the phenomena you study.

- For a systematic approach, time, freedom and (other) resources are necessary (see Chapter 5).

As we shall see, there are different ways of doing social research. First, though, we can develop a preliminary general definition of social research derived from our discussion so far (see Box 1.1).

BOX 1.1

Definition of social research

Social research is the systematic analysis of research questions by using empirical methods (e.g. of asking, observing, analyzing data etc.). Its aim is to make empirically grounded statements that can be generalized or to test such statements. Various approaches can be distinguished and also a number of fields of application (health, education, poverty etc.). Various aims can be pursued, ranging from an exact description of a phenomenon to its explanation or to the evaluation of an intervention or institution.

The Tasks of Social Research

We can distinguish three main tasks for social research. To do so, we use the criterion of how the results of social research may be used.

Knowledge: Description, Understanding and Explanation of Phenomena

A central task of social research originates from scientific interests, which means that the production of knowledge is prioritized. Once a new phenomenon, e.g. a new disease, arises, a detailed description of its features (symptoms, progression, frequency etc.) on the basis of data and their analysis becomes necessary. The first step can be a detailed description of the circumstances under which it occurs or an analysis of the subjective experiences of the patients. This will help us to understand the contexts, effects and meanings of the disease. Later, we can look for concrete explanations and test which factors trigger the symptoms or the disease, which circumstances or medications have specific influences on its course, etc. For these three steps – (a) description, (b) understanding, and (c) explanation – the scientific interest in new knowledge is dominant. Such research contributes to basic research in that area. Here science and scientists remain the target group for the research and its results.

Practice-Oriented Research: Applied and Participative Research

Increasingly, social research is being conducted in practical contexts such as hospitals or schools. Here, research questions focus on practices – those of teachers, nurses or physicians – in institutions. Or they focus on the specific conditions of work in these institutions – routines in the hospital or teacher–student relations, for example. The results of applied research of this kind are also produced according to rules of scientific analysis. However, they should become relevant for the practice field and for the solution of problems in practice.

A special case here is participatory action research. Here the changes initiated by the researcher in the field of study do not come only after the end of the study and the communication of its results. The intention is rather to initiate change *during* the process of research and by the very fact that the study is being done. Take, for example, a study of nursing with migrants. A participatory action research study would not set out merely to describe the everyday routines of nursing with migrants. Rather it would initiate the process of research immediately in those everyday routines. It would then feed back to participants the information gathered in the research process.

This changes the relationship between researcher and participant. A relation which is usually monologic in traditional research (e.g. the interviewees unfold their views, the researchers listen) becomes dialogic (the interviewees unfold their views, the researchers listen and make suggestions for how to change the situation). A subject–object relation turns into a relation between two subjects – the researcher and the participant. The evaluation of the research and its results is no longer focused solely on the usual scientific criteria (as will be discussed in Chapter 11). Rather, the question of the usefulness of the research and its results for the participant becomes a main criterion. Research is no longer just a knowledge process for the researchers, but rather a process of knowledge, learning and change on both sides.

Basis for Political and Practical Decisions

Since the middle of the twentieth century, social research has become more important as a basis for decisions in practical and political contexts. In most countries, regular surveys in various areas are common practice; reports on health, on poverty, and on the situation of the elderly and of youth and children are produced, often commissioned by government. In many cases, such monitoring does not involve extra research, but rather summarizes existing research and results in the field. But as the PISA studies or the HBSC study (Hurrelmann et al. 2003) show, in areas like health, education and youth, additional studies do sometimes contribute to the basis of these reports. In the HBSC study, representative data about 11 to 15-year-old adolescents in the population are collected. At the same time, case studies with purposefully selected cases are included. Where data from representative studies are not available or cannot be expected, sometimes only case studies provide the data basis.

In many areas, decisions about establishing, prolonging or continuing services, programs or institutions are based on evaluations of existing examples or experimental programs (for evaluation see Chapter 5 and Flick 2006). Here, social research not only provides data and results as a basis for decisions, but also makes assessments and evaluations – by, for example, examining whether one type of school is more successful in reaching its goals than a different type.

Table 1.3 summarizes the tasks and research areas of social research outlined above, using the context of health as an example.

What Can You Achieve with Social Research?

In the areas just mentioned, we can use social research to:

- explore issues, fields and phenomena and provide first descriptions
- discover new relations by collecting and analyzing data
- provide empirical data and analyses as a basis for developing theories
- test existing theories and stocks of knowledge empirically
- document the effects of interventions, treatments, programs etc. in an empirically based way
- provide knowledge (i.e. data, analyses and results) as an empirically grounded basis for political, administrative and practical decision-making.

Table 1.3   Tasks and research areas of social research

Research area	Features	Aims	Example	Studies refer to:
Basic research	Development or testing of theories	General statements without a specific link to practices	Trust in social relationships	Random sample of students or unspecific groups
Applied research	Development or testing of theories in practical fields	Statements referring the particular field	Trust in doctor–patient relations	Doctors and patients in a specific field
Participatory action research	Analyzing fields and changing them at the same time	Intervention in the field under study	Analysis and improvement of nursing for migrants	Patients with a specific ethnic background, for example, who are (not sufficiently) supported by existing home care services
Evaluation	Collection and analysis of data as a basis for assessing the success and failure of an intervention	Assessment of institutional services and changes	Improvement of the trust relations between doctors and patients in a specific field with better information	Patients in a specific field
Health monitoring	Documentation of health-related data	Stocktaking of developments and changes in the health status of the population	Frequencies of occupational diseases	Routine data of health insurance

What Is Social Research Unable To Do and What Can You Do with It?

Social research has its limits. For example, the aim of developing a single grand theory to explain society and the phenomena within it, which also withstands empirical testing, could not be achieved. And there is no one method for studying all relevant phenomena. Moreover, social research cannot be relied upon to provide immediate solutions for current, urgent problems. On all three levels, we have to rein in our expectations of social research and pursue more realistic aims.

What we can aim to do is develop, and even test empirically, a number of theories. They can be used to explain certain social phenomena. We can also continue to develop a range of social science methods. Researchers can then select the appropriate methods and apply them to the problems they wish to study. Finally, social research provides knowledge about details and relations, which can be employed for developing solutions for societal problems.

Quantitative and Qualitative Research

We need now to turn to the distinction between qualitative and quantitative research. This distinction will feature frequently throughout this book. The notions of 'qualitative research' and 'quantitative research' are umbrella terms for a number of approaches, methods and theoretical backgrounds on each side. That is, each of these two terms in fact covers a wide range of procedures, methods and approaches. Nevertheless, they are useful. Here, therefore, we develop an outline of the two approaches (for more details see Flick 2009 and Bryman 2008) and consider what characterizes each.

Quantitative Research

Quantitative research can be characterized as follows. In studying a phenomenon (e.g. stress of students), you will start from a concept (e.g. a concept of stress), which you spell out theoretically beforehand (e.g. in a model of stress, which you set up or take from the literature). For the empirical study, you will formulate a hypothesis (or several hypotheses), which you will test (e.g. that for students in humanities, university is more stressful than for students in the natural sciences). In the empirical project, the procedure of measurement has high relevance for finding out differences among persons concerning the characteristics you study (e.g. there are students with more and less stress).

In most cases, we cannot expose a theoretical concept immediately to measurement. Rather, we have to find indicators that permit a measurement in place of the concept. We may say that the concept has to be *operationalized* in these indicators. In our example, you could operationalize stress before an exam by using physiological indicators (e.g. higher blood pressure) and then apply blood pressure measurements. More often researchers operationalize research through using specific questions (e.g. 'Before exams, I feel often under pressure') with specific alternatives of answering (like in the example in Figure 1.1).

Data collection is designed in a standardized way (e.g. all participants in a study may be interviewed under the same circumstances and in the same way). The methodological ideal is the kind of scientific measurement achieved in the

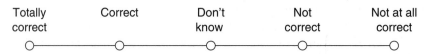

Figure 1.1 Alternatives for answering on Likert scale

natural sciences. By standardization of the data collection and of the research situation, the criteria of reliability, validity and objectivity (see Chapter 11) can be met.

Quantitative research is interested in causalities – for example, in showing that stress before an exam is caused by the exam and not by other circumstances. Therefore, you will create a situation for your research in which the influences of other circumstances can be excluded as far as possible. For this purpose, instruments are tested for the consistency of their measurement, for example in repeated applications. The aim of the study is to achieve generalizable results: that is, your results should be valid beyond the situation in which they were measured (the students also feel the stress or have the higher blood pressure before exams when they are not studied for research purposes). The results from the group of students that participated need to be transferable to students in general. Therefore, you will draw a sample, which you select according to criteria of representativity – the ideal case is a random sample (see Chapter 5 for this) – from the population of all students. This will mean that you can generalize from the sample to the population. Thus the single participants are relevant not as individuals (how does the student Joe Bauer experience stress before exams?) but rather as typical examples. It is not so much the students' entire situation, but rather their specific (e.g. physiological) reactions to a certain condition (a coming exam), that are relevant.

The emphasis on measurement, as in the natural sciences, relates to an important research aim, namely replicability – i.e. the measurement has principally to be able to be repeated, and then, provided the object under examination has not itself changed, to produce the same results. In our example: if you measure blood pressure for the same student before the exam repeatedly, the measured values must be the same – except if there are good reasons for a difference, for example if blood pressure rises as the exam gets closer.

Quantitative research works with numbers. To return to our example: because measurement produces a specific figure for blood pressure, the alternatives for answering in Figure 1.1 can be transformed into numbers from 1 to 5. These numbers make possible a statistical analysis of the data (see Bryman 2008 for a more detailed presentation of these features of quantitative research). Kromrey (2006, p. 34) defines the 'strategy of the so-called quantitative research' as 'a strictly goal-oriented procedure, which aims for the "objectivity" of its results by a standardization of all steps as far as possible and which postulates intersubjective verifiability as the central norm for quality assurance'.

The participants may experience the research situation as follows. They are relevant as members of a specific group, from which they were selected randomly. They are confronted with a number of predefined questions, for which they have a number of also predefined answers, of which they are expected to choose only one. Information beyond these answers, as well as their own assumptions, subjective states or queries and comments on the questions or the issue, are not part of the research situation.

Qualitative Research

Qualitative research sets itself other priorities. Here you normally do not necessarily start from a theoretical model of the issue you study and refrain from hypotheses and operationalization. Also, qualitative research is not modeled on measurement as found in the natural sciences. Finally, you will be interested neither in standardizing the research situation as far as possible nor in guaranteeing representativity by random sampling of participants.

Instead, qualitative researchers select participants purposively and integrate small numbers of cases according to their relevance. Data collection is designed much more openly and aims at a comprehensive picture made possible by reconstructing the case under study. Thus fewer questions and answers are defined in advanced; there is greater use of open questions. The participants are expected to answer these questions spontaneously and in their own words. Often, researchers work with narratives of personal life histories.

Qualitative research addresses issues by using one of the following three approaches. It aims (a) at grasping the subjective meaning of issues from the perspectives of the participants (for example, what does it mean for interviewees to experience their university studies as a burden?). Often, (b) latent meanings of a situation are in focus (for example, which are the unconscious aspects or the underlying conflicts that influence the experience of stress for the student?). It is less relevant to study a cause and its effect than to describe or reconstruct the complexity of situations. In many cases, (c) social practices and the life world of the participants are described. The aim is less to test what is known (e.g. an existing theory or hypothesis) than to discover new aspects in the situation under study and to develop hypotheses or a theory from these discoveries. Therefore, the research situation is not standardized; rather it is designed to be as open as possible. A few cases are studied, but these are analyzed extensively in their complexity. Generalization is an aim not so much on a statistical level (generalization to the level of the population for example) as on a theoretical level (for a more detailed presentation of these features see Flick 2009).

The participants in a study may experience the research situation as follows. They are involved in the study as individuals, who are expected to contribute their experiences and views from their particular life situations. There is scope for what they see as essential, for approaching questions differently and for providing different kinds of answers with different levels of detail. The research situation is designed more as a dialogue, in which probing, new aspects and their own estimations find their place.

Table 1.4 Differences between quantitative and qualitative research

	Quantitative research	Qualitative research
Theory	As a starting point to be tested	As an end point to be developed
Case selection	Oriented on (statistical) representativity, ideally random sampling	Purposive according to the theoretical fruitfulness of the case
Data collection	Standardized	Open
Analysis of data	Statistical	Interpretative
Generalization	In a statistical sense to the population	In a theoretical sense

Differences between Quantitative and Qualitative Research

From the above outlines of features of both approaches, some of the main differences in assessing what is under study (issue, field and persons) have become evident. These are summarized in Table 1.4.

Common Aspects of Quantitative and Qualitative Research

Desp_____ _____ferences, the two approaches have some points in common. In both _____s, you:

- w_____ _____ically by using empirical methods (see Chapters 7 and 8)
- _____izing your findings – to situations other than the research situation _____ other than the participants in the study (see Chapter 11)
- _____ research questions, for which the selected methods should be _____e Chapter 2)
- _____these questions using a planned and systematic procedure (see _____
- _____ _____our process of research for ethical acceptability and appropriate-ness _____ter 12)
- h_____ _____our process of research transparent (i.e. understandable for the reader) in presenting the results and the ways that lead to them (see Chapter 13).

Advantages and Disadvantages

An advantage of quantitative research is that it allows the study of a large number of cases for certain aspects in a relatively short time and its results have a high degree of generalizability. The disadvantage is that the aspects that are studied are not necessarily the relevant aspects for the participants and that the context of the meanings linked to what is studied cannot be sufficiently taken into account.

An advantage of qualitative research is that detailed and exact analyses of a few cases can be produced, in which the participants have much more freedom to determine what is relevant for them and to present it in its contexts. The disadvantage is that these analyses often require a lot of time and you can generalize results to the broad masses in only a very limited way.

Synergies and Combinations

The strengths and weaknesses just mentioned can provide the basis for deciding which methodological alternative you should select for your specific research question (see Chapter 6). At the same time, we should remember that it is possible to combine qualitative and quantitative research (as is explored in more detail in Chapter 10) with the aim of compensating for the limitations and weaknesses of each approach and producing synergies between them.

Doing Research On-site and Doing it Online: New Opportunities and Challenges for Social Research

In the last decade or so a new trend has arisen which has considerably extended the reach of social research. With the development of the Internet, both qualitative and quantitative approaches can now be used in new contexts.

Traditionally, interviews, surveys and observations have mostly been done on-site. You make appointments with your participants, meet them at a specific time and location, and interact with them face to face or send them your questionnaire by mail and they return it in the same way. This kind of research has its limitations. Sometimes, practical reasons will make these encounters difficult: participants live far away, are not ready to meet researchers, or are relevant for your study as members of a virtual community.

These limitations can sometimes be overcome if you decide to do your study online. Quantitative and qualitative methods have been adapted to online research. E-mail or online interviews, online surveys and virtual ethnography are now part of the methodological toolkit of social researchers. This means not so much (or, at least, not only) that you apply social science methods to study (the use of) the Internet, but rather that you use the Internet to apply your methods for answering your research questions. In particular the new forms of communication in the context of Web 2.0 provide new options for communicating in and about social research. They also facilitate doing research collaboratively (see Chapter 9 for details).

Social Research between Frustration and Challenge: Why and How Research Can Be Fun

For many students, completing courses in research methods and statistics seems to be nothing more than an unpleasant duty; it seems you have to go through this, even if you do not know why and for what purpose. To learn methods can be exhausting and painful. If the whole enterprise leads to a difficult written test at the end, sometimes any excitement is submerged by the stress of the exam. To apply methods can be time consuming and challenging.

However, the systematic nature of the procedures and the concrete access to practical issues in empirical research in the studies and the later professional work (as a sociologist, social worker and the like) may provide new insights. You may discover new insights in the analysis of your data. Interviews, life histories or participant observation can provide insights into concrete life situations or into how institutions function. Sometimes these insights come as surprises, which may give you the chance to overcome your prejudices and limited perspectives on how people live and work. And you will learn a lot about how life histories develop or about what happens in practical work in institutions or in the field.

In most research processes you will learn a lot not only about the participants, but also about yourself – especially if you work with issues like health, stress in the university, existential problems in cases of social discrimination etc. in concrete life situations. In particular in the context of theoretically ambitious studies and their contents, working with empirical data can form not only an instructive alternative or complement to theory, but also a concrete link between the theory and everyday problems and life situations.

Working with other people can be an enriching experience, and if you have the chance to do your research among a group of people – a research team or a group of students – that will be a good way out of the isolation students sometimes experience. For many students, work with technical devices, computers, programs and data can be satisfying and a lot of fun. For example, using the communication forms in Web 2.0 for your research purposes will provide new experiences of social networking and practical experiences with what is up to date in the context of using new media in a professional way. And in the end you will have concrete products at hand: examples, results, what they have in common and how they are different for a variety of people, and so on.

Finally, to work on an empirical project requires working on one issue in a sustained way. This is good experience, given that many students' experiences today are characterized more by 'bits and pieces' work. Empirical research in your fields of study can also be a test of how much you like those fields. If this test ends positively, that can reassure you in your decision to become, for example, a social worker or a psychologist.

Landmarks in the Field of Social Research

Knowledge about social research helps in two ways. It can provide the starting point and basis for doing your own empirical study, for example in the context of a thesis or of later professional work in sociology, education, social work etc. And it is also necessary for understanding and assessing existing research and perhaps for being able to build an argument on such research. For both, we can formulate a number of guideline questions, which allow a basic assessment of research (in the planning of your own or in reading other researchers' studies). These are shown in Box 1.2.

BOX 1.2

Guideline questions for an orientation in the field of social research

1. What is studied exactly?

   - What is the issue and what is the research question of the study?

2. How is it assured that the research really investigates what is supposed to be studied?

   - How is the study planned, which design is applied or constructed, how are biases prevented?

3. What is represented in what is studied?

   - Which claims of generalization are made and how are they fulfilled?

4. Is the execution of the study ethically sound and theoretically grounded?

   - How are the participants protected from any misuse of the data referring to them?
   - What is the theoretical perspective of the study?

5. Which methodological claims are made and fulfilled?

   - Which criteria are applied?

6. Does the presentation of results and of the ways they were produced make transparent for the reader how the results came about and how the researchers proceeded?

   - Is the study transparent and consistent in its presentation?

7. Is the chosen procedure convincing?

   - Are the design and methods appropriate for the issue under study?

8. Does the study achieve the degree of generalization that was expected?

These guideline questions can be asked regardless of the specific methodology that has been chosen and can be applied to the various methodological alternatives.

They are relevant for both qualitative and quantitative studies and can be used for assessing a case study as well as for a representative survey of the population of a country. They offer a framework for observations as well as for interviewing or for the use of existing data and documents (see Chapter 7 for this in more detail).

Key Points

- Social research is more systematic in its approach than everyday knowledge.
- Social research can have various tasks: research may be focused on knowledge, practice and consulting.
- Quantitative research and qualitative research offer different approaches. Each has strengths and limitations in what can be studied.
- Quantitative research and qualitative research can mutually complement each other.
- Both can be applied on-site and online.
- We can identify common features across the various approaches.

Further Reading

The first and fourth texts listed below provide more details of quantitative research and include some chapters on qualitative methods, too. The second and the third books give more insights into the variety of qualitative research methods.

Bryman, A. (2008) *Social Research Methods*, 3rd edn. Oxford: Oxford University Press.

Flick, U. (2009) *An Introduction to Qualitative Research*, 4th edn. London: Sage.

Flick, U., Kardorff, E. v. and Steinke, I. (eds) (2004) *A Companion to Qualitative Research*. London: Sage.

Neuman, W.L. (2000) *Social Research Methods: Qualitative and Quantitative Approaches*, 4th edn. Boston: Allyn and Bacon.

CHAPTER 2
FROM RESEARCH IDEA TO RESEARCH QUESTION

Chapter Overview

Chapter Objectives

This chapter is designed to help you:

- recognize the starting points for social research
- appreciate where research questions come from
- understand how research questions differ between qualitative and quantitative research
- understand the use of hypotheses.

Table 2.1 Navigator for Chapter 2

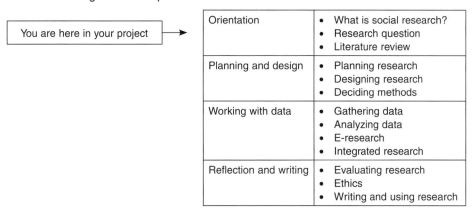

You are here in your project →	Orientation	• What is social research? • Research question • Literature review
	Planning and design	• Planning research • Designing research • Deciding methods
	Working with data	• Gathering data • Analyzing data • E-research • Integrated research
	Reflection and writing	• Evaluating research • Ethics • Writing and using research

This chapter seeks to show how research questions for empirical studies emerge from general interests and from the personal and social backgrounds of the researcher. For this purpose, let's look first at some examples.

Starting Points for Research

The literature of the history of social research recounts many examples of how ideas for research have emerged and been developed into research questions. For example, Marie Jahoda (1995; see also Fleck 2004, p. 59) has described the origins of her study with Paul Lazarsfeld and Hans Zeisel on *Marienthal: The Sociology of an Unemployed Community* (Jahoda et al. 1933/1971). The impulse for the study came in the late 1920s from Otto Bauer, leader of the Austrian Social Democratic Party. The background to the study included the Great Depression of 1929 and also the political interests and orientation of the researchers. As a result, the researchers developed the idea of studying how a community changes in response to mass unemployment. From this general idea they formulated research questions concerning the attitude of the population towards unemployment and the social consequences of unemployment.

Another example, this time from the 1950s, is provided by Hollingshead and Redlich's (1958) study of social class and mental illness. Their study stemmed from the general observation that 'Americans prefer to avoid the two facts studied in this book: social class and mental illness' (1958, p. 3). From this starting point they proceeded to explore possible relationships between social class and mental illness (and its treatment). For example, people with a lower social status might be more at risk of becoming mentally ill and their chance of receiving good treatment for their illness might be lower compared to people with a higher social status. From their general interest, the authors developed two research questions: '(1) Is mental illness related to class in our society? (2) Does a psychiatric patient's position in the status system affect how he [*sic*] is treated for his illness?' (1958, p. 10).

They then elaborated these two questions into five working hypotheses (1958, p. 11):

1. The prevalence of treated mental illness is related significantly to an individual's position in the class structure.

2. The types of diagnosed psychiatric disorders are connected significantly to the class structure.

3. The kind of psychiatric treatment administered by psychiatrists is associated with the patient's position in the class structure.

4. Social and psychodynamic factors in the development of psychiatric disorders correlate with an individual's position in the class structure.

5. Mobility in the class structure is associated with the development of psychiatric difficulties.

To test these hypotheses, Hollingshead and Redlich conducted a community study in a city of 24,000 people. They included all psychiatric patients diagnosed within a certain period, using a questionnaire about their illness and their social status. They also interviewed health professionals.

A contrasting example, also from the mid-twentieth century, is provided by a study by Glaser and Strauss (1965). Following their own experience of their mothers dying in hospital, they developed the idea of studying 'awareness of dying'. The authors (1965, pp. 286–7) described in some detail how these experiences stimulated their interest in the processes of communicating with and about dying persons and what they later described as 'awareness contexts'. Here the background for developing the research idea, interest and question was very much a personal one – the recent autobiographical experiences of the researchers.

And – to give one more example – Hochschild (1983, p. ix) has described how early experiences as a child of her family's home and social life became the source of her later 'interest in how people manage emotions'. Her parents worked for the US Foreign Service. This provided Hochschild with opportunities to see and interpret the different forms of smiles – and their meanings – produced by diplomats from different cultural backgrounds. Hochschild learned from these experiences that emotional expressions, such as smiles and handshakes, conveyed messages on several levels – from person to person and also between the countries the people represented. This led, much later, to her specific research interest:

> I wanted to discover what it is that we act upon. And so I decided to explore the idea that emotion functions as a messenger from the self, an agent that gives us an instant report on the connection between what we are seeing and what we had expected to see and tells us what we feel ready to do about it. (1983, p. x)

From that interest she developed a study (*The Managed Heart*) of two types of public-contact workers (flight attendants and bill collectors), showing how work functioned to induce or suppress emotions when the workers were in contact with their clients.

If we compare the examples above, we can see that they show diverse sources for developing research interests, ideas and subsequently research questions. They range from very personal experiences (Glaser and Strauss) to social experiences and circumstances (Hochschild), through social observations (Hollingshead and Redlich), to societal problems and political commissioning (Jahoda et al.). In each case, a general curiosity arose, which the researchers pursued and subsequently formulated in concrete terms.

Research, then, can take various starting points. In particular:

- Research problems are often discovered in everyday life. For example, in the everyday life of an institution someone may discover that, say, waiting times emerge in specific situations. In order to find out what determines waiting times and, perhaps, how they might be reduced, systematic research may be undertaken.

- Second, there may be a lack of data and empirical insights about a specific problem – for example, the health situation of young people in Germany – or about a specific subgroup – for example, adolescents living on the street.

- A third source for identifying a research problem may be the literature. For example, a theory might have been developed which requires testing empirically. Or analysis of the existing literature may reveal that gaps exist in the knowledge about a problem. Empirical research may be designed to close such gaps.

- Fourth, research problems may grow out of previous studies producing new questions or leaving some questions unanswered.

Origins of Research Questions

We can illustrate the development of research questions by using two recent examples. They concern health behavior and the health of adolescents living on the street.

The 'Health Behavior in Social Context' Study of the World Health Organization (WHO)

In the 'Health Behavior in Social Context' (HBSC) study, children and adolescents from 36 countries were interviewed, using a standardized questionnaire, concerning their health status and behavior. This research was conducted in order to produce a health report for the young generation and thus to contribute to an improvement in illness prevention and health promotion for this age group. In Germany, for example, this survey has been repeatedly run since 1993 – most recently in 2006 (see Hurrelmann et al. 2003; Richter et al. 2008). Hurrelmann et al. have described the aims of this study as follows:

> **In this youth health survey, several questions shall be answered: descriptive questions about physical, mental and social health and about the health behavior; in the focus is the question, how far health relevant life styles are linked to subjective health; and how far personal and social risk and protective factors can be identified for the prevention of health problems together with their subjective representation in physical and in mental respects. (2003, p. 2)**

For this study in Germany, adolescents aged 11, 13 and 15 years were interviewed in schools. For the international study, a representative sample was drawn (see Chapter 5), comprising about 23,000 adolescents in different areas of Germany. For the German study, a subsample of 5650 adolescents was drawn randomly from this sample. This subsample was asked to answer a questionnaire about their subjective health, risks of accidents and violence, the use of substances (tobacco, drugs and alcohol), eating, physical activity, peer and family and school. The research question for this study resulted from the interest in developing a representative overview of the health situation and the health relevant behavior of adolescents in Germany and in comparison with other countries.

Health on the Street: Homeless Adolescents

A different approach to a similar topic is provided by our second example. The study just discussed has provided a good overview of the health situation of the average young person in Germany and other countries. However, such a broad study cannot focus on particular (mainly very small) subgroups. The reasons for this are the use of random sampling and also the fact that the access to the participants was via schools. Adolescents living on the street, who attend school rarely if at all, were not represented in such a sample. For analyzing the specific situation and the health behavior and knowledge of this group, a different approach was required. Accordingly, in our second example (see Flick and Röhnsch 2007; 2008), adolescents were selected purposefully at the specific meeting points and hangouts of homeless adolescents and asked for interviews. Participants were aged between 14 and 20 and had no (regular) housing. To gain a more comprehensive understanding of their health knowledge and behavior under the conditions of 'the street', we not only interviewed them but also followed them through phases of their everyday lives, using participant observation. The topics of the interviews were similar to our first example above, with additional questions about the specific situation of living on the street and about how the participants entered street life.

In the first part of the study, the sampling and the interviews did not focus on illness. The second part of the study focused on the situation of chronically ill homeless adolescents. In addition to interviewing adolescents with various chronic diseases (from asthma to skin diseases and hepatitis), we conducted expert interviews with physicians and social workers in order to obtain their views of the service situation for this target group.

In both the above examples, the health and social situations of adolescents were studied – either of youth in Germany in general, or of a specific subgroup with particularly stressful conditions of living. In both cases, the results should be useful for helping to prevent health problems in the target groups and to improve the design of services for them.

Characteristics of Research Questions

Research questions may be regarded from different angles. From an external point of view, they should address a socially relevant issue. In our examples, the issues are the health situation of and the support for youth – and in particular the deficits in both. Are there particularly strong or frequent health problems, and are there service gaps for particular subgroups or for adolescents in general?

Answering the research questions should lead to some kind of progress – through, for example, providing new insights or new suggestions for how to solve the problem under study. Thus documentation of the changes in the health situation across repeated studies can progress the development of knowledge (as in the youth health survey). If you are studying an issue that to date has been analyzed only generally, progress may result from studying this issue with a specific subgroup (as in our second example).

Seen more from the internal point of view, i.e. of science itself, research questions should be theoretically based, i.e. embedded in a specific research perspective. In the youth health survey, for example, the basis was provided by a model of the links between social structures, the social position of the individuals in those structures, the social and material environments they live in, and behavioral and physiological factors. These links influence the likelihood of suffering from illness and harm, with their respective social consequences (see Richter et al. 2008, p. 14). From this theoretical model, the concrete research questions in the project and then the items in the questionnaire were derived. In the example of the homeless adolescents, the theoretical background was provided by the approach of social representations (see Flick 1998a; 1998b). The core assumption of this approach is that, depending on social context conditions in different social groups, specific forms and contents of knowledge are developed which occur alongside group specific practices. A further assumption is that topics have specific contents and meanings for each group and its members. These assumptions formed the background for developing the general research questions, which focused on the lived experience of homelessness and the meaning of health in it, and also the specific questions in the interviews.

Research questions should also be suitable for study through the methods of social research. A research question should be formulated in such a way that you can apply one or more of the available methods for answering them – if necessary after adapting or modifying one of them. (We will examine this point further in Chapters 7 and 8.) For example, the research questions of the youth health survey could be investigated by using the questionnaire method. In the second example, the research questions are studied by using two methods, namely (episodic and expert) interviews and participant observation. (These methods will be discussed in detail in Chapter 7.)

Important qualities of research questions are their specificity and their focus. That is, you should formulate your research questions so that they are (a) clear and (b) goal directed, so as to facilitate the exact decisions to be made concerning who or what should be investigated. Note that research questions define not only exactly what to study and how, but also which aspects of an issue may remain excluded. This does not mean that a study cannot pursue several subquestions; it means only that you should ensure that your research questions are not fuzzy and that your study is not overloaded with too many research questions.

Overall, a number of possible basic research questions in social research can be distinguished, notably:

1. What type is it?

2. What is its structure?

3. How frequent is it?

4. What are the causes?

5. What are its processes?

6. What are its consequences?

7. What are people's strategies?

These research questions can be studied at various levels (such as knowledge, practices, situations or institutions) and for different units (for example, persons, groups or communities). Generally speaking, we can differentiate between research questions oriented towards describing states and those describing processes. In the first case, you should describe a certain given state: what types of knowledge about an issue exist in a population? How often can each type of knowledge be identified? In the second case, the aim is to describe how something develops or changes: how has this state come about? Which causes or strategies have led to this state? How is this state maintained – by which structure? What are the causes of such a change? Which processes of development can be observed? What are the consequences of such a change? Which strategies are applied in promoting change?

We can apply these two major types of research questions, i.e. those concerning states and those concerning processes, to a variety of study units (see Flick 2009, pp. 101–2; Lofland and Lofland 1984). For example:

8. Meanings

9. Practices

10. Episodes

11. Encounters

12. Roles

13. Relationships

14. Groups

15. Organizations

16. Lifestyles

We can now begin to differentiate between quantitative and qualitative research in relation to the above lists. The former is more interested in frequencies (and distributions) of phenomena and the reasons for them, whereas qualitative research focuses more on the meanings linked to certain phenomena or on the processes that reveal how people deal with them. In the case of the research projects discussed above, the youth health survey asks for frequencies (item 3 in the first list) and structures (2) in dealing with health in a specific group (14 – here adolescents). The second example focuses on meanings (8) and practices (9) at the level of the participants' strategies (7) with a focus on the types (1) of meanings and the adolescents' practices.

Good Research Questions, Bad Research Questions

Obviously you need not only to have a research question, but also to have a good one. Here we will consider what tends to distinguish good research questions from bad ones.

Good Questions

What characterizes a good research question? First of all, it should be an actual question. For example, 'The living situation of immigrants from Eastern Europe' is not a research question but an area of interest. 'What characterizes the living situation of immigrants from Eastern Europe?' is a question, but it is too broad and unspecific for orienting a research project. It addresses a variety of subgroups implicitly – and supposes that immigrants from say Poland and Russia are in the same situation. Also the term 'living situation' is too broad; it would be better to focus on a specific aspect of the living situation, for example health problems and the use of professional services. An example might then be: 'What characterizes the health problems and the use of professional services of immigrants from Russia?'

There are three main types of research question. (1) Exploratory questions focus on a given situation or a change, for example: 'Has the health situation of homeless adolescents changed in the last 10 years?' (2) Descriptive questions aim at a description of a certain situation, state or process, for example: 'Do homeless adolescents come from broken families?' or 'How do adolescents find themselves homeless?' (3) Explanatory questions focus on a relation. This means that more than just a state of affairs is investigated (so one goes further than asking a question such as 'What characterizes … ?'); rather, a factor or an influence is examined in relation to that situation. For example: 'Is a lack of sufficient specialized health services a major cause of more serious medical problems among homeless adolescents?'

Bad Research Questions

Neuman (2000, p. 144) has characterized what he calls 'bad research questions'. He identifies five types of such questions: (1) questions that cannot be empirically tested or are non-scientific questions, for example, 'Should adolescents live on the streets'; (2) statements that include general topics but not a research question, for example, 'Treatment of drug and alcohol abuse of homeless adolescents'; (3) statements that include a set of variables but no questions, for example, 'Homelessness and health'; (4) questions that are too vague or ambitious, for example, 'How can we prevent homelessness among adolescents?'; (5) questions that still need to be more specific, for example, 'Has the health situation of homeless adolescents become worse?'

As these examples may show, it is important to have a research question that really is a question (not a statement) that can be answered. It should be as focused and specific as possible instead of being vague and unspecific. All the elements of a research question should be clearly spelled out instead of remaining broad and full of implicit assumptions. To test your research question before you do your study, reflect on what possible answers to that question would look like.

The Use of Hypotheses

The more explicit and focused your research question is, the easier it is to develop a hypothesis from it. A hypothesis formulates a relation, which then will be tested empirically. (We saw examples of hypotheses in the case study above of Hollingshead and Redlich's study of social class and mental illness.)

Such relations may, for example, be statements taking the form of 'if, then' or 'the more of one, the more of the other'. The first type of relation is found in a hypothesis like: 'If adolescents come from a lower social class, their risk of certain diseases is much higher.' The second form of relation is illustrated by the following hypothesis: 'The lower the social class adolescents come from, the more often they will fall victim to specific diseases.'

Hypotheses should clarify:

- for which area they are valid (are they assumed to be valid always and everywhere or only under some specific local and temporal conditions?)
- to which area of objects or individuals they apply (e.g. humanity as a whole, or just men, or just women younger than 30 years etc.)
- whether they apply to all objects or individuals in this area
- to which issues they apply, i.e. features of the individuals in the object area.

The example of Hollingshead and Redlich's (1958, p. 10) first hypothesis helps to illustrate these features. Their hypothesis was: 'The prevalence of treated mental illness is related significantly to an individual's position in the class structure.' The two issues are 'social class' and 'illness risk'. They have not delimited their hypothesis to specific local or temporal conditions, but assumed that it should be valid for all the people in a specific social situation (social class).

Furthermore, hypotheses should be clearly formulated in terms of the concepts they use. In our example, it has to be specified what is counted as 'mental illness' (e.g. which diagnoses are used to identify this feature). It should also be defined what 'treated' means (for example, only people who are in treatment with medications, or also those who receive consultations?). Finally, the phrase 'position in the class structure' should be defined.

Hypotheses should also be embedded in a theoretical framework. The authors in our example refer to a number of other studies and theoretical works in which the class structure of America in the 1950s was defined, and do the same for 'mental illness'.

Hypotheses should be specific, i.e. all predictions included should be made explicit. In our example, the authors did not look at a general relation between illness and social situation; instead they had a specific focus on mental illness and on the position in a hierarchy of five social classes, which they had carefully identified and defined beforehand.

Hypotheses should be formulated in relation to the available methods and have empirical links (how and with which methods can they be tested?). In our example, the hypothesis was formulated such that diagnostic instruments could be used for identifying the illness situation of the participants and that household surveys could be used for identifying their position in the social class structure.

Just as the research questions that characterize quantitative research may be distinguished from those that characterize qualitative research, so a distinction between the two types of research may be made in terms of the role of hypotheses. Quantitative research should always start from a hypothesis. The procedures in quantitative research are normally oriented towards testing the hypotheses formulated in advance. This means that you should look for empirical pieces of evidence, which allow hypotheses to be either confirmed or contradicted.

Whereas quantitative research starts from hypotheses, they play a minor role in qualitative research. In qualitative research, the aim is not to test a hypothesis that was formulated in advance. In some cases, in the process of research, working hypotheses may be formulated. For example, first observations of differences in reacting to a symptom of skin diseases by male and female adolescents living on the street may lead to a working hypothesis that reactions to illness in this context are gendered. Such a working hypothesis will provide an orientation, for which you will search for evidence or counter-examples. But the aim will not be to test this hypothesis in the way you test a hypothesis in a quantitative study. In qualitative research, the use of the word 'hypothesis' has more in common with how you would use this term in everyday life than with the principles of testing hypotheses in quantitative research mentioned above.

Each form of social research should start from a clear research question. Different types of research questions suggest one or the other methodological procedure or may only be answered with specific methods. Hypotheses play various roles: in quantitative research they form an indispensable starting point, in qualitative research sometimes a heuristic tool.

Checklist for Formulating Research Questions

Box 2.1 lists points that you should consider when formulating your research question(s). You can use these guideline questions both for planning your own study and for assessing existing studies by other researchers.

BOX 2.1

Checklist for formulating research questions

1. Does your study have a research question, which is spelled out clearly?
2. You should be aware of where your research questions come from and what you want to achieve with them.

- Is your interest in the contents of the research question the main motivation?
- Or is answering the research question more a means to an end, like achieving an academic degree?

---

3. How many research questions has your study?

   - Are there too many?
   - Which is the main question?

4. Can your research question be answered?

   - What could an answer look like?

5. Can your research question be answered empirically?

   - Who can provide insights for that?
   - Can you reach these people?
   - Where can you find such people?
   - Which situations can give you insights for answering your research questions, and are these situations accessible?

6. How clearly is your research question formulated?
7. What are the methodological consequences of the research question?

   - What resources are needed (e.g. how much time is needed)?

8. If necessary for the type of study you chose, did you formulate hypotheses?

   - Are they formulated clearly, in a well-defined and testable way?

9. Can they be tested? By which methods?

Key Points

- **Research questions may be developed from practical problems, they may be rooted in the researcher's personal background, or they may arise from social problems.**
- **Research questions can aim at representative results or at specific subgroups of society.**
- **Research questions should be embedded theoretically and be ready to be empirically studied. Above all, they should be specific and focused.**
- **Quantitative research is based on hypotheses, which are empirically tested. When qualitative research uses hypotheses, it will be based on a different conception of hypotheses, i.e. as working hypotheses.**

▨ ▨ Further Reading ▨

The first and the last texts listed below go into more detail about research questions in standardized research; the other three references discuss this more for qualitative studies.

Bryman, A. (2008) *Social Research Methods*, 3rd edn. Oxford: Oxford University Press.

Flick, U. (2008) *Designing Qualitative Research*. London: Sage. Chapter 1.

Flick, U. (2009) *An Introduction to Qualitative Research*, 4th edn. London: Sage. Chapter 9.

Lofland, J. and Lofland, L.H. (1984) *Analyzing Social Settings*, 2nd edn. Belmont: Wadsworth.

Neuman, W.L. (2000) *Social Research Methods: Qualitative and Quantitative Approaches*, 4th edn. Boston: Allyn and Bacon.

CHAPTER 3
READING AND REVIEWING THE LITERATURE

Chapter Overview

Chapter Objectives

This chapter is designed to help you:

- appreciate the relevance of existing literature for planning your own research project
- recognize that you should be familiar with methodological literature as well as research findings in your area of social research
- understand how to find the relevant literature for your research project.

Table 3.1   Navigator for Chapter 3

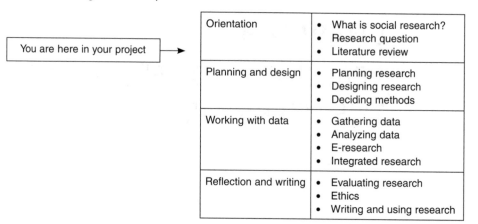

Orientation	• What is social research? • Research question • Literature review
Planning and design	• Planning research • Designing research • Deciding methods
Working with data	• Gathering data • Analyzing data • E-research • Integrated research
Reflection and writing	• Evaluating research • Ethics • Writing and using research

The Scope of a Literature Review

In general, you should begin your research by reading. You should search, find and read what has been published so far about your issue, about the field of your research, and about the methods you wish to apply in your study. (Research methods will be discussed in detail in Chapters 6–10.)

It is also helpful to read to understand the basics of social research (discussed in Chapter 1) and the overall process in which it is applied (discussed in Chapter 4).

Of course, you cannot read everything that has been said about social research. Fortunately, that is not necessary! However, you should find out what is necessary and helpful for doing a research project on your chosen issue and research question.

Sometimes, you may come across the notion that a qualitative study need not be based on knowledge of the existing theoretical or empirical literature. This notion is, however, based on an outdated conception of what it means to develop a theory from empirical data. Today, there is a consensus amongst qualitative, as well as quantitative, researchers that you should be familiar with the ground on which you move and wish to make progress; finding new insights needs to be based on knowing what is known already.

What Do We Mean by 'Literature'?

Types of Literature

When you start researching the issue you have selected, you can search for and find different types of literature and evidence. First, you may find articles in the press. Newspapers and magazines may from time to time take up that issue, perhaps in order to sensationalize it. This kind of literature will help to show what kind of attention the public pays to your issue and perhaps its relevance in public discourse. However, you should be careful not to treat such publications as if they were scientific literature.

Primary and Secondary Sources

You should take care to distinguish between different types of sources. There are primary sources and secondary sources. An example here may explain this distinction. Autobiographies are written by the persons themselves. Biographies are written by an author about a person, sometimes without knowing him or her personally (e.g. if it is a historical person). If we transfer this distinction to scientific literature, a monograph about a theory is a primary source. The same is the case for an article or a book describing the empirical results of a study, when it was written by the researchers who did the study. A textbook summarizing the various theories in a field or giving an overview of the research in a field is a secondary source. Consider too a third example for clarifying this distinction: original documents like death certificates are primary sources, whereas official statistics summarizing causes of death in their frequencies and distribution in groups are secondary sources. The difference rests on how immediate is the access to the reported fact: primary sources are more immediate, whereas in secondary sources usually several primary sources have been summarized, condensed, elaborated or reworked by others.

Original Works and Reviews

Amongst scientific articles, we can distinguish between articles reporting research results for the first time (e.g. Flick and Röhnsch 2007, which reports findings from our interviews with homeless adolescents) and review articles (e.g. Kelly and Caputo 2007, which reviews several studies and gives an overview of health and homeless youth in Canada). Similarly, we can distinguish between original publications about a theory and textbooks that summarize theories across a field.

Amongst review articles, we can further distinguish between narrative and systematic reviews. A narrative review gives an account of the literature in the sense of a general overview (as in Kelly and Caputo 2007) including different types of literature (research, government reports etc.). A systematic review has a stronger focus on research papers, which have been selected according to specific criteria, and has a narrower focus on one aspect of a general issue. An example of a systematic review is the work by Burra et al. (2009) in which a defined range of databases was searched for articles that met a number of criteria predefined in order to assess studies of homeless adults and cognitive functioning. The method of searching (and the choice of databases, criteria, periods of publication etc.) is specified in order to make the review systematic, replicable, and assessable in itself.

An alternative form of summarizing studies is meta-analysis. Again existing research is reviewed, but here the focus is on the effect of a specific variable and how this can be identified in the studies under analysis. For example, Coldwell and Bender (2007) conducted a meta-analysis of studies about the effectiveness of a specific treatment for homeless people with severe mental illness.

Gray Literature

In addition to what is published about your specific issue in books and scientific journals, for example, you should look for 'gray' literature, such as practice reports or reflections of practitioners about their work with this target group. These may be reflections in essay form, and sometimes also empirical reports based on numbers of clients, diagnoses, treatment outcomes and the like. Gray literature is defined as 'literature (often of a scientific or technical nature) that is not available through the usual bibliographic sources such as databases or indexes. It can be both in print and, increasingly, electronic formats' (University Library 2009). Examples are technical reports, preprints, working papers, government documents or conference proceedings. This type of literature will often give you more immediate access to ongoing research or debates as well as institutional ways of documenting and treating social problems. Thus, gray literature can be a valuable first hand source for your study.

Finding Literature

In general, it depends on your topic where you should search for and will find relevant literature. If you want to find out whether your usual library holds the literature you are looking for, you can simply go to the library and check the catalogue. This can be time-consuming and frustrating if the book is not in stock. If you want to find out which library holds the book (or journal) you are looking for, you can access the library's OPAC via the Internet. Therefore, you should go to the homepage of one or more libraries. Alternatively you can use a link to several libraries at the same time. Examples are copac.ac.uk for 24 of the major university libraries and the British Library, or www.ubka. uni-karlsruhe.de/hylib/en/kvk.html for most of the German university libraries and also many in the UK and US. There you can find an exhaustive overview of the existing books or the information for completing your reference lists. Many books are now available as e-books, which you can obtain via your library even from home or from your office.

For journal articles, you can use search engines like wok.mimas.ac.uk. This will lead you to Thomson Reuters' *Social Sciences Citation Index* (also accessible through http://thomsonreuters.com) which you can search by authors, titles, keywords and so on. Other electronic databases that you can use if they fit your issue include for example PubMed and MEDLINE. PubMed comprises more than 20 million citations for biomedical literature from MEDLINE, life science journals and online books. Citations may include links to full-text content from PubMed Central and publisher websites (http://www.ncbi.nlm.nih.gov/pubmed). These are databases that document the publications in journals in the field of health and medicine. 'Athens' is an access management system developed by Eduserv that simplifies access to the electronic resources that your organization has subscribed to. Eduserv is a not-for-profit professional IT services group (www. athensams.net/myathen). If you want to read the whole article, you may need to buy the right to download it from the publisher of the journal or book. More and more articles are available online and for free in open access repositories (e.g. the Social Science Open Access Repository at http://www.ssoar.info/); 'open access' means that everybody can use this literature without paying for access.

You may also use online publication services organized by publishing houses such as Sage (the publisher of this book). At online.sagepub.com you can search all the journals published by this publisher, read abstracts, and get the exact reference dates for free. If you want to read the whole article, you will need to subscribe to the service or the journal, or to buy the article from the homepage (or see whether your library has subscribed to the journal in question).

Of course, a first step in finding your way into the literature can be to use an Internet search engine such as Google, Google Scholar, Intute or AltaVista. That is, however, a first step only and certainly should not be the only one.

Areas of Literature

You will need to review the literature in several areas, notably:

- theoretical literature about the topic of your study
- methodological literature about how to do your research and how to use the methods you choose
- empirical literature about previous research in the field of your study or similar fields
- theoretical and empirical literature to help contextualize, compare and generalize your findings.

Let us examine these areas one by one.

Reviewing Theoretical Literature

Theoretical literature means works about the concepts, definitions and theories used in your field of investigation. Reviewing the theoretical literature in your area of research should help you answer such questions as:

- What is already known about this issue in particular, or the area in general?
- Which theories are used and discussed in this area?
- What concepts are used or debated?
- What are the theoretical or methodological debates or controversies in this field?
- What questions remain open?
- What has not been studied yet?

Here you should synthesize the discussion and the concepts and theories that are used in the field you study. The end point should be that it becomes clear which of these have informed your research interest, your study and its design.

We can distinguish several forms of theories. There are those that conceptualize your issue – such as theories of homelessness in our example – and those that define your research perspective, such as social representations (see Flick 1998a). The latter posit that there are different forms of knowledge about an issue linked to different social backgrounds and that these differences are a starting point for analyzing the issue itself.

Reviewing Methodological Literature

Before deciding on a specific method for your study, you should read the relevant methodological literature. If you want to use, say, focus groups (discussed in Chapter 7) in a qualitative study, you should obtain a detailed overview of the current state of qualitative research, for example by reading a textbook or an introduction to the field. Next you should identify the relevant publications about your method of choice by reading a specialized book, some chapters about it, and prior examples of research that has this method. This will allow you to select your specific method(s) with an appreciation of the existing alternatives. It will also prepare you for the more technical steps of planning to use the method and help you to avoid the pitfalls mentioned in the literature. Such understanding will help you to compose a detailed and concise account of why and how you used your method in your study, when you write your report later on.

Overall, reviewing the methodological literature in your area of research should help you to answer such questions as:

- What are the methodological traditions, alternatives or controversies here?
- Are there any contradictory ways of using the methods, which you could take as a starting point?

Reviewing Empirical Literature

In the next step, you should review and summarize the empirical research that has been done in your field of interest. This should allow you to contextualize your approach and, later, your findings and to see both in perspective.

Reviewing the empirical literature in your area of research should help you to answer such questions as:

- What are the methods that are used or debated here?
- Are there any contradictory results and findings, which you could take as a starting point?

Reading Empirical Studies

When you are reading existing studies, it is important to be able to assess them critically – in terms of both their methods and their results. You should consider, in particular, how far the study has achieved its aims, and how far the study meets appropriate methodological standards in collecting and analyzing data. The checklist in Box 3.1 is designed to help you make critical assessments of the literature you read.

BOX 3.1

Landmarks for assessing existing empirical studies

1. Have the researchers or authors clearly defined the aim and purpose of their study and why they conducted it?
2. What is the research question of the study?
3. Did the author review, integrate and summarize the relevant background literature?
4. Which theoretical perspective is the study based on, and has it been explicitly formulated?
5. Which design was applied in the study? Does it fit the research question that was formulated?
6. Which form of sampling was applied? Was it appropriate to the aims and the research question?
7. Which methods of data collection were applied?

---

8. How far have ethical issues been taken into account (for example, informed consent and data protection)?
9. Which methods have been applied for analyzing the data? Is it clear how they were used and maybe modified?
10. Do methods of data collection and analysis fit together?
11. Which approaches and criteria did the researchers apply for assessing their own ways of proceeding?
12. Have the results been discussed and classified through reference to earlier studies and the theoretical literature about the issue of the study?
13. Does the study define its area of validity and its limits? Have issues of generalization been addressed?

Using the Literature

Ways of Argumentation

There are several ways of using the literature you have found. First, we should distinguish between, on the one hand, listing literature and, on the other, reviewing or analyzing it. Merely listing what you found and where will not be very helpful. In a review or an analysis of the literature you will go further than this by ordering the material and producing a critical assessment of it, involving the selection and weighting of the literature.

The outcomes of your analysis may include a synthesis of the range of literature you draw on and some conclusions. These conclusions should lead the readers to your own research question and research plan and provide a rationale for both.

In most cases, it will not be necessary to give a complete account of what has been published in an area. Rather, you should include what is relevant for your project, for justifying and for planning it.

Sometimes it is difficult to decide when to stop working with the literature. One suggestion here is to continue reading and perhaps summarizing new literature while doing the project. You will in any case have to come back to the literature when discussing your own findings. Another suggestion is that you should set up your research plan after reviewing the literature and then, from the moment you start your empirical work, try not to be distracted by new literature and not to revise your project continuously.

A concise definition of a literature review's contents is provided by Hart:

> **The selection of available documents (both published and unpublished) on the topic, which contain information, ideas, data, and evidence written from a particular standpoint to fulfil certain aims or express certain views on the nature of the topic and how it is to be investigated, and the effective evaluation of these documents in relation to the research being proposed. (1998, p. 13)**

You should demonstrate in the way you present the literature used in your study that you have conducted a skillful search into the existing literature. It should also be evident from your literature review that you have a good command of the subject area and that you understand the issue, the methods you use, and the state of the art of the research in your field.

Documentation and Referencing

It is important to develop a way of documenting what you have read – both the sources and the content. For the latter, you should take notes from the major topics of an article or a book you read and derive from your reading some keywords that you can use for further searches. You should always look at the reference list of what you read as an inspiration for further reading. You can take your notes electronically by writing them in a file with your word processor, for example, or by using commercial software tools like Microsoft OneNote (www.office.microsoft.com/en-us/onenote) or the 'free service for managing and discovering scholarly references' called 'citeulike' (http://www. citeulike.org). These tools allow you to store your search results and notes including the sources, that is where you found your information. Alternatively you can make notes manually on index cards. Be sure to note the source of anything you found noteworthy, so that you can come back to the original article and retrieve the context of an argument or concept.

You also need to decide on a system of referencing your literature in your text and in your reference list. You may, for example, take the way I have referred to other sources in this book and the reference list at the end of it as a model for your own use of literature. This means referring to other authors' works *in the text* as in the following examples:

1. As Allmark (2002) holds ....

2. Such an assessment normally considers three aspects: 'scientific quality, the welfare of participants and ...' (Allmark 2002, p. 9).

3. Gaiser and Schreiner (2009, p. 14) have listed a number of questions ....

4. Flick et al. (2010, p. 755) hold that ....

More generally, this means that you refer to other authors' works by using the format of author's name, followed by the year of the publication in brackets (as in example 1). When you use a direct quote of the authors (their own words), you will have to add the page number (as in example 2). When you refer to a work by two authors, you mention both authors names linked with 'and', the year of publication and the page number (as in example 3). If you refer to a work of three or more authors, you mention the first author's name and add 'et al.' and the year and page number (as in example 4).

In the *list of references* at the end of your work, you will mention the material you used as follows:

1. *Book.* Name(s) and initials of the author(s), year in brackets, book title in italics, publication place, publisher. Example:

   Gaiser, T.J. and Schreiner, A.E. (2009) *A Guide to Conducting Online Research.* London: Sage.

2. *Book chapter.* Name(s) and initials of the author(s), year in brackets, chapter title, 'in' initial and name of editor, '(ed.)', book title in italics, publication place, publisher, first–last page numbers of the chapter. Example:

   Harré, R. (1998) 'The Epistemology of Social Representations', in U. Flick (ed.), *Psychology of the Social: Representations in Knowledge and Language.* Cambridge: Cambridge University Press. pp. 129–37.

3. *Journal article.* Name(s) and initials of the author(s), year in brackets, article title, journal title in italics, volume number, first–last page numbers of the article. Examples:

   Allmark, P. (2002) 'The Ethics of Research with Children', *Nurse Researcher,* 10: 7–19. Flick, U., Garms-Homolová, V. and Röhnsch, G. (2010) '"When they Sleep, they Sleep": Daytime Activities and Sleep Disorders in Nursing Homes', *Journal of Health Psychology,* 15: 755–64.

4. *Internet source.* Name(s) and initials of the author(s), year in brackets, article title, journal title in italics, volume number, link/URL, date at which you accessed the source. Example:

   Bampton, R. and Cowton, C.J. (2002) 'The E-Interview', *Forum Qualitative Social Research,* 3 (2), www.qualitative-research.net/fqs/fqs-eng.htm (accessed 22 February 2005).

Alternatively, you may use footnotes for references. Which format you use will depend on preferences – your own and those of your supervisor or faculty. The major point here is that you must work systematically: every journal article must be referenced in the same format and every book cited consistently.

You can also use bibliographic software like EndNote (www.endnote.com) or ProCite (www.procite.com) for administering your literature. It will take some time to learn how to use the software, and you should begin using it early in your work and continue to use it while reviewing the literature.

Plagiarism and How To Avoid It

In recent years, the topic of plagiarism has attracted increasing attention in the media and in universities. This is a serious issue, not least as it has become technically much easier to copy and use other people's work.

What Is Plagiarism?

Plagiarism means that you simply use formulations by other authors without acknowledging them and making it evident that you have quoted them. There are three main forms of plagiarism (see Neville 2010, p. 29): (1) to copy other people's work (i.e. ideas and/or formulations) without quoting the authors; (2) to blend your own arguments with the ideas and words of other people without referring to them; and (3) to paraphrase other authors' formulations without referring to them and pretending it was your own work.

Inadvertent Plagiarism

Plagiarism can occur for several reasons (see Birnbaum and Goscillo 2009). The most obvious one is that people intend to use someone else's ideas and/ or formulations and to pretend that they were their own ideas or formulations. In this case, they would be aware of their plagiarism. This can also be seen as an intentional deceit. However, there may be other reasons, for example that someone does not know what plagiarism is, or is insecure about how to quote correctly, or is careless in the use of other people's materials. This is referred to as 'inadvertent plagiarism', which in the end will have the same consequences as intentional plagiarism.

Why You Should Avoid Plagiarism

In general, plagiarism offends the rules of good practice in scientific work and it is illegal. Plagiarism detection software is more frequently used now for identifying the use of other authors' formulations without quoting the authors explicitly. Once it is detected, the student or researcher will face very serious consequences, such as failing in their thesis or being removed from the university.

How To Avoid Plagiarism

There are several ways to avoid plagiarism (including inadvertent plagiarism). The first is to pay sufficient attention to including a full list of all the references you have used in writing your thesis. The second is to be very thorough in quoting when you use other people's words. Thus you should put all other authors' wordings you use in quotation marks. You should also use suspension points (ellipsis) when you leave certain words out of a quote, and you should indicate when you add a word by putting it in brackets: for example, 'social research ... [is] valuable'. If you take a sentence from another author and paraphrase it, so that the same content and ideas are still the basis of your formulations, and you do not mention the original author and source, this still constitutes plagiarism. If you take a quotation from a text in which another text was already quoted, you should notify this secondary quotation: for example, '(Author 2, as cited in Author 1, pp. 182–93)'. Both should go in the references.

To avoid plagiarism, you should take your own thoughts and formulations as the basis of your thesis, document your sources carefully, and keep notes of where you have found and read something. Finally, you should use more than one source for developing your arguments. (See Birnbaum and Goscillo's 2009 overview of the issues.)

Checklist for Finding, Assessing and Reviewing Literature

In composing a literature review for an empirical project in social research, you should consider the questions provided in the checklist in Box 3.2.

BOX 3.2

Checklist for the use of literature in social research

1. Is your literature review up to date?
2. Is your literature review connected to the issue of your study?
3. Is your literature review and your writing about it systematic?
4. Does it cover the most important theories, concepts and definitions?
5. Is it based on the most relevant studies in your field of research and about your issue?
6. Did you document how and where you searched for literature?
7. Do your research question and design result from your review of the literature?
8. Are they consistent with it?
9. Have you handled quotations and sources carefully?
10. Did you summarize or synthesize the literature you found?
11. Did you take care to avoid plagiarism?

Key Points

- In social research, the search and analysis of existing literature are the most important steps.
- There are several points in the research process where the use of literature can be helpful and necessary.
- In planning research, in analyzing materials, in writing about findings, you should make use of existing literature about (a) other research, (b) theories, and (c) the methods you use in your study.

The first book listed below is the most comprehensive overview of how to do a literature search for your research, where to look, and how to proceed. The second provides the most comprehensive overview of how to do a literature review for your study, which pitfalls to avoid, and how to write about what you find. The third one explains how to use references and avoid plagiarism. The final one provides information about forms of gray literature and how to use it.

Hart, C. (2001) *Doing a Literature Search*. London: Sage.

Hart, C. (1998) *Doing a Literature Review*. London: Sage.

Neville, C. (2010) *Complete Guide to Referencing and Avoiding Plagiarism*. Maidenhead: Open University Press.

University Library (2009) 'Gray Literature', California State University, Long Beach, www.csulb.edu/library/subj/gray_literature/ (accessed 17 August 2010).

PART II
PLANNING AND DESIGN

Part I of this book was designed to help orient you towards doing your research project. Part II guides you through key steps in the early phases of the project itself, whether it be qualitative or quantitative. Chapter 4 offers an overview of the major steps of the research process. This provides the foundations for planning your research project – the subject of Chapter 5. The first practical step in giving your plans a shape is to write a proposal and design a timescale. For this step it will be helpful to know more about which designs, and which forms of sampling, are used in social research – and the implications of these for your project.

Your project plan will become more concrete as you decide which methods you wish to apply. Chapter 6 outlines the decisions you need to take in the research process when choosing your method, the form of sampling, or the type of research. This should lead you to the reflective stage, half-way through the process, in which you consider again the implications of your research plan, before you start actually to apply concrete methods and begin to work with data.

CHAPTER 4
PLANNING SOCIAL RESEARCH: STEPS IN THE RESEARCH PROCESS

Chapter Overview

Chapter Objectives

This chapter is designed to help you:

- **develop an overview of the process of social research**
- **appreciate, from the point of view of planning, what qualitative and quantitative research have in common and also how they differ**
- **develop an understanding of which steps in the research process you need to take into account when planning your project.**

Table 4.1   Navigator for Chapter 4

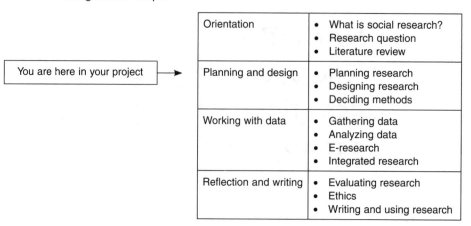

	Orientation	• What is social research? • Research question • Literature review
You are here in your project ⟶	Planning and design	• Planning research • Designing research • Deciding methods
	Working with data	• Gathering data • Analyzing data • E-research • Integrated research
	Reflection and writing	• Evaluating research • Ethics • Writing and using research

Overview of the Research Process

In quantitative research, the research process is planned primarily in a linear way: one step follows another in sequence. In qualitative research, the process is less linear: some of these steps are more closely interlinked, while some are omitted or located at a different stage of the process. This chapter provides an outline of the research processes for both approaches.

The Research Process in Quantitative Research

Some of the processes outlined in this chapter are rather abstract. To understand them, it will help to have a concrete case. Imagine as an example that members of a hospital have noticed that, in its everyday routines, waiting times are too long. For analyzing when and under what conditions delays occur, and for finding a possible solution for the problem, the institution can go two ways: either it commissions a systematic study of situations in which waiting times are produced by a researcher from outside (e.g. a sociologist or psychologist); or someone on the team is commissioned with this task.

Step 1: selection of a research problem

Every research project begins with the identification and selection of a research problem. We have seen in Chapter 2 that the potential sources of research problems are diverse. In our example here, the motivation for the research is a practical problem.

Step 2: systematic searching of the literature

As the next step, a systematic review of the literature is required. This should cover three areas, namely:

- theories about the issue or theoretically relevant literature (see Chapter 3)
- other studies about this or similar issues
- overviews of the relevant literature on research methods in general or on specific methods (see Chapter 6).

In our example, the researchers should look for theoretical models concerning how waiting times emerge and concerning routines in institutions of this kind. They should also focus on empirical studies about the organization of processes in hospitals and comparable service enterprises.

Step 3: formulation of the research question

It is not enough to identify a research problem. For virtually all research problems, one could study a number of research questions – but not all at the same time. Thus, the next steps are: to decide on a specific research question; to formulate it in detail; and, above all, to narrow it down.

In our example the research question could be either 'When do waiting times occur particularly often?' or 'What characterizes situations in which waiting times occur?' Depending on the research questions, qualitative or quantitative research or a specific qualitative or quantitative method will be (more) appropriate (see Chapter 2).

Step 4: formulating a hypothesis

In standardized research, the next step is to formulate a hypothesis. In our example, a hypothesis could be: 'Waiting times occur more often after the weekend compared to other days in the week.' A hypothesis formulates a relation in a way that can be tested (see Chapter 2).

Step 5: operationalization

To test a hypothesis, you first have to operationalize it. This means that you transform it into entities that can be measured or observed or into questions that can be answered. In our example, you should operationalize the term 'waiting time' and define more concretely how to measure it. How much time (e.g. more than 10 minutes) is seen as waiting time? When should one start to measure waiting time? At the same time, for our hypothesis, we should define what is meant by 'after the weekend' (e.g. the time from 9.00 to 12.00 a.m. on Mondays).

Step 6: developing a project plan or research design

The next step is to develop a project plan and a research design for your study. First you choose one of the usual designs, and then define how to standardize and control the processes in your study so that you can interpret any relations you find in an unambiguous way. In our example, you could test our hypothesis first by comparing waiting times at the beginning of the week with those on days like Thursday and Friday (see Chapter 5).

Step 7: sampling

In the next step, you need to define which groups, cases or fields should be integrated into your study. Such decisions of selecting empirical units are made by applying sampling procedures. In our example, you could take a period of four weeks and include all wards of a hospital on Mondays and Thursdays. To define in which wards you collect the data on both days, you can use a randomized procedure (see Chapter 5).

Step 8: selecting the appropriate methods

Next, you need to select appropriate methods for collecting and analyzing data. Here you have three basic alternatives:

- First you can select one of the existing methods. For example, you may use a questionnaire which has been applied successfully by other researchers.
- Often, you will have to modify an existing method. For example, you may skip some questions of that questionnaire or add new ones.
- If that is not sufficient for the study you are planning, the third option is to develop your own method, such as a new questionnaire, or a new methodology, such as a new form of interviewing (see Chapter 7).

In our example, observations in the selected wards would provide time measures of how long patients wait after admission to the hospital for the beginning of assessment or treatment in each ward. At the same time you may interview team members in the ward using a questionnaire addressing how often such waiting times occur according to their experience and what they see as reasons (see Chapter 8).

Step 9: access to the research site

Once you have finished the planning of your study on the methodological level, the next step – especially if you are conducting applied research – is to find a site in which you can do the study. Here, normally four tasks have to be solved. First, if your research is expected to take place in an institution, you have to organize access to the institution as a whole. Second, you should gain access to individuals in the institution who should participate. Third,

you should clarify issues of permission. Fourth, questions of how t̶[...]
participants from any misuse of the data and of anonymity have
answered.

Consider again our example. You have first to find and select appropriat[...]
hospitals (i.e. that are relevant for the research question). In each hospital, the
director's (and perhaps the staff council's) agreement is required before you
can approach single wards and their managers. Once they have agreed to join
the study, you must persuade individual members of the institution to participate in the study – according to the sample that is intended (for example, your
sample should include not only trainees but also experienced doctors and
nurses, maybe even in leading positions). With respect to data protection, you
should clarify how to prevent the identification of single participants within
the institution and of the institution from the outside. For example, you could
develop a system of nicknames or develop a different form of anonymization.
Finally, it should be defined who is allowed to see the data and in what form,
and who is not allowed.

Step 10: data collection

After finishing these methodological preparations, you are ready to start
collecting your data. Basically, you can choose between three main alternatives (see Chapter 7). You may do a survey in one form or another (e.g. with
a questionnaire). You may also do observations (in our example with a
measurement of waiting times). A third alternative is to analyze existing
documents (in our example, documentation of treatment routines could be
analyzed for waiting times, which can be found or reconstructed from those
documents).

Step 11: documentation of data

Before you can analyze your data, you have to decide how to document them.
A survey can be filled in by the participants or alternatively can be completed
by the researcher based on the respondents' answers. The form of documentation will have an influence on the contents and the quality of the data.
Therefore it should be identical for all participants.

The next step is to edit the data. Take the example of questionnaires. First,
the questionnaires themselves need to be entered onto your database.
Questionnaires often include questions with open answers and the respondents could write down their answers in their own words. Then, these answers
have to be coded. This means the answers have to be summarized into
a number of types of answers and each of these types has to be allocated to a
number. This elaboration of the data has an influence on their quality and
should be done in an identical way for each case (each questionnaire, each
observation). This makes the standardization of data and procedures possible
(see Chapter 7).

the data

...stitutes a major step in any project. In standardized studies,
...a is essential. This requires filing responses into categories
...ce or allocated to numerical values (like the alternatives of
...l to 5 in Figure 1.1). If you cannot define the categories in
...(statements, observations) have now to be categorized. This
...similar statements are summarized in a category. This leads
...nt of a category system (see Chapter 8 for more details).
...e study, coding and categorization are followed by statistical
...ample, you could refer the average extension of the measured
...e day of the week when they were measured, or differentiate
them for the wards in which they were measured. Responses in questionnaires are
analyzed for their frequencies and distribution in different professional groups,
for example.

Step 13: interpretation of results

Not every statistical analysis produces meaningful results. How you interpret
any relations that you found in the data therefore becomes very important.
Note that when a statistical analysis shows that certain events occur together
or that they correlate in their frequencies or intensities, this does not provide
any explanation for why this is the case and what that means in concrete
terms. If you show in our example that waiting times on Mondays are much
longer than those on Thursdays, this result does not provide any explanation
why this is so. If estimations of waiting times differ between nurses and physicians, we need to find an explanation for this finding (see Chapter 8).

Step 14: discussion of the findings and their interpretations

The analysis and interpretation of data and results are followed by their discussion. This means that findings are linked to existing literature about the issue (or
the methodology used) and to other relevant studies. Could our study find
anything new? Has it confirmed what was known already, or did contradictions
to existing results emerge? What does it mean if the hypotheses could not be
verified that waiting times occur more often or are more extended after the
weekend, and if this result is different from what was found in other studies?
How do the team members' perceptions of the problem found here differ from
the results of similar surveys by other researchers? In the context of such a discussion you will continue to look for explanations for what you found in your data.

Step 15: evaluation and generalization

From a methodological point of view, this is particularly relevant. You will
critically assess your results and the methods that led to them, which means
checking their reliability and validity (see Chapter 11 for more details). At the

same time you should check what kind of generalization the results justify, asking: can they be transferred to other fields, to other samples, to a specific population (e.g. all nurses, all wards, all hospitals; or all hospitals, physicians etc. of a specific type)? A major element here is to make transparent what the limits of the results are: what could not be found or confirmed, what limits are set for transferability to other institutions, for example (see Chapter 11).

Step 16: presentation of the results and the study

Whether the results of a study are recognized depends mainly on the way in which the results are presented. This means first summarizing the study and its main results and then writing (a report, article, book etc.) about it. Often it is also necessary to select the important information (and to leave out what is less important) due to limits of space and of the reading capacities of potential audiences. In presenting results and the process, it is also important that you manage to make the process of the study transparent for the readers and thus allow them to assess this process and its results (see Chapter 13).

Step 17: using the results

In applied fields of research – such as health – the question arises of how to use the results. This means formulating implications or recommendations. For example, how can you develop suggestions for changing the routines in the ward from analyzing the waiting times in the everyday life of the ward? Using the results can also mean applying them in practical contexts – e.g. that a specific theoretical model (used in the study) is applied in some wards. Finally, 'use' can mean to test the results against the conditions in the practical work and thus to evaluate them critically.

Step 18: develop new research questions

A major outcome of an empirical study is the formulation of new research questions or hypotheses for analyzing the questions that remained unanswered, so that the research in the field can progress.

Step 19: a new study

The new research questions may then lead to a new study.

Summary

These steps of the research process in standardized research can be seen as a linear process as they usually follow one after the other. In practice, however, the process is often more recursive: you will find you often need to go back and revise a step when it becomes evident that an earlier decision does not work in practice. Table 4.2 summarizes the steps of the research process in standardized research. You can use this outline of the research process in standardized or

Table 4.2 Steps of the process in standardized research

1. Selection of a research problem
2. Systematic searching the literature
3. Formulation of the research question
4. Formulating a hypothesis
5. Operationalization
6. Developing a project plan or research design
7. Sampling
8. Selecting the appropriate methods
9. Access to the research site
10. Data collection
11. Documentation of data
12. Analyzing the data
13. Interpretation of results
14. Discussion of the findings and their interpretations
15. Evaluation and generalization
16. Presentation of the results and the study
17. Using the results
18. Developing new research questions
19. A new study

quantitative research for planning your empirical study. It can also be helpful as a framework for reading and assessing existing empirical studies.

The Research Process in Non-standardized Qualitative Research

As we have seen, the process of conducting standardized research may be broken down into a linear sequence of conceptual, methodological and empirical steps. The single steps can be presented and applied one after the other and are more or less independent of each other. In qualitative research, these phases may also be relevant, but they are more closely connected. These connections are illustrated in the following discussion; the step numbers are specified in Table 4.3.

Steps 1–6: selection of a research problem, searching the literature, research question, access

Some of the steps of the process outlined above for standardized research also apply to non-standardized research. In particular, you will have to select a research problem, to formulate a research question, to systematically search the literature and to gain access to the research site here as well before you can collect and analyze data. If we take our example again, you will also formulate a research question if you do a qualitative study: for example, what is characteristic for situations in which waiting times occur (see above). You will review the literature and seek permission for accessing the field. However, you will not formulate a hypothesis to be tested.

Step 7: sampling, collection, documentation and analysis of data

In qualitative research, the remaining parts of the research process tend to be more interrelated than in standardized research. Glaser and Strauss (1967) developed this conception of the research process in their grounded theory approach (see also Strauss and Corbin 1990 and Strauss 1987). The aim of grounded theory within qualitative research makes it very different from standardized research. The aim is to do empirical research in order to use the data and their analysis to develop a theory of the issue under study. Thus theory is not a starting point for research, but rather the intended outcome of the study.

This has consequences for the planning and the steps in the research process. The grounded theory approach gives priority to the data and the field under study over theoretical assumptions. Theories are less applied to the subject being studied. Rather, they are 'discovered' and formulated in working with the field and the empirical data to be found in it. People to be studied are selected according to their relevance to the research topic. They are not (randomly) selected to construct a (statistically) representative sample of a general population. The aim is not to reduce complexity by breaking it down into variables, but rather to increase complexity by including context. Methods also have to be appropriate to the issue under study and have to be chosen accordingly. This approach focuses strongly on the interpretation of data no matter how they were collected. Here the question of which method to use for collecting data becomes minor. Decisions on the data to be integrated and the methods to be used for this are based on the state of the developing theory after analyzing the data already at hand at that moment (see Chapter 8).

In the documentation of data, recording is normally the first step. Interviews, for example, are recorded on tape, mp3 or video. In observations, field notes or protocols are written, sometimes based on video recordings. For interviews, transcription, i.e. making a written text of what was recorded acoustically, is the next step (see Chapter 7).

In qualitative research, interpretation mainly involves analysis of interview statements, events or actions documented in field notes made from observations. Here, you will also look for explanations: why some statements occur in specific contexts together with other statements, or why they occur more often under certain conditions (see Chapter 8).

In our example, researchers would begin with not very structured observations in one ward and talk to members (staff, patients, administrative people etc.) more or less formally. After analyzing their first data, they will select and include another ward and continue observations and conversations there and analyze the resulting materials. They will continue to include further cases and make comparisons among all cases so far included.

Step 8–13: discussion, generalization, use of results and new
research questions

As with standardized research, collection and analysis of the data (see Chapters 7
and 8) will lead to a discussion of the results and their validity and reliability
(see Chapter 11). However, generalization here is meant less in a statistical
than in a theoretical way. Presenting and using the results and developing new
research questions will be the final steps here, too.

The Process of Social Research: Quantitative and Qualitative Research Compared

Qualitative research is compatible with the traditional, linear logic of empirical
(quantitative or standardized) research only to an extent. Interlinking the
empirical steps according to the model of Glaser and Strauss (1967) tends
to be more appropriate to the character of qualitative research, which is
more oriented towards exploring and discovering what is new. Figure 4.1
summarizes the differences between the two approaches. In quantitative
research, you have a linear (step-by-step) process starting from theory and
ending with the validation of the theory based on testing it. Sampling is
usually finished before data collection begins – which means you have fixed
your sampling frame before you send out a questionnaire, for example. It
only makes sense to begin interpreting the data – for example a statistical
analysis – once the data collection has been finished (see Chapters 7 and 8).
Therefore, these steps can be seen as forming a sequence and you will
work through them one after the other, as represented in the upper half of
Figure 4.1.

In qualitative research, these steps are more interlinked. Sampling decisions
are taken during data collection, and interpretation of the data should begin
immediately with the first data – for example, the first interview. From analyzing these data, you may arrive at new decisions, such as whom to interview
next (thus, in this example, the process of sampling continues). You will also
immediately start to compare your data – for example, the second with the
first interview and so on. The aim here is to develop a theory from the empirical material and analysis, where the starting point was preliminary assumptions about the issue you want to study. This process is represented in the
lower part of Figure 4.1.

Despite this interlinkage of some essential steps in the process of the
research, you can also see the qualitative or non-standardized research process
to some extent as forming a sequence of decisions (see Flick 2009). These
decisions refer to selecting the specific method(s) of data collection and analysis
to be applied, the sampling procedure used in the concrete study (see below),
and the ways of documenting and presenting the results.

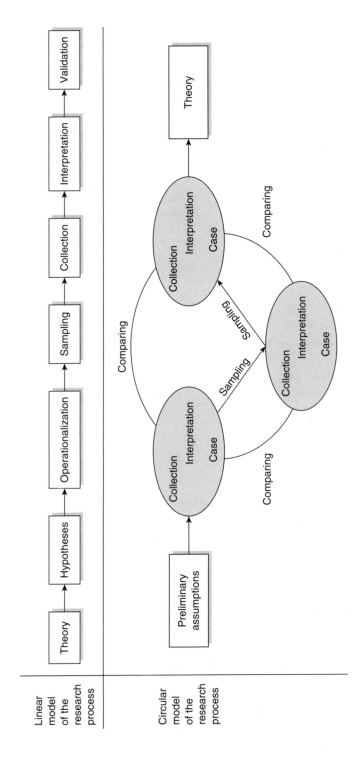

Figure 4.1 Process models of standardized and non-standardized research (Flick 2009, p. 95)

Table 4.3   Steps of the process in standardized and non-standardized research

Standardized research	Non-standardized research
1. Selection of a research problem	1. Selection of a research problem
2. Systematic searching the literature	2. Systematic searching the literature
3. Formulation of the research question	3. Formulation of the research question
4. Formulating a hypothesis	4. Developing a project plan or research design
5. Operationalization	5. Selecting the appropriate methods
6. Developing a project plan or research design	6. Access to the research site
7. Sampling	7. Sampling, data collection, documentation of data, analysis of data, comparison, sampling, data collection, documentation of data, analysis of data, comparison …
8. Selecting the appropriate methods	
9. Access to the research site	
10. Data collection	
11. Documentation of data	
12. Analyzing the data	
13. Interpretation of results	
14. Discussion of the findings and their interpretations	8. Discussion of the findings and their interpretations
15. Evaluation and generalization	9. Evaluation and generalization
16. Presentation of the results and the study	10. Presentation of the results and the study
17. Using the results	11. Using the results
18. Developing new research questions	12. Developing new research questions
19. A new study	13. A new study

Table 4.3 juxtaposes the concepts of the research process of standardized and non-standardized research as outlined in this chapter in a comparative way. This indicates the main differences in the research processes between qualitative and quantitative research. These mainly involve the degree of standardization of procedures. This table also provides a basis for planning the steps of your own project and for developing an adequate design for your study (see Chapter 5 for more detail on this).

Checklist for Planning an Empirical Study

For planning your own empirical project, you should take into account the aspects shown in Box 4.1 and find answers to the questions that arise. This checklist may help you in planning your own study, but you can also use it for assessing the existing studies of other researchers.

BOX 4.1

Checklist for planning an empirical study

1. Be aware which steps in the research process are appropriate for the kind of study you plan.
2. Seek to establish whether the existing knowledge and research about your issue are sufficient for planning and doing a standardized study in which you will test hypotheses.
3. Or seek to clarify whether the empirical and theoretical knowledge about the issue of your study is so limited or has so many gaps that it makes sense to plan and do a non-standardized qualitative study.
4. Check the procedures in your plan for their soundness. Does the methodological plan of your study fit (a) the aims of your study, (b) its theoretical background, and (c) the state of research?
5. Will this kind of research process be compatible with the issue you want to study and with the field in which you intend to do your research?

Key Points

- **Quantitative and qualitative studies run through some similar and some different steps in the research process.**
- **Quantitative research is planned in a linear process.**
- **In qualitative research, in many cases the steps in the research process will be interlinked.**
- **Having a firm grasp of the steps that comprise the research process in each case will give you a basis for planning your own study.**

■ ■ Further Reading ■

Overviews of planning social research in a quantitative approach are discussed in the first and last textbooks, while the other two focus on this issue for qualitative studies.

Bryman, A. (2008) *Social Research Methods*, 3rd edn. Oxford: Oxford University Press.

Flick, U. (2004) 'Design and Process in Qualitative Research', in U. Flick, E. v. Kardorff and I. Steinke (eds), *A Companion to Qualitative Research*. London: Sage. pp. 146–52.

Flick, U. (2009) *An Introduction to Qualitative Research*, 4th edn. London: Sage. Part 3.

Neuman, W.L. (2000) *Social Research Methods: Qualitative and Quantitative Approaches*, 4th edn. Boston: Allyn and Bacon.

CHAPTER 5
DESIGNING SOCIAL RESEARCH

Chapter Overview

Chapter Objectives

This chapter is designed to help you:

- understand how and why to write a proposal and develop a timescale
- develop an overview of the most important research designs
- understand the procedures for selecting study participants
- appreciate the special features of evaluational research.

Table 5.1 Navigator for Chapter 5

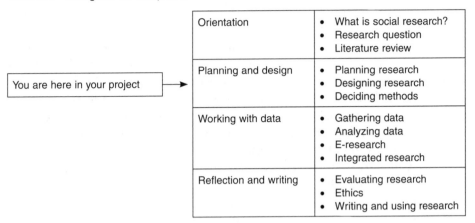

Orientation	• What is social research? • Research question • Literature review
Planning and design	• Planning research • Designing research • Deciding methods
Working with data	• Gathering data • Analyzing data • E-research • Integrated research
Reflection and writing	• Evaluating research • Ethics • Writing and using research

You are here in your project →

Chapter 4 provided an outline of the research process. We can now use this to provide a foundation for research planning.

Writing a Proposal for a Research Project

Planning social research becomes more concrete when you are preparing the final thesis in a university program. In most cases, you will need a proposal for enrolling for your thesis as well as for applying for a grant. If this is not required, writing a proposal can nevertheless be an important and helpful step for planning your project and for estimating whether it is realistic under the given conditions like time – but also the skills you have. A proposal for an empirical project should include topics and subitems as follows (see Table 5.2).

In the introduction you should briefly outline the background of the project (why you intend to do it) and the relevance of the topic. In the description of the research problem, you should summarize the state of the art in research and in the literature and derive your own research interest from the gaps that became evident in this summary. What emphasis you should put on each of the points will depend on the type of study you plan. For a quantitative study, the literature review will be more extensive than for a qualitative study. The purpose of the study and the aim of doing it should be briefly described. A major point in any proposal is the research question (see Chapter 2), if possible and necessary divided into major questions and subquestions.

Whether or not it is necessary to formulate a hypothesis will depend on the type of research you intend to do. For a quantitative study, this step should always be included. In any case, you need to describe the methodological procedures you intend to apply. For qualitative research, you should give a short justification of why you will use qualitative methods and why you will work with this specific method. In quantitative research, such a justification is often not seen as necessary. The research strategy – an exploratory, a hypotheses testing or an evaluative approach – should be described as well. In the proposal, you should outline the research design (see below) in its main features: which sample will be included, how big will it be, and on which comparative perspective is it based? In the next step, your proposal should include a short description and justification of which methods you intend to use for collecting your data (see Chapters 6 and 7) and for analyzing them (see Chapters 6 and 8) and how you will assess the quality of your study (see Chapter 11). In many contexts, it is a requirement that a proposal covers the ethical issues (data protection, non-maleficence, informed consent etc.: see Chapter 12) and demonstrates how the researchers intend to take them into account in doing their project.

In this context, you should consider what results you expect from your study and what will be their relevance in the light of earlier results and practical issues (see Chapters 1 and 13). You will elaborate the state of research in writing your thesis or the final report of your research in more detail. Nevertheless, I would strongly recommend that you get a first overview of the literature while planning your project in order to ensure that you don't adopt a research question which has already been answered before to a sufficient extent. Finally, you should briefly discuss the practical conditions of doing your study. For this purpose, it will be helpful to develop a timescale (see below) and to outline your own experience with research. At the end, a preliminary list of references should be added.

Spelling out the topics listed in Table 5.2 is helpful for developing your research project (and the thesis based on it) and should make successful work more likely.

Table 5.2 Model for a proposal structure

1. Introduction
2. Research problem
   (a) Existing literature
   (b) Gaps in the existing research
   (c) Research interest
3. Purpose of the study
4. Research questions
5. Methods and procedures
   (a) Characteristics of qualitative research and why it is appropriate here
   (b) Research strategy
   (c) Research design

Table 5.2 (Continued)

> (i) Sampling
> (ii) Comparison
> (iii) Expected number of participants, cases, sites, documents
>
> (d) Methods of data collection
> (e) Methods of data analysis
> (f) Quality issues

6. Ethical issues

7. Expected results

8. Significance, relevance, practical implications of the study

9. Preliminary pilot findings, earlier research, experience of the researcher(s)

10. Your own experience with doing social research

11. Timeline, proposed budget

12. References

Developing a Timescale

A timescale for your project should outline both the steps required in the research process (see Chapter 4) and the time estimated for each step. You may also indicate milestones, which means the outcomes that are to be expected when each step is completed. In Box 5.1 you will find an example of a timescale for a qualitative study using interviews and participant observation (it comes from our study on homeless adolescents' health concepts, see Flick and Röhnsch 2007). Such a timescale can have two functions. In a proposal forming an application for funding, it will demonstrate how much time is needed and for what in order to convince the funding agency that the budget you ask for is justified. In designing the research (see below), the timescale will help to orient you towards planning the project.

BOX 5.1

Timescale for a research project (Flick and Röhnsch 2007)

Work step	Month of project																							
	[1]	[2]	[3]	[4]	[5]	[6]	[7]	[8]	[9]	[10]	[11]	[12]	[13]	[14]	[15]	[16]	[17]	[18]	[19]	[20]	[21]	[22]	[23]	[24]
Literature research	■	■	■	📖																				
Development of instruments and pre-test		■	■																					

Work step	Month of project																							
	[1]	[2]	[3]	[4]	[5]	[6]	[7]	[8]	[9]	[10]	[11]	[12]	[13]	[14]	[15]	[16]	[17]	[18]	[19]	[20]	[21]	[22]	[23]	[24]
Fieldwork: finding participants and data collection (e.g. interviews)				■	■	■																		
Transcription					■	■	■	■	■															
Fieldwork: participant observation				■	■	■	■	■																
Writing observation protocols				■	■	■	■	■	■															
Analysis of interviews							■	■	■	■	■	■	■	■	■	■	📖							
Analysis of observation protocols									■	■	■	■	■	■	■	■	■	■						
Linking back the results to the literature																■	■	■	■	■				
Final report and publications																			■	■	■	■		📖

📖 = Milestones

For making the research (and, beforehand, the proposal) work, the following guidelines should be kept in mind:

- You should try to make the design of your research and the methods as explicit, clear and detailed as possible.
- The research questions, and the relevance of planned procedures and expected data and results for answering them, should also be as explicit and clear as possible.
- The study and the expected results and implications should be placed in their academic and practical contexts.
- Ethics and procedures should be reflected as far as possible.

- Methods should be made explicit not only in the how (of their use) but also in the why (of their selection).

- Ensure that plans, timelines, existing experiences and competences, methods and resources all fit into a sound program for your research.

Designing a Study

A central concept in research planning is the research design, which Ragin defines as follows:

> Research design is a plan for collecting and analyzing evidence that will make it possible for the investigator to answer whatever questions he or she has posed. The design of an investigation touches almost all aspects of the research, from the minute details of data collection to the selection of the techniques of data analysis. (1994, p. 191)

When you construct or use a specific research design, the aims are first to make answering the research question possible and to control the procedures. 'Control' here refers to the means of keeping the conditions of the study constant, so that differences in the replies of two participants can be rooted in their own differences (in their attitudes, for example) and do not result from the fact that the participants were asked in different ways. This in turn requires you to keep the conditions of the study constant and to define your sampling procedures (who is selected and why: see below).

In quantitative research, another aim of research designs is to control external variables. This refers to factors which are not part of the relations that are studied but influence the phenomenon under study. If you study the effects of a medication on the course of a certain disease, you should make sure that other factors (e.g. specific features of some patients, or eating during the treatment) do not influence the course of the disease. One way to control such external variables is to use homogeneous samples (see below). Thus you will select patients who are very similar in their most relevant characteristics (e.g. men of 50–55 years with specific professions). The disadvantage of such a homogeneous sample is that you can only generalize the results to people who also fulfill the criteria of the sample (men of 50–55 years with specific professions). It is more consistent to draw a random sample (see below). The disadvantage here is that the sample will need to be rather sizeable if specific features (of subgroups of people) are to be represented in it.

A second way of controlling external influences is to use consistent methods of data collection. This means that the data are collected from all participants in the same way in order to guarantee that differences in the results come from differences in the participants' attitudes and not from differences in the data collection situation. Some of the most common designs in empirical research will be presented below.

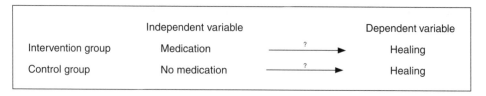

Figure 5.1   Control group design

Research Designs in Standardized Research

Control group designs

Let us again begin with an example. In the practice of a hospital, it might be observed that for patients who received a certain medication, the symptoms are reduced and have disappeared by the end of the treatment. This indicates that healing has occurred. To discover whether the improvement of the patients' state is caused by the medication under study, control group designs are often applied. In such a design the medicament is labeled the independent variable. The improvement in the patient's state that it produces is the dependent variable. Note that the term 'dependent' variable refers to the variable which is caused or changed by another variable (the independent variable). In our example, the healing depends on giving the medication. Thus the medication is labeled independent, as it is not influenced by the other variable in this setting; the healing has no effect on the medication.

To find out whether such a relation really exists – that the healing depends on the medication (and not on something else) – you will apply a control group design. Two groups of patients are selected; the members of these groups are comparable in features like diagnoses, age and gender. The intervention group receives the medicament under study. The control group is not given the medicament or receives a placebo (a pill without substance and effects). After the end of the treatment in the first group, you can compare the two groups for whether the treatment was more successful here than in the control group. If in the end both groups show the same changes, the effect cannot be attributed to the medication (see Figure 5.1).

Experimental designs

Control group designs also form the basis of experimental research. Here, to continue our example, the aim is less to find out the effects of a medicament than to test the effects of taking it. Experiments consist of goal-directed acts upon study groups in order to analyze the effects of these acts. An experimental design includes at least two experimental groups, to which the participants are randomly allocated. The independent variable is manipulated by the researcher (Diekmann 2007, p. 337).

In an experimental study, in contrast to a control group design, the medication (independent variable) is given or changed for research purposes. In order to be sure that an observed effect (of healing for example – dependent variable) does not come from the patient knowing 'I am treated', participants are not informed in such a study as to whether they are given the medication or a placebo without effect. Because the patient does not know whether he or she has received medication or a placebo, this design is also called a blind test.

If, in our example, a clear difference becomes evident – that the healing effects in the intervention group can be documented for significantly more patients than in the control group – this could still be due to another influence. It might not be the medication in itself that produces the healing effect, but rather the attention by nurses or doctors associated with the administration of the pill. To be able to exclude this influence, in many medication trials a double blind test is applied. Here both groups receive treatments, the intervention group with the medication and the control group with a placebo, which look identical. To avoid any influence by the nurses or doctors giving the medication – for example, any subconscious signals sending the message that the placebo is without effect anyway – you would not inform the doctors and nurses which is the pill and which the placebo. Neither patients nor doctors and nurses know who has received the medication and who was given the placebo. Thus this design is called a double blind test.

To exclude the influences of other variables as far as possible, experiments are often conducted in laboratories. They are run not in the service routines or in the everyday life of the hospital, but in an artificially designed surrounding. This allows control or exclusion of any external influences as far as possible. The disadvantage is that the results are difficult to transfer to contexts outside the laboratory – i.e. to everyday life.

Pre–post design

Another way of excluding external influencing variables is to do a pre–post measurement with both groups. First the initial situation is measured in both groups (pre-test measurement). Then the study group is given the treatment (intervention). Afterwards, in both groups, the post-test situation is documented. A problem here is that the first measurement might influence the second one, for example due to a learning effect. This means that experience with the tests, measurements or questions might facilitate the reaction in the second measurement – e.g. a question can be answered more easily (see Figure 5.2).

Cross-sectional and longitudinal studies

The designs presented so far aim at controlling the conditions of the study. This allows capturing the state at the moment of the study. Most studies are planned to take a picture of the moment: interviews or surveys, say, are done at one moment in time, for example to analyze the attitude of a specific group

| Pre-test | Intervention | Post-test |

Figure 5.2   Pre–post design

(the French) towards a specific object (a political party). Such picturing is based on a cross-sectional design: a measurement is done to capture the state at a specific moment. In most cases you take a comparative perspective, for example by comparing the attitudes of several subgroups – e.g. those who voted for one political party and those who voted for another party in an election.

However, if processes, courses or developments form the focus of the study, such a cross-sectional design will not be sufficient. Instead you should plan a longitudinal study for documenting a development – for example the attitudes of one or more groups over the years. This attitude is measured repeatedly: for example, the same instruments are used every two years with the same samples in order to find out how attitudes towards a specific political party have changed. If you repeat such surveys not just once but several times, you can produce time series or trend analyses for documenting long term changes in political attitudes.

Longitudinal studies are also interesting if you want to study the influence of a specific event on attitudes or the life course. An example is how the mental illness of a family member develops and how it influences the other family members' attitude to mental illness in general over the years. A problem in this context could be that this process of changing attitudes can only be covered in a comprehensive way when the attitude has been measured for the first time before the event occurred. If this is not possible, often a retrospective study is done instead: after the disease has been diagnosed, the family members are asked about which changes in their attitude to mental illness they had before the illness and which they have now.

Non-standardized Research Designs

Qualitative or non-standardized research pays less attention to research designs and even less to controlling conditions by constructing specific designs. In general, the use of the term 'research design' here refers to planning a study: how to plan data collection and analysis and how to select empirical 'material' (situations, cases, individuals etc.) in order to be able to answer the research question in the available time and with the available resources.

The literature on research designs in qualitative research (see also Flick 2004b, 2008b or 2009, Chapter 12) addresses the issue from two angles. Creswell (1998) presents a number of basic models of qualitative research from which the researchers can select one for their concrete study. Maxwell (2005) discusses the parts of which a research design is constructed. (See Flick 2009, Chapter 12 for more details of what follows.)

Case studies

The aim of case studies is precise description or reconstruction of cases (for more detail see Ragin and Becker 1992). The term 'case' is understood rather broadly here. You can take persons, social communities (e.g. families), organizations, and institutions (e.g. a nursing home) as the subject of a case analysis. Your main problem then will be to identify a case that would be significant for your research question and to clarify what else belongs to the case and what methodological approaches its reconstruction requires. If your case study is concerned with the chronic illness of a child, you have to clarify, for instance, whether it is enough to observe the child in the treatment environment. Do you need to integrate an observation of the family and its everyday life? Is it necessary to interview the teachers and/or fellow pupils?

Comparative studies

Often, rather than observe some single case as a whole and in all its complexity, you will instead observe a multiplicity of cases, focusing on particular aspects. For example, you might compare the specific content of the expert knowledge of a number of people in respect of a concrete experience of illness. Or you might compare biographies of people with a specific illness and the subsequent course of life. Here arises the question of the selection of cases in the groups to be compared.

A further problem is what degree of standardization or constancy is required for those conditions that you are not focusing on. For example, to be able to show cultural differences in the views of health among Portuguese and German women in one study we conducted, we selected interview partners from both cultures. We had to ensure that in as many respects as possible they lived under at least very similar conditions (e.g. big city life, comparable professions, income and level of education) in order to be able to relate differences to the comparative dimension of 'culture' (see Flick 2000b).

Retrospective studies

Case reconstruction is characteristic of a great number of biographical investigations that examine a series of case analyses in a comparative, typology-oriented or contrastive manner (see Chapter 8). Biographical research is an example of a retrospective research design in which, retrospectively from the point in time when the research is carried out, certain events and processes are analyzed in respect of their meaning for individual or collective life histories. Design questions in relation to retrospective research involve the selection of informants who will be meaningful for the process to be investigated. They also involve defining appropriate groups for comparison, justifying the boundaries of the time to be investigated, checking the research question, and deciding which (historical) sources and documents (see Chapter 7) should be used in addition to interviews. Another issue is how to consider the influences of present views on the perception and evaluation of earlier experiences.

Snapshots: analysis of state and process at the time of the investigation

Qualitative research will often focus on snapshots. For example, you might collect different manifestations of the expertise that exists in a particular field at the time of the research in interviews and compare them to one another. Even if certain examples from earlier periods of time affect the interviews, your research does not aim primarily at the retrospective reconstruction of a process. It is concerned rather with giving a description of circumstances at the time of the research.

Longitudinal studies

Qualitative research may involve longitudinal studies, in which one returns to analyze a process or state again at later times of data collection. Interviews are applied repeatedly and observations are extended over sometimes a very long period.

Figure 5.3 presents the basic designs of qualitative research again.

In what follows, I will examine one aspect of planning empirical studies in more detail, namely the question of how to select the participants for a study so that the insights produced will be (generally) valid and representative. Either you start from a big group (e.g. German youth) which cannot be studied empirically in its entirety, and select the cases you study so that the results can later be generalized to the original group or population. This addresses the issue of statistical sampling in quantitative research. Or you want to select those cases which are particularly relevant for answering your research question. This addresses the issue of purposive sampling in qualitative research.

Sampling

Most empirical studies involve making a selection from a group for which propositions will be advanced at the end. If you study the professional stress of nurses, you will address a selection from all the nurses (in the UK, for example) which is too big a group to be studied. All the nurses are the basic population, from which you will draw a sample for your study.

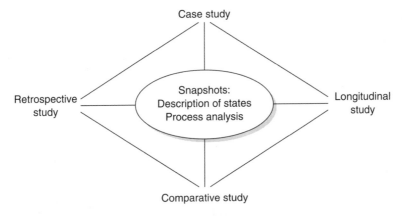

Figure 5.3   Basic designs in qualitative research (Flick 2009, p. 140)

> **The population is the mass of individuals, cases, events to which the statements of the study will refer and which has to be delimited unambiguously beforehand with regards to the research question and the operationalization. (Kromrey 2006, p. 269)**

In exceptional cases you can use the strategy of complete collection, which means all cases of a population are included in the study. The other extreme is to select and study one person in a single case study (see above). In most studies, a sample will be drawn according to one or other of the procedures described below and the results are then generalized to the population. Arguments against complete collection and for sampling are that the latter saves you time and money and allows more accuracy.

Here you should distinguish between sampling elements and the empirical units. The latter refers to the units which you include in your data collection. For example, the sampling elements are several hospitals in which you want to study the emergence of waiting times. The empirical units are specific situations in these hospitals in which waiting times occur or are to be expected, e.g. situations of preparing for surgery. The problem of sampling arises in qualitative and in quantitative studies in a similar way, but it is addressed differently: statistical sampling is typical of quantitative research, while qualitative researchers apply procedures of purposive or theoretical sampling.

Sampling in Quantitative Research

There are a number of requirements for a sample. The sample should be a minimized representation of the population in terms of the heterogeneity of the elements and the representativeness of the variables. The elements of the sample have to be defined. The population should be clear and empirically defined. This means the population has to be clearly limited. Here, we find two alternatives for sampling: random and non-random procedures.

Simple random samples

Often you do not know enough about the constitution or features of the population to make a purposive selection such that the sample is a minimized representation of the population. In such cases it is suggested to draw a random sample. Here, we can distinguish between simple and complex random sampling. An example of simple random sampling is selecting from a card index. The elements of a population are documented in a list or a card index; for example, all inhabitants of a town are registered in a card index at the residents' registration office. You can use this card index for drawing a simple or a systematic random sample. A simple random sample results when every element in the sample is drawn independently in a random process from the population. One example here is to use a lottery drum: all postcards in a competition are in a lottery drum and are drawn one after the other. Each time the cards are mixed again before the next is drawn. If we transfer this principle to drawing a sample from a residents' registration file, you would give a number to every entry in this file and make a ticket for each number. All the tickets are mixed in a lottery drum. One after the other you would draw numbers until your sample is complete. This process can be simulated with a computer.

For very large populations, systematic sampling is suggested. The first choice (the first case, the first index card) is selected randomly (by having a throw or by randomly picking a number from a random number table). The other elements to be included in the sample are defined systematically. For example, from a population of 100,000, you draw a sample of 1000 elements. The first number is selected randomly between 1 and 100, e.g. 37. Then, you include systematically every 100th case in the sample (i.e. the cases 137, 237, 337, ..., 99,937).

One disadvantage of such a simple random sample is the difficulty in representing relevant small subpopulations in the sample. In such sampling you will also neglect the context of the single case, i.e. its features beyond the main criterion for its selection, and will lose that for the analyses. To give an example for the first disadvantage: in a population of nurses from which you want to draw a sample, you find an ethnic minority which could be of particular interest for your study. In simple random sampling, the chances are very limited that members of that subgroup will be included at all or in sufficient number. Context information (concerning, say, ethnic minorities) cannot be taken into account systematically in a simple random sample without neglecting its principle.

Systematic random sampling: stratified and cluster sampling

Therefore, more complex or systematic forms of random sampling may be applied by drawing a stratified sample. The intention often is to be able to analyze the data in the sample separately for specific groups – e.g. to compare the data of the ethnic minority with those of all participants. Accordingly, you will divide the population into several subpopulations (in our example according to the members' ethnic background). From each of these subpopulations you will then draw a (in most cases simple) random sample. In our example, you would divide the population of the nurses according to their ethnic backgrounds and then draw a random sample from the subgroups of the British, Turkish, African, Korean etc. nurses. If you apply the same sampling procedure to every group and if you take into account the proportion of each subgroup in the population, you will receive a proportionally stratified sample. In the sample, the percentage of each subgroup is exactly the same as in the population. In our example: if you know that the proportion of Turkish nurses is 20% of all nurses and that of the Koreans is 5%, you will draw random samples for each of these groups in the population until you have 20% Turkish and 5% Korean nurses in your sample.

In small samples, the consequence here is that the real number of cases with a Korean background will be very small – for example, one case in a sample size of $n = 20$. This is not sufficient for statistical analyses comparing Korean and other nurses. As a solution, you could extend the sample so that in every subsample there will be enough cases, which will increase the financial and time resources necessary for the study. An alternative is to build a disproportionate stratified sample; this would balance the under-representation of a subsample. The sample is drawn in such a way that for every subsample the same number of cases is included. In our example, you would aim at a sample size of 20 cases and in each subgroup you would apply random sampling until you have five cases for each group (British, Turkish, African, Korean nurses).

For taking contexts more strongly into account than in simple random samples, cluster sampling can be applied. In research in schools, you will select the students not as empirical elements but in subgroups like school classes, in which you will collect data and make statements for every member (the individual students). The students are the empirical elements (to whom you apply a questionnaire), the classes are the sampling elements. You will only talk of a cluster sample when the empirical units are not the clusters themselves (i.e. the classes) but their single members (the pupils).

You can also draw samples in stages, working on a number of levels. For example, you will first make an overview of the location of all schools for nursing, from which you draw a simple random sample. Then you will divide the selected schools into units roughly of the same size, e.g. classes. From all of these classes, you draw another random sample. This sample is then divided into subgroups according to their performance, for example (such as all students with an average grade of better than 5, all with grades between 4 and 2, and all with 2 and worse). From these subgroups you will again draw a random sample, which finally constitutes the group of those treated with a questionnaire.

The big advantage of random sampling is that the samples drawn in this way are representative for all features of the empirical elements. A non-random sample can only claim to be representative for the features according to which it was drawn.

Non-random sampling: haphazard, purposive and quota sampling

It is not always possible or even desirable to draw a random sample. Nevertheless, sampling should be as systematic as possible. A relatively unsystematic method of sampling is haphazard sampling. Here we do not have a defined sampling plan or framework, according to which we decide which elements of the population are integrated in the sample. An example is the person-on-the-street interview, in which everyone passing by at a specific moment and ready to be interviewed is integrated in the sample. The decision is taken haphazardly, i.e. not according to defined criteria.

A different strategy is purposive sampling. For example, you do a study in which experts will be interviewed, and define criteria according to which someone is an expert for the issue of the study or not. Then you will search for individuals who meet these criteria. If their number is big enough, you can apply a questionnaire to them, which will be analyzed statistically. The sampling from the population of all experts for this issue is not random. Due to the applied criteria, this is not a haphazard sampling either. In most cases, however, you have to assume that the experts are typical cases (of experts). Then the problem arises, how to decide whether the individual case is a typical case or not. Often, this definition is set by the researchers. For this definition, they need enough knowledge about the population to be able to decide whether a case is typical or not. Whether experts are typical experts for this issue can often only be decided at the end of the study by comparing them with other experts. Therefore the sampling here is often done by using substitute criteria – e.g. professional experience in a specific position. But this again assumes a link between expertise and professional experience.

In addition, you may apply the concentration principle. This means you focus in the sampling on those cases which are particularly important for the issue of the study. The cases are selected according to their relevance – either the very rare cases, which have the strongest influence on the process under study, or those cases that can be found most often, for example.

Survey research often uses the technique of quota sampling. Here, specific features (e.g. age and gender) are defined by which the participants should be characterized. For these features, you will then define quotas of the values of these features, which will be represented in the sample at the end. For example, the distribution of gender might be four to six, i.e. in 10 interviews four men and six women will be included. Age groups might be distributed in a way that in 10 interviews two participants are younger than 30 years, three are older than 60, and five are between 30 and 60 years. In these quotas, you will then search participants haphazardly – i.e. not randomly. If this procedure works, some conditions should be specified. The distribution of the quota features (in our example age and gender) in the population has to be known. A sufficient relation between the quota features and the features to be studied (e.g. health behavior) has to be given or assumed. The quota features have to be easy to assess.

Finally, you can use the principle of snowballing: that is, you ask your way from the first participant to the next ('Who do you think could be relevant for this study, too?'). Often, for practical reasons, this is the best or only way to arrive at a sample. The representativity of this sample, however, is rather limited.

Sampling Strategies in Qualitative Research

In qualitative research, some of the sampling strategies discussed in the previous paragraphs are applied. Others, however, such as random sampling, are seldom found. Here as well you can use quotas (of age or gender) or haphazard or purposive sampling (of experts for example). Principles of snowballing or of concentration are used as well. Some unique principles can refine and systematize these approaches for the specific aims of qualitative research.

Theoretical sampling

If the aim of the research is to develop a theory, strategies of sampling are likely to be based on 'theoretical sampling' as developed by Glaser and Strauss (1967). Decisions about choosing and putting together empirical material (cases, groups, institutions etc.) are made in the process of collecting and interpreting data. Glaser and Strauss describe this strategy as follows:

> **Theoretical sampling is the process of data collection for generating theory whereby the analyst jointly collects, codes and analyses his data and decides what data to collect next and where to find them, in order to develop his theory as it emerges. This process of data collection is controlled by the emerging theory. (1967, p. 45)**

Here you select individuals, groups and so on according to their (expected) level of new insights for the developing theory in relation to the state of theory elaboration so far. Sampling decisions aim at the material that promises the greatest insights, viewed in the light of the material already used, and the knowledge drawn from it. The main question for selecting data is: '*What* groups or subgroups does one turn to *next* in data collection? And for *what* theoretical purpose? ... The possibilities of multiple comparisons are infinite, and so groups must be chosen according to theoretical criteria' (1967, p. 47).

Sampling and the integration of further material are complete when the 'theoretical saturation' of a category or group of cases has been reached (i.e. nothing new emerges any more). In contrast to a statistically oriented sampling, theoretical sampling does not refer to a population whose extent and features are already known. You also cannot define in advance how big the sample to

Table 5.3 Theoretical and statistical sampling

Theoretical sampling	Statistical sampling
Extent of the basic population is not known in advance	Extent of the basic population is known in advance
Features of the basic population are not known in advance	Distribution of features in the basic population can be estimated
Repeated drawing of sampling elements with criteria to be defined again in each step	One-shot drawing of a sample following a plan defined in advance
Sample size is not defined in advance	Sample size is defined in advance
Sampling is finished when theoretical saturation has been reached	Sampling is finished when the whole sample has been studied

Source: Wiedemann 1995, p. 441

be studied has to be. The features of both the population and the sample can only be defined at the end of the empirical study on the basis of the theory that was developed in it.

The main features of theoretical and statistical sampling strategies are compared in Table 5.3.

Purposive sampling

Patton (2002) suggests the following variants of purposive sampling:

- Extreme cases, which are characterized by a particularly long process of development or by the failure or success of an intervention.

- Typical cases, which are typical for the average or the majority of potential cases. Here, the field is explored rather from the inside, from the center.

- Maximum variation sampling includes a few cases which are as different as possible, for analyzing the variety and diversity in the field.

- Intensity sampling includes cases which have a different intensity of the relevant features, processes or experiences or for which you assume such differences. Either way, you will include and compare cases with the highest intensity or with different intensities.

- Critical cases, which show the relations under study particularly clearly or which are very relevant for the functioning of a program under study. Here, you often look for advice from experts about which cases to choose.

- Politically important or sensitive cases can be useful for making positive results widely known.

- Convenience sampling refers to choosing those cases that are most easily accessible under given circumstances. This can reduce the effort in sampling. Sometimes this is the only way to do a study with limited resources of time and with difficulties in applying a more systematic strategy of sampling.

Summary

Sampling refers to strategies for assuring that you have the 'right' cases in your study. 'Right' means that they allow generalization from the sample to the population because the sample is representative of the population. For example, the results from a questionnaire study with a sample of youth should be able to be generalized to youth in Germany. 'Right' can also mean that you have found and included the most instructive cases in your interviews – that you have the range of health experiences of homeless adolescents, rather than that your results are valid for youth in Germany in general (see the examples in Chapter 2).

These sampling strategies are a major step in research planning. Some research designs will need one or the other form of sampling. Experiments, control group or double blind studies need random sampling to be successful. For a non-standardized, theory developing qualitative study, strategies of theoretical or purposive sampling are more appropriate. The same is the case for the models of the research process that we discussed earlier: random and similar forms of sampling are more suitable for the process model of quantitative research; theoretical and purposive sampling are better suited to the qualitative research process.

Evaluation

What has been said so far refers to empirical research as a whole. Let us now focus on one specific area of social research, namely evaluation. Here, the focus is on the assessment of interventions with empirical methods. Evaluation research was developed in the context of social politics in the US and has since been extended to education, health, therapy and politics in general. Several phases can be distinguished (see Guba and Lincoln 1989). The first phase (early twentieth century) was strongly oriented towards measurement (of performance in school, similar to natural science research). The second phase (1920–1940) focused on the exact description of processes (e.g. of promoting pupils' performance). The third phase (1950s–1970s) saw evaluation essentially as assessment and made it an instrument of the state's welfare and social policy. The focus was extended to the use and usefulness of the results obtained in this way, in addition to the scientific quality of the evaluation. The fourth phase (since the 1980s) has been characterized by the concept of responsivity, with a shift in emphasis from scientific quality (as a main criterion) to usefulness of evaluation.

This shift is embedded in a turn to qualitative and more dialogical methods of evaluation:

> **Evaluation practices based in a value-critical framework decenter [the] conception of the aim, nature, and place of social inquiry in social life. They do so by redefining social inquiry as a dialogical and reflective process of democratic discussion and philosophical critique. (Schwandt 2002, p. 151)**

Evaluation in general still addresses the question of how and with what efforts the aims (of an intervention, for example) are reached, and which undesirable side effects occur. Thus evaluation is the use of research methods with the aim of empirically grounded assessments of interventions and their success and consequences. Evaluations are often commissioned to researchers. Commissioned evaluations aim at answering the issue of assessment in a transparent and unambiguous way. An essential here is that the results are elaborated and presented in such a way that non-experts (of research) can also understand them (see Chapter 13).

We can distinguish between self-evaluation and external evaluation. In the first case an institution organizes the evaluation of one of its programs or departments by hiring employees for this purpose. In external evaluation, an independent research team or institute will be asked to do the evaluation, which may lead to more reliable and independent results. If you intend to do an evaluation, you will not only need skills in research methods but also have communicative competencies for successfully negotiating your way in and through the institution. A further distinction here is between summative and formative evaluation. The first is located after the end of a program and focuses on its outcomes; the latter addresses the introduction and proceedings of the program.

Checklist for Designing an Empirical Study

For planning your own empirical project, you should take into account the aspects shown in Box 5.2 and find answers to the questions that arise. This checklist may help you in planning your own study and also for assessing the existing studies of other researchers

---

BOX 5.2

Checklist for designing an empirical study

1. Write a proposal for your project to indicate which steps it should run through.
2. Develop a timescale for your project in order to ascertain whether you can manage it in the available or given timeframe.
3. Do the proposal and the timescale cover the main steps of your project?
4. Is the design you chose adequate for the aims of your study and for the conditions in the field you study?
5. Is the form of sampling you want to apply appropriate for reaching the goals of your study and also for reaching the target groups of your study?
6. If you do an evaluation – is your research plan adequate for this purpose?

▓ ▓ Further Reading ▓

Issues of designing social research in a quantitative approach are discussed by the first and last textbooks, while the other two focus on this issue for qualitative studies.

Bryman, A. (2008) *Social Research Methods*, 3rd edn. Oxford: Oxford University Press.

Flick, U. (2008) *Designing Qualitative Research*. London: Sage.

Flick, U. (2009) *An Introduction to Qualitative Research*, 4th edn. London: Sage. Part 3.

Neuman, W.L. (2000) *Social Research Methods*: *Qualitative and Quantitative Approaches*, 4th edn. Boston: Allyn and Bacon.

CHAPTER 6
DECIDING ON YOUR METHODS

Chapter Overview

Chapter Objectives

This chapter is designed to help you:

- understand the series of decisions required in the research process
- appreciate that selecting a specific method of data collection is an important decision – though only one of many
- see how your decisions concerning methods are related to more general issues concerning (a) your research, (b) the conditions in the field, and (c) available knowledge about the issue.

Table 6.1   Navigator for Chapter 6

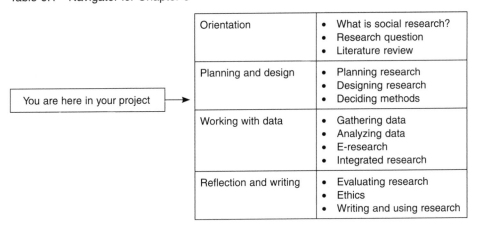

	Orientation	• What is social research? • Research question • Literature review
You are here in your project →	Planning and design	• Planning research • Designing research • Deciding methods
	Working with data	• Gathering data • Analyzing data • E-research • Integrated research
	Reflection and writing	• Evaluating research • Ethics • Writing and using research

Decisions in the Research Process

In Chapter 4, I outlined the steps involved in quantitative and qualitative research processes. In the chapters that follow, the most important methods will be discussed in more detail (see Chapters 7 and 8). Both qualitative and quantitative research entails a series of decisions you will need to take – from defining your research question to collecting and analyzing data and finally to presenting your results. Each decision will have implications for subsequent stages in your research project.

Overviews of methods in social research rarely provide much advice on the choice of specific research methods. This chapter aims to make good that lack.

Decisions in Standardized Research

Selecting the Research Problem

The first decision you need to make concerns the selection of a research problem. This will have major implications for the subsequent procedures. Bortz and Döring (2006) have formulated a number of criteria for evaluating research problems or ideas for studies. These can be used to inform your decision. Their criteria are:

- Precision in the formulation of the problem: how vaguely or exactly is the idea articulated? How clear are the concepts on which it is based?

- Can the problem be studied empirically? Can the ideas be addressed empirically, or are they based on religious, metaphysical or philosophical content (e.g. concerning the meaning of life)? And how likely is it that sufficient potential participants can be reached without excessive effort?

- Scientific scope: has the topic already been studied so comprehensively that no new insights can be expected from further investigations?

- Ethical criteria: would the study violate any ethical principles (as discussed in Chapter 12) or, seen the other way around, is the study ethically justified?

These criteria will help both to assess your research ideas and to justify your selection.

BOX 6.1

Decision quant-1: research problem

Your decision at this point concerns the research problem as such and those aspects of it that will be in the foreground of your study. They should be oriented to your interests and to how far you can formulate them empirically. Furthermore, you should assess whether the existing knowledge about the problem is sufficient for doing a standardized study and whether you will be able to access a sufficient number of participants. Decisions at this stage will subsequently have an influence on your methodological decisions.

Aims of the Study

Quantitative studies usually aim at testing an assumption that has been formulated in advance in the form of a hypothesis. Here the aim will be to assess the connections between variables or to identify the causes of specific events. One should be careful here not to assert a relationship or causal link between variables without evidence to justify the assertion. Thus there will need to be a strong emphasis, when planning and designing the study, on standardizing as many conditions as possible and on defining variables.

It is important to distinguish between independent and dependent variables (see also Chapter 5). The 'causing' condition is labeled the 'independent variable' and the consequences the 'dependent variable'. For example, an infection will be the cause of certain symptoms. The symptoms occur due to the infection. Thus they depend on the existence of the infection and are therefore treated as dependent variables. The infection is independent of the symptoms: it just occurs. It is therefore treated as the independent variable. Sometimes this relation is not so immediate. Other factors may play a role: for example, not everyone exposed to an infection falls ill; some people have more dramatic symptoms due to an infection; and others have less dramatic symptoms despite the same infection. Thus one must suppose that other variables are relevant. These are called intervening variables. This term is a label for those other influences on the connection between independent and dependent variables. In our example, the social situation of the infected persons can be such an intervening variable. (For example, socially disadvantaged people may be more likely to develop stronger symptoms than people in better living situations.) Testing the relationship between the independent and dependent variables can be your aim – in our example, the relation between infection and disease (as seen from the symptoms) and thus the identification of the infection as the cause of the disease. In this example it will be important to control the influence of the intervening variable.

Another aim of a quantitative study can be to describe a state or situation – e.g. the frequency of a disease in the population or in various subpopulations. Such studies are known as 'population description studies', as distinct from 'hypothesis testing studies' (Bortz and Döring 2006, p. 51). When the state of research and the theoretical literature are not sufficiently developed for you to formulate hypotheses that you can test empirically, you may first conduct an exploratory study. In this kind of study you may develop concepts, explore a field, and end up by forming hypotheses based on the exploration of the field.

BOX 6.2

Decision quant-2: aims

Your decision on the type of study you will pursue should be determined by your research interest and the state of the research before your study. The relevant question at this stage is: how far is your decision determined by the issue and the field you study? Or is it (mainly) influenced by your general methodological orientation?

Theoretical Framework

Theoretical questions can become an issue for decisions on a number of levels. You should take as your starting point a specific theoretical model of the issue that you intend to study. Often a number of alternative models will be available. For example, if your study concerns coping behavior in the case of a disease, there are several different models of coping behavior to select from. Moreover, the study can be planned within the framework of a general theoretical model or a research program. For example, in the case of studying coping behavior, one might adopt a rational choice approach.

BOX 6.3

Decision quant-3: theoretical framework

If you decide to use a theoretical framework, this will have a number of methodological consequences. Deciding on a specific theoretical model of the research issue will set the frame for how
to operationalize the relevant features of this issue in your study. A relevant question in this context
is how far the theoretical framework is compatible with your research question, or the issue. These
decisions should be oriented to the issue under study, and the field in which you study it.

If, for example, you study quality of life according to one of the theoretical models developed
about people living on their own in relative health and independence, this will lead to such
operationalizations as questions about people's ability to walk certain distances, for example. If
you want to study this issue (quality of life) in a nursing home with frail and old people, you will
have to consider whether such questions and the theoretical models in the background are
appropriate for this context.

Formulating the Research Question

For the success of any study, it is important to limit the chosen research problem
to a research question that is manageable. For example, if you are interested in
the research problem 'Health of senior citizens', this is not yet a research
question, as it is too vast and vague. To turn it into a research question, you will
have to focus on the parts of the problem formulation. Which aspect of health
do you want to study? What kind of senior citizens are the focus of your study?
What is the link between health and older people? Then you may arrive at a
question like: 'Which factors delimit the autonomy of people over 65 with
depression living in big cities and in rural contexts?' Here the elements of your
research question are clearly defined and you can start to consider how you will
do your sampling and data collection for approaching this question empirically.
If you want to do a quantitative study, you should reflect on whether there will
be enough people for you to address and whether they will be capable of filling
in a survey etc., and how this survey will cover issues of autonomy, of limitations, of living conditions (city, countryside) and of depression (see Chapter 2
for more examples and distinctions between good and bad research questions).

BOX 6.4

Decision quant-4: research question

The decision on a research question will have implications for (a) what will become the issue of
your study, (b) which aspects you will omit, and (c) which methods you can apply in your study.

At this stage, it is important that the formulation of your research question helps you to orient your research. It is also important how far your research question is helpful for stimulating new insights about your research issue so that your study does not simply reproduce knowledge already available from other research.

Resources

A key factor is the cost of a study. Without detailed knowledge about the project, an estimate of the cost will be difficult to make. In general, the higher the methodological standards, the greater the cost. Denscombe (2007, p. 27) mentions in this context that commercial survey institutes in Britain inform their customers that for a certain price a specific level of exactness in measurement and sampling can be expected, and that higher levels will incur higher prices. Accordingly, Hoinville et al. state in the case of sampling that 'In practice, the complexity of the competing factors of resources and accuracy means that the decision on sample size tends to be based on experience and good judgment rather than relying on a strict mathematical formula' (1985, p. 73).

BOX 6.5

Decision quant-5: resources

Your decision in this context generally refers to weighing your available resources (money, time, experience, wo/manpower) against methodological claims (of exactness and scope of the sampling, for example) so that you can make your project work with realistic claims.

Sampling and Building of Comparative Groups

Sampling in quantitative research mostly rests on concern for the representativeness of the studied persons, situations, institutions or phenomena for the wider population. Often one will construct comparative groups so that they match each other as far as possible (for example, the study group will be constructed like the control group as much as possible). The aim here is to control and standardize as many features of the group as possible; then differences between groups can be traced back to the variable that you are studying. The most consistent approach is random sampling, in which the allocation to the study group or the control group is also done randomly (see Chapter 5). However, strictly random sampling is not always the best or most appropriate way. Depending on the issue and field you study, quota or cluster sampling may be more appropriate (see Chapter 5), as the focus of strictly random sampling may be insufficiently specific.

BOX 6.6

Decision quant-6: sampling and comparison

Your decisions here are related to the question of the appropriateness of a specific form of sampling. How far does this allow taking specific target groups of your study sufficiently into account?

Methods

Decisions concerning methods need to be made on a series of levels. The first concerns the character of the data you wish to work with. Ask yourself whether you can use existing data (e.g. routine data on health insurance) for your own analysis. Here, one has to consider the question of accessibility of data (for example, not every health insurance company is ready to make its data available for research purposes). Sometimes data protection issues also form obstacles. There will also be questions about the suitability of the data: in particular, you should check whether the issue you are interested in is indeed covered by the data and whether the way the data are classified permits the necessary analysis (see Chapter 7).

Next you should decide between survey and observation. For example, when collecting data about the relevant phenomena, are you interested more in knowledge and attitudes or in practices?

The next decision to be made is whether for data collection you use an existing instrument or develop a new one. The advantages of the first alternative are that these methods are mostly well tested and that you can more easily link your data to other studies. For example, in quality of life research, existing questionnaires are often used; similarly, in attitude research, interactions are often analyzed with available inventories in observations. However, you should check whether the existing instrument covers the aspects that are relevant for your own study and whether it is appropriate for your specific target group.

Developing your own instrument enables you to adapt it to the concrete circumstances of your study. In this case, you should reflect on whether the existing theoretical or empirical knowledge is developed enough for you to formulate the 'right' questions or observational categories. Finally, pre-testing and checking the reliability and validity (as discussed in Chapter 11) of the instrument are necessary before you can actually apply it.

In analyzing quantitative data, existing statistical packages like SPSS are most often used. Here you should decide which kinds of relational analyses are best for answering your research question. Also you should check in advance which tests you should apply to your data – for example, plausibility checks (are there contradictory responses in the dataset, like 20-year-old pensioners?) or checks for missing data (see Chapters 7 and 8)

BOX 6.7

Decision quant-7: methods

Your decision here is between using existing data or instruments and collecting your own data, perhaps with instruments developed specifically for your study. This decision should be related to your research questions, the conditions in the field, and the existing knowledge about the issue under study. Finally, your decisions can be a matter of your resources – such as the time available.

Degree of Standardization and Control

Quantitative research is based on (a) standardizing the research situation and the research procedures and (b) controlling as many conditions as possible. In most cases, variables are defined that are linked in hypotheses for testing these connections. Analytic units are defined (for example, every patient attending a general practitioner's surgery). Concrete measures are defined for the single variables (for example, the time that each patient waits before he or she is called into the treatment room to see the doctor). These are defined before entering the field and are then applied to every case in an identical way. This is intended to ensure the standardization of the research and the control over the conditions in the research situation as far as possible.

BOX 6.8

Decision quant-8: standardization and control

Your decisions in this context refer to how far you can or should advance with standardizing and controlling. Experimental studies are most systematic when seen from a methodological point of view. However they cannot be applied to every field and every issue. Other study forms are less standardized and controlled, but can more easily fit the conditions in the field under study. The decisions you take in this context concerning more or less standardization and control should be defined both by the conditions in the field and by the aims of your study.

Generalization

Generalization usually involves inference from a small number (of people in the study) to a larger number (of people that could have been studied). Accordingly, generalization may be seen as a numerical or statistical problem. It is closely linked to the question of the (statistical) representativeness of the sample that you have studied for the population that you assumed (as discussed in Chapters 5 and 11). Note here that the 'population' does not necessarily refer to the whole population of a country; in many studies, the term will refer to rather more limited basic populations.

BOX 6.9

Decision quant-9: generalization

Deciding on the specific target population for the purposes of generalization will have consequences for the research design and for the methods that you apply. This decision should be driven by the aims of your study in general and by the conditions in the study field. The general question here is how appropriate is the intended generalization to (a) the issue of your study, (b) the field, and (c) the participants.

Presentation

Who do you want to address with your research and its results? What will be the audience and target group when it comes to presenting your findings? Here, we can distinguish between (a) academic, (b) general, and (c) political audiences. If your study will in the end be presented in a thesis (a master's thesis for example), it will be more important that you demonstrate specific methodological competences than if the results are meant to draw the attention of the general public to a social problem. If your research and its results are intended to have an influence on political decision-making, their presentation will need to be concise, easily understandable, and focused on the essential results (see Chapter 13).

BOX 6.10

Decision quant-10: presentation

Your decisions at this stage concern what kinds of information you should select for the audience you want to address. A second issue is what style of presentation is appropriate for this purpose.

Decisions in Qualitative Research

Selection of the Research Problem

Many factors affect the choice of research problem in qualitative research. It may be that the theoretical literature or empirical research to date is lacking in some way. Alternatively, one might choose a qualitative approach because the participants in question would be difficult to reach through quantitative methods. Another factor influencing the choice may be that the number of potential participants (e.g. people with a specific but rare diagnosis) is small (though not too small). Or one may wish to explore a field to discover something new. The decision over the choice of problem will also involve a consideration of ethical issues (discussed in Chapter 12).

BOX 6.11

Decision qual-1: research problem

Questions you should focus on here are: what is new about the problem under consideration; which aspects of it can be researched empirically and discovered; the limitations of existing research; and whether a sufficient number of participants can be accessed. Your decisions at this stage will influence the methodological steps that you take later in the project.

Aims of the Study

Maxwell (2005, p. 16) has distinguished different types of research aims. There are (a) personal aims such as completing a master's or doctoral thesis; (b) practical aims such as finding out whether a specific program or service works; and (c) research aims concerning the desire for general knowledge on a specific issue.

Qualitative studies often have the aim of developing grounded theory according to the approach of Glaser and Strauss (1967). However, this is an ambitious and demanding aim. If you are writing a bachelor degree thesis, this aim may well be unrealistic: you may not have the time or experience required. It may be more realistic to aim instead to provide a detailed description or evaluation of some ongoing practices. Overall, qualitative research may aim to provide description or evaluation or to develop theory.

BOX 6.12

Decision qual-2: aims

Your decision concerns which aims you can *realistically* pursue with your study.

Theoretical Framework

In qualitative research, it may be that you do not use a theoretical model of the issue under study to provide a starting point for determining the actual questions you use (or those you ask in an interview). Nevertheless, studies should be related to previous theoretical and empirical work on the issue in question. The current state of extant research should influence your subsequent methodological and empirical procedures. In qualitative research there may be a number of frameworks for studying an issue: for example, it may be that you can analyze either (a) subjective views and experiences or (b) interactions related to the topic in question.

BOX 6.13

Decision qual-3: theoretical framework

When you decide the research perspective and the substantive points of the research, you will in effect be committing yourself to proceeding in certain ways. In doing so, you should take as your points of reference the knowledge available to you and the conditions in the field you study.

Formulating the Research Question

We can distinguish between (a) research questions where the answers focus on the possible confirmation of an assumption or a hypothesis, and (b) questions designed to discover new aspects. Strauss (1987) calls the latter 'generative questions'. He defines them as 'Questions that stimulate the line of investigation in profitable directions; they lead to hypotheses, useful comparisons, the collection of certain classes of data, even to general lines of attack on potentially important problems' (1987, p. 22).

In qualitative research, Maxwell (2005) has proposed alternative distinctions. He distinguishes first between generalizing and particularizing questions, and second between questions that focus on distinctions and those that focus on the description of processes. Generalizing questions place the issue under study in a wider context – for example, as the biography of a person or a group could be understood against the background of a political turmoil. Particularizing questions foreground some specific aspect – for example, a specific event, such as the onset of illness. Questions focusing on distinction address differences in the knowledge of people – say several patients' differences in knowing about their illness. Questions focusing on describing a process look at how such knowledge develops in a group of patients in the progress of their illness.

BOX 6.14

Decision qual-4: research question

Selecting a research question entails decisions about both what exactly you will be studying and also what you will be excluding from your study. This will have implications subsequently for your choice of methods for data collection and analysis.

Resources

When one is elaborating a research design, the resources required (time, persons, technologies, competencies, experiences) are often underestimated. In research proposals, it is common to see a mismatch between work packages envisaged and the personal resources that have been requested. To plan a project realistically, you need to assess accurately the work to be undertaken.

For example, for an interview lasting 90 minutes, it is recommended that you allow an equivalent amount of time for recruiting the interviewee, organizing the appointment etc. For calculating the time needed for transcribing the interviewees, estimates vary according to the degree of exactness of the transcription rules that are applied. Morse (1998, pp. 81–2), for example, suggests that for fast-writing transcribers, the length of the tape containing the interview recording be multiplied by a factor of four. If checking the finished transcript against the tape is also included, the length of the tape should be multiplied by a total of six. For the complete calculation of the project she advises doubling the time, to allow for unforeseen difficulties and 'catastrophes'. Example plans for calculating time schedules or empirical projects may be found in Marshall and Rossman (2006, pp. 177–80) and Flick (2008b).

BOX 6.15

Decision qual-5: resources

In decisions in this context, you should above all take the relation of available resources and the aims or the planned efforts of the study into account. This should help you to ensure that the data you collect is not too complex and differentiated for you to be able to analyze them in the time available.

Sampling and Building of Comparative Groups

Decisions about sampling in qualitative research above all refer to persons or situations in data collection. Sampling decisions become relevant again for the parts of the collected material that you will address with extended interpretations when analyzing your data. For the presentation of your research, sampling concerns what you present as exemplary results or interpretations (see Flick 2009, p. 115). Sampling decisions here are not normally taken according to abstract criteria (as in random sampling), but rather according to substantive criteria referring to concrete cases or case groups.

A major task for the sampling decisions is to build comparative groups. Here you need to decide on what level you want to do your comparisons. For example, will your focus be the differences and similarities between persons and institutions, or between situations and phenomena?

BOX 6.16

Decision qual-6: sampling and comparison

Here you make decisions about the persons, groups or situations that you will include in your study. The decisions should be oriented on the relevance of who or what you select for your study. They should also be oriented on having enough diversity in the phenomena you study. If that is your topic, you should look for people with a *specific* illness experience (and not just people who are sick in some way or another). At the same time your selection should provide for some diversity, for example people living in different social circumstance with this illness experience and not just people living under the same conditions.

Methods

The central distinction here is between (a) direct analysis of what occurs and (b) analysis of reports about what has occurred. The former will involve (participant) observation or interaction studies. In the latter case, you will work with interviews with or narratives of the participants. You can decide between different degrees of openness or structuredness: data collection can rely on questions formulated in advance or on narratives; observation is either structured or open and participant. The analysis of data can be oriented on categories (sometimes defined in advance) or on the development of the text (of the narrative or of the interaction protocol: see Chapters 7 and 8).

Degree of Standardization and Control

Miles and Huberman (1994, pp. 16–18) distinguish between tight and loose research designs in qualitative research. Tight research designs involve narrowly restricted questions and strictly determined selection procedures. The degree of openness in the field of investigation and the empirical material will remain limited. The authors see such designs as appropriate when researchers lack experience of qualitative research, when the research operates on the basis of narrowly defined constructs, or when it is restricted to the investigation of particular relationships in familiar contexts. In such cases, they see loose designs as a detour to the desired result. Loose designs are characterized by less defined concepts and have, in the beginning, hardly any fixed methodological procedures. Tight designs make it easier to decide which data are relevant for the investigation. They make it easier to compare and summarize data from different interviews or observations.

Generalization

With qualitative research, aims may vary – for example, between (a) providing a detailed analysis of a single case in as many of its aspects as possible, or (b) comparing several cases, or (c) developing a typology of different cases. The generalization involved is likely to be theoretical rather than numerical. The important consideration is more likely to be the diversity of cases considered or the theoretical scope of the case studies than the number of cases included. To develop a theory can be a form of generalization on various levels as well. This theory can refer to the substantive area that was studied (e.g. a theory of trust in counseling relationships). Generalization can be advanced by developing a formal theory focusing on broader contexts (e.g. a theory of interpersonal trust related to various contexts). This distinction between substantive theory and formal theory was suggested by Glaser and Strauss (1967).

BOX 6.19

Decision qual-9: generalization

Your decision concerning the kind of generalization that you aim for will have implications for planning your study and in particular for your selection of cases. This decision should take account of the aims of your study and at the same time the question of what is possible in the field that you study. It should take account of the situation of the possible participants. More generally, the question arises of how appropriate the type of generalization that you are aiming at will be for the field under study.

Presentation

Finally you should take into account in your planning the questions of presentation. Will the empirical material form the basis for an essay or a narrative with a more illustrative function? Or is your aim to provide a systematic study of the cases under study and the variations between them? You need to consider here the assessment criteria that will be applied for your thesis. In general, the question will be how to relate concrete statements and evidence to more general or deepening interpretations so that your inferences are substantiated in a clear and convincing way. (Questions of presentation will be discussed in more detail in Chapter 13.)

BOX 6.20

Decision qual-10: presentation

You should carefully decide how you will present your research. It is important that you not only present some results. You should also make transparent how you entered the field, how

---

you got in touch with the relevant people, and how you arrived at gathering the data you needed for your analysis. It is also important that your readers have access to the way you gathered your data and to how you analyzed them. The path from the original data to the more general (comparative, analytic) statements and conclusions should be elucidated with examples in the methods section of your report and with enough original material (quotes) in its results section. Illustrations with sample materials but also with charts or tables can be very helpful here.

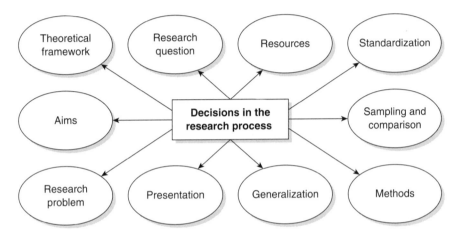

Figure 6.1   Decisions in the research process

Decisions within Quantitative and Qualitative Research

In standardized research, the decision process outlined in the first part of this chapter is intended to help select the alternatives in the procedure and to apply them to a greater or lesser extent to the issue of your study. Each of the decisions delimits the perspective you take on what you study and defines which parts of this issue you can cover in your data and in their analysis. In qualitative research as well as in quantitative research, we can describe the process as a series of decisions. Planning a research project involves making a series of decisions that serve to foreground some aspects and exclude others. The decisions require consideration of interrelated questions concerning your field of study, the issue to be researched, the theoretical context, and the methodology involved.

The decisions discussed in this chapter so far are summarized in Table 6.2. These decisions (displayed in Figure 6.1) will inform the shaping of the research design and of the research process in its further steps.

Table 6.2 Decisions in quantitative and qualitative research

Decision	Quantitative study	Qualitative study
Research problem	Enough existing knowledge? Enough participants accessible?	What is new about the problem? Enough participants accessible?
Aims	Study type Research interest State of the research	Knowledge interest and practical aims?
Theoretical framework	Model as a basis for operationalization?	Research perspective taken?
Research questions	Helpful for working with the research problem?	Delimiting the research question?
Resources	Methodological claims in relation to money, time etc.	Is it possible to analyze the collected data in the time framework?
Sampling and comparison	Appropriateness of sampling: are your target groups sufficiently taken into account?	Diversity of the phenomena in the sample?
Methods	Your own or existing methods? New or existing data?	Openness and structure of the data coming from the methods?
Standardization and control	Limits of standardization in the field	Comparability of the differences in groups or fields?
Generalization	How far is a generalization intended?	How far can a generalization be intended?
Presentation	Condensation of the essential aspects?	Understandability and transparency of the procedures?

Deciding between Qualitative and Standardized Research

The following factors provide starting points for deciding between qualitative and quantitative approaches to your empirical project:

- The issue you study and its features should be your major points of reference for such a decision.

- Theoretical approaches have implications for selecting your methodological approaches.

- Your concrete research question will play a major role in defining how you focus your issue conceptually and how you cover it empirically.

- Methodological decisions between qualitative and quantitative methods and designs should be derived from the points of reference just mentioned above. They should not be based simply on the belief that only one or the other version of social research is scientific, acceptable or credible.

- A main reference should be the resources available. (With regard to time, however, note that doing a qualitative analysis consistently and carefully in most cases takes as long as a quantitative study.) Under 'resources' here are included your own methodological knowledge and competences.

Overall, your decision between qualitative and quantitative methodologies should be driven more by your research interest and the features of the field and issue you study than by prior methodological preferences. If it is not possible to decide unequivocally between the two approaches, there may be a case for using a combination of the two (as is discussed further in Chapter 10).

Deciding between Doing Research On-site or Online

As will be discussed further in Chapter 9, quantitative and qualitative approaches may take the form of e-research. You may, for example, conduct a survey, not by mailing out copies of a questionnaire and waiting for them to be returned by post, but doing it on the Internet. You may also consider doing your interviews online instead of face to face. The arguments outlined in the literature concerning the advantages and disadvantages of doing research projects online compared to the traditional way are discussed in detail in Chapter 9.

Deciding on Specific Approaches to Research

Textbooks on social research often provide little help concerning the choice between specific methods for a project. Most books treat each single method or research design separately and describe their features and problems in isolation. In most cases, they fail to provide a comparative presentation, either of methodological alternatives or of the bases for selecting methods appropriate for the research issue in question.

In medicine or psychotherapy, it is usual to check the appropriateness of a certain treatment for specific problems and groups of people. This raises the question of 'indication': one asks whether a specific treatment is 'indicated' (i.e. is appropriate) for a specific problem in a specific case. Similarly in social research we can ask when (in terms of, for example, the research question, field and issue) qualitative methods are indicated and when quantitative methods are indicated instead. For example, it is common practice to study 'quality of life' for people living with a chronic illness. You will find a number of established instruments to measure quality of life (e.g. the SF-36) which are regularly applied for measuring

Table 6.3 Indication of research methods

Psychotherapy and medicine			Social research		
Which disease, symptoms, diagnosis, population	**indicate**	which treatment or therapy?	Which issue, population, research question, knowledge of issue and population	**indicate**	which method or methods?

1. When is a particular method appropriate and indicated?
2. When is which combination of methods appropriate and indicated?
3. How do you make a rational decision for or against certain methods?

quality of life of different populations. The question of indication becomes relevant if you want to use this instrument to study the quality of life of say a population of very old people living in a nursing home who are suffering from a number of diseases (and not just one) and are somewhat disoriented. Then you will see that this well-established instrument finds its limits in the specific features of this target groups: as Mallinson (2002) has shown, the application of this instrument is not at all clear for such a population and the concrete situation in which they are living. The research question – 'What is the quality of life of old people with multiple morbidity in nursing homes?' – is an appropriate one. However, to answer it you may need other methods than the established SF-36 due to the concrete conditions under which you will study it. For this population, a different method (e.g. an open interview) may be more indicated than the common method. This may be different if you study the question of quality of life for a more general population. Then there may be no need to use very open methods and to start from a very open approach in order to develop theories and instruments. Here, enough knowledge about the issue and the population is available to apply standardized and well-established methods. Table 6.3 illustrates this comparison diagrammatically (for more details about this in qualitative research see Flick 2009, Chapter 29).

Reflection Halfway through the Process

Before considering in detail the most common methods available for doing a research project, you might be advised to step back for a moment and reflect on the process of planning so far. Table 6.4 provides a list of guideline questions for examining the consistency and adequacy of your planning to date. Reflecting on these questions will provide a solid foundation for choosing your methods for collecting and analyzing your data.

Table 6.4 Guideline questions for reflecting on your own research project

Issue	Guideline questions	Relevant aspects
Relevance	What is your study important for?	• What theoretical and empirical progress of knowledge do you expect from your results? • What practical relevance do you see for your results?
Clarity	How clearly is your study conceptualized?	• How clear are the aims of your study? • How clearly is the research question formulated?
Background knowledge	What are the bases of your study and of doing it?	• Did you check the state of research and the knowledge about the issue of your research? Do both justify a standardized, hypotheses testing study? Or is there enough of a gap for justifying a qualitative study? • Which methodological skill do you have for doing the study?
Feasibility	Can the study be realized?	• Are your resources (e.g. time) sufficient for doing the study? • Did you clarify the access to the field and the participants? How likely is the possibility of organizing this access? • Are there (enough) people who can answer your questions?
Scope	Is the approach planned too narrowly?	• Will you include cases, groups, events etc. in sufficient diversity? • Will the response rate and the readiness to participate be great enough? • Which generalization can you achieve with your results?
Quality	Which quality claims can be formulated for the results?	• Will you be able to apply the methods consistently? • Will the participants' statements be reliable? • Will the data be sound enough to do the intended analysis with them?
Neutrality	How can you avoid biases and being one-sided?	• Can you approach the field and the participants in an unbiased way, even if you do not share their points of view? • Can you avoid acting for or against certain participants in a one-sided way? • Can you accept the limits of your methodological procedures?
Ethics	Is your research ethically sound?	• Can you proceed in your research without deceiving the participants or doing harm to them? • How can you guarantee anonymity, data protection and confidentiality?

Checklist for Choosing a Specific Method

For selecting your concrete methods, you can take the points in Box 6.21 as an orientation. These questions can be relevant for planning your own project and for assessing the existing studies of other researchers.

BOX 6.21

Checklist for choosing a specific method

1. How far does your methodological approach fit the aims and theoretical starting points of your study?
2. Do your methods of data collection fit those of analyzing your data?
3. Do your data fit the level of scaling and the calculations you will do with them?
4. Are the methods of analysis to be used appropriate to the level of complexity of the data?
5. What implications do the methods (from sampling to collection and analysis) selected have for the issue of the study and on what is covered in it?
6. Is your decision on certain procedures grounded in the issue and field you study or based on your methodological preferences?
7. Have you assessed which approach(es) are 'indicated'?

Key Points

- In doing social research, whether qualitative or quantitative, you face decisions at each of the steps outlined in Chapter 4.

- The decisions are interrelated. The method of data collection should be taken into account when you decide how to do your analysis.

- The aims of your research – for example, who you want to reach and maybe convince with your results – and the framework conditions (e.g. the resources available and the characteristics of the people or groups and fields you study) also play a role.

- Decisions between qualitative and quantitative approaches should be driven by the issue you study and by your resources.

- The same applies to the decision of whether to conduct your project online or not.

- Checking the 'indication' of research methods provides a starting point for the decisions discussed in this chapter.

■ ■ Further Reading ■

The first and last texts listed below take a more integrative approach to the selection of research methods, while the second and third references adopt a qualitative perspective.

Bryman, A. (2008) *Social Research Methods*, 3rd edn. Oxford: Oxford University Press.
Flick, U. (2009) *An Introduction to Qualitative Research*, 4th edn. London: Sage.
Miles, M.B. and Huberman, A.M. (1994) *Qualitative Data Analysis: An Expanded Sourcebook*, 2nd edn. Thousand Oaks, CA: Sage.
Punch, K. (1998) *Introduction to Social Research*. London: Sage.

PART III
WORKING WITH DATA

The central part of a research project consists of collecting and analyzing data. This third part of the book explains these processes.

Chapter 7 introduces three main forms of data collection. The first is the use of questionnaires or interviews; the second is the use of observation; and the third is documentary research. Chapter 8 focuses on three major forms of data analysis. The first is content analysis; the second is descriptive statistics; and the third is interpretative analysis for qualitative data. Case studies are discussed at the end. And Chapter 9 considers the use in research of the Internet, especially for online surveys and interviews and virtual ethnography.

Every method has its limitations and so it can be fruitful to combine methods. Chapter 10 outlines ways to do this through mixed method research, triangulation, and integrated research.

CHAPTER 7
GATHERING DATA: QUANTITATIVE AND QUALITATIVE APPROACHES

Chapter Overview

Chapter Objectives

This chapter is designed to help you:

- understand a range of social research methods for collecting data
- appreciate the similarities and differences, with regard to methods, between qualitative and quantitative research
- assess the methods available to you and what you can achieve with them.

Table 7.1 Navigator for Chapter 7

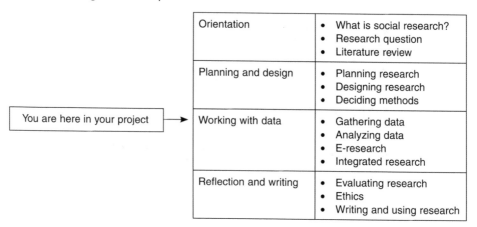

Orientation	• What is social research? • Research question • Literature review
Planning and design	• Planning research • Designing research • Deciding methods
Working with data	• Gathering data • Analyzing data • E-research • Integrated research
Reflection and writing	• Evaluating research • Ethics • Writing and using research

You are here in your project → Working with data

In social research, there are three main forms of data collection: you can collect data through asking people (through surveys and interviews), observing, or studying documents. This chapter outlines each of these methods in turn.

Surveys and Interviews

By way of preparation for understanding the alternatives for asking people, please respond to the questionnaire given in Box 7.1.

BOX 7.1

Questionnaire

Please fill in the following excerpt of a questionnaire for assessing the stress caused by studying according to the following instruction:

'We ask you to answer some questions about your personal situation and about features of your university. Please circle without hesitation how far each of the areas mentioned in the questions is stressful and satisfying for you. Very stressful is indicated by the value 5 in the stress scale, very satisfying by the value 5 in the satisfaction scale. Not stressful or satisfying is indicated by 1 on the respective scale. If one of the areas for you is only stressful or only satisfying, please circle only one of the scales (stressful or satisfying).' If you circle 0, that means this area is neither stressful/nor satisfying for you.

Stressful   Satisfying
5----4----3----2----1----0----1----2----3----4----5

	Stressful	Satisfying
To study at this university means a limitation of my behavior for me	5----4----3----2----1----0----1----2----3----4----5	
To do exams is for me	5----4----3----2----1----0----1----2----3----4----5	
At the university, contacts often happen	5----4----3----2----1----0----1----2----3----4----5	
At the university, contacts rarely happen	5----4----3----2----1----0----1----2----3----4----5	
The professors and lecturers hardly bother about my studies or my work	5----4----3----2----1----0----1----2----3----4----5	
To spend much (leisure) time for my studies is for me	5----4----3----2----1----0----1----2----3----4----5	
Often I have to decide between family/friends and studying	5----4----3----2----1----0----1----2----3----4----5	
Sometimes I have to do things at the university I do not agree with	5----4----3----2----1----0----1----2----3----4----5	
Much is expected from me	5----4----3----2----1----0----1----2----3----4----5	

Now – again by way of preparation – please use the material in Box 7.2 to interview one of your peer students.

BOX 7.2

Interview about everyday life and studying

I would like to do an interview with you about the issue 'everyday life and studying'. It is important that you answer according to your subjective point of view and express your opinions. I will ask you several questions concerning situations in which you have experience with studying and ask you to recount those situations for me.

First of all I would like to know …

1. What was your first experience with studying here? Could you please give me a concrete example about this?
2. Please tell me about the course of your day yesterday and when your studies played a role in it.
3. When you look at what you do in your time off, what role does your study play in it? Please give me a concrete example for this.

4. If you look at your life in general, do you have the feeling that studying takes a bigger part of it than you expected? Can you outline this by giving me an example?
5. What do you link to the word 'stress'?
6. When you look back: what was your first experience with stress as a student? Could you tell me about' this situation?

What do you find are the differences between these two experiences? Which exercise do you feel would cover the respondent's situation better? Which form gave more room for the respondent's own views? Which one do you think produces the clearer data?

The two research instruments in Boxes 7.1 and 7.2 are adapted from a questionnaire often used for studying stress at the workplace and an episodic interview. They represent contrasting forms of asking people about their situation. The main difference lies in the degree of standardization of the procedure: the questionnaire comes with a predefined list of questions and answers, while the interview is more open ended. In the interview, the questions can be varied in their sequence and interviewees can use their words and decide what they want to refer to in their responses. Below, we discuss both methods in more detail.

Standardized Surveys: Questionnaires

Most surveys are based on questionnaires. These may be answered either in written form or orally in a face-to-face interrogation with a researcher noting the answers. A characteristic of questionnaires is their extensive standardization. The researchers will determine the formulation and sequencing of questions and possible answers. Sometimes a number of open or free text questions, which the respondents may answer in their own words, are included too.

Questionnaire studies aim at receiving comparable answers from all participants. Therefore, the questions as well as the interview situation are designed in an identical way for all participants. When one is constructing a questionnaire, rules for formulating questions and arranging their sequence should be applied.

Question wording

Here, there are three main issues: how to formulate a question, which kinds of question and possible answers are appropriate, and the purpose for asking the questions. Questions should collect, directly or indirectly, the respondents' reasons for a specific behavior or attitude and show their state of information concerning the issue under examination.

How instructive is the information received will depend both on the type of question and on its position in the questionnaire. It will also depend on whether (a) the questions fit the respondent's frame of reference and (b) the respondent's and the interviewer's frames of reference correspond. Finally, the situation, in which a question is asked and should be answered, plays a major role.

If you wish to identify the interviewee's frame of reference, you should ask for reasons to be given (e.g. 'Why did you choose this issue for your studies?'). You will need to take the interviewee's state of information into account: if questions are too complex, they are likely to be misunderstood and produce diffuse answers. Accordingly you should translate complex issues into concrete, clearly understandable questions. Where possible, use colloquial language. Note here that it may not make much sense to incorporate the language of your hypothesis directly into your questions.

Be careful to avoid multidimensional questions, for example: 'How and when did you discover that … ?'. If questions include several dimensions, their comparability will be reduced, because respondents may pick up different dimensions in a question. Also avoid questions with a bias, which suggests a specific answer (suggestive questions), or with certain assumptions. For example, if you are studying burnout processes, the question 'How burnt out by your job do you feel?' assumes that the respondent already feels burnt out. Instead, you should find out through a prior question whether this is in fact the case. Questions should be as short and simple as possible and aligned to the respondent's frame of reference as closely as possible. Double negations should be avoided. So too should unclear or technical terms. For example, rather than ask 'What is your subjective definition of health?', ask 'What do you associate with the word "health"?'.

You should also recognize that the features of the event you are studying will influence the quality of the answers provided. The further in the past an event is, the less exact the answers will be. The more respondents are interested in an issue, the more detailed and accurate the answers will be. The more frightening an event has been for respondents, the more likely it is they will have forgotten it. The more something is linked to social rejection (e.g. times spent in psychiatric wards), the less a person will talk or make statements about it. The higher the value of something (e.g. income, status), the more likely it is that the responses will include overestimates. For closed questions with two possible answers, it is more likely that the second will be given. For questions with a list of possible answers ('list questions'), a person who does not know the answer is likely to select an answer from the lowest third of the list: this is known as the 'position effect'. These and other problems of how to formulate and position a question are dealt with in detail by Neuman (2000, Chapter 10).

		Degree of agreement				
		Not at all				Full
A	Science and technology will be able to solve environmental problems	1	2	3	4	5
B	More economic growth is the most important precondition for solving environmental problems	1	2	3	4	5

Figure 7.1   Five-step answer scale (excerpt from Diekmann 2007, p. 212)

Some texts (e.g. Bortz and Döring 2006, pp. 244–6) provide checklists for assessing standardized oral or written questions. Such checklists include guiding points such as:

- Are all the questions necessary?
- Does the questionnaire include redundant questions?
- Which questions are superfluous?
- Are all the questions formulated easily and clearly?
- Are there negative questions, with answers that could be ambiguous?
- Are the questions formulated too general?
- Will the interviewee be potentially able to answer the questions?
- Is there a risk that the questions will be embarrassing for the interviewee?
- Might the result be influenced by the position of the questions?
- Are questions formulated in a suggestive way?
- Are the opening questions adequately formulated and has the questionnaire a properly reflected end?

Types of questions and of possible answers

Questions can be distinguished according to how they can be answered. Open questions do not come with answers defined in advance, while closed questions already specify the alternatives for answering them. Such alternatives may be specified in the wording of the question (e.g. 'Are most nurses satisfied or unsatisfied by their work?'), which permits only a limited number of answers (in our example, two). A closed question may limit the number of possible answers by use of a scale of agreement, as shown in Figure 7.1. An alternative is to present different possibilities for answering, as illustrated in Box 7.3.

BOX 7.3

Ways of defining possible answers

1. The first alternative is to use a scale. One example is the Likert scale, which includes five possible answers, one of which is neutral ('don't know'). This might be used for the statement, '*Most nurses are unhappy with their work.*'

Totally correct	Correct	Don't know	Not correct	Not at all correct
O———	———O———	———O———	———O———	———O

2. Often, simple questions are presented and multi-step rating scales presented for answering them: '*How happy are you with your work?*'

Very satisfied   A bit satisfied   A bit unsatisfied   Very unsatisfied

O———O———O———O———O———O———O

Satisfied   Neither   Unsatisfied

3. A third option is to present several possible answers to the question, '*What do you think? Why are nurses unhappy with their work?*' (multiple answers possible).

- Unfavorable hours of working ☐
- Poor pay ☐
- Emotional stress ☐
- Stress with colleagues ☐

It is also possible to present a situation. Here you would list several possible answers to the question, 'What would you do in such a situation?' Or you could ask questions relating to how some other person would react in this situation. Sometimes questionnaires include control questions, which readdress the issues of earlier questions using a different wording. Questions can also be asked indirectly: for example, 'Many people think that nursing as a profession is underrated in our society. Do you think this, too?' Thus you can avoid a direct confrontation with a possibly delicate issue whilst still receiving the interviewee's opinion.

Positioning of questions

Questions may influence each other. That is, how some question is answered may be influenced by the question asked immediately before. This is known as the 'halo effect'. The links between two questions are not necessarily designed deliberately. In general, it is suggested that you group questions from the most general at the start to the most concrete at the end.

Suggestions for how to formulate questions

Porst (2000) has provided '10 commandments' of question wording for surveys. These are given in Box 7.4. His starting point is as follows:

> **Why questions have to be 'good', i.e. methodically and technically faultless, should be self-evident: bad questions lead to bad data and no procedure of weighing and no method of analyzing the data can make good results from bad data. (2000, p. 2)**

The 'commandments' are designed to ensure that questions are clearly formulated and do not over-challenge or confuse respondents. Porst intends these rules to provide an orientation only: 'most of the rules leave room for interpretation and sometimes ... are even in competition to each other and thus cannot be applied a hundred percent at the same time' (2000, p. 2).

BOX 7.4

The '10 commandments' of question wording (Porst 2000)

1. You shall use simple unambiguous concepts which are understood by all respondents in the same way!
2. You shall avoid long and complex questions!
3. You shall avoid hypothetical questions!
4. You shall avoid double stimuli and negations!
5. You shall avoid assumptions and suggestive questions!
6. You shall avoid questions aiming at information many respondents presumably will not have available!
7. You shall use questions with a clear reference to time!
8. You shall use answer categories which are exhaustive and disjunct (free of overlap)!
9. You shall assure that the context of a question does not impact on answering it!
10. You shall define unclear concepts!

 Practical issues

Often questionnaires are distributed and recipients are asked to send them back within a certain time. In this case, the questionnaire will need to be accompanied by a letter providing sufficient information about the study, explaining its importance, and encouraging the recipient to participate. A major problem is the response rate (i.e. the number of questionnaires which are actually filled in and sent back). It is not only necessary that enough questionnaires are returned (50% would be quite a good ratio here); in addition, enough of those returned must have been filled in *completely*.

Finally you should check how far the distribution of the returned questionnaires corresponds to the distribution in the original sample. To use a simple example: the proportion of men to women in a population is two to one. The selection of the sample and the mailout of the questionnaires have taken this proportion into account. If the proportion that characterizes the distribution in the returned questionnaires is completely different from the proportion in the original sample, the results of the study can be generalized to the population in only a very limited way. An alternative is to decide not to mail out the questionnaires, but instead to do a standardized survey with an interviewer, who visits the participants. This may improve the return of questionnaires, though it will be much more time consuming and expensive.

Example: a youth health survey

The youth health survey has already been described in Chapter 2. It is based on a questionnaire covering the topics in Box 7.5 (see Richter 2003).

BOX 7.5

Topics in the youth health survey

- Demographic information: gender, age, family structure, location, form and grade of school, socioeconomic status, ethnic background.
- Subjective health: psychosomatic complaints, mental health, allergies, life satisfaction etc.
- Risk of accidents and violence: accident injuries, mugging (perpetrator and victim), participation in fights, use of substances (tobacco, alcohol, illegal drugs).
- Eating behavior and diets: eating habits, body-mass-index diets etc.
- Physical activity: sports, physical efforts, inactivity because of television and computer etc.
- Social resources: number of friends, support by parents and peers, family situation, living conditions etc.
- School: performance requirements, quality of teaching, support by parents, fellow students and teachers, friends at school, involvement in the school etc.
- Peer group and leisure activities: frequency of meetings, use of media, membership in associations and organizations etc.

Summary

Questionnaires are appropriate for a study when (a) the knowledge about the issue allows you to formulate a sufficient number of questions in an unambiguous way, and (b) a large number of participants will be involved. Questionnaires are highly standardized. The sequence and formulation of questions are defined in advance, as are the possible answers. Questionnaires are often sent out which may produce problems with the response rates.

Non-standardized Inquiries: Interviews and Focus Groups

We turn now to consider alternative forms of interviews. There are semi-structured interviews: these are based on an interview guide with (sometimes different types of) questions to be answered more or less openly and extensively. There are also narrative-based interviews, which focus on inviting the interviewees to recount (aspects of) their life history. Also we find interviews mixing both questions and narrative stimuli. Finally, there are interviews applied to groups rather than single participants. Focus groups are another form of collecting verbal data. Below we consider some of these types in more detail.

Semi-structured interviews

For semi-structured interviews, a number of questions are prepared that between them cover the intended scope of the interview. For this purpose, you will need to develop an interview guide as an orientation for the interviewers. In contrast to questionnaires, interviewers can deviate from the sequence of the questions. They also do not necessarily stick to the exact formulation of the questions when asking them. The aim of the interview is to obtain the individual views of the interviewees on an issue. Thus questions should initiate a dialogue between interviewer and interviewee. Again in contrast to questionnaires, in an interview you will not present a list of possible answers. Rather, the interviewees are expected to reply as freely and as extensively as they wish. If their answers are not rich enough, the interviewer should probe further.

In constructing an interview guide and doing the interview, four criteria are helpful. These have been provided (initially for focused interviews) by Merton and Kendall (1946). They focus on:

- non-direction in the relation with the interviewee
- specificity of the views and definition of the situation from their point of view
- covering a broad range of meanings of the issue
- the depth and personal context shown by the interviewee.

For this purpose, in most cases a variety of questions are applied. Questions may be open ('What do you link to the word "health"?') or semi-structured ('If you think about what you eat, what role does health play in this context?'). Only rarely are structured questions used, which present a statement that the interviewee is expected to agree with or to reject (e.g. 'Many children are eating in too unbalanced a way. In your everyday life as a teacher, is this your impression too?'). Such statements almost have a suggestive character, though they are used sometimes in this context to stimulate the interviewees to reflect about their position or maybe also to make them explicitly express their distinction from the question or statement. Other elements in a semi-structured interview – such as presenting a fictitious case story with questions referring to it (also known as the 'vignette' technique) – can have a similar function.

Decisive for the success of a semi-structured interview is that the interviewer probes at apposite moments and leads the discussion of the issue into greater depth. At the same time, interviewers should ask all the questions in the interview that are relevant for its issue. Open questions should allow room for the specific, personal views of the interviewees and also avoid influencing them. Such open questions should be combined with more focused questions, which are intended to lead the interviewees beyond general, superficial answers and also to introduce issues that the interviewees would not have mentioned spontaneously.

The construction of an interview should of course be linked closely to the aims and the target group of the research. Expert interviews (see Bogner et al. 2009), for example, focus not so much on the personalities of the interviewees, but rather on the need to retrieve their expertise in a specific area. In contrast, if you interview patients about their illness, the people themselves and their personal experiences will be of greater interest. Accordingly, in the first case the experts will be asked more focused questions, while in the second case the patients will be asked more open questions. In all applications of semi-structured interviews, it is only in the interview situation that you can decide when and how extensively to probe. For this purpose, it can be helpful first to do interview training before the data collection. This will consists of role-plays of practice interviews and of comments by others.

Narrative interviews

A different path to discovering the subjective views of participants is found in the narrative interview. Here, it is not questions that are central. Instead, the interviewees are invited to present longer, coherent accounts (say, of their lives as a whole, or of their disease and its course) in the form of a narrative. The method is prominent in biographical research. Hermanns describes its basic principle of collecting data as follows:

> **In the narrative interview, the informant is asked to present the history of an area of interest, in which the interviewee participated, in an extempore narrative … The interviewer's task is to make the informant tell the story of the area of interest in question as a consistent story of all relevant events from its beginning to its end. (1995, p. 183)**

The narrative interview comprises several parts – in particular (a) the interviewee's main narrative, following a 'generative narrative question', (b) the stage of narrative probing in which narrative fragments that were not exhaustively detailed before are completed, and (c) the final stage of the interview (known as the 'balancing phase'), consisting of questions that take the interviewees as experts and theoreticians of themselves.

If you aim to elicit a narrative that is relevant to your research question, you must formulate the generative narrative question broadly yet at the same time sufficiently specifically to produce the desired focus. The interest may relate to the informant's life history in general. In this case, the generative narrative question will be rather generalized: for example, 'I would like to ask you to begin with your life history.' Or the interest may lie in some specific, temporal and topical aspect of the informant's biography, e.g. a phase of professional reorientation and its consequences. An example of the type of generative question required here is:

> I want to ask you to tell me how the story of your life occurred. The best way to do this would be for you to start from your birth, with the little child that you once were, and then tell all the things that happened one after the other until today. You can take your time in doing this, and also give details, because for me everything is of interest that is important for you. (1995, p. 182)

It is important to ensure that the first question really is a narrative generative question and that the interviewer does not impede the interviewee's storytelling with questions or directive or evaluating interventions. A major test of validity here is the question of whether a narrative really was presented by the interviewee. Here you should take into account that 'It is always only "the story of" that can be narrated, not a state or an always recurring routine' (1995, p. 183).

There is a problem presented here by the role expectations of the parties involved. They include a systematic violation of the usual expectations surrounding an 'interview', because the main part of the narrative interview does not consist of questions in the traditional way. At the same time, expectations pertaining to the situation 'everyday narrative' are also violated, as the extensive space for narration that the interviewee is given here in a unilateral way hardly ever occurs in everyday situations. This can produce difficulties for both parties involved. Here, interview training focused on active listening and a clarification of the specific character of the interview situation for the interviewee is necessary.

The narrative interview aims to access interviewees' subjective experiences through three means, namely:

1. The opening question, which aims to stimulate not simply a narrative, but specifically a narrative about the interesting topical area and period in the interviewee's biography.

2. The orientation of the scope for the interviewees in the main narrative part, which enables them to tell their stories perhaps for several hours.

3. The postponing of concrete, structuring, thematically deepening interventions in the interview until the final part, when the interviewer is supposed to pick up issues briefly mentioned and to ask focused questions. This means that any structuring activities of the interviewer are located at the end of the interview and even more so at the beginning.

The episodic interview

Both methods presented so far choose one approach – either questions and answers, or narrative stimulus and telling life histories – as the major approach to an issue under study. For many research questions, however, it is necessary to use a method that combines both principles – narratives and interrogation – equally. The episodic interview (see Flick 2008a; 2009) starts from the assumption that individuals' experiences about a certain area or issue are stored in the forms of narrative-episodic and semantic knowledge. While the first form is focused closely on experiences and linked to concrete situations and circumstances, the second form of knowledge contains abstracted, generalized assumptions and connections. In the first case, the course of the situation in its context is the central unit, around which knowledge is organized. In the second case, concepts and their interrelations form the central units. In order to cover both parts of knowledge about an issue, the method collects narrative-episodic knowledge in narratives and semantic knowledge in concrete and focused questions.

The aim is systematic connection of the two kinds of data (i.e. narratives and answers) and thus of the two kinds of knowledge they make accessible. The episodic interview gives space for context-related presentations in the form of narratives, as they address experiences in their original context more immediately compared to other forms of presentation. At the same time, narratives can elucidate more about processes of constructing realities on the part of the interviewees than other approaches that focus on more abstract concepts and answers.

The focus in the interview is on situations and episodes, in which the interviewee has had experiences that are relevant for the issue of the study. Which form of presentation (description or narrative) is chosen for the single situation, as well as the selection of situations, can be decided by the interviewees according to their subjective relevance for the issue. The aim of the episodic interview is to permit the interviewee for each substantial area to present experiences in a general or comparative form, and at the same time to recount relevant situations and episodes. Planning, doing and analyzing episodic interviews includes the following steps (see Flick 2000a). As a preparation, you should develop an interview guide, which includes narrative stimuli and questions for the areas and aspects you see as relevant for the issue of your study. At the beginning of the interview, you should introduce the principle of the interview, explaining that you will repeatedly invite the interviewee to recount specific situations. The general problem of interviews based on narratives is relevant here, too; some people have more problems with narrating than others. Therefore it is very important that you explain the principle of recounting situations to the interviewees. Interviewees should be encouraged to recount relevant situations, rather then merely mention them. You should take care that the interviewee has understood and accepted the method. An example of such an introduction to the interview principle is: 'In this interview, I will ask you a number of times to tell me situations in which you have had experiences with the topic of health.'

With the opening questions, you invite the interviewees to present their subjective definition of the issue of the research and to recount relevant situations. Examples of such questions are: 'What does "health" mean for you? What do you link with the word "health"?', or 'What has influenced your ideas of health in a particular way? Could you please tell me a situation which makes this clear for me?' Which exemplary situation they choose and recount for this purpose is always a decision of the interviewees. You can subsequently analyze both the selection and the account of the situation that each interviewee focuses on.

The next part of the interview will focus on the role or relevance of the issue under study for the participants' everyday lives. For this purpose, you can ask them to recount how a day (e.g. yesterday) went and what relevance the issue had on that day. If a multitude of situations is mentioned, you should pick up the most interesting ones and probe for a more detailed presentation. Again it is interesting for the analysis to identity which situations the interviewees pick up themselves for recounting. An example of a question addressing changes in the relevance of the issue is: 'Do you have the impression that your idea of health has changed during your professional life? Could you please recount a situation for me which shows this change?'

Next you will ask the interviewees to outline their personal relation to major aspects of the issue under study. For example, 'What does it mean for you to promote health as part of your work? Could you please tell me a situation of this kind?' You should ask the interviewee to illustrate these examples of personal experiences and subjective concepts as substantially and comprehensively as possible by probing if necessary.

In the final part of the interview, you will ask the interviewees to talk about more general aspects of the focal issue and to present their personal views in this context. This is meant to extend the scope of the interview. You should try as much as possible to link these general answers with the more personal and concrete examples used before so that possible discrepancies and contradictions become visible. An example of such a generalizing question is: 'Who do you think is responsible for your health? Is there a situation for which you can outline this?'

As in other interviews, the final question should ask the respondent for aspects missing from the questions or ask whether there is anything that should be added (e.g. 'Is there anything else …?').

Immediately after the interview, you should complete a sheet on which you document socio-demographic information about the interviewee and features of the particular interview situation. Any disturbances and anything mentioned about the issue of the interview after the recording device was turned off should be noted as well, provided that is ethically acceptable (see Flick 2009, p. 299 for an example of such a documentary sheet).

Example: health concepts of homeless adolescents

In Chapter 2, the study on the health concepts of homeless adolescents was described. Our interviews with the adolescents were based on the episodic interview and covered the areas in Box 7.6, for which some examples of questions and narrative stimuli are presented.

Excerpts from an interview guide for an episodic interview

Health concepts: general and individual definition of health, relevance, possible influences

- First of all, I would like to ask you to tell me what life in your family was like. What made you turn to living on the street? Can you tell me of a situation which explains this for me?
- Now let's turn to our topic. What is that for you – health?
- How do you decide that you are healthy? Can you please tell me about a situation which helps me to understand this?

Links of factors and risks in the life world to health concepts and practices

- If you think of how you live these days, is there anything which influences your health? Can you tell me about a situation which explains this for me?
- Do you see any relation between your current housing situation and your health? Can you tell me about a situation which explains this for me?
- How do you deal with illness? Can you tell me of a situation which explains this for me?
- Do you think that your financial situation has an influence on your health? How? Can you give me a situation for this?

Risk behavior and secondary prevention as part of health practices

- Do you think that you sometimes risk your health by what you do? Is there a situation you can tell me about?
- If you think of drugs and alcohol, what do you use? Please give a situation when you do this.

Illness experiences and dealing with them

- When you do not feel well, what are your major problems? How do you think this problem [mentioned by the interviewee] comes about?

Focus groups and group discussions

An alternative to interviewing individuals is to use group interviews in which several participants are asked the same question and they answer one after the other. Alternatively – and more commonly – a group may be used as an interaction community. Since the 1950s, group discussions have been used mainly in German speaking areas and, in parallel, focus groups were used in the Anglo-Saxon world. In both cases, data collection is based on inaugurating a discussion in a group about the issue of the study. For example, pupils discuss their experiences with violence and how they deal with it, or students evaluate the quality of their courses and of the teaching in focus groups.

The starting point for using this method is that these discussions can make apparent how attitudes or evaluations are developed and changed. Participants are likely to express more and go further in their statements than in single interviews. The dynamics of the groups become an essential part of the data and of their collection.

For group discussions, a variety of forms of group can be used. You can start from a natural group (i.e. a group that exists in everyday life beyond the research), or from a real group (which is confronted in its everyday life by the issue of the study), or from artificial groups (set up for the research according to specific criteria). You can also distinguish between homogeneous and heterogeneous groups. In homogeneous groups, the members are similar in essential dimensions with respect to the research question: for example, they may have a similar professional background. In heterogeneous groups, the members should differ in the features that are relevant for the research question. Focus groups and group discussions can be moderated in different ways. You can refrain from any form of moderation, or do some formal steering (setting up a list of speakers), or do a more substantial moderation (by introducing topics or intervening with some provoking questions). One starts a focus group or a group discussion with a discussion stimulus, which can be a provoking question, a comic or a text, or the presentation of a short film.

In general you should be aware that running focus groups may require a lot of organizational effort (in coordinating the date of the meeting, for example). Afterwards it is the various groups that can be compared rather than all participants across the groups. Thus you should compare the various groups with each other, rather than the single members. You should use this method only if you have good reasons because of the research question and not because you expect to save some time compared to single interviews (see also Chapter 11).

Conclusion

The methods presented so far aim at collecting verbal data – whether by interviewing individuals, by inviting them to recount autobiographical experience, or by having groups discussing an issue. These methods make the knowledge about practices and processes accessible, but do not give immediate access to practices and processes in their course.

Observation

More direct access to practices and processes is provided by the use of observations. Here we can also distinguish several concepts regarding the role of the researcher:

- Covert and overt observation: how far are the observed persons or fields informed that they are observed?

- Non-participant and participant observation: how far do the observers become active parts of the field that is observed?

- Systematic and unsystematic observation: is a more or less standardized observation scheme applied or are the processes observed more openly?

- Observation in natural or artificial settings: do the researchers enter the relevant fields, or do they 'transfer' the interactions to a specific room (a laboratory) for improving the quality of the observations?

- Introspection or observation of others: in most cases, observation will focus on other people. What role does the researcher's reflecting introspection have in making the interpretations of the observed more solid?

- Standardized and non-standardized observation: in most cases, complex situations are now observed with open and adapted methods. However, approaches using observation categories defined in advance for observing a sample of situations are also applied.

- Experimental and non-experimental observation: in the first case, you will intervene specifically and observe the consequences of such an intervention.

Standardized Observations

Bortz and Döring describe this approach as follows:

> **The observation plan of a standardized observation exactly defines what to observe and how to protocol what was observed. The events to observe are known in principle and can be dismantled in single elements or segments, which are exclusively the issue or the observer's attention. (2006, p. 270)**

For standardized observation, you will draw a sample either of events or of time. The first alternative is oriented to certain events (e.g. a certain activity) in their frequency in the period of observation or in the frequency of occurrence in combination with other events: how often do girls answer in a mathematics class, or how often do they do so after a specific question is asked? To answer these questions, a whole class is observed and the frequency of the events is noted. An alternative is to draw a time sample. Here, the observation is segmented in fixed periods in which you observe or maybe change the object of observation – for example, in five minute intervals, which are randomly sampled from the observation period (mathematics class). The observations are done with a standardized observation scheme, often after training for the observers in dealing with the situation and the instrument. Observations can be documented with video and then be noted off the tape. A problem can be that the camera (or the observation scheme) does not cover the essentials of the situation. In time sampling, the relevant events may occur outside the selected periods.

This basic situation of social science observation – the researchers observe the field, and the people in it, by using a sample and confine themselves to noting the processes – can be extended in several directions in research practice.

Experiments

In experimental research, especially in psychology, observation may be focused on a deliberate intervention in one group, which is then compared to a second group in which this intervention is absent. For example, in school observations, the teacher may apply an intervention reducing aggression in one group – e.g. a teaching unit about de-escalation in situations of conflict. Then, in a second group, this intervention is not applied. Both groups will then be observed in their behavior in the next situation of conflict that occurs and compared. If the groups are set up by random sampling, this will be an experimental study. If the groups already exist (two seventh grades) this is a quasi-experimental study. The observation is applied according to the principles mentioned earlier – e.g. in sampling times or persons. The researchers will do a non-participant observation and use an observation protocol for documenting behaviors defined as relevant in advance. In our example, the data will still be collected in a field observation (in class). This will make standardization of the research situation more complicated. Therefore observation in the laboratory, i.e. an artificial situation under controlled conditions, is the alternative to observing in the natural context of teaching situations.

Participant Observation

A contrasting form of data collection is provided by participant observation. Here, the researcher's distance from the observed situation is reduced. Their participation over an extended period in the field that is studied becomes an essential instrument of data collection. At the same time, the observation is much less standardized. Here, you will also do some sampling of the situations that are observed, but not in the sense of time sampling as described above. Rather, you will select situations, persons and events according to how far the interesting phenomenon becomes accessible in this selection. The principal procedure can be summarized in Jörgensen's words by 'a logic and process of inquiry that is open-ended, flexible, opportunistic, and requires constant redefinition of what is problematic, based on facts gathered in concrete settings of human existence' (1989, p. 13).

Participant observation can be understood as a two-part process. First, the researchers are supposed to become participants and find access to the field and the persons in it. Second, the observation itself becomes more concrete and more strongly oriented to the essential aspects of the research question. Here we can distinguish three phases (see Spradley 1980, p. 34). First, descriptive observation for orienting in the study field is supposed to provide rather unspecific descriptions, to cover the complexity of the field as far as possible and to make research questions more concrete. Second, focused observation is more and more limited to the processes and problems that are particularly relevant for the research question. Selective observation at the end of data collection is supposed to find further evidence and examples for the processes identified in the second step. The documentation mostly consists of detailed field notes of protocols of situations. Whenever possible, research ethics (see Chapter 12) demand that observations are conducted openly, so that the observed people know that they are observed and have agreed beforehand to being observed. Third, for (participant) observation, the problem often is that certain issues are not immediately accessible at the level of practice, but only or mainly become 'visible' in interactions when people talk about the issues. Some topics are only an issue in conversations with the research or in *ad hoc* interviews. However, the results of a participant observation will be more fruitful when more insights come from protocols of activities and fewer come from reports about activities. Nevertheless, conversations, interrogations and other data sources will always comprise a big part of the knowledge process in participant observation.

Ethnography

Recently, the more general strategy of ethnography has tended to replace participant observation. However, observation and participation are interlinked with other procedures in this strategy as well:

> **In its most characteristic form it involves the ethnographer participating, overtly or covertly, in people's daily lives for an extended period of time, watching what happens, listening to what is said, asking questions – in fact, collecting whatever data are available to throw light on the issues that are the focus of the research. (Hammersley and Atkinson 1995, p. 1)**

This strategy will help you adapt data collection to your research question and to conditions in the field most consistently. Methods are subordinated to the research practice in the field. There is a strong emphasis on exploring a field or phenomenon. You will collect mostly unstructured data instead of using categories defined in advance and an observation scheme. For this purpose, a few cases are involved (or even a single case). Data analysis focuses on interpretation of meanings and functions of practices, statements and processes (see Hammersley and Atkinson 1995, p. 110–11). Lüders sees the central defining features of ethnography as follows:

> **first [there is] the risk and the moments of the research process which cannot be planned and are situational, coincidental and individual ... Second, the researcher's skillful activity in each situation becomes more important ... Third, ethnography ... transforms into a strategy of research which includes as many options of collecting data as can be imagined and are justifiable. (1995, pp. 320–1; see also Lüders, 2004a)**

Conclusion

The observational methods described above vary in the distance the researchers maintain to the field that is observed; the alternatives are to participate or just to observe from the outside. Furthermore the methods differ in the degree of control of the conditions of the study exerted by the researchers. Control is strongest in the laboratory experiment and weakest in participant observation. They can also be distinguished by the standardization of the research situations – again, most limited in participant observation and strongest for the experiment. In general, for observation, the idea guiding data collection is that it provides more immediate access to practices and routines compared to interviews and surveys. However, in most cases, conversations, statements and questions or sometimes *ad hoc* interviews are involved in observations.

Working with Documents

The methods presented so far have in common that you will *produce* data with them – data such as answers in a survey, or a narrative in an interview, or the observations and descriptions in the field or laboratory. As an alternative, you can use already *existing* materials, e.g. documents resulting from an institutional process. These can be texts or images, which can be analyzed in a qualitative or quantitative way depending on the research question. The analysis of documents can refer to existing materials – like diaries – which have not yet been used as data in other contexts. Sometimes they refer to existing datasets from other contexts – like official statistics, which have been produced not for research but for purposes of documentation.

The term 'secondary analysis' means that you <u>analyze data that were not collected for your own research project</u>. Instead, you use existing datasets that were <u>produced for other purposes</u>.

Kinds of secondary analyses

Here we can distinguish between reanalyzing data from other research projects and data produced for purposes other than research. In the second category, we find data from federal bureaux of statistics which are collected, elaborated and analyzed for monitoring purposes. They can be used for a number of research questions. In the first category, you will find data produced and analyzed by other researchers in studying a specific issue that now can be used again by other researchers for their own research questions. This can be organized through the direct cooperation of researchers with other researchers. But there are also several institutions which collect datasets from research projects and provide them for other researchers, who pay for the right to use these data. Examples of such institutions are GESIS in Germany and GALLUP in the US. In several contexts, datasets are elaborated as 'public use files' and made available to interested researchers for further work with them.

Selecting and weighting secondary data

The advantage of analyzing secondary data is that <u>you do not need to collect data and so can save time</u>. However, you should consider some questions and problems arising when you use secondary data. First, you should check whether these data fit your research question: do they include the information necessary to answer it? Second, you should assess whether the form of elaboration in which the data are available corresponds to the aims of your study. A simple example will illustrate: if your research question refers to a distribution of age in one-year steps but the available dataset has classified the studied people in age groups (for example in five-year steps) and if this classification cannot be traced back to the single value in years, this might produce problems in the usability of the data for your purpose. A second example: many epidemiological studies have been based on death cause statistics in local health authorities for reconstructing the frequencies of certain diseases as death causes. Here, in many cases, it was not the single death certificate which was used as data but the classification done by the single health authority. Here again the problem results that the classification of different death causes (or diseases) in categories will not necessarily be the same as the researchers needed or would have applied for their study and research question. Mistakes made in allocating a single case to a category cannot be assessed in such a dataset (see Chapter 8). The more general problem is that the data are available in aggregated form only, i.e. elaborated and processed, and that the original raw data are not accessible.

Qualitative Analysis of Documents

Alternatively, you may use existing documents for a qualitative analysis. The following definition outlines what is generally understood as 'documents':

> **Documents are *standardized artifacts*, in so far as they typically occur in particular *formats*: as notes, case reports, contracts, drafts, death certificates, remarks, diaries, statistics, annual reports, certificates, judgments, letters or expert opinions. (Wolff 2004, p. 284)**

Again you can use documents produced for your study. For example you might ask a group of people to write a diary over the next 12 months and then analyze and compare what was noted in these diaries. Or you might use existing documents, for example the diaries written by a specific group of people (e.g. patients with a specific diagnosis) in their everyday lives independent of the research. Documents are mostly available as texts (in printed form) and more and more also or exclusively in electronic form (e.g. in a database).

Many official or private documents are meant only for a limited circle of recipients who are authorized to access them or who are addressed by them. Official documents allow conclusions about what their authors or the institutions they represent do or intend, or how they evaluate. Documents are produced for a certain purpose – e.g. for substantiating a decision or for convincing a person or an authority. But that also means that documents represent issues only in a limited way. When analyzing them for research purposes, you should always consider who has produced a document, for whom, and for what purpose. How documents are designed is a part of their meaning; how something is presented influences which effects are produced with a document.

From a practical point of view, the first step is to identify the relevant documents. For analyzing official records, you have to find out where they are stored and whether they are accessible for research purposes. Then you have to make the appropriate selection: which of the existing records will you concretely use and why (see also Rapley 2008)?

Visual Data: Photo and Film

Visual data, such as photos, film and videos, have attracted increasing attention as documents to be used in research (see Knoblauch et al. 2006). Again, we can distinguish two approaches: cameras can be used as instruments for data collection and images can be produced for research purposes; or existing images can be selected for the research and analyzed. An approach can be to analyze the photos in family albums and the family's or the individual's history as documented in these photos over time. In research with families or institutions, the analysis of self-presentations in photos or images of the members displayed on the walls of rooms can give insights into the structures of the social field (see Banks 2008). Media analyses also address films or TV series for analyzing the presentation of certain problems and how a society deals with them (see Denzin 2004 for this).

Conclusion

When you use existing materials (texts, images, datasets) for your study, you will save time at the data collection stage, since this is limited to selecting from the existing material. But you should not underestimate the obstacles arising from such material: photos, texts and statistics have their own structure that is often strongly influenced by who produced them and for what purpose. If this structure is not compatible with the demands for data arising from your own research question, this may produce selectivity problems. To solve these problems can sometimes be more expensive and time consuming than to collect your own data. Thus, to use secondary data in particular and existing materials in general is only suggested if the research question gives you good reasons to do so.

Obtaining and Documenting Information

Social research is based on data collected with empirical methods. In general we can distinguish two major groups of methods. Quantitative methods aim at covering the phenomena under study in their frequencies or distributions and therefore work with big numbers of cases in data collection. Numbers are in the foreground. For example, you could collect how often waiting times in the hospital occur, what the average time is that a patient waits (unnecessarily) before a treatment, and how this is distributed over the week.

Qualitative methods are more interested in an exact description of processes and views and therefore often work with small numbers of cases. In the foreground are texts – e.g. transcribed interviews. In our example you would collect data about how situations occur in which patients wait (unnecessarily), what subjective explanations the staff have for this, or how single patients experience these situations of waiting.

Data collection in qualitative research pursues different aims, and is grounded on different principles, from quantitative research. Quantitative research is devoted to the ideals of measurement and works with numbers, scales and index construction. Qualitative research is more oriented to producing protocols of its research issues and to documenting and reconstructing them. Before we turn to methods of analyzing data (see Chapter 8), we will briefly consider these aims and principles.

Measurement

For quantitative methods, a measurement is assumed; in a time measure, for example, the duration of an event is identified with a measurement instrument (a watch). This is fairly unproblematic if there is an established unit (e.g. a minute, a centimetre) and a means of measurement to identify how many of these units are given in the concrete case (e.g. 15 minutes of waiting time). However, often this unit does not exist for the objects social science is interested in and has to be defined by the researcher. To measure then is to allocate a number to a certain object or event. Three problems are linked to this allocation. First, the number comes to represent the object or its feature in the further progress of the research – in other words, the object itself is no longer part of the process. In addition, different numerical values represent differences and relations between the objects. For example, extensions of waiting time before an operation are measured in minutes. In this case, you can assume that two minutes are always two minutes and four minutes are twice as long as two minutes. Another example illustrates the other two problems, namely unambiguousness and significance. The subjective distress of the patient has to be translated into a numerical value first. If 'extremely stressful' equals 4, 'very stressful' equals 3 and 'stressful' equals 2 on a scale, you can assume neither that the distance between 2 and 3 is as big as that between 3 and 4, nor that a value of 2 always represents the same degree of subjective distress. This is the question of the unambiguousness of measurement values. Finally, you cannot assume in this example that a value of 4 here represents double the value of 2. This is the problem of significance. That raises questions about which mathematical operations make sense based on the measurements made.

Scaling

The allocation of numerical values to an object or an event leads to the construction of a scale. Here, four kinds of scales are distinguished.

A nominal scale allocates objects with identical features to identical numerical values. For example, male as gender might be labeled with 1, female as gender with 2. A relation between the values does not exist.

In ordinal scales, a relation of ordering exists between the values. If, in our example, the degree of the patients' subjective distress is labeled as 4 when the situation is extremely stressful, 3 when it is very stressful and 2 when it is stressful, this represents an order between the different degrees of subjective distress. But here, the distances between the values are not necessarily the same.

In an interval scale, in contrast, the distances between two values are always the same. An example is the Fahrenheit temperature scale.

Table 7.2　Kinds of scale

Kind of scale	Possible statements	Examples	Answers and values
Nominal scale	Equality differences	Gender	☐ Male ☐ Female
		Professional groups	☐ Physician ☐ Teacher
		Satisfied by the treatment	☐ Yes ☐ No
Ordinal scale	Bigger–smaller relations	Social status	☐ Upper class ☐ Middle class ☐ Working class
		School grades	☐ Very good ☐ Good ☐ Satisfying ☐ Sufficient ☐ Failed
Interval scale	Sameness of differences	Temperature (°F)	☐ 36 °F ☐ 37 °F ☐ 38 °F
		Calendar, time intervals (e.g. of sickness leave per year)	☐ One day ☐ Two days ☐ Three days
Ratio scale	Sameness of relations	Weight	☐ One kilogram ☐ Two kilograms ☐ Three kilograms
		Length	☐ One centimetre ☐ Two centimetres ☐ Three centimetres

A ratio scale is given if not only the distances between values are the same, but you can assume that two units of distance represent twice the distance of one unit. Examples are measurements of length or weight: the distance between 2 kg and 3 kg is the same as the distance between 5 kg and 6 kg, and 6 kg is twice as heavy as 3 kg. A ratio scale furthermore has a fixed point zero. Ratio scales are seldom found in the social sciences and their research.

The kind of scale determines which calculations are justified for each scale (see Chapter 8). Table 7.2 summarizes the various kinds of scale.

Counting

If you want to count certain objects, this assumes that the objects to be counted are equal in their major features: that is, that you are not 'comparing apples and oranges'. If you want to count people, activities or situations, the sameness as a precondition of the countability has to be produced in advance. People are characterized by strong individuality and diversity. They can be counted if they can be classified according to specific features – e.g. their ages. The age is already defined as a number. For other, more qualitative features, first a classification in numerical form has to be done beforehand. Someone is either male or female. People can be helpful in varying degrees (not at all, a bit, average, very or extraordinarily helpful). To be able to count such a feature, the characteristic has to be classified and labeled with a numerical value (not at all helpful is classified as 1, a bit helpful as 2 etc.). Then you can count these features and relate them to others using numerical values. A precondition is that a feature like helpfulness can be classified with such categories. For this purpose, it must be possible to define categories exactly (e.g. what does 'a bit helpful' or 'not all helpful' mean?). Categories should be able to describe the feature in an exhaustive way (it must be possible to allocate all possible forms of helpfulness to these categories).

Constructing an Index

For quantitative features like age, all persons with a certain value (age) are summarized (e.g. all 25-year-olds) or allocated to specific age groups (e.g. the 20- to 30-year-olds). Often, more complex features have to be counted. Many studies start from the social status of a person (e.g. for finding out whether people with a high social status fall ill less often than people with low social status). The social status is constructed from various single features – the state of education, the profession, the income, the situation of housing. This means an index is constructed in which these single features are combined. Counting then is applied to this index. The parts of the index can have the same weight or can be weighted differently, e.g. when income counts twice as much as the other parts of the social state. In the research on quality of life (see for example Guggenmoos-Holzmann et al. 1995) a variety of quality of life indices have been established.

Protocols

While quantitative research is based on measurement and counting, qualitative research tends to refrain from using such numerical values. Rather, the first step is to produce a protocol of the events and of the context in which they occurred. The protocol should be as detailed, comprehensive and exact as possible. For observations, you will produce detailed descriptions of situations and of their contexts. Interviews are recorded on tape or on mp3 players and this is complemented by memory protocols of the interview situation. Interactions are documented on audio or video tape in order to make possible a repeated and more or less unfiltered access to the raw data. Whereas in interviews the data are produced with methods (questions lead to answers or narratives, which are produced specifically for the research), several other approaches in qualitative research, like ethnography or conversation analysis (see Chapter 8 and Flick 2009 for more details), restrict themselves to recording and proto-colling everyday life situations, without intervening with questions for example. Quantitative research produces a specific condensation of the data already in the data collection by delimiting them to specific questions and possible answers. Qualitative research is first interested in less condensed data. Reduction of the information here is part of the analysis. The original data should remain available in an unfiltered way and accessible repeatedly.

Documentation

Documentation of the data has a specific relevance here. A comprehensive recording is seen as most important for qualitative research. Therefore audio or video recording has priority over making notes of answers or practices only at a glance. Only where technical recording devices are in the way of the method – when they prevent the researcher from participating and from integrating into the field in participant observation, for example – is the preference still for field notes and protocols made after the observation (see Flick 2009, Chapter 22 for more details). A detailed and comprehensive recording leads in most cases to a similarly exact transcript of the data. This should include as much as possible of the context information for the interviewees' statements. Here again, an unobstructed view of the reality under study is seen as highly relevant.

Exactness in documenting the events is a precondition for a detailed inter-pretation of the statements and occurrences grounded in the data.

Reconstruction

In the analysis and interpretation of the data, it becomes possible to recon-struct – asking, for example, how does or did something occur, or what views the participants had on this occurrence. In a detailed reconstruction of case trajectories, data are obtained which then will be the subject of comparison. This comparison does not work with numbers, but nevertheless is intended to arrive at generalizing statements. For example, reconstructions of single trajec-tories lead to constructing types of processes and detailed descriptions of these types. Here it is less important how often these types can be identified. Rather the question is how far these types cover the range of existing trajectories and allow inferences about when and under what conditions each type is relevant.

Summary

The two kinds of methods – quantitative and qualitative – are often character-ized as 'standardized' and 'non-standardized methods' respectively because an essential difference is their degree of standardization of the procedures. Analyzing data from a questionnaire in a quantitative and statistical way makes sense only when the data collection was standardized by uniform question wording and sequence and uniform alternatives for answering them. This requires that every participant is under exactly the same conditions in answering the questions. Qualitative studies in contrast are often most fruitful when the procedures are less standardized and are applied in a flexible way so that new and unexpected aspects become relevant. At the same time, specific attention is paid to including context information: the participants' answers are not meant to speak as facts for themselves. Rather they should be embedded in a longer narrative or extended presentation. This will then allow insights into the subjective meaning of what has been presented and thus make clear in which contexts the interviewees themselves understand their statements.

Checklist for Designing Data Collection

In doing your empirical project in social research, you should consider the points in Box 7.7 for selecting and conceptualizing methods of data collection. These questions can be helpful for doing your own study and also for assessing the studies of other researchers.

BOX 7.7

Checklist for designing data collection

1. What are the major aspects that should be covered by the data collection?
2. Is the focus more on practices referring to an issue or more on knowledge about it?
3. Do existing data already include the relevant information, so that it is not necessary to collect your own data?
4. Do the existing data and their content, their degree of detailing, fit your own research question?
5. What is the intention for the data in their later analysis? Are the data provided by the actual method of data collection appropriate for this kind of analysis (in their exactness, structure and level of scaling)?
6. What scope for idiosyncrasies (of the contents or the way of presenting them by the participants) do the selected methods offer, and what scope is necessary for answering the research question?
7. What degree of exactness in documenting and transcribing qualitative data is necessary for answering the research question?

■ ■ Further Reading ■

The first and fourth of the texts listed below provide a comprehensive overview of social research methods with a stronger focus on quantitative methods; the second and third concentrate more on qualitative methods.

Bryman, A. (2008) *Social Research Methods,* 3rd edn. Oxford: Oxford University Press.

Flick, U. (2009) *An Introduction to Qualitative Research,* 4th edn. London: Sage.

Flick, U. (ed.) (2007) *The Sage Qualitative Research Kit,* 8 vols. London: Sage.

Neuman, W.L. (2000) *Social Research Methods: Qualitative and Quantitative Approaches,* 4th edn. Boston: Allyn and Bacon.

CHAPTER 8
ANALYZING QUANTITATIVE AND QUALITATIVE DATA

Chapter Overview

Chapter Objectives

This chapter is designed to help you:

- understand some major methods of data analysis in social research
- understand the similarities and differences between the procedures of qualitative and quantitative data analysis
- be able to assess which methods are available for your research and what they can provide.

Table 8.1 Navigator for Chapter 8

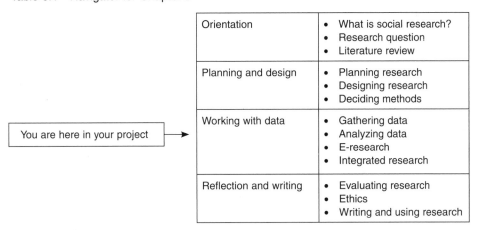

Orientation	• What is social research? • Research question • Literature review
Planning and design	• Planning research • Designing research • Deciding methods
Working with data	• Gathering data • Analyzing data • E-research • Integrated research
Reflection and writing	• Evaluating research • Ethics • Writing and using research

You are here in your project →

The previous chapter discussed selected methods of data collection. In this chapter, we turn to describing methods for analyzing the data that has been collected. We first consider quantitative and qualitative content analysis. We then focus on quantifying analyses for standardized data. Finally, we look at interpretative methods for analyzing qualitative data from interviews and participant observations.

Content Analysis

Content analysis is a classical procedure for analyzing text material of whatever origin, from media products to interview data. It is 'an empirical method for systematic, inter-subjectively transparent description of substantial and formal features of messages' (Früh 1991, p. 25). The method is based on using categories derived from theoretical models. One normally applies such categories to texts, rather than develop them from the material itself – though one may of course revise the categories in the light of the texts under analysis. Content analysis aims at classifying the content of texts by allocating statements, sentences or words to a system of categories.

Below we distinguish quantitative and qualitative content analyses.

Quantitative Content Analysis

Analyzing newspaper articles

While *qualitative* content analysis is seen as a method of *analyzing* for example data from interviews, some sources see *quantitative* content analysis rather as a specific method for *collecting* data (e.g. Bortz and Döring 2006). Schnell et al. (2008, p. 407) see the method as 'a mixture of "analytic technique" and data collection procedure'. It is used for collecting and classifying information, e.g. in newspaper articles. We find as a definition:

> **Quantitative content analysis captures single features of text by categorizing parts of the text in categories, which are operationalizations of the interesting features. The frequencies of the single categories inform about the features of the analyzed text. (Bortz and Döring 2006, p. 149)**

In the foreground of such analyses are the questions: (a) what characterizes the communication about a specific issue in certain media, and (b) what impact does this have on the addressees? Communication according to this model can be defined according to the formula of Laswell (1938): WHO (communicator) SAYS (writes, mentions in form of signs ...) WHAT (message) in WHICH CHANNEL (medium) to WHOM (receiver) and WITH WHAT EFFECT?

The methodological core of content analysis is the category system used to classify the materials you study. The allocation of a passage in the text to a category is described as coding. A crucial step is that you select the right materials (the sample that is drawn from the text) and the correct units for your analysis. Which texts from which newspaper and on which publishing days should you select? Will you analyze single words, or will you allocate whole sentences or paragraphs to the categories?

Analytic strategies

We can distinguish several analytic strategies. In simple frequency analyses, you ask how often certain concepts are mentioned in the texts you analyze. This method is used for inferring the medial presence of a topic in the daily newspapers: e.g. how often was the topic 'health fund' an issue in the most important German press releases in the period under study (see Table 8.2)?

In a contingency analysis, you do not seek only the frequency of concepts (and thus of topics) in the relevant period in the press. Contingency analysis is interested in which other concepts appear at the same time: for example, how often is the issue 'health fund' mentioned together with 'caring deficits' or 'costs' (see Table 8.3)?

Quantitative content analysis of other texts

Quantitative content analysis is often used for analyzing newspaper articles. However, you can use it as a method for analyzing interviews or other materials that have been produced for research purposes.

Steps in quantitative content analysis

We can distinguish several steps in the analysis. First you will decide which texts are relevant for the purpose of your study. The next step is to draw a sample from

Table 8.2 Frequency analysis in content analysis

	Health fund
Newspaper A 20.10.2008	
Newspaper B 20.10.2008	
Newspaper A 21.10.2008	
Newspaper B 21.10.2008	
Newspaper A 22.10.2008	
Newspaper B 22.10.2008	
Newspaper A 23.10.2008	
Newspaper B 23.10.2008	

Table 8.3 Contingency analysis in content analysis

	Health fund	Caring deficits	Costs	Interest of health insurers
Newspaper A 20.10.2008				
Newspaper B 20.10.2008				
Newspaper A 21.10.2008				
Newspaper B 21.10.2008				
Newspaper A 22.10.2008				
Newspaper B 22.10.2008				
Newspaper A 23.10.2008				
Newspaper B 23.10.2008				

these texts before you define the counting unit (all or certain words, groups of words, sentences, complete articles, headlines etc.). From the research question and from its theoretical background, you will next derive a system of categories. These should be (a) mutually exclusive (clearly distinguishing), (b) exhaustive, (c) precise, (d) based on discrete dimensions, and (e) independent of each other.

The classification of texts with categories aims mainly at reducing the material. The category system can consist of concepts and subconcepts. Often, a dictionary is established that includes the names of categories and the definitions and rules for allocating words to categories. For applying the categories to texts, coding rules are defined. Coders collect the analytic units by applying the categories that were defined before. Coders are trained for this purpose and the coding system is checked in a pre-test for its reliability (correspondence of allocation by different coders). Then statistical analyses are applied for identifying how often certain words in total or in connection with other words appear in the text and for analyzing the distribution of categories and contents (see below).

Problems of quantitative content analysis

Problems in quantitative content analysis arise from the necessary isolation of single words or passages, which are thus taken out of their context. Texts are decomposed in their elements, which then can be used as empirical units. This makes it more difficult to grasp any meaning or coherence of and in texts.

For example, there have been attempts to identify changes in attitudes towards the elderly by analyzing newspaper articles using the frequencies with which certain words (e.g. 'frail' or 'experience') appear together with 'age' or 'old people'. If the concepts or the frequencies in which they are used together with 'age' and 'old people' are changing, this is used to infer changes in attitudes towards aging.

Thus the application of content analysis is often rather reductionist. This may result from strong standardization and the use of small analytical units (e.g. a single word) in order to provide repeatability, stability and exactness of the analysis. Repeatability refers to the degree to which classifications of the material are completed in the same way by several analysts. Stability means that the method of classification of content does not vary over time. Exactness indicates how far the coding of a text corresponds with the norm of coding or the standard coding.

A strength of quantitative content analysis is that you can analyze large amounts of data with it. The procedures can be standardized to a high degree. Frequencies and distributions of statements, attitudes etc. can be calculated. The weakness of quantitative content analysis is that one rules out the analysis of single cases right from the beginning: the single text and its structure or particularity as a whole are not taken into account. The context of words is rather neglected. How far the analysis of frequencies or topics in texts is sufficient for answering substantive research questions has been debated since the early days of research with content analysis.

Qualitative Content Analysis

Against the background of the limitations of quantifying approaches, Mayring (1983) has developed his approach of a qualitative content analysis.

The procedure of qualitative content analysis

The first step here is to define the material (e.g. to select the interviews or those parts that are relevant for answering the research question). Then you will analyze the situation of data collection (how was the material generated, who was involved, who was present in the interview situation, where the documents to be analyzed come from, and so on). You will continue by formally characterizing the material (was the material documented with a recording or a protocol? Was there an influence on the transcription of the text when it was edited? and so on). Then, you will define the direction of the analysis for the selected texts and 'what one actually wants to interpret out of them' (1983, p. 45).

In the next step, the research question is further defined on the basis of theories. A precondition is that the 'research question of the analysis must be clearly defined in advance, must be linked theoretically to earlier research on the issue and generally has to be differentiated in sub-questions' (1983, p. 47). After that, you will select the analytic technique (see below) and define the units. The 'coding unit' defines what is 'the smallest element of material which may be analyzed, the minimal part of the text which may fall under a category'; the 'contextual unit' defines what is the largest element in the text which may fall under a category; the 'analytic unit' defines which passages 'are analyzed one after the other'. Now you conduct the actual analyses before you interpret their final results with respect to the research question. In the end, you will ask and answer questions of validity (see Figure 8.1).

Techniques of qualitative content analysis

The concrete methical procedure essentially involves three techniques. In *summarizing content analysis*, you will paraphrase the material so that you can skip less relevant passages and paraphrases with the same meanings (this is the first reduction) and bundle and summarize similar paraphrases (the second reduction). For example, in an interview with an unemployed teacher, the statement 'and actually, quite the reverse, I was well very, very keen on finally teaching for the first time' (1983, p. 59) was paraphrased as 'quite the reverse, very keen on practice' and generalized as 'rather looking forward to practice'. The statement 'therefore, I have already waited for it, to go to a seminar school, until I finally could teach there for the first time' was paraphrased as 'waited to teach finally' and generalized as 'looking forward to practice'. Owing to the similarity of the two generalizations, the second one then is skipped and reduced with other statements to 'practice not experienced as shock but as big fun' (1983, p. 59).

Explicative content analysis works in the opposite way. It clarifies diffuse, ambiguous or contradictory passages by involving contextual material in the analysis. Definitions taken from dictionaries or based on the grammar are used or formulated. 'Narrow context analysis' picks up additional statements from the text in order to explicate the passages to be analyzed, whereas 'wide context analysis' seeks information outside the text (about the author, the generative situations, from theories). On this basis, an 'explicating paraphrase' is formulated and tested.

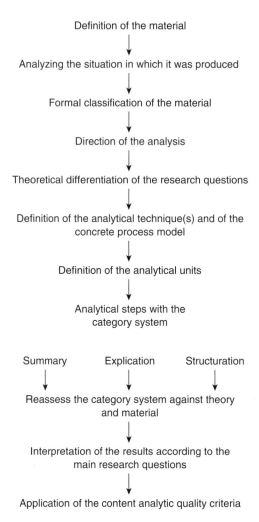

Definition of the material

↓

Analyzing the situation in which it was produced

↓

Formal classification of the material

↓

Direction of the analysis

↓

Theoretical differentiation of the research questions

↓

Definition of the analytical technique(s) and of the
concrete process model

↓

Definition of the analytical units

↓

Analytical steps with the
category system

Summary   Explication   Structuration

↓   ↓   ↓

Reassess the category system against theory
and material

↓

Interpretation of the results according to the
main research questions

↓

Application of the content analytic quality criteria

Figure 8.1   General content analytic process model (Source: Mayring 1983, p. 49)

For example: in an interview, a teacher expressed her difficulties in teaching by stating that she – unlike successful colleagues – was no 'entertainer type' (1983, p. 109). In order to find out what she wished to express by using this concept, definitions of 'entertainer' were assembled from two dictionaries. Then the features of a teacher who fits this description were sought from statements made by the teacher in the interview. Further passages were consulted. Based on the descriptions of such colleagues included in these passages, an 'explicating paraphrase can be formulated: an entertainer type is somebody who plays the part of an extroverted, spirited, sparkling, and self-assured human being' (1983, p. 74). This explication was assessed again by applying it to the direct context in which the concept was used.

With *structuring content analysis*, you look for types or formal structures in the material. You can look for and find four kinds of structures. You may find specific topics or domains which characterize the texts (content structures) – for example, xenophobic statements in interviews are always linked to issues of violence and crime. Or you find an internal structure on a formal level which characterizes the material – for example, every text begins with an example and then an explanation of the example follows. Scaling structuring means that you find varying degrees of a feature in the material – e.g. texts which express xenophobia in a stronger way than other texts in the material. Finally you may find typifying structures – e.g. that interviews with female participants are systematically different from those with male participants in how the main questions are answered.

Structuring *content analysis* has been described as follows:

> **According to formal aspects, an internal structure can be filtered out (formal structuring); material can be extracted and condensed to certain domains of content (structuring as regards content). One can look for single salient features in the material and describe them more exactly (typifying structuring); finally, the material may be rated according to dimensions in the form of scales (scaling structuring). (1983, pp. 53–4)**

Problems of qualitative content analysis

The schematic elaboration of the procedures makes this method look more transparent, less ambiguous, and easier to handle than other qualitative methods of analysis. This is because of the reduction it allows, as outlined above. The method is mainly suitable for reducing large amounts of text and analyzes on their surface (What is said in them?). Often, however, the application of the rules given by Mayring proves at least as time consuming as in other procedures. The quick categorization of text based on theories may obscure the view of the contents, rather than facilitate analyzing the text in its depth and underlying meanings. Interpretation of the text (How is something said? What is its meaning?) is applied rather schematically with this method, especially when the technique of explicative content analysis is used. Another problem is the use of paraphrases, which are used not only to explain the basic text but also to replace it – mainly in summarizing content analysis. The more quantitative a content analysis is oriented and applied, the more it reduces the meaning of the text to frequencies and parallel appearance of certain words or word sequences.

Example of a Content Analysis

The example in Box 8.1 is a thematic content analysis of journals.

BOX 8.1

Age and health in journals: example of a content analysis

In this study (Walter et al. 2006), four journals, two medical and two nursing journals, were content analyzed. We selected articles which focused on the topics of health, age, aging, old or very old people, and prevention and health promotion for the elderly. For this purpose, (1) the content of the title of the articles, (2) the abstract and (3) the whole article were analyzed.

The number of selected articles shows that representations of health, of aging and of old people as well as the areas of prevention and health promotion for the elderly are hardly an issue in the four journals. Of the 3028 issues of the journals in the years 1970–2001, only 83 articles explicitly address representations of health; 216 (7.1%) address representations of aging and old people, and 131 (4.3%) mention prevention and health promotion for the elderly, over a period of three decades and in four major journals.

For a more detailed content analysis, 283 publications from 1970 to 2001 were available. The relevance of the issues of aging and of the elderly in the medical and nursing journals was rather low. The distribution of the 216 publications over the period 1970–2001 shows in particular that the general practitioners journal and the nursing journal pick up this topic, whereas the other two refer to it more seldom. In the 1970s only 37 (17.1%) articles could be identified which addressed aging; in the 1980s 71 (32.9%) and in the 1990s 91 (42.1%) referred to that topic. Three of the journals paid more attention to it over time, and only the second nursing journal picked it up in the 1970s more frequently.

In the majority of the 131 identified articles, prevention and health promotion for the elderly are mentioned according to the distinction of primary, secondary and tertiary prevention. Only 12% of the 131 articles address health promotion according to the Ottawa Charta of the World Health Organization (1986).

The quantitative part of prevention and health promotion for elder people in most of the articles is below 10%. This means that the topic mostly is only mentioned in one to three sentences. This already shows the marginal relevance of prevention and health promotion in the journals that were studied.

Often, prevention and health promotion are not mentioned explicitly in the selected medical and nursing journals in Germany. This applies in particular to the nursing journals, which use prophylactic aids as a term instead.

All in all, the distribution of the identified publication over the decade shows the following. Representations of health were an issue in the medical and nursing journals in the 1990s less frequently compared to the 1970s. Images of aging and of old people have been increasingly an issue over the decades, but without having much relevance. Also the issues of prevention and health promotion are mentioned more and more. This shows the growing importance of these topics over time but also that they are still mentioned in a very limited way.

Quantitative Data Analysis

In the first part of this chapter, quantitative and then qualitative approaches to content analysis have been presented. In the next step we will consider

Table 8.4 Data matrix 1

Study unit		Variable				
	Gender	Age	Profession	School degree	Question 1: grade of consent	Question 2: grade of consent
Case 1	M	21	Student	High school	5	3
Case 2	F	28	Sales person	Grammar school	3	4
Case 3	M	–	Taxi driver	Public school	1	1
Case 4	F	25	Physician	Without	2	5
...						

Table 8.5 Data matrix 2

Study unit	Variable					
	V1	V2	V3	V4	V5	V6
01	2	21	4	4	5	3
02	1	28	1	2	3	4
03	2	999	3	3	1	1
04	1	25	5	1	2	5
...						

general aspects of quantitative data analysis, before I then turn to qualitative interpretative analyses.

Elaboration of the Data

Before you can analyze questionnaire data, you have first to elaborate them. This includes constructing a data matrix, i.e. a compilation of all variables for every study unit, more specifically of all responses for every case (see Table 8.4), which you will transform into numerical values (see Table 8.5). The questionnaire in our example begins with four questions about the demographic characteristics of the respondents (gender, age, profession, school degree) before substantive questions follow. A code plan was developed in advance, showing which number is code for which possible answer. For gender, female is coded with 1, male with 2. School degree is coded from 'without' to 'high school' with values of 1–4, and the current profession in a similar way. For the answers to questions 1 and 2, the values are taken from the scale (see the example in Figure 7.1). The cases are given an identification number and the variables are labeled with numbers (e.g. age in Table 8.4 becomes variable V2 in Table 8.5).

In this context, coding means allocating numerical values to answers. In this data matrix, you will enter all responses from every questionnaire. If open questions (without a defined scale of answers) are used, the answers (the text noted by the participant at this point) have to be allocated to categories, which then can be labeled with numerical values.

Cleaning the Data

In the next step, one needs to clean the data. First, you should test in the first frequency calculation whether data have be entered in the wrong column. If, for example, only 10 possible values were defined for 'profession' but several cases have values of 25 or 35, this indicates that maybe age values were coded in the column for profession. Such mistakes in columns have to be checked and corrected. Then, missing data have to be checked. In Table 8.4, for case 3, the age is missing and was coded with '999' for missing value in Table 8.5. You should also do a plausibility check for the data. In Table 8.4, you will find entries in case 4 which are at least unlikely (a physician without a school degree and with an age of 25). Here you should also check whether this is a coding error or if a combination of these answers really can be found in the questionnaires. Perhaps these answer have to be treated as 'missing'. After this assessment of the data, which can be quite time consuming for big datasets, and after correcting all identified errors, you can analyze the data on various levels of complexity.

Univariate Analyses: Referring to One Variable

A common way of demonstrating commonalities and differences for a certain feature or for a variable is to calculate its distribution in the sample that is studied.

Frequencies

If there are, say, four possible answers, you can first calculate their relative frequencies by dividing the number of cases in one category by the number of cases in the sample. If you want to calculate the percentage of the frequency, the result of this division is multiplied by 100. If, say, 27 of a sample of 100 people ticked 'public school' as highest degree, the relative frequency of public school as school degree is 0.27 and the percentage is 27%. Finally, you can calculate the cumulated relative percentage. If in our example another 33 persons have indicated 'grammar school' and 20 persons 'no degree' and 20 persons 'high school', you can rank order the values according to the level of the degrees. From cumulating (or adding) the single values, you can see for example that here the relative frequency of people with not more than a grammar school degree is 0.80 and the relative percentage is 80% (see Table 8.6).

Table 8.6   Frequency distribution of the variable 'school degree'

Category		Number of cases	Relative frequency	Percentage	Cumulated relative frequency	Cumulated percentage
No degree	1	20	0.20	20%	0.20	20%
Public school	2	27	0.27	27%	0.47	47%
Grammar school	3	33	0.33	33%	0.80	80%
High school	4	20	0.20	20%	1.00	100%

For demonstrating the distribution of answers in a sample, you can go two ways: on the one hand you can identify the central tendency, or on the other hand the dispersion.

Central tendency

The most prominent measure for the central tendency is the arithmetic mean, which is calculated by dividing the sum of the observed values by the number of cases. A familiar example is school grades. A student has the grades 1, 1, 4, 3 and 5 in his degree. For calculating the mean, you will add the single grades and divide that by the number of subjects (the sum is 14, the number of subjects is 5, which makes a mean of 2.8). For calculating means, you need data on the level of interval scales (the distances between the values have to be equal – see Chapter 7). If your data only consist of an ordinal scale, you can calculate the central tendency with the mode or with the median.

The mode is the value that occurs most frequently. The mode in our grades example is 3 (as it occurs most often). The median is the midpoint of a distribution, which means where the cumulated relative frequency reaches 50%. This means the distribution is separated such that 50% of the values are under and 50% are over the median. In our example of the school degrees (see Table 8.6), the median would be a little higher than 'public school' as almost 50% of the respondents have the values 'public school and less' and a little more than 50% have 'grammar school and more'.

Dispersion

Measures of central tendency will not tell you everything about a distribution. The example of the mean of two school grades may demonstrate this. A grade of 3 and a grade of 4 have a mean of 3.5. The same applies to the grades of 1 and 6. The dispersion of the grades is much lower in the first case (both values are close to each other) than in the second case (where the distance between the values is much bigger). For taking this dispersion into account, the first way is to calculate the range of the values. This is the difference between the minimum and the maximum value. For this purpose, you will subtract the minimum from the maximum values. In our example, in the first case (grades of 3 and 4), the range is 1. In the other case (grades of 1 and 6), it is 5.

The range is still strongly influenced by outliers, as it is only based on minimum and maximum values; it does not take the frequency of the values between those outliers into account. By defining the quartiles and the distance between quartiles you can analyze the distribution of the values more exactly. Quartiles define the limiting points which distinguish the quarters of a value distribution. Accordingly, there are the quartiles Q_1–Q_4: 25% of the values are less than or equal to the value of the first quartile Q_1, 50% are less than or equal to the second quartile Q_2, and 75% are less than or equal to the third quartile Q_3. The second quartile is equivalent to the median and separates the second and third quarters of the values. The interquartile range is the difference between the third and the first quartiles.

If the measured values are expressed on an interval or a ratio scale, you can calculate the dispersion by calculating the *standard deviation* and the *variance*. The standard deviation is the average amount of variation around the mean and the variance is the squared value of the standard deviation. These measures shed light on the distribution of the single values in the sample. With the calculations discussed so far, you can identify the central tendency in the data, what are the average values in a variable, and how the values are distributed in the dataset.

Analyses Referring to Two Variables: Correlations and Bivariate Analyses

If you want to identify the connections between two variables, you may calculate their correlation. Correlation means that a change in the value of one variable is associated with a change in the other variable. Three forms of correlation can be distinguished: a positive correlation (when variable 1 has a high value, variable 2 also has a high value); a negative correlation (when variable 1 has a high value, variable 2 has a low value and vice versa); and the absence of a correlation (you cannot say what will be the value of variable 2 if the value of variable 1 is high or low). The correlation coefficient varies between −1 (a strongly negative correlation), and +1 (a strongly positive correlation), and a value of 0 indicates the absence of a correlation. For example, you will find a correlation between education and income (more education is associated with higher income).

Correlations need to be interpreted: a correlation does not by itself indicate which of the variables is causal (for example, does more education lead to more income, or does a higher income make more education more likely?). Furthermore, a correlation does not establish a causal connection. In our example, perhaps another variable (e.g. the social status of the family of origin) is the reason for the high values for education and income: the two are consequences of the third variable and are not in a causal relation with each other. On the level of calculations, you may find meaningless connections in calculations (e.g. links between good weather and income).

Table 8.7   Bivariate analysis

Civil rights	Middle class	Working class
High	37%	45%
Low	63%	55%
N	120	120

Source: Schnell et al. 2008, p. 446 (Copyright: Methoden der empirischen Sozialforschung, p. 446, Tabelle 9-4, Schnell et al., 3rd edn (2005) Oldenbourg Wissenschaftsverlag GmbH)

Table 8.8   Multivariate analysis

	Colored		White	
Civil rights	Middle class	Working class	Middle class	Working class
High	70%	50%	30%	20%
Low	30%	50%	70%	80%
N	20	100	100	20

Source: Schnell et al. 2008, p. 447 (Copyright: Methoden der empirischen Sozialforschung, p. 447, Tabelle 9-5, Schnell et al., 3rd edn (2005) Oldenbourg Wissenschaftsverlag GmbH)

Often the issues under study are more complex than can be represented through bilateral correlation. Schnell et al. (2008, pp. 446–7) demonstrate this by using an example of Rosenberg (1968). Here attitudes towards civil rights were surveyed and linked to the social class of the respondents: middle class versus working class, and liberal attitude (given a high value) versus conservative attitude (a low value). A survey of 240 people (half of them working class and half of them middle class) led to the values in Table 8.7. This gives the impression that working class people, more than members of the middle class, have a positive attitude to civil rights.

Analyses with More Than Two Variables: Multivariate Analyses

If you intend to show the relations between more than two variables, you should apply a multivariate analysis. If we take our last example and further differentiate for the respondents' color, this study leads to the distributions shown in Table 8.8.

Here we see that taking the third variable (color) into account leads to a different picture. The differences between the two classes in both parts of the table are stronger (20% and 10%) than in the first table which did not consider color (only 8%). Furthermore, the relation in both groups is inverted. In Table 8.7, in both subgroups, a bigger portion of the middle class members gave a higher value to civil rights than the working class. Now, in Table 8.8, the relation is different in both subgroups: the higher the social class, the more positive the attitude to civil rights. We see a higher estimation of civil rights in 70% of 'coloured' middle class compared to 50% of working class, and in 30% in white middle class compared to 20% in working class instead of 37% of middle class compared to 45% of working class in Table 8.7.

Discovery of relations

Methods of multivariate analysis can also be used for testing relations, especially differences between groups, if the data are on interval or ratio levels. Multiple regression, for example, starts by analyzing the differences between means in groups and shows how far a set of variables explains the dependent variable, in the sense of predicting values of the dependent variable on the grounds of information about independent variables. In addition, the regression measures the direction and strength of the effect of each variable on a dependent variable (see Neuman 2000, p. 337).

Software packages like SPSS facilitate such multivariate analyses. Nevertheless, the following should be borne in mind:

> It is typical for this and other multivariate methods that they hardly produce unambiguous solutions; rather, there are a number of models and parameters to choose in a cluster analysis, which can lead to differing results also independent of the optimal numbers of clusters to be defined. That leads to the general problems that these procedures now can be used quite easily with the current software packages for statistical analyses. However the question of which model to choose and the interpretation of the results that are produced still require firm methodological skills and refined theoretical considerations referring to the issue of the studies. (Weischer 2007, p. 392)

Testing Associations and Differences

To find relationships between variables in the data is often not sufficient for answering a research question. Rather it becomes necessary to test whether the observed relationships occur by chance and how strong the observed relationships between two variables are. It might be also necessary to know whether one variable is the cause of the other or if both are mutual conditions for each other. For answering such questions you can apply a significance test. Then you basically test whether a result was to be expected or whether it represents a relationship between two variables that is above chance.

If, say, you want to study pupil absence from school because of illness and to find out whether there is a relationship to gender, you can count the frequencies of absence for boys and girls. If you find that 76% of the documented absences occur for female students, this may be remarkable at first sight and seems to indicate a relationship between gender and absence. However, if in the school that is studied and in the sample that was drawn three-quarters of the students are girls, it can be expected that also 75% of the absences apply to girls. That means that you should test whether there is enough difference between the measured value (in our example 76%) and the expected value (in our example 75%) that you can derive a relationship between the variables – here gender and times of absence. By comparing the expected and the observed values you will test the null hypothesis: there is no relation between the variables above chance. If in our example the value of 76% has been observed, you can test in a significance test (e.g. the chi-square test) whether the difference between expected and observed values is big enough for confirming a relation between gender and absence. For this purpose, several significance tests are available that can be applied depending on the type of data that were measured. These include the t-test and Mann–Whitney test.

In the t-test, two datasets are compared for their differences – e.g. measures at two times or measures of two subgroups, such as either (a) the grades of a school class at the beginning and at the end of a term or (b) the grades of two classes at the end of term. With the t-test, a statistical significance test is applied, in which the means and the standard deviations of both datasets are taken for calculating the probability that the differences between the two datasets are accidental. Here also you will assume that the null hypothesis is correct – that there are no real differences and that observed differences occur by chance – until the statistical test demonstrates that the probability is big enough that the differences found are above chance. The latter is the case when you can show that there is a probability of less than 5% that differences are accidental. The t-test can be applied to small samples and also to samples with different sizes – like school classes of 18 and 25 students in our example. This test requires interval data.

The Mann–Whitney U-test can be applied to ordinal data. Here, you will do a rank ordering of the cases in both groups and an overall ranking of all cases in both groups. The position of the members of each group in this overall ranking will be the basis for calculating and testing the statistical significance of the differences between the two groups.

Quantitative Analyses of Relations: A Conclusion

The procedures for analyzing relations outlined above highlight either the central tendency in the data or the distribution of values in the data. They also calculate the relations between two or more variables and test the significance of the relations that were found.

Table 8.9 summarizes the approaches of quantitative analysis, the types of variables that each requires, and the usual tests for relations that can be applied.

The above overview has presented only some basic principles of quantitative analyses. For applying and studying them more extensively, you should consult a more comprehensive textbook of quantitative research and of statistics (e.g. Bryman 2008 or Neuman 2000).

Interpretative Analysis

Interpretations are also relevant in quantitative analysis. Interrelations, which can be found through calculations, e.g. correlations of two variables, are

Table 8.9 Variable types and appropriate descriptive-statistical tests

Variable types	Central tendency	Dispersion	Statistical tests
Nominal	Mode	Frequency distribution	Chi-square
Ordinal	Median	Range	Mann–Whitney *U*-test
Interval	Mean	Standard deviation	*t*-test

Source: after Denscombe 2007, p. 271

interpreted by looking for a substantive explanation for these numerical relations. However, the subject of the interpretations is not so much the data themselves but rather the calculations made with them and their results. In the methods that are presented in what follows, interpretation refers immediately to the data and is the actual analysis (see Flick 2009 for more details).

Analyses for Generating Theories Coding in Grounded Theory Research

In the development of a grounded theory from empirical material, coding is the method for analyzing data that have been collected for this purpose. This approach was introduced by Glaser and Strauss (1967) and further elaborated by Glaser (1978), Strauss (1987) and Strauss and Corbin (1990/1998/2008) or Charmaz (2006). In the process of interpretation, a number of 'procedures' for working with text can be differentiated. They are termed 'open coding', 'axial coding' and 'selective coding'. You should see these procedures neither as clearly distinguishable procedures nor as sequential phases in a linear process. Rather, they are different ways of handling textual material between which the researchers move back and forth if necessary and which they combine (see also Chapter 31 in Flick 2009).

Whereas the process of interpretation begins with open coding, towards the end of the whole analytical process *selective* coding comes more to the fore. Coding here is understood as representing the operations by which data are broken down, conceptualized, and put back together in new ways. It is the central process by which theories are built from data (Strauss and Corbin 1990/1998, p. 3). According to this understanding, coding includes the constant comparison of phenomena, cases, concepts and so on and the formulation of questions that are addressed to the text. Starting from the data, the process of coding leads to the development of theories through a process of abstraction.

Open coding aims at expressing data and phenomena in the form of concepts. For this purpose, data are first disentangled ('segmented'). 'Units of meaning' classify expressions (single words, short sequences of words) in order to attach annotations and 'concepts' (codes) to them.

This procedure cannot be applied to the whole text of an interview or of an observation protocol. Rather, you will use it for particularly instructive or perhaps extremely unclear passages. Often the beginning of a text is the starting point for the coding. This procedure serves to elaborate a deeper understanding of the text. Possible sources for labeling codes are concepts borrowed from social science literature (*constructed* codes) or taken from interviewees' expressions (*in vivo* codes). Of the two types of codes, the latter is preferred because codes then are closer to the studied material. The categories found in this way are then further developed. To this end the properties belonging to a category are labeled and dimensionalized. This means they are located along a continuum in order to define the category more precisely regarding its content. Open coding may be applied in various degrees of detail. You can code a text line by line, sentence by sentence, or paragraph by paragraph. A code can also be linked to a whole text (a protocol, a case etc.).

For open coding, and indeed for the other coding strategies, it is suggested that you regularly address the text with the following list of so-called basic questions (Strauss and Corbin 1998):

- *What?* What is the issue here? Which phenomenon is mentioned?
- *Who?* Which persons or actors are involved? Which roles do they play? How do they interact?
- *How?* Which aspects of the phenomenon are mentioned (or not mentioned)?
- *When? How long? Where?* Time, course, and location.
- *How much? How strong?* Aspects of intensity.
- *Why?* Which reasons are given or can be reconstructed?
- *What for?* With what intention, to which purpose?
- *By which?* Means, tactics, and strategies for reaching the goal.

By asking these questions, you may open up the text. They may be applied either to particular passages or to entire texts.

After a number of substantive categories have been identified, the next step is to refine and differentiate the categories that result from open coding. As a second step, Strauss and Corbin suggest completing a more formal coding for identifying and classifying links between substantive categories. In *axial coding*, the relations between categories are elaborated. In order to formulate such relations, Strauss and Corbin (1998, p. 127) suggest a coding paradigm model, which is symbolized in Figure 8.2.

This serves to clarify the relations between a phenomenon, its causes and consequences, its context, and the strategies of those involved. The coding paradigm outlines possible relations between phenomena and concepts. It is used to facilitate the discovery or establishment of structures of relations between phenomena, between concepts, and between categories. Here, as well,

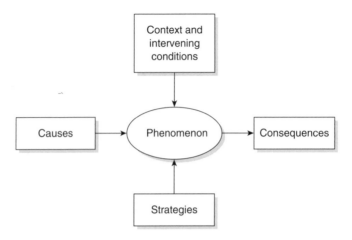

Figure 8.2 The paradigm model

the questions addressed to the text and the comparative strategies mentioned above are employed once again in a complementary way. You will move continuously back and forth between inductive thinking (developing concepts, categories and relations from the text) and deductive thinking. The latter means testing the concepts, categories and relations against the text, especially against passages or cases that are different from those from which they were developed.

In the third step, i.e. *selective coding*, you will focus on elaborating the potential core concepts or core variables. This leads to an elaboration or formulation of the *story of the case*. In any case, the result should be *one* central category and *one* central phenomenon. You should develop the core category again in its features and dimensions and link it to other categories (all of them, if possible) by using the parts and relations of the coding paradigm. The analysis and the development of the theory aim at discovering patterns in the data as well as the conditions under which these apply. Grouping the data according to the coding paradigm gives specificity to the theory and will enable you to say, 'Under these conditions (listing them) this happens; whereas under these conditions, this is what occurs' (Strauss and Corbin 1990, p. 131).

Finally, you will formulate the theory in greater detail and again check it against the data. The procedure of interpreting data, like the integration of additional material, ends at the point where *theoretical saturation* has been reached. This means that further coding, enrichment of categories, and so on no longer provide or promise new knowledge. At the same time, the procedure is flexible enough that you can re-enter the same source texts and the same codes from open coding with a different research question and aim at developing and formulating a grounded theory of a different issue.

Box 8.2 provides a case study of this method in operation.

BOX 8.2

Example: 'awareness of dying'

The following represents an important early example of a study that pursued the goal of developing theory from qualitative research in the field. Barney Glaser and Anselm Strauss worked from the 1960s as pioneers of qualitative research and of grounded theory in the context of medical sociology. They did this study in several hospitals in the United States around San Francisco. Their research question asked what influenced various people's interaction with dying people and how the knowledge that the person would die soon determined the interaction with that person. More concretely, they studied which forms of interaction between the dying person and the clinical staff in the hospital, between the staff and the relatives, and between relatives and the dying person could be noted.

The starting point of the research was the observation that, when the researchers' relatives were in the hospital, the staff in hospitals (at that time) seemed not to inform patients with a terminal disease and their relatives about the state or the life expectancy of the patient. Rather the possibility that the patient might die or die soon was treated as a taboo. This general observation and the questions it raised were taken as a starting point for a more systematic observation and interviews in one hospital. These data were analyzed and used to develop categories. That was also the background for deciding to include another hospital and to continue the data collection and analysis there.

Both hospitals – as cases – were directly compared for similarities and differences. The results of such comparison were used to decide which hospital to use next, until finally six hospitals were included in the study. These included a teaching hospital, a Veterans' Affairs hospital, two county hospitals, a private Catholic hospital, and a state hospital. Wards included among others geriatrics, cancer, intensive care, pediatrics and neurosurgery, in which the fieldworkers stayed two to four weeks each. The data from each of these units (different wards in one hospital, similar wards in different hospitals, hospitals amongst each other) were contrasted and compared in order to show similarities and differences.

At the end of the study, comparable situations and contexts outside hospitals and health care were included as another dimension of comparison. Analyzing and comparing the data allowed a theoretical model to be developed, which then was transferred to other fields in order to develop it further. The result of this study was a theory of awareness contexts as ways of dealing with the information and with the patients' need to know more about their situation.

This method aims at a consistent breaking down of texts. Combining a consistently open coding with more and more focused procedures can contribute to a more profound understanding of the contents and meanings of text – one that goes beyond paraphrasing and summarizing it (which were the main approaches of qualitative content analysis discussed above). The advantage is that the interpretation of texts here becomes methodologically realized and manageable. It differs from other methods of interpreting texts because it leaves the level of the pure texts during the interpretation in order to develop categories and relations, and thus theories.

One problem with this approach is that the distinction between method and art becomes hazy. This makes it in some places difficult to teach or learn as a method. Often, the extent of the advantages and strengths of the method becomes clear only whilst applying it. If the numbers of codes and possible comparisons become too great, it is suggested to set up lists of priorities: which codes have to be further elaborated in all cases, which appear to be less instructive, and which can be omitted when you take your research question as a point of reference?

Thematic Coding

If you want to keep the reference to interviewees, for example, as a (single) case when using a coding procedure, the alternative is to use thematic coding (see Flick 2009, Chapter 23). Here you start your analysis with case studies for which you will develop a thematic structure (what characterizes across several substantive areas how the interviewee deals with health? Can you identify issues running through these ways of handling the areas?). In thematic coding you will first analyze the cases in your study in a number of case studies. For a first orientation you should develop a short description of each case, which you can continually check and modify throughout the further interpretation of the case if necessary. This description will include a statement which is typical for the interview, a short characterization of the interviewee with respect to the research question (e.g. age, profession, number of children, if relevant for your issue of research), and the major topics mentioned in the interview with respect to the issue under study. This short description first is a heuristic tool for the following analysis.

In Strauss's (1987) procedure, you will code material also across single cases in a comparative way from the beginning. In thematic coding, you will go more into the depth of the material by focusing on the single case in the next step (for example, looking at a single interview as a whole). This single-case analysis has several aims: it preserves the meaningful relations that the respective person deals with in the topic of the study, which is why a case study is done for all interviews; and it develops a system of categories for the analysis for the single case.

In the further elaboration of this system of categories (similar to Strauss), first apply open coding and then selective coding. With selective coding here you will aim less at developing a grounded core category across all cases than at generating thematic domains and categories for the single case first.

After the first case analysis, you will cross-check the categories you have developed with the thematic domains that are linked to the single cases. A thematic structure results from this cross-check, which underlies the analysis of further cases in order to increase their comparability.

· The structure you developed from the first cases should be continually assessed for all further cases. You should modify it if new or contradictory aspects emerge and use it to analyze all cases that are part of the interpretation. For a fine interpretation of the thematic domains, single passages of the text (e.g. narratives of situations) are analyzed in greater detail. The coding paradigm suggested by Strauss (1987, pp. 27–8; see above) is taken as a starting point. The result of this process complemented by a step of selective coding is a case-oriented display of the way it specifically deals with the issue of the study, including constant topics (e.g. strangeness of technology) that can be found in the viewpoints across different domains (e.g. work, leisure, household).

The thematic structure developed will also serve for comparing cases and groups (that is, for elaborating correspondences and differences between the various groups in the study). Thus, you analyze and assess the social distribution of perspectives on the issue under study.

This procedure is helpful above all for studies in which theoretically based group comparisons are conducted in relation to a specific issue. Therefore, the scope for a theory to be developed is more limited than in Strauss's (1987) procedure.

Hermeneutic Procedures

In qualitative research, one makes great efforts when collecting the data to be able to understand and analyze statements in their context afterwards. Therefore, in interviews, open questions are asked. In analyzing the data, open coding is used for this purpose, in the first step at least. The analytic methods just discussed, as well as qualitative content analysis, increasingly depart from the original wording of the text: statements assume a new order according to the categories or – in Glaser and Strauss's method – the theories that are developed. More consequently oriented to the Gestalt of the text are methods guided by the principle of sequential analysis.

Narrative analyses

For analyzing narrative interviews, Schütze suggests as a 'first analytic step [i.e. formal text analysis] … to eliminate all non-narrative passages from the text and then to segment the "purified" narrative text for its formal sections' (1983, p. 286). A structural description of the contents follows, specifying the different parts of narratives ('temporally limited process structures of the life course on the basis of formal narrative connectors': Riemann and Schütze 1987, p. 348), such as 'and then' or pauses. The analytic abstraction – as a third step – moves away from the specific details of the life segments. Instead its intention is to elaborate 'the biographical shaping *in toto*, i.e., the life historical sequence of experience-dominant processual structures in the individual life periods up to the presently dominant processual structure' (1983, p. 286).

Only after this reconstruction of patterns of process do you integrate the other, non-narrative parts of the interview into the analysis. Finally, the case analyses produced in this way are compared and contrasted with each other. The aim is less to reconstruct the narrators' subjective interpretations of their lives than to reconstruct the 'interrelation of factual process courses' (1983, p. 284).

Thus Rosenthal and Fischer-Rosenthal (2004) accordingly suggest analyzing narrative interviews in five steps, as follows:

1. analysis of biographical data (data of events)
2. text and thematic field analysis (sequential analysis of textual segments from the self-presentation in the interview)
3. reconstruction of the case history (life as lived)
4. detailed analysis of individual textual locations
5. contrasting the life story as narrated with life as lived
6. formation of types.

Lucius-Hoene and Deppermann (2002) have proposed an alternative procedure. They describe the following steps, in which they move from a structural (rough) analysis to a fine analysis of the material. First, structural analysis identifies presentational segments in the text (transitions, sections, life-historical ruptures, thematic changes) in order to derive an internal structure of the text. Furthermore, some interview passages are selected for the fine analysis at this stage. Ideally, you should select a passage from the beginning of the interview, which is not too long and represents a clear episode completely in narrative form. Excerpts should be small enough and distinct in their topic and determined in their logic of action and their narrative structure.

The fine analysis should proceed with a selected excerpt in a strictly sequential fine segmentation (one that proceeds word by word, sentence by sentence, without jumping back and forth in the text). In addition, structural aspects of the text that go beyond the single sentences (which function has the passage as part of a longer narrative?) should be considered at the same time.

As a heuristic of analyzing a text, the authors suggest a number of questions (2002, p. 321):

- What is presented?
- How is it presented?
- For which purpose is this presented – and not something else?
- For which purpose is this presented now – and not at a different moment?
- For which purpose is this presented in this way – and not in a different way?

Finally, you will elaborate a case structure by collecting, bundling and comparing recurrent findings, core concepts and more abstract structural features in different passages of the sequential analysis. For example, you may develop a typology based on analyzing several narratives. Or you may identify turning points in several narratives about illness experiences, which show some kind of regularity. Or you may identify that several narrators turn to very abstract language when they address the aspect of terminality in their illness narrative.

What do the methods for analyzing narrative data discussed above have in common? They take the overall form of the narrative as a starting point for the interpretation of statements, which are seen in the context of the process of the narrative. Furthermore, they include a formal analysis of the material: which passages of the text are narrative passages, which other forms of text can be found?

In these methods, the narrative has a varying importance for analyzing the issues under study. If something is presented in the interview in the form of a narrative, Schütze sees this as an indicator that it has happened in the way it is told. Other authors, however, see narratives as a specifically instructive form of presentation of events and experiences and analyze them as such. Sometimes the assumption is made that narratives as a form of constructing events can be met in everyday life and knowledge as well. Thus, this mode of construction can be used for research purposes in a particularly fruitful way. Combining a formal analysis with a sequential procedure in the interpretation of presentations and experiences is typical for narrative analyses in general.

However, particular approaches deriving from Schütze exaggerate the quality of reality in narratives. The influence of the presentation on what is recounted is underestimated; the possible inference from narrative to factual events in life histories is overestimated. Only in very rare examples are narrative analyses combined with other methodological approaches in order to overcome their limitations. A second problem is how closely analyses stick to individual cases. The time and effort spent analyzing individual cases restricts studies from going beyond the reconstruction and comparison of a few cases.

Objective hermeneutics

Objective hermeneutics was originally formulated for analyzing natural interactions (e.g. family conversations). Subsequently the approach has been used to analyze all sorts of other documents, including even works of art and photographs. This approach makes a basic distinction between (a) the subjective meaning that a statement or activity has for one or more participants and (b) its objective meaning. The latter is understood by using the concept of a 'latent structure of meaning'. This structure can be examined only by using the framework of a multi-step scientific procedure of interpretation. Owing to its orientation to such structures, the label 'structural hermeneutics' has also been used.

Analyses in objective hermeneutics must be 'strictly sequential': that is, you should follow the temporal course of the events or the text in conducting the interpretation. You should work as one of a group of analysts working on the same text. First, the members define the case to be analyzed and on which level it is to be located. It could for example be defined as a statement or activity of a specific person, or of someone who performs a certain role in an institutional context, or of a member of the human species.

This definition is followed by a sequential *rough analysis* aimed at analyzing the external contexts in which a statement is embedded in order to take the influence of such contexts into account. The focus of this rough analysis is mainly on considerations about the nature of the concrete action problem for which the studied action or interaction offers a solution. First, you will develop case structure hypotheses, which you may falsify in later steps, and the rough structure of the text and of the case. The specification of the external context or the interactional embedding of the case serves to answer questions about how the data came about.

In the following sequential *fine analysis*, the interpretation of interactions proceeds on nine levels (Oevermann et al. 1979, pp. 394–402):

1. explication of the context, which immediately precedes an interaction

2. paraphrasing the meaning of an interaction according to the verbatim text of the accompanying verbalization

3. explication of the interacting subject's intention

4. explication of the objective motives of the interaction and of its objective consequences

5. explication of the function of the interaction for the distribution of interaction roles

6. characterization of the linguistic features of the interaction

7. exploration of the interpreted interaction for constant communicative figures

8. explication of general relations

9. independent test of the general hypotheses that were formulated at the preceding level on the basis of interaction sequences from further cases.

The procedure at levels 4 and 5 focuses on reconstructing the objective context of a statement by constructing possible contexts in thought experiments and then excluding them again one after the other. Here, the analysis of the subjective meanings of statements and actions plays a minor role. The interpreters reflect about the consequences that the statement they have just analyzed might have for the next turn in the interaction. They ask, what could the protagonist say or do next? This produces a variety of possible alternatives of how the interaction *might* proceed. Then the next *actual* statement is analyzed. It is compared with those possible alternatives which might have occurred (but which did not in fact do so). By increasingly excluding such alternatives and by reflecting why the protagonists did not choose them, the analysts elaborate the structure of the case. This structure is finally generalized to the case as a whole. For this purpose, it is tested against further material from the case – which means subsequent actions and interactions in the text.

Here, the analysis of the subjective meanings of statements and actions plays a minor role. The procedure at level 4 is oriented towards interpretations using the framework of conversation analysis (see below), whereas at level 5 the focus is on the formal linguistic (syntactic, semantic or pragmatic) features of the text. At level 6 the focus is on the formal linguistic (syntactic, semantic or pragmatic) features of the text.

Levels 7 to 9 strive for an increasing generalization of the structures that have been found (e.g. an examination is made of whether the forms of communication found in the text can be repeatedly found as general forms – i.e. communicative figures – and also in other situations). These figures and structures are treated as hypotheses and are tested step by step against further material.

According to Wernet (2006), interpretative practices are oriented on five principles:

1. *Freedom of context.* According to this, a statement is analyzed independent of the specific context in which it was made. Therefore, thought experimental contexts that are compatible with the text (p. 23) are formulated. This clarifies which meanings the statement could have, after which an interpretation referring to the concrete context follows.

2. *Literality.* According to this, the statement has to be interpreted in the way it was actually made and not how the speaker possibly meant it – in particular when a mistake is made. 'The principle of literality makes a direct interpretative approach to the difference between manifest meanings and latent meaning structures of a text' (p. 25).

3. *Sequential analysis.* Here you do not search for content in the text, but interpret its process step by step. 'For the sequential analysis, it is absolutely important *not* to consider the text that follows a sequence that is currently being interpreted' (p. 28).

4. *Extensiveness.* This means to include a multitude of interpretations (meanings the text might have).

5. *Parsimony.* 'The principle of parsimony … defines that only those interpretations may be formulated which are forced by the text that is interpreted without any additional assumption about the case' (p. 35).

Following these principles should guarantee that your text is analyzed in a comprehensive way – without either drawing on additional assumptions outside the material, or reading something into the text that is not documented in it.

Objective hermeneutics was developed for analyzing *everyday language* interactions, which are available in recorded and transcribed form as material for interpretation. The sequential analysis seeks to reconstruct the layering of social meanings from the process of the actions. When the empirical material is available as a tape or video recording and as transcript, you can analyze them step by step from the beginning to the end. Therefore, always begin the analysis with the opening sequence of the interaction. When one is analyzing interviews using this approach, the problem arises that interviewees do not always report events and processes in their chronological order. For example, the interviewees may recount certain phases in their lives and then refer to them during their narrative of events, which have to be located earlier. In the narrative interview too, and particularly in the semi-structured interview, events and experiences are not recounted in chronological order. When using a sequence analytic method for analyzing interviews, you first have to reconstruct the sequential order of the story – or of the action system under study – from the interviewee's statements. Therefore, rearrange the events reported in the interview in the temporal order in which they occurred. Then orient the sequential analysis to this order of occurrence, rather than the temporal course in the interview: 'The beginning of a sequential analysis is not the analysis of the opening of the conversation in the first interview but the analysis of those actions and events reported by the interviewee which are the earliest "documents" of the case history' (Schneider 1988, p. 234).

A consequence of this approach is that the sequential analytical procedure has developed into a program with clearly demarcated methodological steps. A further consequence of this is that it is made clear that subjective views provide only *one* form of access to social phenomena: what an individual sees as the meaning of his or her illness is one level, and this maybe is mainly linked to issues of how to cope with it. There are also social meanings, of that same illness, which are perhaps more linked to stigmatizing it than to coping with it. (On this in a different context see Silverman 2001.) Another aspect is the call for conducting group interpretations in order to increase the variety of the versions and perspectives brought to the text and to use the group to validate interpretations that have been made.

A problem with this approach is that, because of the great effort involved in the method, it is often limited to single case studies. The leap to general statements is often made without any intermediate steps. Furthermore, the understanding of the method as art, which can hardly be transformed into didactic elaboration and mediation, makes it more difficult to apply generally (for general skepticism see Denzin 1988).

BOX 8.3

Example: counselor–client interactions

Sahle (1987) has used this procedure to study the interactions of social workers with their clients. Additionally, she interviewed the social workers. She presents four case studies. In each case, the author has extensively interpreted the opening sequence of the interactions in order to elaborate the 'structure formula' for the interaction, which is then tested against a passage randomly sampled from the further text. From the analyses she derives hypotheses about the professional self-concept of the social workers and then tests them in the interviews. In a very short comparison, Sahle relates the case studies to each other and finally discusses her results with the social workers who were involved.

Conversation analysis

When applying this method, you will be less interested in interpreting the content of texts than in analyzing the formal procedures with which people communicate and with which specific situations are produced. Classic studies have analyzed the organization of turn-taking in conversations or explained how closings in conversations were initiated by the participants. Basic assumptions of conversation analysis are that (a) interaction proceeds in an orderly way and (b) nothing in it should be regarded as random. The context of interaction influences this interaction; the participants of therapy interaction act according to that framework, and the therapist talks like a therapist should do. At the same time, this sort of talking also produces and reproduces this context: by talking like a therapist should do, the therapist contributes to making this situation a therapy and to preventing it turning into a different format of talk – like gossip for example. The decision about what is relevant in social interaction and thus for the interpretation can only be made through the interpretation and not by *ex ante* settings. Drew (1995, pp. 70–2) has formulated a series of methodological precepts for conversation analysis (CA). He suggests focusing on how talk is organized and in particular on how the speakers organize turn-taking in the conversation. Another focus is on errors and how they are repaired by the speakers. CA looks for patterns of talk and of its organization by comparing several examples of conversations. In presenting the analysis of a conversation, it is important that you give enough examples in verbatim quotes that readers can assess your analysis. For example, if you analyze counseling, you could look at the opening interactions and at how the two participants arrive at defining the issue which the consultation will be about. By comparing several examples, you could show patterns of organizing an issue for the conversation and thus a consultation with a focus.

The procedure of conversation analysis of the material itself involves the following steps. First, you identify a certain statement or series of statements in transcripts as a potential element of order in the respective genre of conversation. The second step is that you assemble a collection of cases in which this element of order can be found. You will then specify how this element is used as a means for producing order in interactions and for which problem in the organization of interactions it is the answer (see Bergmann 2004). This is followed by an analysis of the methods with which those organizational problems are dealt with more generally. Thus, a frequent starting point for conversation analyses is to enquire into how certain conversations are opened and which linguistic practices are applied for ending those conversations in an ordered way.

Research in conversation analysis originally concentrated on everyday conversations (e.g. telephone calls, gossip or family conversations in which there is no specific distribution of roles). Increasingly, however, it has become occupied with specific role distributions and asymmetries as found in, for example, counseling conversation, doctor–patient interactions, and trials (i.e. conversations occurring in specific institutional contexts). The approach has also been extended to include analysis of written texts, mass media or reports, i.e. text in a broader sense (Bergmann 2004).

Discourse analysis

Discourse analysis has been developed from different backgrounds, one of which was conversation analysis. There are various versions of discourse analysis now available. Discursive psychology, as developed by Edwards and Potter (1992), Harré (1998) and Potter and Wetherell (1998), is interested in showing how, in conversations, 'participants' conversational versions of events (memories, descriptions, formulations) are constructed to do communicative interactive work' (Edwards and Potter 1992, p. 16). There is a special emphasis on the construction of versions of the events in reports and presentations. The 'interpretative repertoires', which are used in such constructions, are analyzed. Interpretative repertoires are ways of talking about a specific issue. They are called repertoires as it is assumed that these ways are not completely spontaneous, but that people apply certain ways of talking about an issue. At the same time, for example, the way an issue is treated in the press sets up such repertoires (for example, if a specific ethnic minority is always talked about by referring to violence and crime).

Willig (2003) has described research process in discourse analysis in several steps. After selecting texts and talk occurring in natural contexts, which have to be described first, you will carefully read the transcripts. Coding and then analyzing the material follows from guide questions like: why am I reading this passage in this way? What features of the text produce this reading? The analysis focuses on context, variability and constructions in the text and, finally, on the interpretative repertoires used in the texts. The last step, according to Willig, is writing up a discourse analytic research. Writing should be part of the analysis and return the researcher back to the empirical material.

Features of interpretative methods

Common to the hermeneutical methods discussed above is that they focus on the temporal-logical structure of the text and take this as a starting point of the interpretation. Thus, they stick more closely to the text than the methods based on categories, which we discussed before. The relation of content and formal aspects is shaped here in different ways. In narrative analyses, the formal difference between narrative and argumentative passages in interviews informs decisions over which passages receive how much interpretative attention and how credible the contents are. In objective hermeneutic analyses, in contrast, the formal analysis of the texts is a rather subordinate level of interpretation. Conversation analysis mainly focuses on formal aspects, which are used to design conversations – e.g. counseling conversations – and how this is employed for negotiating the specific contents of a topic. Discourse analysis again makes a turn in analyzing text and talk for contents and formal aspects.

Case Studies and Typologies

In Chapter 5, case studies were discussed as one of the basic designs in non-standardized research. The methods of data interpretation discussed so far work with case studies in various phases of treating the material. Hermeneutic methods mostly produce a case study in the first stage, consisting of a single interaction, document or interview. Comparing the cases is a later step.

In the approach of Glaser and Strauss, however, the single case (the interview, a document or an interaction) is given less attention. When they talk of 'case', they mean instead the field or issue of the study as a whole. This approach starts immediately by comparing interviewees or specific situations.

Producing and Reading Case Studies

Sometimes, for example in the evaluation of an institution, a case study may be the *result* of the research. In other approaches, case studies form the beginning, before comparison becomes more central. A third possibility is to use case studies for illustrating a basically comparative study, in order to highlight links between the different issues studied in the research. In this sense, we included a number of case studies in addition to a thematically structured comparative presentation in our study on health and illness concepts of homeless adolescents (see Flick and Röhnsch 2008).

An essential point in the production and assessment of case studies is the localization of the case and its analysis. What does the case represent and what do you intend to show by analyzing it? Is the presentation about the single person (or institution etc.) *per se*? Does it represent the person as typical for a specific subgroup in the study, or does it represent a specific professional perspective (e.g. the physicians in this field)? What were the criteria for selecting this specific case – for the data collection, for the analysis and for the presentation?

Constructing Typologies

Typologies are constructed in quantitative research, too. However, this step of condensing and presenting results is more often part of qualitative research. Kelle and Kluge (2010) have made some suggestions for how to apply this, which can be used for developing the following procedure.

The first step is either to construct case studies for the cases that are included in the research or, alternatively, to begin with analyses referring to certain issues. This is followed by systematic comparisons (of cases or referring to issues).

The next step is to define relevant dimensions of comparison. Consider what is the focus of the intended comparison – for example, the contents of the concepts of health that had been mentioned on the one hand and age and gender on the other. This may reveal here which substantial dimension characterized the ranges of health concepts that were mentioned and how the various dimensions can be allocated in the differentiation of the age of the cases or what can be found more for male or more for female interviewees.

The next step is to group the cases (according to the substantial dimension and/or age) and to analyze empirical regularities (e.g. certain concepts can mainly be found for younger girls, other concepts more for older boys).

As far as possible, the range of statements should be documented and delimited in order to develop a contrastive framework for single statements. This can be the result of compiling all relevant statements and ordering them along a dimension. In the example of Gerhardt (1988) on family rehabilitation after the husband has fallen chronically ill, this feature space consists of the range of activities found for the husband (professional work; at home) and for the wives (professional work; at home) and the combinations that result from the four possibilities in the concrete cases. In Gerhardt's study, four types result from this: dual career (both professionally working), traditional (husband working, wife at home), rational (reversed when the husband can no longer work professionally) and unemployment (when no one is working). Gerhardt has compared these four types to see in which circumstance rehabilitation of the chronically ill husband was most successful.

The next step in the construction of a typology is to analyze substantive meanings. Therefore, you will again analyze the cases in the different types for which meanings for one's own practices can be identified in the interviews and which regularities become visible for this.

Finally you will characterize the constructed types, exploring which features or combinations of features characterize the cases that have been allocated to the various types: what do they have in common, what distinguishes the cases in the different types? It may be necessary to remove cases strongly deviating from the single type, to further combine groups in order to reduce the variety, or to differentiate into more groups in the case of strong differences within the types constructed so far.

This procedure involves analyzing cases systematically, comparing them, and defining a typology. The typology may refer to the cases as a whole, which means to allocate for example interviewees to the different types. It may also refer to specific topics, which leads to a typology of how the interviewed adolescents manage sexual risks in their street lives and to a typology referring to their utilization of medical support in the case of health problems. The allocation of the interviewees to these two typologies will not necessarily be identical.

Checklist for Analyzing Data

If you conduct an empirical project, it will help to consider the questions in Box 8.4 for the analysis of your data. These questions can be used for doing your own study or for assessing the research of other researchers.

BOX 8.4

Checklist for data analysis

1. Is the method of analysis you chose appropriate to the data you collected?
2. Does it meet the complexity of the data?
3. Does the nature of the data permit you to apply the analytic structure that you chose?
4. Does the kind of analysis allow reducing the complexity of the data in a way that the results become easily understandable?
5. Can you answer your research question with the form of analysis you chose?
6. What is the research question or the aspect of it that is intended to be the focus of the analysis?
7. Can your analysis assess whether your result came up by chance or if it is a singular result?
8. Are your quantitative results statistically significant?
9. Do any regularities (e.g. a typology) become visible in the qualitative results?
10. How does your analysis consider deviant cases or data?

| **Key Points** |

- Content analysis works with texts – in a quantitative way in analyzing newspapers, for example, and in a qualitative way also in analyzing interviews and other data.
- Quantitative analysis starts with elaborating, evaluating and cleaning data.

- The next step is the descriptive analysis of frequencies, distributions, central tendencies and dispersions in the data.

- Quantitative analyses can focus on one, two or more variables and their relationships.

- Relationships found in this way are tested for their statistical significance with different tests.

- Qualitative analyses can aim at developing a theory by applying various methods of coding the data.

- They also can focus on analyzing narratives for the processes and life histories represented in them.

- The analysis of interactions is an option in analyzing qualitative data.

- Qualitative analysis moves between case-oriented and comparative analysis with the aim of developing typologies.

■ ■ Further Reading ■

The following texts provide more detailed discussion of the issues covered in this chapter.

Bryman, A. (2008) *Social Research Methods*, 3rd edn. Oxford: Oxford University Press.

Flick, U. (ed.) (2007) *The Sage Qualitative Research Kit*, 8 vols. London: Sage.

Flick, U. (2009) *An Introduction to Qualitative Research*, 4th edn. London: Sage.

Flick, U., Kardorff, E. v. and Steinke, I. (eds) (2004) *A Companion to Qualitative Research*. London: Sage.

CHAPTER 9
E-RESEARCH: DOING SOCIAL RESEARCH ONLINE

Chapter Overview

Chapter Objectives

This chapter is designed to help you:

- understand the use of the Internet in social research
- appreciate the advantages of using the Internet as a support for your study
- understand how traditional approaches to social research can be transferred to Internet-based research
- recognize the limits of doing social research online.

Table 9.1   Navigator for Chapter 9

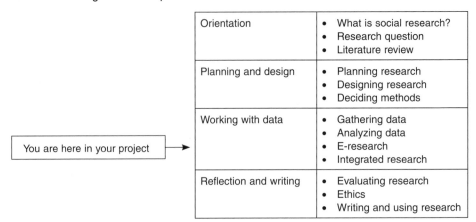

Orientation	• What is social research? • Research question • Literature review
Planning and design	• Planning research • Designing research • Deciding methods
Working with data	• Gathering data • Analyzing data • E-research • Integrated research
Reflection and writing	• Evaluating research • Ethics • Writing and using research

You are here in your project →

What Is E-Research and Why Do It?

The Internet has become a part of many people's lives in one way or another. It can be interesting, therefore, to study (a) who is using the Internet and (b) for what purposes, and (c) who is not using the Internet. If you were to pursue such questions, you would be making the Internet an *issue* of your research.

In such studies you could of course apply the methods we discussed in the preceding chapters in a traditional way. You could, for example, distribute a questionnaire or do face-to-face interviews in your student community or a sample of the general population. This would be helpful, especially for pursuing the third of the questions itemized above – i.e. who is *not* using the Internet.

Besides becoming an issue of your research in this way, the Internet has become an important instrument for doing research – sometimes on issues not directly linked to the Internet itself. Research that uses the Internet as an instrument for doing social research is sometimes called 'e-research' and it is on this that we focus in this chapter. Here we find traditional methods of social research transferred, and sometimes adapted, to e-research. Examples include online surveys, online and e-mail interviews, online focus groups, virtual ethnography and the like.

There are two sets of preliminary questions to ask yourself before embarking on e-research. (1) Do you like working with computers and using the Internet and its various forms of communication? Do you feel comfortable working in this context? (2) Do you have the technical skills to create and use online tools (e.g. a survey or an interview)? If not, do you have the necessary support for doing so? If your answer to such questions is 'no', you might prefer a different method for your research project.

Sampling and Access

As in general research, so in e-research: the concept of sampling involves a wider population from which you draw a sample, and so your sample of actual participants represents some larger group of potential participants. In e-research, however, you may have the problem of a double reality. To take a simple example: if you wish to study trends in book purchasing and you use an online shop like Amazon to find your participants, you will be using a very selective approach: you cannot necessarily equate the clients of this shop with those of (a) offline bookshops or even (b) other shops on the Internet. Thus in this example it will be difficult to draw conclusions from a sample (of Internet bookshop users) to a population of book buyers in general. This example entails questions not only of how representative online samples are for real-world populations, but also of access – where you will find participants, how you will contact them, and so on.

Here we may consider a number of forms of access for an online survey (see below) aiming at a random sample (see Baur and Florian 2009). They are:

- web surveys without scientific claims

- open web surveys with no limitations on who is expected to take part; everyone is invited (through, say, a banner on a website) and may even be able to participate several times over

- self-recruited volunteer panels that address potential participants drawn to a certain issue

- intercept surveys that draw a random sample of all people who visit a certain webpage and then invite the members of that sample to participate in a survey

- list-based surveys that use institutions with a complete e-mail list of its members (e.g. a university with all its students and employees), all of whom are invited to participate (or from which a random sample is drawn)

- mixed mode surveys that use a random sample of the population; members of the sample may then choose between paper and online questionnaires for their participation

- a panel of the population recruited beforehand, drawn from a random sample of the population and where, if members of this sample do not have access to the Internet, the researchers will provide them with access.

These alternatives differ with regard to where you find your population to draw a sample from and also how far you can realize the idea of random sampling in this context. The population can consist either of the users of a website or Internet portal or of the general population of a country. In the latter case, you have to take into account that Internet users constitute a selection from the general population: by no means everyone uses the Internet. For example,

Internet users tend to be younger than the average population and are more likely to have received a higher education. This may lead to problems of *under-coverage* in your Internet sample compared to the general population: that is, certain groups of the population (e.g. older people or those without children) will be systematically under-represented in your Internet-based sample. At the same time, you may face *over-coverage* as a problem: people who are not in your target group or sample may respond to your questionnaire, sometimes without revealing their identity, which then makes it difficult to exclude them from your dataset. Or some people fill in your questionnaire several times. Other problems include non-response to certain items/questions or respondents who drop out, for example after answering the first group (or page) of questions and then losing interest or because of a breakdown in the Internet connection.

Another problem of access is what and how much you will really know about your participants if you use people's e-mail address or the nickname they use in discussion groups or chatrooms for identifying them. In some cases, you will know no more about them or have to rely on the information they give you about their gender, age, location and so on. This may raise questions about the reliability of such demographic information and lead to problems of contextualizing the statements in the later interview. As Markham asks: 'What does it mean to interview someone for almost two hours before realizing (s)he is not the gender the researcher thought (s)he was?' (2004, p. 360).

In addition, using e-mail address as the identifier for participants in your study may raise other issues. Many people use more than one e-mail address or several Internet providers at the same time. In contrast, several people within the same household may use the same computer (see Bryman 2008, p. 647).

Several responses to these problems of sampling have been suggested. One is that not every study needs a sample as closely representative of the 'population at large' as possible: this applies to online research as well as offline (Hewson et al. 2003). Qualitative studies follow a different logic of sampling, and maybe it does make sense to study the shopping trends of amazon.com clients (in our example above) for some purpose. So such a sample may be adequate as long as you refrain from generalizing your results to inadequate populations (e.g. book buyers in general). You need to be careful in generalizing your results to other populations and to reflect on what is adequate and what is not. Finally, for some studies and research questions, it may not be a problem that participants respond repeatedly or use unclear identities as this may represent typical user practices on the Internet. The questions and issues mentioned by Gaiser and Schreiner in this context may be helpful:

> **Consider who you want in the study and where you are going to find them. Who is likely to frequent your type of online environment? How can you get participants to participate in your site? How might a researcher best engage a particular population? What technologies do sample participants use or are more likely to use? (2009, p. 15)**

In general, as in other forms of survey, you should consider two steps for increasing the response rate. Before you send a questionnaire to potential participants, you should contact them and ask for their permission to include them in your study. You should follow up non-respondents at least once (Bryman 2008, p. 648).

Online Surveys, Interviews and Focus Groups

The three basic methods for gathering participants' statements – namely drawing on opinions, stories and other forms of verbal data – have been transferred to e-research.

Online Surveys

There are several assessments of online surveys. Most research using the Internet is quantitative and consists of online surveys, web-based questionnaires, or Internet experiments (see Hewson et al. 2003). It has been estimated that at least a third of all surveys worldwide are online surveys (Evans and Mathur 2005, p. 196) and the trend is upwards. Bryman (2008) discusses e-mail surveys and web surveys. The first, as the name suggests, is sent by e-mail to recipients selected in advance. The questionnaire is attached to an e-mail with the expectation that the recipients answer the questions and send the questionnaire back as an attachment to their reply e-mail. An alternative is to send the questionnaire embedded in the e-mail itself, and the answers are given by adding an 'x' to the questions or by writing text into the e-mail and send it back by touching the reply button. Although the latter version may be easier to handle for the respondent, some e-mail programs may produce problems with the formatting. Web surveys are more flexible in formatting the whole questionnaire and the answer options. Questionnaires can be designed appealingly and it is easier to include filter questions or skip questions (the answer directs the participant to different questions to refer to next, or questions are left out after a specific answer). Participants may be addressed by placing a banner similar to an advertisement on a webpage and respondents can click on the questionnaire and fill it in. There are also software tools and services available on the Internet which can facilitate doing your online survey; many companies offer these services professionally (which means you have to pay for them). If you search 'Google survey' you will end up at along list of such services like Survey Monkey or Bristol Online Surveys (http://www.survey.bris.ac.uk).

Compared to postal questionnaire surveys, online surveys have a number of advantages. These include:

- *Low cost*. As you will not have to print your questionnaire, you can save money on envelopes and stamps. The questionnaires you receive back are already 'in' the computer and more easily transferred into the statistics software.

- *Time*. Online questionnaires come back more quickly than postal questionnaires.

- *Ease of use*. Online questionnaires are easier to format and easier to navigate for the participant (see above).

- *Lack of spatial restrictions*. You can reach people over long distances without waiting for the questionnaire to travel back and forth.

- *Response rate*. The number of unanswered questions in most cases is lower with online surveys, while open questions tend to be answered in a more detailed way and the answers are already given in a digital format.

However, there are also a number of disadvantages of online questionnaires compared to traditional surveys. The response rates can be lower in some cases; you will only reach populations that are already online (see above). There is skepticism about anonymity, especially on the part of potential participants; this may reduce the motivation to respond. Alternatively, people sometimes reply more than once (see Bryman 2008, p. 648; Hewson et al. 2003, p. 43).

BOX 9.1

Case study: longitudinal monitoring of students' quality assessments

At the university of Potsdam, an online panel was established to monitor student biographies, course evaluations, and assessments of the study program quality, in a longitudinal perspective. Students were invited to join the online panel through online and offline contacts. Students were contacted before they started their studies and before enrolling for the programs and were motivated by a lottery for participants. Nevertheless, of the 18,000 students of the university, only 700 were in the panel after a year. The research team took careful precautions to guarantee the anonymity of the participants and to be able to link data from the several waves of survey (see Pohlenz et al. 2009 for details).

Sue (2007, pp. 20–1) has outlined a research timeline for online surveys to be completed in 13 weeks. The first three weeks are devoted to writing the study objectives, reviewing the literature, and revising the objectives. The next three weeks are devoted to selecting survey software and developing, pre-testing and revising the questionnaire. In week 7, the actual data collection is run and incoming responses are monitored. Weeks 8 and 9 focus on reminding non-respondents and analyzing the data. In the remaining four weeks you will write first and second drafts of research reports and present them. This timeline looks very tight, in particular in the part where the research is run – but it at least gives an initial indication of how to progress.

Online Interviews

You can organize online interviewing in several ways. You may use a *synchronous* form. This means that you contact your participant while you are both online at the same time – for example in a chatroom where you can directly exchange questions and answers. This comes closest to the verbal exchange in a face-to-face interview. Alternatively, you can organize online interviews in an *asynchronous* form, which means you send your questions to the participants and they send their answers back later: here you are not necessarily online at the same time. The latter version is mostly done through e-mail exchanges and comes close to what you do in a questionnaire study. You can also use messaging services like Skype to establish an *immediate* dialogue in the format of question and answer. If the technical resources are available, you can even establish a video dialogue in which you see your respondent and vice versa.

Each of these alternatives needs technical resources (like a camera, a fast broadband connection and the like) on both sides. Mann and Stewart (2000, p. 129) following Baym (1995) see five questions as important to consider for computer-mediated interaction in interviews. They are:

1. What is the purpose of the interaction/interview? This will influence the interest of possible participants in whether or not to become involved in the study.

2. What is the temporal structure of the research? Are synchronous or asynchronous methods used, and will there be a series of interactions in the research or not?

3. What are the possibilities and limitations of the software which will influence the interaction?

4. What are the characteristics of the interviewer and the participants? What about their experience of and attitude to using technology? What about their knowledge of the topics, writing skills, insights etc.? Is one-to-one interaction or researcher–group interaction planned? Has there been any interaction between researcher and participant before? How is the structure of the group addressed by the research (by hierarchy, gender, age, ethnicity, social status etc.)?

5. What is the external context of the research – the inter/national culture and/or communities of meaning that are involved? How do their communicative practices outside the research influence the latter?

If you do your interviews in an asynchronous form, the delay between question and answer may influence the quality of your data and the thread of the interview may get lost. When running the interview itself, you can either send one question or a couple of questions, wait for the answers, and then probe (as in a face-to-face interview), or continue sending the next questions. If there is a longer delay before answers come, you can send a reminder (after a few days for example). Bampton and Cowton (2002) view a decline in the length and quality of responses, as well as a tendency for answers to come more slowly, as a sign of fading interest on the part of the participant and the signal for the interview to come to an end.

The advantages mentioned for interviewing online are the same as for online research in general. You may save time and costs and can reach people over big distances. An additional advantage is the greater anonymity for the participant, in particular in e-mail interviews. If you choose a video call, the anonymity for the participant is no longer given as it is in the e-mail interview, where only statements are exchanged as text. At the same time, you can more easily contextualize statements in paralinguistic contexts like facial expressions. The disadvantages are doubts about the 'real' identities (who am I talking to), the loss in direct rapport with the participants, and the problems in probing when answers remain unclear. The latter applies more to e-mail interviews, which come closer to the situation of filling in a questionnaire (see Salmons 2010 for more details of planning and doing online interviews in a synchronous way).

Online Focus Groups

There has been particular interest in online focus groups. Again, one can distinguish between synchronous (or real-time) and asynchronous (non-real-time) groups. The first type of online focus group requires that all participants are online at the same time. They may participate via a chatroom or by using specific conferencing software. The latter option requires all participants to have this software on their computers or to be provided with it. Besides the technical problems this may cause, many people may hesitate to receive and install software for the purpose of taking part in a study. Asynchronous focus groups do not require that all participants are online at the same time (and this prevents the problems of coordination).

For online focus groups to work, ready access for the participants is required. Mann and Stewart (2000, pp. 103–5) describe in some detail the software you can use for setting up synchronous focus groups ('conferencing software'). They also describe the alternatives of how to design websites, and how these can facilitate access for those who are intended to participate and exclude others not intended to have access. The authors also discuss how the concepts of naturalness and neutrality concerning the venue of a focus group also apply online. For example, it is important that the participants can take part in the discussions from their computers at home or at their workplace, rather than from a special research site. As a beginning, it is important to create a welcome message, which invites the participants, explains the procedures and what is expected from the participants, and describes what the rules of communication among the participants should be (e.g. 'please be polite to everyone') and so on (see 2000, p. 108 for an example). The researcher should – as with any focus group – create a permissive environment.

The advantages of doing focus groups online are that you may save time and costs, as you will not have to set up your group at the same time and place and you will save transcription costs as data already come in digital form. Other advantages are that there is greater anonymity for the participants and that group dynamics play a smaller role compared to real-world focus groups: it is less likely here that participants will dominate the group or suppress other participants' contribution.

At the same time, there are disadvantages. An asynchronous group may take a long time to respond. Also contributions may 'come late': discussion may already have moved on, when respondents after some time refer to an earlier state of discussion. The tendency for non-response may be higher than in face-to-face interviews. Technical requirements and problems (for example, connection difficulties) may influence the data quality as well the process of an asynchronous discussion.

Virtual Ethnography

If you transfer methods of surveying or individual or group interviews to e-research, you turn to the Internet as a *tool* to study people you could not otherwise reach. But you can also see the Internet as a *place* or as a *way of being* (for these three perspectives see Markham 2004). In these cases, you can study the Internet as a form of milieu or culture in which people develop specific forms of communication or, sometimes, specific identities. This requires a transfer of ethnographic methods to Internet research and to studying the ways of communication and self-presentation on the Internet: 'Reaching understandings of participants' sense of self and of the meanings they give to their online participation requires spending time with participants to observe what they do online as well as what they say they do' (Kendall 1999, p. 62). Box 9.2 provides a case study of ethnography online.

BOX 9.2

Case study: virtual ethnography

In her study, Hine (2000) took a widely discussed trial (the Louise Woodward case – a British au pair who was tried for the death of a child she was responsible for in Boston) as a starting point. She wanted to find out how this case was constructed on the Internet by analyzing webpages concerned with this issue. She also interviewed web authors by e-mail about their intentions and experiences and analyzed the discussions in newsgroups in which 10 or more interventions referring to the case had been posted. She used www.dejanews.com for finding newsgroups. At this site, all newsgroup postings are stored and can be searched by using keywords. Her search was limited to one month in 1998.

Hine posted a message to several of the newsgroups which had dealt with the issue more intensively. However, the response was rather limited, as other researchers had obviously found repeatedly (2000, p. 79). Hine also set up her own homepage and mentioned it while contacting prospective participants or in posting messages about her research. She did this to make herself and her research transparent for potential participants.

In summarizing her results, she stated that:

> The ethnography constituted by my experiences, my materials and the writings I produce on the topic is definitely incomplete … In particular, the ethnography is partial in relation to its choice of particular applications of the Internet to study. I set out to study 'the Internet', without having made a specific decision as to which applications I intended to look at in detail. (2000, p. 80)

Nevertheless, Hine produced interesting results of how people dealt with the issue of the trial on the Internet. Her thoughts and discussions on virtual ethnography are very instructive beyond her own study. However, they also show the limitations of transferring ethnography – or, more generally, qualitative research – to online research, as Bryman's critical comment illustrates: 'Studies like these are clearly inviting us to consider the nature of the Internet as a domain for investigation, but they also invite us to consider the nature and the adaptiveness of our research methods' (2008, p. 636).

In general, interest in doing ethnographies of the Internet – also called 'netnographies' (Kozinets 2010) – is increasing. Often forms of interviewing are used, as opposed to ethnographic methods in the strict sense of the term.

Analyzing Internet Documents and Interactions

Bergmann and Meier (2004) go one step further. Starting from a conversation analytic background, they suggest analyzing the formal parts of interaction on the web. Conversation analysis is interested in the linguistic and interactive tools (like taking turns, repairing, opening up closings: see Chapter 8) that people use when they communicate about an issue. In a similar way, the authors suggest that you identify the traces online communication leaves for understanding how communication is practically produced on the web. Thus they use electronic process data, that is 'all data that are generated in the course of computer-assisted communication processes and work activities – either automatically or on the basis of adjustments by the user' (2004, p. 244). These data are not simply ready to hand: rather they must be reconstructed on the basis of a detailed and ongoing documentation of what is happening on the screen (and, if possible, in front of it) when someone sends an e-mail, for example. This includes the comments of the sender while typing an e-mail, and paralinguistic aspects like laughing and so on. It is important to document the temporal structure of computer-mediated communication. Here you can use special software (like Lotus ScreenCam) that allows filming of what is happening on the computer screen together with recording the interaction in front of the screen with video, for example.

Similarly, you may take webpages as a medium of online interaction and analyze them for their content and for the means that are used for communicating these contents. You can use qualitative methods for such a study – like a hermeneutic approach or qualitative content analysis – or approach these objects with quantitative methods like content analysis, or by analyzing the frequencies with which they are addressed or used.

A specific feature of webpages is the intertextuality of documents on the web, organized and symbolized by (electronic) links from one text (or one page) to other texts. This kind of cross-referencing goes beyond the traditional definition and boundaries of a text and links a large number of single pages (or texts) to one big (sometimes endless) text. Many webpages constantly update, change, disappear and reappear on the web. It is necessary therefore to always mention the date you accessed a page when referring to it as a source. As with other forms of analyzing documents as means of interaction, you should ask: who produced this webpages, for whom, and with what intentions? Which means are used to reach these goals?

E-Research Today: Using Web 2.0

The approaches mentioned so far have been made possible by the development of the Internet, or web, over the last couple of decades. More recently, from around 2005 onwards, a set of new developments has changed forms of communication on the web again. Together they are usually referred to as 'Web 2.0'. New forms of communicating (blogs for example) and of social networking sites (like Facebook, YouTube, or Twitter) have become public and widely used.

Again, these developments can be an issue for research (who uses them and for what purposes?). They can also be used as instruments for doing research as well, together with other Web 2.0 developments. A recent study (RIN 2010) has focused on the use of Web 2.0 tools in particular for research purposes and on who is already using them and what developments this will lead to.

What is Web 2.0?

The following definition highlights what is characteristic for Web 2.0 and what makes it relevant for research purposes:

> Web 2.0 encompasses a variety of different meanings that include an increased emphasis on user-generated content, data and content sharing and collaborative effort, together with the use of various kinds of social software, new ways of interacting with web-based applications, and the use of the web as a platform for generating, re-purposing and consuming content. (Anderson 2007, quoted in RIN 2010, p. 14)

A central feature is the way communication and the production of knowledge are organized:

> Web 2.0 services emphasize decentralized and collective generation, assessment and organization of information, often with new forms of technological intermediation. (2010, p. 14)

How Can You Make Use of Web 2.0 for Your Own Research?

For using this approach in the context of social research, the sharing of information is a central issue. This involves (a) retrieving information (publications for example), (b) making information accessible (sharing of data, public datasets etc.) and (c) publishing research (results, reports etc.). Thus the main issue is how these new media are used to organize and facilitate scholarly communication. You can use these media for collaborative research by sharing your data and experiences with other researchers. So you could work on the same datasets with other people, use blogs for this purpose, and make your results public in this context.

The variety of developments is evident in what was studied in the research mentioned above:

> We include common forms such as blogs and wikis, widely adopted generic services such as video-sharing, bookmarking or reference-sharing, and social networking systems offered by commercial providers. In addition, we investigated services provided by actors such as publishers and libraries, and some individual open access publishers and aggregators, along with some more specialised tools adapted for specific workflows or research communities. (2010, p. 14)

Examples of applying these forms of communication are to use and contribute to public wikis (the best known may be Wikipedia, but there are other examples) or private wikis set up for a specific purpose. Other forms are to write blogs or comment on blogs, to post presentations, slides, images or videos publicly. These forms can be used for working in collaborative teams in one institution or across several institutions (see also http://www.oii.ox.ac.uk/microsites/oess/ for more information in this area in general).

Communicating (about) Your Research

A major issue in this context is the use of open access software, and even more the use of open access online journals for one's own publications, for seeking existing publications and for commenting on other people's publications. There are also commercial services like SlideShare (www.slideshare.net), where slide presentations can be made public as a more informal way of communicating about research and findings. And finally, there is a strong trend towards open access repositories making literature available online and for free (e.g. the Social Science Open Access Repository at http://www.ssoar.info/).

These developments will change social research in the near future by making new forms of collaboration, of retrieving information and of publishing results and reports easier.

Checklist for Designing Social Research Online

When you do your research project on the Internet, you should consider the questions listed in Box 9.3. These questions can be helpful for doing your own study online, but also for assessing other researchers' online studies.

BOX 9.3

Checklist for designing social research online

1. Why do you wish to do your research online as opposed to on-site?
2. Is your target group a population specifically linked to the Internet, which thus makes an online study necessary?
3. Is your target population likely to have the Internet access required for participating in your study?
4. Do the advantages of applying your methods online outweigh the disadvantages?
5. Do you have the necessary computer skills for designing your instruments and administering the project online?
6. What is the potential of Web 2.0 communication for doing your research?

Key Points

- Survey, interviews, observation and documentary research are the major methods in social research that have been transferred to online research.

- Online research requires computer and Internet literacy on the part of researchers, but also on the part of the potential participants.

- Sampling issues are doubled here: what inferences can you make from your online sample to (a) populations in the virtual world and (b) real-world populations?
- It may be difficult to preserve the specific characteristics of a method when using it online – for example, to prevent an e-mail interview from becoming an e-mail questionnaire.
- For analyzing online communication as a research topic, methods need to be further developed.
- New forms of online communication support and change the way of doing and publishing research.

▓ ▓ Further Reading ▓

The four texts listed below provide a helpful overview of e-research.

Flick, U. (2009) *An Introduction to Qualitative Research*, 4th edn. London: Sage. Chapter 20.

Gaiser, T.J. and Schreiner, A.E. (2009) *A Guide to Conducting Online Research*. London: Sage.

Hewson, C., Yule, P., Laurent, D. and Vogel, C. (2003) *Internet Research Methods: A Practical Guide for the Social and Behavioral Sciences*. London: Sage.

RIN (2010) 'If You Build It, Will They Come? How Researchers Perceive and Use Web 2.0', http://www.rin.ac.uk/our-work/communicating-and-disseminating-research/use-and-relevance-web-20-researchers (accessed 21 August 2010).

Salmons, J. (2010) *Online Interviews in Real Time*. London: Sage.

CHAPTER 10
INTEGRATED SOCIAL RESEARCH: COMBINING DIFFERENT RESEARCH APPROACHES

Chapter Overview

Chapter Objectives

This chapter is designed to help you:

- understand the limits of social research
- appreciate the arguments for combining various procedures in a research project
- understand the concept of triangulation
- understand the idea of integrated social research
- see that combining methods can be productive, if you use them to collect or analyze data on different levels.

Table 10.1 Navigator for Chapter 10

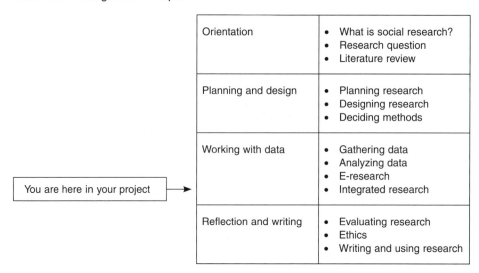

Orientation	• What is social research? • Research question • Literature review
Planning and design	• Planning research • Designing research • Deciding methods
Working with data	• Gathering data • Analyzing data • E-research • Integrated research
Reflection and writing	• Evaluating research • Ethics • Writing and using research

You are here in your project →

For all the value of social research, it should be recognized that it has its limits. One cannot study everything – for ethical (see Chapter 12), for methodological and sometimes for practical reasons. Research projects limited to single methods are particularly limited. This chapter is designed both to make those limitations clearer and to show how using a combination of methods can expand the range of what is possible in research.

Limits of Quantitative Research

Let us first consider the main limitations of standardized research.

Limits of Representativeness

To ensure that studies are representative, researchers need to draw appropriate samples. Yet this is easier said than done. In many cases, you will find that biases in the sample arise. For example, you may find that you cannot reach some of the potential participants: they may have moved away or died, for example, or they may refuse to take part in your study. In particular, the increasing number of telephone surveys in the context of market research may result in resistance from potential participants. Sometimes an increase in funding for a particular area of research results in participants being approached too often and so refusing. As a result, obtaining a representative sample may require considerable effort.

Limits of Standardized Surveys

Standardized surveys are intended to collect views on the issues under study, independently of both the situation in which data are collected and the person of the interviewer. That is the aim, whether you are using questionnaires to be completed by the participant or standardized interviews with a catalogue of questions to be asked by an interviewer. Yet there are difficulties with these methods. Interviewees' characteristics – for example, their age or gender – can influence the way they approach questions in an interview situation (e.g. Bryman 2008, pp. 210–11). Responses may be influenced by ideas about their social desirability: interviewees may ask themselves, which answer is expected from me? Which opinion would I rather not express? Another problem is that respondents might answer all questions with consistently positive (or consistently negative) answers.

In addition, there is the problem that respondents may interpret questions differently from each other. Can you, for example, assume that everybody who ticks 'agree completely' for a question has understood it in the same way as all the others giving the same answer, and that this answer represents the same attitude in every case? Do interviewee and interviewer share the same meaning of the words in the question? Both would be a precondition for summarizing identical answers under the same category.

Limits of Structured Observation

For structured observation that uses an observation scheme or guidelines with predefined categories, there are also limitations. Such instruments may force an inappropriate or irrelevant framework upon the setting that you observe. Structured observation documents behaviors rather than underlying intentions, and in general pays too little attention to their context (2008, p. 269).

Limits of Quantitative Content Analysis

Content analyses are only as good as the documents that you study with them. Moreover, it is difficult to develop a category system that does not to some extent depend on the interpretation of the coder. Underlying or latent meanings are very difficult to capture through content analysis: such analysis usually remains at a surface level. Also, it is difficult to identify the reasons behind certain statements. Finally, this method has been criticized for its lack of theoretical reference (see Bryman 2008, p. 291 for these points).

Limits in Analyzing Secondary Data

The main limitation of secondary (statistical or routine) data is that researchers may be only partly familiar with the data. You may be over-challenged by the complexity of the data (their volume, their internal structure etc.). In addition, you will have little control over the quality of the data (how exact was the documentation in the statistics, who conducted the error control or data cleaning and how?). Moreover, sometimes entries or values that are important for your research question may be missing (2008, p. 300). In many cases, it will be impossible for you to go back to the raw data, as the data are accessible only in aggregated form (summaries, calculations, distributions). If you use official statistics as data, you will need to ensure that category labels are not misleading and that your definitions are the same as those used in data collection.

Limits of Standardized Research

Standardized research has the advantage that it works with a large number of cases and a clearly structured data basis. Thus it often provides representative results. The price for this, however, is that data collection and analysis have to be strongly structured and focused in advance. The scope for new aspects, for the specific experiences of individual participants and for taking concrete contexts into account in data collection remains very limited. The data available for the analysis then are significantly reduced in richness due to the way they were collected (e.g. participants may be limited to five alternative responses). Subjective views that fall outside the range anticipated when you designed your instruments will be difficult to handle. This may limit what you are able to study through standardized methods.

Limits of Qualitative Research

Qualitative research also has its limitations, as described below.

Limits of Theoretical Sampling

If you use theoretical sampling, you will adapt the selection of material as much as possible to the existing gaps in knowledge. Additional cases are then selected according to which aspects of the research question the analysis has not answered so far. The problem here is that neither the beginning nor the end of selecting material can be defined and planned in advance. Unless you can apply this strategy with much sensitivity, experience and flexibility, the scope of the material that you then analyze, and the generalizability of your results, may remain rather limited.

Limits of Interviewing

When you use prepared questions as the core of your interviews, there is a danger that they might omit points that are in fact essential for the interviewees. However, compared to questionnaire studies, you can make this an issue more easily and can repair it more easily. Despite the use of an interview schedule, you will be able to predict what happens in your interviews in a relatively limited way. This also refers to how comparable the situations in your interviews will be. The flexibility in doing the interview permits more sensitivity for the interviewee, but reduces the comparability of the collected data at the same time. Narratives are even more oriented to the single case when you collect your data. Therefore the path from the single interviewee to (theoretically) generalized statements is even longer. The quality of your data will depend very much on your 'success' in the interview situation: do you manage to mediate between what the interviewee mentions and your questions, or to initiate narratives which include the aspects that are relevant for your study? In any case, the data will be limited to reports about an event or an activity and will not give you direct access to them.

Limits of Participant Observation

The strength of participant observation is that you as observer are really involved in the events. Because of your participation, you will have insights into the internal perspective of the setting. As in other forms of observation, participant observation has access only to what happens during the time the researchers participate and observe. What happened before or beyond the setting or concrete situations remains closed to observation and can be covered only through more or less formal conversations. The proximity to what is studied is both the strength and the weakness of the method at the same time. In many reports (e.g. Sprenger 1989), it is evident that the research situation may overwhelm the researchers; their distance from the situation or people that are observed is then endangered. At the same time, there is the question of how situations, and access to them, are selected. We may ask: how far do the periods in which you make your observations enable you to gain the insights you seek? Do your observations actually elucidate the issue you are researching and show its relevance to the field?

Limits of Qualitative Content Analysis

Compared to quantitative content analysis, there will in qualitative research be a stronger consideration of context and the meaning of texts. Compared to other interpretative or hermeneutic approaches, an analysis will be achieved which is much more based on rules and pragmatism. Often the rules that are formulated for a content analysis are as demanding in their application as other methods. The need to interpret text when classifying may make it difficult to maintain procedural clarity. It puts the promised procedural clarity of the method and its rules in perspective again. Categorization of the material employing categories derived externally or from theories, rather than from the material itself, may direct the researchers' focus more to the content than to exploration of the meanings and depth of the text. Interpretation of text through analytic methods, such as objective hermeneutics or grounded theory analysis, plays a role in qualitative content analysis only in a rather schematic way – in explicative content analysis (as outlined in Chapter 8). Another problem is that in qualitative content analysis one often works with paraphrases: these may be useful for explaining the original material, but cause problems if used in place of original material for content analysis.

Limits of Qualitative Analyses of Documents

The advantage of documents is that they are often already available, as they have been produced for purposes other than the research. Institutions produce records, notes, statements and other documents that you can use for your research. Again, however, you face the problem that you cannot influence the quality of the data (production). Documents may have other points of focus and different contents than required for answering your research questions. Sometimes documents have not been produced systematically enough to permit their comparison across institutions. Finally, problems of access to specific documents may arise.

Limits of Non-standardized Research

Qualitative research also has important limitations. The very openness, flexibility and richness of qualitative research may make it difficult to make comparisons between data or to see the big picture – 'the wood for the trees'.

Qualitative research may also intrude into the lives and the private spheres of the participants more than standardized research does. For example, if a disease has led to a stressful situation in one's life, it may be easier to answer some questions in a questionnaire than to recount in a narrative interview the whole process of becoming ill.

Overall, we can see from the above summary of the typical limitations associated with single research methods that both qualitative and standardized research have their limits. We can now consider whether these limits can be overcome by combining different methods.

Combining Different Approaches

At the end of Chapter 6, the importance of deciding between qualitative and quantitative research was highlighted. For many research problems, however, a decision may lead to narrowing the perspective on the issue under study. The number of research problems that require a *combination* of qualitative and quantitative approaches, and thus of several perspectives on what is studied, is growing. Therefore, we will consider approaches for (a) combining methods within either qualitative or quantitative research and also for (b) combining qualitative and quantitative research within the same study. Bryman (1988; 1992) has identified 11 ways of integrating quantitative and qualitative research as follows:

1. The logic of triangulation means checking qualitative findings against quantitative results.

2. Qualitative research can support quantitative research.

3. Quantitative research can support qualitative research.

4. Integration may provide a more general picture of the issue under study.

5. Structural features are analyzed with quantitative methods and processual aspects with qualitative approaches.

6. The perspective of the researchers drives quantitative approaches, while qualitative research emphasizes the viewpoints of the participants.

7. The problem of generality can be solved for qualitative research by adding quantitative findings.

8. Qualitative findings may facilitate the interpretation of relationships between variables in quantitative datasets.

9. The relationship between micro and macro levels in an area under study can be clarified by combining qualitative and quantitative research.

10. Using qualitative or quantitative research can be appropriate at different stages of the research process.

11. Hybrid forms may use qualitative research in quasi-experimental designs (see Bryman 1992, pp. 59–61).

Overall, this classification includes a broad range of variants. Items 5, 6 and 7 rest on the idea that qualitative research captures different aspects than quantitative research. Theoretical considerations are not very prominent in the list of 11 variants Bryman identifies, as the focus is more on the pragmatics of research.

Triangulation

In the social sciences, triangulation means to view a research issue from at least two vantage points. Mostly, the analysis from two or more points is realized by using several methodological approaches. As a strategy for grounding empirical research and its results (see Chapter 11), triangulation has attracted a lot of attention in the context of qualitative research. In particular, the conceptualization provided by Denzin has proved popular (1970/1989). Denzin initially understood triangulation as a strategy of validation (see Chapter 11), but then developed a broader concept. As a result, Denzin has distinguished four forms of triangulation:

- *Triangulation of data* combines data drawn from different sources and at different times, in different places or from different people.

- *Investigator triangulation* is characterized by the use of different observers or interviewers to balance out the subjective influences of individuals.

- *Triangulation of theories* means 'approaching data with multiple perspectives and hypotheses in mind … Various theoretical points of view could be placed side by side to assess their utility and power' (1970, p. 297).

- Denzin's central concept is *methodological triangulation* 'within method' (e.g. through using different subscales within a questionnaire) and 'between method'. 'To summarize, methodological triangulation involves a complex process of playing each method off against the other so as to maximize the validity of field efforts' (1970, p. 304).

From these forms, we can develop the definition of triangulation provided in Box 10.1.

BOX 10.1

Definition of triangulation

Triangulation means that you take different perspectives on an issue you study or in answering your research questions. These perspectives can be substantiated through using several methods or several theoretical approaches. Furthermore, triangulation may refer to combining different sorts of data against the background of the theoretical perspectives which you apply to the data. As far as possible, you should treat these perspectives on an equal footing. At the same time, triangulation (of different methods or of data sorts) should provide additional knowledge. For example, triangulation should produce knowledge on different levels, which means it goes beyond the knowledge made possible by one approach and thus contributes to promoting quality in research.

Triangulation within Qualitative Research

Triangulation can involve combining different qualitative approaches. The case in Box 10.2 illustrates the definition of triangulation provided in Box 10.1.

BOX 10.2

Triangulation within qualitative research: case study

In Chapter 2, I mentioned our study on the situation of homeless adolescents with chronic illness (Flick and Röhnsch 2007; 2008). In this study we combined three methodological approaches: (a) participant observations in the everyday lives of the adolescents; (b) episodic interviews with the adolescents about their concepts of health and illness and their experiences with the health system; and (c) expert interviews with social workers and physicians about the health care situation of adolescents living under these circumstances. Thus, we achieved triangulation between methods and between different kinds of data (statements and observations). We also achieved within-method triangulation, since the episodic interviews combined two approaches ('questions' and 'narrative stimuli') leading to two sorts of data ('answers' and 'narratives') (see Chapter 7). At the same time, different theoretical approaches were brought together: (a) an approach oriented towards interactions and practices in the group under observation; (b) an approach more based on narrative theories in the interviews with the adolescents; and (c) an approach focused on expert knowledge as a specific form of knowledge in the expert interviews.

Triangulation within Quantitative Research

Similarly, you can use triangulation for combining several quantitative approaches. For example, you can use several subscales in a questionnaire, or combine several questionnaires, or complement questionnaires with standardized observations.

Triangulation of Qualitative and Quantitative Research

Finally, triangulation may involve the combination of qualitative and quantitative research. Triangulation of qualitative and quantitative research often becomes concrete at the level of the results produced. It is on that level that Kelle and Erzberger (2004) focus in their discussion of combining the two approaches. They discuss three alternatives:

1. Results may *converge*. That is, the results confirm each other. They may also partly confirm each other and support the same conclusions. For example, statements

from a representative survey with standardized questionnaires may align with statements from semi-structured interviews with a part of the sample in the survey.

2. Results may focus on different aspects of an issue (e.g. the subjective meanings of a specific illness and its social distribution in the population), but be *complementary* to each other and lead to a fuller picture. For example, interviews may provide results that complement (through, say, deepening, detailing, explaining or extending) findings obtained from questionnaire data.

3. Results may be *divergent* or *contradictory*. For example, in interviews, you receive different views from those provided by questionnaires. You could then take this as the starting point for further theoretical or empirical clarification of the divergence and the reasons behind it.

In all three alternatives, similar questions arise. For example: how far did you take into account the specific theoretical background of the two methods that you used in collecting and analyzing your data? Are any differences simply the result of the differing understanding of realities and issues in qualitative and quantitative approaches? Should convergences that go too far make you skeptical, rather than seeing them as a simple confirmation of the one by the other result? And finally: how far are the two approaches and their results seen as equally relevant and independent findings, so that using the concept of triangulation is justified? How far is one of the approaches reduced to a subordinate role, such as merely making plausible the results of the other, more dominant, approach?

Mixed Methods

When bridges are built in the other direction – i.e. when coming *from* quantitative research – the term 'mixed methods' tends to be preferred to 'triangulation'. Supporters of mixed methodologies are interested in combining qualitative and quantitative research pragmatically, seeking to end the 'paradigm wars' between the two approaches. Tashakkori and Teddlie (2003b, p. ix) declare this approach to be a 'third methodological movement'. They see quantitative research as the first movement. For them, qualitative research is the second movement, and mixed methods research is the third movement – one that resolves all of the conflicts and differences between the first and the second movements.

Mixed Methods Designs

When using mixed methods in your own project, the issue of how to design a mixed methods study will be most interesting on a practical level. Creswell (2003) has distinguished three forms of mixed methods design, namely:

1. Phase designs, in which qualitative and quantitative methods are applied separately one after the other (no matter in what order). Such designs can include two or more phases.

2. Dominant/less-dominant design, which is mainly committed to one of the approaches and uses the other only marginally.

3. Mixed methodology designs, which link the two approaches in all phases of the research process.

For the mixed methodologies approach, Tashakkori and Teddlie (2003a), Creswell (2003) and Creswell et al. (2003) have suggested a more elaborate version of designs that combine qualitative and quantitative research. Creswell et al. (2003, p. 211) see mixed methods as designs in their own right in the social sciences, and use the following definition:

> A *mixed methods study* involves the collection or analysis of both quantitative and/or qualitative data in a single study in which the data are collected concurrently or sequentially, are given a priority, and involve the integration of the data at one or more stages in the process of research. (2003, p. 212)

Overall, mixed methods have been used increasingly since the end of the 1990s for overcoming the tensions between qualitative and quantitative research. Here, a rather pragmatic methodological approach is chosen.

Integrated Social Research

As we shall see, the concept of *integrated* research goes a step further than the concepts that have been discussed so far. This concept draws on the range of methodological alternatives and approaches outlined in this book.

Relevance of Integrated Social Research

An argument for integrated research was advanced in the mid twentieth century by Barton and Lazarsfeld (1955). The authors refer to the ability of qualitative research with small numbers of cases to make visible the relations, causes, effects and dynamics of social processes that cannot be found through statistical analyses of larger samples. According to their view, qualitative and quantitative research will be used at different stages of a research project. Qualitative research would mainly be used at the beginning, though it can also be employed subsequently for the interpretation and clarification of statistical analyses.

The debate about qualitative or quantitative research, which was originally informed by epistemological and philosophical standpoints (see Becker 1996 or Bryman 1988 for overviews), has shifted towards issues of research practice

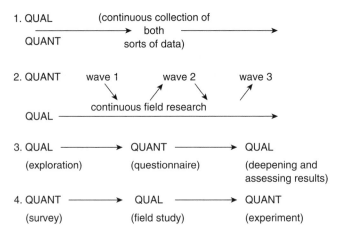

Figure 10.1   Research designs for the integration of qualitative and quantitative research (adapted from Miles and Huberman 1994, p. 41)

concerning the appropriateness of each approach. Wilson states that for the relation of the two methodological traditions, 'qualitative and quantitative approaches are complementary rather than competitive methods [and the] use of a particular method … rather must be based on the nature of the actual research problem at hand' (1982, p. 501).

Procedures of Integrated Social Research

1. In a first step, you should consider how developed is the state of knowledge about the issue of your research and which empirical approaches are required, perhaps in combination.

2. Following the approach of integrated social research, you will take the different theoretical positions and distinctions of the approaches into account when you plan your concrete methodological procedures.

3. In planning a study in integrated social research, you can take the different designs suggested by Miles and Huberman (1994, p. 41) as an orientation, as illustrated in Figure 10.1. In the first design, you pursue both strategies in parallel. In the second design, one strategy (for example, continuous observation of the field) will provide a basis. You can use this basis for planning the waves of a survey. The several waves are related to the observation from which these waves are derived and shaped. In the third combination, you will begin with a qualitative method, e.g. a semi-structured interview. These interviews are followed by a questionnaire study as an intermediate step, before you deepen and assess the results from both steps in a second qualitative phase. In the fourth design, you will do a complementary field study in order to add more depth to the results of a survey in the first step. The last step is an experimental intervention in the field for testing the results of the first two steps.

4. The methodological approaches of collecting and analyzing data are based on the concepts of methodological and data triangulation formulated by Denzin.

5. Finally, the presentation of results (see Chapter 13) reflects the combination of research approaches – by combining case studies with overviews in tables or charts, for example.

It is useful here to consider an example of integrated research. Box 10.3 outlines one such case.

BOX 10.3

Integrated social research: an example

In a running study about the issues of sleep and sleep disorders in institutional everyday life in nursing homes (see Flick et al. 2010; Garms-Homolová et al. 2010), we take different perspectives towards this problem in analyzing its relevance for the routines of care and for the development of diseases. In a number of nursing facilities, we analyze routine data in a longitudinal perspective. Repeated assessments of around 4000 nursing home residents are analyzed three times after one-year periods. We look for interrelations between sleep problems documented in them and the numbers and intensities of diseases in this period. Parallel to such secondary analyses, we do interviews with nurses and physicians in the same facilities and complement them with interviews of relatives of residents in this context. These interviews focus on the perception of the problem in the caring routines and how these problems are dealt with. The design is oriented on the second suggestion by Miles and Huberman (1994; see Figure 10.1). This study allows analysis of the issue on two levels: (a) the reality of caring and (b) the professional perception of the problem. For this purpose, it combines two methodological perspectives: a quantitative secondary analysis of routine data, and a qualitative primary collection and analysis of interviews. On the methodological level, a triangulation of several approaches is realized. This research project is an example of integrated social research not only because the results of qualitative and quantitative analyses are referred to each other, but also because the two approaches are integrated within a comprehensive design.

Overall, the approach of integrated social research can take us beyond some of the limitations of one-sided research. It uses for this goal the theoretical and methodological triangulation of several approaches in a complex design for making possible a more comprehensive understanding of the issue under study.

E-Research as Complementary Strategy

Often the Internet is used as a context for social research because of the limitations of traditional forms of social research. Some of these limitations are practical ones concerning costs and time. However, there are also more general limitations. For example, you can reach people over greater distances when you use a web survey instead of a paper survey. You will reach some people only via the Internet, e.g. as members of a specific online community (see Chapter 9). At the same time, limitations of e-research have been identified. They include limited response rates, unclear sampling frames, restriction of samples to people who use the Internet, and so on.

To overcome these limitations, several authors suggest combining paper and web surveys (see Bryman 2008, pp. 651–2). This can be done in two ways. Either you run your study in two phases, sending out a questionnaire by mail to a sample and sending a second electronically to another sample via the Internet. Or you offer your respondents in a postal questionnaire survey the option to complete the questionnaire either on paper or online. In both cases, you combine the advantages of the two forms of research. Similarly you could complement face-to-face interviews with online interviews (or focus groups). All in all, e-research extends the options for which methods to mix or which perspectives to triangulate or integrate in your study.

Pragmatism and the Issue as Points of Reference

The preceding parts of this chapter have demonstrated that a rhetoric of strict separation (or incompatibility) between single research approaches has its limits. The point of reference for choosing and combining research approaches should be the requirements of the issue under study, rather than single-sided methodological certainties and claims. Combinations can mean that you link qualitative and quantitative research as well as triangulating different qualitative or different quantitative approaches. At the same time, you should see the combination of research approaches pragmatically. That is, you can ask yourself: what is necessary for a sufficiently comprehensive understanding of the issues you study? What is possible under the given circumstances of your own resources and in the field you study? When is it worth making the extra effort of combining methods? For making such a decision, consider whether the different methods will really focus on different aspects or levels or whether they will merely capture the same in very similar ways.

It is helpful here to differentiate between various possible levels of research, such as the four that follow, each of which are explained through examples.

Subjective Meaning and Social Structure

For understanding the subjective meaning of a phenomenon – for example of a disease – patients are interviewed. This is complemented by analyzing the frequency and distribution of the disease in the population or in subpopulations with different social backgrounds (see Flick 1998b).

State and Process

The situation and the current practices of adolescents living on the street are analyzed for issues of health and illness by using participant observation as an approach. This description of a state is combined with interviews revealing which processes in the single adolescents' biographies have led them into their current situation (see Flick and Röhnsch 2007).

Knowledge and Practices

Counselors' subjective theories of trust held in relations to clients are reconstructed in interviews. These are juxtaposed with conversation analyses of consultations done by these counselors with clients in order to find out how trust is built up or impeded (see Flick 1992).

Knowledge and Routines

Nurses' knowledge about the effects of sleep problems on the health of nursing home residents is analyzed in interviews. In addition, routine data are analyzed which are based on diagnoses of certain diseases and documentations of sleep disorders (see Flick et al. 2010).

Integrated Social Research and Its Limits

At the beginning of this chapter we discussed the limitations of social research, beginning with the limitations of single methods. This sought to show that no single method by itself can provide comprehensive access to a phenomenon under study or always be relied upon to provide the appropriate approach. It should also have become clear that quantitative and qualitative approaches in general each have their limitations.

One step towards overcoming the specific limitations of particular methods or approaches is the combination or integrated use of a number of methods. This does not altogether solve the problem of the limitation of research, since each of the methods used remains selective in what it can capture. However, combination or integration can make a research project less restrictive in what it can achieve.

Beyond these limitations, there remain fundamental limits to social research. In addition to the ethical questions discussed in Chapter 12, there are issues that cannot be 'translated' into empirical concepts or approaches. For example, it is not very realistic to try to study the meaning of life empirically! (You can, of course, ask participants in a study what for them personally would be the meaning of their lives – but the phenomenon 'meaning of life' in a comprehensive sense will escape an empirical study.) Furthermore, social research reaches its limits when *immediate* solutions are expected. That this is less a methodological than a fundamental problem should have become evident in Chapter 1.

Checklist for Designing Combinations of Methods

When deciding on using and combining several methods, you should consider the questions listed in Box 10.4. These questions can be used to inform the planning of your own study and also for assessing the studies of other researchers.

BOX 10.4

Checklist for designing combinations of methods

1. What are the limits of the single method which can be overcome by combining several methods?
2. What is the extra gain in knowledge that you can expect from combining the methods?
3. Do the methods really address different levels or qualities in the data, so as to justify their combination?
4. Can the extra effort required for combining methods be accommodated in your framework of research (resources, time etc.)?
5. Are these efforts proportionate for the gain in knowledge they make possible?
6. Are the combined methods compatible with each other?
7. How should you sequence the methods you will use? How will sequencing affect the study?
8. How far are the methods applied according to their characteristics, so that their specific strengths are taken into account?

Key Points

- Every method has its limitations in what it can grasp and how it can do so.
- Distinct limits can be identified for quantitative research and for qualitative research.
- Combinations of research strategies can help to overcome such limits.

- Triangulation, mixed methods and integrated social research provide ways of combining methods.
- Combinations should be grounded in the issue under study and in the additional gain of knowledge they make possible.

▨ ▨ Further Reading ▨

The first two books address the approach of triangulation, whereas the other works focus on mixed methods research.

Denzin, N.K. (1989) *The Research Act: A Theoretical Introduction to Sociological Methods*, 3rd edn. Englewood Cliffs, NJ: Prentice Hall.

Flick, U. (2008) *Managing Quality in Qualitative Research*. London: Sage.

Kelle, U. and Erzberger, C. (2004) 'Quantitative and Qualitative Methods: No Confrontation', in U. Flick, E. v. Kardorff and I. Steinke (eds), *A Companion to Qualitative Research*. London: Sage. pp. 172–7.

Tashakkori, A. and Teddlie, Ch. (eds) (2003) *Handbook of Mixed Methods in Social and Behavioral Research*. Thousand Oaks, CA: Sage.

PART IV
REFLECTION AND WRITING

Successful social research involves much more than merely applying research methods. It is also important to reflect on how methods have been applied – and to make your procedures transparent to others. This final part of the book, therefore, focuses on issues of reflection and writing.

First, we consider quality assessment in quantitative and qualitative research, and then focus on these questions in the context of e-research (Chapter 11).

Second, we discuss research ethics and what it means to make a research project ethically sound. In the process we consider codes of ethics and ethics committees, as well as specific problems of e-research in this context (Chapter 12).

The final chapter considers how to write up research and results in a transparent way, how to feed them back to participants, and how to use data and results in practical or political contexts (Chapter 13).

CHAPTER 11
WHAT IS GOOD RESEARCH? EVALUATING YOUR RESEARCH PROJECT

Chapter Overview

Chapter Objectives

This chapter is designed to help you:

- identify the most important criteria for evaluating empirical research
- recognize that these criteria were originally developed for standardized research
- recognize that for qualitative research, other criteria and approaches of evaluation are applicable
- recognize that generalization of results forms a major part in the assessment of social research
- distinguish between quantitative and qualitative research with regard to approaches to evaluation.

Table 11.1   Navigator for Chapter 11

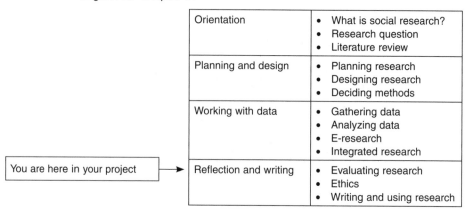

Orientation	• What is social research? • Research question • Literature review
Planning and design	• Planning research • Designing research • Deciding methods
Working with data	• Gathering data • Analyzing data • E-research • Integrated research
Reflection and writing	• Evaluating research • Ethics • Writing and using research

You are here in your project →

Evaluating Empirical Studies

As well as the question of the utility of empirical research, we also need to examine its quality. Here we need to assess whether the methods you applied are reliable, and also how far the results you have obtained can claim validity and objectivity. The last is essentially a question of how far the results could have been obtained by other researchers and are independent from the researcher who did the study. For assessing the quality of empirical research, criteria have been formulated to facilitate assessment of the methodological procedures that led to the results. Here we can ask whether one uniform set of criteria is adequate for every form of empirical research, or whether we should differentiate between criteria that are appropriate for qualitative or quantitative research. Accordingly, in this chapter we first will discuss the criteria of reliability, validity and objectivity, which are generally accepted in quantitative research, and then consider specific approaches in qualitative research.

A fundamental question here is how far results can be generalized. That is, how far may they be transferred to other situations beyond the research situation? Here again, we should ask whether procedures of or claims for generalization should be formulated in a unified way for all sorts of empirical research or whether we need differentiated approaches.

Quality and Evaluation of Quantitative Research

Reliability

The first generally accepted criterion for assessing studies originates from test theory: 'The reliability ... indicates the degree of exactness in measurement (precision) of an instrument. The reliability is the higher the smaller the part of error E linked to a measurement value X is' (Bortz and Döring 2006, p. 196). We can assess the reliability of a measurement in different ways.

Retest reliability

For assessing retest reliability, you will need to apply a measurement (for example, a test or a questionnaire) *twice* to the same sample and then calculate the correlation between the results of the two applications. In the ideal case, you will obtain identical results. This presupposes, however, that the attribute that was measured is stable in itself and has not changed between the two measurement times. When one is repeating performance tests, differences in the results can arise from a change in performance in the meantime (for example, because of additional knowledge that was obtained). Differences in the measurements can result because on the second occasion questions are recognized by participants and learning effects may occur.

Parallel test reliability

For assessing parallel test reliability, you will need to apply two different instruments, so that you operationalize the same construct in parallel. For example, if you wish to find out how reliable a specific intelligence test is, you can apply a second test in parallel. If the first one has measured the intelligence in a reliable way, the second test should produce the same result – i.e. the same intelligence quotient. 'The more alike the results of the two tests, the less error effects obviously are involved' (Bortz and Döring 2006, p. 197).

Split half

In a test or a questionnaire, you can calculate the resulting scores for each half of the items (questions) and then compare the two scores. But then the results will depend on the method of splitting the instruments in two halves (for example, the first and the second half of the questions, even and uneven numbers of the questions, random allocation of questions to one or the other half). For excluding effects of the position of the questions, the internal consistency is calculated. For doing this you will treat each question separately like independent tests and compute the correlation between the results, i.e. the answers given to the various questions.

Inter-coder reliability

When you use content analysis, you can calculate inter-coder reliability to assess the extent to which different analysts allocate the same statements to the same categories and hence the reliability of the category system and its application.

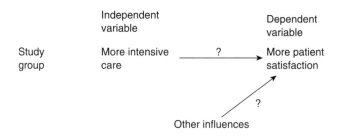

Figure 11.1 Internal validity

Validity

Validity is assessed both for research designs and for measurement instruments.

Validity of research designs

In the case of research designs, the focus will be on the evaluation of results. You will need to check the *internal* validity of a research design. Internal validity characterizes how far the results of a study can be analyzed unambiguously. If you want to study the effects of an intervention, you should check whether changes in the dependent variables can be traced to changes in the independent variable or whether they may result from changes in some other variable (see Figure 11.1).

Consider, for example, the case of a research project on intensive care, in which the introduction of more intensive care constitutes the independent variable, the satisfaction of the patients the dependent variable. If you wish to study the hypothesis 'more intensive care leads to more satisfaction of the patients', you should clarify how the relation between intensive care and satisfaction can be measured unambiguously. For assessing the internal validity, you will try to exclude other influences: how far other conditions have changed in parallel to increasing the intensity of care, and how far the increase in the patients' satisfaction comes from these conditions.

For assuring internal validity, conditions need to be isolated and controlled. A way to assess the effect of an intervention is to apply a control group design (see Chapter 5). In our example, in a second group, as comparable as possible to the first, the intervention would not be introduced – that is, the intensity of care would not be increased. Then one could check whether the effect found in the study group – i.e. the increase in the patients' satisfaction – is evident.

> **Internal validity is achieved if the changes in the dependent variables can be unambiguously traced back to the influence of the independent variable, i.e. if there are no better alternative explanations beyond the study hypothesis. (Bortz and Döring 2006, p. 53)**

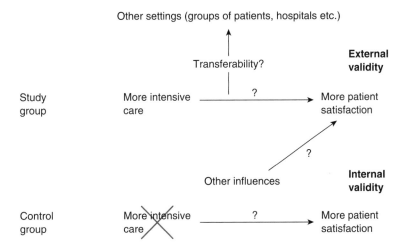

Figure 11.2   External validity

Internal validity is best achieved in the laboratory and in experimental research. However, this is at the expense of the second form of validity of a research design, namely *external* validity. Here, the general question is: how far can we transfer results beyond the situations and persons for which they were produced, to situations and persons outside the research? For example, can we transfer a relation between the intensity of care and the patients' satisfaction to other wards, hospitals or situations of care in general, or is it only valid under the concrete conditions under which it was studied and found (see Figure 11.2)?

There is a difficulty here. Although in the laboratory and under more or less controlled conditions, internal validity will be high, external validity will in contrast be rather limited. In research in the field and under natural conditions, external validity is higher and internal validity is lower, as here the control of conditions is possible only in a very limited way: 'External validity is achieved when the result found in studying a sample can be generalized to other people, situations or points in time' (Bortz and Döring 2006, p. 53). To meet both criteria in one research design at the same time and to the same extent is seen as difficult (Bortz and Döring 2006). Here we face a dilemma of empirical research, which is difficult to solve in a research design.

External and internal validity are assessed for research designs. Validity, however, is also assessed for measurement instruments.

Validity of measurement instruments

The issue of the validity of a research instrument can be summarized in the question: does the method measure what it is supposed to measure? To answer this question, you can apply various forms of validity checks, namely (a) content validity, (b) criterion validity and (c) construct validity.

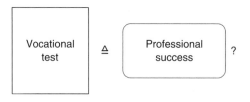

Figure 11.3   Criterion validity

Content validity is achieved when the method or measurement instrument captures the issue under study in its essential aspects and in an exhaustive way. You can check this yourself based on your subjective judgment – by reflecting on how far your instrument covers all the important aspects of your issue and whether it does so in a way that is appropriate to this issue. Even better is to have the measurement instrument assessed by experts or laypeople. Errors should catch the eye in such assessments. Thus the term 'face validity' is used for this assessment. To continue our example: consider whether you would document the caring intensity in the relevant situations of the day routines in a hospital or only in a specific situation – for example at the admission of patients.

Criterion validity is achieved if the result of a measurement corresponds with an external criterion. This will be case, for example, if the results of vocational testing correspond with the professional success of the tested person (see Figure 11.3). Such external criteria can be defined in parallel, which allows you to check the concurrent validity. This means that you apply a second measurement at the same time. For example, you do the test and at the same time observe the candidate's behavior in a discussion group. Then you compare the results of the two measurements – how far the part of the vocational test on communicative skills corresponds to the communication in the group. Alternatively, you check the measurement later, in which case the predictive validity will be assessed – for example, do the results of a vocational test allow the prediction of professional success?

One problem here is that the external criterion has to be valid itself if it is going to be used as a means for checking measurements. Here, you have to take the differential validity into account: concordance between the test score and the external criterion can be different in different populations. If we again take our example, the communicative behavior in the discussion groups may be systematically different for male and female participants, whereas the original test mainly focused on general aspects of vocational qualification. Then the relation between the test score and the external criterion will be different for the two gender subgroups. Methods in general should be able to capture differences in various groups.

Finally, *construct validity* should be assessed. Here you will check whether the construct that is captured by your method is linked sufficiently closely to variables that can be theoretically justified. You will also check here how far

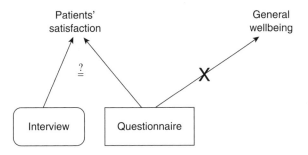

Figure 11.4   Construct validity

the construct allows hypotheses to be derived that can be tested empirically. One way to assess construct validity is to use various measurements: constructs are measured with several methods. When several methods measure the same construct with corresponding results, *convergent validity* is given. For example, you may study the patients' satisfaction with a questionnaire and an interview. When both methods produce results which confirm each other, this shows the convergent validity of your construct. This would indicate your theoretical concept of 'patients' satisfaction' is valid and your study meets this criterion of validity. *Discriminant validity* refers to the question of how far your measurements are able to distinguish the construct you study from other constructs. In our example, you would assess how far your theoretical concept and your measurements really capture the patients' satisfaction with the care. Or do they just capture a general state of wellbeing instead of specific satisfaction with aspects of the care situation? In that case, your concept of 'patients' satisfaction' is not valid and your study misses this criterion of validity (see Figure 11.4).

Validity of indices

An index will need to be constructed when something cannot be directly observed or measured (see Chapter 7), because several aspects of a theoretical construct are integrated in it. For example, patients' general satisfaction with their stay in a hospital cannot be measured directly. Such satisfaction includes satisfaction with the treatment, with the staff's friendliness, with the food, with the atmosphere and so on. For measuring the construct 'general satisfaction' you would have to select one or more indicators. In order to reduce the biases in the measurement of complex constructs as far as possible, several indicators should be used in order to increase the quality of measurement. (For example, grading a school essay combines evaluations of orthography, of style, of content and of form – either in equal shares or with different weights because the style is seen as more important than the number of spelling mistakes.)

In a similar way, one would try to derive patients' satisfaction from various indicators. For example, you could use an instrument for assessing quality of life, a questionnaire for measuring satisfaction with the service by the hospital staff, and another questionnaire addressing satisfaction with the infrastructure of the hospital. Then the question is how to weight the single variables. For example, in constructing a patient satisfaction index, how much weight should be given to the questionnaire results about the staff service compared to, say, the results concerning the quality of life in the hospital?

A further problem here is that if you want to assess the validity of the index, the included variables – e.g. quality of life, satisfaction with staff – themselves have to be measured in a valid way so that the index as a whole can be valid. Thus validity assessments become relevant on two levels here: on the level of the single indicator, and on the level of the index constructed with these indicators. 'The quality of an index essentially depends on how far all the relevant dimensions have been selected and weighed appropriately' (Bortz and Döring 2006, p. 144). For indices, overall validity is composed of the validity of (a) single items or questions, (b) the scales constructed with these items and (c) the weighting of the components.

The construction of an index is based on the use of several indicators for measuring a value which cannot be directly observed or measured. This raises specific problems concerning the validity of indices. Thus you should check whether

- the relevant dimensions have been selected and weighted appropriately
- the instruments for measuring the selected indicators are valid
- the items in the indicators are valid.

Validity addresses different aspects for checking the quality of study results. If you consider external validity, this already includes aspects of the transferability and generalization of results.

Objectivity

The objectivity of instruments, such as tests or questionnaires, depends on the extent to which the application of the instrument is independent of the person applying it. If several researchers apply the same method to the same persons, the results have to be identical. Three forms may be distinguished:

- Objectivity in the data *collection* concerns how far the answers or test results of the participant are independent of the interviewer or person of the researcher. This will be obtained by standardization of the data collection (standardized instructions for applying the instrument and standardized conditions in the situation of the data collection).

- Objectivity of the *analysis* concerns how far the classification of answers in a questionnaire or test are independent of the person who does the classification in the concrete case (for example, by allocating an answer to a specific score).

- Objectivity of the *interpretation* means that any interpretation of statements or scores in a test should be independent of the persons of the researchers and their subjective views or values. Thus norm values (for example, age, gender or education) may be identified with representative samples, which can be used for classifying the achievement or values of the participant in the concrete study.

Achieving objectivity of an instrument or a study principally requires standardization of the ways in which data are collected, analyzed and interpreted. This will exclude the subjective or individual influences of the researcher or the concrete situation in which data were collected.

Quality and Evaluation of Qualitative Research

The criteria discussed so far are well established for quantitative research. They are based more or less on the standardization of the research situation. Sometimes it has been suggested that the classical criteria of empirical social research – reliability, validity and objectivity – may also be applied to qualitative research (see Kirk and Miller 1986). This raises the question of how far these criteria, with their strong emphasis on standardization of procedures and the exclusion of communicative influences by the research, can do justice to qualitative research and its procedures, which are mainly based on communication, interaction and the researcher's subjective interpretations. Often these bases are seen not as biases but as strengths or even preconditions of the research. Accordingly, Glaser and Strauss

> **raise doubts as to the applicability of the canons of quantitative research as criteria for judging the credibility of substantive theory based on qualitative research. They suggest rather that criteria of judgement be based on generic elements of qualitative methods for collecting, analyzing and presenting data and for the way in which people read qualitative analyses. (1965, p. 5)**

In the light of such skepticism, a series of attempts has been made over time to initiate a debate about criteria in qualitative research (see Flick 2009, Chapter 28). One also finds a number of attempts to develop 'method-appropriate criteria' (see Flick 2008a) in order to replace criteria like validity and reliability.

Reformulation of Traditional Criteria

Suggestions for reformulating the concept of reliability with a more procedural emphasis have focused on the question of how data are produced. A requirement is that (a) statements by participants and (b) interpretation by the researcher should be clearly distinguishable. Finally, a way to increase the reliability of the whole process is to document it in a detailed and reflexive way. This refers mainly to documenting and reflecting on the decisions taken in the research process – showing which ones were taken and why (see Chapter 6 for decision-making in the research process).

The concept of validity also requires reformulation. One suggestion is that researchers should scrutinize interview situations for any signs of strategic communication. That means that the interviewee did not openly respond to the questions but was selective or reluctant to give the answers. That leads to a question of how far you can trust the statements of the interviewee. You should also check whether a form of communication occurred in the interview which is not adequate for the interview situation. For example, if the interview produced a therapy-like conversation, this should raise doubts about the validity of the interviewee's statements (Legewie 1987).

A second suggestion is to check the validity by integrating the participants as individuals or groups in the further research process. One way is to include communicative validation at a second meeting, after an interview has been conducted and transcribed (for concrete suggestions see Flick 2009, p. 159). Sometimes communicative validation has been discussed for validating the interpretations of texts. Because of the ethical problems in confronting participants with interpretations of their statements, this form of communicative validation is only seldom applied. For a more general application of communicative validation, two questions remain to be answered, namely:

- How can one design the methodological procedure in communicative validation (or member checks) in a way that does justice to the issues under study and to the viewpoints of the participants?

- How can one answer the question of validity beyond the participants' agreement to the data and interpretations?

Mishler (1990) goes one step further in reformulating the concept of validity. He starts from the *process* of validating (rather than the *state* of validity). He defines 'validation as the social construction of knowledge' (1990, p. 417) by which we 'evaluate the "trustworthiness" of reported observations, interpretations, and generalisations' (1990, p. 419).

Method-Appropriate Criteria

The criteria used for assessing objectivity need to be appropriate to the methods of qualitative research. Beyond the already mentioned communicative validation and triangulation (see Chapter 10), we find a number of suggestions for new criteria in American discussion (see Flick 2009, Chapter 29; 2008a).

For example Lincoln and Guba (1985) have proposed (a) trustworthiness, (b) credibility, (c) dependability, (d) transferability and (e) confirmability as appropriate criteria for qualitative research. Of these, trustworthiness is considered most important. Lincoln and Guba have outlined five strategies for increasing the credibility of qualitative research:

- activities for increasing the likelihood that credible results will be produced by a 'prolonged engagement' and 'persistent observation' in the field and the triangulation of different methods, researchers and data
- 'peer debriefing': regular meetings with other people who are not involved in the research in order to disclose one's own blind spots and to discuss working hypotheses and results with them
- the analysis of negative cases in the sense of analytic induction
- appropriateness of the terms of reference of interpretations and their assessment
- 'member checks' in the sense of communicative validation of data and interpretations with members of the fields under study.

For assessing dependability a process of auditing is suggested, based on the procedure of audits in the domain of accounting. The aim is to produce an auditing trail (Guba and Lincoln 1989) covering:

- the raw data, their collection and recording
- data reduction and results of syntheses by summarizing, theoretical notes, memos and so on, summaries, short descriptions of cases etc.
- reconstruction of data and results of syntheses according to the structure of categories (themes, definitions, relationships), findings (interpretations and inferences), and the reports produced with their integration of concepts and links to the existing literature
- process notes, i.e. methodological notes and decisions concerning the production of trustworthiness and credibility of findings
- materials concerning intentions and dispositions like the concepts of research, personal notes, and the expectations of the participants
- information about the development of the instruments including the pilot version and preliminary plans.

The question of transferability of results has been discussed already in the context of external validity. We will address it again below in relation to evaluation.

Generalization

In quantitative research, the extent to which results can be generalized may be checked in two ways: by assessing external validity, one would (a) assure that the results found for the sample are valid for the population and also (b) test how far they can be transferred to other, comparable populations. Bortz and Döring hold that 'generalizability in quantitative research is achieved by the inference from a random sample (or sample parameters) to populations (or population parameters), which is founded in probability theory' (2006, p. 335).

Various sampling procedures (see Chapter 5) may be used to ensure this. One procedure is to use a random sample, in which every element in the population has the same chance to be an element in the sample. This procedure enables the exclusion of any biases resulting from the disproportionally weighted distribution of features in the sample compared to the population. Thus the sample is representative for the population. An inference from the sample to the population concerning the validity of the results is therefore justified. Other procedures aim at representing the distribution in the population in a more focused way, as, for example, when you draw a stratified sample. Then you will take into account that your population consists of several subgroups, which are unevenly distributed. You will try to cover that distribution in your sample. This allows you to generalize your findings from the sample to the population.

Generalization can be checked by assessing the external validity of a study (see above). This generalization is based on the degree of similarity between the participants in the study and the populations for which the study and its results are supposed to be valid. Accordingly, Campbell (1986) uses the term 'proximal similarity' rather than external validity: in the dimensions that are relevant for the study and its results, the sample should be as similar as possible to the population to which the results are to be transferred.

Generalization in Qualitative Research

In quantitative research, generalization is primarily a numerical problem, to be solved by statistical means. In qualitative research, this question is more difficult. At root there is the familiar issue of generalization: a limited number of cases which have been selected according to specific criteria, or sometimes a single case, have been studied and the results are claimed to be valid beyond the material in the study. The case or the cases are taken as representative of more general situations, conditions or relations. Yet the question of generalizability in qualitative research often arises in a fundamentally different way. In some qualitative research the aim is to develop theory from empirical material (according to Glaser and Strauss 1967) – in which case the question is raised as to how far the resulting theory may be applied to other contexts.

Accordingly, one approach for evaluating qualitative research is to ask what measures have been taken to define or extend the area of validity of empirical results (and indeed of any theories developed from them). Starting points are the analysis of cases and the inferences from them to more general statements. The problem here is that the starting point is often an analysis focused on a specific context or a concrete case, addressing the specific conditions, relations, processes etc. It is often precisely the reference to a specific context that gives qualitative research its value. Yet if one then proceeds to generalize, the specific context is lost and one must consider how far the findings are valid independent of the original context.

In highlighting this dilemma, Lincoln and Guba (1985) have suggested that 'the only generalization is: there is no generalization'. Yet in terms of the 'transferability of findings from one context to another' and 'fittingness as to the degree of comparability of different contexts', they outline criteria for judging the generalization of findings beyond a given context. A first step is to clarify the degree of generalization the research is aiming at and which it is possible to attain. A second step involves the cautious integration of different cases and contexts in which the relations under study are empirically analyzed. The generalizability of the results is often closely linked to the way the sampling is done. Theoretical sampling, for example, offers a way of designing the variation of the conditions under which a phenomenon is studied as broadly as possible. The third step consists of the systematic comparison of the collected material.

The constant comparative method

In the process of developing theories, Glaser (1969) suggests the 'constant comparative method' as a procedure for interpreting texts. It consists of four stages: '(1) comparing incidents applicable to each category, (2) integrating categories and their properties, (3) delimiting the theory, and (4) writing the theory' (1969, p. 220). For Glaser, the systematic circularity of this process is an essential feature:

> **Although this method is a continuous growth process – each stage after a time transforms itself into the next – previous stages remain in operation throughout the analysis and provide continuous development to the following stage until the analysis is terminated. (1969, p. 220)**

This procedure becomes a method of *constant* comparison when interpreters take care that they compare coding over and over again with codes and classifications that have already been made. Material which has already been coded is not finished with after its classification: rather it is continually integrated into the further process of comparison.

Contrasting cases and ideal type analysis

The process of constant comparison may be systematized further through strategies of contrasting cases. Gerhardt (1988) has made the most consistent suggestions based on the construction of ideal types. This strategy involves several steps. After reconstructing and contrasting the cases with one another, types are constructed. Then 'pure' cases are tracked down. Compared with these ideal types of processes, the understanding of the individual case can be made more systematic. After constructing further types (see Chapter 8), this process culminates in a structural understanding (i.e. the understanding of relationships pointing beyond the individual case).

The main instruments here are (a) the *minimal* comparison of cases that are as similar as possible, and (b) the *maximal* comparison of cases that are as different as possible. They are compared for differences and correspondences.

Generalization in qualitative research involves the gradual transfer of findings from case studies and their context to more general and abstract relations – for example in the form of a typology. The expressiveness of such patterns can then be specified according to how far different theoretical and methodological perspectives on the issue – if possible by different researchers – have been triangulated and how negative cases were handled. The degree of generalization claimed for a study should also be taken into consideration. Then, the question of whether the intended level of generalization has been reached provides a further criterion for evaluating the qualitative research project in question.

Standards and Quality in E-Research

All that has been said in this chapter about the criteria and quality of quantitative and qualitative research in principle applies to e-research as well as to traditional research. However, some issues of quality can be raised here with a specific focus on e-research. For example, in e-research the question of generalization refers not only to how far you can infer from a sample of online users (that were part of a survey) to the population of Internet users in general, but also to how far that specific online sample relates to populations beyond the Internet. There are also specific issues of data protection to take into account. For this reason, extra 'standards for quality assurance for online surveys' have been formulated (see ADM 2001) which are helpful for assessing (your) research with this specific approach (see also Chapter 9 for some of these issues).

Checklist for Evaluating a Research Project

For the evaluation of an empirical project in social research, the questions in Box 11.1 are designed to inform your practice. These aspects are relevant for evaluating your own research as well as for assessing other researchers' studies.

BOX 11.1

Checklist for evaluating a research project

1. In a quantitative study, have the criteria of (a) reliability, (b) validity and (c) objectivity been checked?
2. In a qualitative study, which criteria or approaches for assessment of quality have been applied?
3. How far have you made the study and the assessment of its quality transparent and explicit in the presentation of the results and of the procedures?
4. What did you do with deviant results or negative cases?
5. How have you examined the generalizability of your results? What were the aims in this, and how were they reached?

Key Points

- **For evaluating quantitative research, the established criteria are reliability, validity and objectivity.**

- **In qualitative research, these criteria in most cases cannot be applied immediately. Rather they have first to be reformulated. A number of suggestions have been made for how to reformulate these criteria for qualitative research.**

- **In addition, method-appropriate criteria have been developed for qualitative research.**

- **Generalization in quantitative research is based on (statistical) inference from the sample to the population.**

- **In qualitative research, in contrast, theoretical generalization may be the aim.**

- **In qualitative research, the building of typologies and the contrasting of cases play a major role.**

▬ ▬ Further Reading ▬

The first and third references below discuss quality issues in quantitative research; the second and fourth cover quality in qualitative research.

Campbell, D.T. and Russo, M.J. (2001) *Social Measurement*. London: Sage.

Flick, U. (2008) *Managing Quality in Qualitative Research*. London: Sage.

May, T. (2001) *Social Research: Issues, Methods and Process*. Maidenhead: Open University Press. Chapter 1.

Seale, C. (1999) *The Quality of Qualitative Research*. London: Sage.

CHAPTER 12
ETHICAL ISSUES IN SOCIAL RESEARCH

Chapter Overview

Chapter Objectives

This chapter is designed to help you:

- see how ethical issues are involved in social research projects
- develop your sensitivity to ethical questions in social research
- appreciate the complexity of ethical considerations
- plan and conduct your research project within an ethical framework.

Table 12.1   Navigator for Chapter 12

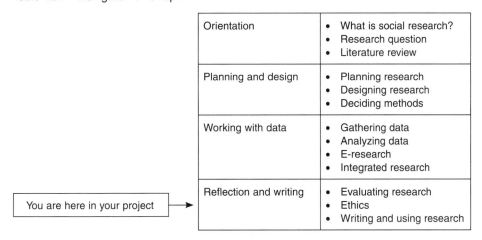

Orientation	• What is social research? • Research question • Literature review
Planning and design	• Planning research • Designing research • Deciding methods
Working with data	• Gathering data • Analyzing data • E-research • Integrated research
Reflection and writing	• Evaluating research • Ethics • Writing and using research

You are here in your project →

In Chapter 10, we considered the limitations of social research. There the main focus was on methodological or technical limitations. We considered such questions as: what can we grasp with one method, what is missed by it, how can we overcome this by using several methods? We also considered a more fundamental limitation, asking: when should you rather refrain from doing your research?

This chapter also focuses on limitations to social research, though of a different sort. We explore such questions as: which ethical problems should be taken into account in research? Which ethical boundaries are touched and how can you approach ethical issues in doing your social research project? As we shall see, these questions involve us in some very general rules and problems.

Principles of Ethically Acceptable Research

Definitions of Research Ethics

Ethical issues are relevant to research in general. They are especially relevant in medical and nursing research. Here we find the following definition of research ethics, which can be applicable to other research areas too:

> **Research ethics addresses the question of which ethically relevant issues caused by the intervention of researchers can be expected to impact on the people with or about whom they research. It is concerned in addition with the steps taken to protect those who participate in the research, if this is necessary. (Schnell and Heinritz 2006, p. 17)**

Principles

In the context of the social sciences, Murphy and Dingwall (2001, p. 339) have developed an 'ethical theory' that provides a useful framework for this chapter. Their theory is based on four principles:

- *Non-maleficence* – researchers should avoid harming participants.

- *Beneficence* – research on human subjects should produce some positive and identifiable benefit rather than simply be carried out for its own sake.

- *Autonomy or self-determination* – research participants' values and decisions should be respected.

- *Justice* – all people should be treated equally.

We shall examine in more detail below how these principles apply in social research.

In addition, Schnell and Heinritz (2006, pp. 21–4), working in the context of health sciences, have developed a set of principles specifically concerning the ethics of research. Their eight principles are listed in Box 12.1.

BOX 12.1

Principles of research ethics (Schnell and Heinritz 2006, pp. 21–4)

1. Researchers have to be able to justify why research about their issue is necessary at all.
2. Researchers must be able to explain what the aim of their research is and under what circumstances subjects participate in it.
3. Researchers must be able to explicate the methodological procedures in their projects.
4. Researchers must be able to estimate whether their research acts will have ethically relevant positive or negative consequences for the participants.
5. Researchers must assess the possible violations and damages arising from doing their project – and be able to do so *before* they begin the project.
6. Researchers have to take steps to prevent violations and damages identified according to principle 5.
7. Researchers must not make false statements about the usefulness of their research.
8. Researchers have to respect the current regulations of data protection.

Overall, such principles aim to ensure that researchers are able to make their procedures transparent (necessity, aims, methods of the study), that they can avoid or eliminate any harm or deception for the participants, and that they take care of data protection.

Informed Consent

Informed Consent as a General Principle

It should be self-evident that studies should generally involve only people who (a) have been informed about being studied and (b) are participating voluntarily. Principles of informed consent and of voluntary participation for social research are to be found in the code of ethics of the German Sociological Association. For example:

> A general rule for participation in sociological investigations is that it is voluntary and that it takes place on the basis of the fullest possible information about the goals and methods of the particular piece of research. The principle of informed consent cannot always be applied in practice, for instance if comprehensive pre-information would distort the results of the research in an unjustifiable way. In such cases an attempt must be made to use other possible modes of informed consent. (Ethik-Kodex 1993: I B2)

There are of course some difficulties here. As mentioned in the quote, informing participants beforehand may contradict the aims of a study. Also there are research settings in which it is not possible to inform all people who might become part of the research in advance. For example, in observations in open spaces (marketplaces, train stations etc.) many people just passing by might become part of the observation for very short moments. For these people, it will be very difficult to obtain their consent. If, however, this is not the case, and consent *can* practically be obtained, you should never refrain from doing so. Accordingly it is generally assumed that informed consent is a precondition for participating in research. For applying this principle in concrete terms, you can find some criteria in the literature:

- The consent should be given by someone competent to do so.
- The person giving the consent should be adequately informed.
- The consent is given voluntarily (Allmark 2002, p. 13).

Informed Consent in Researching Vulnerable Groups

Research with people who are, for special reasons, unable to give their consent raises specific ethical problems. These people are termed vulnerable groups:

> Vulnerable ... subjects are people who, because of their age or their limited cognitive abilities, cannot give their informed consent or who, because of their specific situation, would be particularly stressed or even endangered by their participation in a research project. (Schnell and Heinritz 2006, p. 43)

How then to proceed, if you want to do research with people not able or not seen as able to understand your concrete procedures or to assess them and to decide independently? Examples include small children, or people who are very old or who suffer from dementia or mental problems (for research with vulnerable people see Liamputtong 2007). In such cases, you could ask other people to give the consent as substitutes – the children's parents, family members or responsible medical or nursing staff in the case of the aged or ill persons. But do you then still meet the criteria of informed consent? Can you always assume that these other persons will take the same perspective as the participants you want to study? If you apply the principle of informed consent in a very strict sense in such cases, research is not permitted with these groups of participants, and thus research about relevant issues from the viewpoint of those concerned would be forgone. If you are conducting research involving vulnerable people, you should certainly not ignore the principle of informed consent. You should establish a way in which informed consent can be obtained either from or for the participants: consider carefully who is able to give this consent either together with or for them. However, these are tradeoffs that can only be made for a specific study and not generally. There is no general rule on how to manage this problem: you will have to think for your particular study and your particular target group about how to solve this dilemma between doing necessary research and avoiding any mistreatment of your participants.

Confidentiality, Anonymity and Data Protection

Box 12.2 provides an example of a form developed for the author's own research projects. It is helpful to consider it here as a way to focus both on the issues of informed consent (discussed above) and on anonymity and data protection for the participants.

The form should be completed and signed by both the researcher and the participant. Sometimes an oral agreement can be used as a substitute for the written contract if the participant does not want to sign it. Note that the form specifies a certain period after which the participants can withdraw their consent. Furthermore, the form specifies who will have access to the data and whether the data can be used for teaching after anonymization.

BOX 12.2

Agreement about data protection for scientific interviews

- Participation in the interview is voluntary. It has the following purpose:

[issue of the study]

- Responsible for doing the interview and analyzing it are:

  Interviewer:
  [name]
  [name of institution]
  Supervisor of the project:
  [name]
  [name and address of institution]
  The responsible persons will ensure that all data will be treated confidentially and only for the purpose agreed herewith.
- The interviewee agrees that the interview will be recorded and scientifically analyzed. After finishing the recording he or she can ask for erasure of particular parts of the interview from the recording.
- For assuring data protection, the following agreements are made (please delete what is not accepted):

  The material will be processed according to the following agreement about data protection:

  Recording

  1. The recording of the interview will be stored in a locked cabinet and in password protected storage media by the interviewers or supervisors and erased after the end of the study or after two years at the latest.
  2. Only the interviewer and the members of the project team will have access to the recording for analyzing the data.
  3. In addition the recording can be used for teaching purposes. (All participants in the seminar will be obliged to maintain the data protection.)

  Analysis and archiving

  1. For the analysis, the recording will be transcribed. Names and locations mentioned by the interviewee will be anonymized in the transcript – as far as necessary.
  2. In publications, it is guaranteed that an identification of the interviewee will not possible.
- The interviewer or the supervisor of the project holds the copyright for the interviews.
- The interviewee may revoke his or her declaration of consent completely or partially within 14 days.

Location, date:
Interviewer:
Interviewee:

In case of an oral agreement:
I confirm that I informed the interviewee about the purpose of the data collection, explained the details of this agreement about data protection, and obtained his or her agreement.

Location, date:
Interviewer:

Confidentiality and anonymity may be particularly relevant if the research involves several participants in a specific, very small, setting. If you interview employees in the same enterprise or family members independently of each other it will be necessary to ensure confidentiality not only with respect to the public beyond that setting, but also within it. Readers of a publication should not be able to identify the individuals who participated as an interviewee, for example. Therefore, you should change personal data such as names, addresses, workplaces etc. so that inferences to persons etc. become impossible or, at the very least, are hampered. Accordingly the researcher has to ensure that the other participants cannot identify their colleagues in the presentation of their common workplace or in what the researcher reveals about their study. For this purpose, a consistent anonymization of the data and a parsimonious use of context information are necessary.

If children are interviewed, parents often want to know what their children said in the interviews – which may be problematic for interviews referring to relations of parents to children or to conflicts among them. To avoid this problem, it may be necessary to inform the parents beforehand when such information cannot be given to them.

It is particularly important to store the data (questionnaires, recordings, transcripts, field notes, interpretations etc.) physically in a safe and locked way (data safes, cupboards that can be locked for example), so that nobody gains access to the data who is not supposed to have this access (see Lüders 2004b). The same precautions have to be taken if the data are stored electronically – which means that they are password protected at least, and that the number of persons having access to the site is strictly limited.

How to Avoid Harm for Participants

The risk of harm for participants is a major ethical issue in social research. If, for example, you ask in an interview or a questionnaire how people live with their chronic illness and cope with it, you will confront your respondents with the severity of their illness and maybe with the limits to or lack of their life expectancy, again or additionally. This might cause a crisis or lead to extra stress for the interviewees. Is it ethically correct to produce such a risk for the participants in the research?

A specific problem arises in testing the effects of medications (or other forms of intervention) in randomized control studies (see Chapters 5 and 11). Here people with a diagnosis are randomly allocated to an intervention group (receiving treatment with the medication) and to a control group (receiving instead a placebo without effect, which means no treatment). Is it ethically justified to deprive this second group of a treatment, or to give it to them only after the end of the study? Should you do randomized studies in such cases – in particular, if it is about a serious or life threatening disease? (See Thomson et al. 2004 for this issue.)

The examples just given are drawn from medical research. However, the need to avoid harm applies to *all* research, not just medical studies. According to the code of ethics of the German Sociological Association:

> **Persons who are observed, questioned or involved in some other way in investigations, for example in connection with the analysis of personal documents, shall not be subject to any disadvantages or dangers as a result of the research. All risks that exceed what is normal in everyday life must be explained to the parties concerned. The anonymity of interviewees or informants must be protected. (Ethik-Kodex 1993: I B 5)**

Demands on the Participants Resulting from the Research

Research projects always make demands on participants (see Wolff 2004). For example, participants may be required to sacrifice time to complete a questionnaire or to answer the interviewers' questions. In addition, they may be expected to deal with embarrassing questions and issues and to give the researchers access to their privacy.

From an ethical point of view, you should reflect on whether the demands your research would make on participants are reasonable – especially in the light of their specific situations. For example, you should consider whether a confrontation with their own life history and illness in an interview or survey might even intensify your participants' illness.

Rule of Economy of Demands and Stress

If you are requesting personal information, you should always consider whether you really need the whole life history (in a narrative interview for example) for answering your research question, or whether responses to more focused questions might be sufficient. However, we can observe a trend in standardized research to add this questionnaire to the data collection or to include that question in the survey. This leads, on the one hand, to an extension of the datasets in the single study. On the other hand, I see this as a demonstration that questions of economy are not only an issue for qualitative research. In both contexts, you should check what are justifiable demands on the participants, what is already stressful and no longer justified as a demand, and when harming the participants begins.

Codes of Ethics

Many scientific associations have published codes of ethics. They are formulated for regulating the relations between researchers and the people and fields they study. Sometimes they also regulate how therapists or caregivers should work with their clients or patients, as in psychology and nursing. Some of them refer to specific questions of the research in the area, as in research with children in education. Examples of codes of scientific associations, available on the Internet, include:

- The British Psychological Society (BPS) has published a Code of Conduct, Ethical Principles, and Guidelines (www.bps.org.uk/the-society/ethics-rules-charter-code-of-conduct/ethics-rules-charter-code-of-conduct_home.cfm).

- The British Sociological Association (BSA) has formulated a Statement of Ethical Practice (www.britsoc.co.uk).

- The American Sociological Association (ASA) refers to its Code of Ethics (www.asanet.org/members/ecoderev.html).

- The Social Research Association (SRA) has formulated Ethical Guidelines (www.the-sra.org.uk/Ethicals.htm).

- The German Sociological Association (GSA) has developed a Code of Ethics (www.soziologie.de/index_english.htm).

Such codes of ethics demand that research be pursued only under the condition of informed consent and without harming the participants. This includes a requirement that the research does not intrude on the participants' privacy in inappropriate ways and that the participants are not deceived about the research aims.

Ethics Committees

Professional associations, hospitals and universities typically have ethics committees to ensure that ethical standards are met.

> **Ethics committees are in charge of assessing whether researchers have made enough ethical considerations before beginning the research they plan. For this purpose, ethics committees have two instruments. They can decide about projects by accepting or rejecting them. Secondly they can become active in consulting researchers and discuss with them suggestions for the ethical planning of a project. (Schnell and Heinritz 2006, p. 18)**

For this purpose, the committees assess proposed research designs and methods before they are applied to human beings. Such assessments normally consider three aspects (see Allmark 2002, p. 9): (a) scientific quality; (b) the welfare of participants; and (c) respect for the dignity and rights of participants.

A relevant question for ethics committees is whether a research project will provide new insights to add to existing knowledge. A project that merely duplicates earlier results can be seen as unethical – in particular, research that repeatedly does the same studies again (see for example Department of Health 2001). Here, the question is raised of how the stress for the participants is justified by the benefits to science and the novelty of results. Exceptions are studies with the explicit aim to test whether it is possible to replicate findings from earlier studies.

In considering the quality of research, we can see a source of conflict. To be able to judge the quality of research, the members of the ethics committee should have the necessary knowledge to assess a research proposal on a methodological level. In effect, this may mean that the members of the committee or at least some of the members should be researchers themselves. Yet if you talk for a while with researchers about their experiences with ethics committees and with proposals submitted to them, you will come across many stories about how a research proposal was rejected because the members did not understand its premise, or lacked the methodological background of the applicant, or simply disliked the style of research. Thus ethics committees may in practice end up rejecting research proposals for non-ethical reasons. Such a reservation can be particularly strong when a qualitative research proposal is confronted by committees or members who think only in natural science categories, or where experimental research is confronted by committees mainly thinking in interpretative categories.

In assessments by ethics committees, questions of welfare often involve weighing the risks (for the participants) against the benefits (of new knowledge and insights about a problem or of finding a new solution to an existing problem). For example if you want to find out the effects of a medication in a control group study (see Chapter 5), this means that you will give the participants in the control group a placebo rather than the medicine under study. If the control group is to be comparable to the study group, you will need people for it who are also in need of a treatment with the medication. Thus the dilemma arises between depriving the control group members of a possible treatment (at least for the moment) and otherwise being unable to study the effects of this medication adequately (see Thomson et al. 2004). Again, we find a potential conflict here: weighing the risks and benefits is often relative rather than absolute and clear.

The dignity and rights of the participants pertain to issues of (a) consent given by the participant, (b) sufficient information provided as a basis for giving consent, and (c) the need for consent to be voluntary (Allmark 2002, p. 13). Beyond this, researchers need to guarantee participants' confidentiality. This requires that the information about them will be used only in ways that make it impossible for other persons to identify the participants or for any institution to use it against the interests of the participants.

Ethics committees review and canonize the principles discussed here. For a detailed discussion of such principles, see Hopf (2004) and Murphy and Dingwall (2001).

Rules of Good Scientific Practice

Unfortunately, researchers have sometimes been guilty of concealing their results (for examples see Black 2006). Because of this, the German Research Council has developed proposals for safeguarding good scientific practice. These are outlined in Box 12.3 and are available (in English) at http://www. dfg.de/antragstellung/gwp/index.html. These rules define standards concerning honesty in using data, scientific fraud, and the documentation of original data (completed questionnaires, recordings and transcripts of interviews etc.).

BOX 12.3

Rules for good scientific practice (excerpt) (Deutsche Forschungsgemeinschaft 1998)

Recommendation 1
Rules of good scientific practice shall include principles for the following matters (in general, and specified for individual disciplines as necessary):

- fundamentals of scientific work, such as

  - observing professional standards
  - documenting results
  - consistently questioning one's own findings
  - practising strict honesty with regard to the contributions of partners, competitors, and predecessors

- cooperation and leadership responsibility in working groups ...
- mentorship for young scientists and scholars (recommendation 4)
- securing and storing primary data (recommendation 7)
- scientific publications (recommendation 11).

Recommendation 7
Primary data as the basis for publications shall be securely stored for ten years in a durable form in the institution of their origin.

Recommendation 8
Universities and research institutes shall establish procedures for dealing with allegations of scientific misconduct. They must be approved by the responsible corporate body. Taking account of relevant legal regulations including the law on disciplinary actions, they should include the following elements:

- a definition of categories of action which seriously deviate from good scientific practice [recommendation 1] and are held to be scientific misconduct, for instance the fabrication and falsification of data, plagiarism, or breach of confidence as a reviewer or superior
- jurisdiction, rules of procedure (including rules for the burden of proof), and time limits for inquiries and investigations conducted to ascertain the facts

- the rights of the involved parties to be heard, and to discretion, and rules for the exclusion of conflicts of interest
- sanctions depending on the seriousness of proven misconduct
- the jurisdiction for determining sanctions.

Recommendation 11
Authors of scientific publications are always jointly responsible for their content. A so-called 'honorary authorship' is inadmissible.

Research Ethics: Cases and Mass Research

Ethical principles in social research apply to qualitative as well as quantitative research – even though the concrete questions and details involved may be very different. Data protection and anonymization may be more easily guaranteed for a single participant in the random sampling and statistical analysis of data than for a participant in a qualitative study with purposive sampling and (a few) expert interviews. Note, in particular, that if you plan a survey with repeated data collection from the same people in the first instance, you will need to store the real contact data of the participants so that you can return to them. There is a risk here of inadvertently infringing participants' rights to anonymity and data protection. Contact data and questionnaire responses will need to be separated.

Research Ethics in Online Research

Gaiser and Schreiner (2009, p. 14) have listed a number of questions to consider from an ethical point of view if you are planning an online study. They are:

- Can participant security be guaranteed? Anonymity? Protection of the data?
- Can someone ever really be anonymous online? And if not, how might this impact on the overall study design?
- Can someone 'see' a participant's information, when s/he participates?
- Can someone unassociated with the study access data on a hard drive?
- Should there be informed consent to participate? If so, how might online security issues impact on the informed consent?
- If a study design calls for participant observations, is it okay to 'lurk'? Is it always okay? If not then when? What are the determining factors?
- Is it ever okay to deceive online? What constitutes online deception?

This list shows how general issues of research ethics are relevant for online as well as traditional research.

Conclusion

We may finish with two general points concerning the ethical principles in research. First, we should remember that research entails questions of integrity and objectivity. As the German Sociological Association states:

> Sociologists strive for scientific integrity and objectivity in pursuing their profession. They are committed to the best standards that are possible in research, teaching and other professional practices. If they make discipline specific judgments, they will represent their field of work, the state of knowledge, their disciplinary expertise, their methods and their experience unambiguously and appropriately. In presenting or publishing sociological insights, the results are presented without any biasing omission of important results. Details of the theories, methods and research designs that are important for assessing the results of the research and of the limits of their validity are reported to the best of the researchers' knowledge. Sociologists should mention all their funding sources in their publications. They guarantee that their findings are not biased by the specific interests of their sponsors. (Ethik-Kodex 1993: I A 1–3)

This quotation refers specifically to 'sociologists'. It may be applied, however, to social researchers in general.

Second, questions of research ethics are raised in *any* kind of social research and with *all* sorts of methods. No methodological approach is free of ethical problems, even though these differ between methods:

> Research methods are not ethically neutral. That applies to qualitative, quantitative and triangulated methods in the same way. Criteria for assessing the quality of research at least implicitly ask for ethical issues as well. (Schnell and Heinritz 2006, p. 16)

Checklist for Taking Ethical Issues into Account

In pursuing an empirical project in social research, you should consider the ethical questions in Box 12.4. These questions can be applied to the planning of your own study and in a similar way to the evaluation of other researchers' existing studies.

BOX 12.4

Checklist for taking ethical issues into account in social research

1. How will you put the principle of informed consent into practice?
2. Have you informed all participants that they are taking part in a study or are involved in it?

---

3. How will you ensure that the participants do not suffer any disadvantages or damages from the study or from taking part in it?

4. How will you make sure that the participants in a control group do not suffer any disadvantage from the intervention they did not receive?

5. How will you guarantee the voluntariness of the participation?

6. How will you ensure that children or cognitively impaired people have agreed to being interviewed (for example) – i.e. that not merely the consent of parents or caregivers was obtained?

7. How will you organize the anonymization of the data and how will you deal with the issues of data protection in the study?

8. How will you take these issues into account for the storage of the data and in presenting the results?

9. Have you checked your method of proceeding against the relevant ethical code(s)?

10. If so, which problems became evident here?

11. Is a statement from an ethics committee necessary for your study and if so have you obtained it?

12. How will the project conform to requirements formulated in this process?

13. What is the novelty in the expected results, which justifies doing your project?

14. Can you specify the expected results?

Key Points

- **Every research project should be planned and assessed according to ethical principles.**

- **Voluntariness of participation, anonymity, data protection, and avoidance of harm for the participants are preconditions.**

- **Informed consent should be obtained for every research project. Exceptions from this have to be justified rigorously.**

- **Codes of ethics provide an orientation for taking ethical principles into account and applying them.**

- **Ethics committees seek to ensure that ethical principles are upheld.**

- **For qualitative and quantitative research, ethical questions may be raised in different ways.**

■ ■ Further Reading ■

The following resources provide further discussion on the ethics of social research.

Bryman, A. (2008) *Social Research Methods*, 3rd edn. Oxford: Oxford University Press.

Flick, U. (2009) *An Introduction to Qualitative Research*, 4th edn. London: Sage. Chapter 4.

Hopf, C. (2004) 'Research Ethics and Qualitative Research: An Overview', in U. Flick, E. v. Kardorff and I. Steinke (eds), *A Companion to Qualitative Research*. London: Sage. pp. 334–9.

Mertens, D. and Ginsberg, P.E. (eds) (2009) *Handbook of Research Ethics*. London: Sage.

CHAPTER 13
WRITING RESEARCH AND USING RESULTS

Chapter Overview

Chapter Objectives

This chapter is designed to help you:

- recognize that presentation of results and methods is an integral part of social research projects
- know which forms of presentation are appropriate to (a) qualitative and (b) quantitative projects
- know which factors to consider when presenting results to (a) participants and (b) interested institutions and other audiences.

Table 13.1   Navigator for Chapter 13

Orientation	• What is social research? • Research question • Literature review
Planning and design	• Planning research • Designing research • Deciding methods
Working with data	• Gathering data • Analyzing data • E-research • Integrated research
Reflection and writing	• Evaluating research • Ethics • Writing and using research

You are here in your project ⟶

Essentially, social research consists of three steps: (1) planning a study; (2) working with data; and (3) communicating the results. According to Wolff, communication (in the form of a 'text') is integral to social science:

> **To do social science means mainly to produce texts ... Research experiences have to be transformed into texts and to be understood on the basis of texts. A research process has findings only when and as far as these can be found in a report, no matter whether and which experiences were made by those who were involved in the research. The observability and practical objectivity of social science phenomena is constituted in texts and nowhere else. (1987, p. 333)**

When you communicate your research findings, you should aim to make the process that led you to them transparent to the reader. In the process, you should aim to demonstrate that your findings are not arbitrary, singular or question-able – but rather that they are based on evidence. This chapter considers the relevance of research, the utilization of its results, and their elaboration and presentation.

Goals of Writing Social Research

When you report your research, you may have various aims. For example:

1. to document your results

2. to show how you proceeded during your research – how you arrived at your results

3. to present results in such a way that you can achieve specific objectives – for example, to obtain a qualification, to influence a process (such as through

evidence-based policy-making) or to show something fundamentally new in your scientific field

3. to legitimize the research in some way – by showing that the results are not arbitrary, but rigorously based on data.

Writing Quantitative Research

In quantitative research, a research report will normally include the following elements:

1. the research problem

2. the conceptual framework

3. the research question

4. the method of data collection

5. analysis of the data

6. conclusions

7. discussion of the results.

When presenting your research, you should include statements referring to each of these points. They should permit an assessment of your methodology, the robustness of your results and their relationship to previous literature and research.

The Empirical Procedure

When writing about your empirical procedure, you should answer the following questions for your readers (see Neuman 2000, p. 472):

1. What type of study (e.g. experiment, survey) have you conducted?

2. Exactly how did you collect data (e.g. study design, type of survey, time and location of data collection, experimental design used)?

3. How were variables measured? Are the measures reliable and valid?

4. What is your sample? How many subjects or respondents are involved in your study? How did you select them?

5. How did you deal with ethical issues and specific concerns of the design?

The essential point is to allow the reader to evaluate your study. This will make it possible to assess the relevance and reliability of your results.

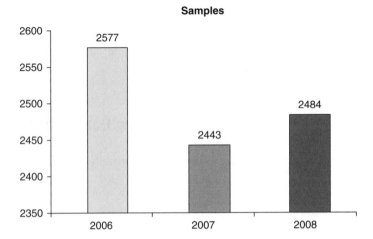

Figure 13.1   Bar chart

Elaboration of Results

Often researchers face the problem that a study may produce a multitude of findings. Here the first step is to provide a number of detailed findings. You can then distill, extrapolate or construct the fundamental results that emerge from the detailed findings. For example, you may do more to sort the data into classes.

Maybe even the researchers themselves feel confused by the multitude of findings produced in their study. In this case, they need to develop a framework for the continuing analysis. For example, they may focus on the distribution of data or they may adopt a comparative perspective (focusing, for example, on the differences between two subgroups in the sample). Above all, the researchers will need to be selective. As Neuman explains:

> Researchers make choices in how to present the data. When analyzing the data, they look at dozens of univariate, bivariate, and multivariate tables and statistics to get a feel for the data. This does not mean that every statistic or table is in a final report. Rather, the researcher selects the minimum number of charts or tables that fully inform the reader and rarely presents the raw data himself. Data analysis techniques should summarize the data and test hypotheses (e.g. frequency distributions, tables with means and standard deviations, correlations and other statistics). (2000, p. 472)

Presenting Results

Frequencies and numbers can often be presented more clearly in charts than in words. Consider, for example, Figure 13.1, which presents the

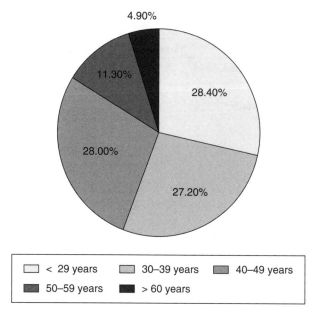

Figure 13.2 Pie chart

sample sizes in a longitudinal study at three times of measurement (2006, 2007, 2008).

An alternative is to use pie charts. Figure 13.2 provides an example in which the age distribution of homeless people in Germany is summarized in age groups (e.g. 30–39 years).

A third means of presentation is to use tables. Table 13.2 provides an example. Here, the frequencies of responses to the question of how to prevent diseases are summarized according to the age of children, who could give more than one answer.

These examples demonstrate how you can present findings visually so that they become apparent for readers 'at first sight'. The three methods above are not, of course, the only methods available; they are included here merely to illustrate the usefulness of visual presentation.

Evidence

In many areas of research, the notion of evidence-based practice has become very important. This emphasizes the need to distinguish reliable from less reliable scientific results. Here we can consider the example of medical practice. In evidence-based medicine, a medication is tested in a specific form of research before it is introduced in regular medical routines. Greenhalgh gives as a definition:

Table 13.2   Prevention with regard to health (extract from results) (%, multiple answers possible)

Categories	5-year-old	8-year-old	12-year-old	16-year-old
Healthy eating, fruit, vegetables, tea, juice	28	56	83	88
Vitamins, minerals	–	8	29	16
Take care of clothing, dress warmly	24	24	33	8
Moving, sports	20	32	38	76
Outdoor, fresh air	12	20	17	16
Not smoking	–	–	25	32
No alcohol	–	–	13	12
Little or no stress	–	–	–	4
Relax, sleep	–	4	4	8
Not getting infected, avoid contact with ill people	–	4	4	12

Source: Schmidt and Fröhling 1998, p. 39

> **Evidence-based medicine is the use of mathematical estimates of the risk of benefit and harm, derived from high-quality research on population samples, to inform clinical decision making in the diagnosis, investigation or management of individual patients. The defining feature of evidence-based medicine, then, is the use of figures derived from research on *populations* to inform decisions about *individuals*. (2006, p. 1)**

Here, double blind tests (see Chapter 5) are applied, which are also labeled randomized controlled studies (RCTs). Participants in a medication study are allocated randomly to the treatment group (with the medication) and a control group (with a placebo) for testing the effect of the medication by comparing the two groups. For the existence of evidence in the area of the epidemiology of diseases (e.g. lung cancer) in relation to certain risk factors (e.g. smoking), Stark and Guggenmoos-Holzmann hold:

> **If certain criteria of scientific evidence are fulfilled, a causal relation between the influential variable (risk factor) and the target variable (disease) is generally accepted. As major criteria we find:**
>
> - **A strong correlation between influential and target variable exists.**
> - **The results could be confirmed in several studies (reproducibility).**
> - **A dose–effect relation between influential and target variable exists.**
> - **The temporal course of cause and effect is logical.**
> - **The results are biologically plausible.**
> - **If the risk factor is eliminated, the illness risk is reduced. (2003, p. 417)**

Thus, a very specific understanding of what evidence is and, moreover, what kind of research can produce such evidence, has been developed. More generally, evidence-based practice means that professional practice and decision-making in the single case should be based on research and results, i.e. on evidence. This scientific foundation of professional practice should replace decision-making based on anecdote ('I knew a similar case …'), or what is just fashionable in the press.

Here we may note two implications of the development just mentioned. First, this understanding of evidence and of research threatens to push back other approaches of research and to challenge their relevance. Consequently we find several suggestions for classifying types of evidence. Such classification ranges from meta-analyses, based on randomized studies, as the most accepted form, to case studies and expert evaluations, which are the forms with the least acceptance (see Chapter 3).

Second, other disciplines – like social work, education, nursing and others – have also been developing evidence-based practice in their field. The trend towards evidence basing threatens to question other forms of research. There is a problem here: what makes a lot of sense in assessing the effect of medications is not necessarily justified for social research in general. Other forms to be replaced by evidence are concepts of cost minimizing etc. (Greenhalgh 2006, pp. 9–11). The challenge is to develop a broader understanding of what evidence is. Thus analyzing life histories of cancer patients, for example, will not meet the criteria of evidence basing in the sense outlined above – but will produce helpful evidence when it comes to understanding how people live with cancer and how they try to cope with it.

Writing Qualitative Research

For qualitative research, many commentators have expressed doubts that we can use the same approach as for quantitative research. Lofland (1976) and Neuman (2000, p. 474) have proposed an alternative structure for reporting qualitative research:

1. introduction

    (a) most general aspects of the situation
    (b) main contours of the general situation
    (c) how materials were collected
    (d) details about the setting
    (e) how the report is organized

2. the situation

    (a) analytical categories
    (b) contrast between situation and other situations
    (c) development of situation over time

3. strategies of interaction

4. summary and implications.

This structure provides a possible framework for your report. The advantage is that you then will go from more general aspects of your issue of research to the more concrete procedures and finally to the findings you obtained. Thus, this structure contributes to leading your readers through your report and directing them to the central points you want to make about your findings.

The Empirical Procedure

For qualitative projects, the presentation of the empirical procedures is often chronological, providing in the process insights into the field or situation under study. Van Maanen (1988) distinguishes three forms of presentation, namely (a) 'realist', (b) 'confessional' and (c) 'impressionist' tales.

In *realist tales*, one reports observations as facts, or documents them by using quotations from statements or interviews. Emphasis is laid on the *typical* forms of what is studied (see Flick et al. 2010 as an example). Therefore, you will analyze and present many details. Viewpoints of the members of a field or of interviewees are emphasized in the presentation: how did they experience their own life in its course? What is health for the interviewees? The interpretation does not stop at subjective viewpoints but goes beyond them by various and far-reaching interpretations.

Confessional tales are characterized by the personalized authorship and authority of the researcher as an expert. Here, the authors express the role that they played in what was observed, in their interpretations, and also in the formulations that are used. The authors' viewpoints are treated as an issue in the presentation, alongside the problems, breakdowns, mistakes, etc. (1988, p. 79) in the field. Nevertheless, authors will attempt here to present their findings as *grounded* in the issue that they studied. Such reports combine descriptions of the studied object and of the experiences of studying it. An example of this kind of report is Frank's book *The Wounded Storyteller* (1997).

Impressionist tales take the form of dramatic recall. The aim is to place the audience imaginatively in the research situation, including the specific characteristics of the field and of the data collection. A good example for this kind of report is Geertz's (1973) analysis of the Balinese cockfight.

Results

Qualitative studies can produce various forms of results. They may range from detailed case studies to typologies (e.g. several types of health concepts) or to the frequency and distribution of statements in a category system. In qualitative research one may again be able to condense information in the form of

Table 13.3 Sample I: Street youth by age and gender

Age (years)	Gender		
	Male N = 12	Female N = 12	
14	–	3	3
15	1	3	4
16	2	2	4
17	2	1	3
18	4	2	6
19	3	–	3
20	–	1	1
Mean	17.5	16.0	16.75

Source: Flick and Röhnsch 2008

Table 13.4 Sample II: Chronically ill street youth by age groups and gender

Age (years)	Gender		Total N = 12
	Male N = 6	Female N = 6	
14–17	1	3	4
18–25	5	3	8
Mean	21.5	16.8	19.2

Source: Flick and Röhnsch 2008

Table 13.5 Health concepts of the street youth interviewees

Health concept	Street youth				
	Total	Male	Female	General	Chronically ill
Health as physical and mental wellbeing	14	9	5	9	5
Health as absence of illness and of complaints	11	4	7	4	7
Health as result of certain practices	7	2	5	7	–
Health as functionality	4	3	1	4	–
N	36	18	18	24	12

Source: Flick and Röhnsch 2008

tables – for example about the composition of a sample regarding gender and age in years (see Table 13.3) or age groups and gender (see Table 13.4).

In qualitative research, this has mostly the aim of contextualizing the single statements and their interpretations (see Table 13.5, which summarizes the health definitions given by the adolescents in both samples displayed in Tables 13.3 and 13.4 according to gender and subgroups).

of result (or outcome) of a qualitative study may be the
ory. The presentation of such a theory requires, according
, four components:

ry.
ptual level, with description kept secondary.
ation of relationships among categories, with levels of
so kept clear.
variations and their relevant conditions, consequences,
ng the broader ones. (1990, p. 229)

esearch will highlight the core concepts and lines of
developed. Visualization in the form of conceptual
networks, trajectories and so on is a means to give the presentation more
pregnancy. The suggestions of Lofland (1974) for presenting findings in the
form of theories lead us in a similar direction. He mentions as criteria for
writing the same criteria as for evaluating such reports, namely ensuring
that:

(1) The report was organized by means of a *generic* conceptual framework; (2) the
generic framework employed was *novel*; (3) the framework was *elaborated* or
developed in and through the report; (4) the framework was *eventful* in the sense
of being abundantly documented with qualitative data; (5) the framework was
interpenetrated with the empirical materials. (1974, p. 102)

In qualitative research one again faces the problem of selecting essentials from
a multitude of data and relationships that the study has identified. Here you
have to find a balance in your report between providing insight into, on the
one hand, the occurrences and conditions in the field and, on the other, the
data and the more general issues you can derive from such insights and details.
This is necessary for making your results accessible and transparent for the
readers. One way is to combine topic-related summaries and structures with
case studies, which go beyond those topics and show commonalities between
the topics.

Evidence in Qualitative Research

The concept of evidence according to the evidence-based approaches outlined
above cannot be transferred to qualitative research without problems.
However, the question has to be asked of how to define evidence in the use of
qualitative methods, and what role qualitative research can play in this development (see Denzin and Lincoln 2005; Morse et al. 2001). The discussion
includes the suggestion of linking several studies – in the sense of meta-
analyses – and also extending and transferring results to practical contexts as a

from of 'test' (Morse 2001). For example, we found in one of our studies (Flick et al. 2010) three types of knowledge about the link between residents' sleeping problems at night and the lack of daytime activities in the nursing home for nurses. One of them was rather limited; one of them was much more developed. We can use these results for training nurses and then assess whether this intervention changes their practices and reduces the intensities of sleeping problems. In this way, practice provides a kind of 'test' concerning the evidence of our findings.

Issues of Writing

There are some general issues concerning the writing of research, regardless of the type of research project. In producing a text, researchers need to consider their potential readers or audience:

> **Making your work clearer involves considerations of audience: who is it supposed to be clearer to? Who will read what you write? What do they have to know so that they will not misread or find what you say obscure or unintelligible? You will write one way for the people you work with closely on a joint project, another way for professional colleagues in other specialities and disciplines, and differently yet for the 'intelligent layman'. (Becker 1986, p. 18)**

The choice of audience will have implications for the style of presentation. One needs to ask, what can you assume as already existing knowledge and available terminologies on the part of the readers? How complex and detailed should the account be? Which forms of simplification are specifically necessary for my audience?

Feeding Back Results to Participants

In practice-oriented research, feedback of preliminary or final results to the participants is often expected – particularly if the results are likely to be used for evaluation or decision-making. In this case you will need to consider how to present your research transparently in a form that the participants will find accessible. Furthermore you should take into account the dynamics in the field – what the results may initiate or change in this context. When describing how she fed back the results and evaluations in her studies in the context of police research, Mensching (2006) used the term 'mediating work': her research had to be presented very sensitively in order to avoid being either too challenging or too simplistic. You must also ensure that you protect the single participants from being identified from the results – even by their colleagues. See Box 13.1.

Feedback of results to participants

In our study on health professionals' social representations about health and aging (Flick et al. 2004), we organized the feedback of our results to our participants as follows. After episodic interviews with the single participants about their health concepts and ideas and experiences with prevention and health promotion, and after analyzing the data, we did focus groups with general practitioners and home care nurses. The results of the study were reported back to the participants for collecting their comments to the findings. Then we discussed practical implications with them concerning any improvement in the routines and practices in home care nursing and medicine.

In order to avoid discussion in groups becoming too general or heterogeneous, we selected a concrete part of the data as a stimulus for opening up the more comprehensive discussions. For this purpose we selected the results concerning the barriers to a stronger orientation of one's own practice towards prevention. The results about the readiness for and resistance to more prevention on the part of the professionals and of the patients were presented. First, we gave an overview of the barriers that had been mentioned. Then the participants were asked to rank these barriers for their relevance, before discussing this relevance for their own professional practice and for the role about health in it. When this discussion abated, we asked the participants to make suggestions about how to overcome the barriers discussed before, and again to discuss these suggestions. At the end, we had not only the evaluations of the results of the initial interviews but also a list of comments and suggestions from every group. These lists could be analyzed and integrated in the final results of the study.

Using Data in Debate

The specific problems of using data in debates has been highlighted by Lüders (2006). There are questions concerning how far the data and the conclusions drawn from them are credible and can be trusted:

> From the viewpoint of the political administration ... the question simply is: can we also rely on the data and the results in the classical understanding of reliability and at least internal validity? ... The questions of credibility and of trust refer not merely to the problem of whether the data are reliable and valid for the units that were studied, but mainly to the problem of the transferability to similar contexts. (2006, p. 456)

This issue is heightened when the data come from a qualitative study with very few cases and where political initiatives may be based on the results. Here, the issue is the robustness of the results in the process of argumentation and the implications that follow.

When in a small qualitative study with seven cases in two areas of a country the result is that juvenile intensive offenders – and in these seven cases the concept is adequate – keep the responsible organizations (police, legal services, child and youth services, mental services for children and adolescents, schools etc.) so busy that no one has an overview anymore, then this result is first valid for these seven cases without doubt. The *politically* relevant question, however, is: are the results robust enough that a process is inaugurated using them to redefine the institutional responsibilities in the country for such a constellation – and how is this defined? – with all the necessary effort, extending even to changing the laws? This also refers to the risks linked to those changes, for example of conflict between interest groups that are concerned and the possible advantage handed to the political opposition in parliament. (2006, pp. 458–9)

Lillis (2002, p. 36) has argued in a different context (i.e. market research) that the movement from the data to practical suggestions or implications entails three steps:

- The first step focuses on what the participants (in qualitative studies) think and mean. By analogy, you can see what the numbers in a quantitative study say (what correlates with what for example). That refers to the report about the research and the immediate results.

- The second step in both cases relates to what patterns emerge and what they mean. That is mainly based on the interpretation of the data and results by the researchers.

- The third step asks for the implications for the commissioner of the study and thus for the applicability of the results for them.

For research-based consultation, we should distinguish between those suggestions which (1) are grounded in the research alone, (2) involve knowledge about the relevant market beyond the results and (3) additionally take the commissioners' specific product or service into account (2002, p. 38). Suggestions will only rarely be based on the empirical results alone: if they are to have any effect, they will have to take into account the current political situation and the specific mandate of the institution.

Utilization of Results

It should be recognized that the results of a research project will not necessarily be taken up one-to-one in the different contexts in which they are read. Rather they will be the subject of further interpretation. Studies about the utilization of social science research results (e.g. Beck and Bonß 1989) have shown that various processes of using, reinterpreting, evaluating and selecting occur in utilization:

> Since the results of the social science utilization research, we know that the utilization of scientific knowledge more or less occurs according to the logic of the respective field of practice – in our case the logic of political administration in a way that is often rather confusing for the scientists. (Lüders 2006, p. 453)

As we have seen in Chapter 11, the evaluation of the research is no longer conducted using only the internal criteria of sciences alone. Rather it becomes evident that the 'quality criteria and checks of the research ... are no longer exclusively defined out of the disciplines and with "peer reviews", but that additional or even competing social, political and economic criteria emerge from the contexts of application (of the results)' (Weingart 2001, p. 15).

If social science and its results are intended to have practical, political or other forms of impact, such processes must be taken into account. The results and the scientific quality of research alone will not prove decisive. Rather, results have to be elaborated and presented in such a way that they become relevant and understandable for the specific context of discussion and application.

> One is made aware that scientific knowledge is always presented scientific knowledge. And the consequence is that a 'logic of presentation' has to be considered as well as a 'logic of research'. How researchers' constitution of experiences is linked to the way those experiences are saved in presentations has only begun to become an issue for reflection and research. (Bude 1989, p. 527)

Checklist for Presenting Empirical Procedures

When presenting an empirical project in social research you should take the aspects listed in Box 13.2 into account. These questions again are relevant not only for writing your own report but also for assessing how other researchers presented their research.

BOX 13.2

Checklist for presenting empirical procedures

1. Have the aims of the project been made clear?
2. Has the research question been explicitly formulated and grounded?
3. Is it evident why particular persons or situations have been involved in the study and what the methodological approach of the sampling is?
4. Is it evident how the data were collected, for example by presenting example questions?
5. Is it transparent how data collection proceeded and which special occurrences played a role – perhaps for the quality of the data?

---

6. Will the readers be able to understand how the data were analyzed?
7. Have questions (criteria and strategies) of quality assurance in the research been addressed?
8. Have the results been condensed so that their essentials become evident for the readers?
9. Have consequences been drawn from the study and the results and discussed?
10. Is the report easy to read and understand and has the text been complemented by illustrations?
11. Did you provide enough evidence (e.g. quotations or extracts from the calculations) to enable the readers to evaluate your results?

Key Points

- Social research and its results become accessible only through the form of writing that you choose.

- The aim is to make transparent to readers both how the researchers proceeded and what results they have obtained.

- There is a need to select and weigh what you found in order to direct your readers' attention to what is essential in the results.

- Quantitative and qualitative research differ in the ways they present their findings and the processes that have led to them. However, the two types of research also have some aims in common.

- Particular needs of elaborating data and results pertain to political or administrative consultations and the feedback presented to participants.

- The utilization of results often follows logics other than those of research and researchers.

Further Reading

The works listed below provide further discussion of the issues of writing and presenting social research and evidence. The final two books in the list focus on how to display quantitative research.

Becker, H.S. (1986) *Writing for Social Scientists.* Chicago: University of Chicago Press.

Flick, U. (2009) *An Introduction to Qualitative Research*, 4th edn. London: Sage. Chapter 30.

Greenhalgh, T. (2006) *How to Read a Paper: The Basics of Evidence-Based Medicine.* Oxford: Blackwell-Wiley.

Matt, E. (2004) 'The Presentation of Qualitative Research', in U. Flick, E. v. Kardorff and I. Steinke (eds), *A Companion to Qualitative Research*. London: Sage. pp. 326–30.

Neuman, W.L. (2000) *Social Research Methods: Qualitative and Quantitative Approaches*, 4th edn. Boston: Allyn and Bacon.

Tufte, E.R. (1990) *Envisioning Information*. Cheshire: Graphics.

Tufte, E.R. (2001) *Visual Display of Quantitative Information*. Cheshire: Graphics.

Glossary

Applied research   Different from basic research, studies are done in specific practical fields and theories are tested for contexts of use in practice (e.g. the hospital).

Assessment   (In medical or psychological contexts) measurement of the (cognitive) performance or the health and illness status of patients, for example.

Audit   Strategy to assess a process (in accounting or in research) in all its steps and components.

Background theories   Theories that inform social research approaches through their conceptualization of reality or research.

Basic research   Research that starts from a specific theory in order to test its validity without restriction to a specific field of application or topic.

Bivariate analysis   Calculations showing the relation between two variables.

Burnout   A syndrome of exhaustion by one's own profession, often caused by high stress and a lack of positive feedback.

Categorization   Allocation of certain events to a category. Summarizing several identical or similar events under a concept.

Central tendency   Average in a distribution (e.g. mean, median).

Closed question   A finite range of answers are presented, often in the form of a scale of answer possibilities.

Code of ethics   A set of rules of good practice in research (or interventions) established by professional associations or by institutions as an orientation for their members.

Coding   Development of concepts in the context of grounded theory. For example, to label pieces of data and allocate other pieces of data to them (and the label). In quantitative research, coding means to allocate a number to an answer.

Coding paradigm   A set of basic relations for linking categories and phenomena among each other in grounded theory research.

Communicative validation   Criterion for validity for which the consent of the study participants is obtained for data that were collected, for interpretations or for results.

Complete collection   Form of sampling that includes all elements of a population defined in advance.

Constant comparative method   Part of grounded theory methodology focusing on comparing all elements in the data with each other. For example, statements from an interview about a specific issue are compared with all the statements about this issue in other interviews and also with what was said about other issues in the same and other interviews.

Constructionism/constructivism   A variety of epistemologies in which the social reality is seen as the result of constructive processes (activities or the members or processes in their minds). For example, living with an illness can be influenced by the way the individuals see their illness, what meaning they ascribe to it, and how this illness is seen by other members of their social world. On each of these levels, illness and living with it are socially constructed.

Context sensitivity   Methods that take the context of a statement or observation into account.

Contingency analysis   Analysis of how often certain concepts appear together with other concepts in the study period in the press.

Control group design   A design that includes two groups, of which one (the control group) will not receive the treatment that is studied in order to control whether the effects that were observed in the treatment group also occur without treatment or whether they can be really referred to the treatment.

Conversation analysis   Study of language (use) for formal aspects (for example, how a conversation is started or ended, how turns from one to the other speaker are organized).

Correlation   General concept for describing relations between variables – e.g. number of divorces and amount of income.

Covert observation   A form of observation in which the observers do not inform the field and its members about the fact they are doing observations for research purposes. This can be criticized from an ethical point of view.

Data protection   Conduct or means that guarantees the anonymity of research participants. To make sure that data do not end up in or are passed on to the hands of unauthorized persons or institutions.

Deduction   The logical reference from the general to the particular or, put in other words, from the theory to that which can be observed empirically.

Dependent variable   Variable that belongs to the 'then' part of a (if–then) hypothesis and which shows the effects of the independent variable (cause, effects).

Description   Studies provide (only) an exact representation of a relation or of the facts and circumstances.

Dispersion   A measure for the variation in the measurements.

Double blind test   Empirical study in which participants and researchers do not know the aim of the study. A 'blind' researcher does not know whether he or she is in contact with a member of the study group or the control group. This avoids the participants being unconsciously influenced.

Episode   A shorter situation in which something specific happens, for example an illness episode.

Epistemology   Theories of knowledge and perception in science.

Ethics committees   Committees in universities, or sometimes also in professional associations, that assess research proposals (for dissertations or funding) for their ethical soundness. If necessary, these committees pursue violations of ethical standards.

Ethnography   A research strategy combining different methods, but based on participation, observation and writing about a field under study. For example, for studying how homeless adolescents deal with health issues, a participant observation in their community may be combined with interviewing the adolescents. The overall image of details from this participation, observation and interviewing is unfolded in a written text about the field. The way of writing gives the representation of the field a specific form.

Ethnomethodology   Theoretical approach interested in analyzing the methods people use in their everyday life to make communication and routines work.

Evaluation research   The use of research methods with a focus on assessing a treatment or intervention for demonstrating the success or the reasons for failure of a treatment or intervention.

Everyday theory   Theories that are developed and used in everyday practices for finding explanations and making predictions.

Evidence-based practices   Interventions (in medicine, social work, nursing etc.) that are based on results of research done according to specific standards.

Experiment   An empirical study in which certain conditions are produced deliberately and observed in their effects. Participants are distributed randomly to experimental and control groups.

Explanation   Identification of regularities and relations in the experience and behavior by assuming external causes and testing their effects.

External validity   A criterion of validity focusing on the transferability of results to other situations beyond the research situation.

External variables   Influences other than those to be studied.

Factor analysis   A form of statistical analysis, focusing on identifying a limited number of basic factors and summarizing them so that they can explain the relations in a field.

Falsification   Disproof of a hypothesis.

Field notes   Notes taken by the researcher about their thoughts and observations when they are in the field 'environment' they are researching.

Field research   Studies done not in a laboratory but in practical fields – like a hospital – in order to analyze the phenomena under study under real conditions.

Focus groups   Research method used in market and other forms of research, in which a group is invited to discuss the issue of a study for research purposes.

Generalizability   The degree to which the results derived from a sample can be transferred to the population.

Generalization   Transfer of research results to situations and populations that were not part of the research situation.

Grounded theory   Theories developed from analyzing empirical material or from studying a field or process.

Hermeneutics The study of interpretations of texts in the humanities. Hermeneutical interpretation seeks to arrive at valid interpretations of the meaning of a text. There is an emphasis on the multiplicity of meanings in a text, and on the interpreter's foreknowledge of the subject matter of a text.

Heuristic Something that is used for reaching a certain goal.

Homogeneous sample A form of sampling in which all elements of the sample have the same features (e.g. age and profession).

Hypothesis Assumption that is formulated for study purposes (mostly coming from the literature or an existing theory) in order to test it empirically in the course of the study. Often formulated as 'if–then' statements.

Ideal type Pure cases that can represent the phenomenon under study in a specifically typical way.

Independent variable Variable that belongs to the 'if' part of a (if–then) hypothesis.

Index construction A combination of several single indicators, which are collected and analyzed together (e.g. the social states is composed from the states of education, profession and income).

Indication Decision about when exactly (under what conditions) a specific method (or combination of methods) should be used.

Indicator Something representing a specific phenomenon that is not directly accessible.

Induction Reference from the specific to the general or, in other words, from empirical observation to theory.

Informed consent The agreement by the participants in a study to be involved in it that is based on information about the research.

Internal validity Form of validity that defines how unambiguously a relation that was measured can be captured (how far biases coming from external variables can be excluded).

Intervening variable A third variable that influences the relation between independent and dependent variables.

Interview Systematic form of asking people for research purposes – either in an open form with an interview schedule or in a standardized form similar to a questionnaire.

In vivo code   A form of coding based on concepts taken from an interviewee's statements.

Key person   A person that will make access to the field under study (or to certain persons in it) possible or easier for the researcher.

Likert scale   Five-step scale for measuring attitudes, for which certain statements are presented and agreement with those statements is collected.

Longitudinal study   A design in which the researchers return repeatedly, after some time, to the field and the participants to do interviews several times again in order to analyze development and changes.

Market research   Use of research methods in analyzing the market for specific products.

Measurement   Allocation of a number to a certain object or event in dependence of their degree according to defined rules.

Member check   Assessment of results (or of data) by asking the participants for their consensus.

Mixed methodologies   An approach combining qualitative and quantitative methods in a pragmatic manner.

Multivariate analysis   Calculation of the relations between more than two variables.

Narrative   A story told by a sequence of words, actions or images, and more generally the organization of the information within that story.

Narrative analysis   Study of narrative data which takes the context of the whole narrative into account.

Narrative interview   A specific form of interview based on one extensive narrative. Instead of asking questions, the interviewer asks participants to tell the story of their lives (or their illness for example) as a whole, without interrupting them with questions.

Objective hermeneutics   A way of doing research by analyzing texts for identifying latent structures of meaning underlying those texts and explaining the phenomena that are the issues of the text and the research. For example, analyzing the transcript of a family interaction can lead to identifying and elaborating an implicit conflict underlying the communication of the members in this interaction and other occasions. This conflict as a latent structure of meaning shapes the members' interaction without them being aware of it.

Objectivity   Criterion for assessing whether a research situation (the application of methods and their outcome) is independent of the single researcher.

Open question   A form of questions in a questionnaire for which no pre-formulated responses are provided and which can be answered using keywords or a little paragraph written by the respondent.

Operationalization   Means for empirically covering the degrees of a feature, for which you will define methods of data collection and measurement.

Parallel test reliability   A criterion of reliability of an instrument which is tested by applying a second measurement instrument in parallel.

Paraphrase   A reformulation of the core of the information included in a specific sentence or statement.

Participant observation   A specific form of research in which the researcher becomes a member of the field under study in order to make observations.

Participative research   A form of research in which the study participants are integrated in designing the study. The aim is change through research.

Participatory action research   Research that intends to produce changes in the field under study. This is to be achieved by planning the interviews in a specific way and by feeding back results to the participants. The members in the field are made active participants in designing the research process.

Patients' career   The stages of a series of treatments of a chronic illness in several institutions.

Peer debriefing   A criterion of validity for which colleagues' comments about the results of a study are obtained.

Peer review   Assessment (of papers before publication) by colleagues from the same discipline acting as reviewers.

Population   Aggregate of all possible study objects about which a statement is intended (e.g. nurses). Research studies mostly include selections (samples) from this population and results are generalized from samples to populations.

Pragmatic test of theories   A form of theory assessment in everyday life, when people test their implicit theories by looking at how far they can be used for explaining certain relations.

Pre-test Application of a methodological instrument (questionnaire or category system) with the aim of testing it before its use in the main study.

Principle of openness A principle in qualitative research, according to which researchers will mostly refrain from formulating hypotheses and formulate (interview) questions as openly as possible in order to come as close as possible to the views of the participants.

Protocol A detailed process documentation of an observation or of a group discussion. In the first case, it is based on the researchers' field notes; in the second case, interactions in the group are recorded and transcribed, often complemented by researchers' notes about the features of communication in the group.

Qualitative methods Research methods aiming at a detailed description of processes and views that are therefore used with small numbers of cases in the data collection.

Quantitative methods Research methods aiming at covering the phenomena under study in their frequencies and distribution and thus working with large numbers in the data collection.

Questionnaire A defined list of questions presented to every participant of a study in an identical way either written or orally. The participants are asked to respond to these questions mostly by giving them a limited number of alternative answers.

Random sample Sample drawn according to a random principle from a complete list of all elements in a population (e.g. every third entry in a page of the telephone directory), so that every element in the population has the same chance to be integrated in the study. The opposite of purposive or theoretical sampling.

Reactivity Influences on persons in a study due to their knowledge about being studied.

Reconstruction Identification of continuous topics or basic conflicts in, for example, a patient's life history.

Reliability A standard criterion in standardized/quantitative research, which is based on repeated application of a test for assessing whether the results are the same in both cases.

Representative sample A sample that corresponds to the major features of the population: for example, a representative sample of all Germans corresponds in its features (e.g. age structure) to the features of the German population.

Representativeness   A concept referring to the generalization of research and results. It is understood either in a statistical way (e.g. is the population represented in the sample in the distribution of features such as age, gender, employment?) or in a theoretical way (e.g. are the study and its results covering the theoretically relevant aspects of the issue?).

Research design   A systematic plan for a research project specifying whom to integrate in the research (sampling), whom or what to compare for which dimensions etc.

Research methods   Everyday techniques such as asking, observing, understanding etc., but used in a systematic way in order to collect and analyze data.

Response rate   The number or share of questionnaires that are filled in and returned in a study.

Sample   Selection of study participants from a population according to specific rules.

Sampling   Selection of cases or materials for the study from a larger population or variety of possibilities.

Scaling   The allocation of numerical values to an object or event.

Secondary data   Data that have not been produced for the current study, but are available from other studies or from (for example) the documentation of administrative routines.

Segmenting   Decomposition of a text into the smallest meaningful elements.

Semi-structured interview   A set of questions formulated in advance, which can be asked in a variable sequence and perhaps slightly reformulated in the interview in order to allow the interviewees to unfold their views on certain issues.

Sequential analysis   Analysis of a text that proceeds from the beginning to the end along the line of development in the text, rather than by categorizing it.

Significant relation   A relation that (statistically) is stronger than the estimation of its non-existence.

Standard deviation   Root drawn from the variance.

Standardization   Control of a research situation by defining and delimiting as many features of it as necessary or possible.

Study design The plan according to which a study will be conducted, specifying the selection of participants, the kind and aims of the planned comparisons and the quality criteria for evaluating the results.

Survey Representative poll.

Systematic review A way of reviewing the literature in a field that follows specific rules, is replicable and transparent in its approach, and provides a comprehensive overview of the research in the field.

Thematic coding An approach involving analysis of data in a comparative way for certain topics after case studies (of interviews for example) have been done.

Theoretical sampling The sampling procedure in grounded theory research, where cases, groups or materials are sampled according to their relevance for the theory that is developed, and against the background of what is already the state of knowledge after a certain number of cases have been collected and analyzed.

Theoretical saturation The point in grounded theory research at which more data about a theoretical category do not produce any further theoretical insights.

Theory development The use of empirical observations to derive a new theory.

Theory test The assessment of the validity of an existing theory on the basis of empirical observations.

Transcription Transformation of recorded materials (conversations, interviews, visual materials etc.) into text for analysis.

Triangulation The combination of different methods, theories, data and/or researchers in the study of one issue.

Typology A form of systematization of empirical observation by differentiating several types of a phenomenon, allowing the bundling of single observations.

Utilization research Studies analyzing how research results are adopted in practical contexts.

Validity A standard criterion in standardized/quantitative research, for which you will check for example whether confounding influences affected the relations under study (internal validity) or how far the results are transferable to situations beyond the current research situation (external validity).

Variance   Sum of the square deviation of the values from the mean.

Verstehen   German word for 'to understand'. It describes an approach to understanding a phenomenon more comprehensively than reducing it to one explanation (for example a cause–effect relation). For example, to understand how people live with their chronic illness, a detailed description of their everyday life may be necessary, rather than merely identifying a specific variable (e.g. social support) for explaining the degree of success in their coping behavior.

Virtual ethnography   Ethnography through the Internet – e.g. participation in a blog or discussion group.

Vulnerable population   People in a specific situation (for example, social discrimination, risks, illness) that require particular sensitiveness when they are being studied.

Working hypothesis   An assumption that is made for orienting the work in progress. Different from hypotheses in general, these are not tested in a standardized way.

References

ADM (2001) *Standards for Quality Assurance for Online Surveys*, http://www.adm-ev.de/index.php?id=2&L=1 (accessed 2 July 2010).

Allmark, P. (2002) 'The Ethics of Research with Children', *Nurse Researcher*, 10: 7–19.

Anderson, P. (2007) *What is Web 2.0? Ideas, technologies and implications for education*. JISC Technology and Standards Watch, February, 2007. Bristol: JISC. www.jisc.ac.uk/media/documents/techwatch/tsw0701b.pdf (accessed 29 October 2010)

Bampton, R. and Cowton, C.J. (2002) 'The E-Interview', *Forum Qualitative Social Research*, 3 (2), www.qualitative-research.net/fqs/fqs-eng.htm (accessed 22 February 2005).

Banks, M. (2008) *Using Visual Data in Qualitative Research*. London: Sage.

Barton, A.H. and Lazarsfeld, P.F. (1955) 'Some Functions of Qualitative Analysis in Social Research', *Frankfurter Beiträge zur Soziologie*. I. Frankfurt a. M.: Europäische Verlagsanstalt. pp. 321–61.

Baur, N. and Florian, M. (2009) 'Stichprobenprobleme bei Online-Umfragen', in N. Jackob, H. Schoen and T. Zerback (eds), *Sozialforschung im Internet: Methodologie und Praxis der Online-Befragung*. Wiesbaden: VS-Verlag. pp. 109–28.

Baym, N.K. (1995) 'The Emergence of Community in Computer-Mediated Communication', in S. Jones (ed.), *Cybersociety: Computer-Mediated Communication and Community*. London: Sage. pp. 138–63.

Beck, U. and Bonß, W. (eds) (1989) *Weder Sozialtechnologie noch Aufklärung? Analysen zur Verwendung sozialwissenschaftlichen Wissens*. Frankfurt: Suhrkamp.

Becker, H.S. (1986) *Writing for Social Scientists*. Chicago: University of Chicago Press.

Becker, H.S. (1996) 'The Epistemology of Qualitative Research', in R. Jessor, A. Colby and R.A. Shweder (eds), *Ethnography and Human Development*. Chicago: University of Chicago Press. pp. 53–72.

Bergmann, J. (2004) 'Conversation Analysis', in U. Flick, E. v. Kardorff and I. Steinke (eds), *A Companion to Qualitative Research*. London: Sage. pp. 296–302.

Bergmann, J. and Meier, C. (2004) 'Electronic Process Data and Their Analysis', in U. Flick, E. v. Kardorff and I. Steinke (eds), *A Companion to Qualitative Research*. London: Sage. pp. 243–7.

Birnbaum, D. and Goscillo, H. (2009) 'Avoiding Plagiarism', http://clover.slavic.pitt.edu/~tales/plagiarism.html.

Black, A. (2006) 'Fraud in Medical Research: A Frightening, All-Too-Common Trend on the Rise', *Natural News*, http://www.naturalnews.com/019353.html (accessed 1 September 2010).

Bogner, A., Littig, B. and Menz, W. (eds) (2009) *Interviewing Experts*. Basingstoke: Palgrave Macmillan.

Bortz, J. and Döring, N. (2006) *Forschungsmethoden und Evaluation für Sozialwissenschaftler*, 3rd edn. Berlin: Springer.

Bryman, A. (1988) *Quantity and Quality in Social Research*. London: Unwin Hyman.

Bryman, A. (1992) 'Quantitative and Qualitative Research: Further Reflections on Their Integration', in J. Brannen (ed.), *Mixing Methods: Quantitative and Qualitative Research*. Aldershot: Avebury. pp. 57–80.

Bryman, A. (2008) *Social Research Methods*, 3rd edn. Oxford: Oxford University Press.

Bude, H. (1989) 'Der Essay als Form der Darstellung sozialwissenschaftlicher Erkenntnisse', *Kölner Zeitschrift für Soziologie und Sozialpsychologie*, 41: 526–39.

Burra, T.A., Stergiopoulos, V. and Rourke, S.B. (2009) 'A Systematic Review of Cognitive Deficits in Homeless Adults: Implications for Service Delivery', *Canadian Journal of Psychiatry*, 54: 123–33.

Campbell, D. (1986) 'Relabeling Internal and External Validity for Applied Social Sciences', in W.M.K. Trochin (ed.), *Advances in Quasiexperimental Design Analysis*, pp. 67–77.

Campbell, D.T. and Jean Russo, M. (2001) *Social Measurement*. London: Sage.

Charmaz, K. (2006) *Constructing Grounded Theory: A Practical Guide through Qualitative Analysis*. London. Sage.

Coldwell, C.M. and Bender, W.S. (2007) 'The Effectiveness of Assertive Community Treatment for Homeless Populations with Severe Mental Illness: A Meta-Analysis', *American Journal of Psychiatry*, 164: 393–9.

Creswell, J.W. (1998) *Qualitative Inquiry and Research Design: Choosing among Five Traditions*. Thousand Oaks, CA: Sage.

Creswell, J.W. (2003) *Research Design: Qualitative, Quantitative, and Mixed Methods Approaches*. Thousand Oaks, CA: Sage.

Creswell, J.W., Plano Clark, Vicki, L., Gutman, Michelle, L. and Hanson, W.E. (2003) 'Advanced Mixed Methods Research Design', in A. Tashakkori and C. Teddlie (eds), *Handbook of Mixed Methods in Social and Behavioral Research*. Thousand Oaks, CA: Sage. pp. 209–40.

Denscombe, M. (2007) *The Good Research Guide: For Small-Scale Social Research Projects*, 3rd edn. Maidenhead: McGraw Hill.

Denzin, N.K. (1970/1989) *The Research Act*, 3rd edn. Englewood Cliffs, NJ: Prentice Hall.

Denzin, N.K. (1988) *Interpretive Biography*. London: Sage.

Denzin, N.K. (2004) 'Reading Film: Using Photos and Video as Social Science Material', in U. Flick, E. v. Kardorff and I. Steinke (eds), *A Companion to Qualitative Research*. London: Sage. pp. 234–47.

Denzin, N. and Lincoln, Y.S. (2005) 'Introduction: The Discipline and Practice of Qualitative Research', in N. Denzin and Y.S. Lincoln (eds), *Handbook of Qualitative Research*, 3rd edn. London: Sage. pp. 1–32.

Department of Health (2001) *Research Governance Framework for Health and Social Care*. London: Department of Health.

Deutsche Forschungsgemeinschaft (DFG) (1998) *Vorschläge zur Sicherung guter wissenschaftlicher Praxis: Empfehlungen der Kommission 'Selbstkontrolle in der Wissenschaft'*. Denkschrift. Weinheim: Wiley-VCH.

Diekmann, A. (2007) *Empirische Sozialforschung*. Reinbek: Rowohlt.

Drew, P. (1995) 'Conversation Analysis', in J.A. Smith, R. Harré and L. v. Langenhove (eds), *Rethinking Methods in Psychology*. London: Sage. pp. 64–79.

Edwards, D. and Potter, J. (1992) *Discursive Psychology*. London: Sage.

Ethik-Kodex (1993) 'Ethik-Kodex der Deutschen Gesellschaft für Soziologie und des Berufsverbandes Deutscher Soziologen', *DGS-Informationen*, 1/93: 13–19.

Evans, J.R. and Mathur, A. (2005) 'The Value of Online Surveys', *Internet Research*, 15: 195–219.

Fleck, C. (2004) 'Marie Jahoda', in U. Flick, E. v. Kardorff and I. Steinke (eds), *A Companion to Qualitative Research*. London: Sage. pp. 58–62.

Flick, U. (1992) 'Knowledge in the Definition of Social Situations: Actualization of Subjective Theories about Trust in Counseling', in M. v. Cranach, W. Doise and G. Mugny (eds), *Social Representations and the Social Bases of Knowledge*. Bern: Huber. pp. 64–8.

Flick, U. (ed.) (1998a) *Psychology of the Social: Representations in Knowledge and Language*. Cambridge: Cambridge University Press.

Flick, U. (1998b) 'The Social Construction of Individual and Public Health: Contributions of Social Representations Theory to a Social Science of Health', *Social Science Information*, 37: 639–62.

Flick, U. (2000a) 'Episodic Interviewing', in M. Bauer and G. Gaskell (eds), *Qualitative Researching with Text, Image and Sound: A Practical Handbook*. London: Sage. pp. 75–92.

Flick, U. (2000b) 'Qualitative Inquiries into Social Representations of Health', *Journal of Health Psychology*, 5: 309–18.

Flick, U. (2004) 'Design and Process in Qualitative Research', in U. Flick, E. v. Kardorff and I. Steinke (eds), *A Companion to Qualitative Research*. London: Sage. pp. 146–52.

Flick, U. (ed.) (2006) *Qualitative Evaluationsforschung: Konzepte, Methoden, Anwendungen*. Reinbek: Rowohlt.

Flick, U. (ed.) (2007) *The Sage Qualitative Research Kit*, 8 vols. London: Sage.

Flick, U. (2008a) *Managing Quality in Qualitative Research*. London: Sage.

Flick, U. (2008b) *Designing Qualitative Research*. London: Sage.

Flick, U. (2009) *An Introduction to Qualitative Research*, 4th edn. London: Sage.

Flick, U. and Röhnsch, G. (2007) 'Idealization and Neglect: Health Concepts of Homeless Adolescents', *Journal of Health Psychology*, 12: 737–50.

Flick, U. and Röhnsch, G. (2008) *Gesundheit und Krankheit auf der Straße: Vorstellungen und Erfahrungsweisen obdachloser Jugendlicher*. Weinheim: Juventa.

Flick, U., Kardorff, E. v. and Steinke, I. (eds) (2004) *A Companion to Qualitative Research*. London: Sage.

Flick, U., Garms-Homolová, V. and Röhnsch, G. (2010) '"When They Sleep, They Sleep": Daytime Activities and Sleep Disorders in Nursing Homes', *Journal of Health Psychology*, 15: 755–64.

Frank, A. (1997) *The Wounded Storyteller: Body, Illness, and Ethics*. Chicago: University of Chicago Press.

Früh, W. (1991) *Inhaltsanalyse: Theorie und Praxis*, 3rd edn. München: Ölschläger.

Gaiser, T.J. and Schreiner, A.E. (2009) *A Guide to Conducting Online Research*. London: Sage.

Garms-Homolová, V., Flick, U. and Röhnsch, G. (2010) 'Sleep Disorders and Activities in Long Term Care Facilities: A Vicious Cycle?', *Journal of Health Psychology*, 15: 744–54.

Geertz, C. (1973) *The Interpretation of Cultures: Selected Essays*. New York: Basic.

Gerhardt, U. (1988) 'Qualitative Sociology in the Federal Republic of Germany', *Qualitative Sociology*, 11: 29–43.

Glaser, B.G. (1969) 'The Constant Comparative Method of Qualitative Analysis', in G.J. McCall and J.L. Simmons (eds), *Issues in Participant Observation*. Reading, MA: Addison-Wesley.

Glaser, B.G. (1978) *Theoretical Sensitivity*. Mill Valley, CA: University of California.

Glaser, B.G. and Strauss, A.L. (1965) *Awareness of Dying*. Chicago: Aldine.

Glaser, B.G. and Strauss, A.L. (1967) *The Discovery of Grounded Theory: Strategies for Qualitative Research*. New York: Aldine.

Greenhalgh, T. (2006) *How to Read a Paper: The Basics of Evidence-Based Medicine*. Oxford: Blackwell-Wiley.

Guba, E.G. and Lincoln, Y.S. (1989) *Fourth Generation Evaluation*. Newbury Park, CA: Sage.

Guggenmoos-Holzmann, I., Bloomfield, K., Brenner, H. and Flick, U. (eds) (1995) *Quality of Life and Health: Concepts, Methods and Applications*. Berlin: Blackwell Science.

Hammersley, M. and Atkinson, P. (1995) *Ethnography: Principles in Practice*, 2nd edn. London: Routledge.

Harré, R. (1998) 'The Epistemology of Social Representations', in U. Flick (ed.), *Psychology of the Social: Representations in Knowledge and Language*. Cambridge: Cambridge University Press. pp. 129–37.

Hart, C. (1998) *Doing a Literature Review*. London: Sage.

Hart, C. (2001) *Doing a Literature Search*. London: Sage.

Hermanns, H. (1995) 'Narratives Interview', in U. Flick, E. v. Kardorff, H. Keupp, L. v. Rosenstiel and S. Wolff (eds), *Handbuch Qualitative Sozialforschung*, 2nd edn. Munich: Psychologie Verlags Union. pp. 182–5.

Hewson, C., Yule, P., Laurent, D. and Vogel, C. (2003) *Internet Research Methods: A Practical Guide for the Social and Behavioural Sciences*. London: Sage.

Hine, C. (2000) *Virtual Ethnography*. London: Sage.

Hochschild, A.R. (1983) *The Managed Heart*. Berkeley, CA: University of California Press.

Hoinville, G. et al. (1985) *Survey Research Practice*. Aldershot: Gower.

Hollingshead, A.B. and Redlich, F.C. (1958) *Social Class and Mental Illness: A Community Sample*. Wiley.

Hopf, C. (2004) 'Research Ethics and Qualitative Research: An Overview', in U. Flick, E. v. Kardorff and I. Steinke (eds), *A Companion to Qualitative Research*. London: Sage. pp. 334–9.

Hurrelmann, K., Klocke, A., Melzer, W. and Ravens-Sieberer, U. (2003*) Konzept und ausgewählte Ergebnisse der Studie*, http://www.hbsc-germany.de/pdf/artikel_hurrelmann_klocke_melzer_urs.pdf (accessed 30 June 2008).

Jahoda, M. (1995) 'Jahoda, M., Lazarsfeld, P. and Zeisel, H. (1933): Die Arbeitslosen von Marienthal', in U. Flick, E. v. Kardorff, H. Keupp, L. v. Rosenstiel and S. Wolff (eds), *Handbuch Qualitative Sozialforschung*, 2nd edn. München: Psychologie Verlags Union. pp. 119–22.

Jahoda, M., Lazarsfeld, P.F. and Zeisel, H. (1933/1971) *Marienthal: The Sociology of an Unemployed Community*. Chicago: Aldine-Atherton.

Jörgensen, D.L. (1989) *Participant Observation: A Methodology for Human Studies*. London: Sage.

Kelle, U. and Erzberger, C. (2004) 'Quantitative and Qualitative Methods: No Confrontation', in U. Flick, E. v. Kardorff and I. Steinke (eds), *A Companion to Qualitative Research*. London: Sage. pp. 172–7.

Kelle, U. and Kluge, S. (2010) *Vom Einzelfall zum Typus: Fallvergleich und Fallkontrastierung in der qualitativen Sozialforschung*. Wiesbaden: VS-Verlag.

Kelly, K. and Caputo, T. (2007) 'Health and Street/Homeless Youth', *Journal of Health Psychology*, 12: 726–36.

Kendall, L. (1999) 'Recontextualising Cyberspace: Methodological Considerations for On-Line Research', in S. Jones (ed.), *Doing Internet Research: Critical Issues and Methods for Examining the Net*. London: Sage. pp. 57–74.

Kirk, J.L. and Miller, M. (1986) *Reliability and Validity in Qualitative Research*. Beverly Hills, CA: Sage.

Knoblauch, H., Schnettler, B., Raab, J. and Soeffner, H.-G. (eds) (2006) *Video Analysis: Methodology and Methods*. Frankfurt: Lang.

Kozinets, R.V. (2010) *Netography: Doing Ethnographic Research Online*. London: Sage.

Kromrey, H. (2006) *Empirische Sozialforschung: Modelle und Methoden der standardisierten Datenerhebung und Datenauswertung*. Opladen: Leske and Budrich/UTB.

Laswell, H.D. (1938) 'A Provisional Classification of Symbol Data', *Psychiatry*, 1: 197–204.

Legewie, H. (1987) 'Interpretation und Validierung biographischer Interviews', in G. Jüttemann and H. Thomae (eds), *Biographie und Psychologie*. Berlin: Springer. pp. 138–50.

Liamputtong, P. (2007) *Researching the Vulnerable: A Guide to Sensitive Research Methods*. Thousand Oaks, CA: Sage.

Lillis, G. (2002) *Delivering Results in Qualitative Market Research*, vol. 7 of the *Qualitative Market Research Kit*. London: Sage.

Lincoln, Y.S. and Guba, E.G. (1985) *Naturalistic Inquiry*. London: Sage.

Lofland, J.H. (1974) 'Styles of Reporting Qualitative Field Research', *American Sociologist*, 9: 101–11.

Lofland, J. (1976) *Doing Social Life: The Qualitative Study of Human Interaction in Natural Settings*. New York: Wiley.

Lofland, J. and Lofland, L.H. (1984) *Analyzing Social Settings*, 2nd edn. Belmont, CA: Wadsworth.

Lucius-Hoene, G. and Deppermann, A. (2002) *Rekonstruktion narrativer Identität: Ein Arbeitsbuch zur Analyse narrativer Interviews*. Opladen: Leske and Budrich.

Lüders, C. (1995) 'Von der Teilnehmenden Beobachtung zur ethnographischen Beschreiibung: Ein Literaturbericht', in E. König and P. Zedler (eds), *Bilanz qualitativer Forschung*, vol. 1. Weinheim: Deutscher Studienverlag. pp. 311–42.

Lüders, C. (2004a) 'Field Observation and Ethnography', in U. Flick, E. v. Kardorff and I. Steinke (eds), *A Companion to Qualitative Research*. London: Sage. pp. 222–30.

Lüders, C. (2004b) 'The Challenges of Qualitative Research', in U. Flick, E. v. Kardorff and I. Steinke (eds), *A Companion to Qualitative Research*. London: Sage. pp. 359–64.

Lüders, C. (2006) 'Qualitative Daten als Grundlage der Politikberatung', in U. Flick (ed.), *Qualitative Evaluationsforschung: Konzepte, Methoden, Umsetzungen*. Reinbek: Rowohlt. pp. 444–62.

Mallinson, S. (2002) 'Listening to Respondents: A Qualitative Assessment of the Short-Form 36 Health Status Questionnaire', *Social Science and Medicine*, 54: 11–21.

Mann, C. and Stewart, F. (2000) *Internet Communication and Qualitative Research: A Handbook for Researching Online*. London: Sage.

Markham, A.M. (2004) 'The Internet as Research Context Research', in C. Seale, G. Gobo, J. Gubrium and D. Silverman (eds), *Qualitative Research Practice*. London: Sage. pp. 358–74.

Marshall, C. and Rossman, G.B. (2006) *Designing Qualitative Research*, 4th edn. Thousand Oaks, CA: Sage.

Maxwell, J.A. (2005) *Qualitative Research Design: An Interactive Approach*, 2nd edn. Thousand Oaks, CA: Sage.

May, T. (2001) *Social Research: Issues, Methods and Process*. Maidenhead: Open University Press.

Mayring, P. (1983) *Qualitative Inhaltsanalyse: Grundlagen und Techniken*. Weinheim: Deutscher Studien Verlag.

Mensching, A. (2006) 'Zwischen Überforderung und Banalisierung: zu den Schwierigkeiten der Vermittlungsarbeit im Rahmen qualitativer Evaluationsforschung', in U. Flick (ed.), *Qualitative Evaluationsforschung: Konzepte, Methoden, Umsetzungen*. Reinbek: Rowohlt. pp. 339–60.

Mertens, D. and Ginsberg, P.E. (eds) (2009) *Handbook of Research Ethics*. London. Sage.

Merton, R.K. and Kendall, P.L. (1946) 'The Focused Interview', *American Journal of Sociology*, 51: 541–57.

Miles, M.B. and Huberman, A.M. (1994) *Qualitative Data Analysis: A Sourcebook of New Methods*, 2nd edn. Newbury Park, CA: Sage.

Mishler, E.G. (1990) 'Validation in Inquiry-Guided Research: The Role of Exemplars in Narrative Studies', *Harvard Educational Review*, 60: 415–42.

Morse, J.M. (1998) 'Designing Funded Qualitative Research', in N. Denzin and Y.S. Lincoln (eds), *Strategies of Qualitative Research*. London: Sage. pp. 56–85.

Morse, J.M. (2001) 'Qualitative Verification: Strategies for Extending the Findings of a Research Project', in J.M. Morse, J. Swanson and A. Kuzel (eds), *The Nature of Evidence in Qualitative Inquiry*. Newbury Park, CA: Sage. pp. 203–21.

Morse, J.M., Swanson, J. and Kuzel, A.J. (eds) (2001) *The Nature of Qualitative Evidence*. Thousand Oaks, CA: Sage.

Murphy, E. and Dingwall, R. (2001) 'The Ethics of Ethnography', in P. Atkinson, A. Coffey, S. Delamont, J. Lofland and L. Lofland (eds), *Handbook of Ethnography*. London: Sage. pp. 339–51.

Neuman, W.L. (2000) *Social Research Methods: Qualitative and Quantitative Approaches*, 4th edn. Boston: Allyn and Bacon.

Neville, C. (2010) *Complete Guide to Referencing and Avoiding Plagiarism*. Maidenhead: Open University Press.

Oevermann, U., Allert, T., Konau, E. and Krambeck, J. (1979) 'Die Methodologie einer "objektiven Hermeneutik" und ihre allgemeine forschungslogische Bedeutung in den Sozialwissenschaften', in H.G. Soeffner (ed.), *Interpretative Verfahren in den Sozial- und Textwissenschaften*. Stuttgart: Metzler. pp. 352–433.

Patton, M.Q. (2002) *Qualitative Evaluation and Research Methods*, 3rd edn. London: Sage.

Pohlenz, P., Hagenmüller, J.-P. and Niedermeier, F. (2009) 'Ein Online-Panel zur Analyse von Studienbiographien: Qualitätssicherung von Lehre und Studium durch webbasierte Sozialforschung', in N. Jackob, H. Schoen and T. Zerback (eds), *Sozialforschung im Internet: Methodologie und Praxis der Online-Befragung*. Wiesbaden: VS-Verlag. pp. 233–44.

Porst, R. (2000) 'Question Wording: Zur Formulierung von Fragebogen-Fragen', *ZUMA How-to-Reihe*, no. 2, http://www.gesis.org/fileadmin/upload/forschung/publikationen/gesis_reihen/howto/how-to2rp.pdf (accessed 17 March 2009).

Potter, J. and Wetherell, M. (1998) 'Social Representations, Discourse Analysis, and Racism', in U. Flick (ed.), *Psychology of the Social: Representations in Knowledge and Language*. Cambridge: Cambridge University Press. pp. 177–200.

Punch, K. (1998) *Introduction to Social Research*. London: Sage.

Ragin, C.C. (1994) *Constructing Social Research*. Thousand Oaks, CA: Pine Forge.

Ragin, C.C. and Becker, H.S. (eds) (1992) *What Is a Case? Exploring the Foundations of Social Inquiry*. Cambridge: Cambridge University Press.

Rapley, T. (2008) *Doing Conversation, Discourse and Document Analysis*. London: Sage.

Richter, M. (2003) 'Anlage und Methode des Jugendgesundheitssurveys', in K. Hurrelmann, A. Klocke, W. Melzer and U. Ravens-Sieberer (eds), *Jugendgesundheitssurvey: Internationale Vergleichsstudie im Auftrag der Weltgesundheitsorganisation WHO*. Weinheim: Juventa. pp. 9–18.

Richter, M., Hurrelmann, K., Klocke, A., Melzer, W. and Ravens-Sieberer, U. (eds) (2008) *Gesundheit, Ungleichheit und jugendliche Lebenswelten: Ergebnisse der zweiten internationalen Vergleichsstudie im Auftrag der Weltgesundheitsorganisation WHO*. Weinheim: Juventa.

Riemann, G. and Schütze, F. (1987) 'Trajectory as a Basic Theoretical Concept for Analyzing Suffering and Disorderly Social Processes', in D. Maines (ed.), *Social Organization and Social Process: Essays in Honor of Anselm Strauss*. New York: Aldine de Gruyter. pp. 333–57.

RIN (2010) 'If You Build It, Will They Come? How Researchers Perceive and Use Web 2.0', http://www.rin.ac.uk/our-work/communicating-and-disseminating-research/use-and-relevance-web-20-researchers (accessed 21 August 2010).

Rosenberg, M. (1968) *The Logic of Survey Analysis*. New York: Basic.

Rosenthal, G. and Fischer-Rosenthal, W. (2004) 'The Analysis of Biographical-Narrative Interviews', in U. Flick, E. v. Kardorff and I. Steinke (eds), *A Companion to Qualitative Research*. London: Sage. pp. 259–65.

Sahle, R. (1987) *Gabe, Almosen, Hilfe.* Opladen: Westdeutscher Verlag.

Salmons, J. (2010) *Online Interviews in Real Time*. London: Sage.

Schmidt, L. and Fröhling, H. (1998) 'Gesundheits- und Krankheitsvorstellungen von Kindern und Jugendlichen', in U. Flick (ed.), *Wann fühlen wir uns gesund? Subjektive Vorstellungen von Gesundheit und Krankheit.* Weinheim: Juventa. pp. 33–44.

Schneider, G. (1988) 'Hermeneutische Strukturanalyse von qualitativen Interviews', *Kölner Zeitschrift für Soziologie und Sozialpsychologie*, 40: 223–44.

Schnell, M.W. and Heinritz, C. (2006) *Forschungsethik: Ein Grundlagen- und Arbeitsbuch mit Beispielen aus der Gesundheits- und Pflegewissenschaft.* Bern: Huber.

Schnell, R., Hill, P.B. and Esser, E. (2008) *Methoden der empirischen Sozialforschung.* München: Oldenbourg.

Schütze, F. (1983) 'Biographieforschung und Narratives Interview', *Neue Praxis*, 3: 283–93.

Schwandt, T.A. (2002) *Evaluation Practice Reconsidered*. New York: Lang.

Silverman, D. (2001) *Interpreting Qualitative Data: Methods for Analysing Talk, Text and Interaction*, 2nd edn. London: Sage.

Spradley, J.P. (1980) *Participant Observation*. New York: Rinehart and Winston.

Sprenger, A. (1989) 'Teilnehmende Beobachtung in prekären Handlungssituationen: Das Beispiel Intensivstation', in R. Aster, H. Merkens and M. Repp (eds), *Teilnehmende Beobachtung: Werkstattberichte und methodologische Reflexionen.* Frankfurt: Campus. pp. 35–56.

Stark, K. and Guggenmoos-Holzmann, I. (2003) 'Wissenschaftliche Ergebnisse deuten und nutzen', in F.W. Schwartz (ed.), *Das Public Health Buch.* Heidelberg: Elsevier, Urban and Fischer. pp. 393–418.

Strauss, A.L. (1987) *Qualitative Analysis for Social Scientists*. Cambridge: Cambridge University Press.

Strauss, A.L. and Corbin, J. (1990/1998/2008) *Basics of Qualitative Research*, 2nd edn 1998, 3rd edn 2008. London: Sage.

Sue, V.M. (2007) *Conducting Online Surveys*. London: Sage.

Tashakkori, A. and Teddlie, Ch. (eds) (2003a) *Handbook of Mixed Methods in Social and Behavioral Research*. Thousand Oaks, CA: Sage.

Tashakkori, A. and Teddlie, Ch. (2003b) 'Major Issues and Controversies in the Use of Mixed Methods in Social and Behavioral Research', in A. Tashakkori and Ch. Teddlie (eds), *Handbook of Mixed Methods in Social and Behavioral Research*. Thousand Oaks, CA: Sage. pp. 3–50.

Thomson, H., Hoskins, R., Petticrew, M., Ogilvie, D., Craig, N., Quinn, T. and Lindsay, G. (2004) 'Evaluating the Health Effects of Social Interventions', *BMJ*, 328: 282–5.

Tufte, E.R. (1990) *Envisioning Information*. Cheshire: Graphics.

Tufte, E.R. (2001) *Visual Display of Quantitative Information*. Cheshire: Graphics.

University Library (2009) 'Gray Literature', California State University, Long Beach, www.csulb.edu/library/subj/gray_literature (accessed 17 August 2010).

Van Maanen, J. (1988) *Tales of the Field: On Writing Ethnography*. Chicago: University of Chicago Press.

Walter, U., Flick, U., Fischer, C., Neuber, A. and Schwartz, F.W. (2006) *Alt und gesund? Altersbilder und Präventionskonzepte in der ärztlichen und pflegerischen Praxis.* Wiesbaden: VS-Verlag.

Weingart, P. (2001) *Die Stunde der Wahrheit? Zum Verhältnis der Wissenschaft zu Politik, Wirtschaft und Medien in der Wissensgesellschaft.* Weilerswist: Velbrück.

Weischer, C. (2007) *Sozialforschung: Theorie und Praxis*. Konstanz: UVK-UTB.

Wernet, A. (2006) *Einführung in die Interpretationspraxis der Objektiven Hermeneutik*, 2nd edn. Wiesbaden: VS-Verlag.

Wiedemann, P.M. (1995) 'Gegenstandsnahe Theoriebildung', in U. Flick, E. v. Kardorff, H. Keupp, L. v. Rosenstiel and S. Wolff (eds), *Handbuch Qualitative Sozialforschung*, 2nd edn. Munich: Psychologie Verlags Union. pp. 440–5.

Willig, C. (2003) *Introducing Qualitative Research in Psychology: Adventures in Theory and Method*. Buckinghamshire: Open University.

Wilson, T.P. (1982) 'Quantitative "oder" qualitative Methoden in der Sozialforschung', *Kölner Zeitschrift für Soziologie und Sozialpsychologie*, 34: 487–508.

Wolff, S. (1987) 'Rapport und Report: Über einige Probleme bei der Erstellung plausibler ethnographischer Texte', in W. v. d. Ohe (ed.), *Kulturanthropologie: Beiträge zum Neubeginn einer Disziplin*. Berlin. Reimer. pp. 333–64.

Wolff, S. (2004) 'Analysis of Documents and Records', in U. Flick, E. v. Kardorff and I. Steinke (eds), *A Companion to Qualitative Research*. London: Sage. pp. 284–90.

World Health Organization (1986) *Ottawa Charta for Health Promotion. First International Conference on Health Promotion, Ottawa*. www.who.int/hpr/docs/ottawa.html.

Name Index

Subject Index

Tables and Figures are indicated by page numbers in **bold**.